Step by Step

Microsoft®

MICROSOFT® VISUAL C++® .NET STEP BY STEP

Julian Templeman
Andy Olsen

Microsoft® .net™

PUBLISHED BY
Microsoft Press
A Division of Microsoft Corporation
One Microsoft Way
Redmond, Washington 98052-6399

Library of Congress Cataloging-in-Publication Data
Templeman, Julian.
Microsoft Visual C++ .NET Step by Step / Julian Templeman.
p. cm.
Includes index.
ISBN 0-7356-1567-5
1. C++ (Computer program language) 2. Microsoft Visual C++. I. Title.

QA76.73.C153 T455 2002
005.2'768--dc21 2001058666

Printed and bound in the United States of America.

2 3 4 5 6 7 8 9 QWT 7 6 5 4 3 2

Distributed in Canada by Penguin Books Canada Limited.

A CIP catalogue record for this book is available from the British Library.

Microsoft Press books are available through booksellers and distributors worldwide. For further information about international editions, contact your local Microsoft Corporation office or contact Microsoft Press International directly at fax (425) 936-7329. Visit our Web site at www.microsoft.com/mspress. Send comments to *mspinput@microsoft.com.*

Acquisitions Editor: Danielle Bird
Project Editor: Rebecca McKay

Body Part No. X08-42186

Contents

Introduction

In the past few months, much of people's attention has focused on the many new features that have been introduced along with Microsoft .NET, such as the major changes to Microsoft Visual Basic, the introduction of C#, the new ASP.NET and ADO.NET models, and the increased use of XML. C++ developers need not feel left out, however, because a lot of new features in this latest version of Microsoft Visual C++ make C++ a first class member of the .NET family of programming languages.

This book provides you with an introduction to the new, .NET-specific features that Microsoft has added to Visual C++ to support .NET development. This new functionality is called the Managed Extensions to C++, and as well as providing C++ programmers with access to all the functionality in the .NET class libraries, it also lets you interoperate with existing C++ code, as well with COM objects and the Win32 API.

System Requirements

You'll need the following hardware and software to complete the exercises in this book:

To complete the exercises in this book, you'll need to have Microsoft Visual Studio .NET installed. Microsoft Visual Studio .NET is available in various editions, you'll need one of the following:

- Visual C++ .NET Standard
- Visual Studio .NET Professional
- Visual Studio .NET Enterprise

The Visual Studio .NET software isn't included with this book. You must purchase it separately and install it before you can complete the exercises in this book.

You'll also need a computer capable of running Microsoft Visual Studio .NET. For complete details, check the product package, or check the Microsoft Visual Studio Web site at *http://msdn.microsoft.com/vstudio/*.

Installing and Using the Practice Files

The companion CD inside the back cover of this book contains the practice files that you'll use as you perform the exercises in the book. By using the practice files, you won't waste time creating objects that aren't relevant to the exercise. Instead, you can concentrate on learning object-oriented programming with the Managed Extensions to C++. The files and the step-by-step instructions in the lessons also let you learn by doing, which is an easy and effective way to acquire and remember new skills.

important

Before you break the seal on the *Microsoft Visual C++ .NET Step by Step* companion CD package, be sure that this book matches your version of the software. This book is designed for use with Microsoft Visual Studio .NET Professional Edition for the Windows operating systems. To find out what software you're running, you can check the product package or you can start the software, and then click About Microsoft Development Environment in the Help menu at the top of the screen.

Installing the Practice Files

Follow these steps to install the practice files on your computer's hard disk so that you can use them with the exercises in this book.

1 Remove the companion CD from the package inside the back cover of this book and insert the CD in your CD-ROM drive.

note

On some computers, the starting menu screen might launch automatically when you close the CD-ROM drive. In this case, follow the instructions on the screen, skipping steps 2 through 5.

2 Double-click the My Computer icon on the Desktop.

3 Double-click the icon for your CD-ROM drive.

4 Double-click StartCD.exe.

A starting menu screen appears, with options that allow you to view, browse, and install the contents of the CD-ROM and to access the Microsoft Press technical support Web site.

5 Click "Install Practice Files." Click OK in the initial message box.

The setup program window appears with the recommended options preselected for you. For best results in using the practice files with this book, accept these preselected settings.

6 When the files have been installed, remove the CD from your CD-ROM drive and replace it in the package inside the back cover of the book.

   A folder called *Microsoft Visual C++ .NET Step by Step* has been created on your hard disk, and the practice files have been placed in that folder.

Uninstalling the Practice Files

Follow these steps to remove the practice files from your computer. These steps are written for the Windows XP Professional operating system. If you are using a different version of Windows, refer to your Windows Help documentation for removing programs.

1. Click Start, and then click Control Panel.
2. In Control Panel, click Add Or Remove Programs.
3. In the Add Or Remove Programs window, click *Microsoft Visual C++ .NET Step By Step* in the Currently Installed Programs list.
4. Click Change/Remove. The Confirm File Deletion dialog appears.
5. Click Yes to delete the practice files.
6. Click Close to close the Add Or Remove Programs window.
7. Close Control Panel.

Conventions and Features in this Book

This book presents information using conventions designed to make the information more readable and easier to follow. The book also includes features that contribute to a deeper understanding of the material.

Conventions

- Each exercise is a series of tasks. Each task is presented as a series of numbered steps. If a task has only one step, the step is indicated by a round bullet.
- Notes labeled "tip" provide more information for completing a step successfully.
- Notes labeled "important" alert you to information you need to check before continuing.
- Text that you are to type appears in bold.
- Terms are displayed in italics the first time they are defined.
- A plus sign (+) between two key names means that you must press those keys at the same time. For example, "Press Alt+Tab" means that you hold down the Alt key while you press Tab.

Other Features of This Book

- You can learn special techniques, background information, or features related to the information being discussed by reading the shaded sidebars that appear throughout the lessons. These sidebars often highlight difficult terminology or suggest future areas for exploration.
- You can get a quick reminder of how to perform the tasks you learned by reading the Quick Reference at the end of a lesson.

Corrections, Comments, and Help

Every effort has been made to ensure the accuracy of this book and the contents of the practice files on the companion CD. Microsoft Press provides corrections and additional content for its books through the World Wide Web at

http://mspress.microsoft.com/support/

If you have problems, comments, or ideas regarding this book or the companion CD, please send them to Microsoft Press.

Send e-mail to	mspinput@microsoft.com
Or send postal mail to	Microsoft Press Attn: Step by Step Series Editor One Microsoft Way Redmond, WA 98052-6399

Please note that support for the Visual Studio .NET software product itself is not offered through the preceding address. For help using Visual Studio .NET, visit *http://support.microsoft.com*.

Visit the Microsoft Press World Wide Web Site

You are also invited to visit the Microsoft Press World Wide Web site at the following location: www.microsoft.com/mspress

You'll find descriptions for the complete line of Microsoft Press books, information about ordering titles, notice of special features and events, additional content for Microsoft Press books, and much more.

You can also find out the latest in Visual Studio .NET software developments and news from Microsoft Corporation by visiting the following World Wide Web site: http://msdn.microsoft.com/vstudio/nextgen/

PART 1

Getting Started with C++

CHAPTER 1

Hello, C++!

In this chapter, you'll learn about

- ✔ *C++ characteristics*
- ✔ *C++ functions*
- ✔ *C++ keywords and identifiers*
- ✔ *Creating a C++ program*

Welcome to the exciting world of programming .NET with Microsoft Visual C++. This chapter introduces the C++ language and simple input/output (I/O) using the C++ standard library console (text-based) facilities.

What is a C++ program? Well, it contains exactly the same elements as any other computer program—data to store your information and blocks of code that manipulate that data. Whether your previous experience is with Microsoft Visual Basic or with 40-year-old COBOL, the basic elements will be familiar. Much mystery surrounds the practice of C++ programming, but most of it is unwarranted and unnecessary.

Let's start with some basic ground rules for C++:

C++ is a strongly typed language.

If you have a variable that has been declared able to store apples, you can store only apples in it. However, this is not as grim as it sounds. C++ contains many features for providing implicit conversions where necessary. This strong type checking eliminates many common programming bugs because it explicitly disallows any data type conversions that could result in data loss.

C++ is an efficient language.

If you write code that needs to execute quickly (sorting lists or performing complex mathematics, for example), C++ should be your language of choice.

C++ is an object-oriented language.

Modern programmers like the many advantages of object-oriented programming. (See Chapter 2 for more information on object-oriented programming.) C++ is one of the premier languages for such use.

C++ is based on C (as you might suspect).

C is a well-established language. Although C++ includes some strange features—specifically to maintain its compatibility with C—it probably wouldn't be as popular as it is without this compatibility.

C++ is a case-sensitive language.

If the compiler warns you about an undeclared variable, you probably typed an uppercase character instead of a lowercase character (or vice versa).

Your First C++ Program

Let's get our hands dirty with a simple C++ program. Of course, no book on C++ would be complete without including the clichéd "Hello, World!" program, so let's start with that.

```
#include <iostream>
using namespace std;

int main()
{
    cout << "Hello, World!" << endl;
    return 0;
}
```

This short program illustrates some fundamental C++ concepts:

- The first line uses the directive *#include* to tell the C++ compiler to copy in the file named iostream at the beginning of the program. Why is this inclusion necessary? A golden rule of C++ is that *everything*, must be declared before it is used, including the output stream named *cout* used later in the program. (The *cout* output stream causes output to go to the console.) So why not just declare *cout* explicitly in this file? Since the iostream file is a separate unit, it can be included in any other program, thus making it easy to reuse the declarations. In a nutshell, it saves a lot of typing for the programmer.

- The second line (`using...`) tells the compiler that the standard C++ library is to be used (hence the word *std*—an abbreviation of *standard*). Many different libraries could be used in a single project; the *using* statement lets us tell the compiler which library we mean to use.

- The rest of the program is an example of a C++ function. All blocks of code in C++ are called functions—there's no such thing as a procedure or subroutine. Each C++ function contains the header part (the first line of this program) and function body (all the text between the braces { and }). The header part shows the return value of the function (in this case *int*, short for integer), the name of the function (*main*), and the list of parameters inside round brackets. This example has no parameters, so the round brackets are empty—but the brackets still must be there.
- All statements in C++ are terminated with a semicolon.

Of the seven lines of text in the example program, only two contain C++ statements: the *cout* line and the *return* line. The *cout* line outputs characters to the console. The syntax for using *cout* is the word *cout* followed by a << operator, followed by the items you want to output. (The *endl* stream manipulation operator inserts a new-line character in the stream.)

You can output many items by using a single *cout* statement—just separate any extra items with further << operators, as shown here:

```
cout << "Hello" << ", " << "World" << endl;
```

Alternatively, you can use several *cout* statements to give exactly the same effect:

```
cout << "Hello";
cout << ", ";
cout << "World";
cout << endl;
```

As you might expect, programmers tend to prefer the single statement version.

The *main* Function

Why is this example's only function named *main*? The simple answer is that the example won't compile if the function isn't named *main*. However, it might be more useful to explain how the language works.

A normal C++ program contains many functions (and also many classes—see Chapter 2). How does the compiler know which function should be called first? Obviously, the compiler can't be allowed to just randomly choose a function! The rule is that the compiler will always generate code that looks for a function named *main*. If you omit the *main* function, the compiler reports an error and doesn't create a finished executable program.

Free-Format Languages

The C++ language is *freeformat*, which means that the compiler ignores all spaces, carriage returns, new-line characters, tabs, form feeds, and so on. Collectively these characters are referred to as *white space*. The only time the compiler recognizes white space is if it occurs inside a string.

Free-format languages give the programmer great scope for using tab or space indenting as a way of organizing program layout. Statements inside a block of code—such as a *for* loop or an *if* statement—are typically indented slightly (often four characters). This indentation helps the programmer's eye more easily pick out the contents of the block.

This gives rise to one of the most common (and least useful) arguments in the C++ community—how do you indent the braces? Should they be indented with the code or should they be left hanging at the beginning of the *if* or the *for* statement? There is no right or wrong answer to this question (although some hardened C++ developers might disagree), but a consistent use of either style will help make your program readable. As far as the compiler is concerned, your entire program could be written on one line!

So the compiler will expect a function named *main*. Is that all there is to it? Well, not quite. There are some additional items—such as the return type and parameters being correct—but in the case of *main* some of the C++ rules are relaxed. In particular, *main* can take parameters that represent the command-line arguments, but you can omit them if you don't want to use the command line.

C++ Keywords and Identifiers

A C++ *keyword* (also called a *reserved word*) is a special item of text that the compiler expects to be used in a particular way. The keywords used in the example program are *using*, *namespace*, and *return*. You're not allowed to use these keywords as variable or function names—the compiler would report an error if you did so.

An *identifier* is any name that the programmer uses to represent variables and functions. An identifier must start with a letter and must contain only letters, numbers, or underscores. The following are legal C++ identifiers:

- *My_variable*
- *AReallyLongName*

The following are not legal C++ identifiers:

Identifier	Reason for being invalid
0800Number	Must not start with a number
You+Me	Must contain only letters, numbers, and underscores
return	Must not be a reserved word

Compiler Error or Linker Error?

To be absolutely correct, it is the linker that reports the error. You'll find more on compiler and linker errors later in this chapter.

Outside of these restrictions, any identifier will work. (Oddly enough, the identifier *main* is not a reserved keyword; you can define a variable named *main* within the program—but this is not recommended!) Some choices are not recommended. For example:

Identifier	Reason it's not recommended
main	Could be confused with the function *main*
INT	Too close to the reserved word *int*
B4ugotxtme	Just too cryptic!
_identifier1	An underscore at the beginning is possible but not recommended

Creating an Executable Program—Theory

Several stages are required to build an executable program; Microsoft Visual Studio .NET helps by automating them. To examine and understand these stages, however, let's look at them briefly. You'll see these stages again later in the chapter when we build our first program.

Editing the Program Source Files

Before you can create a program, you must write something! Visual Studio .NET provides an integrated C++ editor, complete with color syntax highlighting and IntelliSense to show function parameter information and word completion.

Compiling the Source Files

The C++ compiler is the tool for converting textual source files into machine code object files that have an .obj file extension. (*Object* in this sense is not to be confused with *object–oriented.*) The compiler is invoked inside the Visual Studio .NET environment, and any errors or warnings are displayed in the environment.

The object files produced, however, are *not* executable files. They are incomplete, lacking references to any functions not contained with the source files for the particular compilation.

Linking the Object Files

The final step in producing an executable file is to link together all object files that make up a particular project. This linking includes not only object files produced from your own source code, but also object files from system libraries such as the C++ standard library or the Microsoft Foundation Class (MFC) library.

Link errors tend to be less helpful than compile errors. Compile errors will give the file name and the line number of the error; the linker will give only the name of the object file, so a bit of detective work is often required.

System and Class Libraries

System and class libraries often have many .obj files associated with them. Handling all of a library's object files in a project would soon become onerous, so .obj files are frequently combined into .lib library files for convenience.

Running and Testing the Program

Although linking might be the final step in creating an executable file, it's not the last step in development. You still need to test and run the program.

For many development environments, this is often the most difficult part of the program development cycle. However, Visual Studio .NET has yet another ace up its sleeve—the integrated debugger. The debugger has a rich set of features to allow easy run-time debugging, such as setting breakpoints and variable watches.

Creating an Executable Program—Practice

- Start up Microsoft Visual Studio .NET. An invitingly blank window should be displayed.

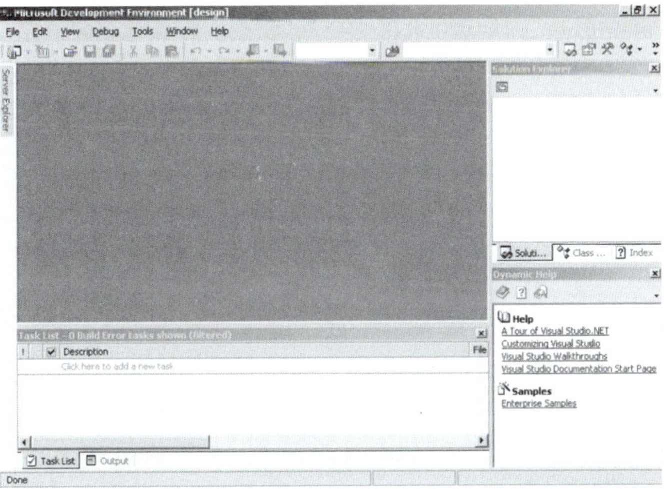

This window is the powerful Visual Studio .NET integrated development environment (IDE). It contains all the tools you'll need to create full-featured, easy-to-use applications.

Creating a Project

The first task is to create a new project for the "Hello, World!" program. To create a project, follow these steps:

1. Under the File menu, click New, and then click Project. (Alternatively, you can press Ctrl+Shift+N.)

   The New Project dialog box will be displayed.

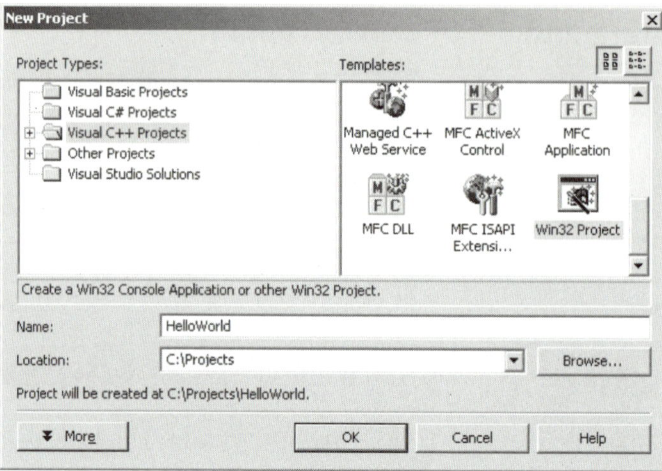

2 Select Visual C++ in the Project Types box, select Win32 Project in the Templates box, and then type **HelloWorld** in the Name box.

3 Choose a location for your new project in the Location box, either by typing a directory path in the Location box, or by clicking Browse and navigating to the appropriate directory.

4 Click OK to start the Win32 Application Wizard.

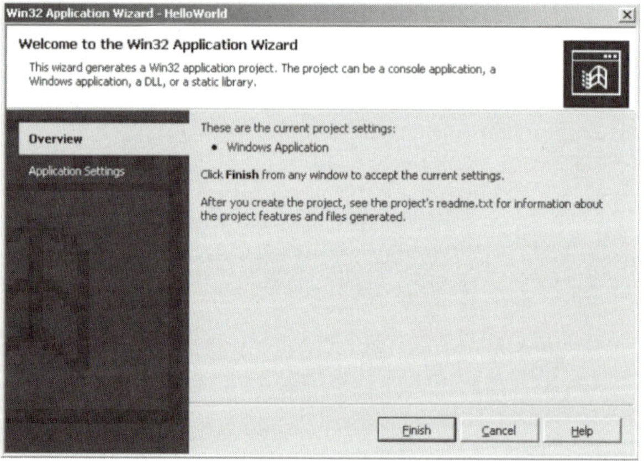

For this project, you need to create a console project. This simple, text-based interface (similar to an MS-DOS screen from years ago) will be adequate for our purposes. Unfortunately, the wizard quite reasonably assumes that you want to create a Windows program, so you must change the default wizard settings.

1 Click on Application Settings text just underneath the Overview text.

The right side of the dialog box changes to show the current wizard settings.

2 Under Application Type, select Console Application, and then select Empty Project under Additional Options.

3 Click Finish to create the project.

The wizard correctly initializes all the compiler settings for a console project. If you're not sure this has actually happened, right-click the HelloWorld icon in Solution Explorer and select Properties on the shortcut menu. (Press Ctrl+R or select Solution Explorer from the View menu if you don't see Solution Explorer.)

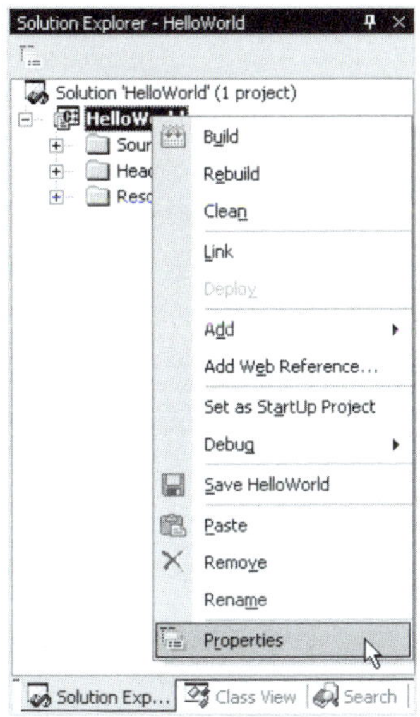

Click the Linker folder in the left list box, click the System category, and then examine the Configuration Properties in the right box. You will see that the *SubSystem* property has been set to console.

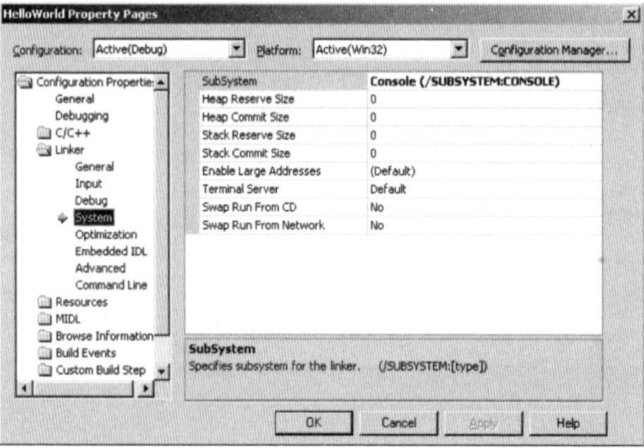

Adding a C++ Source File to the Project

An empty project is not particularly exciting on its own, so let's add a new C++ source file. As always in Visual Studio .NET, you have many ways to do the same thing.

1 Either click the Add New Item icon or right-click the HelloWorld icon in Solution Explorer.

2 Click Add, and then click Add New Item to open the Add New Item dialog box.

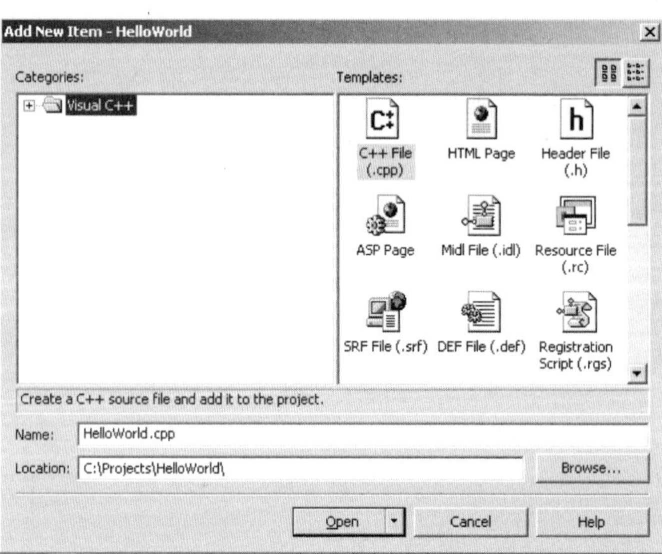

3 Select C++ File (.cpp) from the Templates list on the right, type **HelloWorld.cpp** in the Name box, and then click Open.

Visual Studio .NET creates an empty source code file and adds it to the project for you.

Now it's time to put the mouse down, pick up the keyboard, and start typing some C++ code.

Adding C++ Code to the Source File

- Type in the source code for the program, as shown here.

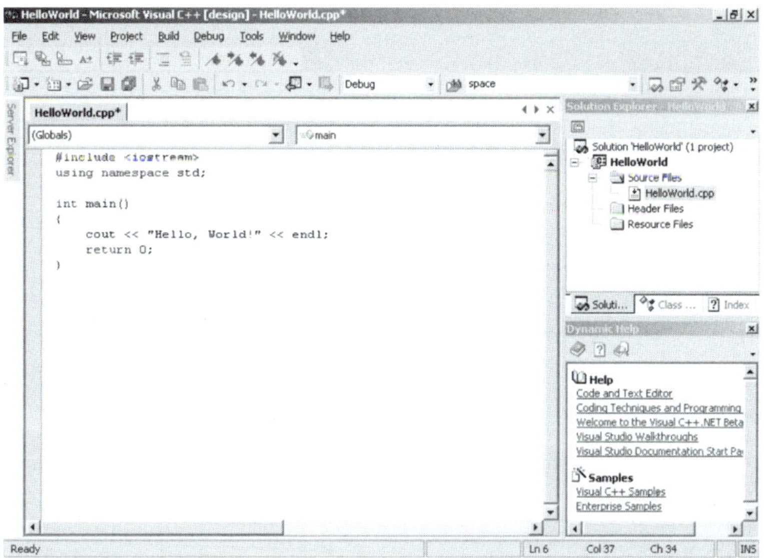

Notice that the keywords automatically turn blue (providing you spell them correctly).

Building the Executable

The next step is to build the executable. The term *build* in Visual Studio .NET refers to compiling and linking the program. Visual Studio .NET compiles any source files that have changed since the last build and—if no compile errors were generated—performs a link.

- To build the executable, select Build from the Build menu or press Ctrl+Shift+B. An Output window displaying the build progress will appear near the bottom of the Visual Studio .NET. If no errors are encountered, the message *Build: 1 succeeded, 0 failed, 0 skipped* should appear in the Output window.

If any problems occurr, the Output Window will contain a list of errors and warnings, as shown here.

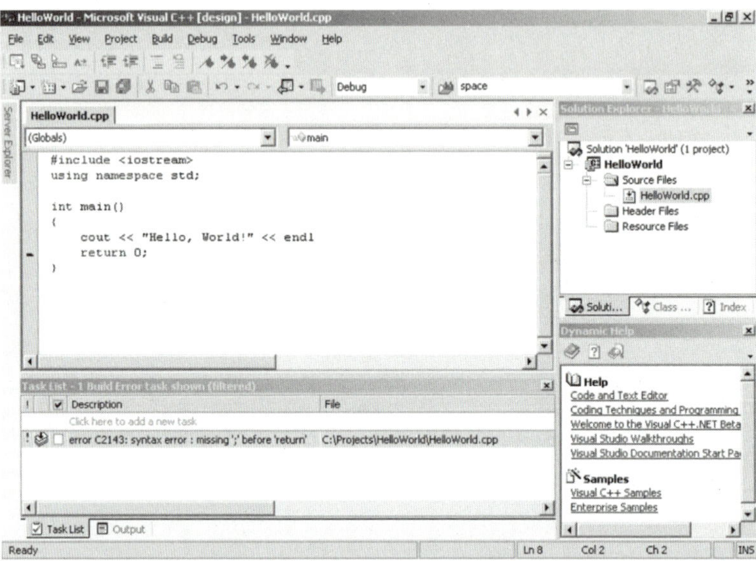

If the error or warning is generated by the compiler and not the linker, double-click on the error line in the Output window to place the cursor at the line in the source file where the compiler encountered the error. Fix the error (you might have misspelled a keyword or forgotten a semicolon), and rebuild the project.

How Should You Treat Warnings?

Always treat warnings as errors—in other words, get rid of them. Warnings are there for a reason—they mean your code is not correct.

Executing the Program

Once you've eliminated all errors and you've successfully built the project, you can finally execute the program. Choose Start from the Debug menu to run the program. You'll probably be disappointed with the result, however. Your program seems to run, but flashes into and then out of existence too quickly to see. Why is this? You haven't put any code in the program to pause execution. To fix the problem, add the following line before the *return* statement:

```
cin.ignore();
```

Build the program and run it again. Now you will see the output of your program, paused in all its glory, waiting for you to press Enter.

Conclusion

Although the example in this chapter isn't the most exciting program ever written, it demonstrated some key C++ development points. It introduced the IDE, the ability to compile and link a program, and served as an introduction to the C++ language.

Now there's no turning back. Every new C++ and Visual Studio .NET feature that you learn about will fire your imagination to learn more and be productive. Software development can be an exciting world.

Finally, don't forget to have some fun. Go back and try a few variations on the example program, click a few menus, and become familiar with the environment. You have nothing to lose.

Chapter 1 Quick Reference

To	Do this
Create a new project in Visual Studio .NET	Use the File, New, Project menu item; or press Ctrl+Shift+N.
Add a file to a project	Use the File, New, File menu item; or press Ctrl+N.
Build a Visual Studio .NET project	Use the Build, Build menu item; or press Ctrl+Shift+B.
Execute a program from withinVisual Studio .NET	Use the Debug, Start Without Debugging menu item; or press Ctrl+F5.

Introducing Object-Oriented Programming

In this chapter, you'll learn

- ✔ *The key concepts of object-oriented programming*
- ✔ *How these concepts are supported by C++ language constructs*
- ✔ *About the major development benefits of object-oriented programming*
- ✔ *How to create and use simple classes*

What is Object-Oriented Programming?

Object-oriented programming (OOP) has the advantage of being a natural paradigm in which to develop systems. We perceive the world as consisting of objects: tables, chairs, computers, cars, bank accounts, rugby matches, and overdrafts. It is also a natural human trait to try and organize these objects, arranging them into some form of classification, choosing to highlight certain features of objects in preference to others. So dogs and cats are mammals, toasters and refrigerators are appliances, rugby and tennis are sports, Jaguars and Fords are cars, trucks and cars are vehicles, and so on.

There can be many levels to these categories, and many ways to classify the objects in the world. How people classify things depends to a large extent on what they want to do with them and the features that are salient to these desires. For example, an electrical engineer is likely to have different, and in some ways deeper and richer, categories for household appliances than a teacher might have. While grouping objects into classification schemes, we also tend to highlight certain attributes of objects in preference to others. For example, a car's color might not matter in an engineer's mind, but it might figure heavily in a Ferrari salesperson's mental model of car classifications.

This idea (of building hierarchies of related objects) is used in object-oriented programming. As long ago as the 1960s, researchers realized that many computer program model entities can be named and their properties and behavior can be described. They noticed that programs deal with bank accounts, arrays, files, and users, which are analogous to objects in the real world.

Object-oriented development can crudely be characterized as identifying the relevant objects, organizing them into hierarchies, adding the attributes to the objects that describe the relevant features in the problem context, and adding the functions (methods) to the objects to perform the required tasks on the object. The details are a little more complicated, but essentially it is a simple and natural process.

Yet simple and natural doesn't necessarily mean easy, because a collection of objects could be classified in virtually countless ways. The ability to identify the important attributes of objects and to form good abstractions and appropriate hierarchies is key. Even within the context of a problem domain, it's sometimes hard to determine the correct levels of abstraction and suitable classification hierarchies. Just deciding which class or grouping an object belongs to can be very difficult. As Wittgenstein (1953) pointed out, some objects will bear more of a family resemblance to a concept than others; for example, rugby and tennis are more obviously sports than chess and synchronized swimming.

Features of Object-Oriented Programming Languages

I've already said that object-oriented development means defining and building hierarchies of objects, and defining their properties and behavior. You can do this to a certain extent in any programming language, just the same as you could, theoretically, take a trip across the Rockies in a golf cart, but it is much easier to do object-oriented programming if you use a language that is designed to support object-oriented programming methods.

Object-oriented programming languages—such as C++ and C#—are characterized by three key features—encapsulation, inheritance, and polymorphism—that support this natural process of identifying and classifying objects.

Encapsulation

One of the problems faced by software developers is that the systems we are developing are getting increasingly larger and increasingly more complex. Encapsulation helps by breaking a program down into small, self-contained entities. For example, if you're building an accounting system, you'll probably need objects to represent accounts and invoices. Once you've developed the *Account* class, you no longer need to worry about the details of the implementation of the class. You can use the class anywhere in your program in much the same way you would use a built-in type, such as integer. The class will expose the essential features of the *Account* object while hiding the implementation details.

The account's name and the state of its balance are some of the attributes of the object the client is interested in and needs to know. Details of how the account name is stored—whether an array of 50 characters or a string object, or the fact that the account's balance is maintained as a currency variable—are irrelevant to the client. The process of hiding the data structures and implementation details of an object from other objects in the system is called data hiding, and it prevents the other objects from accessing details they don't need to know about.

Encapsulation makes large programs easier to comprehend; data hiding makes them more robust.

Objects can interact with other objects only through the publicly exposed attributes and methods of the object. The more attributes and methods publicly exposed, the more difficult it will be to modify the class without affecting the code that uses the class. A hidden variable could be changed from a *long* to a *double*, without affecting the code that uses objects created (instantiated) from that class. The programmer would have to worry only about the methods in the class that accessed that variable, rather than worrying about all the places in the program that an object instantiated from that class might be called. Chapter 6 covers the details of how C++ supports encapsulation.

Inheritance

The natural tendency for humans to classify objects into hierarchies is useful from a programmer's perspective and is supported in most object-oriented languages, including C++, by inheritance.

Inheritance provides two advantages to the C++ programmer. First, and most important, it lets them build hierarchies that express the relationships between types. Suppose that you have two classes, *SavingsAccount* and *CheckAccount*, both of which are derived from the parent *Account* class. If you have a function that requires an *Account* as an argument, you can pass it a *SavingsAccount* or a *CheckAccount*, because both classes are types of *Account*. *Account* is a general classification, and *CheckAccount* and *SavingsAccount* are more specific types.

The second feature is that classes can inherit features from the more general features of classes higher in the hierarchy. Instead of developing new classes from scratch, new classes can inherit the functionality of existing classes and then modify or extend this functionality. The parent class from which the new class inherits is known as the base class and the new class is known as the derived class.

One of the major tasks facing a developer is finding appropriate classifications for the objects and classes for their program. For example, if you need to develop classes for a driving game, it makes more sense for you to develop a general car class and then use this class as a base class for specific car types such as Jaguar or Ford. These derived classes would then extend or modify the general car class by adding new attributes and methods or by overriding existing methods. Decomposing objects into sub-objects—for example, a car consists of an engine and a chassis—simplifies the development effort. As a result, each of the objects is simpler and therefore easier to design and implement than the collective whole. Chapter 7 covers inheritance in more depth.

Polymorphism

The third feature of object-oriented programming languages is polymorphism, which is Greek for "many forms." It is quite a hard concept to define, so I'll use some examples to show you what polymorphism is, and leave the precise definitions to more academic writers.

Polymorphism essentially means that classes can have the same behavior, but implement it in different ways. Consider several different types of vehicle: they all need to be started, so in programming terms we could say that all vehicles have "start" functionality. Exactly *how* starting is implemented depends on the vehicle: if it is a Model T Ford, it'll mean cranking the starting handle, but if it is a modern car, it'll mean turning the key in the ignition, and if it is a steam locomotive, it'll be a very different and more complex process.

As another example, consider the *SavingsAccount* and *CheckAccount* types I mentioned earlier. All types derived from *Account* share certain functionality, such as the ability to deposit, withdraw, and query the balance. They might implement them in different ways, because *CheckAccount* might permit an overdraft while *SavingsAccount* might give interest, but they all work the same way. This means that if I'm passed an *Account*, it doesn't matter exactly what type of account it is, I can still deposit funds, withdraw funds, and query the balance.

This is useful in programming terms, because it gives you the ability to work with generic object types—accounts and vehicles—when you're not concerned with the way in which each class implements functionality.

Classes and Objects

Up to this point in the chapter, the terms "class" and "object" have been used fairly interchangeably. However, classes and objects aren't the same thing, and we need to clarify the differences between these terms. As the name implies, object-oriented programming is about objects. An object is composed of data that describes the object and the operations that can be performed on the object. However, when you create a program in C++, you declare and define classes, not objects.

A class is a user-defined type; it encapsulates both the data and the methods that work on that data. With the exception of static functions, you cannot use classes directly. A class is much more like a template, which is used to create (instantiate) objects. Just as you have to declare an *integer* variable before you can use it, you also have to instantiate an object of the class before it can be used.

For example, you would not declare and define an animal object. Instead, you would declare and define an animal class and its attributes and methods. The class represents the concept, so that the *Animal* class does not represent a specific animal but the class of all animals. When you want to use an *Animal* object, you have to instantiate an animal object from the class. The class can be considered as the abstract representation of an entity, while the instantiation of the class—the object—is the concrete representation.

The Benefits of Object-Oriented Programming to the Developmental Life Cycle

There are three key benefits to object-oriented programming: comprehensibility, reusability, and extensibility. Breaking code down into classes helps to impose a structure as programs get larger and larger. The ideal is to assemble object-oriented systems from prewritten classes, and to make the required modifications to support the new requirements by using inheritance to derive new classes from the existing classes. The existing classes are used as building blocks and not altered in any way. Creating systems from reusable components naturally leads to higher productivity, which is probably the most frequently cited benefit of object-oriented approaches. Object-oriented development should also result in higher quality systems. Classes that are being reused—having been tested and developed on earlier projects—are likely to contain fewer bugs than classes developed from scratch. Over the passage of time, bugs have been found and fixed in these classes, whereas a class that starts from scratch has yet to pass through the same bug detection and fixing process.

The features of object-oriented programming also provide benefits. Encapsulation makes it easier to scale up from small systems to large systems. To a large extent, regardless of the size of the system, the developer is simply creating objects. Large systems might require more objects than small systems, but the level of complexity facing the developer is not significantly increased. Inheritance helps to improve the flexibility and extensibility of systems, hence reducing their costs to maintain. Deriving new classes from existing classes provides additional functionality, and allows the extension of the software without altering the existing classes.

Finally, data hiding also leads to more secure systems. The state of an object can be modified only by its publicly exposed methods; this increases the predictability of object behavior.

A Simple Example

This example will show you how to:

- Create a class
- Instantiate objects from the class
- Access member functions and attributes of the class

1. Start Microsoft Visual Studio .NET.
2. From the File menu, select New, and then select Project.

   The New Project dialog box appears.
3. Set the Project Type to Visual C++ Projects.
4. Set the Template to Managed C++ Application.
5. Type **animals** in the Name text box.
6. Set the Location to C:\Projects. Click OK.

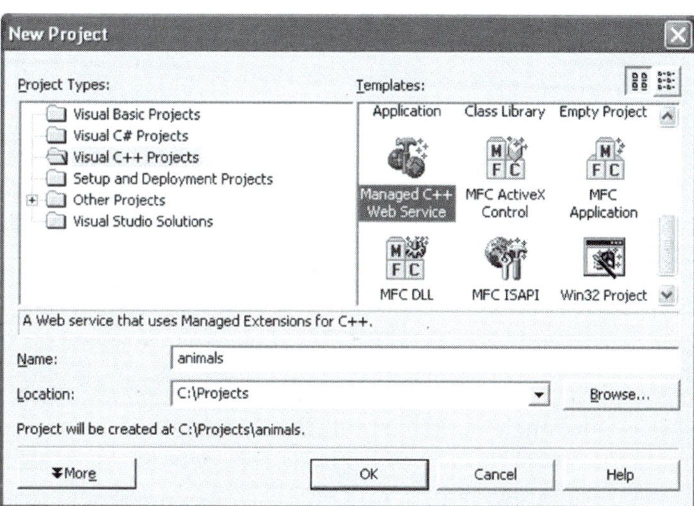

7 In the Solution Explorer window, double-click on the animals.cpp file in the Source Files folder.

8 Add the following line immediately after the *#include <stdafx.h>* line at the top of the file:

```
#include <string.h>
```

This includes the definitions that you need in order to be able to use the *string* data type.

9 Immediately under the *using namespace System;* line, add the following class definition:

```
__gc class animal
{
    int     legs;
    String *strName;
};
```

To declare a class in C++, you use the keyword *class* followed by a name for the class, such as "animal" in this example, then list of all the class's member variables, functions, and methods between an opening brace ({) and a closing brace (}).

So far, you have created an *animal* class with an *integer* variable for the number of its legs and a *string* variable for its name. As it stands, no other program or class will be able to access these variables. The members of a class—data and methods—are private by default and can only be accessed by methods of the class itself. C++ provides three access modifiers—*public:*, *private:*, and *protected*—to specify the visibility of the various members of the class.

10 Add the keyword *public:* on a new line between the opening brace and the first variable declaration.

```
__gc class animal
{
public:
    int     legs;
    String *strName;
};
```

This makes both the variables accessible. However, it is not usually a good idea to allow other classes and parts of your program access to the variables of a class. As discussed above in the section on encapsulation, it is better to keep the implementation details of a class hidden from users of that class and to control the access to the class's data through functions. In this example, the keyword *private:* will be used to prevent direct access to the *String* variable of the class. The *integer* variable legs will be left with public access, simply to show how it can then be directly accessed by the main program.

11 Add the keyword *private:* between the first *integer* variable and the second *String* variable.

```
__gc class animal
{
public:
    int     legs;
private:
    String *strName;
};
```

To provide access to the private *String* variable, public accessor functions and methods need to be added to the class to allow other functions to manipulate its value.

12 After the declaration of the *integer* variable and before the private access modifier, add the following method declarations or implementations lines:

```
    void SetName(String *Name)
        { strName->Copy(Name); };
    String* GetName() { return strName; };
```

Because these methods are small functions, it was easiest to declare and implement them as in-line functions.

The *animal* class is now complete. The syntax of the declaration is:

```
class classname
{
```

```
Access control keywords (Public: Private: or Protected:)
The declaration of class variables and methods
}
```


You have probably noticed the *__gc* keyword. This is one of the Managed Extensions for C++ that simplifies the interaction with .NET Framework components. By placing *__gc* in front of the *class* keyword, the class becomes a managed class. When the object is instantiated, it will be created on the common language run-time heap, and the new operator will return the memory address of this object. The lifetime of an object instantiated from the class will be managed by the .NET developer platform. When the object falls out of scope, the memory used will be garbage-collected, and no explicit calls to delete will have to be made. This is a reference type variable because the variable does not actually contain the object but a pointer to the memory where the object is.

However, there are performance issues to consider when using reference types. The memory has to be allocated from the managed heap, which could force a garbage collection to occur. In addition, reference types have to be accessed via their pointers, affecting both the size and speed of the compiled application.

Because of this, .NET also supports value types. Value type objects are created on the stack. The variable contains the object itself rather than a pointer to the object. Hence, the variable does not have to be dereferenced to manipulate the object and that, of course, improves performance. To declare a value type class, the *__value* keyword should be used instead of the *__gc* keyword. In this case, the variables would have been created on the stack. Instead of declaring pointers for this class and then creating the objects on the Common Language Runtime heap by using the new operator, the objects would have been declared in the same way as the built-in C++ types and the member variables accessed by the dot operator rather than via the dereferencing operator.

Now that the *animal* class has been constructed, it can be used by the program just as the program would use a built-in type.

1. In the *main* function, delete the following line:

   ```
   Console::WriteLine(S"Hello World");
   ```

2. Declare and create two *animal* objects in your *main* function:

   ```
   animal    *Cat, *Dog;
   Cat = new animal;
   Dog = new animal;
   ```

   The keyword *new*, followed by the class of the object being created, creates the object on the Common Language Runtime heap rather than the stack. The memory address of the created object is returned and stored in the pointer.

3 Use the member function to assign the names "Cat" and "Dog" to the respective *Cat* and *Dog* objects and set the *legs* variable for both objects to 4.

```
Cat->SetName("Cat");
Cat->legs = 4;
Dog->SetName("Dog");
Dog->legs = 4;
```

To access the member variables and functions, you have to dereference the pointer either by using the dereferencing operator, an asterisk (*) followed by the dot notation—for example, (*Cat).legs—or by the shorthand operator for indirect access, a minus sign and right angle bracket (->).

4 Having created a couple of *animal* objects and assigned data to them, you are now going to display that data on the screen. Add the following lines:

```
Console::WriteLine("Animal 1");
Console::Write("Name: ");
Console::WriteLine(Cat->GetName());
Console::Write("Legs: ");
Console::WriteLine(Cat->legs);
Console::WriteLine();

Console::WriteLine("Animal 2");
Console::Write("Name: ");
Console::WriteLine(Dog->GetName());
Console::Write("Legs: ");
Console::WriteLine(Dog->legs);
Console::WriteLine();
```

5 Build the application. Select Build from the Build menu bar or use the keyboard shortcut Ctrl+Shift+B.

In case you've had any problems putting the program together from the fragments in the preceding steps, the entire program is listed here:

```
// This is the main project file for VC++ application
// project generated using an Application Wizard.

#include "stdafx.h"
#include <string.h>

#using <mscorlib.dll>
#include <tchar.h>

using namespace System;
```

```
__gc class animal
{
public:
    int     legs;

    void SetName(String *Name)
        { strName = strName->Copy(Name); };
    String* GetName() { return strName; };
private:
    String  *strName;
};

// This is the entry point for this application
int _tmain(void)
{
    // TODO: Please replace the sample code below with
    // your own.
    animal *Cat, *Dog;

    Cat = new animal;
    Dog = new animal;

    Cat->SetName("Cat");
    Cat->legs = 4;
    Dog->SetName("Dog");
    Dog->legs = 4;

    Console::WriteLine("Animal 1");
    Console::Write("Name ");
    Console::WriteLine(Cat->GetName());
    Console::Write("Legs ");
    Console::WriteLine(Cat->legs);
    Console::WriteLine();

    Console::WriteLine("Animal 2");
    Console::Write("Name ");
    Console::WriteLine(Dog->GetName());
    Console::Write("Legs ");
    Console::WriteLine(Dog->legs);
    Console::WriteLine();
    return 0;
}
```

6 If the build was successful, run the application by selecting Debug, Start Without Debugging or the keyboard shortcut Ctrl+F5.

Quick Reference

To	Do this
Create a class	Use the keyword *class*
Control the visibility of variables and methods	Use the access control keywords *public:*, *private:*, or *protected:*
Declare a reference type class	Place the *__gc* keyword before the class specifier
Declare a value type class	Place the *__value* keyword before the class specifier

Instantiate a reference type class object	Declare a pointer of the class type for the object.
	Use the *new* keyword followed by the name of the class to create the object on the Common Language Runtime heap, and assign the returned pointer to the object pointer declared above. For example:
	`HeapClass *pObject1;`
	`pObject1 = new HeapClass;`

Instantiate a value type class object	Define the object by stating its *class* followed by the variable name for the object. For example: `ValueClass    object1;`

CHAPTER

3

Variables and Operators

In this chapter, you'll learn how to

- ✔ *Declare (create) variables*
- ✔ *Use the built-in C++ data types*
- ✔ *Create user-defined types*
- ✔ *Add member variables to a class*
- ✔ *Use the Microsoft .NET Framework* String *class*
- ✔ *Assign values to a variable*
- ✔ *Create expressions using the C++ operators*
- ✔ *Cast (change) the type of a variable*

In the previous chapter, we looked at the advantages of object-oriented programming and developed a simple program to illustrate the creation and use of classes.

In this chapter, we will take a closer look at how to create and use variables, the fundamental data types of C++, how to access and use classes from the .NET Framework, and the creation of expressions using the C++ operators.

What Is a Variable?

Variables are locations in memory where data can be temporarily stored for use by the program. They have a name, type, and value. The value of the variable can be changed during the execution of the program, hence the name variable. Before a variable can be used, it must be declared: Its type has to be specified and it has to be given a name. The type of a variable defines the allowable range of values that the type can hold and the operations that can be performed on the variable.

The Fundamental Data Types

C++ has a built-in set of data types, as shown in the table below.

Type	Description	Range	
bool	A Boolean type which can contain true or false	true	false
char	A character type which can hold ASCII values	–128	127
short	An integral type; stores whole numbers	–32,768 unsigned—0	32,767 65,536
int	An integral type; stores whole numbers	–2,147,483,648 unsigned—0	2,147,483,647 4,294,967,295
long	An integral type like the *int*, except that on many compilers, it's twice the size	In Microsoft Visual C++, the long is the same size as the *int* and therefore can only store the same size variables	
__int8	A Microsoft specific integral type, synonymous with the *char* data type		
__int16	A Microsoft specific integral type, synonymous with the short data type		
__int32	A Microsoft specific integral type, synonymous with the *int* data type		
__int64	A Microsoft specific integral type that stores whole numbers	–9,223,372, 036,854, 775,808	9,223,372, 036,854, 775,807
float	Stores floating point numbers, for example, 3.7b	In Visual C++, the float stores up to six decimal places	
double	Stores floating point numbers like the float but with greater precision and hence more accuracy.	The double can store up to 15 decimal places	
wchar_t	A wide character or multibyte character type		

From these types built-in types, you can construct other types, as we'll see in this and later chapters:

- Pointer types, for example, *int**
- Array types, for example, *int[]*
- Reference types, for example, double&

Or you can construct user-defined types by creating data structures and classes; see the section on user-defined types below.

Declaring a Variable

As mentioned above, variables have to be declared before they can be used. A simple declaration consists of a type, followed by one or more variable names separated by commas and terminated by a semicolon. For example:

```
int     nPrimeNumber;
double  x, y, z;
```

Each variable can be given a qualifier before the type (for example, unsigned). You can also place an initializer after the variable name in order to give it an initial value (for example, int i = 0). The qualifier and the initializer are optional and do not have to appear in the declaration, but the base type and variable name must be present. The declaration is terminated by the semicolon:

```
[qualifier] type name [initializer];

unsigned int i;        // An unsigned integer variable i, note the
                       //   qualifier limiting the variable to
                       //   positive numbers.
long lSalary = 0;      // A long variable initialized to zero.
double y;              // A double variable without qualifier or
                       //   initializer
```

Declaring the variable enables the compiler to:

- Allocate enough memory to store the variable of that type and to associate the name of the variable with that memory location.
- Reserve the name of the variable to prevent it from being used by other variables within the same function.
- Ensure that the variable is used in a way consistent with its type. For example, if you have declared a variable as a *char*, you can't store the value 3.7 in it.

Variable Naming

A C++ variable name can be any combination of letters, numbers, and underscores as long as the first character of the variable is a letter or underscore. Although C++ does not place any restrictions on your choice of variable names, you should use meaningful variable names and be consistent in your naming conventions to increase the readability of your code. C++ is case-sensitive, meaning uppercase and lowercase letters are considered different; for example, myvariable and myVariable are two separate variables. However, it's not a good idea to differentiate variables solely on the basis of case in order to avoid confusion. It would be easy to type a letter in the wrong case and end up using a completely wrong variable!

note

Do not create identifiers that begin with two underscores or an underscore followed by a capital letter, (for example, _A). Microsoft uses this naming convention to specify macros and Microsoft-specific keywords, so starting your variables with these combinations could lead to name conflicts.

Declaring Multiple Variables

You can declare several variables of the same type in the same statement simply by separating them with commas:

```
int x = 10, y, z = 11;
```

This statement creates three integers called x, y, and z. The first integer is initialized to 10 and the third to 11, while the second is not initialized.

Assigning Values to Variables

You assign a value to a variable by using the assignment operator = (an equal sign). The value on the right side of the operator is stored in the variable on the left side. When assigning a value to a variable, the value must belong to the same type as the variable, be a type for which C++ will perform an assignment conversion (such as between float and integral types), or be explicitly cast to the correct type.

> **note**
>
> Assignment conversions occur when variables on opposite sides of an equal sign are of different types, and the compiler can convert between the two types without any possible loss of data. For instance, assigning an integer to a double will result in an assignment conversion because all the compiler has to do is to add '.0' to the integer to make the conversion.
>
> You may occasionally need to tell the compiler to perform a conversion which it otherwise wouldn't do. For example dividing two integers will result in an integer result: if you want a floating point result, you can tell the compiler to convert one of the values to a double, like this:
>
> ```
> double result = double(640) / 480;
> ```
>
> You give the name of the type to convert to, followed by the value in parentheses. This process is called casting, and it can be rather dangerous because you're telling the compiler to apply a conversion, and you'd better be sure you're correct:
>
> ```
> int x;
> float y;
> double z;
> x = 1;
> z = x;
> y = 3.56;
> x = y;          // Assignment conversion from float to int
>                 // results in loss of data.
>                 // The integer 3 is stored in the variable x.
> ```
>
> The compiler will generate the warning "C4244: '=' conversion from 'float' to 'int' possible loss of data." The reason for this is that the assignment to an integer will lose the fractional part, so 3.56 will be truncated to 3.

Arrays

An array is a collection of data-storage locations, each of which holds the same type of data—such as all integers or all doubles—but only one type. Arrays are very useful when you want to represent a collection of values, such as the number of days in each month or the names of company employees. Each storage location is called an element of the array. Elements of the array are accessed by referring to an offset from the array name. The array elements start at zero (0) and continue up to one less than the array bound:

```
int     nArray[10];  // Declare an array of ten integers.
int     x;
nArray[0] = 23;      // The first element in the array starts at
                     // the offset 0
nArray[9] = 21;      // The last element in the array starts at
                     // the offset 9
x = nArray[0];
```

Writing past the end of the array is a serious problem and the cause of many bugs in C++ programs. When accessing an array element, the compiler calculates the offset from the start of the array. If you're writing to an array element and you give an invalid index so that the calculated offset is beyond the end of the array, the compiler will overwrite whatever happens to be in that memory location.

Pointers

A pointer is a variable that holds the memory address of another variable or function, and this means that you can use a pointer to refer indirectly to a variable.

> **note**
>
> Why are pointers useful? The first, and most pragmatic reason, is that they have been part of the C family of languages right since the start and they're very widely used, so you'll need to know something about them. There are many other reasons though, and I've summarized a couple of the most important ones in this note.
>
> First, pointers are one of the main ways that arguments are passed to functions. Arguments are usually passed by value – as a copy – so you can't modify the value and expect it to get back to the calling code. Pointers let you pass arguments in such a way that you can modify them.
>
> Second, some operations on series of data – such as values in arrays – can be performed very efficiently using pointers.

Although a pointer variable contains an address and therefore can store a memory address of any data type, pointer variables are declared to be data type specific. A pointer to an integral data type (*int*) can't store the address of a double. The pointer variable is declared in the same way as the data type variable, but the pointer operator * (an asterisk) is appended to the data type:

```
int* pi;             // pointer to an int
double* pd;          // pointer to a double
char* pc;            // pointer to a char
```

Every variable has an address and that address can be obtained using the address of operator, an ampersand (&). The address of the variable can be stored in a pointer variable and using that pointer, the contents of that variable can be manipulated by using the dereference operator * (an asterisk):

```
int x = 10, y = 0;
int* pX = NULL;  // Declare an integer pointer.
pX = &x;          // Store the address of the integer variable x.
y = *pX;          // Use the dereference operator to assign the
                  // value of x to y.
*pX = 20;         // Use the dereference operator to assign 20 to x.
```

In the last two lines of the code, *pX can be read as "what pX points to." Chapters 7 and 8 will discuss pointers in more detail.

References

A reference variable is an alias for another variable. All reference variables must be initialized when declared. From then on, any changes made to the referenced variable will be made to the aliased variable. Reference variables are particularly important when passing variables to functions; this topic will be covered in Chapter 4, but here's an example:

```
int     x = 10;
int&    y = x;        // declare y as reference to x.
Y = 4;                // Changes the value of x to 4.
```

Constants

Like variables, constants are named data-storage locations. However, unlike a variable, the value of a constant can't be changed after it has been declared. It has to be initialized when it is created and can't be assigned a new value later. C++ has two types of constants: literal and symbolic.

A literal constant is simply a value typed into the program. The statements below assign the literals 40 and "Dog" to the respective variables *NoOfEmployees* and *strName*:

```
NoOfEmployees = 40;
strName = "Dog";
```

A symbolic constant is a constant that is represented by a name. It is defined in exactly the same way as a variable, but the qualifier must start with the keyword *const* and the variable must be initialized. After declaration, the constant name can be used anywhere a variable of that type could be used:

```
const unsigned long NoOfFullTimeEmployees = 49;
const unsigned long NoOfPartTimeEmployees = 234;
unsigned int NoOfEmployees;
NoOfEmployees = NoOfFullTimeEmployees + NoOfPartTimeEmployees;
```

There are a couple of advantages to using symbolic constants rather than literal ones:

- The symbolic names make the program more readable. The symbolic constant *NoOfFullTimeEmployees* is more meaningful than the literal constant 49.
- It is easier to change a single symbolic constant declaration than to find and replace all occurrences of a literal in a program.

However, this can be taken too far. It is not necessary to replace all literals with constants. There are some constants which are intuitively obvious to everyone and which are not going to change; for example, the number of days in a week or months in a year. These values can be left as literals without reducing the readability or maintainability of the code.

Enumerations

In situations where a variable can only take on a specific set of values, such as colors or gender, enumerations allow you to create new types and to declare variables whose values are restricted to the enumerated set.

Enumerations are declared by the keyword *enum*, followed by the type name, an opening brace ({), the enumerated values separated by commas, a closing brace (}), and a semicolon (;). Variables are then declared as an enumerated type, and they can only receive one of the enumerated values:

```
enum WorkDays { Monday, Tuesday, Wednesday, Thursday, Friday };
const int Saturday = 7;
WorkDays WorkingDay;
WorkingDay = Thursday;      // Thursday is a member of the WorkDays
                            // enumerated type and therefore can be
                            // assigned to the WorkDays variable.
WorkingDay = Saturday;      // Although Saturday is an integer
```

```
                          // constant, it is not part of the
                          // enumerated type WorkDays and
                          // therefore can't be assigned to the
                          // WorkDays variable.
```

Typedefs

A typedef is a user-defined synonym for an existing type. To create a synonym for a type, you use the keyword *typedef* followed by the name of the type and the new name you are defining. Because typedef is a C++ statement, you also need a closing semicolon:

```
typedef unsigned int positiveNumber;
```

The typedef above declares *positiveNumber* to be a synonym of *unsigned int* and can be used in a declaration instead of the actual type name:

```
positiveNumber      one, two;
```

Adding Member Variables to Classes

1 Start Microsoft Visual Studio .NET, and select New from the File menu, then select Project.

  The New Project dialog box appears.

2 Set the Project Type to Visual C++ Projects, and set the Template to Managed C++ Application.

3 Type **variables** in the Name text box and set the Location to C:\Projects. Click OK.

  From the Project menu, select Add Class. The Add Class dialog box appears.

4 Set the Template to Generic C++ Class. Click Open.

  The **Generic C++ Class Wizard** dialog box appears.

5 Type **animal** in the Class Name text box. Note how default names for the header and source files are created automatically.

6 Leave the Base Class text box blank.

7 In the Access list, select Public. (Note that Public is the default so it should already be selected.)

8 Check the Virtual Destructor check box.

  (Class destructors will be explained in Chapter 7.)

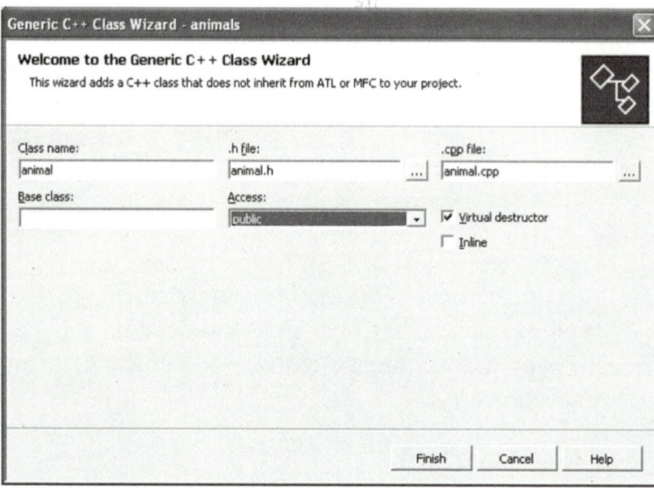

9. Click Finish.

   Note that the source code for the new class, animal.cpp, has been loaded into the main window. In the Solution Explorer, the animal.cpp file has been added to the Source Files folder and the header file, animal.h, has been added to the Header Files folder. In the Class View window, if you expand the Animals Project node, you will see that the new *animal* class has been added to the project. If you expand the *animal* class, you will see the default constructor, *animal(void)*, and destructor, *~animal(void)*, for the class.

10. In the Class View window, right-click on the *animal* class and select Add, then select Add Variable.
11. Accept the default Access modifier public.
12. Select int from the Variable Type drop-down menu.
13. Type **legs** in the Variable name text box.

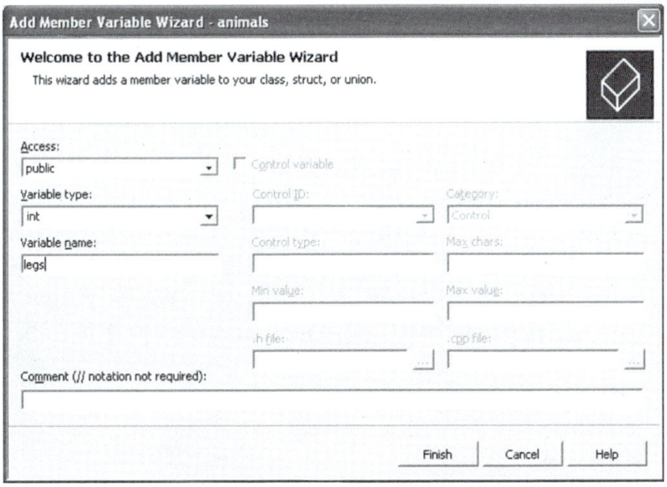

14 Click Finish.

In this exercise you've seen how to create a new class using Visual Studio and how to add members to it.

The .NET Framework String Class

The *String* class is not a built-in data type like *int* or long, but part of the .NET Framework. Because *String* isn't a built-in type, you have to include some files in your project before the compiler will let you use it. Add the following two lines to the top of your project:

```
#using <mscorlib.dll>
using namespace System;
```

The '#using' line tells the compiler to look in the file mscorlib.dll for details of the *String* class. Mscorlib.dll is the library file that contains the core .NET components, and you'll meet it a lot during the course of this book. The second 'using' line makes it easier to use certain .NET classes; just type the line in as it is for now, and you'll find out more about namespaces in Chapter 15.

The *String* class contains a large number of methods to simplify manipulating strings.

note

Although the *String* class is a very powerful class, once you initialize a *String* object, it is immutable: it can't be changed after it is created. The member functions of the *String* class that appear to alter Strings, such as *Insert* and *Replace*, actually return a new *String* object which contains the modification(s). This makes these *String* class methods very inefficient when making repeated modifications to a string. If you need to make repeated changes to a string, you should use the *StringBuilder* class. You will have to include the mscorlib.dll assembly and the *System.Text* namespace to simplify member access.

Operators And Expressions

Expressions are built using operators that work with data—the operands—to give a result. For example:

```
Remuneration = Salary + Bonus;
```

In the above example, the addition operator + (a plus sign) is used to add the operands Salary and Bonus, and the assignment operator is used to store the total in the *Remuneration* variable.

Assignment Operators

An assignment expression is used to assign a value to a variable. All expressions return a value when evaluated and the value of the assignment expression is the new value of the object on the left side. This makes it possible to assign the same value to a group of variables. For example:

```
NoOfMammals = NoOfDogs = NoOfCats = 0;
```

In the above example, all three variables—*NoOfMammals*, *NoOfDogs*, and *NoOfCats*—are set to zero.

Arithmetic Operators

C++ has 12 arithmetic operators, five of which operate like the standard mathematical operators: the addition operator + (a plus sign), the subtraction operator - (a minus sign), the multiplication operator * (an asterisk), the division operator / (a slash), and the modulus operator % (a percentage sign), which returns the remainder after division:

```
Result = 4 + 2 - 3;  // Result = 3
Result = 4 * 5;      // Result = 20
Remainder = 7 % 3;   // Remainder = 1
```

In addition, there are a number of arithmetic assignment operators: the addition assignment operator += (a plus sign with an equal sign), the subtraction assignment operator -= (a minus sign with an equal sign), the multiplication assignment operator *= (an asterisk with an equal sign), the division assignment operator /= (a slash with an equal sign), and the modulus assignment operator %= (a percentage sign with an equal sign). These operators are shorthand forms that combine the corresponding mathematical operation with the assignment operation. For example:

`A = A + 5;` could be expressed as `A += 5;`

Instead of using the addition operator to add 5 to the value of the variable A, and then using the assignment operator to assign the new value to the variable A, you can just use the addition assignment operator to add 5 to the value of the variable A and assign the new value. The addition assignment operator is a shortcut operator. There is no difference between the two statements. In both statements, an addition is performed, followed by an assignment. The second form is just a shorter way of expressing a frequently used statement.

The increment and decrement operators are similar shorthand operators, but these operators only add or subtract 1 from the value of the variable:

```
A++; // Adds 1 to the value of the variable A.
A--; // Subtracts 1 from the value of the variable A.
```

There are two forms of the increment and decrement operators: the prefix form ++A or --A, and the postfix forms A++ or A--. Both forms add or subtract 1 to the variable. In the prefix form, the mathematical operation is performed before the variable's role in the expression is evaluated; in the postfix form the variable is incremented or decremented after the variable has been used in the expression. For example:

```
int a , b, c;
a = b = c = 0;
b = ++a,   // a = 1, b = 1
c = a++;   // c = 1, a = 2
```

In the code fragment above, the final values of the variables are a = 2, b = 1, and c = 1. The prefix increment operator expression added 1 to the value of *a* before assigning the value of the variable *a* to the variable *b*. The postfix increment operator expression assigned the value of the variable *a* to the variable *c* and then incremented the value of the variable *a* by 1.

note

When working with objects, the prefix versions of the increment and decrement operators are more efficient than the postfix versions because a temporary copy of the object doesn't have to be made for use in the expression before incrementing or decrementing the object.

Relational and Logical Operators

Relational operators are used to compare two values or expressions, returning a true or false value. C++ has six relational operators: the greater than operator > (a right angle bracket), the greater than or equal operator >= (a right angle bracket with an equal sign), the less than operator < (a left angle bracket), the less than or equal operator <= (a left angle bracket with an equal sign), the equal operator == (two equal signs), and the not equal operator != (an exclamation point with an equal sign):

```
a > b   // returns true if a is greater than b.
a >= b  // returns true if a is greater than or equal to b.
a < b   // returns true if a is less than b.
a <= b  // returns true if a is less than or equal to b.
a == b  // returns true if a is equal to b.
a != b  // returns true if a is not equal to b.
```

A logical operator is used to relate two relational expressions. C++ has three logical operators: the and operator && (two ampersands), the logical OR operator ||, and the not operator ! (an exclamation point). The and operator relates two expressions both of which must be true for the operator to return a true value. The OR operator returns true if either of the two expressions evaluates to true:

```
a && b                // returns true if both a and b are true
(a > b) && (a < c)    // returns true if a is greater than b and a
                      // is less than c
a || b                // returns true if either a or b are true
(a > b) || (a < c)    // returns true if either a is greater than b
                      // or a is less than c
```

The evaluation of a relational expression stops as soon as the logical value of the whole expression is determined. For example, the expression expr1 && expr2 is true only if both expr1 and expr2 are true. If expr1 is false, then the final value of the expression must be false, and therefore expr2 is not evaluated.

The not operator returns the negation of the Boolean value of its operand:

```
!a      // If a is true the not operator will return false, if a is
        // false the not operator will return true.
```

These operators are most often used in *decision* or *loop* structures, which will be discussed in Chapter 5.

Bitwise Operators

C++ has six bitwise operators: the and operator & (an ampersand), the bitwise OR operator |, the exclusive OR operator ^ (a caret), the complement operator ~ (a tilde), the right shift operator >> (two right angle brackets), and the left shift operator << (two left angle brackets). These operators work on the individual bits of the byte and can only be applied to integral operands—char, short, int, and long. The bitwise and operator compares the bits of two operands; if the bit in the same position for each operand is 1, the resulting bit is 1; if however either bit is zero, the resulting bit is set to zero. This operator is often used to mask off bits.

The bitwise OR operator compares the bits of two operands: if either bit is 1, the corresponding bit of the result is 1, and if both bits are zero, the corresponding bit of the result is set to zero. The bitwise OR operator is often used to turn bits/flags/options on.

The exclusive OR operator sets the result bit to 1, only if one of the operands has the corresponding bit set to 1. If the corresponding bit of both operands is 1 or 0, the bit is set to 0.

The complement operator reverses the bit setting of the operand. If the bit is 1 it is set to 0; if the bit is 0 it is set to 1.

The left shift operator moves the bit pattern of its left operand to the left by the number of bits specified by its right operand. The bits vacated by the left shift are filled with zeros. The right shift operator moves the bit pattern of its right operand to the right by the number of bits specified by its right operand. If the variable is an unsigned data type the vacated bits will be filled with zeros; if the variable is signed the vacated bits will be filled with the sign bit:

```
int a;
a = 5;
a = a << 2;     // The bits of a will be shifted two bits to the left
                // and the value of 20 assigned to a
a = 5;
a = a >> 2;     // The bits of a will be shifted two bits to the
                // right and the value of 1 assigned to a
```

The Ternary Operator

The ternary operator ? (a question mark) is an inline *if* statement. (See Chapter 5 for more information.) The expression to the left of the ternary operator is evaluated: If it is true, the value or expression between the ternary operator and the colon is returned. If it is false, the value or expression after the colon is returned:

```
int a;
bool b;
b = true;
a = b ? 1 : 2;// b is true, so a is assigned 1.
b = false;
a = b ? 1 : 2;// b is false, so a is assigned 2.
```

The Sizeof Operator

The sizeof operator returns the size of the C++ data type, either built-in or user-defined in bytes. For example, *sizeof(int)*; and *sizeof(animal)*.

Type Casting

C++ supports the C style cast operator, where the type you wish to convert the expression to is placed in parentheses in front of the expression; for example, *(float) 7*. It also supports four new cast operators:

- static_cast<type>
- const_cast<type>
- dynamic_cast<type>
- reinterpret_cast<type>

The static_cast<type> changes the data type of the variable. For example, if an expression needs to convert an integer into a floating point number for a calculation, the number should be cast using the *static_cast<double>* operator. The dynamic_cast<type> is used to cast objects down or across the inheritance hierarchy (covered in Chapter 7). The const_cast<type> changes the const-ness of the variable. The reinterpret_cast<type> allows any pointer to be converted into a pointer of another type. For example:

```
int a = 10;
double b;
b = (double) a;                 // old C style cast operator
b = static_cast<double>(a);     // C++ static_cast operator
```

Operator Precedence and Associativity

There are two ways in which the expression 2 + 3 * 4 could be evaluated: It could be evaluated as (2 + 3) * 4, giving a value of 20 or it could be evaluated as 2 + (3*4), giving a value of 14.

The rules of operator precedence allow an unambiguous evaluation of expressions. Operators higher in the hierarchy are given precedence over operators lower in the hierarchy. Because the * operator is higher than the + operator, the second interpretation of the above expression, 2 + (3 * 4), would be evaluated. In situations where two operators are at the same level in the hierarchy, the order of evaluation proceeds from left to right. Hence, 2 * 3 / 2 * 3 would be evaluated as ((2 * 3) / 2) * 3 giving a value of 9. Parentheses can be used to group operators and override the precedence hierarchy. For example, (2 * 3) / (2* 3) giving a value of 1. Ideally, you should use parentheses even when they are not strictly required simply to clarify your intentions. The following table shows the hierarchy of precedence from highest to lowest. Operators in the same row of the table share the same level of precedence.

<table>
<tr><th>Operator</th><th>Name</th></tr>
<tr><td>::</td><td>Scope resolution</td></tr>
<tr><td>. -> [] () ++ --</td><td>Member selection, subscripting, function calls, postfix increment, postfix decrement</td></tr>
<tr><td>sizeof() ++ --
^ ! - + & * new
delete delete[]
static_cast<type>
const_cast<type>
dynamic_cast<type>
reinterpret_cast<type></td><td>Sizeof(), prefix increment, prefix decrement, complement, not, unary minus, unary plus, address of, dereference, new, delete, delete[], casting operators</td></tr>
<tr><td>.* ->*</td><td>Pointer to member operator</td></tr>
<tr><td>* / %</td><td>Multiply, divide, modulus</td></tr>
<tr><td>+ -</td><td>Add, subtract</td></tr>
<tr><td>>> <<</td><td>Right shift, left shift</td></tr>
<tr><td>< <= > >=</td><td>Relational operators (inequality)</td></tr>
<tr><td>== !=</td><td>Equality, inequality</td></tr>
<tr><td>&</td><td>Bitwise and</td></tr>
<tr><td>|</td><td>Bitwise OR</td></tr>
<tr><td>&&</td><td>Logical and</td></tr>
<tr><td>||</td><td>Logical OR</td></tr>
<tr><td>? :</td><td>Ternary operator</td></tr>
<tr><td>= += -= *= /= %
= <<= >>= &= |= ^=</td><td>Assignment operators</td></tr>
<tr><td>,</td><td>Comma</td></tr>
</table>

Chapter 3 Quick Reference

To	Do This

Declare a variable	Specify the type followed by space(s), then the variable name followed by a semicolon.
	For example:
	`int    number1;`
	`long   longNumber1;`

Assign values to a variable	Use the assign operator =.
Group homogenous data together	Use an array
Prevent data from being changed	Make the variable a constant. For example: `const int x = 10;`
Restrict the values a variable can accept to a small set	Declare an enumerated constant and declare the variable to be of that type.
Add member variables to a class	Use the Generic C++ Class Wizard.
Access a *String* class	Use the .NET class *String*.
Find the size of an object or type	Use the sizeof() operator.
Convert one data type to another	Use the static_cast<type>() operator.
Override default operator precedence or make the code more readable	Use parentheses to group operators.

CHAPTER

4

Using Functions

In this chapter, you'll learn how to

- ✔ *Declare function prototypes*
- ✔ *Define function bodies*
- ✔ *Call functions*
- ✔ *Deal with local and global variable scope*
- ✔ *Define and use overloaded functions*

By now, you should be fairly comfortable with basic C++ syntax. You've seen how to declare variables, write statements, use operators, and perform simple console output. However, as your programs start to get larger, you need to organize your code to cope with the growing complexity.

In this chapter, you will learn how to divide a Microsoft Visual C++ program into functions. First, you'll see how to declare function prototypes to introduce the functions to the compiler. Next, you'll see how to define function bodies to carry out the required processing; for example, you might write a function to calculate the expected growth on an investment, or to get the user's password from a Login screen. Finally, you'll see how to call a function from elsewhere in your program.

Why Use Functions?

There are many good reasons for dividing a program into functions:

- Each function is usually quite short and discrete. It's easier to write a program as a series of functions because you can concentrate on one function at a time.
- It's also easier to read and debug a program that contains lots of small functions because you don't have to remember what the whole program is doing.
- Functions are reusable. Once you've written a function, you can call it whenever you need it in your program. This reduces coding effort, and therefore improves developer productivity.

Declaring Function Prototypes

A function prototype is a single-line statement that introduces the name of a function to the compiler. The prototype also indicates what types of parameters can be passed into the function, and what type of value the function returns.

Declaring a Simple Function Prototype

The following example shows a simple function prototype:

```
void DisplayWelcome();
```

In this example, the name of the function is *DisplayWelcome*. The parentheses are required to indicate that this is a function. The parentheses are empty in this example, which means that the function doesn't take any parameters. The *void* keyword at the beginning of the function prototype indicates that the function doesn't return a value either—presumably, the function just displays a welcome message on the screen.

note

Some programming languages differentiate between functions (which return a value) and subroutines (which do not return a value). For example, Microsoft Visual Basic .NET uses the *Function* keyword for functions and the *Sub* keyword for subroutines. Visual C++ just has functions; use the *void* return type if the function doesn't return a value.

Notice the semicolon at the end of the function prototype. This is a statement terminator, and it marks the end of the function prototype. A function prototype doesn't tell you what the function does; it just tells you the function signature.

In this exercise, you will declare a simple function prototype in a Visual C++ application. The function will not take any parameters, and will not return a value either.

1. Start Microsoft Visual Studio .NET and open a new Managed C++ Application project named InvestmentPlanner.
2. From the View menu, select the menu command Solution Explorer.
3. In Solution Explorer, double-click InvestmentPlanner.cpp to view the code in this file.
4. At the top of the file, immediately under the *using namespace System;* line, add the following function prototype:

   ```
   void DisplayWelcome();
   ```

   This is the function prototype you saw earlier. You place function prototypes near the top of the source file, so that they are visible to the rest of the code in the file.
5. From the Build menu, select the menu command Build to build your program. There's no point in running the program yet, because you haven't implemented or called the *DisplayWelcome* function You'll do that later in this chapter.

Declaring Parameters in a Function Prototype

Functions can take parameters to make them more generic. You must declare the data types for these parameters in the function prototype.

In this exercise, you will declare a function prototype that uses parameters.

1. Open the Managed C++ Application project you created in the previous exercise.
2. Add the following function prototype:

   ```
   void DisplayProjectedValue(double amount, int years, double
   rate);
   ```

   This function prototype declares a function named *DisplayProjectedValue*. The function takes three parameters: a *double*, an *int*, and another *double*. The compiler uses this information to ensure that the function is always called with the correct number and types of parameters.

tip

Parameter names are optional in the function prototype. Strictly speaking, you could omit the parameter names and just specify the parameter types. However, parameter names help to convey the meaning of the parameters, so it's good practice to use them.

3 Build your program.

Declaring the Return Type in a Function Prototype

As well as specifying input parameters for a function, you must also specify a return type for the function. As you saw earlier, the *void* return type indicates that the function does not return a value.

In this exercise, you will see how to specify a non-*void* return type for a function.

1 Open the Managed C++ Application project from the previous exercise.

2 Add the following function prototype:

```
double GetInvestmentAmount();
```

This function prototype declares a function named *GetInvestmentAmount*. The function doesn't take any parameters, but it returns a *double*.

3 Add another function prototype as follows:

```
int GetInvestmentPeriod(int min, int max);
```

This example shows how to declare a function that takes parameters and returns a value. The *GetInvestmentPeriod* function takes two *int* parameters, and also returns an *int*.

note

The parameter types and return type are independent of each other. The fact that the *GetInvestmentPeriod* parameters and return type are all *int* is entirely coincidental. It's quite easy to imagine a function whose parameter types and return type are different.
For example:

```
double CalculateAverageValue(int number1, int number2);
```

4 Build your program.

Declaring Default Values for Function Parameters

When you declare a function prototype, you can specify default values for some or all of its parameters. This is useful for parameters that usually have the same value each time the function is called. Specifying a default value for a function parameter means you can omit the parameter value when you call the function; the compiler will substitute the default value on your behalf.

In this exercise, you will define default parameters in one of the function prototypes you declared earlier.

1. Open the Managed C++ Application project from the previous exercise.
2. Find the following function prototype:

```
int GetInvestmentPeriod(int min, int max);
```

3. Modify the function prototype as follows to define default parameter values:

```
int GetInvestmentPeriod(int min=10, int max=25);
```

   This function prototype has two parameters named *min* and *max*. The parameters are followed by an = sign, then a default value. We have defined a default value of 10 for the *min* parameter and a default value of 25 for the *max* parameter. You'll see how to call this function later in this chapter.

4. Build your program.

Defining Function Bodies

In the previous section, you learned how to declare function prototypes. As you saw, a function prototype specifies the name of a function, its parameter list, and its return type. However, function prototypes do not contain any executable statements; they do not indicate what the function will do when it is called.

To provide the behavior for a function, you must define a function body. The function body contains executable statements to perform the desired operations in the function.

In this part of the chapter, you will define function bodies for all the function prototypes introduced earlier.

Defining a Simple Function Body

The following example shows a simple function body, corresponding to the *DisplayWelcome* function prototype you saw earlier:

```
void DisplayWelcome()
```

```
{
  Console::WriteLine(S"-------------------------------------");
    Console::WriteLine(
        S"Welcome to your friendly Investment Planner");
  Console::WriteLine(S"-------------------------------------");
    return;
}
```

Notice that the first line of the function body is identical to the function prototype, except that there is no semicolon. This first line is known as the function header.

After the function header, a pair of braces ({}) encloses the executable statements for the function body. In this example, the *DisplayWelcome* function displays a simple welcome message on the screen. Later in this chapter, you'll see more complex functions that perform Console input and mathematical calculations.

The *return* keyword at the end of the function causes flow of control to return to the calling function. In this example, the *return* keyword is superfluous because the closing brace of the function acts as an implicit return. However, you can use *return* in other locations in a function, such as within an *if* statement, to return prematurely from a function. You'll see more about the *if* statement in Chapter 5.

In this exercise, you will add the *DisplayWelcome* function body to your Visual C++ application.

1. Open the Managed C++ Application project you created earlier in this chapter.
2. Locate the end of the *main* function. On the next line, define the *DisplayWelcome* function body as follows:

```
void DisplayWelcome()
{
    Console::WriteLine(S"--------------------------------");
     Console::WriteLine(
          S"Welcome to your friendly Investment Planner");
    Console::WriteLine(S"--------------------------------");
     return;
}
```

3 Build your program. You shouldn't get any compiler errors.

note

You can define function bodies in any order in Visual C++. For example, you can place the *DisplayWelcome* function body before or after the *main* function body. However, functions cannot be nested. You can't define one function body inside the braces ({}) of another function.

Defining a Function Body that Uses Parameters

When you define a function body that uses parameters, you must define exactly the same number and types of parameters as in the function prototype. This is quite reasonable—the whole point of the function prototype is to introduce the exact signature of the function.

tip

The function body can use different parameter names than the prototype because the parameter names in the prototype are there just for documentation. However, for consistency, you should use the same parameter names in the prototype and the function body.

In this exercise, you will define a function body for the *DisplayProjectedValue* function. You saw the prototype for this function earlier:

```
void DisplayProjectedValue(double amount, int years, double rate);
```

The function body will have the same signature as the prototype and will calculate the projected value of an investment after a specified number of years at a particular growth rate.

1. Open the Managed C++ Application project from the previous exercise.
2. Scroll to the end of the program, and add the following code. This is the start of the *DisplayProjectedValue* function body:

```
void DisplayProjectedValue(double amount, int years, double
   rate)
{
```

3. Next, define some local variables within the function:

```
    double rateFraction = 1 + (rate/100);
    double finalAmount = amount * Math::Pow(rateFraction,
        years);
    finalAmount = Math::Round(finalAmount, 2);
```

Here, the *rateFraction* variable holds the growth rate as a fractional value. For example, if the rate is 6 percent, then *rateFraction* will be 1.06.

The expression *Math::Pow(rateFraction, years)* shows how to raise a number to a power in Visual C++. For example, *Math::Pow(1.06, 3)* is equivalent to 1.06 * 1.06 * 1.06.

The expression *Math::Round(finalAmount, 2)* rounds *finalAmount* to two decimal places. For example, if *finalAmount* is 1000.775, the rounded value will be 1000.78.

4 Now add the following statements to the function to display the result of the calculations:

```
    Console::Write(S"Investment amount: ");
    Console::WriteLine(amount);

    Console::Write(S"Growth rate [%]: ");
    Console::WriteLine(rate);

    Console::Write(S"Period [years]: ");
    Console::WriteLine(years);

    Console::Write(
        S"Projected final value of investment: ");
    Console::WriteLine(finalAmount);

    return;
}
```

5 Build your program.

Defining a Function Body that Returns a Value

When you define a function with a non-*void* return type, you must return an appropriate value from the function. To return a value, use the *return* keyword followed by the value you want to return.

note

If you forget to return a value, you'll get a compiler error on the closing brace of the function. This is the point where the compiler realizes you haven't returned a value from the function.

In this exercise, you will define a function body for the *GetInvestmentAmount* function. This is the prototype for the function, as you saw earlier:

```
double GetInvestmentAmount();
```

The function will ask the user how much money they want to invest. The function will return this value as a *double* data type.

You will also define a function body for the *GetInvestmentPeriod* function. The prototype for this function is:

```
int GetInvestmentPeriod(int min=10, int max=25);
```

The function will ask the user how long they want to invest their money and will return this value as an *int* data type.

1 Open the Managed C++ Application project from the previous exercise.

2 Scroll to the end of the program, and define the *GetInvestmentAmount* function body as follows:

```
double GetInvestmentAmount()
{
    Console::Write(
        S"How much money do you want to invest? ");

    String __gc * input = Console::ReadLine();
    double amount = input->ToDouble(0);

    return amount;
}
```

The first statement displays a prompt message on the Console, asking the user how much money they want to invest. The *Console::ReadLine* function call reads a line of text from the Console keyboard, and the result is assigned to a *String* variable. (You'll learn what the *__gc* syntax means in a later chapter.)

The *input->ToDouble* function call parses the string and converts it to a *double* value. The *return* statement returns this value back to the calling function.

tip

You can declare local variables anywhere in a function. For example, here the *input* and *amount* variables are declared halfway down the *GetInvestmentAmount* function. Typically, you should declare variables at the point where they are first needed in the function. This is different from the C programming language, where you have to declare local variables at the start of a block.

3. Now add the following function body:

```
int GetInvestmentPeriod(int min, int max)
{
    Console::Write(S"Over how many years [");
    Console::Write(S"min=");
    Console::Write(min);
    Console::Write(S", max=");
    Console::Write(max);
    Console::Write(S"] ? ");

    String __gc * input = Console::ReadLine();
    int years = input->ToInt32(0);

    return years;
}
```

The *Console::Write* function calls ask the user to enter a value between *min* and *max*; these values are supplied as parameters into the *GetInvestmentPeriod* function.

The *Console::ReadLine* function call reads the user's input as a *String*, and the *input->ToInt32* function call converts this value into a 32-bit integer. The *return* statement returns this value to the calling function.

note

The function prototype for *GetInvestmentPeriod* declared default values for the *min* and *max* parameters. The default value for *min* is 10, and the default value for *max* is 25. Default values are only specified in the function prototype—you don't mention these default values in the function body. If you accidentally define the default values in the function body as well as in the function prototype, you'll get a compiler error at the function body.

4 Build your program.

Calling Functions

Now that you have defined all the function bodies in the sample application, the last step is to call the functions at the appropriate place in the application.

To call a function, specify its name followed by a pair of parentheses. For example, you can call the *DisplayWelcome* function as follows:

```
DisplayWelcome();
```


This is a simple example because the function doesn't take any parameters or return a value.

If you want to call a function that returns a value, you can assign the return value to a variable. The following example calls the *GetInvestmentAmount* function, and assigns the return value (a *double*) to a local variable named *sum*:

```
double sum = GetInvestmentAmount();
```

> **note**
>
> You can ignore the return value from a function if you want. When you call the function, leave out the assignment operator on the left side of the function name. The function still returns the value, but the value is discarded.

If you want to call a function that takes parameters, pass the parameter values between the parentheses in the function call. The following example calls the *DisplayProjectedValue* function, passing in three literal values as parameters:

```
DisplayProjectedValue(10000, 25, 6.0);
```

> **note**
>
> You don't specify the parameter data types when you call a function. Just provide the parameter values.

The following example shows how to call a function that takes parameters and returns a value. In this example, we call the *GetInvestmentPeriod* function to get a value between 5 and 25. We assign the return value to a local *int* variable named *period*:

```
int period = GetInvestmentPeriod(5, 25);
```

Calling Functions in the Sample Application

In this exercise, you will extend your sample application to include the function calls you've just seen.

1. Open the Managed C++ Application project you created earlier in this chapter.
2. Locate the *main* function. Just after the opening brace ({) of the *main* function, add the following statement. This calls the *DisplayWelcome* function:

```
DisplayWelcome();
```

3. Next, add the following statements to display an illustration of investment growth. The *DisplayProjectedValue* function call will display the value of 10,000 after 25 years, at a growth rate of 6 percent:

```
Console::WriteLine(S"\nIllustration...");
DisplayProjectedValue(10000, 25, 6.0);
```

4. Next, add the following statements to ask the user how much they want to invest and for how long. The *GetInvestmentAmount* and *GetInvestmentPeriod* function calls return these values:

```
Console::WriteLine(
   S"\nEnter details for your investment:");
double sum = GetInvestmentAmount();
int period = GetInvestmentPeriod(5, 25);
```

note

The *GetInvestmentPeriod* function has default values for each of its parameters (the first parameter has a default value of 10, and the second parameter has a default value of 25). You can use these default values when you call the function. For example, the following function call uses the default value for the second parameter:

```
int period = GetInvestmentPeriod(5);    // First parameter is5; second
parameter defaults to 25
```

If you use a default value for a parameter, you must use the default values for each subsequent parameter in the parameter list. For example, the following function call is invalid:

```
int period = GetInvestmentPeriod(, 20);    // Try to use default value
for just the first parameter - illegal.
```

5. Finally, add the following statements to calculate and display the projected

final value of this investment, assuming a growth rate of 6 percent:

```
Console::WriteLine(S"\nYour plan...");
DisplayProjectedValue(sum, period, 6.0);
```

6 Build your program, and fix any compiler errors.

Stepping Through the Application with the Debugger

In this exercise, you will step through the application with the debugger. This will help you understand how the flow of control passes from one function to another in your application.

This exercise will also illustrate the concept of variable scope. You will see how local variables in a function come into scope during the function's execution, and disappear from scope at the end of the function.

1 Open the Managed C++ Application project from the previous exercise.

2 Locate the *main* function.

3 Insert a debug breakpoint by clicking in the gray border to the left of the code. Click next to the *DisplayWelcome* function call, and you should see a red dot appear in the border:

```
(Globals)                                   wmain
// This is the entry point for this application
#ifdef _UNICODE
int wmain(void)
#else
int main(void)
#endif
{
    DisplayWelcome();

    Console::WriteLine(S"\nIllustration...");
    DisplayProjectedValue(10000, 25, 6.0);

    Console::WriteLine(S"\nEnter details for your investment:");
    double sum = GetInvestmentAmount();
    int period = GetInvestmentPeriod(5, 25);

    Console::WriteLine(S"\nYour plan...");
    DisplayProjectedValue(sum, period, 6.0);

    return 0;
}
```

4 Start the debugging session by pressing F5. Once the program has loaded, it will execute and stop at the breakpoint in the *main* function:

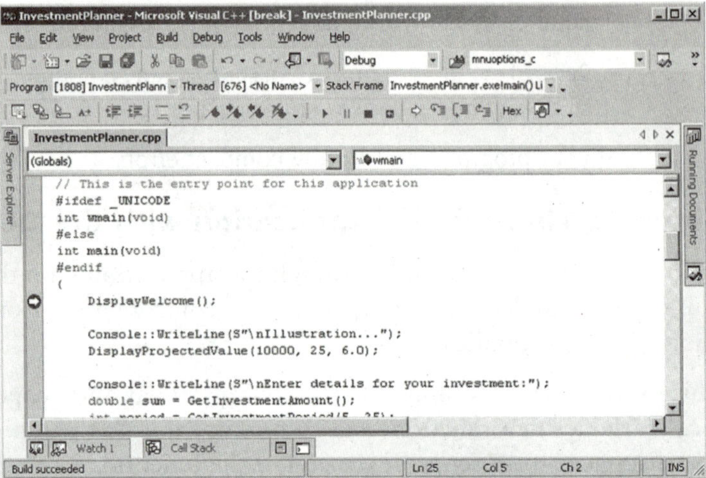

A yellow arrow appears in the margin, next to the *DisplayWelcome* function call. The yellow arrow indicates that this is the next statement to be executed.

5 Press F11 to step into the *DisplayWelcome* function. This debugger calls the *DisplayWelcome* function, and displays a yellow arrow at the start of that function:

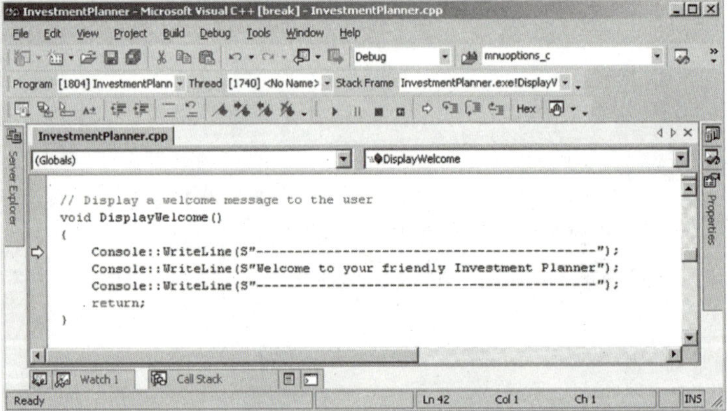

6 Press F10 several times to step over each statement one at a time in the *DisplayWelcome* function. This will cause a welcome message to be displayed in the Console window. At the end of the function, the debugger will return you to the *main* function. The yellow arrow indicates the next statement to execute in *main*:

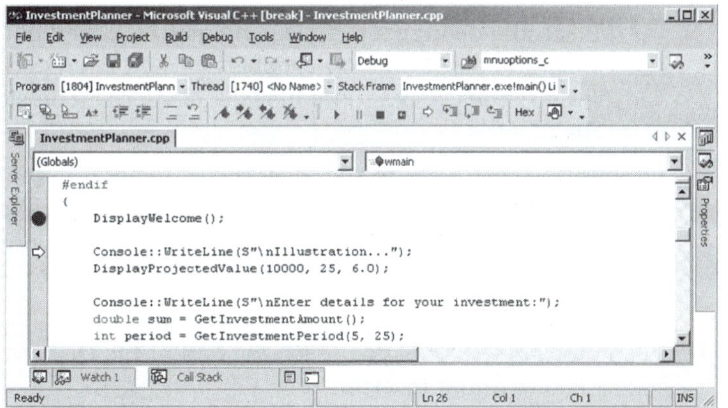

7 Press F10 to step over the *Console::WriteLine* function. The debugger executes the *Console::WriteLine* function, but doesn't take you through it step by step. The yellow arrow moves on to the *DisplayProjectedValue* function call in *main*.

8 Press F11 to step into the *DisplayProjectedValue* function. From the Debug menu, select Windows, then Locals. This displays the local variables in this function:

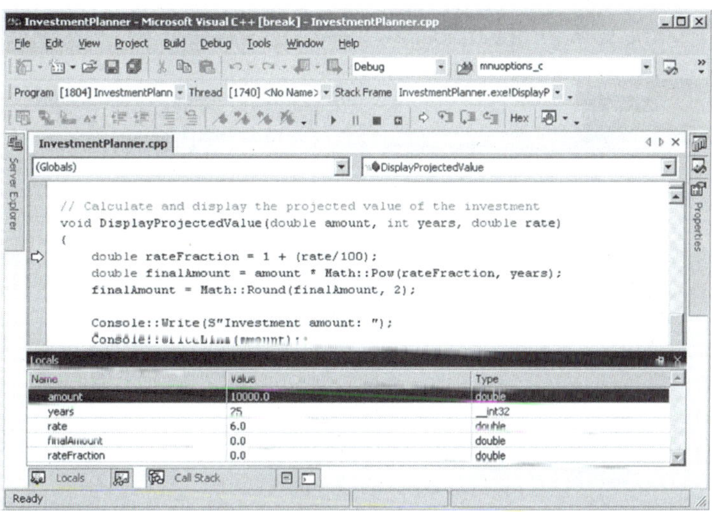

The Locals window displays five local variables. The first three variables—*amount*, *years*, and *rate*—are the function parameters. These variables are already initialized with the values you passed into the function.

The last two variables—*finalAmount* and *rateFraction*—do not have meaningful values. This is because the variables haven't been assigned a value yet. In fact, the debugger is misleading us a little here because the *finalAmount* and *rateFraction* variables haven't been declared yet. These variables don't really exist until the variable declaration statements further on in the function.

9 Press F10 several times to step over the statements in the *DisplayProjectedValue* function. Observe how the *finalAmount* and *rateFraction* variables change during the function (the debugger displays changed values in red, for prominence). Take a look at the Console window to see what is displayed.

10 Keep pressing F10 until you reach the end of the *DisplayProjectedValue* function, and return to *main*.

11 In *main*, press F10 to step over the *Console::WriteLine* statement.

12 Press F11 to step into the *GetInvestmentAmount* function. Step through the statements in this function. When the debugger executes the *ReadLine* statement, the Console window appears and you are asked to enter a number. Enter a number such as 20, and press Enter.

13 Keep stepping through the *GetInvestmentAmount* function until you return to *main*.

14 Press F10 one more time, and then examine the local variables in *main*. Notice that the return value from *GetInvestmentAmount* has been assigned to the *sum* local variable in *main*:

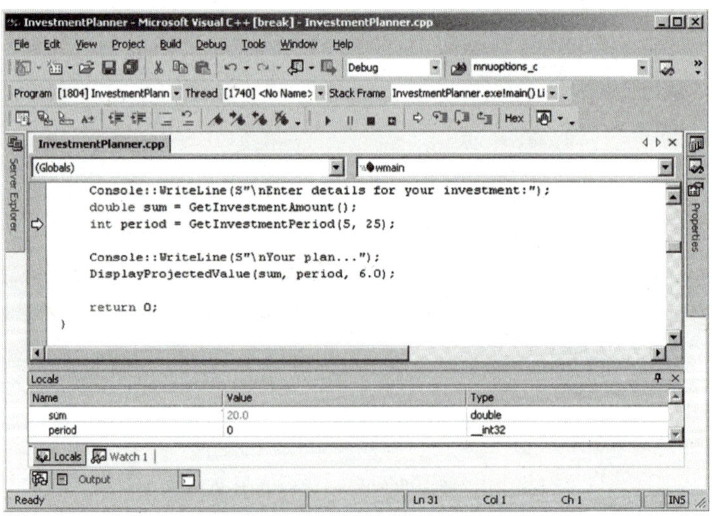

15 Continue stepping through the application in this manner until the application terminates.

tip

If the debugger takes you into a function that you are not interested in stepping through, press Shift+F11 to step out of the function. If you just want to run the application without stopping at all, press F5.

Local and Global Scope

As you saw in the previous exercise, each function defines its own scope for local variables. The local variables are created during function execution, and are automatically destroyed at the end of the function. This means you can quite happily have variables with the same name in different functions, without interference.

It is also possible to declare variables globally, outside of any function. Global variables are visible in all function bodies that come after the global variable definition in your source file. You can use global variables as a rudimentary way of sharing information between multiple functions.

caution

Global variables are generally considered bad programming practice, especially in object-oriented languages such as C++. Global variables have too much visibility: If a global variable gets corrupted, it's difficult to pinpoint where the problem occurred. Global variables also introduce too much dependency between functions.

For these reasons, you should use global variables sparingly. A better way of sharing information between functions is to pass parameters and return values, as you saw earlier in this chapter.

In this exercise, you will define a global variable in your application. You will use this global variable in several functions to illustrate its global scope.

1. Open the Managed C++ Application project you created earlier in this chapter.
2. Before the start of the *main* function, define a global integer variable named *numberOfYourFunctionsCalled*, as follows:

```
// Define and initialize a global integer variable
int numberOfYourFunctionsCalled = 0;

// This is the entry point for this application
#ifdef _UNICODE
int wmain(void)
#else
int main(void)
#endif
{
    DisplayWelcome();

    Console::WriteLine(S"\nIllustration...");
```

3 Find the *DisplayWelcome* function in your code. At the start of this function, increment the *numberOfYourFunctionsCalled* variable as follows:

```
// Display a welcome message to the user
void DisplayWelcome()
{
    numberOfYourFunctionsCalled++;

    Console::WriteLine(S"------------------------------------------");
    Console::WriteLine(S"Welcome to your friendly Investment Planner");
    Console::WriteLine(S"------------------------------------------");
    return;
}
```

4 Add a similar statement to the start of every function in your application.

5 Modify the *main* function. At the end of this function, just before the *return* statement, display the value of the *numberOfYourFunctionsCalled* variable:

```
int wmain(void)
#else
int main(void)
#endif
{
    DisplayWelcome();

    Console::WriteLine(S"\nIllustration...");
    DisplayProjectedValue(10000, 25, 6.0);

    Console::WriteLine(S"\nEnter details for your investment:");
    double sum = GetInvestmentAmount();
    int period = GetInvestmentPeriod(5, 25);

    Console::WriteLine(S"\nYour plan...");
    DisplayProjectedValue(sum, period, 6.0);

    Console::Write(S"\nNumber of your functions called: ");
    Console::WriteLine(numberOfYourFunctionsCalled);

    return 0;
}
```

6 Build and run your program. How many of your functions are called during the program?

Function Overloading

Visual C++ lets you provide many functions with the same name, as long as each function has a different parameter list. This is known as function overloading. Function overloading is useful if you have several different ways of performing a particular operation, based on different input parameters.

For example, you might want to provide an *average* function to find the average value of two *double* values, and another *average* function to find the average value of an array of integers. You can define two functions to support these requirements. Give each function the same name, *average*, to emphasize the common purpose of these functions. Define different parameter lists for the functions, to differentiate one from another:

```
double average(double number1, double number2);
double average(int array[], int arraySize);
```

You must still implement both of these functions—there is no magic here! When you call the *average* function, the compiler deduces which version of the function to call based on the parameter values you supply.

note

If you define overloaded functions, the functions must have a different parameter list. If you define overloaded functions that differ only in their return type, you'll get a compiler error.

In this exercise, you will define an overloaded version of the *DisplayProjectedValue* function. The new version will calculate a random growth rate between 0 and 20 percent, rather than use a specific growth rate.

1. Open the Managed C++ Application project you created earlier in this chapter.
2. Add the following function prototype at the start of your code, near the other function prototypes:

   ```
   void DisplayProjectedValue(double amount, int years);
   ```

3. In the *main* function, locate the second call to the *DisplayProjectedValue* function. Modify the function call so that you only pass two parameters into the function:

   ```
   DisplayProjectedValue(sum, period);
   ```

4. At the end of the program, define the new *DisplayProjectedValue* function body as follows:

```
void DisplayProjectedValue(double amount, int years)
{
    Random __gc * r = new Random();
    int randomRate = r->Next(0, 20);
    DisplayProjectedValue(amount, years, randomRate);
}
```

   This function uses the *Random* class to calculate a random number between 0 and 20. The function passes the random number into the original version of the *DisplayProjectedValue* function to calculate the value of the investment using this random rate.

5. Define breakpoints at the start of both of the *DisplayProjectedValue* functions.
6. Build the program, and start it in the debugger.
7. Observe which versions of *DisplayProjectedValue* are called as your program executes. See what random number the program uses for your growth rate.
8. Run the program several times to verify that the growth rate really is random.

Chapter 4 Quick Reference

To	Do This
Declare a function prototype	Specify the return type of the function, followed by the function name, followed by the parameter list enclosed in parentheses. Remember the semicolon at the end of the function prototype. For example: `double MyFunction(int p1, short p2);`
Define default parameters	Define default parameters in the function prototype, if required. Use an = operator, followed by the default value. For example: `double MyFunction(int p1, short p2=100);`

Define a function body	Specify the return type of the function, followed by the function name, followed by the parameter list enclosed in parentheses. Do not specify default parameters here. Define the function body within braces. For example:
	`double MyFunction(int p1, short p2)`
	`{`
	`    int n = p1 + p2;`
	`    ...`
	`}`

Return a value from a function	Use the *return* keyword, followed by the value you want to return. For example: `return (p1 + p2) / 2.00;`
Call a function	Specify the function name, and pass parameter values within parentheses. If the function returns a value, you can assign it to a variable. For example: `double result = MyFunction(100, 175);`

Define and use global variables	Define the global variable outside of any function. Use the variable in any subsequent function in the source file. For example:
	`int myGlobal = 0;`
	`void MyFunction()`
	`{`
	`    myGlobal++;`
	`    ...`
	`}`

Define and use overloaded functions	Define several functions with the same name but different parameter lists. Implement each function. Call the version you want, using appropriate parameter values. For example:
	`// Prototypes`
	`void MyFunction(int p1);`
	`void MyFunction(double p1, double p2);`
	`...`
	`// Function calls`
	`MyFunction(100);`
	`MyFunction(2.5, 7.5);`
	`...`
	`// Function bodies`
	`void MyFunction(int p1)`
	`{`
	`    ...`
	`}`
	`void MyFunction(double p1, double p2)`
	`{`
	`    ...`
	`}`

Decision and Loop Statements

In this chapter, you'll learn how to

- ✔ *Make decisions by using the* if *statement*
- ✔ *Make multi-way decisions by using the* switch *statement*
- ✔ *Perform loops by using the* while, for, *and* do-while *statements*
- ✔ *Perform unconditional jumps in a loop by using the* break *and* continue *statements*

All high-level languages provide keywords that enable you to make decisions and perform loops. C++ is no exception. C++ provides the *if* statement and the *switch* statement for making decisions, and the *while*, *for*, and *do-while* statements for performing loops. In addition, C++ provides the *break* statement to exit a loop immediately, and the *continue* statement to return to the start of the loop for the next iteration.

In this chapter, you will see how to use these statements to control the flow of execution through a Microsoft Visual C++ application.

Making Decisions with the *if* Statement

The most common way to make a decision in Visual C++ is to use the *if* statement. You can use the *if* statement to perform a one-way test, a two-way test, a multi-way test, or a nested test. Let's consider a simple one way test first.

Performing One-Way Tests

The following illustration shows a simple one-way test:

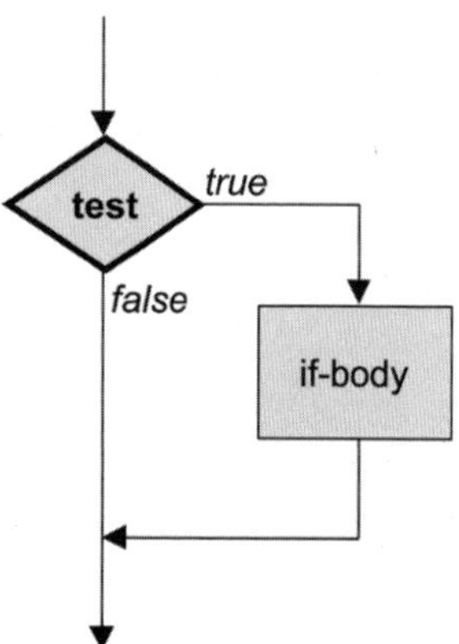

The following example shows how to define a one-way test in Visual C++:

```
if (number < 0)
    Console::WriteLine(S"The number is negative");
Console::WriteLine(S"The end");
```

The *if* keyword is followed by a conditional expression, enclosed in parentheses (the parentheses are mandatory). If the conditional expression evaluates to true, the next statement is executed—the message *The number is negative* will be displayed. Note that the message *The end* will always be executed, regardless of the outcome of the test, because it is outside the *if*-body.

note

There is no semicolon after the closing parenthesis in the *if*-test. One of the most common programming errors in C++ is to put one in by mistake:

```
if (number < 0);    // Note the spurious semicolon
```

This is equivalent to the following statement, which is probably not what you intended:

```
if (number < 0)
    ;   // Null if-body - do nothing if number < 0
```

If you want to include more than one statement in the *if*-body, enclose the *if*-body in braces ({}) as follows:

```
if (number < 0)
{
    Console::Write(S"The number ");
    Console::Write(number);
    Console::WriteLine(S" is negative");
}
Console::WriteLine(S"The end");
```


tip

It's good practice to enclose the *if*-body in braces, even if it only comprises a single statement. This is defensive programming, in case you (or another developer) add more statements to the *if*-body in the future.

In this exercise, you will create a new application to perform one-way tests. As this chapter progresses, you will extend the application to use more complex decision-making constructs and to perform loops.

For now, the application will ask the user to enter a date, then it will perform simple validation and display the date in a user-friendly format on the console.

1 Start Microsoft Visual Studio .NET and open a new Managed C++ Application project.

2 At the top of the file, immediately under the *using namespace System;* line, add the following function prototypes (you will implement all these functions during this chapter):

```
int GetYear();
```

```
int GetMonth();
int GetDay(int year, int month);
void DisplayDate(int year, int month, int day);
```

3 At the end of the file, after the end of the *main* function, implement the *GetYear* function as follows:

```
int GetYear()
{
    Console::Write(S"Year? ");
    String * input = Console::ReadLine();
    int year = input->ToInt32(0);
    return year;
}
```

4 Implement the *GetMonth* function as follows (this is a simplified implementation; later in this chapter, you will enhance the function to ensure the user enters a valid month):

```
int GetMonth()
{
    Console::Write(S"Month? ");
    String * input = Console::ReadLine();
    int month = input->ToInt32(0);
    return month;
}
```

5 Implement the *GetDay* function as follows (you will enhance this function later to ensure the user enters a valid day in the given year and month):

```
int GetDay(int year, int month)
{
    Console::Write(S"Day? ");
    String * input = Console::ReadLine();
    int day = input->ToInt32(0);
    return day;
}
```

6 Implement the *DisplayDate* function as follows to display the date as three numbers (later, you will enhance this function to display the date in a more user-friendly format):

```
void DisplayDate(int year, int month, int day)
{
    Console::WriteLine(S"\nThis is the date you entered:");
    Console::Write(year);
    Console::Write(S"-");
```

```
    Console::Write(month);
    Console::Write(S"-");
    Console::Write(day);
    Console::WriteLine();
}
```

7 Finally, add the following code inside the *main* method. This code asks the user to enter a year, month, and day. If the date passes a simplified validation test, the date is displayed on the console. If the date is invalid, it is not displayed at all:

```
Console::WriteLine(S"Welcome to your calendar assistant");
Console::WriteLine(S"\nPlease enter a date");
int year = GetYear();
int month = GetMonth();
int day = GetDay(year, month);

// Simplified test for now - assume there are 31 days in
// every month :-)
if (month >= 1 && month <= 12 && day >= 1 && day <= 31)
{
    DisplayDate(year, month, day);
}
Console::WriteLine(S"\nThe end\n");
```


note

This *if* statement combines several tests by using the logical *and* operator *&&*. As you learned in Chapter 3, logical tests are performed from left to right. Testing stops as soon as the final outcome is known for sure. For example, if the month is 0, there is no point performing the other tests—the date is definitely invalid. This is known as shortcut evaluation.

8 Build the program, and fix any compiler errors that you might have.

9 Run the program. Enter valid numbers for the year, month, and day (for example, 2001, 12, and 31). The program displays the following messages:

```
Welcome to your calendar assistant

Please enter a date
Year? 2001
Month? 12
Day? 31

This is the date you entered:
2001-12-31

The end

Press any key to continue
```

Notice that the program displays the date because it is valid. The message The end is also displayed at the end of the program.

10 Run the program again, but this time enter an invalid date (for example, 2001, 0, and 31). The program displays the following messages:

```
Welcome to your calendar assistant

Please enter a date
Year? 2001
Month? 0
Day? 31

The end

Press any key to continue
```

Notice that the program doesn't display the date because the date is invalid. Instead, the program just displays The end at the end of the program. You can make the program more user-friendly by displaying an error message if the date is invalid. To do this, use a two-way test.

Performing Two-Way Tests

The following illustration shows a simple two-way test:

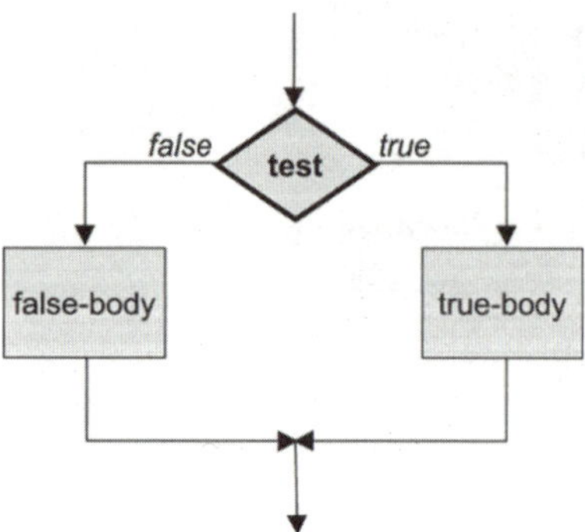

The following code shows how to define a two-way test for the Calendar Assistant application:

```
if (month >= 1 && month <= 12 && day >= 1 && day <= 31)
{
    DisplayDate(year, month, day);
}
else
{
    Console::WriteLine(S"Invalid date");
}
Console::WriteLine(S"\nThe end\n");
```

The *else*-body defines what action to perform if the test condition fails.

In this exercise, you will enhance your Calendar Assistant application to display an error message if an invalid date is entered.

1. Open the Managed C++ Application project from the previous exercise.
2. Modify the *main* function so that it uses an *if-else* statement to test for valid or invalid dates:

```
if (month >= 1 && month <= 12 && day >= 1 && day <= 31)
{
    DisplayDate(year, month, day);
}
else
{
    Console::WriteLine(S"Invalid date");
}
Console::WriteLine(S"\nThe end\n");
```

3. Build and run the program. Enter an invalid date, such as 2001, 0, and 31. The program now displays an error message, as follows:

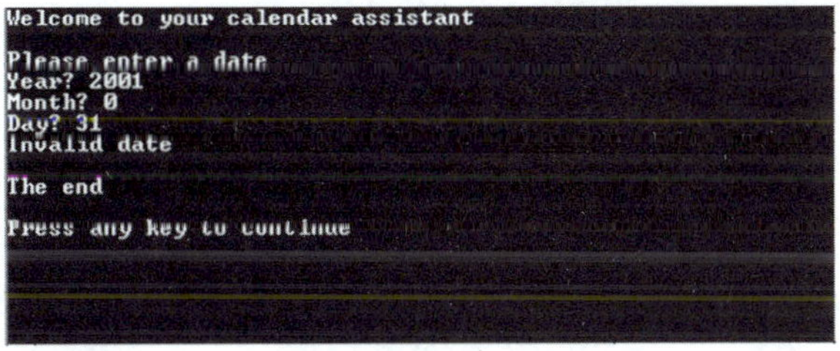

```
Welcome to your calendar assistant

Please enter a date
Year? 2001
Month? 0
Day? 31
Invalid date

The end

Press any key to continue
```

Performing Multi-Way Tests

You can arrange *if-else* statements in a cascading fashion to achieve multi-way decision making. The following illustration shows multi-way testing in a flowchart:

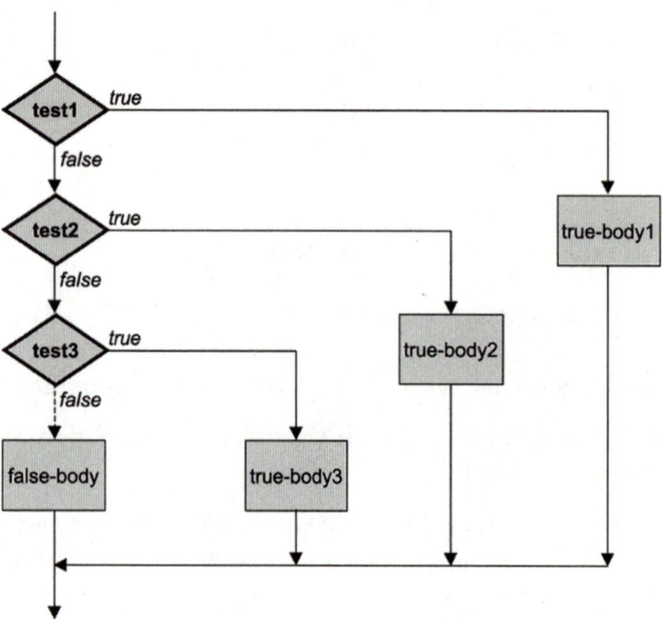

The following code shows how to use a multi-way test to determine the maximum number of days (*maxDay*) in a month:

```
int maxDay;
if (month == 4 || month == 6 || month == 9 || month == 11)
{
    maxDay = 30;
}
else if (month == 2)
{
    maxDay = 28;
}
else
{
    maxDay = 31;
}
```

If the month is April, June, September, or November, *maxDay* is set to 30. If the month is February, *maxDay* is set to 28. (We'll ignore leap years for now!) If the month is anything else, *maxDay* is set to 31.

> **note**
>
> There is a space between the keywords *else* and *if* because they are distinct keywords. This is unlike Microsoft Visual Basic .NET, which has the single keyword *ElseIf*.

In this exercise, you will enhance your Calendar Assistant application to display the maximum number of days in the user's chosen month.

1. Open the Managed C++ Application project from the previous exercise.
2. Modify the *GetDay* function so that it uses an *if-else-if* statement to determine the maximum allowable number of days:

```
int GetDay(int year, int month)
{
    int maxDay;
    if (month == 4 || month == 6 || month == 9 || month ==
11)
    {
        maxDay = 30;
    }
    else if (month == 2)
    {
        maxDay = 28;
    }
    else
    {
        maxDay = 31;
    }
    Console::Write(S"Day [1 to ");
    Console::Write(maxDay);
    Console::Write(S"]? ");

    String * input = Console::ReadLine();
    int day = input->ToInt32(0);
    return day;
}
```

3. Build and run the program. Enter the year **2001** and the month **1**.

   The program prompts you to enter a day between 1 and 31:

```
Welcome to your calendar assistant

Please enter a date
Year? 2001
Month? 1
Day [1 to 31]? _
```

Enter a valid day, and close the Console window when the date is displayed.

4 Run the program again. Enter the year **2001** and the month **2**. The program prompts you to enter a day between 1 and 28:

```
Welcome to your calendar assistant

Please enter a date
Year? 2001
Month? 2
Day [1 to 28]?
```

Enter a valid day, and close the Console window when the date is displayed. (Don't worry about the date validation in *main*. You will remove this later, and replace it with more comprehensive validation in the *GetMonth* and *GetDay* functions.)

Performing Nested Tests

You can perform nested tests, as shown in the following illustration:

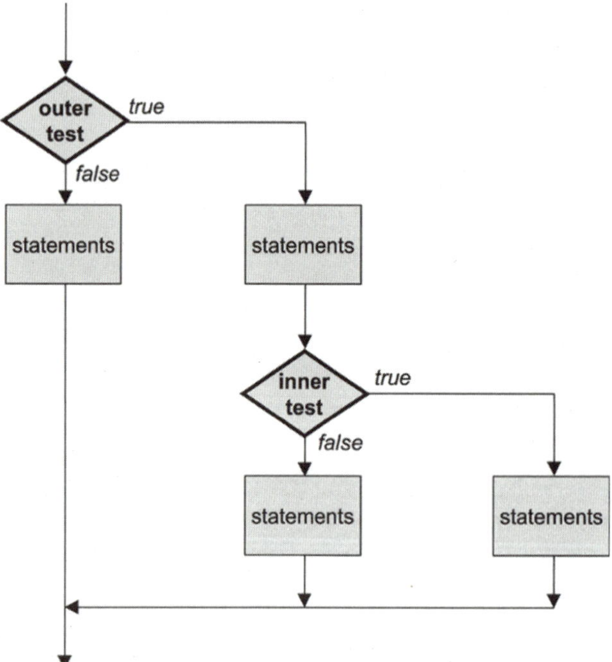

The following code shows how to use nested tests to process leap years correctly in the Calendar Assistant application:

```
int maxDay;
if (month == 4 || month == 6 || month == 9 || month == 11)
{
    maxDay = 30;
}
else if (month == 2)
{
    bool isLeapYear = (year % 4 == 0 && year % 100 != 0) || (year %
400 == 0);
    if (isLeapYear)
    {
        maxDay = 29;
    }
    else
    {
        maxDay = 28;
    }
}
else
{
    maxDay = 31;
}
```


If the month is February, we define a *bool* variable to determine if the year is a leap year. A year is a leap year if it is evenly divisible by 4 but not evenly divisible by 100 (except years that are evenly divisible by 400, which are leap years). The following table shows some examples of leap years and non-leap years.

Year	Leap year?
1996	Yes
1997	No
1900	No
2000	Yes

We then use a nested *if* statement to test the *bool* variable *isLeapYear*, so that we can assign an appropriate value to *maxDay*.

> **note**
>
> There is no explicit test in the nested *if* statement. The condition *if (isLeapYear)* is equivalent to *if (isLeapYear != false)*.

In this exercise, you will enhance your Calendar Assistant application to deal correctly with leap years.

1. Open the Managed C++ Application project from the previous exercise.
2. Modify the *GetDay* function as just described to test for leap years.
3. Build and run the program. Enter the year **1996** and the month **2**. The program prompts you to enter a day between 1 and 29. Enter a valid day, and close the Console window when the date is displayed.
4. Run the program again. Enter the year **1997** and the month **2**. Verify that the program prompts you to enter a day between 1 and 28.
5. Run the program several more times, using the test data from the previous table.

Making Decisions with the *switch* Statement

Now that you have seen how the *if* statement works, let's take a look at the *switch* statement. The *switch* statement enables you to test a single variable, and to execute one of several branches depending on its value.

Defining Simple *switch* Statements

The following illustration shows how the *switch* statement works:

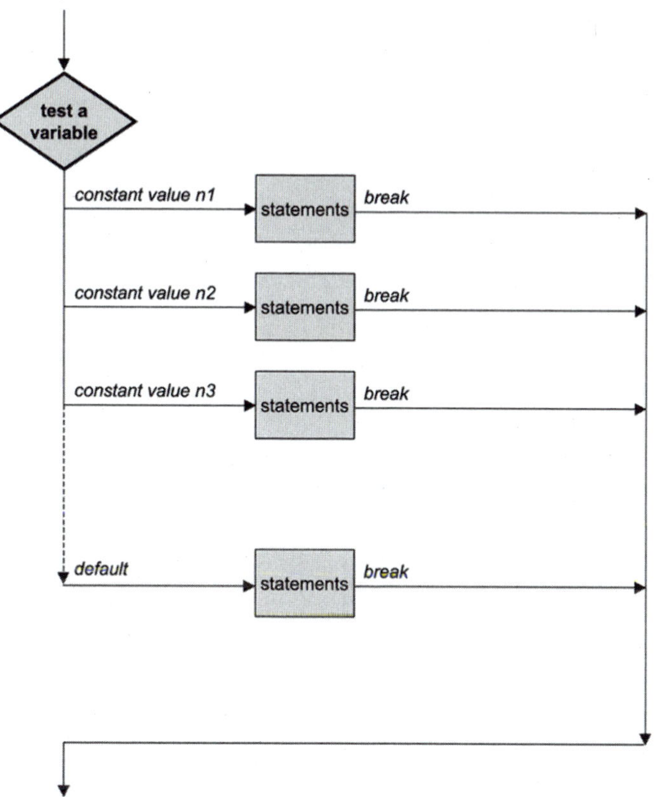

The following example shows the syntax for the *switch* statement. The *switch* statement tests the *numberOfSides* in a shape, and displays a message to describe that shape:

```
int numberOfSides;    // Number of sides in a shape
...
switch (numberOfSides)
{
    case 3:  Console::Write(S"Triangle");      break;
    case 4:  Console::Write(S"Quadrilateral"); break;
    case 5:  Console::Write(S"Pentagon");      break;
    case 6:  Console::Write(S"Hexagon");       break;
    case 7:  Console::Write(S"Septagon");      break;
    case 8:  Console::Write(S"Octagon");       break;
    case 9:  Console::Write(S"Nonagon");       break;
    case 10: Console::Write(S"Decagon");       break;
    default: Console::Write(S"Polygon");       break;
}
```

The *switch* keyword is followed by an expression in parentheses, (The expression must evaluate to an integer-based value, a character, or an enumeration value.) Next, a series of *case* branches are defined within braces.

note

Each *case* label specifies a single constant number. You can't specify multiple values, and you can't define a range of values.

Each *case* branch can contain any number of statements. At the end of each branch, use a *break* statement to exit the *switch* statement.

note

There is no need to use braces within each *case* branch. The *break* statement marks the end of each *case* branch.

You can define an optional *default* branch in the *switch* statement. The *default* branch will be executed if the expression doesn't match any of the *case* labels.

tip

It's good practice to define a *default* branch, even if you don't have any specific processing to perform. Including the *default* branch shows that you haven't just forgotten it. Also, the *default* branch can help you trap unexpected values and display a suitable warning to the user.

In this exercise, you will enhance your Calendar Assistant application to display the month as a string such as *January*, *February*, and so on.

1. Open the Managed C++ Application project from the previous exercise.
2. Modify the *DisplayDate* function. Rather than displaying the month as an integer, use a *switch* statement to display the month as a string instead:

```
switch (month)
{
    case 1:  Console::Write(S" January ");   break;
    case 2:  Console::Write(S" February "); break;
    case 3:  Console::Write(S" March ");     break;
```

```
        case 4:  Console::Write(S" April ");     break;
        case 5:  Console::Write(S" May ");       break;
        case 6:  Console::Write(S" June ");      break;
        case 7:  Console::Write(S" July ");      break;
        case 8:  Console::Write(S" August ");    break;
        case 9:  Console::Write(S" September "); break;
        case 10: Console::Write(S" October ");   break;
        case 11: Console::Write(S" November ");  break;
        case 12: Console::Write(S" December ");  break;
        default: Console::Write(S" Unknown ");   break;
    }
```

3. Build the program.
4. Run the program several times, and enter a different month each time. Verify that the program displays the correct month name each time.

Defining Fall-Through in a *switch* Statement

If you omit the *break* statement at the end of a *case* branch, flow of control continues on to the next statement. This is called fall-through.

The following example illustrates why this might be useful. This example tests a lowercase letter to see if it is a vowel or a consonant:

```
char lowercaseLetter;   // Single lowercase letter, for example 'a'
…
switch (lowercaseLetter)
{
    case 'a':
    case 'e':
    case 'i':
    case 'o':
    case 'u':  Console::Write(S"Vowel"); break;

    default:   Console::Write(S"Consonant"); break;
}
```

There is no *break* statement in the first four *case* labels. Flow of control passes on to the next executable statement to display the message *Vowel*. The *default* branch deals with all the other letters and displays the message *Consonant*.

Using Fall-Through in a *switch* Statement

In this exercise, you will enhance your Calendar Assistant application to display the season for the user's date.

1. Open the Managed C++ Application project from the previous exercise.
2. Modify the *DisplayDate* function. After displaying the year, month, and day, add the following code to display the season:

```
switch (month)
{
    case 12:
    case 1:
    case 2:  Console::WriteLine(S" [Winter]"); break;

    case 3:
    case 4:
    case 5:  Console::WriteLine(S" [Spring]"); break;

    case 6:
    case 7:
    case 8:  Console::WriteLine(S" [Summer]"); break;

    case 9:
    case 10:
    case 11: Console::WriteLine(S" [Fall]"); break;
}
```

3. Build the program.
4. Run the program several times, and enter a different month each time. Verify that the program displays the correct season name each time.

Performing Loops

For the rest of this chapter, we will see how to perform loops in Visual C++. We'll also see how to perform unconditional jumps in a loop by using the *break* and *continue* statements.

Visual C++ has three loop constructs: the *while* loop, the *for* loop, and the *do-while* loop. Let's look at the *while* loop first.

Using *while* Loops

The following illustration shows a simple *while* loop:

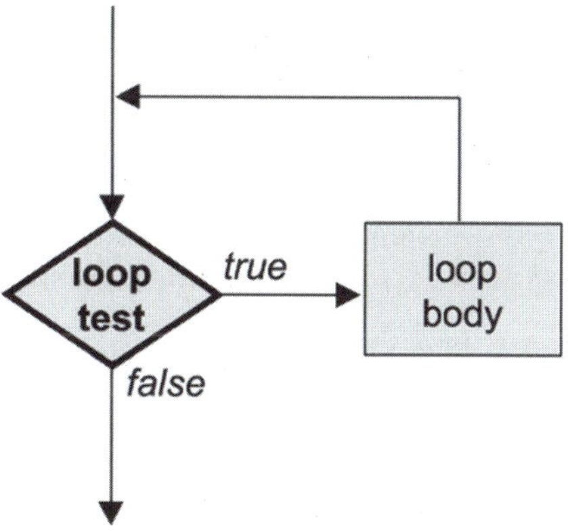

The following example shows how to write a simple *while* loop in Visual C++:

```
int count = 1;
while (count <= 5)
{
    Console::WriteLine(count * count);
    count++;
}
Console::WriteLine(S"The end");
```

The *while* keyword is followed by a conditional expression, enclosed in parentheses. (The parentheses are mandatory.) If the conditional expression evaluates to *true*, the *while* body is executed. After the loop body has been executed, control returns to the *while* statement and the conditional expression is tested again. This sequence continues until the test evaluates to *false*.

tip

Remember to include some kind of update statement in the loop, so that the loop will terminate eventually. The update statement in the example above is *count++*, to increment the loop counter. If you don't provide an update statement the loop will iterate forever.

The example above displays the following output:

```
1
4
9
16
25
The end
Press any key to continue_
```

In this exercise, you will enhance your Calendar Assistant application so that the user can enter five dates.

1. Open the Managed C++ Application project from the previous exercise.
2. Modify the code in the *main* function to enable the user to enter five dates:

```
Console::WriteLine(S"Welcome to your calendar assistant");

int count = 1;     // Declare and initialize the loop counter
    while (count <= 5)    // Test the loop counter
    {
        Console::Write(S"\nPlease enter date ");
        Console::WriteLine(count);

        int year = GetYear();
        int month = GetMonth();
        int day = GetDay(year, month);
        DisplayDate(year, month, day);

        count++;    // Increment the loop counter
    }
```

3. Build and run the program. The program prompts you to enter the first date. After you have entered this date, the program prompts you to enter the second date. This continues until you have entered five dates, at which point the program closes:

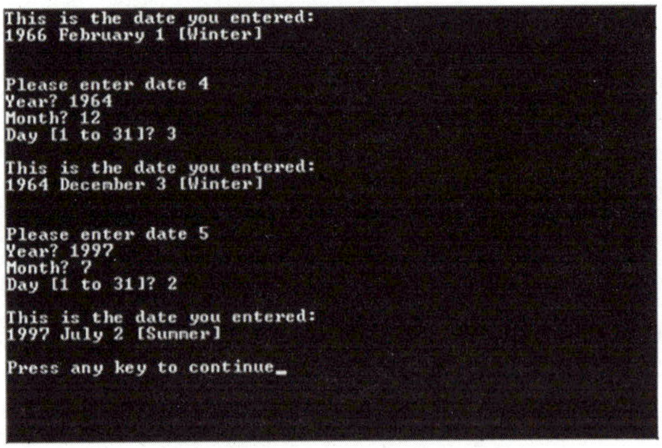

```
This is the date you entered:
1966 February 1 [Winter]

Please enter date 4
Year? 1964
Month? 12
Day [1 to 31]? 3

This is the date you entered:
1964 December 3 [Winter]

Please enter date 5
Year? 1997
Month? 7
Day [1 to 31]? 2

This is the date you entered:
1997 July 2 [Summer]

Press any key to continue_
```

Using *for* Loops

The *for* loop is an alternative to the *while* loop. The flowchart in the following illustration shows a simple *for* loop:

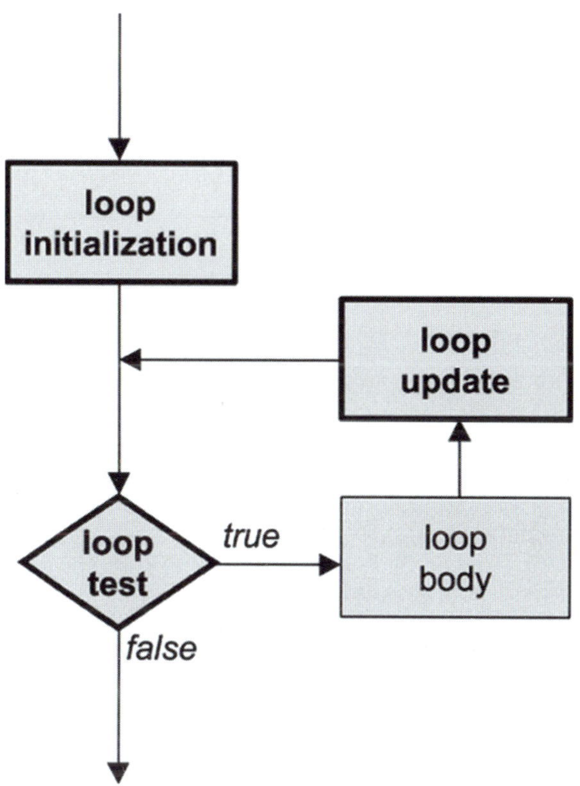

The following example shows how to write a simple *for* loop in Visual C++. This example has exactly the same effect as the *while* loop you saw earlier:

```
for (int count = 1; count <= 5; count++)
{
    Console::WriteLine(count * count);
}
Console::WriteLine(S"The end");
```

The parentheses after the *for* keyword contain three expressions separated by semicolons. The first expression performs loop initialization, such as setting loop counters (the initialization expression is performed once only, at the start of the loop).

note

You can declare loop variables in the first expression of the *for* statement. The example above illustrates this technique. The *count* variable is local to the *for* statement, and goes out of scope when the loop terminates.

The second expression in the *for* statement defines a test. If the test evaluates to *true*, the loop body is executed. After the loop body has been executed, the final expression in the *for* statement is executed; this performs loop update operations, such as incrementing loop counters.

note

The *for* statement is very flexible. You can omit any of the three expressions in the *for* construct, as long as you retain the semicolon separators. You can even omit all three expressions, as in *for(; ;)*. This represents an infinite loop.

The preceding example displays the following output:

```
1
4
9
16
25
The end
Press any key to continue_
```

In this exercise, you will modify your Calendar Assistant application so that it uses a *for* loop rather than a *while* loop to obtain five dates from the user.

1. Open the Managed C++ Application project from the previous exercise.
2. Modify the code in the *main* function to use a *for* loop rather than a *while* loop:

```
Console::WriteLine(S"Welcome to your calendar assistant");

for(int count = 1; count <= 5; count++)
{
    Console::Write(S"\nPlease enter date ");
    Console::WriteLine(count);

    int year = GetYear();
    int month = GetMonth();
```

```
        int day = GetDay(year, month);
        DisplayDate(year, month, day);
    }
```

Notice there is no *count++* statement after displaying the date because the *for* statement takes care of incrementing the loop counter.

3 Build and run the program. The program asks you to enter five dates, as before.

Using *do-while* Loops

The third and final loop construct in Visual C++ is the *do-while* loop. The *do-while* loop is fundamentally different from the *while* loop and the *for* loop because the test comes at the end of the loop body. This means the loop body is always executed at least once in a *do-while* loop.

The following illustration shows a simple *do-while* loop:

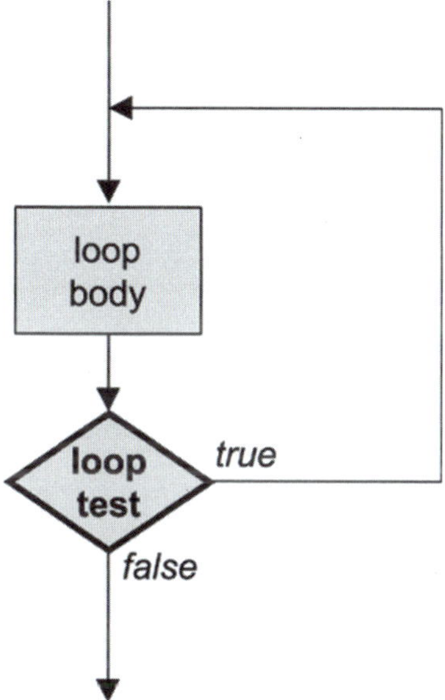

The following example shows how to write a simple *do-while* loop in Visual C++. This example generates random numbers between 1 and 6 inclusive to simulate a die, and counts how many throws are needed to get a 6:

```
Random * r = new Random();
int randomNumber;
int throws = 0;
do
{
```

```
        randomNumber = r->Next(1, 7);
        Console::WriteLine(randomNumber);
        throws++;
    }
    while (randomNumber != 6);

    Console::Write(S"You took ");
    Console::Write(throws);
    Console::WriteLine(" tries to get a 6");
```

The loop starts with the *do* keyword, followed by the loop body, followed by the *while* keyword and the test condition. A semicolon is required after the closing parenthesis of the test condition.

The example above displays the following output:

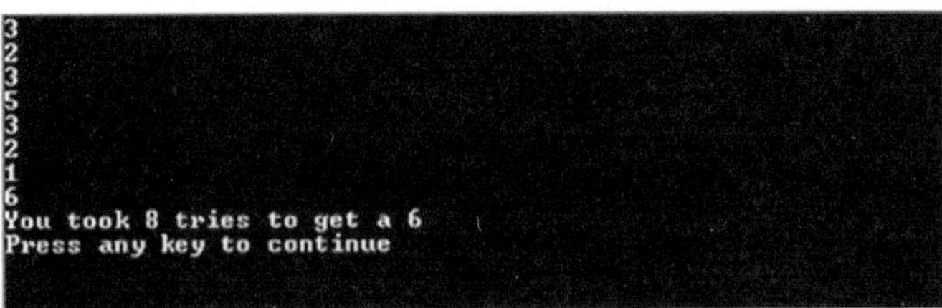

In this exercise, you will modify your Calendar Assistant application so that it performs input validation. This is a typical use of the *do-while* loop.

1 Open the Managed C++ Application project from the previous exercise.

2 Modify the *GetMonth* function as follows, so that it forces the user to enter a valid month:

```
int GetMonth()
{
    int month = 0;
    do
    {
        Console::Write(S"Month [1 to 12]? ");
        String * input = Console::ReadLine();
        month = input->ToInt32(0);
    }
    while (month < 1 || month > 12);
    return month;
}
```

3 Modify the *GetDay* function as follows, so that it forces the user to enter a valid day:

```
int GetDay(int year, int month)
{
    int day = 0;
    int maxDay;

    // Calculate maxDay, as before (code not shown here) … …
…

    do
    {
        Console::Write(S"Day [1 to ");
        Console::Write(maxDay);
        Console::Write(S"]? ");
        String * input = Console::ReadLine();
        day = input->ToInt32(0);
    }
    while (day < 1 || day > maxDay);
    return day;
}
```

4 Build and run the program.

5 Try to enter an invalid month. The program keeps asking you to enter another month until you enter a value between 1 and 12 inclusive.

6 Try to enter an invalid day. The program keeps asking you to enter another day until you enter a valid number (which depends on your chosen year and month).

Performing Unconditional Jumps

Visual C++ provides two keywords—*break* and *continue*—that enable you to jump unconditionally in a loop. The *break* statement causes you to exit the loop immediately. The *continue* statement abandons the current iteration, and goes back to the top of the loop ready for the next iteration.

tip

The *break* and *continue* statements can make it difficult to understand the logical flow through a loop. Use *break* and *continue* sparingly to avoid complicating your code unnecessarily.

In this exercise, you will modify the main loop in your Calendar Assistant application. You will give the user the chance to break from the loop prematurely, skip the current date and continue on to the next one, or display the current date as normal.

1. Open the Managed C++ Application project from the previous exercise.
2. Modify the *main* function as follows to enable the user to *break* or *continue* if desired:

```
Console::WriteLine(S"Welcome to your calendar assistant");
for (int count = 1; count <= 5; count++)
{
    Console::Write(S"\nPlease enter date ");
    Console::WriteLine(count);
    int year = GetYear();
    int month = GetMonth();
    int day = GetDay(year, month);

    Console::Write(S"Press B (break), C (continue), or
                   S"anything else to display date ");
    String * input = Console::ReadLine();
    if (input->Equals(S"B"))
    {
        break;
    }
    else if (input->Equals(S"C"))
    {
        continue;
    }
    DisplayDate(year, month, day);
}
```

3. Build and run the program.
4. After you have entered the first date, you will be asked whether you want to break or continue. Press X (or any other key except B or C) to display the date as normal.
5. Enter the second date, and then press C. This causes the *continue* statement to be executed, which abandons the current iteration without displaying your date. Instead, you are asked to enter the third date.
6. Enter the third date, and then press B. This causes the *break* statement to be executed, which terminates the entire loop.

Chapter 5 Quick Reference

To	Do This

Perform a one-way test	Use the *if* keyword, followed by a test enclosed in parentheses. You must enclose the *if*-body in braces if it contains more than one statement.
	For example:
	`if (n < 0)`
	`{`
	`    Console::Write(S"The number ");`
	`    Console::Write(n);`
	`    Console::WriteLine(S" is negative");`
	`}`

Perform a two-way test	Use an *if-else* construct. For example:
	`if (n < 0)`
	`{`
	`    Console::Write(S"Negative");`
	`}`
	`else`
	`{`
	`    Console::Write(S"Not negative");`
	`}`

Perform a multi-way test	Use an *if-else-if* construct. For example:
	`if (n < 0)`
	`{`
	`    Console::Write(S"Negative");`
	`}`
	`else if (n == 0)`
	`{`
	`    Console::Write(S"Zero");`
	`}`
	`else`
	`{`
	`    Console::Write(S"Positive");`
	`}`

(continued)

(continues)

<table>
<tr><td>Test a single expression against a finite set of constant values</td><td>Use the switch keyword, followed by an integral expression enclosed in parentheses. Define case branches for each value you want to test against, and a default branch for all other values. Use the break statement to close a branch. For example:
<pre>
int dayNumber; // 0=Sun, 1=Mon, etc.
...
switch (dayNumber)
{
case 0:
case 6:
     Console::Write(S"Weekend");
    break;
 default:
     Console::Write(S"Weekday");
    break;
}
</pre></td></tr>
<tr><td>Perform iteration by using the while loop</td><td>Use the while keyword, followed by a test enclosed in parentheses. For example:
<pre>
int n = 10;
while (n >= 0)
{
    Console::WriteLine(n);
    n--;
}
</pre></td></tr>
<tr><td>Perform iteration by using the for loop</td><td>Use the for keyword, followed by a pair of parentheses. Within the parentheses, define an initialization expression, followed by a test expression, followed by an update expression. Use semicolons to separate these expressions.
For example:
<pre>
for (int n = 10; n >= 0; n--)
{
    Console::WriteLine(n);
}
</pre></td></tr>
<tr><td>Perform iteration by using the do-while loop</td><td>Use the do keyword, followed by the loop body, followed by the while keyword and the test condition. Terminate the loop with a semicolon.
For example:
<pre>
int n;
do
{
    String * input =
Console::ReadLine();
    n = input->ToInt32(0);
}
while (n > 100);
</pre></td></tr>
</table>

To terminate a loop prematurely	Use the *break* statement inside any loop. For example:

```
for (int n = 0; n < 1000; n++)
{
        int square = n * n;
        if (square > 3500)
        {
            break;
        }
        Console::WriteLine(square);
}
```

To abandon a loop iteration and continue with the next iteration	Use the *continue* statement inside any loop. For example:

```
for (int n = 0; n < 1000; n++)
{
        int square = n * n;
        if (square % 2 == 0)
        {
            continue;
        }
        Console::WriteLine(square);
}
```

PART 2

More About Object-Oriented Programming

CHAPTER

6

More About Classes and Objects

In this chapter, you'll learn how to

- ✔ *Organize classes into header files and source files*
- ✔ *Create and destroy objects*
- ✔ *Define constructors to initialize an object and a destructor to deinitialize an object*
- ✔ *Define class-wide members by using the* static *keyword*
- ✔ *Define relationships between different objects in an application*

As you saw in Chapter 2, C++ is an object-oriented programming language. You define classes to represent the important types of entity in your application, and create objects as instances of these classes. For example, a Human Resources application might define classes such as *Employee* and *Contract*. When the application is running, it might create a new *Employee* object every time a new employee joins the company, and create a new *Contract* object to describe the employee's terms of employment.

This chapter builds on the introduction to classes and objects in Chapter 2. In this chapter, you will see how to organize classes into header files and source files. This enables you to keep a clean separation between a class definition and its implementation. You will also learn how to provide constructors to initialize new objects when they are created. Likewise, you will provide destructors to tidy up objects just before they are destroyed.

Most of the data members and member functions in a class are "instance members" because they pertain to specific instances of the class. It is also possible to define "class members," which pertain to the class as a whole. You will see how to define class members in this chapter using the *static* keyword.

Finally, you will see how to create object relationships in C++. This is an important object-oriented concept because it allows objects to communicate with each other in a running application.

Organizing Classes into Header Files and Source Files

In Chapter 2, you saw how to define a simple class and implement all its member functions inline. Consider the following class, which represents a credit card account:

```
class CreditCardAccount
{
public:
    void PrintStatement()
    {
        Console::Write("Credit card balance: ");
        Console::WriteLine(currentBalance);
    }
private:
    double currentBalance;
};
```

Managed Classes vs. Unmanaged Classes

Chapter 2 used the *__gc* keyword in class definitions. This creates a managed class, which means the Microsoft Visual Studio .NET Framework garbage collector automatically destroys unused objects in your program.

You will learn all about managed classes in Chapter 8. Before learning about managed classes, however, it is important to understand how unmanaged classes work. With an unmanaged class, you have to delete objects explicitly in your own code. This chapter describes how to use unmanaged classes.

The *CreditCardAccount* class in the above example contains a single member function named *PrintStatement*. This function has been declared *public*, so it can be accessed by other parts of the program. The class also contains a single data member named *currentBalance*, which has been declared *private* to preserve encapsulation.

Notice that the class definition contains the full body of the *PrintStatement* function, not just its prototype. This is known as an inline function. Inline functions are fine for simple classes but can cause too much clutter in bigger classes. Imagine a class containing 30 functions; the class definition would be very long, and it would be difficult to pick out the function signatures in the class.

The solution is to divide the class definition into two parts: a header file and a source file, as shown in the following graphic.

```
class CreditCardAccount
{
public:
    void PrintStatement();
private:
    double currentBalance;
};
```

CreditCardAccount.h

```
#include "CreditCardAccount.h"

void CreditCardAccount::PrintStatement()
{
    Console::Write("Credit card balance: ");
    Console::WriteLine(currentBalance);
}
```

CreditCardAccount.cpp

note

You can use any filenames and file extensions you like for the header file and source file. Most developers use the same name as the class, with the file extensions .h and .cpp.

The header file, CreditCardAccount.h, contains the class definition. Notice that the class definition now contains function prototypes, rather than function bodies. This makes the header file easier to read, because the function signatures are more prominent.

The source file, CreditCardAccount.cpp, contains all the function bodies for the class. Each function must be prefixed by the name of the class to which it belongs, followed by two colons as follows:

```
void CreditCardAccount::PrintStatement()
{
    ... function body ...
}
```

The double-colon syntax (::) is the C++ scope resolution operator. In this example, the scope resolution operator tells us that the *PrintStatement* function belongs to the *CreditCardAccount* class.

> **note**
>
> You must provide a *#include* statement at the start of the source file to include the header file for the class. For example, CreditCardAccount.cpp has a *#include* statement to include CreditCardAccount.h. The compiler needs the information in this header file so it can compile the function bodies in the source file.

Defining a Class in a Header File

In this exercise, you will create a new application and define a *CreditCardAccount* class in a header file (you will implement the class in the following exercise).

1. Start Visual Studio .NET and open a new Managed C++ Application project named CreditOrganizer.
2. Select the menu item Project, then choose Add New Item.
3. In the Add New Item dialog box, select the template Header File (.h). In the Name field, type **CreditCardAccount.h**, and click Open.

   Visual Studio .NET creates an empty header file.

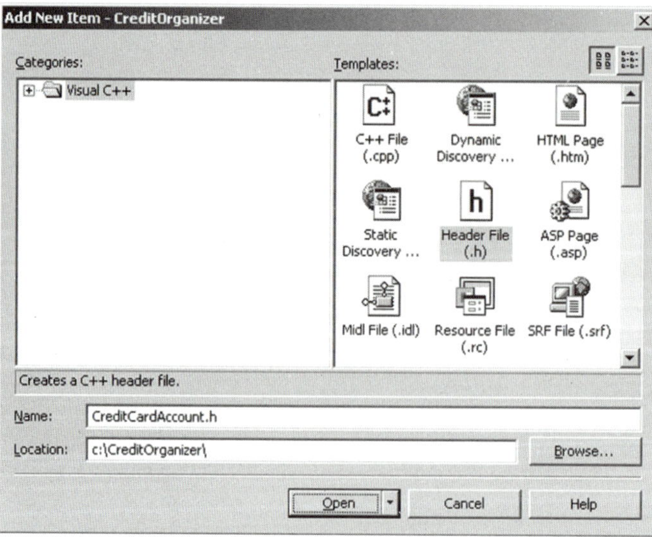

4 Type the following code in the header file to define the *CreditCardAccount* class:

```
class CreditCardAccount
{
public:
    bool MakePurchase(double amount);
    void MakeRepayment(double amount);
    void PrintStatement();

private:
    long accountNumber;
    double currentBalance;
    double creditLimit;
};
```

Every credit card account has a unique account number, a current balance, and a credit limit. The *MakePurchase* member function will enable you to make a purchase on the credit card; this function will return *true* if the purchase is allowed, or *false* if the purchase would cause the credit limit to be exceeded. The *MakeRepayment* member function will repay some or all of the outstanding balance. The *PrintStatement* member function will display a statement for the account.

5 Build the program and fix any compiler errors.

Implementing a Class in a Source File

In this exercise, you will implement the *CreditCardAccount* class in a source file.

1 Continue using the Managed C++ Application project from the previous exercise.

2 Select the menu item Project, then choose Add New Item.

3 In the Add New Item dialog box, select the template Source File (.cpp). In the Name field, type **CreditCardAccount.cpp**, and click Open.

Visual Studio .NET creates an empty source file.

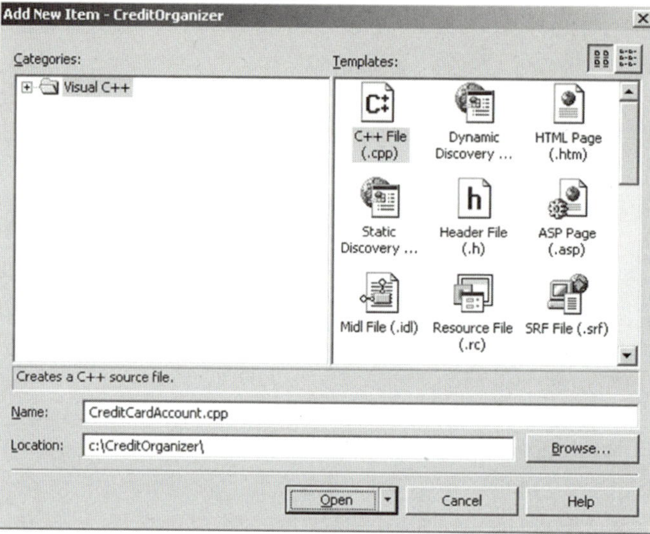

4 Add two *#include* statements at the start of the file, as follows:

```
#include "stdafx.h"
#include "CreditCardAccount.h"
```

The file stdafx.h is a header file that can include other standard header files; you include stdafx.h at the start of every source file in your project.

CreditCardAccount.h contains the class definition for *CreditCardAccount*. You include this header file here, so that the compiler can check your implementation of the *CreditCardAccount* class.

5 Add the following code so that you can use classes and data types defined in the *System* namespace:

```
#using <mscorlib.dll>
using namespace System;
```

The *using <mscorlib.dll>* preprocessor directive imports the Microsoft Intermediate Language (MSIL) file mscorlib.dll, so that you can use managed data and managed constructs defined in this DLL file.

The *using namespace System* statement enables you to use classes and data types defined in the *System* namespace. Specifically, you will use the *Console* class to display messages on the console.

6 Implement the *CreditCardAccount::MakePurchase* member function as follows:

```
bool CreditCardAccount::MakePurchase(double amount)
{
    if (currentBalance + amount > creditLimit)
```

```
        {
            return false;
        }
        else
        {
            currentBalance += amount;
            return true;
        }
}
```

This function is called when the card owner attempts to make a purchase using the credit card. The *amount* parameter indicates the amount of the purchase. The function tests whether the purchase would exceed the *creditLimit* data member and returns *false* in this case. Otherwise, the function adds the *amount* to the *currentBalance* data member and returns *true*.

note

Member functions have unrestricted access to all the members in the class, including *private* members.

7 Implement the *CreditCardAccount::MakeRepayment* member function as follows:

```
void CreditCardAccount::MakeRepayment(double amount)
{
    currentBalance -= amount;
}
```

This function allows the user to pay off some or all of the outstanding balance.

8 Implement the *CreditCardAccount::PrintStatement* member function as follows:

```
void CreditCardAccount::PrintStatement()
{
    Console::Write("Account number: ");
    Console::WriteLine(accountNumber);

    Console::Write("Current balance: ");
    Console::WriteLine(currentBalance);
}
```

This function displays information about the current state of the account.

9 Build the program and fix any compiler errors.

Creating and Destroying Objects

Once you have defined and implemented a class, you are ready to start creating and destroying objects. The way you create and destroy an object in Microsoft Visual C++ depends on whether the class is a managed class or an unmanaged class. In this chapter, we will just consider unmanaged classes—managed classes are discussed in Chapter 8.

The following code shows how to create an object, call its public member functions, and delete the object when it is no longer needed:

```
CreditCardAccount  * myAccount;     // Declare a pointer
myAccount = new CreditCardAccount; // Create a new
                                   // CreditCardAccount object
myAccount->MakePurchase(100);      // Use -> operator to invoke
                                   // member functions
myAccount->MakeRepayment(70);
myAccount->PrintStatement();
...
delete myAccount;                  // Explicitly delete object
                                   // when not needed
```

The *new* operator creates a new object of the *CreditCardAccount* class and returns a pointer to this new object. The pointer is used with the -> operator to invoke various member functions on the new object. When the object is no longer needed, you must explicitly destroy the object using the *delete* operator.

> **note**
>
> If you forget to delete an object of an unmanaged class, the garbage collector doesn't help you out. The object remains allocated in memory. This constitutes a memory leak and is one of the most common problems in traditional C++ applications. Another common error is to delete an object too soon. If you try to use the object after it has been deleted, your program will cause a run-time exception.

In this exercise, you will create a new *CreditCardAccount* object, invoke its member functions, and delete the object when it is no longer required.

1 Continue using the Managed C++ Application project from the previous exercise.

2 If the Solution Explorer isn't visible, select the menu item View, then choose Solution Explorer.

3 In the Solution Explorer window, find the source file CreditOrganizer.cpp. Double-click this file to display it in the Code View.

4 Just after the *#include "stdafx.h"* line, add another *#include* directive as follows:

```
#include "CreditCardAccount.h"
```

This enables you to create and use *CreditCardAccount* objects in this source file.

5 Add the following code to the *main* function:

```
CreditCardAccount * myAccount;      // Declare a pointer
myAccount = new CreditCardAccount; // Create a new
                                    //CreditCardAccount
                                    // object
myAccount->MakePurchase(1000);      // Use -> operator to
                                    // invoke member func-
tions
myAccount->MakeRepayment(700);
myAccount->PrintStatement();
delete myAccount;                   // Explicitly delete
                                    // object when not needed
```

6 Build the program and fix any compiler errors.

7 Run the program by pressing Ctrl+F5. The program creates a *CreditCardAccount* object, makes a purchase and a repayment, and prints a statement. However, the statement displays seemingly random numbers for the account number and current balance:

The reason for this result is that the *CreditCardAccount* object is not initialized when it is created. The data members in the object take on whatever values happen to be in memory where the object is located.

To resolve this problem, you can define a constructor in the *CreditCardAccount* class. The constructor will initialize new objects when they are created. You can also define a destructor in the class to tidy up objects just before they are destroyed.

Defining Constructors and Destructors

In this section, you will see how to define constructors and destructors for a class. Let's start at the beginning with constructors.

Defining Constructors

A constructor is a special member function that is called automatically when an object is created. The purpose of the constructor is to initialize the object to bring it into an operational state.

You declare the prototype for the constructor in the class definition. The following example declares a simple constructor for the *CreditCardAccount* class:

```
class CreditCardAccount
{
public:
    CreditCardAccount();
    // ... Other members, as before
};
```

There are several important points to notice here. First, the constructor must have the same name as the class; this is how the compiler recognizes it as the constructor. Also, the constructor cannot specify a return type, not even *void*. If you do specify a return type for a constructor, you will get a compiler error.

You can implement the constructor in the source file as follows:

```
CreditCardAccount::CreditCardAccount()
{
    accountNumber = 1234;
    currentBalance = 0;
    creditLimit = 3000;
}
```

This simple constructor will initialize every new *CreditCardAccount* object with the same values. A more realistic approach is to define a constructor that takes parameters to allow each object to be initialized with different values.

note

You can provide any number of constructors in a class, as long as each constructor has a distinct parameter list. This is an example of function overloading.

In this exercise, you will add a constructor to your *CreditCardAccount* class. The constructor will take two parameters specifying the account number and credit limit for the new account. The current balance will always be initialized to 0 for each new account, so there is no need to supply a parameter for this data member.

1 Continue using the Managed C++ Application project from the previous exercise.

2 Open CreditCardAccount.h, and declare a *public* constructor as follows:

```
class CreditCardAccount
{
public:
    CreditCardAccount(long number, double limit);
    // ... Other members, as before
};
```

tip

Make sure the constructor is *public*. If you make it *private* by mistake, you will not be able to create *CreditCardAccount* objects in your program.

3 Open CreditCardAccount.cpp, and implement the constructor as follows:

```
CreditCardAccount::CreditCardAccount(long number, double
limit)
{
    accountNumber = number;
    creditLimit = limit;
    currentBalance = 0.0;
}
```

note

There is an alternative syntax for initializing data members in a constructor using a member initialization list as follows:

```
CreditCardAccount::CreditCardAccount(long number, double
limit)
      : accountNumber(number), creditLimit (limit),
currentBalance(0.0)
{
}
```

The colon on the second line is followed by a comma-separated list of data members. For each data member, an initial value is provided in parentheses.

For simple initialization, it doesn't matter whether you use a member initialization list or simply initialize members in the constructor body. However, there are some situations where you have to use a member initialization list. You'll see such an example in Chapter 7, when you learn about inheritance.

4 Open CreditOrganizer.cpp. Modify the statement that creates the *CreditCardAccount* object, as follows:

```
myAccount = new CreditCardAccount(12345, 2500);
```

This statement creates a new *CreditCardAccount* object and passes the values 12345 and 2500 into the *CreditCardAccount* constructor. The constructor uses these parameter values to initialize the *accountNumber* and *creditLimit* data members, respectively.

5 Build the program and fix any compiler errors.

6 Run the program. The program now displays meaningful information for the *CreditCardAccount* object:

```
Account number: 12345
Current balance: 300
Press any key to continue
```

Defining Destructors

A destructor is a special member function that is called automatically when an object is about to be destroyed. The purpose of the destructor is to tidy up the object. For example, the destructor might deallocate additional memory allocated by the object, release resources owned by the object, close database connections opened by the object, and so on.

> **note**
>
> Only unmanaged classes have destructors. In managed classes, the .NET garbage collector deals with clearing up unused objects; you don't play a part in object destruction and so you don't supply a destructor.

You declare the prototype for the destructor in the class definition. The following example declares the destructor for the *CreditCardAccount* class:

```
class CreditCardAccount
{
public:
    ~CreditCardAccount();
    // ... Other members, as before
};
```

The destructor starts with a tilde (~) and has the same name as the class. The destructor does not have a return type and cannot take any parameters. This implies you can only have one destructor in a class.

You can implement the destructor in the source file as follows:

```
CreditCardAccount::~CreditCardAccount()
{
    Console::Write("Account being destroyed: ");
    Console::WriteLine(accountNumber);
    Console::Write("Closing balance: ");
    Console::WriteLine(currentBalance);
}
```

This simple destructor displays status information about a *CreditCardAccount* object just before it is destroyed.

In this exercise, you will add a destructor to your *CreditCardAccount* class. The destructor will display a status message describing the object that is being destroyed.

1 Continue using the Managed C++ Application project from the previous exercise.

2 Open CreditCardAccount.h, and declare a *public* destructor as follows:

```
class CreditCardAccount
{
public:
    ~CreditCardAccount();
    // ... Other members, as before
};
```

> **tip**
> Make sure the destructor is *public*, just like the constructor.

3 Open CreditCardAccount.cpp, and implement the destructor as follows:

```
CreditCardAccount::~CreditCardAccount()
{
    Console::Write("Account being destroyed: ");
    Console::WriteLine(accountNumber);
    Console::Write("Closing balance: ");
    Console::WriteLine(currentBalance);
}
```

4 Build the program and fix any compiler errors.

5 Run the program. As before, the program creates a *CreditCardAccount* object, invokes its member functions, and then deletes it. When the *CreditCardAccount* object is deleted, the destructor is called implicitly to display the closing status of the *CreditCardAccount* object:

```
Account number: 12345
Current balance: 300
Account being destroyed: 12345
Closing balance: 300
Press any key to continue_
```

Defining Class-Wide Members

The data members and member functions currently defined in the *CreditCardAccount* class are instance members. Each *CreditCardAccount* instance has its own *accountNumber*, *currentBalance*, and *creditLimit*. Likewise, when you invoke the member functions *MakePurchase*, *MakeRepayment*, and *PrintStatement*, you must specify which *CreditCardAccount* instance you are using, as shown in the following figure:

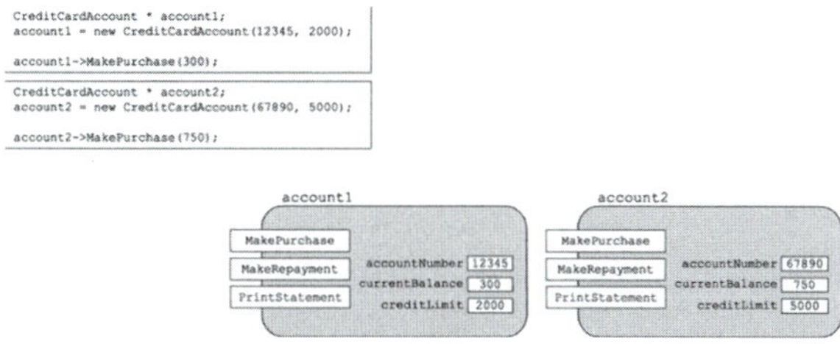

C++ also lets you define class-wide members, which pertain to the entire class rather than to a specific instance. For example, you can define a class-wide data member named *numberOfAccounts* to count how many *CreditCardAccount* instances have been created. Similarly, you can provide a class-wide member function named *GetNumberOfAccounts* to retrieve this count, as shown here:

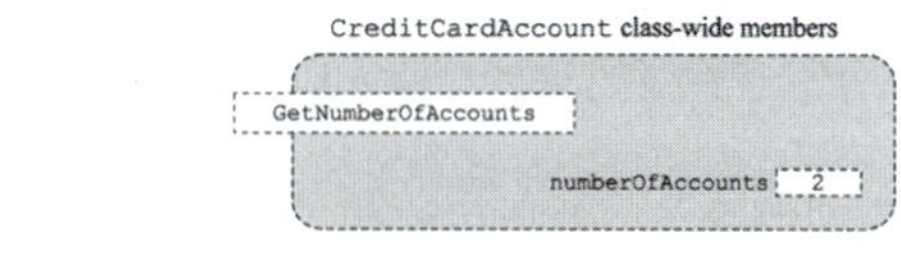

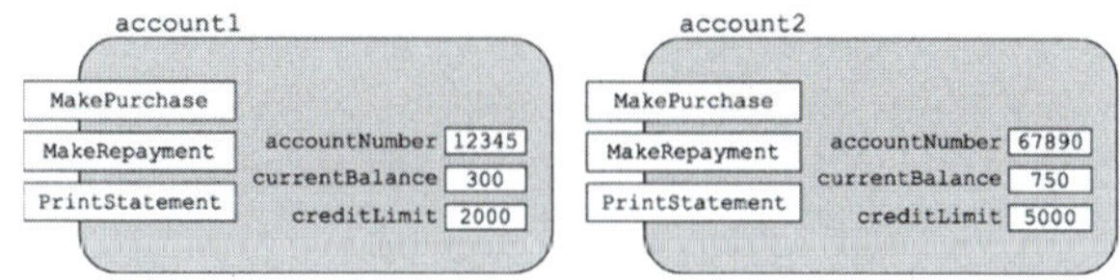

Let's see how to define class-wide data members and member functions.

Defining Class-Wide Data Members

To define a class-wide data member, use the *static* keyword as follows:

```
class CreditCardAccount
{
private:
    static int numberOfAccounts;                    // Declare class-
                                                    // wide data member
```

```
    // ... Other members, as before
};
```

This declaration tells the compiler there will be a class-wide data member named *numberOfAccounts*. However, the declaration does not allocate any storage for *numberOfAccounts*. You must do this yourself by adding the following statement in the source file CreditCardAccount.cpp:

```
int CreditCardAccount::numberOfAccounts = 0;    // Define class-wide
                                                // data member
```

This statement allocates permanent storage for the *numberOfAccounts* variable. This variable will be available for the entire lifetime of the program, even before any *CreditCardAccount* objects have been created.

> **note**
>
> If you do not initialize *numberOfAccounts* explicitly, the default initial value is 0. If you forget to define *numberOfAccounts* altogether, you will get a link error when you try to build the program. The link error tells you that *numberOfAccounts* hasn't been defined.

In this exercise, you will add a *static numberOfAccounts* data member to the *CreditCardAccount* class. You will increment this data member every time a new *CreditCardAccount* object is created.

1. Continue using the Managed C++ Application project from the previous exercise.
2. Open CreditCardAccount.h, and declare the *static numberOfAccounts* data member as follows:

    ```
    class CreditCardAccount
    {
    private:
        static int numberOfAccounts;
        // ... Other members, as before
    };
    ```

3. Open CreditCardAccount.cpp, and define the *numberOfAccounts* data member as follows:

    ```
    int CreditCardAccount::numberOfAccounts = 0;
    ```

note

Add this statement after all the *#include* directives but outside of any function body.

4 Modify the *CreditCardAccount* constructor, so that it increments *numberOfAccounts* every time a new *CreditCardAccount* object is created:

```
CreditCardAccount::CreditCardAccount(long number, double
limit)
{
    accountNumber = number;
    creditLimit = limit;
    currentBalance = 0.0;

    numberOfAccounts++;
    Console::Write("Number of accounts created: ");
    Console::WriteLine(numberOfAccounts);
}
```

5 Open CreditOrganizer.cpp. Modify the *main* function, so that it creates and uses several *CreditCardAccount* objects:

```
Console::WriteLine("Creating first object");
CreditCardAccount * account1;
account1 = new CreditCardAccount(12345, 2000);
account1->MakePurchase(300);
account1->PrintStatement();

Console::WriteLine("\nCreating second object");
CreditCardAccount * account2;
account2 = new CreditCardAccount(67890, 5000);
account2->MakePurchase(750);
account2->PrintStatement();

Console::WriteLine("\nDestroying objects");
delete account1;
delete account2;
```

6 Build the program and fix any compiler errors.

7 Run the program.

Every time a new *CreditCardAccount* object is created, the program increments *numberOfAccounts* and displays its latest value:

```
Creating first object
Number of accounts created: 1
Account number: 12345
Current balance: 300

Creating second object
Number of accounts created: 2
Account number: 67890
Current balance: 750

Destroying objects
Account being destroyed: 12345
Closing balance: 300
Account being destroyed: 67890
Closing balance: 750
Press any key to continue
```

Defining Class-Wide Member Functions

To define a class-wide member function, use the *static* keyword in the function declaration as follows:

```
class CreditCardAccount
{
public:
    static int GetNumberOfAccounts();
    // ... Other members, as before
};
```

Implement the function in the source file as follows:

```
int CreditCardAccount::GetNumberOfAccounts()
{
    return numberOfAccounts;
}
```

note

A *static* member function can only access *static* class members. For example, *GetNumberOfAccounts* can access *numberOfAccounts*, but it cannot access *accountNumber*, *currentBalance*, or *creditLimit*.

To call a *static* member function, use the class name rather than a particular instance. For example:

```
int n = CreditCardAccount::GetNumberOfAccounts();
```

This emphasizes the fact that *CreditCardAccount* is a class-wide member function, rather than an instance member function.

note

You have seen the syntax *ClassName::FunctionName* before. Every time you display a message on the Console, you use a statement such as *Console::WriteLine("Hello world")*. This calls the *static* member function *WriteLine* on the *Console* class.

In this exercise, you will define a *static GetNumberOfAccounts* member function in the *CreditCardAccount* class. You will then call this function several times in *main*.

1. Continue using the Managed C++ Application project from the previous exercise.
2. Open CreditCardAccount.h, and declare the *GetNumberOfAccounts* function as follows:

```
class CreditCardAccount
{
public:
    static int GetNumberOfAccounts();
    // ... Other members, as before
};
```

3. Open CreditCardAccount.cpp, and implement the *GetNumberOfAccounts* function as follows:

```
int CreditCardAccount::GetNumberOfAccounts()
{
    return numberOfAccounts;
}
```

4. Open CreditOrganizer.cpp. Modify the *main* function, so that it calls *GetNumberOfAccounts* at various stages during execution:

```
int n = CreditCardAccount::GetNumberOfAccounts();
Console::Write("Number of accounts initially: ");
Console::WriteLine(n);

Console::WriteLine("\nCreating first object");
CreditCardAccount * account1;
account1 = new CreditCardAccount(12345, 2000);
account1->MakePurchase(300);
account1->PrintStatement();

Console::WriteLine("\nCreating second object");
```

```
CreditCardAccount * account2;
account2 = new CreditCardAccount(67890, 5000);
account2->MakePurchase(750);
account2->PrintStatement();

n = CreditCardAccount::GetNumberOfAccounts();
Console::Write("\nNumber of accounts now: ");
Console::WriteLine(n);

Console::WriteLine("\nDestroying objects");
delete account1;
delete account2;
```

5 Build the program and fix any compiler errors.

6 Run the program. The program displays the following messages:

```
Number of accounts initially: 0

Creating first object
Number of accounts created: 1
Account number: 12345
Current balance: 300

Creating second object
Number of accounts created: 2
Account number: 67890
Current balance: 750

Number of accounts now: 2

Destroying objects
Account being destroyed: 12345
Closing balance: 300
Account being destroyed: 67890
Closing balance: 750
Press any key to continue
```

Defining Object Relationships

For the remainder of this chapter, you will see how to define relationships between objects in a Visual C++ application. Visual C++ applications typically contain many objects, which communicate with each other to achieve the overall functionality needed in the application.

To illustrate object relationships, you will add a new class named *LoyaltyScheme* to your credit card application. The *LoyaltyScheme* class will allow credit card owners to accrue bonus points when they use their credit card. The bonus points act as a reward for the customer's loyal use of the credit card.

When a *CreditCardAccount* object is first created, it will not have a *LoyaltyScheme* object. The *LoyaltyScheme* object will be created when the *CreditCardAccount* reaches 50 percent of its credit limit. Subsequently, every $10 spent using the credit card will accrue one bonus point in the

LoyaltyScheme object. When the *CreditCardAccount* object is finally destroyed, the *LoyaltyScheme* object must also be destroyed. The following illustration shows the lifetimes of the *CreditCardAccount* and *LoyaltyScheme* objects:

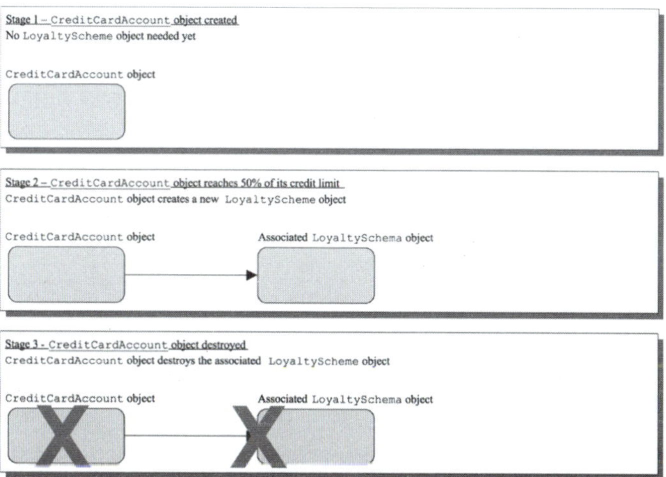

To achieve this functionality, you will complete the following exercises:

- Define the *LoyaltyScheme* class
- Implement the *LoyaltyScheme* class
- Create, use, and destroy *LoyaltyScheme* objects
- Test the application

Defining the *LoyaltyScheme* Class

In this exercise, you will define the *LoyaltyScheme* class in a new header file named LoyaltyScheme.h.

1. Continue using the Managed C++ Application project from the previous exercise.
2. Select the menu item Project, then choose Add New Item.
3. In the Add New Item dialog box, select the template Header File (.h). In the Name field, type **LoyaltyScheme.h** and click Open.
4. Type the following code in the header file to define the *LoyaltyScheme* class:

```
class LoyaltyScheme
{
public:
```

```
    LoyaltyScheme();            // Constructor
    ~LoyaltyScheme();           // Destructor

    void EarnPointsOnAmount(double amountSpent);    // Earn
                                        // one point per $10 spent
    void RedeemPoints(int points); // Redeem points
    int GetPoints();            // Return the value of
                                // totalPoints

private:
    int totalPoints;            // Total points accrued so far
};
```

5 Build the program and fix any compiler errors.

Implementing the *LoyaltyScheme* Class

In this exercise, you will implement the *LoyaltyScheme* class in a new source file named LoyaltyScheme.cpp.

1 Continue using the Managed C++ Application project from the previous exercise.

2 Select the menu item Project, then choose Add New Item.

3 In the Add New Item dialog box, select the template C++ File (.cpp). In the Name field, type **LoyaltyScheme.cpp** and click Open.

Visual Studio .NET creates an empty source file.

4 Add two *#include* statements at the start of the file, as shown here:

```
#include "stdafx.h"
#include "LoyaltyScheme.h"
```

5 Add the following code to expose the *System* namespace:

```
#using <mscorlib.dll>
using namespace System;
```

6 Implement the *LoyaltyScheme* constructor and destructor as follows:

```
LoyaltyScheme::LoyaltyScheme()
{
    Console::WriteLine("Congratulations, you now qualify for"
                       " bonus points");
    totalPoints = 0;
}

LoyaltyScheme::~LoyaltyScheme(void)
```

```
{
    Console::WriteLine("Loyalty scheme now closed");
}
```

7 Implement the *EarnPointsOnAmount* member function as follows:

```
void LoyaltyScheme::EarnPointsOnAmount(double amountSpent)
{
    int points = (int)(amountSpent/10);
    totalPoints += points;
    Console::Write("New bonus points earned: ");
    Console::WriteLine(points);
}
```

The syntax *(int)(amountSpent/10)* divides the amount spent by 10 and converts the value into an *int* data type.

8 Implement the *RedeemPoints* member function as follows:

```
void LoyaltyScheme::RedeemPoints(int points)
{
    if (points <= totalPoints)
    {
        totalPoints -= points;
    }
    else
    {
        totalPoints = 0;
    }
}
```

This function enables the user to redeem some or all of the accrued bonus points.

9 Implement the *GetPoints* member function as follows:

```
int LoyaltyScheme::GetPoints()
{
    return totalPoints;
}
```

10 Build the program and fix any compiler errors.

Creating, Using, and Destroying *LoyaltyScheme* Objects

In this exercise, you will extend the *CreditCardAccount* class to support the loyalty scheme functionality.

1. Continue using the Managed C++ Application project from the previous exercise.
2. Open CreditCardAccount.h. At the start of the file, add a *#include* directive as follows:

   ```
   #include "LoyaltyScheme.h"
   ```

   This will enable you to use the *LoyaltyScheme* class in this header file.
3. Add a *private* data member to the *CreditCardAccount* class, as follows:

   ```
   LoyaltyScheme * ptrLoyaltyScheme;     // Pointer to a
   LoyaltyScheme object
   ```

   This pointer defines an association between a *CreditCardAccount* object and a *LoyaltyScheme* object.
4. Add a *public* member function to the *CreditCardAccount* class, as follows:

   ```
   void RedeemLoyaltyPoints();
   ```

   This function acts as a wrapper to the *RedeemPoints* function in the *LoyaltyScheme* class. When you want to redeem loyalty points, you call *RedeemLoyaltyPoints* on your *CreditCardAccount* object. This function will call *RedeemPoints* on the underlying *LoyaltyScheme* object to do the work.

> **note**
>
> This is an example of delegation. The *CreditCardAccount* object delegates the *RedeemPoints* operation to the *LoyaltyScheme* object.

5. Open CreditCardAccount.cpp, and find the *CreditCardAccount* constructor. Add the following statement in the constructor body:

   ```
   ptrLoyaltyScheme = 0;
   ```

   This statement sets the *ptrLoyaltyScheme* pointer to 0 initially. This is a special value for a pointer because it indicates the pointer does not point to a real object yet. (The *LoyaltyScheme* object won't be created until the credit card balance reaches 50 percent of the credit limit.)
6. Modify the *MakePurchase* function as follows to accrue bonus points when the credit card balance reaches 50 percent of the credit limit:

   ```
   bool CreditCardAccount::MakePurchase(double amount)
   {
       if (currentBalance + amount > creditLimit)
       {
           return false;
       }
   ```

```
        else
        {
            currentBalance += amount;

        // If current balance is 50% (or more) of credit limit...
            if (currentBalance >= creditLimit / 2)
            {
                // If LoyaltyScheme object doesn't exist yet...
                if (ptrLoyaltyScheme == 0)
                {
                    // Create it
                    ptrLoyaltyScheme = new LoyaltyScheme();
                }
                else
                {
        // LoyaltyScheme already exists, so accrue bonus points
                    ptrLoyaltyScheme->EarnPointsOnAmount(
                            amount);
                }
            }
            return true;
        }
    }
```

7 Implement the *RedeemLoyaltyPoints* function as follows. This is a new member function and enables the user to redeem some or all of the loyalty points in the associated *LoyaltyScheme* object:

```
void CreditCardAccount::RedeemLoyaltyPoints()
{
    // If the LoyaltyScheme object doesn't exist yet...
    if (ptrLoyaltyScheme == 0)
    {
        // Display an error message
        Console::WriteLine("Sorry, you do not have a "
                           "loyalty scheme yet");
    }
    else
    {
         // Tell the user how many points are currently
         // available
        Console::Write("Points available: ");
        Console::Write( ptrLoyaltyScheme->GetPoints() );
```

```
            Console::Write(". How many points do you want "
                           "to redeem? ");

            // Ask the user how many points they want to redeem
            String * input = Console::ReadLine();
            int points = input->ToInt32(0);

            // Redeem the points
            ptrLoyaltyScheme->RedeemPoints(points);

            // Tell the user how many points are left
            Console::Write("Points remaining: ");
            Console::WriteLine( ptrLoyaltyScheme->GetPoints() );
    }
}
```

note

It's important to test the *ptrLoyaltyScheme* pointer before you use it. If you forget to test the pointer and the pointer is still 0, your program will cause a NULL pointer exception at run time. This is a very common error in C++ applications.

8 Add the following statement to the *CreditCardAccount* destructor:

```
delete ptrLoyaltyScheme;
```

This statement deletes the *LoyaltyScheme* object because it is no longer needed.

note

When you use *delete*, you do not need to test for a *null* pointer. The *delete* operator has an internal *null* pointer test.

9 Build the program and fix any compiler errors.

Testing the Application

In this exercise, you will modify the code in CreditOrganizer.cpp to test the loyalty scheme functionality.

1 Continue using the Managed C++ Application project from the previous exercise.

2 Open CreditOrganizer.cpp. Modify the *main* function as follows:

```
Console::WriteLine("Creating account object");
CreditCardAccount * account1;
account1 = new CreditCardAccount(12345, 2000);

Console::WriteLine("\nMaking a purchase (300)");
account1->MakePurchase(300);

Console::WriteLine("\nMaking a purchase (700)");
account1->MakePurchase(700);

Console::WriteLine("\nMaking a purchase (500)");
account1->MakePurchase(500);

Console::WriteLine("\nRedeeming points");
account1->RedeemLoyaltyPoints();

Console::WriteLine("\nDeleting account object");
delete account1;
```

3 Build the program and fix any compiler errors.

4 Run the program. The program creates a *CreditCardAccount* object and makes various purchases. Once the credit card balance reaches $1,000, a *LoyaltyScheme* object is created. Subsequent purchases accrue a loyalty point for every $10 spent.

When you try to redeem loyalty points, the program tells you how many points are available and asks how many you want to redeem. Enter a value such as 36. The program tells you how many points are left.

At the end of the program, the *CreditCardAccount* object is deleted. The associated *LoyaltyScheme* object is deleted at the same time.

The following graphic shows the messages displayed on the Console during the program:

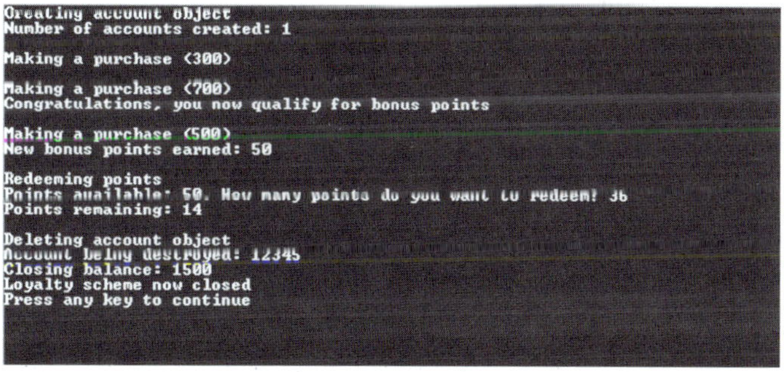

```
Creating account object
Number of accounts created: 1

Making a purchase (300)

Making a purchase (700)
Congratulations, you now qualify for bonus points

Making a purchase (500)
New bonus points earned: 50

Redeeming points
Points available: 50. How many points do you want to redeem? 36
Points remaining: 14

Deleting account object
Account being destroyed: 12345
Closing balance: 1500
Loyalty scheme now closed
Press any key to continue
```

Chapter 6 Quick Reference

To	Do This

Define a class	Add a header file to your project. Define the class in the header file. For example:
	`class MyClass`
	`{`
	`public:`
	`    void MyFunction();`
	`private:`
	`    int myData;`
	`};`

Implement a class	Add a source file to your project. In the source file, use a *#include* statement to include the header file that contains the class definition. Then implement the member functions in the source file. For example:
	`#include "MyHeader.h"`
	`void MyClass::MyFunction()`
	`{`
	`    myData = myData * 2;`
	`}`

Provide a constructor in a class	Declare the constructor in the header file, and implement it in the source file. The constructor must have the same name as the class and cannot return a value. However, a constructor can take parameters. For example:
	`// Header file`
	`class MyClass`
	`{`
	`public:`
	`    MyClass(int n);`
	`    ...`
	`};`
	`// Source file`
	`MyClass::MyClass(int n)`
	`{`
	`    myData = n;`
	`}`

Provide a destructor in a class	Declare the destructor in the header file, and implement it in the source file. The destructor must have the same name as the class, preceded by a tilde (~). The destructor cannot return a value or take any parameters. For example:
	`// Header file`
	`class MyClass`
	`{`
	`public:`
	`    ~MyClass();`
	`    ...`
	`};`
	`// Source file`
	`MyClass::~MyClass()`
	`{`
	`    Console::WriteLine("Goodbye");`
	`}`

Create and destroy objects of an unmanaged class	Create an object using the *new* keyword, passing parameters into the constructor if necessary. Delete the object using the *delete* keyword. For example:
	`MyClass * myObject(100);`
	`myObject->MyFunction();`
	`delete myObject;`

Define class-wide data members	Declare the data member using the *static* keyword. Define the data member in the source file. For example:
	`// Header file`
	`class MyClass`
	`{`
	`private:`
	`    static int myClassData;`
	`    ...`
	`};`
	`// Source file`
	`int MyClass:myClassData = 0;`

(continued)

(continued)

Define and use class-wide member functions	Declare the member function using the *static* keyword. Implement the member function in the source file. Call the function using the syntax *ClassName::FunctionName*. For example:
	`// Header file`
	`class MyClass`
	`{`
	`public:`
	`    static void MyClassFunction();`
	`    ...`
	`};`
	`// Source file`
	`void MyClass::MyClassFunction()`
	`{`
	`    myClassData++;`
	`}`
	`// Client code`
	`MyClass::MyClassFunction();`

Define relationships between objects	Define all the required classes, and use pointers to denote relationships between objects. For example, if an instance of class *A* needs to point to an instance of class *B*:
	`class B`
	`{`
	`    ...`
	`};`
	`class A`
	`{`
	`    ...`
	`private:`
	`    B * pointerToB;`
	`};`

7

Controlling Object Lifetimes

In this chapter, you'll learn

- ✔ *How Microsoft .NET memory management differs from traditional C++ memory management*
- ✔ *How to provide finalizers for your classes*
- ✔ *How to implement a* Dispose *method for your classes*

Now that you know how to create objects in C++ using the *new* operator, you'll learn how object lifetimes are controlled in Managed C++, and see how the Managed approach differs from the traditional new-and-delete approach.

Traditional C++ Memory Management

You've already seen how to create and delete objects dynamically in C++ using the *new* and *delete* operators, but let's review how the system works.

Creating Objects

Objects are created dynamically using the *new* operator, which does three things:

- It allocates memory for the object.
- It calls a constructor to initialize the object.
- It returns you a pointer to the object.

The following code fragment shows how to create an object belonging to the *Account* class:

```
// Create an object to represent Account number 1234567
Account* pa = new Account(1234567);
```

Dynamically created objects have their memory allocated from the heap—the pool of free memory allocated to the process—whereas local variables have their memory allocated on the program's stack. A dynamically created object actually consists of two parts: the object and the pointer you use to access it.

Deleting Objects

Local variables are created on the stack, and they'll be destroyed when they go out of scope. In fact, another name for local variables is automatic variables, which reflects the fact that they are automatically created and destroyed as necessary.

In contrast, unmanaged C++ requires you to manage the lifetime of dynamically created objects yourself. Consider the following code fragment:

```
void someFunction()
{
    // Declare an integer to represent the account number
    long num = 123456;

    // Create an object to represent Account number 1234567
    Account* pa = new Account(num);
}
```

Two variables go out of scope at the closing brace and will be destroyed: the *long num* and the pointer *pa*. The actual *Account* object is not automatically destroyed, but will exist until it is destroyed or until the program finishes.

You destroy objects using the *delete* operator:

```
// Create an object to represent Account number 1234567
Account* pa = new Account(num);

// Use the Account

// Destroy the Account
delete pa;
```

The *delete* operator takes a pointer to the object and performs two operations:

- It executes the class destructor, so you can tidy up the object state.
- It gives the memory back to the operating system.

Advantages and Disadvantages of Manual Memory Allocation

There are advantages and disadvantages with this approach. The main—some people would say the only—advantage of manual memory allocation is that you have very precise control over when an object is destroyed, so you are not using memory for an instant longer than necessary.

A second advantage is the use of destructors: when you destroy an object, code is automatically executed to tidy up the object. This ensures that objects are always properly tidied up without intervention by the programmer.

There are two disadvantages to calling *delete* manually to get rid of unwanted objects: calling it too late (or not at all) and calling it too early.

Neglecting to call *delete* isn't usually fatal to your program, but it can have unwanted consequences. The most common of these is that your program will hang on to memory longer than it needs to, a condition known as *memory leakage*. In some cases this can be fatal. Consider the following code fragment:

```
void lineDraw(int x1, int y1, int x2, int y2)
{
    // Create a Pen to draw the line...
    Pen* p = new Pen(Black, OnePixelWide, Dashed);

    // Call some graphics library function to draw the line
    drawTheLine(p, x1,y1, x2,y2);

    // Forget to delete the Pen
    // delete p;
}
```

Suppose that each *Pen* object is 10 bytes in size and that the *lineDraw* function is called 10,000 times. If the programmer forgets to delete the *Pen*, this one routine will leak 100,000 bytes of memory. In prehistoric times—say, when Microsoft Windows was at version 3.0—computers didn't have much memory, and a badly behaved program could consume all the free memory and crash the system.

Deleting an object too early—or at the wrong time—is a much more serious matter. If an object is deleted too early, someone might try to use it later. This usually results in the program failing. However, it's sometimes difficult to decide just when an object should be released. Here's an example:

```
// Create an object
SomeObject* pObj = new SomeObject();

// Pass it to a function...
aFunction(pObj);

// Use the object
pObj->doSomething();      // BANG!
...
void aFunction(SomeObject* pp)
{
  // Use pp
  pp->doThis();

  // We're done with the object - or are we?
  delete pp;
}
```

The code creates an object, then passes the pointer to a function. The function uses the object through the pointer, then thinks that the object is finished and calls *delete*. When the function returns, the calling code tries to use the object with predictable results.

The problem is deciding who has the responsibility for deleting the object—in other words, who owns the object—and this can be surprisingly hard to determine in large or complex projects.

The .NET Approach

Just as Sun Microsystems did with Java, Microsoft decided that the disadvantages of manual memory allocation far outweighed the advantages. Therefore, Managed C++ uses automatic memory management, as do all .NET languages.

Using the .NET mechanism, you still create objects dynamically using the *new* operator, but the system is responsible for deleting objects, not you. The system keeps track of references to objects, and when an object is no longer being referenced by anyone, it becomes a candidate for garbage collection.

This has more consequences for the programmer than you might at first think:

- Objects are always created using *new*. Unmanaged code lets you create objects on the heap (as automatic variables) or dynamically on the stack. For garbage collection to work, objects have to be accessed through some sort of reference, which in C++ is a pointer.

- You always access class members using pointers.
- You can't tell when an object is going to be garbage collected.

You can still use the *delete* operator to destroy an object manually, because that's an inherent part of the way C++ works, but you typically leave it up to the garbage collector to handle deallocation.

.NET Garbage Collection

The garbage collection mechanism in .NET Framework is very sophisticated, but you don't need to know much about it to use Managed C++. In fact, it's designed to work fine without any intervention from you at all, but if you're interested to know a little more about what's going on, read on.

Memory for objects is allocated from the managed heap, the chunk of memory that the process uses to store dynamically allocated objects. Every allocation takes some space from the heap, and it is possible that at some point heap memory will be exhausted. In theory if this happens, the garbage collector will be invoked to see if there are any unreferenced objects whose memory can be reclaimed to minimize the size of the heap.

In reality it's not quite that simple. Every dynamically created .NET Framework object belongs to a generation: objects created early in an application's lifecycle belong to generation 0, and younger objects are added to later generations. Dividing objects into generations means you don't have to run the garbage collector on all the objects in the heap, and need only consider the age of a particular object.

Garbage collection occurs when generation 0 is full. Dead objects are reclaimed, then any objects that survived the collection are promoted to generation 1, and new objects are added to generation 0 again. The garbage collector improves its efficiency by always running a collection on generation 0 first. If that doesn't free up enough memory, it can move on to run a collection on the next generation. At present, only three generations (0, 1, and 2) are supported by .NET.

You usually let the garbage collector decide when to perform a collection, but you can use the *Collect* static method of the *System::GC* class to force a collection if you know you will have a lot of reclaimable objects in your code. *Collect* lets you run a default collection or specify a particular generation. If you're interested in finding out what generation a particular object belongs to, you can use the *System::GC::GetGeneration* method, passing in an object reference.

Finalizers

All .NET reference types (*__gc* classes in Managed C++) inherit a method called *Finalize* from the ultimate base class, *Object*. *Finalize* allows an object to free up resources and perform other clean-up operations before the object is garbage collected. Any managed class can override *Finalize* if it needs to perform these tasks.

It's important to note that *Finalize* isn't the same as a traditional C++ destructor. Destructors are deterministic, meaning you can always tell when the destructor for an object is going to be called. It might be hard to decide when a destructor will be called in complex code with a lot of pointers and references being passed around, but it is always possible because the destructor is invoked explicitly at some point.

Finalizers, on the other hand, are non-deterministic. You can't tell when the *Finalize* method for an object will be called because that depends on when the object is garbage collected. And although you can force a garbage collection, it is typically up to the system to decide when to do it. This means that you shouldn't put any code into *Finalize* that you rely on being called at a particular point in the program because you can't guarantee that it will happen.

So what do you use *Finalize* for? You use it to release any unmanaged resources that your object holds, such as file handles, window handles, or database connections. You don't need to implement *Finalize* to deal with managed resources because the garbage collector will deal with them.

Although finalizers are not the same as destructors, in Managed C++ you use the normal C++ syntax to write a destructor, and the compiler then writes you a .NET *Finalize* method. This means that a destructor such as this

```
~MyClass()
{
    Console::WriteLine(S"Finalizing...");
}
```

expands to

```
MyClass::Finalize()
{
    Console::WriteLine(S"Finalizing...");
    MyBaseClass::Finalize();
}

virtual ~MyClass()
```

```
{
    System::GC::SuppressFinalize(this);
    A::Finalize();
}
```

The destructor calls the *Finalize* method for class, which contains any code you supplied in the constructor. *Finalize* then calls the finalizer for its base class, if any. The call to *SuppressFinalize* prevents the garbage collector from undertaking any other finalization action. If the destructor has been called in code, the object is explicitly deallocated and you don't want the garbage collector trying to do any finalization itself.

You have to implement finalizers using the C++ destructor syntax. You can't implement *Finalize* directly for a class, and you'll get a compiler error if you try.

> **note**
>
> Implement *Finalize* only on classes that need it because object reclamation during garbage collection takes longer when finalizers have to be called.

Implementing a Finalizer

The following short exercise shows how to implement a finalizer for a managed class:

1. Create a new Managed C++ Application project, and call it TestFinalize.
2. Open the TestFinalize.cpp file and add the definition of a managed class before the *_tmain* function:

```
__gc class Tester
{
public:
    Tester()
    {
        Console::WriteLine(S"Tester constructor");
    }

    ~Tester()
    {
        Console::WriteLine(S"Tester finalizer");
    }
};
```

The class contains code for a constructor and a destructor, so the compiler will generate a *Finalize* method automatically.

3 Create a *Tester* object in the *_tmain* function:

```
int _tmain(void)
{
    Console::WriteLine(S"Finalization Test");

    // Create an object
    Tester* pt = new Tester();

    Console::WriteLine(S"End of Test");
    return 0;
}
```

4 Compile and run the code. You should see the messages from both functions on the console, indicating that both constructor and destructor functions have been called. Note that the destructor message is printed after the "End of Test" message, showing that the object is being destroyed as part of program cleanup.

5 Change the code so that the object is deleted immediately before the "End of Test" message:

```
int _tmain(void)
{
    Console::WriteLine(S"Finalization Test");

    // Create an object
    Tester* pt = new Tester();

    // Delete the object
    delete pt;

    Console::WriteLine(S"End of Test");
    return 0;
}
```

6 Build and run the code. You'll see that the message from the destructor is printed before the "End of Test" message, showing that the object has been destroyed at this point.

A Few Points About *Finalize*

There are three points that you need to be aware of when using finalizers in the .NET rather than the C++ sense. First, objects with finalizers take longer to allocate, and longer to destroy, because the finalizer has to be called.

Second, no guarantee is made as to what order finalizers will be called in, and this can be problematic when using nested objects. Suppose that class A contains a reference to an object of class B; both finalizers will be called when an A object is destroyed, but you can't tell which will be called first. This can cause problems if the class B finalizer is called first, and if class A references the embedded B object in its finalizer. For this reason, you shouldn't refer to embedded objects in finalizers.

Finally, finalizers aren't called on application shutdown for objects that are still being used, such as those being used by background threads, or objects that are created as part of the finalization process. Although all system resources will be freed up when the application exits, objects that don't have their finalizers called might not get a chance to clean up properly.

Using a *Dispose* Method

The .NET Framework uses *Finalize* for cleanup when an object is garbage collected, and this is called through the destructor when C++ objects are destroyed.

Most other .NET languages—especially C# and Microsoft Visual Basic—don't give you any control over object lifetime. These languages offer no equivalent of the C++ destructor, so *Finalize* will be called only when the garbage collector reclaims the object.

What if you want to make sure that an object releases the resources it holds? Putting the code in *Finalize* is a bad idea because you don't know when it will be called. In the past—and in early beta versions of .NET—programmers had to code improvised methods in their classes that clients had to call in order to force object cleanup. Having everyone invent their own version of the same mechanism isn't very efficient, so Microsoft formalized the process and introduced the *IDisposable* interface in beta 2.

note

Interfaces are related to inheritance and covered in detail in the following chapter. This section will show you how to implement a *Dispose* method for your classes, but see the following chapter for details of how interfaces work if you haven't already met them.

Classes that implement *IDisposable* have to implement a *Dispose* method to free unmanaged resources. Clients can explicitly call *Dispose* when they have finished with the object to free up the resources it used, and leave the run time to garbage collect the object at an appropriate point.

You may want to implement *IDisposable* on your classes if:

- A class uses unmanaged resources that the client might want to release at a defined point in the code.
- You want to use a Managed C++ class from other .NET languages.

The following exercise shows how to add *Dispose* support to a class:

1. Continue with the project from the previous exercise.
2. Edit the class definition so that the class inherits from *IDisposable*:

```
__gc class Tester : public IDisposable
```

   If you haven't met inheritance before, see the explanation in Chapter 8.

3. Inheriting from *IDisposable* means that a class must implement a *Dispose* method, so add a *new* method to the class:

```
void Dispose()
{
    Console::WriteLine(S"Tester Dispose");
}
```

   The function has to be called *Dispose*, have no arguments, and have a *void* return type.

4. Arrange to call *Dispose* in the *_tmain* function:

```
int _tmain(void)
{
    Console::WriteLine(S"Finalization Test");

    // Create an object
    Tester* pt = new Tester();

    // Call Dispose
    pt->Dispose();

    Console::WriteLine(S"End of Test");
    return 0;
}
```

5 Build and run the code. You'll see that the *Dispose* method is called before the object is destroyed.

Integrating *Finalize* and *Dispose*

There's potential for serious problems when integrating *Finalize* and *Dispose*. The *Dispose* method releases resources on demand, but the object is still alive. This means someone could try to use the object once it has released its resources, which we don't want to happen.

Another problem is that *Dispose* releases resources on demand, whereas *Finalize* releases them when the object is garbage collected. This means *Finalize* has to know whether resources have already been released by a call to *Dispose*, so that it doesn't try to release them a second time.

The solution is to add a flag to the class that records whether the object's resources have been released. You can check this flag whenever the object is accessed, and throw an exception if the object is accessed after its resources have been released. The following exercise shows you how to do this.

1 Continue with the existing project, and add a private Boolean member to the class:

```
__gc class Tester : public IDisposable
{
    bool bDisposed;
    ...
}
```

2 Set the flag to *false* in the constructor:

```
Tester()
{
    Console::WriteLine(S"Tester constructor");
    bDisposed = false;
}
```

3 Set the flag to *true* in the *Dispose* method to show that resources have been released:

```
void Dispose()
{
    Console::WriteLine(S"Tester Dispose");

    // Release any resources
```

```
    bDisposed = true;
}
```

4 Check the flag in the destructor, and use it to control whether resources are released:

```
~Tester()
{
    Console::WriteLine(S"Tester finalizer");

    if (bDisposed == false)
    {
        Console::WriteLine(S"Releasing resources...");
    }
}
```

5 To show how you would protect against calling a method on an object that has released its resources, add a *public* method to the class:

```
void aMethod()
{
    if (bDisposed) throw new
ObjectDisposedException(S"Tester");

    Console::WriteLine(S"Tester aMethod");
}
```

The method checks whether the flag has been set to *true*. If it has, the code throws an *ObjectDisposedException*, one of the standard exceptions provided in the *System* namespace to handle such an occurrence.

6 Add a call to *aMethod* immediately after the call to *Dispose* in the code:

```
int _tmain(void)
#endif
{
   Console::WriteLine(S"Finalization Test");

    // Create an object
    Tester* pt = new Tester();

    // Call Dispose
    pt->Dispose();
```

```
    // Try calling a method on the object...
    pt->aMethod();

    Console::WriteLine(S"End of Test");
    return 0;
}
```

7 Build and run the code. Calling the method will result in the program failing as the exception is generated, but it does prevent the caller from trying to use an object that has released its resources.

Chapter 7 Quick Reference

To	Do This

Provide a finalizer for a class	Implement a C++ destructor. For example:
	`~MyClass()`
	`{`
	`   // Put cleanup code here`
	`}`

Provide a *Dispose* method for a class	Make your class inherit from the *IDisposable* interface and implement the *Dispose* method. For example:
	`__gc class MyClass : public IDisposable`
	`{`
	`public:`
	`    void Dispose()`
	`    {`
	`        // Put cleanup code here`
	`    }`
	`}`

Integrate *Finalize* and *Dispose*	Provide a Boolean flag that is set when the resources have been released. Set this in *Dispose*, and check it in the destructor.
Ensure that methods aren't called on objects that have had their resources reclaimed	Check the flag that tells you whether the object's resources have been reclaimed. If they have, the object is dead and you should throw an *ObjectDisposedException* to tell the caller that the object is dead.
Force a garbage collection	Call the *System::GC::Collect* method.
Find out what garbage collector generation an object belongs to	Call the *System::GC::GetGeneration* method, passing in a reference to the object.

CHAPTER

8

Inheritance

In this chapter, you'll learn how to

- ✔ *Describe the importance of inheritance in object-oriented programming*
- ✔ *Define a base class*
- ✔ *Define a derived class*
- ✔ *Access base-class members from the derived class*
- ✔ *Use the* virtual *keyword to achieve polymorphism*
- ✔ *Define abstract classes and abstract methods*
- ✔ *Define sealed classes*
- ✔ *Use interfaces*

Inheritance is an important object-oriented concept. Inheritance enables you to define a common base class that captures the similarities between several different classes. The base class contains the common data members and member functions for all these other classes.

You can then define derived classes that inherit all these members, and add new data members and member functions as required. Derived classes can also override some of the methods defined in the base class. This is known as polymorphism, and it is an extremely useful programming technique.

The benefits of inheritance are well documented in the object-oriented community. Inheritance helps you develop applications more quickly because you can reuse functionality defined in the base class. Testing and maintenance are simplified because there is less code in your application. Inheritance also helps you create a more accurate and meaningful model of your system.

In this chapter, you will learn how to use all aspects of inheritance in Microsoft Visual C++. You will see how to define base classes and derived classes, and find out how to use these classes effectively in your application.

Designing an Inheritance Hierarchy

Before you start writing any code to use inheritance in C++, you should spend some time designing the inheritance hierarchy. Identify classes that have common behavior, and consider whether these classes would benefit from using inheritance.

In this chapter, you will define and implement an inheritance hierarchy representing different types of bank accounts. The following illustration shows how the classes will be arranged in the inheritance hierarchy:

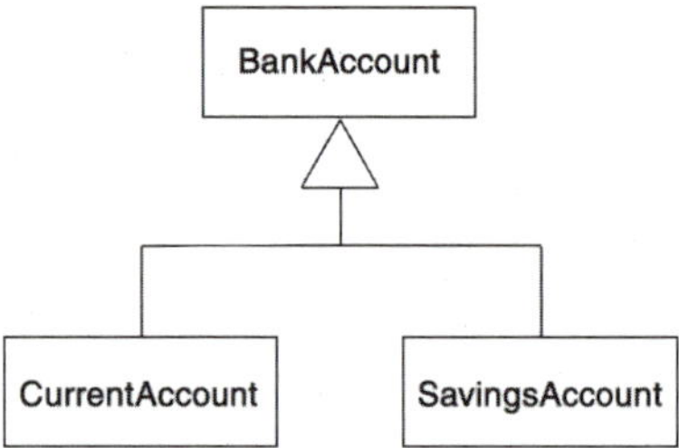

> **note**
>
> This illustration uses Unified Modeling Language (UML) notation to represent inheritance. Each box in this diagram is a class. The arrow pointing to *BankAccount* denotes inheritance in UML.

- *BankAccount* is the base class (also known as the superclass), and defines common data members and member functions that apply for all kinds of bank accounts.
- *CurrentAccount* and *SavingsAccount* are derived classes (also known as subclasses), and represent specific types of bank accounts. These derived classes inherit all the data members and member functions from *BankAccount*, and can add extra data members and member functions as required for different types of bank accounts.
- *CurrentAccount* and *SavingsAccount* can also override member functions defined in *BankAccount*. For example, the *BankAccount* class might have a method named *CanDebit* to indicate whether a

certain amount of money can be debited from the account. The policy rules for allowing debits are different for each type of account; therefore, *CurrentAccount* and *SavingsAccount* can override the *CanDebit* method to perform the required processing for each type of account.

You will define and implement all these classes during this chapter. Let's begin with the base class, *BankAccount*.

Defining a Base Class

C++ provides several keywords you can use in a base class to specify how the base class is exposed to derived classes and the client program. You will learn about these keywords later in this chapter. For the time being, you will create a simple base class that doesn't use any of these inheritance-related language features.

When you define a base class, the best place to start is by defining the common member functions that will be required by all the derived classes. Once you have defined these member functions, add data members to support these member functions. Then provide one or more constructors to initialize these data members.

Inheritance in Managed C++

Inheritance has been part of C++ since Bjarne Stroustrup created the language, but Managed C++ introduces several additional keywords for inheritance. These new keywords make it easier to use inheritance in your Visual C++ application, and also provide conformity with the Common Language Specification in the .NET Framework.

In this exercise, you will create a new application and define the *BankAccount* class. The *BankAccount* class will be the base class for all types of bank accounts in the application.

In *BankAccount*, you will define the common member functions and data members that apply for all types of bank accounts. You will also define a constructor and destructor for this class.

1 Start Microsoft Visual Studio .NET and open a new Managed C++ Application project named BigBank.

2 Select the menu item Project, then choose Add New Item. In the Add New Item dialog box, select the template Header File (.h). In the Name field, type **BankAccount.h** and click Open.

Visual Studio .NET creates an empty header file.

3 Type the following code in the header file to define the *BankAccount* class:

```
#pragma once
#using <mscorlib.dll>
using namespace System;

__gc class BankAccount
{
public:
    BankAccount(String * holder);
    ~BankAccount();
    void Credit(double amount);
    void Debit(double amount);
private:
    String * accountHolder;
    double balance;
};
```

tip

The *#pragma once* compiler directive specifies that this header file will be processed only once by the compiler during a build. This directive is particularly useful for frequently included header files, such as those containing base-class definitions.

If you omit the *#pragma once* directive, you will almost certainly get a compiler error when you try to build the application later on. This is because BankAccount.h will be included in several different places in the application, and the compiler will generate an error if it sees the *BankAccount* class definition more than once.

4 Select the menu item Project, then choose Add New Item. In the Add New Item dialog box, select the template C++ File (.cpp). In the Name field, type **BankAccount.cpp**, and then click Open.

Visual Studio .NET creates an empty source file.

5 Type the following code in the source file to implement the *BankAccount* class:

```
#include "stdafx.h"
#include "BankAccount.h"

BankAccount::BankAccount(String * holder)
:accountHolder(holder), balance(0.0)
{
}

BankAccount::~BankAccount()
{
}

void BankAccount::Credit(double amount)
{
    balance += amount;
    Console::Write(S"After credit, new balance is: ");
    Console::WriteLine(balance);
}

void BankAccount::Debit(double amount)
{
    balance -= amount;
    Console::Write(S"After debit, new balance is: ");
    Console::WriteLine(balance);
}
```

note

The constructor uses a member initialization list to initialize the *BankAccount* data members. This is the preferred syntax for initializing data members in a constructor. Furthermore, it's the only way to invoke superclass constructors; this will become apparent when you define the *CurrentAccount* and *SavingsAccount* classes shortly.

6 Build the program.

Defining a Derived Class

To define a derived class in Managed C++, use the following syntax:

```
__gc class MyDerivedClass : public MyBaseClass
```

```
{
    ...
};
```

The colon in the class definition indicates inheritance. After the colon, you must specify the *public* keyword, followed by the name of the base class. The *public* keyword indicates that *public* members in the base class will remain *public* when they are inherited by your derived class.

> **tip**
>
> If you omit the *public* keyword after the colon, the default access level for inheritance is *private*. Private inheritance is a specialized technique used in unmanaged C++, but it is not supported in Managed C++. Therefore, you'll get a compiler error if you omit the *public* keyword in the class definition.

In this exercise, you will define and implement the *CurrentAccount* class. *CurrentAccount* will inherit from *BankAccount*. This means there is no need to reimplement inherited member functions, such as *Credit* and *Debit*. Likewise, there is no need to redefine inherited data members, such as *accountHolder* and *balance*. All you need to define in *CurrentAccount* are additional member functions and data members, which apply specifically to current accounts.

1. Continue using the Managed C++ Application project from the previous exercise.
2. Select the menu item Project, then choose Add New Item. In the Add New Item dialog box, select the template Header File (.h). In the Name field, type **CurrentAccount.h**, and then click Open.

   Visual Studio .NET creates an empty header file.
3. Type the following code in the header file to define the *CurrentAccount* class:

```
#include "BankAccount.h"

__gc class CurrentAccount : public BankAccount
{
public:
    CurrentAccount(String * holder, double limit);
    ~CurrentAccount();
    void ChangeOverdraftLimit(double newLimit);
private:
```

```
    double overdraftLimit;
};
```

Notice the *#include "BankAccount.h"* directive. This is required because *BankAccount* is the base class of *CurrentAccount*. The compiler needs to know how *BankAccount* is defined in order to compile the *CurrentAccount* class.

Also notice that the *CurrentAccount* constructor takes two parameters; the first parameter will initialize the account holder's name (defined in *BankAccount*), and the second parameter will initialize the *overdraftLimit* (defined in *CurrentAccount*).

4 Select the menu item Project, then choose Add New Item. In the Add New Item dialog box, select the template C++ File (.cpp). In the Name field, type **CurrentAccount.cpp**, and then click Open.

Visual Studio .NET creates an empty source file.

5 Type the following code in the source file to implement the *CurrentAccount* class:

```
#include "stdafx.h"
#include "CurrentAccount.h"

CurrentAccount::CurrentAccount(String * holder, double
limit)
:BankAccount(holder), overdraftLimit(limit)
{
}

CurrentAccount::~CurrentAccount()
{
}

void CurrentAccount::ChangeOverdraftLimit(double newLimit)
{
    overdraftLimit = newLimit;
}
```

The most important point to observe here is the *CurrentAccount* constructor. The member initialization list includes the syntax *BankAccount(holder)*. This syntax calls the constructor in the base class, *BankAccount*, to initialize inherited data members. If you take a look in BankAccount.cpp, you'll see that the *BankAccount* constructor requires a string parameter to set the account holder's name. The balance is always set to 0 initially.

6 Build the program.

note

The derived-class constructor must call the base-class constructor, using the member initialization list syntax. If you forget to call the base-class constructor, the compiler will attempt to call a no-argument constructor in the base class on your behalf; if there isn't a no-argument constructor in the base class, you'll get a compiler error.

Accessing Members of the Base Class

When you define a derived class, you might want to access some of the members in the base class. For example, you might want to call a base-class member function to perform some required operation for you. Similarly, you might want to access a base-class data member so that you can perform a calculation in your derived class.

If the base-class member is *public*, you can access the member in your derived class (or anywhere else in the application, for that matter). However, if the base-class member is *private*, you cannot access it in the derived class. *Private* members can be accessed only by member functions in that class; derived classes do not have access.

To overcome this restriction, C++ provides a third access specifier named *protected*. If you declare a base-class member *protected*, it is accessible to that class and all derived classes. The following example illustrates all three access levels—*public*, *protected*, and *private*:

```
__gc class BankAccount
{
// Public members, visible everywhere
public:
    BankAccount(String * holder);
    ~BankAccount();
    void Credit(double amount);
    void Debit(double amount);

// Protected members, visible in this class and in
// subclasses
protected:
   double balance;

// Private members, just visible in this class
private:
```

```
    String * accountHolder;
};
```

tip

Use the *protected* access specifier with care. Once you define a data member as *protected*, you introduce a dependency between your class and all derived classes. If you change the definition of the *protected* data member (such as changing its data type from *int* to *String**), you will have to modify all derived classes that use this data member.

In this exercise, you will define and implement the *SavingsAccount* class. The *SavingsAccount* class will have an *ApplyInterest* member function, which will add interest to the savings account. The interest will be calculated as a percentage of the current balance. However, the balance is currently declared as a *private* data member in *BankAccount*; you will change this to *protected*, so that derived classes can access the *balance* data member.

1. Continue using the Managed C++ Application project from the previous exercise.
2. Open BankAccount.h, and change the *BankAccount* class definition. Specifically, make the *balance* data member *protected*, rather than *private*.
3. Select the menu item Project, then choose Add New Item. In the Add New Item dialog box, select the template Header File (.h). In the Name field, type **SavingsAccount.h**, and then click Open.

   Visual Studio .NET creates an empty header file.
4. Type the following code in the header file to define the *SavingsAccount* class:

```
#include "BankAccount.h"

__gc class SavingsAccount : public BankAccount
{
public:
    SavingsAccount(String * holder);
    ~SavingsAccount();
    void ApplyInterest();
private:
    static double interestRate = 0.05;    // 5% interest rate
                                          // for all accounts
};
```

Notice the *static interestRate* data member. This enables all savings accounts to share a common interest rate.

> **note**
>
> Static data members of Managed C++ classes must be defined within the class. In other words, you must provide a definition such as *static double interestRate = 0.05;* rather than a declaration such as *static double interestRate;*.

5 Select the menu item Project, then choose Add New Item. In the Add New Item dialog box, select the template C++ File (.cpp). In the Name field, type **SavingsAccount.cpp**, and then click Open.

Visual Studio .NET creates an empty source file.

6 Type the following code in the source file to implement the *SavingsAccount* class:

```
#include "stdafx.h"
#include "SavingsAccount.h"

SavingsAccount::SavingsAccount(String * holder)
:BankAccount(holder)
{
}

SavingsAccount::~SavingsAccount()
{
}

void SavingsAccount::ApplyInterest()
{
    Credit(balance * interestRate);
}
```

Notice that the *ApplyInterest* member function calls the *Credit* member function, which is defined in the base class. It's quite common to call inherited base-class functions to reuse the functionality defined in these functions.

Also notice that *ApplyInterest* uses the *balance* data member, which is defined in the base class. The base class defines *balance* as *protected* to permit this access.

7 Build the program.

Creating Objects

When you define an inheritance hierarchy, the base class acts as a repository for the common member functions and data members supported by all derived classes. However, the base class usually doesn't contain enough information to represent real objects.

Consider the bank account example we've been developing during this chapter. When you walk into a bank to open a bank account, you have to say what type of account you want (checking account or savings account). You can't open just a generic bank account.

In programming terms, this means you should prevent generic *BankAccount* objects from being created. You should allow only derived classes such as *CurrentAccount* and *SavingsAccount* to be instantiated.

To achieve this effect in Managed C++, declare the *BankAccount* class as an abstract class as follows:

```
__gc __abstract class BankAccount
{
    // ... Class body, as before
};
```

In this exercise, you will modify the *BankAccount* class as just described to make it an abstract class. You will then write some code in the *_tmain* function in the application to create and use *CurrentAccount* and *SavingsAccount* objects.

1. Continue using the Managed C++ Application project from the previous exercise.
2. Open BankAccount.h, and change the *BankAccount* class definition. Specifically, add the *__abstract* keyword to make the class abstract.
3. Open BigBank.cpp, which contains the *_tmain* function for the application.
4. At the top of this file, just after the *#include "stdafx.h"* directive, add the following *#include* directives:

```
#include "CurrentAccount.h"
#include "SavingsAccount.h"
```

note

There is no need to explicitly write *#include "BankAccount.h"* because this header file is already included in CurrentAccount.h and SavingsAccount.h.

5. Inside the *_tmain* function, try to create a *BankAccount* object as follows:

```
BankAccount * genericAccount = new BankAccount(S"Emily");
```

6. Build the program. You will get the following compiler error, which confirms the fact that *BankAccount* is an abstract class:

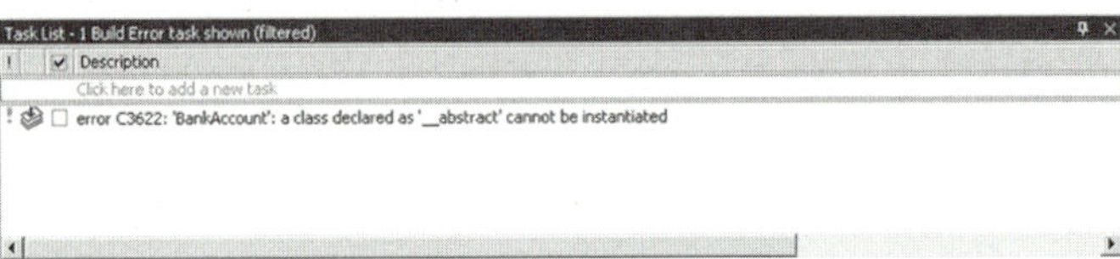

7. Delete the statement you created in Step 5.
8. Add the following code in *_tmain* to create and use a *CurrentAccount* object:

```
CurrentAccount * current = new CurrentAccount(S"Emily",
100);
current->Credit(500);
current->ChangeOverdraftLimit(300);
current->Debit(750);
```

This example shows that the client program can access any *public* members in the base class or derived class. For example, *Credit* and *Debit* are inherited from *BankAccount*, but *ChangeOverdraftLimit* is specific to *CurrentAccount*.

9. Build and run the program. The program displays the following output on the console:

```
After credit, new balance is: 500
After debit, new balance is: -250
Press any key to continue
```

10. Add the following code in *_tmain* to create and use a *SavingsAccount* object:

```
SavingsAccount * savings = new SavingsAccount(S"Thomas");
savings->Credit(500);
savings->Debit(100);
savings->ApplyInterest();
```

This example uses the *Credit* and *Debit* member functions inherited from *BankAccount*, and also the *ApplyInterest* member function that is specific to *SavingsAccount*.

11 Build and run the program. The program displays the following output for *SavingsAccount*:

```
After credit, new balance is: 500
After debit, new balance is: 400
After credit, new balance is: 420
Press any key to continue
```

Overriding Member Functions

When you define a base class, you must consider whether derived classes will need to override any of your base-class member functions. For each member function in the base class, there are three possibilities:

- The base-class function is suitable for all derived classes. Derived classes will never need to override the member function with customized behavior. The *Credit* and *Debit* member functions in *BankAccount* fit this scenario. These functions simply add or subtract money from the *balance*—derived classes do not need to override these member functions. For example:

```
__gc __abstract class BankAccount
{
public:
    void Credit(double amount);   // This function cannot be
                                  //   overridden
    void Debit(double amount);    // Neither can this one
    ...
};
```

- The base-class function performs some task, but derived classes might need to override the function in order to provide customized behavior. To enable a base-class function to be overridden, you must declare the function using the *virtual* keyword in the base-class definition. For example:

```
__gc __abstract class BankAccount
{
public:
    virtual String * ToString();   // This function can be
                                   //   overridden
    ...
};
```

- The base-class function specifies some operation that is required by all derived classes, but each derived class needs to perform the operation in a significantly different way. There is no sensible common behavior you can define in the base class. To achieve this effect, declare the base-class member function using the *virtual* keyword. At the end of the function prototype, use the syntax = *0* as shown below. This indicates that the function isn't implemented in the base class—derived classes must override this function. For example:

```
__gc __abstract class BankAccount
{
public:
    virtual bool CanDebit(double amount) = 0;   // This
                                                 // function
                                                 // must be
                                                 // overridden

    ...
};
```

> **note**
>
> In C++, we use the term "pure virtual function" to describe a function that must be overridden by derived classes. Other programming languages use different terminology and keywords. For example, C# allows you to use the *abstract* keyword for such a method. Microsoft Visual Basic uses the *MustOverride* keyword.

In this exercise, you will define a *ToString* member function in the *BankAccount* class. You will declare this function as *virtual* to give derived classes the opportunity to override the function if they want to.

You will also define a pure virtual function named *CanDebit* in the *BankAccount* class. This forces all derived classes to implement the *CanDebit* function.

1. Continue using the Managed C++ Application project from the previous exercise.
2. Open BankAccount.h, and add the following function declarations to the *BankAccount* class:

```
virtual String * ToString();                // Derived classes
                                            // can override
```

```
virtual bool CanDebit(double amount) = 0; // Derived classes
                                          // must override
```

3 Open BankAccount.cpp, and implement the *ToString* function as follows:

```
String * BankAccount::ToString()
{
    String * result = new String(S"Account holder: ");
    result = String::Concat(result, accountHolder);
    result = String::Concat(result, S", Balance: ");
    result = String::Concat(result, balance.ToString());
    return result;
}
```

4 Modify the *Debit* member function as follows:

```
void BankAccount::Debit(double amount)
{
    if (CanDebit(amount))
    {
        balance -= amount;
        Console::Write(S"Debit succeeded, new balance is: ");
        Console::WriteLine(balance);
    }
    else
    {
        Console::Write(S"Debit refused, balance is still: ");
        Console::WriteLine(balance);
    }
}
```

Notice that *Debit* now calls *CanDebit* to verify that the debit is allowed. *CanDebit* isn't implemented in *BankAccount*, but all derived classes are obliged to provide this function. At run time, the correct version of *CanDebit* will be called depending on the type of bank account being used for the debit operation. This is polymorphism in action!

5 Open CurrentAccount.h, and add the following function declarations to the *CurrentAccount* class:

```
virtual String * ToString();             // Choose to
                                         // override ToString
virtual bool CanDebit(double amount);    // Obliged to
                                         // override CanDebit
```

6 Open CurrentAccount.cpp, and implement the *ToString* function as follows:

```
String * CurrentAccount::ToString()
{
   String * result = __super::ToString();
   result = String::Concat(result, S", Overdraft Limit: ");
   result = String::Concat(result,
    overdraftLimit.ToString());
   return result;
}
```

The *__super::ToString()* syntax calls the *ToString* function in the superclass (*BankAccount*). This returns a string containing the account holder's name and balance. We concatenate the *overdraftLimit* value to this string, and return it.

7 Still in CurrentAccount.cpp, implement the *CanDebit* function as follows:

```
bool CurrentAccount::CanDebit(double amount)
{
    if (amount <= balance + overdraftLimit)
    {
        return true;
    }
    else
    {
        return false;
    }
}
```

8 Open SavingsAccount.h, and add the following function declaration to the *SavingsAccount* class:

```
virtual bool CanDebit(double amount);  // Obliged to over-
ride CanDebit
```

You are obliged to override *CanDebit* because it's a pure virtual function. However, you do not have to override *ToString* because the base class (*BankAccount*) provides a default implementation of this function. The *SavingsAccount* class chooses not to override *ToString*.

9 Open SavingsAccount.cpp, and implement the *CanDebit* function as follows:

```
bool SavingsAccount::CanDebit(double amount)
{
    if (amount <= balance / 10)
    {
        return true;
```

```
        }
        else
        {
            return false;
        }
    }
```

This function enables the user to withdraw one-tenth of the current balance.

10 Open BigBank.cpp, and add the following code to the *_tmain* function:

```
Console::WriteLine(S"Testing the CurrentAccount");
CurrentAccount * current = new CurrentAccount(S"Emily",
100);
current->Credit(500);
current->Debit(600);          // Should be accepted
current->Debit(1);            // Should be declined
Console::WriteLine(current->ToString());

Console::WriteLine(S"\nTesting the SavingsAccount");
SavingsAccount * savings = new SavingsAccount(S"Thomas");
savings->Credit(500);
savings->Debit(50);           // Should be accepted
savings->Debit(46);           // Should be declined
Console::WriteLine(savings->ToString());
```

11 Build and run the program. The program displays the following output on the console:

```
Testing the CurrentAccount
After credit, new balance is: 500
Debit succeeded, new balance is: -100
Debit refused, balance is still: -100
Account holder: Emily, Balance: -100, Overdraft Limit: 100

Testing the SavingsAccount
After credit, new balance is: 500
Debit succeeded, new balance is: 450
Debit refused, balance is still: 450
Account holder: Thomas, Balance: 450
Press any key to continue
```

12 Create a breakpoint on the first statement in the *_tmain* function, and start the program in the debugger. Step through the program one statement at a time to see which functions are called during execution.

Defining Sealed Classes

In Managed C++, you can define a class as "sealed." This means the class cannot be inherited from. This is a useful security measure if your class contains sensitive information, or if it performs operations that you don't want customized in derived classes.

To mark a class as sealed, use the *__sealed* keyword in the class definition as follows:

```
__gc __sealed class MyClass
{
    // ... Class body, as before
};
```

Defining and Using Interfaces

An interface is similar to a class, but all the member functions are pure virtual. Interfaces are useful for defining capabilities for diverse classes in your application. The following example shows you how to define a hypothetical interface in Managed C++:

```
__gc __interface IStorableAsXml
{
    void ReadFromXmlFile(String * XmlFilename);
    void WriteToXmlFile(String * XmlFilename);
};
```

tip

By convention, interface names start with the letter I. This makes it easier to differentiate between interfaces and classes.

Once you have defined the interface, you can implement it in any class that supports the functionality prescribed in the interface. The syntax for implementing an interface is the same as for extending a base class. The following example shows how to implement the *IStorableAsXml* interface in the *SavingsAccount* class:

```
__gc __sealed class SavingsAccount : public BankAccount, public
IStorableAsXml
{
```

```
public:

    // Override functions defined in the interface
    void ReadFromXmlFile(String * XmlFilename){}
    void WriteToXmlFile(String * XmlFilename){}

    // Other members, as before ...
};
```

In this example, *SavingsAccount* inherits from *BankAccount* and implements the *IStorableAsXml* interface. The *SavingsAccount* class is obliged to implement the *ReadFromXmlFile* and *WriteToXmlFile* methods.

Chapter 8 Quick Reference

To	Do This

Define an abstract base class	Use the *__abstract* keyword in the class definition. For example:
	`__gc __abstract class MyBase`
	`{`
	`    ...`
	`};`

Define a derived class	In the derived-class definition, use a colon, followed by *public*, followed by the name of the base class. For example:
	`__gc class MyDerived : public MyBase`
	`{`
	`    ...`
	`};`

Construct derived objects	In the derived-class constructor, use a member initialization list to call the base-class constructor. For example:
	`MyDerived::MyDerived(int bdata, int ddata)`
	`:MyBase(bdata), derivedData(ddata)`
	`{`
	`    ...`
	`}`

Enable derived classes to access members in the base class	Declare the members as *protected* in the base class. For example:
	`__gc __abstract class MyBase`
	`{`
	`protected:`
	`    int dataVisibleToDerivedClass;`
	`    ...`
	`};`

(continued)

(continued)

Define overridable member functions in the base class

Declare the member functions as *virtual* in the base class. For example:

```
__gc __abstract class MyBase
{

protected:
    virtual void myOverridableFunction();
    ...

};
```

Specify base-class member functions that must be overridden by derived classes

Declare the member functions as *virtual* in the base class. After the closing parenthesis, append *=0*. For example:

```
__gc __abstract class MyBase
{
protected:
    virtual void myMustBeOverridden() = 0;
    ...
};
```

Prevent a class from being derived from

Use the *__sealed* keyword in the class definition. For example:

```
__gc __sealed class MySealedClass
{
    ...
};
```

Define an interface

Use the *__interface* keyword. For example:

```
__gc __interface IMyInterface
{
    void function1(int n);
    int function2(double d);
};
```

Implement an interface

Use the same syntax as for inheritance. Implement all the required functions in your class. For example:

```
__gc class MyImplementingClass
        : public IMyInterface
{
public:
    void function1(int n);
    int function2(double d);

    // Other members, as needed ...
};
```

PART 3

.NET Programming Basics

Value Types

In this chapter, you'll learn how to

- ✔ *Distinguish between reference and value types*
- ✔ *Work with structures*
- ✔ *Work with enums*

In Part II, you learned about object-oriented programming and how to apply it within .NET. You've seen how many data types within .NET are represented by classes, and you've learned how to create and use your own classes. However, not every data type in .NET is a class, and now you're going to meet the other fundamental building block of .NET types—the *value type*.

In this chapter, you'll discover what value types are, and how they differ from the reference types you've already met. You will also meet two important value types—structs and enums—that will be useful in your own code.

Reference Types and Value Types

Let's summarize what you've learned about classes so far. Classes are known as reference types because you always access objects by using reference variables. Consider the following line of code:

```
MyClass* pc = new MyClass();
```

In this example, *pc* is a reference variable that lets us refer to the *MyClass* object created by the *new* operator. Accessing objects using references in this way allows the .NET garbage-collection mechanism to reclaim the resources used by an object when no body has a reference to it any more. This feature of .NET makes for efficient memory usage and means that you won't suffer from one of the traditional problems of C++ programs—memory leaks.

The second thing you've learned about classes is that they consist of data members and member functions. Data members represent the state of the object, and it's good practice to make them private to the class. Member functions provide the behavior of the object, and they use the data members to determine how to respond. All operations on objects are done by calling member functions, using the -> operator, as in the following line of code:

```
result = pc->DoOperation();
```

The Need for Value Types

So how are value types different from reference types, and why do we need them? As the name *value type* implies, they have been designed to hold values, such as integers, floating-point numbers, Booleans, and characters. Anything that is basically a wrapper around a simple value—and is less than about 16 bytes in size—is a good candidate for a value type.

We need value types because we want simple values to be used as efficiently as possible, but we also want them to be usable as objects. This is a problem with object-oriented languages, because if basic types are represented as objects, all operations (such as addition and multiplication of integers) have to be done by calling functions, and this isn't efficient at all. On the other hand, if basic types are not represented as objects, operations on them can be very efficient, but we can't use them where objects are needed.

.NET gets around this with value types, which are represented and used as efficiently as built-in types, but which can also be used as objects when necessary. You don't need to know this is happening most of the time. This process, is called *boxing*, is discussed in Chapter 26 in the "Advanced Topics" section.

The following table summarizes the value types provided by the .NET Framework.

Value Type	Description	Managed C++ Equivalent Type
Byte	An 8-bit unsigned integer	*char*
SByte	An 8-bit signed integer	*signed char*
Int16	A 16-bit signed integer	*short*
Int32	A 32-bit signed integer	*int* or *long*
Int64	A 64-bit signed integer	*__int64*
UInt16	A 16-bit unsigned integer	*unsigned short*
UInt32	A 32-bit unsigned integer	*unsigned int* or *unsigned long*
UInt64	A 64-bit unsigned integer	*unsigned __int64*
Single	A single-precision, 32-bit, floating-point number	*float*

Double	A double-precision 64-bit floating-point number	*double*
Boolean	A Boolean value	*bool*
Char	A 16-bit Unicode character	*wchar_t*
Decimal	A 96-bit decimal value	*Decimal*
IntPtr	A signed integer whose size depends on the platform	no built-in type
UIntPtr	An unsigned integer whose size depends on the platform	no built-in type

Note that the C++ equivalents are simply names for the types—aliases, if you like—that are rather more C++ like in nature. Although it is more natural to use the native language equivalents, you could use the underlying .NET types instead. This means that the following two lines of code mean exactly the same thing:

```
int n = 0;               // use managed C++ type
System::Int32 n = 0;     // use .NET native type
```

Properties of Value Types

A value type is a type that inherits from the *System.ValueType* class. Value types have several special properties:

- Value types are stored on the stack (unlike references, which are stored on the run-time heap).
- Instances of value types are always accessed directly (unlike reference types, which are accessed through references). This means that you don't use the *new* operator when creating instances.
- Copying value types copies the value, rather than the reference.

As you can see, value types behave just like the standard built-in types, such as *int* and *char*, and they are just as efficient to use. As mentioned in the previous section, the main difference between value types and built-in types is that value types can also be treated as objects when necessary.

Structures

Structures provide a way to create the compound data or record types that you might have come across in other programming languages. Like classes, structures can contain member functions, data members, properties, delegates, and events, but there's one important difference: structures are value types, not reference types.

This means that if you have a value type that needs to have some internal structure, such as a point with X and Y coordinates, you can implement it using a *struct*. The following exercise shows how to create a structure representing a point, how to create instances of the structure, and how to use the instances in code.

> **note**
>
> Both traditional and Managed C++ use the *struct* keyword to define structures. This chapter discusses the use of .NET structs rather than the traditional version. Declaring .NET structures has the advantages of working within the .NET world and also allows you to exchange structures with other .NET languages.

Creating and Using a Simple Struct

1 Start Visual Studio .NET, and open a new Managed C++ Application project.

2 At the top of the file, immediately under *using namespace System;*, add the following structure definition:

```
// The Point structure definition
__value struct Point
{
public:
    int x, y;
};
```

The *__value* and *struct* keywords start a structure definition, and you'll notice that structures look very similar to classes in the way they are defined. The body of the structure is enclosed in curly brackets and finishes with a semicolon, and the *public* and *private* keywords are used to set the access level for structure members.

Note the use of the *__value* keyword here. This keyword tells the compiler that this is a value type and not a traditional C++ structure. It is important that you remember to use *__value* when defining your structures.

This simple structure represents a point on a graph, so it has two integer data members representing the X and Y coordinates.

3 To create and initialize a *Point* object, add the following line to the *_+ main* function of your application:

```
// Create a Point
Point p1;
// Initialize its members
```

```
p1.x = 10;
p1.y = 20;
```

Note that the code doesn't use the *new* operator. This is because *new* is used to create references to objects, and value types aren't accessed by reference. Instead, a *Point* has been created on the program stack, and you access it directly as *p1*. Because the data members are public at this point, you can access them using the familiar dot notation.

4 Add two lines to print out the value of one of the struct members, like this:

```
Console::Write(S"p1.x is ");
Console::WriteLine(p1.x);
```

If you compile and run the program at this point, you should see the output *p1.x is 10*.

Investigating the Structure

In this exercise, you will run the program under control of the debugger so that you can look at the structure of the value type you have created.

1 If you closed the project, open it again, and open the source file.

2 Insert a debug breakpoint by clicking in the gray border to the left of the code. Click next to the declaration of *p1*. A red dot appears in the border.

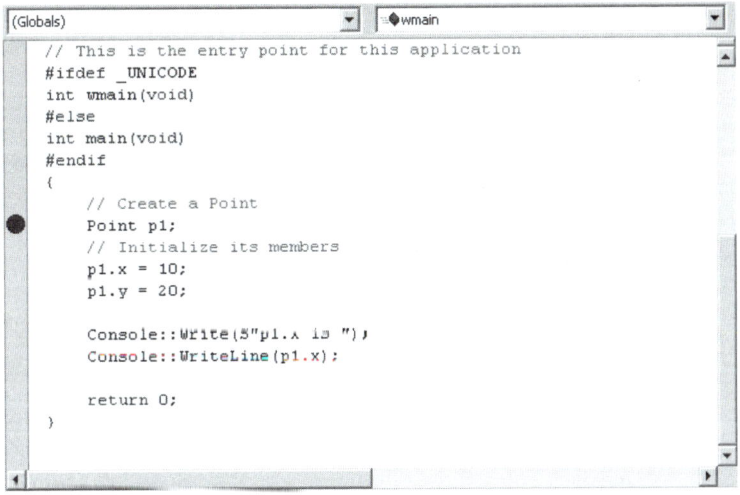

```
(Globals)                                  wmain
// This is the entry point for this application
#ifdef _UNICODE
int wmain(void)
#else
int main(void)
#endif
{
    // Create a Point
    Point p1;
    // Initialize its members
    p1.x = 10;
    p1.y = 20;

    Console::Write(S"p1.x is ");
    Console::WriteLine(p1.x);

    return 0;
}
```

3 Start the debugging session by pressing F5.

Once the program has loaded, it will execute and stops at the breakpoint. You can now use the Locals window at the bottom of the screen to look at the structure of the *Point* type.

4 If the Locals window isn't displayed in debug mode, display it by pressing Ctrl+Alt+V followed by L.

You should see an entry for the variable *p1*. Any type that has internal structure—such as *Point*—will have a plus sign (+) to the left of the variable name.

5 Click on the plus sign to expand the structure. You'll see a display similar to the one shown here.

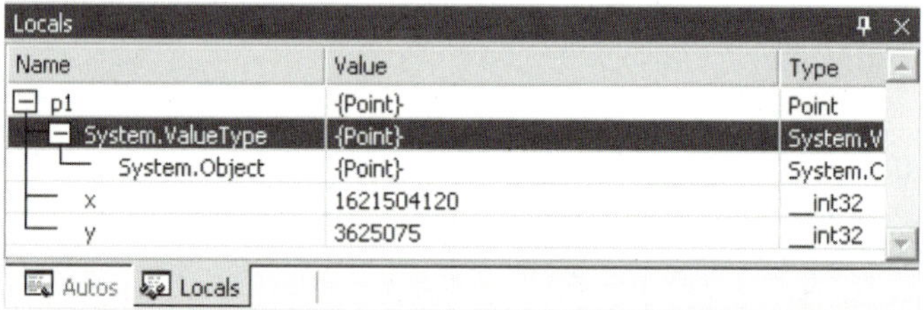

You can see that *p1* has three entries under it. The first shows that it is derived from *System.ValueType*, which is in turn derived from *System.Object*. The other two are the *x* and *y* members, which are both 32-bit integers. At this point in time they haven't been initialized, so they contain random values.

6 Press F10 twice to execute the next two statements.

This will result in *p1* being initialized, and you will see the values of *x* and *y* change to zero. The values also change from black to red in the Locals window, showing that they were changed in the previous execution step.

7 Continue pressing F10 to single-step through the code, examining the changes that occur to *p1*. When you're done, click the Stop Debugging button on the toolbar (a blue square), or press Shift+F5.

Differences Between Structures and Classes

Structures and classes have several fundamental differences:

- You can't initialize members in a structure definition. If you need to provide initialization for a structure type, you have to provide a constructor.
- Structures can't have finalizers because they aren't garbage-collected.
- Inheritance is not applicable to structs, so they can't inherit from anything else and can't be used as a base class.
- Structs can implement interfaces.

Implementing Constructors for a Struct

In this next exercise, you will add a constructor to the *Point* struct so that instances can be initialized on creation.

1 Add the following two lines immediately after the *public* declaration in your *Point* structure definition:

```
Point() { x = 0; y = 0; }
Point(int xVal, int yVal) { x = xVal; y = yVal; }
```

The first constructor takes no arguments and simply sets both data members to zero. A constructor that takes no arguments is called a *default constructor*. The second constructor takes two *int* values and uses them to initialize the *x* and *y* data members. In this case, the arguments are simply being copied into the data members, but it would be simple to add some checking to ensure that the data passed in is correct.

> **note**
> Anyone who has used C++ before will be familiar with the use of default arguments on constructors. You can't use default arguments on managed types in Visual C++, so you need to provide an explicit default constructor.

2 You can now add extra code to your *main* function to create initialized *Points*:

```
Point p1;  // use the default constructor
Point p2(10,20);    // use the second constructor to set x
                    // to 10 and y to 20
```

Using One Struct Inside Another

It is possible—and often useful—to use one struct inside another. Imagine that you have a structure named *Person* for describing a person. The structure contains the name and date of birth, among other data. You could use separate fields for each item, but you could also make the date entries into another struct and refer to it inside *Person*. Here's an example:

```
// A Date structure containing day, month and year
__value struct Date
{
    int dd, mm, yyyy;
};
```

```
// A Person structure containing a Date member
__value struct Person
{
    String* name;
    Date DOB;
};
```

You can see how the *Date* structure contains three members representing the day, month, and year. This is quite general, so you could use this structure in other programs. The *Person* structure contains a *String* reference to hold the name and a *Date* object to hold the date of birth.

In this exercise, you'll use these two classes to investigate how nested structures work.

1 Start Visual Studio .NET, and open a new Managed C++ Application project.

2 At the top of the file, immediately under *using namespace System;*, add the previous structure definitions for *Date* and *Person*.

3 In the *main* function, create a *Person* object. Remember that you don't use *new*, because structures are value types.

```
// Create a Person
Person p1;
```

4 Fill in the values for the fields:

```
// Fill in the name
p1.name = "Fred";
p1.DOB.dd = 10;
p1.DOB.mm = 3;
p1.DOB.yyyy = 1960;
```

Note how nested structure members are accessed. Because the *DOB* member has members of its own, you simply extend the dot notation to another level to access its members. You can continue this nesting to as many levels as you like, although it is unusual to go much deeper than you've done here.

5 You can also initialize all the members of the *Person* in one line. Remove the four initialization lines you entered in Step 4, and then amend the line where you create the *Person*:

```
Person p1 = { "Fred", {10, 3, 1960}};
```

Can you see what is going on here? The data in the curly brackets—called an *aggregate initializer*—provides data for the initialization of the struct. The *Person* struct contains two items, a *String* and a *Date*. Therefore, there are two items in the list. Because *Date* has members of its own, its entries are also enclosed in curly brackets.

> **note**
>
> Use of an aggregate initializer is an alternative to using a constructor and can be useful where there is no checking to be done on the data.

6 If you decide that the date of birth is wrong, you can simply create a new *Date* and copy it into the *Person* object. Try this:

```
// Create a new Date
Date newDOB = {1, 4, 1955};
p1.DOB = newDOB;
```

The new *Date* takes the values specified in the initializer, and it is then copied into the *Person* object, overwriting the values already there.

7 You can see the structure of the *Person* struct by running the program under control of the debugger. Place a breakpoint in the program at the line where *p1* is created by clicking in the gray margin to the left of the code. You should see a red dot appear, marking an active breakpoint.

8 Start the program by pressing F5. Once the program has loaded, it will execute and stop at the breakpoint. You can now use the Locals window at the bottom of the screen to look at the structure of the *Person* type.

9 If the Locals window isn't being displayed in debug mode, display it by pressing Ctrl+Alt+V followed by L.

10 Click the plus sign to the left of *p1* in the Locals window to expand the structure of the *Person*. You'll see that it has *name* and *DOB* members, and if you click the plus sign to the left of *DOB*, you can expand its structure as well.

11 Press F10 to step through the code until all the members are initialized. You will see the members of *p1* displayed in red as each value changes.

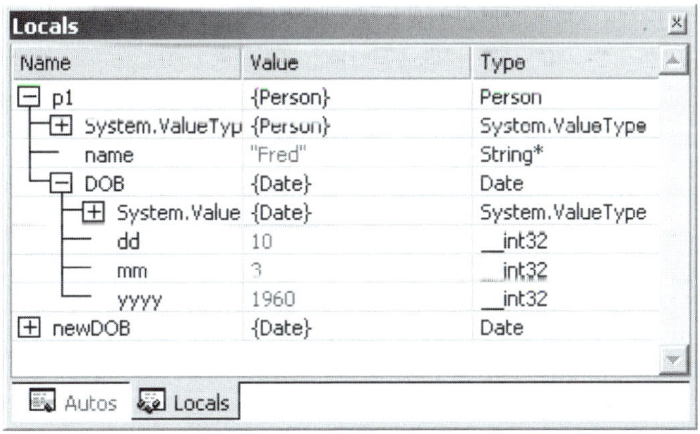

12 When you've finished, press Shift+F5 to stop debugging, or click the Stop Debugging button on the toolbar.

Finally, let's consider nested structs. If you don't want to use the *Date* struct anywhere except inside your *Person* structure, you can define the *Date* structure inside the *Person* structure, as shown here:

```
// A Person structure containing a Date structure
__value struct Person
{
    String* name;
    __value struct Date
    {
        int dd, mm, yyyy;
    };
    Date DOB;
};
```

You create *Person* variables and access their members exactly the same as before. The big difference is that the *Date* structure is now a part of *Person*, and you can't create *Date* variables on their own.

Copying Structs

Because structs are value types, copying them makes a copy of the values they contain. Contrast this behavior with classes, where copying objects results in references being copied:

```
Person p1;
Person p2;
...
p2 = p1;    // p1's data is copied into p2
MyClass m1;
MyClass m2;
...
m2 = m1;    // m2 and m1 now refer to the same object.
            // No data is copied.
```

> **note**
>
> You can't use a *__gc* reference type as a member of a struct, because structs aren't garbage collected; a reference member would have to take part in garbage collection.

Enumerations

An enumeration is a set of named integer constants. Enumerations are especially suitable for representing types that can take one of a set of fixed values, such as the days of the week or the months of the year. Enumerations are value types, and they derive from the abstract *System.Enum* class, which in turn derives from *System.ValueType*.

Creating and Using an Enum

In the following exercise, you will create an enumeration to hold values representing the days of the week, and then use it in a program.

1. Start Visual Studio .NET and open a new Managed C++ Application project.
2. At the top of the file, immediately under *using namespace System;* line, add the following structure definition:

```
// The Weekday enum definition
__value enum WeekDay
{
    Monday, Tuesday, Wednesday, Thursday, Friday,
    Saturday, Sunday
};
```

The *__value* and *enum* keywords start an enum definition, and you'll notice that, once again, enumerations are defined similarly to classes. The body of the enum is enclosed in curly brackets and finishes with a semicolon. Note the use of the *__value* keyword here. It is this keyword that tells the compiler that this is a value type, and not a traditional C++ enum. It is very important that you remember to use *__value* when defining your enumerations.

The enum itself consists of a comma-separated set of names, each of which represents an integer constant.

3. Create enum variables the same as you create any other type. To create and initialize a *WeekDay* object, add the following lines to the *main* function of your application:

```
// Create a WeekDay
WeekDay w = Monday;
```

As with structs, the code doesn't use the *new* operator. An enum named *WeekDay* has been created on the program stack, and you access it directly as *w*. Note how the enum variable is initialized with one of the members of the enumeration. This syntax is how you initialize enum variables and how you can assign to them later on.

4. Try printing out the value of the *WeekDay* object like this:

```
Console::Write("Value of w is ");
Console::WriteLine(w);
```

The value 0 should print out. Each of the named constants making up the enum is given an integer value; by default, these values start from 0 and increase by one for each subsequent member of the enumeration. You can test this by changing the value you initially assign to *w* to be, for example, *Saturday*. When you run the code again, the value 5 should print out.

Even though the value given to an enum is an integer, there is no implicit conversion between enums and integers. If you consider the following lines of code, you'll understand why:

```
//** This code won't compile! **//
// '1' would mean Tuesday
w = 1;
// What would '8' mean?
w = 8;
```

If converting between integers and enums were allowed, it would be possible to put invalid values into the enum. Going the other way is okay, though, because any enum value is a valid integer.

You don't have to rely on the default numeric values that are assigned to the enum members. Suppose you want the integer equivalents of the weekdays to range from 1 through 7 instead of 0 through 6: simply assign 1 to the Monday member:

```
__value enum WeekDay
{
    Monday = 1, Tuesday, Wednesday, Thursday, Friday,
    Saturday, Sunday
};
```

The enumeration will now start with 1, and because you haven't given any other values for the remaining members, they'll be numbered 2 through 7.

If you want, you can give a completely discontinuous series of values for the enum members, as in this example:

```
__value enum StatusCodes
{
    OK=0, FileNotFound=2, AccessDenied=5, InvalidHandle=6,
    OutOfMemory=8
};
```

Using Enums in Programs

In this exercise, you'll see how to use an enum to control program execution by using it in a *switch* statement.

1 Use the same application as in the previous example. If you've closed it, select File, Open Solution to open the project again.

2 After the *WriteLine* statements, add the following switch statement code:

```
// Switch on the weekday
switch(w)
{
case Monday:
    Console::WriteLine("It's a Monday!");
    break;
case Tuesday:
    Console::WriteLine("It's a Tuesday!");
    break;
case Wednesday:
    Console::WriteLine("It's a Wednesday!");
    break;
default:
    Console::WriteLine("It's some other day...");
}
```

You are allowed to use an enum variable as a switch control variable because it's basically an integer. Likewise, you can use the names of enum members as switch case labels because they're also integers. The example code has cases for Monday through Wednesday; everything else is handled by the default case. Remember to put the *break* statements in after the code for each case, or the program won't behave as you expect.

Avoiding Ambiguity

The names of enum members don't have to be unique, but if they aren't, you might need to qualify them with the name of the enum to which they belong, to avoid ambiguity. Suppose that you have two enums declared in your program—*Direction* and *Mood*—both of which have a *Down* member. Here's how you'd have to use them:

```
int myMood = Down;           // ambiguous
int myMood = Mood::Down;     // OK
```

Using Memory Efficiently

By default, enums are *ints*, and therefore are 32 bits in size, which gives you a range of values of -2,147,483,648 through 2,147,483,647. If you're going to use only small values for enum members, memory will be wasted if each variable takes up 32 bits. For this reason, it is possible to base an enum on any integer type; in the case of our *WeekDay* example, all our values can quite happily fit into one byte. You could base the enum on a *char*, as shown here:

```
// WeekDay variables are one byte in size
__value enum WeekDay : char
{
    Monday = 1, Tuesday, Wednesday, Thursday, Friday,
    Saturday, Sunday
};
```

Chapter 9 Quick Reference

To	Do this

Create a struct	Use *__value struct*, followed by the name of the struct, and the body in curly brackets, followed by a semicolon. For example:
	`__value struct`
	`Point3D`
	`{`
	`    int x, y, z;`
	`};`

Initialize struct members	Create a constructor, which is a function that has the same name as the struct. For example:
	`__value struct`
	`Point3D`
	`{`
	`    int x, y, z;`
	`    Point3D(int xVal, int yVal,`
	`    int zVal)`
	`    {`
	`        x=xVal;`
	`        y=yVal;`
	`        z=zVal;`
	`    }`
	`};`
	You can also use an aggregate initializer:
	`Point3D p1 = { 10, 20, 30 };`

Access struct members	Use the dot notation. For example:
	`Point3D p1.x = 10;`
	`myPerson.DOB.dd = 20;`

Create an enum	Use *__value enum*, followed by the name of the enum and the body in curly brackets, followed by a semicolon. For example:
	`__value enum Seasons`
	`{ Spring, Summer,`
	`Autumn, Winter };`

Control the values used for enum members	Assign values to the members in the enum definition. For example.
	`__value enum Seasons`
	`{ Spring=1, Summer,`
	`Autumn, Winter };`

Base enums on other integer types	Put a semicolon and the type name after the enum name. For example:
	`__value enum Seasons`
	` : char { Spring, Summer,`
	`Autumn, Winter };`

Operator Overloading

In this chapter, you'll learn

- ✔ *What operator overloading is*
- ✔ *Which classes must support operator overloading*
- ✔ *What you can and can't overload*
- ✔ *Guidelines for providing overloaded operators*
- ✔ *How to implement operator overloads*

You've already seen how to construct classes and structs, provide member functions in your types, and use these functions in programs. In this chapter, you're going to find out about a special category of member functions called overloaded operator functions, which allow you to add extra functionality so that your types can be used more naturally and intuitively.

note

If you've met operator overloading in C++ before, you need to be aware that overloading is handled completely differently in Managed C++. In fact, Managed C++ types aren't allowed to implement traditional C++ overloaded operators, so you'll need to pay close attention to this chapter to find out how it is now done.

What Is Operator Overloading?

You met the operators provided by the C++ language in Chapter 3. The problem is that those operators work only with the built-in types, and you're starting to use classes and structs to define your own data types. This means that if you want to do an addition operation or a comparison operation on types that you've created, you can't use the + and == operators because the compiler doesn't know how to apply them to your types.

Operator overloading is a C++ feature that lets you define operators to work with your types, and this can often lead to a more natural style of programming, so that instead of writing this:

```
object3 = object1.Add(object2);
```

you can instead write this:

```
object3 = object1 + object2;
```

What Types Need Overloaded Operators?

In general, overloaded operators are needed by classes that wrap simple values. Types can be split into three broad classifications, as shown in the following table:

Classification	Defining characteristics	Examples
Values	Values wrap data; if two objects contain the same data, those objects are identical.	*String*, *Matrix*, *Date*, *Time*
Services	Services have little or no state data. They provide services through their member functions.	*CreditCardCheck*, *AddressLookup*
Entities	Entities have an identity that is unique for each object.	*BankAccount* (identified by account number), *Person* (identified by Social Security number)

Values are the classes for which you will most often find yourself implementing overloaded operators. You can imagine wanting to implement +, >, ==, and other operators for types such as *Date* and *String*, but it is harder to see when you might want them for the other classifications. Service types, which have little or no state, don't tend to need operators: what would comparing two *AddressLookup* objects mean? Entity types might have some operators, but their meaning might not be intuitive. You could use == to check two *BankAccounts* for equality, but what would that mean? There's more on equality later on in the lesson; let's move on to see how operator overloading works.

What Can You Overload?

You learned about the rich set of operators that C++ supports in Chapter 3. You can overload many of these, but there are some restrictions. Traditional C++ won't let you overload several of the more esoteric operators, such as *sizeof* and the member-of dot operator. Managed C++ extends the list, and adds a number of other C++ operators that can't be overloaded, including ->, (), and [].

The main reason for this restriction is that the Common Language Specification (CLS) is designed for use across languages, and as such will support only a set of operators that is useful to all .NET languages, rather than being C++-specific. You'll see later exactly which operators .NET lets you overload.

Rules of Overloading

Several rules apply when overloading operators. The problem is that you can implement operators to mean whatever you like, so some rules are needed to impose some limits, and in addition prevent giving the compiler an impossible job.

- You can have no new operators. Even if you think that %% would make a neat new operator, you can't add new ones.
- You can't change the number of operands taken by an operator. You might think it would be really useful to create a unary / operator, but the division operator always has to have two operands.
- You can't change the precedence or associativity of operators. What this means is that * will always take precedence over +, regardless of what they are actually implemented to mean for a type.

Overloading Operators in Managed Types

Overloading operators in managed types is quite different from how you overload them in traditional C++. The CLS defines the list of arithmetic, logical, and bitwise operators that .NET languages can support, and compiler vendors use the language's native operators to implement these functions.

This means that when you override an operator in a managed C++ type, you don't override the C++ operator, but instead override the underlying CLS functionality.

> **Note**
>
> If you are currently a C++ programmer, be aware that the compiler won't let you implement normal C++ operator overloads in Managed types. You have to use the overloading mechanism described in the following section.

Overloading Value Types

Let's start by adding operator overloading to value types, and then move on to reference types. You already know that value types are the types most likely to need operator overloading.

Overloading Arithmetic Operators

In this exercise you'll see how to implement operators in a value type. The exercise also introduces many of the techniques you'll need to use when adding operator overloading to your own types.

1. Start Visual Studio.NET and open a new Managed C++ Application project.
2. At the top of the file, immediately under the line *using namespace System;*, add the following class definition:

   ```
   // The Dbl class definition
   __value struct Dbl
   {
       double val;
   public:
       Dbl(double v) { val = v; }
       double getVal() { return val; }
   };
   ```

   This simple *Dbl* struct is the one you'll use throughout these exercises. It simply wraps a double, and then provides a constructor for creating and initializing *Dbl* objects and a *get* function for accessing the data member. As you might remember from the previous chapter, the keyword *__value* makes *Dbl* a .NET value type rather than a traditional C++ struct.
3. Create three *Dbl* objects in your *_+main* function:

   ```
   Dbl d1(10.0);
   Dbl d2(20.0);
   Dbl d3(0.0);
   ```

4. Add a call to *Console::WriteLine* to print out the value of *d3*:

   ```
   Console::Write("Value of d3 is");
   Console::WriteLine(d3.getVal());
   ```

   Remember that you have to use the dot operator to reference members of a managed object.
5. Try adding *d1* and *d2* and assigning the result to *d3*. Insert this line into your code immediately before the call to *Console::Write*:

   ```
   d3 = d1 + d2;
   ```

When you try this, you'll find that it doesn't work, and the compiler gives you a C2676 error.

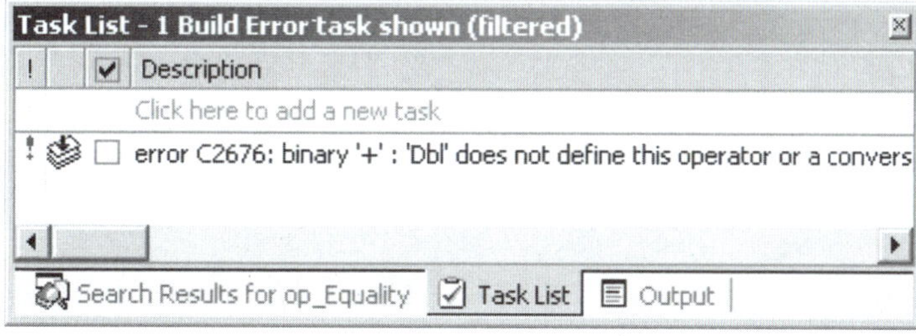

The compiler is telling you that it doesn't have a + operator to use that works with *Dbl* objects, so it can't perform the operation.

6 Implement the + operator for the class by adding the following code to the class definition, immediately after the *getVal* function:

```
// The addition operator for the Dbl struct
static Dbl op_Addition(Dbl lhs, Dbl rhs)
{
    Dbl result(lhs.val + rhs.val);
    return result;
}
```

Let's analyze this function. The keyword *static*, which you met in Chapter 6, tells you that this function belongs to the *Dbl* class as a whole, rather than belonging to any one member of it. The addition operation is implemented by the *op_Addition* function, which is one of the overloadable functions defined in the CLS. The following table lists the operators supported by the CLS, together with their C++ equivalents.

Operation	C++ operator	CLS function
Decrement	—	*op_Decrement*
Increment	++	*op_Increment*
Negate	!	*op_Negation*
Unary minus	-	*op_UnaryNegation*
Unary plus	+	*op_UnaryPlus*
Addition	+	*op_Addition*
Subtraction	-	*op_Subtraction*
Multiplication	*	*op_Multiply*
Division	/	*op_Division*

(continued)

(continued)

<table>
<tr><td>Modulus</td><td>%</td><td>op_Modulus</td></tr>
<tr><td>Assignment</td><td>=</td><td>op_Assign</td></tr>
<tr><td>Equality</td><td>==</td><td>op_Equality</td></tr>
<tr><td>Inequality</td><td>!=</td><td>op_Inequality</td></tr>
<tr><td>Less than</td><td><</td><td>op_LessThan</td></tr>
<tr><td>Less than or equal to</td><td><=</td><td>op_LessThanOrEqual</td></tr>
<tr><td>Greater than</td><td>></td><td>op_GreaterThan</td></tr>
<tr><td>Greater than or equal to</td><td>>=</td><td>op_GreaterThanOrEqual</td></tr>
<tr><td>Logical AND</td><td>&&</td><td>op_LogicalAnd</td></tr>
<tr><td>Logical OR</td><td>||</td><td>op_LogicalOr</td></tr>
<tr><td>Left-shift</td><td><<</td><td>op_LeftShift</td></tr>
<tr><td>Right-shift</td><td>>></td><td>op_RightShift</td></tr>
<tr><td>Bitwise AND</td><td>&</td><td>op_BitwiseAnd</td></tr>
<tr><td>Bitwise OR</td><td>|</td><td>op_BitwiseOr</td></tr>
<tr><td>Exclusive OR</td><td>^</td><td>op_ExclusiveOr</td></tr>
</table>

To overload an operator, you pick the equivalent function from the list and implement it in your class. The arguments a function takes and what it returns depend upon the function: in this case, we're implementing the binary addition operator, so the arguments are going to be two *Dbl* values, and the return type will also be a *Dbl* value.

You can see how the function works: the result of adding two *Dbl* values has to be a third *Dbl*, so you create a third one, initialize it with the contents of the two operands, and return it.

Operator Overloading in Unmanaged C++

If you need to provide overloaded operators in traditional, unmanaged C++, you'll find that operator overloading is done rather differently. Operator overloads use the *operator* keyword to name an overload function, so the addition operator is implemented by a function named *operator+*, the equality operator by one named *operator==*, the increment operator by one called *operator++*, and so on. These functions can either be member functions of the type or global functions that aren't a member of any type.

There is a lot more to operator overloading in unmanaged C++. If you need to know more, consult a book on C++ programming. Bjarne Stroustrup's *The C++ Programming Language* (Addison-Wesley, 1997) is the classic C++ text.

7 Try compiling your program again.

You should find that this time the compilation is successful, because the compiler recognizes that you have implemented the + operator. If you run the program, you should get the answer 30.0 printed out, because of the following two lines.

```
Console::Write("Value of d3 is");
Console::WriteLine(d3.getVal());
```

If your type implements an operator, the compiler maps C++ operators (such as +) onto the equivalent *op_ function* for you. You can also call the operator function explicitly, although there's generally little reason why you'd want to do so. This means that you could replace the addition line, as follows:

```
// d3 = d1 + d2;
d3 = Dbl::op_Addition(d1, d2);
```

A static method is accessed by using the type name followed by the :: operator and the name of the function.

Now that you've seen how to implement the addition operator, it will be simple for you to implement the other arithmetic operators for the class (subtraction, division, multiplication, and modulus).

Overloading Operator Functions

You can also overload the operator functions themselves. For example, suppose you wanted to handle the following addition operations:

```
// Add two Dbl's
d3 = d1 + d2;

// Add a Dbl and an int
d3 = d1 + 5;

// Add an int and a Dbl
d3 = 5 + d2;
```

You can add overrides of the *op_Addition* function to handle this task. The following short exercise shows you how.

1 Find the *op Addition* function in the *Dbl* struct. Add the following two variations after it:

```
// Adding a Dbl and an int
static Dbl op_Addition(Dbl lhs, int rhs)
```

```
{
    Dbl result(lhs.val + rhs);
    return result;
}
// Adding an int and a Dbl
static Dbl op_Addition(int lhs, Dbl rhs)
{
    Dbl result(lhs + rhs.val);
    return result;
}
```

2 Add two more additions to your *main* function to test the new operator functions, plus some calls to *Console::WriteLine* to verify that the additions have worked correctly:

```
// Add two Dbl's
d3 = d1 + d2;
Console::Write("Value of d3 is ");
Console::WriteLine(d3.getVal());

// Add a Dbl and an int
d3 = d1 + 5;
Console::Write("Value of d3 is now ");
Console::WriteLine(d3.getVal());

// Add an int and a Dbl
d3 = 5 + d2;
Console::Write("Value of d3 is now ");
Console::WriteLine(d3.getVal());
```

3 Now for the interesting step: remove (or comment out) those last two operator overloads you added in Step 1, and then recompile the code and run it.

You should find it works exactly the same as it did with the operators in. So what's going on? You can find out by using the debugger.

4 Place a breakpoint in the code by clicking in the gray margin to the left of the code, next to the *d3 = d1 + 5* line.

You should see a red dot in the margin, showing that a breakpoint has been set.

```
    Console::Write("Value of d3 is ");
    Console::WriteLine(d3.getVal());

    // Add a Dbl and an int
    d3 = d1 + 5;
    Console::Write("Value of d3 is now ");
    Console::WriteLine(d3.getVal());

    // Add an int and a Dbl
    d3 = 5 + d2;
    Console::Write("Value of d3 is now ");
    Console::WriteLine(d3.getVal());

    return 0;
}
```

5 Run the program by pressing the F5 key. The program will start up and then stop at the breakpoint. Now press the F11 key to step into the next function to be executed. You might expect this function to be *op_Addition*, but you'd be wrong, because you step into the *Dbl* constructor.

6 Press F11 again and you're finished with the constructor and back to the *d3 = d1 + 5;* line. Press it once more, and you're in *op_Addition,* where you might expect to be.

Why did you get an extra call to the *Dbl* constructor? Because the compiler saw an integer in the code, but it only has an *op_Addition* function that takes two *Dbl* values. However, because the *Dbl* class has a constructor that takes an integer, the compiler has used the constructor to create a temporary *Dbl* object to pass to the function.

If, when you're in the *op_Addition* function, you examine the arguments in the Locals window, you'll see that they are both of type *Dbl*, and that the *rhs* argument has the value 5.0.

You can see that, provided your types implement the correct constructors, you can sometimes use one operator overload to perform several different conversions.

Implementing Logical Operators and Equality

We've now dealt with the arithmetic operators, so let's continue by considering the logical and comparison operators. As you've already seen, C++ provides a set of comparison operators, and they're summarized in the following table:

Operator	Description
==	Equality
!=	Inequality
>	Greater than
>=	Greater than or equal to
<	Less than
<=	Less than or equal to

Implementing these operators is quite simple and follows the model of the addition operator in the previous exercises. Here's how to implement the equality operator, ==:

1 Using the same Dbl project as in the previous exercises, find the *op_Addition* function in your code, and add the following function after it:

```
// The equality operator for the Dbl struct
static bool op_Equality(Dbl lhs, Dbl rhs)
{
    return lhs.val == rhs.val;
}
```

The function follows the same pattern as those you implemented for the arithmetic operators. It is a static member of the *Dbl* type, but this time it returns a Boolean, just as you'd expect a logical operator to do, and it makes its decision by comparing the inner structure of its two operands.

What Is Equality?

Deciding whether to implement == and != depends on the type you're writing, and it might not be a simple decision. For some classes the choice is fairly obvious: take a *Point* type, which has *X* and *Y* members. In this case, == would compare the *X* and *Y* members of two *Points* and return True if they're the same.

What about a *Currency* class, which has a value and a currency type? You might say that two *Currency* objects are the same if both the value and the currency type are identical. Likewise, you could say that the two objects were identical if their values were the same when converted to some underlying base currency, such as dollars or Euros. Both view points are equally valid; it's up to you to choose one and document it.

Additionally, there might be classes for which any notion of equality is artificial. Consider a *BankAccount* class: what would equality mean? Two account objects can't be identical, because they have different, unique account numbers. You might choose some criteria that you could test for equality, or you might decide that equality doesn't apply to *BankAccount* objects.

2 Add some test code to the *main* function to test the new operator:

```
if (d1 == d2)
    Console::WriteLine("d1 and d2 are equal");
else
    Console::WriteLine("d1 and d2 are not equal");
```

As you'd expect, *d1* and *d2* aren't equal, so if you compile and run your program you see the second message.

3 You can take a shortcut when you implement the inequality operator, !=, by making use of the fact that its result is the opposite of whatever == would return for the same operands. This means that you can implement the inequality operator in terms of the equality operator:

```
// The inequality operator for the Dbl struct
static bool op_Inequality(Dbl lhs, Dbl rhs)
{
    return !(lhs == rhs);    // calls op_Equality()
}
```

The function compares its two arguments using the == operator, which causes the *op_Equality* function to be called, and *op_Inequality* then applies the not operator (!) to turn a true result into false, and vice versa.

In this case, using the shortcut doesn't save us any code, but if *op_Equality* ended up checking a lot of data members, this could be a worthwhile shortcut. It will also help if the structure of the class changes, because you'll only have to change the implementation of *op_Equality*.

The other logical operators (<, <=, >, and >=) can be overloaded in a similar manner, and you can make use of the same shortcuts when implementing pairs of operators.

Implementing *Equals*

You've already learned that all types in .NET ultimately inherit from the *Object* class. This class provides several functions that all .NET types inherit, and one in particular is relevant to our discussion of the == and != operators.

The *Object::Equals* method is intended to let types provide a way of comparing content, as opposed to comparing references. This is the same task that you've performed by implementing the == operator, but one of the great attractions of .NET is that managed types can be accessed seamlessly from other languages, and they might well want to use *Equals* to test for equality.

The following exercise shows you how to implement *Equals* for the *Dbl* class.

1 Using the same *Dbl* project as in the previous exercises, find the *op_Inequality* function in your code, and add the following function after it:

```
// The equality operator for the Dbl struct
bool Equals(Object* pOther)
{
    Dbl* s = dynamic_cast<Dbl*>(pOther);
    if (s == 0) return false;

    return s->val == val;
}
```

This is a more complex operator function than others in this chapter, so let's look at it line by line. The first line declares the *Equals* function to take an *Object** as its single argument and return a *bool*. It's important that you declare it exactly this way; otherwise, it won't be an override for the virtual function inherited from the *Object* base class.

The use of *Object** for the argument type means that you can pass a pointer to any managed type into the function, so the first thing you need to do is to make sure that it is actually a *Dbl** that has been passed in. You run this test by using a dynamic cast. You'll remember from Chapter 6 that a dynamic cast is used to do a run-time cast. Here, the cast is from *Object** to *Dbl**. If the cast fails—if the pointer passed in isn't a *Dbl**— the result will be a null pointer. The function checks for this possibility and returns false if it is the case. If the dynamic cast works, you know that you have a *Dbl**; therefore, you can check its content to see if it is the same as that of the object.

2 Calling the *Equals* method from code is more complicated than using the operators we've already met, because of the need to pass in an *Object** pointer. Add the following code to the *main* function after your test of the == operator:

```
if (d1.Equals(__box(d2)))
    Console::WriteLine("d1 and d2 are equal");
else
    Console::WriteLine("d1 and d2 are not equal");
```

This code calls the *Equals* function on *d1* to see whether *d1* is equal to *d2*. *Equals* needs a pointer to an *Object*, so you need somehow to get an *Object** representing *d2*, and this task is done by using keyword the *__box*.

You learned in Chapter 9 how value types are as efficient as built-in types, but they can also be used as reference types when the need arises. Treating a value type as a reference type is done by *boxing* it; boxing is discussed in more detail in Chapter 26, "Working with Unmanaged Code," but it basically involves wrapping an object around a value type. The object wrapper is a reference type, and acts as a box to contain the value.

This process might seem complicated, but you're really providing *Equals* for other .NET languages to use. In managed C++ code you'd usually use == instead, without worrying about boxing.

> **tip**
>
> If you implement *Equals* for a type, it is strongly recommended that you implement the == operator.

Implementing Assignment

The *op_Assign* function provides a way to overload the assignment operator, =. Why would you want to do this? Suppose you have a class that contains a date and time, and you want to make sure that these member variables hold the date and time when the object was created or assigned to. If you don't implement *op_Assign*, the existing values will be copied straight from the right side over to the left side. By implementing the operator, you can customize the copy operation, and ensure that the date and time are updated when the assignment is performed.

The following short exercise shows you how to implement *op_Assign* for the *Dbl* class.

1 Using the same *Dbl* project as in the previous exercises, add three data members to represent the time. In addition, alter the constructor so that the time fields are initialized to the current time:

```
// The Dbl class definition
__value struct Dbl
{
    double val;
    double hr, min, sec;      // creation or assignment time
public:
    Dbl(double v)
    {
        val = v;

        // Create new date and time fields
        DateTime dt = DateTime::get_Now();
        hr = dt.get_Hour();
        min = dt.get_Minute();
        sec = dt.get_Second();
```

```
    }

    double getVal() { return val; }
};
```

The constructor uses a *System::DateTime* object to hold the current time; this object is initialized by a call to the static *DateTime::get_Now* method. The individual fields are then saved into the appropriate members of the object.

2 Now add the assign function to the *Dbl* class:

```
// The assignment operator for the Dbl class
static Dbl op_Assign(Dbl& lhs, const Dbl& rhs)
{
    // Copy over the value
    lhs.val = rhs.val;

    // Create new date and time fields
    DateTime dt = DateTime::get_Now();
    lhs.hr = dt.get_Hour();
    lhs.min = dt.get_Minute();
    lhs.sec = dt.get_Second();

    return lhs;
}
```

You'll notice several things about this function. First is the fact that it uses references for the arguments. You met references in Chapter 3, where you found out that a reference lets you pass values by reference, so that the name you use in the function is a link back to the argument that was passed in. Passing in values by using references is essential when you think how assignment has to work. Let's say you code a line like this:

```
obj2 = obj1;
```

You want *obj2* to contain the values from *obj1* when the function returns. If you pass the arguments by value—without the &—any changes to *lhs* will be lost, because this local variable ceases to exist at the end of the function. Making the arguments to the function references provides a link back to the value that was passed in, so changes made to *lhs* will be persistent. The *rhs* argument is made a *const* reference, because you don't want to make changes to the right side, and the keyword *const* ensures that you can't.

The *val* member is copied over, and then a new set of time members is generated so that the object will reflect the time it was assigned, not the original time it was created.

3 To test the changes, you have to arrange some sort of time delay between creating the object and assigning to it, so that you can see that the times are different. The easiest way to do this is to use the static *Sleep* method from the *System::Thread* class, so add the following code to your *main* method:

```
// Create two objects
Dbl one(0.0);
Dbl two(10.0);

// Sleep for five seconds
System::Threading::Thread::Sleep(5000);

// Do an assignment
one = two;
```

4 The best way to see the result is to run the code under the debugger. Place a breakpoint in the code on the line where the *one* object is created by clicking in the gray margin to the left of the code. You'll see a red dot appear, indicating an active breakpoint.

5 Run the program by pressing F5, and the code runs until the breakpoint is reached. Press F10 to single-step over the creation of the *one* object. Now look in the Locals window, and click the plus sign to the left of *one* to expand it. You see the time values assigned to the object:

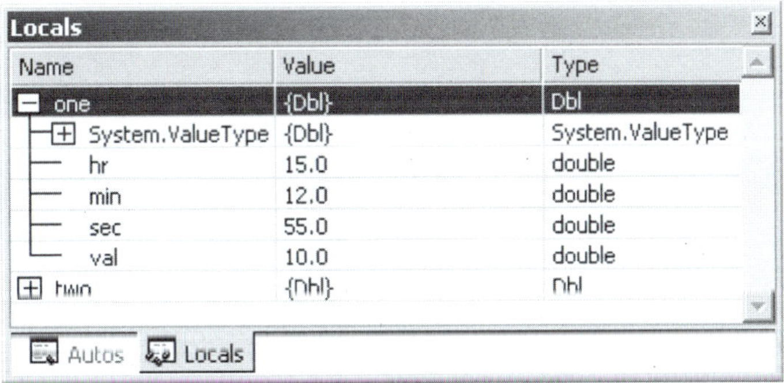

6 Now press F10 to single-step through the code, past the call to *Sleep*. When you pass the assignment, you see that the data members in *one*: *val* takes on the value of the *val* member from *two*, while the time reflects the time the assignment was done.

Implementing Increment and Decrement

As a final example, the exercise in this section shows you how to overload the increment and decrement operators, ++ and —. As you saw in Chapter 3, the built-in ++ and — operators are used to increment and decrement the values of numeric variables. You can overload them for your own numeric types, but you can also overload these operators to provide other functionality. For example, suppose you had a *Date* type that holds day, month, and year values; you could implement ++ and — to add or subtract one day from the current date, adjusting the month and year as appropriate.

The following exercise shows you how to implement the ++ operator for the *Dbl* type that you've been working with in this chapter.

1 Using the same *Dbl* project as in the previous exercises, find the *Equals* function in your code, and add the following code immediately after it:

```
// The increment operator for the Dbl struct
static Dbl op_Increment(Dbl d)
{
    d.val += 1;
    return d;
}
```

The ++ operator is implemented by the *op_Increment* function; the — operator is implemented by *op_Decrement*. The single argument represents the value to be incremented, so one gets added to its value, and then a copy is returned.

2 Use the operator in code like this:

```
// Create a Dbl, and increment it
Dbl d5(1.0);
Console::Write("Initial value of d5 is ");
Console::WriteLine(d5.getVal());

// Increment it
d5++;
Console::Write("Value of d5 is now ");
Console::WriteLine(d5.getVal());
```

The answer 2 should print out, representing the new value of *d5*. Note that even though the function returns a *Dbl*, the return value isn't being used in this example, and you're executing the function only to get its side effect of incrementing the value.

Once you've implemented the increment operator, you'll find it simple to implement decrement as well.

> **note**
>
> You saw in Chapter 3 that there are two forms of the increment and decrement operators: the prefix form that goes before the operand (++x) and the postfix form that follows the operand (x++). When overloading managed types, it isn't possible to distinguish between prefix and postfix operators, so the same *op_Increment* or *op_Decrement* function is called for both. In traditional C++ operator overloading, you can overload both prefix and postfix versions separately.

Overloading Reference Types

You can overload operators for reference types in the same way that you do for value types, but you need to be aware of the issues detailed in this section.

Implementing Overloaded Operators for Reference Types

You already know that reference types are accessed using pointers, which means that the arguments to operator functions for reference types always have to be pointers. So if you were to implement *op_Addition* for a reference type, you would have to code it something like this:

```
// The addition operator for a reference type
static MyRef* op_Addition(MyRef* pLhs, MyRef* pRhs)
{
    MyRef* result = new MyRef(lhs.val + rhs.val);
    return result;
}
```

Calling Overloaded Operators for Reference Types

You can't call overloaded operators implicitly for reference types, so you have to call the overload function directly:

```
// This doesn't work
MyRef* r3 = one + two;

// This does
MyRef* r3 = MyRef::op_Addition(one, two);
```

> **note**
> This limitation might be removed in later versions of Visual C++ .NET.

Guidelines for Providing Overloaded Operators

The most important guideline is *Overloaded operators must make intuitive sense for a class*. For instance, if you have a *String* class, using + to concatenate *Strings* is pretty intuitive. You might get some agreement that -, as in *s2 - s1*, would mean "look for *s1* within *s2*, and if you find it, remove it." But what could the * operator mean when applied to two *Strings*? There's no obvious meaning, and you're only going to confuse people if you provide it. So make sure that the operators you provide for your types are the ones that people expect to find.

The second guideline is *Operator usage must be consistent*. In other words, if you overload ==, make sure you overload != as well. The same goes for < and >, ++ and —, and so on.

> **note**
> The C# compiler enforces consistent overloading, and it will not let you overload one of a pair of operators without also implementing the other. In C++, however, it is up to you to be consistent.

The third guideline is *Don't overload obscure operators or ones that change the semantics of the language*. Operators such as , are obscure, and few people know how they work, so it isn't a good idea to overload them. Other operators, such as the logical AND and OR operators && and ||, can cause problems. In Chapter 3 you learned about the *if* statement and how expressions joined by && and || are only evaluated if necessary. As a result, some expressions in an *if* statement may never be evaluated. If you overload the AND and OR operators, the whole of the expression will have to be evaluated, and this changes the way the *if* works.

Chapter 10 Quick Reference

To	Do this
Overload operators for value types	Implement the appropriate *op_* function as a static member of the type.
Implement equality tests	Overload == and !=, and provide an overload of *Equals* for the benefit of other .NET languages.
Overload operators for reference types	Use pointers for argument and return types.

CHAPTER

11

Exception Handling

In this chapter, you'll learn

- ✔ *What exceptions are*
- ✔ *The different types of exceptions that can be used in Managed C++*
- ✔ *How to generate exceptions*
- ✔ *How to handle exceptions*
- ✔ *How to create your own exception classes*

Now that you know how to construct classes and value types and use them in programming, this chapter introduces you to exception handling, a powerful way of handling errors within C++ programs.

What Are Exceptions?

Exceptions are an error-handling mechanism employed extensively in C++ and several other modern programming languages. Traditionally, error and status information is passed around using function return values and parameters, like this.

```
// Pass status back as return value
bool bOK = doSomething();

// Pass status back in a parameter
int status;
doSomething(arg1, arg2, &status);
```

Although this is a tried and tested way of passing status information around, it suffers from several drawbacks:

- You can't force the programmer to do anything about the error.
- The programmer doesn't even have to check the error code.
- If you're deep down in a series of nested calls, you have to set each status flag and back out manually.
- It is very difficult to pass back status information from something that doesn't take arguments or return a value.

Exceptions provide an alternative error handling mechanism, which gives you three main advantages over traditional return value error handling:

- **Exceptions can't be ignored.** If an exception isn't handled at some point, the program will terminate. This makes exceptions suitable for handling critical errors.
- **Exceptions don't have to be handled at the point where the exception occurs.** An error can occur many levels of function call deep in a program, and there might not be a way to fix the problem at the point where the error occurs. Exceptions let you handle the error anywhere up the call stack (see the sidebar below).
- **Exceptions provide a useful way to signal errors where a return value can't be used.** There are two particular places in C++ where return values can't be used: constructors don't use them, and overloaded operators can't have their return value overloaded to use for error and status information. Exceptions are particularly useful in these situations, because they let you sidestep the normal return-value mechanism.

The Call Stack and Exceptions

At any point in a program, the call stack holds information about which functions have been called to get to the current point. The call stack is used in three main ways by programs: during execution to control calling and returning from functions, by the debugger, and during exception handling.

The handler for an exception can occur in the routine in which the exception was thrown. It can also occur in any routine above it in the call stack, and at run time each routine in the call stack is checked to see if it implements a suitable handler. If nothing suitable has been found by the time the top of the stack has been reached, the program terminates.

In .NET, C++ exceptions have one other significant advantage, in that they can be used across languages. Because exceptions are part of the underlying .NET Framework, it is possible to throw an exception in C++ code and catch it in Microsoft Visual Basic, something that isn't possible outside the .NET environment.

As you would with any other error mechanism, you will tend to trigger exceptions by making errors in your code. However, you can also generate them yourself if necessary, as you'll see shortly.

How Do Exceptions Work?

When an error condition occurs, the programmer can generate an exception using the *throw* keyword, and the exception is tagged with a piece of data that identifies exactly what has happened.

At this point, normal execution stops and the exception-handling code built into the program goes to look for a handler. It looks in the currently executing routine, and if it finds a suitable handler, the handler is executed and the program continues. If no handler is in the current routine, the exception-handling code moves one level up the call stack and checks for a suitable handler. This carries on until either a handler is found, or the top level in the call stack—the *_tmain* function—is reached. If nothing has been found by this time, the program is terminated with an unhandled exception message.

Here's an example of how an unhandled exception appears to you. You've probably seen a lot of these already! Look at the following simple code fragment:

```
Console::WriteLine("Exception Test");
int top = 3;
int bottom = 0;

int result = top / bottom;
Console::Write("Result is ");
Console::WriteLine(result);
```

It's easy to see that this is going to cause a divide-by-zero error, and when it is executed you see the following result:

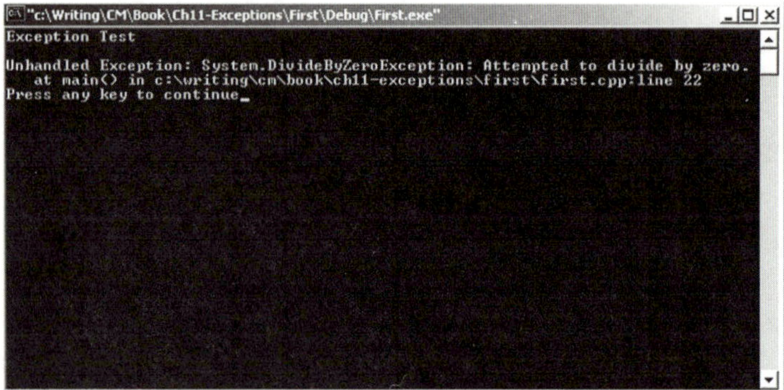

You can see that the divide-by-zero error has resulted in an exception being generated. Because I didn't handle it in the code, the program has been terminated and the final output never makes it to the screen. Note the form of the standard message: it tells you what happened (a System.DivideByZero error), presents an error message, and then gives you a stack trace that tells you where the error occurred (in the *_tmain* function at line 22 in the first.cpp file).

System.DivideByZero denotes the kind of object that was passed in the exception; a lot of exception classes are provided in the System namespace, and it is also common for you to make up your own, based on the System.Exception base class, as you'll see later on.

Exception Types

Exception handling is slightly complicated in that you might encounter three different types of exception handling when using Managed C++: traditional C++ exceptions, Managed C++, and Windows' own Structured Exception Handling (SEH). Traditional C++ exceptions form the basis of all exception handling in C++. Managed C++ adds the ability to use managed types (for example, *__gc* classes and *__value* types) in exceptions, and you can mix them with traditional exceptions. Managed C++ also extends exception handling by adding the concept of a "finally" clause, which I'll discuss later in the chapter. The third sort of exception handling you might encounter is Structured Exception Handling (SEH), a form of exception handling built into Microsoft Windows operating systems that is independent from C++. I won't talk any more about SEH here, except to note that you can interact with it from C++.

Throwing Exceptions

I'll start our exploration of exceptions by discussing how to generate, or *throw*, them. You'll end up generating far more exceptions by accident than by design, but you need to know how to generate your own when errors occur in your application.

What Can You Throw?

Traditional C++ lets you attach any type of object to an exception, so you can use built-in types (such as *int* and *double*) as well as structures and objects. If you throw objects in C++, you usually throw and catch them by reference.

Managed C++ extends this to let you throw and catch pointers to managed types, and you'll most likely be using managed types when you're writing .NET code. This chapter deals almost exclusively with throwing and catching managed types, but be aware that you'll meet other data types that are being used out in the wider C++ world.

How do you know what to throw? There are a large number of exception classes as part of the *System* namespace, all of which derive from *Exception*. A number of those you'll commonly encounter are listed in the following table. You should be able to find the exception class to suit your purposes, and if you can't, it is always possible to derive your own exception classes from *System::Exception*.

Exception Class	Description
System::ApplicationException	Thrown when a non-fatal application error occurs
System::ArgumentException	Thrown when one of the arguments to a function is invalid. Subclasses include *System::ArgumentNullException* and *System::ArgumentOutOfRangeException*.
System::ArithmeticException	Thrown to indicate an error in an arithmetic, casting, or conversion operation. Subclasses include *System::DivideByZeroException* and *System::OverflowException*.
System::Exception	The base class of all exception types
System::IndexOutOfRangeException	Thrown when an array index is out of range
System::InvalidCastException	Thrown when an invalid cast or conversion is attempted
System::MemberAccessException	Thrown when an attempt is made to dynamically access a member that doesn't exist. Subclasses include *System::MissingFieldException* and *System::MissingMethodException*.

(continued)

(continued)

System::NotSupportedException	Thrown when a method is invoked that isn't supported
System::NullReferenceException	Thrown when an attempt is made to dereference a null reference
System::OutOfMemoryException	Thrown when memory cannot be allocated
System::SystemException	The base class for exceptions that the user can be expected to handle. Classes such as *ArgumentException* and *ArithmeticException* are subclasses of *SystemException*.
System::TypeLoadException	Thrown when the CLR cannot find an assembly or a type within an assembly, or cannot load the type. Subclasses include *System::DllNotFoundException*.

The following exercise will show you how to generate an exception; in the next section, you'll go on to see how to catch and process the exception.

1. Start Microsoft Visual Studio .NET and open a new Managed C++ Application project called Throwing.
2. Immediately after the *using namespace System;* line and immediately before *_tmain*, add the following function definition:

```
void func(int a)
{
  if (a <= 0)
    throw new System::ArgumentException(S"Aaargh!");
}
```

   This simple function takes an integer argument, and if its value is less than 0, it throws an exception. In this case I'm creating a new *System::ArgumentException* object, initializing it with a string, and then throwing it.
3. Add code to test out the function by adding this code to the *_tmain* function:

```
Console::WriteLine(S"Throw Test");
Console::WriteLine(S"Calling with a=3");
func(3);
Console::WriteLine(S"Calling with a=0");
func(0);
Console::WriteLine(S"All done");
```

The code calls the function twice, once with a valid value, and once with 0, which should trigger the exception.

4 Compile and run the code, and you should get a screen that looks like this:

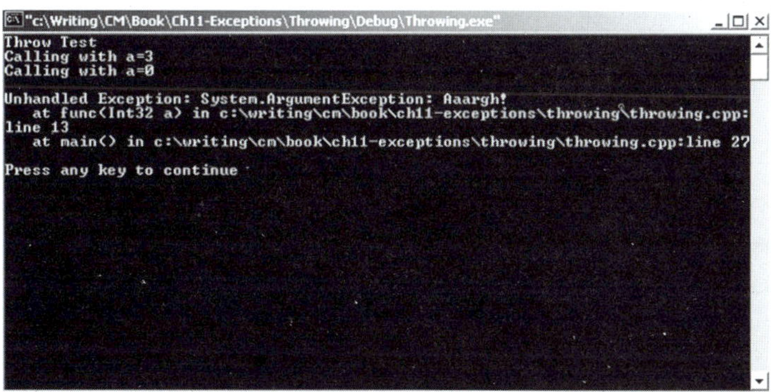

The program has called the function once without incident, but the second call has triggered an exception. As before, you get a message and a stack trace. This time the message is the string used to initialize the exception object, and the stack trace has two levels, showing that the exception was triggered at line 13 in the *func* function, which was called from the *_tmain* function at line 27.

note

The precise line number you get reported in the exception stack trace will depend on exactly how you typed in and formatted your code.

Handling Exceptions

Now that you've seen how to generate exceptions, let's move on to handling them.

Using the *try* and *catch* Construct

Exceptions are caught and processed using the *try* and *catch* construct, which has the following form:

```
try
{
  // code that may fail
}
```

```
catch(TypeOne* pOne)
{
  // handle this exception
}
catch(TypeTwo* pTwo)
{
  // handle this exception
}
```

Code that you suspect might fail is enclosed in a *try* block; this is followed by one or more handlers, in the form of *catch* blocks. Each *catch* block looks a little like a function definition, with *catch* followed by a type in parentheses; this represents the type that will be caught and processed by the *catch* block. In the preceding code, the first *catch* block will handle exceptions tagged with a TypeOne type, while the second block will handle those tagged with a TypeTwo* type.

> **note**
>
> *Try* and *catch* blocks form a single construct: you can't have a *try* without at least one *catch*, you can't have a *catch* without a *try*, and you can't put anything in between them.

You can chain as many *catch* blocks together as there are exception types to catch, as long as you have at least one.

The following exercise will show you the basics of handling exceptions, using the example from the previous exercise as a basis.

1. Reopen the project from the previous example if you've closed it.
2. Modify the *_tmain* function so that it looks like this:

```
Console::WriteLine(S"Throw Test");

try
{
  int n = 3;
  Console::WriteLine(S"Calling with n=3");
  func(n);
  Console::WriteLine(S"Calling with n=0");
  n = 0;
  func(n);
```

```
}
catch(System::ArgumentException* pex)
{
  Console::WriteLine(S"Exception was {0}", pex);
}
Console::WriteLine(S"All done");
```

The calls to the function are enclosed in a *try* block, which is followed by a single *catch* block. When the second call to the function fails, the exception handling mechanism takes over. It can't find a handler in the function where the error originated, so it walks one level up the call stack, and comes out in the *try* block. At this point, the run time wants to go off looking for a handler. As part of this process, it puts the program stack back to where it was at the start of the *try* block; in other words, it unwinds the stack. This means that it destroys any variables that have been created on the stack within the *try* block, so you can't use them in the *catch* block. You need to bear this in mind when writing exception handlers, and declare any variables you need to use in the *catch* block outside the corresponding *try*.

When the stack has been unwound, the code looks at the *catch* blocks associated with this *try* block to see whether there is one that has an argument type that matches what was thrown. In this case, we have a match, so the contents of the *catch* block are executed. If there wasn't a suitable *catch* block, the run time would try to move up another level of the call stack, then would fail and terminate the program.

3 Execute this code. You should see something very similar to the following graphic:

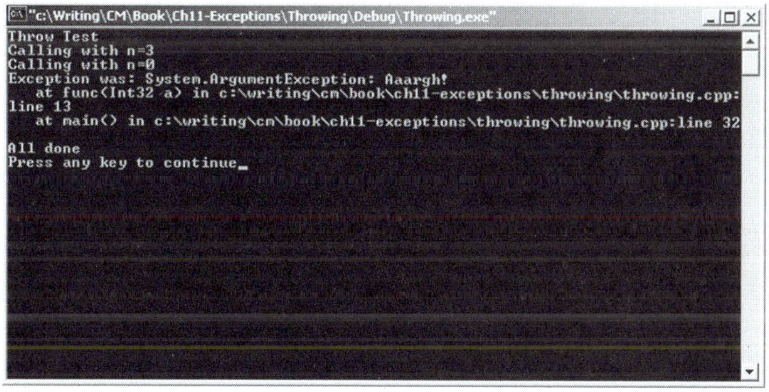

```
"c:\Writing\CM\Book\Ch11-Exceptions\Throwing\Debug\Throwing.exe"
Throw Test
Calling with n=3
Calling with n=0
Exception was: System.ArgumentException: Aaargh!
   at func(Int32 a) in c:\writing\cm\book\ch11-exceptions\throwing\throwing.cpp:
line 13
   at main() in c:\writing\cm\book\ch11-exceptions\throwing\throwing.cpp:line 32

All done
Press any key to continue_
```

The second function call has generated an exception, and this has been caught by the *catch* block, which has printed out "Exception was:" plus the exception details. In contrast to what happened in the previous exercise, the final "All done" message is now printed. This illustrates an important point about exception handling: once a *catch* block has been executed, program execution continues after the *catch* block as if nothing had happened. If there are any other *catch* blocks chained to the one that is executed, they are ignored.

4 Try changing the second call so that it passes in a positive value. You'll find that the *catch* block isn't executed at all. If a *try* block finishes without any exception occurring, execution skips all the *catch* blocks associated with the *try* block.

Customizing Exception Handling

Just printing out the exception object results in the type-plus-message-plus-stack-trace that you saw when the exception was unhandled. You can use properties of the *Exception* class to control what is printed, as shown in the following table:

System::Exception Member	Description
get_Message	Returns a string containing the message associated with this exception
get_StackTrace	Returns a string containing the stack trace details
get_Source	Returns a string containing the name of the object or application that caused the error. By default, this is the name of the assembly.

If you altered the *WriteLine* statement in the *catch* block to read like this:

```
catch(System::ArgumentException* pex)
{
  Console::WriteLine(S"Exception was {0}",
                     pex->get_Message());
}
```

you'd expect to see a result like this:

```
Exception was: Aaargh!
```

In a similar way, you could use *get_StackTrace* to retrieve and print the stack trace information.

Using the Exception Hierarchy

The exception classes form a hierarchy based on *System::Exception*, and you can use this to simplify your exception handling. As an example, consider

System::ArithmeticException, which inherits from *System::Exception* and has subclasses that include *System::DivideByZeroException* and *System::OverflowException*. Now look at the following code:

```
try
{
  // do some arithmetic operation
}
catch(System::ArithmeticException* pex)
{
  // handle this exception
}
catch(System::DivideByZeroException* pex)
{
  // handle this exception
}
```

Suppose a *DivideByZeroException* is thrown. You might expect it to be caught by the second *catch* block, but it will in fact get caught by the first one. This is because, according to the inheritance hierarchy, a *DivideByZeroException is* an *ArithmeticException*, so the type of the first *catch* block matches. To get the behavior you expect when using more than one *catch* block, you need to rank the *catch* blocks from most specific to most general.

tip

The compiler will give you warning C4286 if you get the *catch* blocks in the wrong order. This works for both managed and unmanaged code.

What this means is that if you just want to catch all arithmetic exceptions, you can simply put in a handler for *ArithmeticException* and all exceptions from derived classes will get caught. In the most general case, you can simply add a handler for *Exception*, and all managed exceptions will be caught.

Using Exceptions with Constructors

I mentioned one of the advantages of exceptions earlier in the chapter: they enable you to signal an error where there's no way to return a value. This means that they're very useful for reporting errors in constructors, which, as you now know, don't have a return value.

In the following exercise, you'll see how to define a simple class that uses an exception to report errors from its constructor, and how to check for exceptions when creating objects of this type.

1 Start Visual Studio .NET and start a new Managed C++ Application project called CtorTest.

2 Immediately after the *using namespace System;* line and immediately before *_tmain*, add the following class definition:

```
__gc class Test
{
  String* pv;
public:
  Test(String* pval)
  {
    if (pval == 0 || pval == S"")
      throw new System::ArgumentException(
          "Argument null or blank");
    else
      pval = pv;
  }
};
```

The *__gc* keyword makes this a managed class, which has one simple data member, a pointer to a managed *String*. At construction time, this pointer must not be null or point to a blank string, so the constructor checks the pointer, and throws an exception if the test fails. If the pointer passes the tests, construction continues.

3 Try creating an object in the *_tmain* function, like this:

```
int _tmain(void)
{
  Console::WriteLine(S"Exceptions in Constructors");
  // Create a null pointer to test the exception handling
  String* ps = 0;

  Test* pt = 0;

  // Try creating an object
  try
  {
    pt = new Test(ps);
  }
```

```
    catch(System::ArgumentException* pex)
    {
        Console::WriteLine(S"Exception: {0}",
                            pex->get_Message());
    }

    Console::WriteLine(S"Object construction finished");
    return 0;
}
```

Note that the call to *new* is enclosed in a *try* block. If something is wrong with the *String* pointer (as it is here), the *Test* constructor will throw an exception that will be caught by the *catch* block. Try modifying the declaration of the *ps* string so that it points to a blank string (initialize it with S" "), and then try a non-blank string, to check that the exception is thrown correctly.

Nesting and Rethrowing Exceptions

Now that you've seen how to use the *try* and *catch* construct, let's move on to cover some more advanced uses. The first of these are *nesting* and *rethrowing* exceptions.

As the name implies, nesting exceptions means including one *try* and *catch* construct inside another, and this can provide a useful way to handle error conditions. It works as you might expect:

```
try           // outer try block
{
    try       // inner try block
    {
        // Do something
    }
    catch(SomeException* pex)
    {
        Console::WriteLine(S"Exception: {0}",
                            pex->get_Message());
    }
}
catch(OtherException* pex)
{
    Console::WriteLine(S"Exception: {0}", pex->get_Message());
}
```

If an exception occurs within the inner *try* block and it is of type *SomeException**, it will be handled by the inner *catch* block, and execution will continue after the end of the inner *catch* block as usual. The outer *catch* block will not be executed in this case, because the error has already been adequately handled.

If an exception occurs within the inner *try* block and it is of type *OtherException**, it won't be handled by the inner catch block, and so it will be passed to the outer *try* and *catch* construct, where it is processed by the outer *catch* block.

> **note**
>
> You can nest *try* and *catch* constructs to several levels, but it is unusual to go more than two levels deep, because it can complicate the structure of the code.

Rethrowing an exception means just that: handling an exception in a *catch* block, and then throwing it again so that it can be handled somewhere else. The following exercise shows how to catch an exception and rethrow it.

1. Start Visual Studio .NET , open a new Managed C++ Application project and call it Rethrow.
2. Immediately after the *using namespace System;* line and immediately before *_tmain*, add the following function definition:

```
void func(int a)
{
  try
  {
    if (a <= 0)
      throw new System::ArgumentException(S"Aaargh!");
  }
  catch(System::ArgumentException* pex)
  {
    Console::WriteLine("Exception caught in func()");
  }
}
```

This is basically the same simple function you met at the start of the chapter, which throws a *System::ArgumentException* when it is passed a negative argument. The difference here is that the exception is being caught within the function.

3 Modify the *_tmain* function so that it looks like this:

```
Console::WriteLine(S"Throw Test");

try
{
  int n = 0;
  Console::WriteLine(S"Calling with n=0");
  func(n);
}
catch(System::ArgumentException* pex)
{
  Console::WriteLine(S"Exception caught in _tmain()");
}
Console::WriteLine(S"All done");
```

If you run this code, you'll find that the exception is caught locally in *func*, and the *catch* block in *_tmain* doesn't execute.

4 Modify the definition of *func* so that it rethrows the exception after handling it:

```
void func(int a)
{
  try
  {
    if (a <= 0)
      throw new System::ArgumentException(S"Aargh!");
  }
  catch(System::ArgumentException* pex)
  {
    Console::WriteLine("Exception caught in func()");
    throw;   // rethrow the exception
  }
}
```

Using *throw* without an argument rethrows the current exception, and it can only be used in this way within a *catch* block. At this point, the run time goes off looking for another handler, which means moving up the call stack to the *_tmain* function, where the exception gets caught a second time. If you run this code, you should see the "Exception caught in func()" and "Exception caught in _tmain()" messages printed.

Note that you don't have to rethrow the same exception; it is quite usual to catch one type of exception, handle it, and then rethrow an exception of another type. You'll see an example of this in the following section on creating your own exception types.

The *__finally* Block

Managed C++ adds a new construct to traditional C++ exception handling, the *__finally* block. The purpose of this block is to let you clear up after an exception has occurred, and the following short exercise shows how it works:

1. Reopen the project from the previous example, if you closed it.
2. Modify the *_tmain* function so that it looks like this, adding a *__finally* block after the *catch* block:

```
Console::WriteLine(S"Throw Test");


try
{
  int n = 3;
  Console::WriteLine(S"Calling with n=3");
  func(n);
  Console::WriteLine(S"Calling with n=0");
  n = 0;
  func(n);
}
catch(System::ArgumentException* pex)
{
  Console::WriteLine(S"Exception was {0}", pex);
}
__finally
{
  Console::WriteLine(S"This is the __finally block");
}

Console::WriteLine(S"All done");
```

   If you try executing the code, you'll find that the *__finally* block gets executed after the *catch* block.
3. Modify the *_tmain* function so that the second call doesn't cause an exception, either by changing the value or by commenting it out. When you run the program again, you'll see that the *__finally* block still gets executed, even though there was no error.

   The purpose of this block is to ensure that if you do something in the *try* block—such as opening a file or allocating some memory—you'll be able to tidy up whether an exception occurs or not, because the *__finally* block is always executed when execution leaves a *try* block. This construct gives you a way to clean up that might otherwise require complex coding.

The *catch(...)* Block

C++ has a construct that is sometimes seen in traditional code and is used to catch any exception that goes past. Here's how it works:

```
try
{
  // do some arithmetic operation
}
catch(System::ArithmeticException* pex)
{
  // handle this exception
}
catch(...)
{
  // handle any exception
}
```

If an exception doesn't match the first *catch* block, it will get caught by the second one no matter what type it is. The problem is that you lose any information about the exception, because the *catch(...)* block doesn't have an argument.

If you want this functionality when using managed exceptions, use a *catch* block that has an *Exception** as its argument, as this will catch any managed exception object.

Creating Your Own Exception Types

You've already seen how all the exception types are derived from the *System::Exception* class. If you can't find one in the standard exception hierarchy that suits your needs, you can easily derive your own class from *Exception* and use it in your code. The following exercise shows you how to derive a new exception class, and how to use it in code.

1. Start Visual Studio .NET and open a new Managed C++ Application project called OwnExcept.
2. Add the following class definition immediately after the *using namespace System;* line:

```
// User-defined exception class
```

```
__gc class MyException : public System::Exception
{
public:
  int errNo;
  MyException(String* msg, int num) : Exception(msg),
errNo(num) {}
};
```

The custom exception class is a managed class that inherits from *System::Exception*, and it extends *Exception* by adding a single field to hold an error number. The class constructor takes a message and a number, and passes the message string back to the base class.

> **note**
>
> I've made the *errNo* field public. Although you're normally advised to make all data members of classes private, you can make a case for having public data members in certain circumstances. Once you've created an *Exception* object and passed it back to the client, do you care what the client does with it? Exceptions are "fire and forget" objects, and you're normally not concerned with the integrity of their state once they leave your code in a *throw* statement.

3 Add a function definition immediately after the class definition:

```
void func(int a)

{
  try
  {
    if (a <= 0)
      throw new System::ArgumentException(
          "Negative argument");
  }
  catch(System::ArgumentException* pex)
  {
    Console::WriteLine(S"Caught ArgumentException "
                       S"in func()");
    throw new MyException(pex->get_Message(), 1000);
  }
}
```

The function checks its argument, and throws a *System::ArgumentException* if it finds a negative value. This exception is caught locally, and a message is printed. Now I decide that I *really* want to handle the exception elsewhere, so I create a new *MyException* object and rethrow it, initializing it with the message from the original *ArgumentException*.

4 Test the exception handling by calling the function in the program's *_tmain* routine:

```
int _tmain(void)
{
  Console::WriteLine(S"Custom Exceptions");
  try
  {
    func(0);
  }
  catch(MyException* pex)
  {
    Console::WriteLine(S"Caught MyException in main()");
    Console::WriteLine(S"Message is : {0}",
                          pex->get_Message());
    Console::WriteLine(S"Error number is : {0}",
                          __box(pex->errNo));
  }
  return 0;
}
```

Calling the function with a zero value triggers the exception, which is handled in the function itself, and is then rethrown to be handled here in the _tmain_ function. You can see from the following graphic how the exception has been caught in both in places:

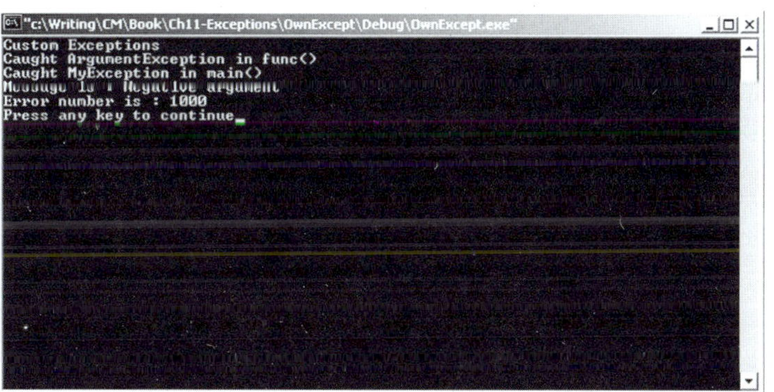

In the preceding code, note that it is necessary to box the error number before it can be used in a call to *WriteLine*. This is because the formatted overloads to *WriteLine* need a list of *Object** pointers, and boxing lets you use a built-in type as an object. See Chapter 25 for more information on boxing.

Using *__value* Classes

In the preceding example, you implemented the custom exception as a managed class (declared using the *__gc* keyword), but it is also possible to use value types (declared with the *__value* keyword) as custom exceptions. The difference comes when you want to use value types as exceptions, because you need to throw a pointer to a managed type.

This is not a problem with *__gc* classes, because you always create them using *new*, and always get a pointer returned. Value types are created on the stack, and you operate on them directly, rather than through pointers. If you want to get a pointer to a value type, you have to *box* it. This wraps, or boxes, the value type in an object, and returns a pointer to it. Here's an example of how you'd use a value type as an exception:

```
__value struct MyExceptionStruct
{
  int errNo;
};

void SomeFunction()
{
  // I want to throw a struct...
  MyExceptionStruct mes = { 1000 };
  throw __box(mes);
}
```

The call to the *__box* function wraps the struct in an object box and returns a pointer to the object, which can then be thrown.

Using *__try_cast* for Dynamic Casting

C++ supports the idea of *casting*, wherein you tell the compiler to convert one type into another in order to use it in an expression. Although casting can be useful, it can also be dangerous, and the *__try_cast* keyword has been introduced in the Managed Extensions to help make the operation safer. The following code fragment shows both safe and unsafe casting:

```
// Define the Vehicle and Car classes
__gc class Vehicle {};
__gc class Car : public Vehicle {};
__gc class Truck : public Vehicle {};
__gc class Bus : public Vehicle {};
...
Car* pc = new Car();         // Create a Car
Vehicle* pv = pc;            // Point to it using a Vehicle pointer -
                             // OK
...
Car* pc2 = pv;               // Copy pv into another Car* pointer -
                              // not OK!
```

The compiler raises an error on the last line, complaining that it can't convert a *Vehicle** to a *Car**. The problem is that a *Vehicle** pointer could point to any *Vehicle*-derived object, such as a *Truck* or a *Bus*. Implicitly casting from a *Car* to a *Vehicle* is fine, because a *Car* is a *Vehicle*; going the other way doesn't work, because not every *Vehicle* is a *Car*.

The way around this is to use the *__try_cast* construct, like this:

```
try
{
  Car* pc2 = __try_cast<Car*>(pv);
}
catch(System::InvalidCastException* pce)
{
  Console::WriteLine("Cast failed");
}
```

At run time, *__try_cast* checks the object on the other end of the pointer to see if it has the same type as the object you are trying to cast to. If it does, the cast works; if it doesn't, an *InvalidCastException* is thrown.

note

Experienced C++ programmers should know that *__try_cast* is almost identical to the *dynamic_cast* construct supported by standard C++, the difference being that *__try_cast* throws an exception if the cast fails.

Using Exceptions Across Languages

One of the great things about managed exceptions in C++ is that they work across languages, so that now you can, for example, throw an exception in C++ and catch it in a Visual Basic application. No longer are exceptions simply a C++ feature, and this ability to harmonize error handling across code written in different languages makes mixed-language programming much easier than it has been in the past.

In the final example in this chapter, you'll create a C++ class in a dynamic link library (DLL), and then use the class in a Visual Basic application.

1. Start Visual Studio .NET and open a new Managed C++ project. This time, choose a Managed C++ Class Library project, which is used when you want to create a DLL rather than an EXE. I called the project MyClass. You can call it what you like, but make a note of the name.

   You'll find that you've created a project that defines a namespace called *MyClass*, containing a single class called *Class1*. It is this class that you will edit, adding a method that can be called from a Visual Basic client.

2. The project will contain a number of files, among them MyClass.h and MyClass.cpp, which are used to hold the definition and implementation of the *Class1* class. Open MyClass.h, and add the *Test* function so that it looks like the following code:

```
// MyClass.h

#pragma once

using namespace System;

namespace MyClass
{
  public __gc class Class1
  {
  public:
    void Test(int n)
    {
      if (n < 0)
        throw new ArgumentException(
            "Argument must be positive");
    }
  };
}
```

The *Test* method should look familiar by now: it simply checks its argument, and throws an exception if it is less than 0.

3 Build the project. You'll end up with a DLL being created in the project's debug directory.

4 Close the project, and create a new Visual Basic Console application project, which I called Tester. Before you can access the C++ DLL you just created, you have to add a reference to it to the project. To do this, click on the Solution Explorer tab, expand the project, and right-click on the References icon:

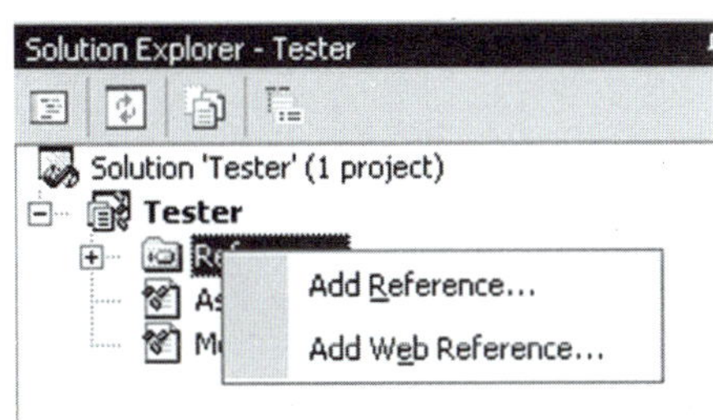

5 Choose Add Reference from the drop-down menu, and when the dialog box appears, click Browse, and search for the DLL you built in step 3. Make sure it is added to the Selected Components pane, and then click OK.

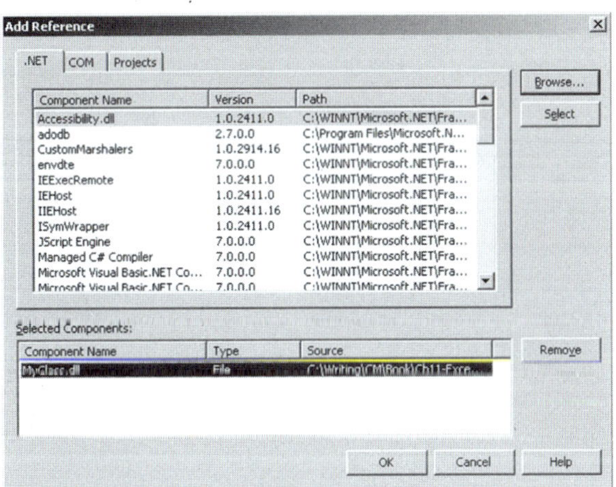

6 Now you can add the code to the project. Edit the *Main* function so it looks like the following code:

```
' Application to demonstrate cross-language exception handling

Imports [MyClass]

Module Module1
  Sub Main()
    Dim obj As New Class1()

    Try
      obj.Test(-1)
    Catch e As ArgumentException
      Console.WriteLine("Exception: " & e.Message)
    End Try

    Console.WriteLine("All done")
  End Sub
End Module
```

The first line imports the *MyClass* namespace into the program. This does the same job as *using namespace* does in C++, so you don't have to fully qualify the name *Class1* when it appears. The first line in the *Main* function creates a new *Class1* object, and is equivalent to creating an object in C++ using *new*. The call to the *Test* function is enclosed in a *Try* and *Catch* block, and you can see the similarity between the way exceptions are handled in Visual Basic and C++; the main difference is that in Visual Basic, the *Catch* blocks are inside the *Try* block.

7 Build the code and execute it. Passing -1 through as the argument will trigger the exception, and you should see the message printed out in the *catch* block.

Chapter 11 Quick Reference

To	Do This
Generate an exception	Use the *throw* keyword, using a pointer to a managed type as the argument, for example: `throw new SomeException();`

Catch an exception	Use the *try* and *catch* construct, surrounding the code that may fail with a *try* block, followed by one or more *catch* blocks, for example:
	`try`
	`{`
	`    // code that might fail`
	`}`
	`catch(SomeException* pce)`
	`{`
	`    // handle the exception`
	`}`

Catch more than one exception	Chain *catch* blocks together, for example:
	`catch(SomeException* pce)`
	`{`
	`    // handle the exception`
	`}`
	`catch(SomeOtherException* pce)`
	`{`
	`    // handle the exception`
	`}`

Catch a family of exceptions	Use the base class of the exceptions you want to catch in the *catch* block, for example, *ArithmeticException* will catch *DivideByZeroException* and several others
Catch every exception	Use a *catch* block that takes *Exception** as a parameter, and this will catch every type that is derived from *Exception*
Handle exceptions at more than one point in a program	Use *throw* to rethrow exceptions from one *catch* block to another
Create your own exceptions	Derive from the *Exception* class, adding your own members

Arrays and Collections

In this chapter, you'll learn how to

- ✔ *Implement arrays in C++*
- ✔ *Create single- and multidimensional arrays*
- ✔ *Create managed arrays*
- ✔ *Use the features of the* System::Array *class with managed arrays*
- ✔ *Use the collection classes provided in the* System::Collections *and* System::Collections::Specialized *namespaces*

This chapter is concerned with data structures. You'll learn about arrays and other collection classes, and how to use them in your programs. In the first part of the chapter, you're going to learn about two sorts of arrays: the native arrays provided by the C++ language, and the managed arrays of Microsoft .NET, which can use functionality inherited from the .NET Framework. You'll find out how they all work, and when one should be used rather than the other.

The second part of the chapter looks more widely at the range of collection classes provided by the .NET Framework, discussing their characteristics and showing you how and when to use them.

Native C++ Arrays

Native arrays are those provided as part of the C++ language. They're based on the arrays that C++ inherits from C, and although they are designed to be fast and efficient, there are drawbacks associated with using them, as you'll see shortly.

This first exercise will introduce you to C++ native arrays by showing you how to create an array of value types, and how to use the array.

1. Open Microsoft Visual Studio .NET and create a new Managed C++ Application project called Trad.
2. Open the source file Trad.cpp and add the following code to the *_tmain* function:

```
int _tmain(void)
{
  Console::WriteLine(S"Traditional Arrays");

  // Create an array
  int arr[10];

  // Fill the array
  for(int i=0; i<10; i++)
    arr[i] = i*2;

  return 0;
}
```

The array is created by giving a type, a name, and a size enclosed in square brackets ([]). Here, the array is named *arr* and it holds ten *ints*. All arrays are created using the same syntax, as shown here:

```
// Create an array of six doubles
double arr[6];
// Create an array of two char*'s
char* arr[2];
```

Here's the first important point about native arrays: once you've created an array, you can't resize it, so you have to know how many elements you're going to need before you start. If you don't know how many elements you're going to need, you might be better off using a .NET array, discussed later in this chapter.

note

The array size has to be known at compile time, so, for example, you can't ask the user for a value and then use that value to specify an array dimension at run time. However, constants are commonly used to specify array dimensions, either using preprocessor *#defines* or *const ints*.

As you can see from the loop in the preceding code, array elements are accessed using square brackets that contain the index. This introduces the second important point about native arrays: indexing starts from zero rather than one, so the valid range of indices for an array is from zero to one less than the size of the array. In other words, for a 10-element array, valid indices are [0] to [9].

3 Add a second loop to print out the array contents.

```
// Fill the array
for(int i=0; i<10; i++)
  arr[i] = i*2;

// Print its contents
for(int j=0; j<10; j++)
  Console::WriteLine(arr[j]);
```

You should find that this prints the values, one to a line, as shown here:

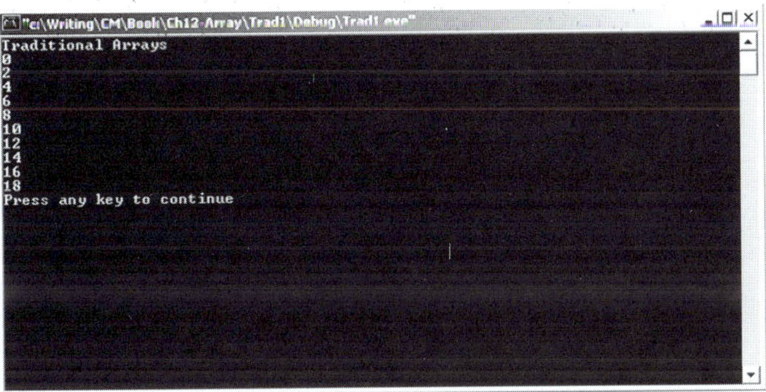

4 What happens if you change the range of the second loop so that it tries to print element [10]? Alter the code in the second loop to look like this:

```
// Print its contents
for(int j=0; j<=10; j++)
  Console::WriteLine(arr[j]);
```

Note the less than or equal to (<=) condition. The effect of this is to try to print 11 elements rather than 10. Compile and run the program, and you should see output similar to the following:

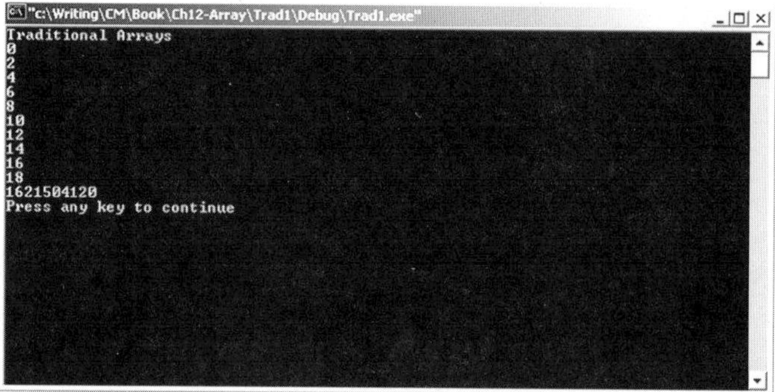

Note the random value that's been printed at the end of the list. This shows you the third important point about native arrays: bounds aren't checked. Native arrays in C++ aren't objects, and therefore have no knowledge of how many elements they contain. It's up to you to keep within the bounds of the array and if you don't, you risk corrupting data or crashing your code.

Passing Arrays to Functions

Passing arrays between functions introduces one complication because of the fact that an array has no knowledge of its size or contents. As you'll see shortly, when you pass an array over to a function, you only pass thc starting address. This means that you have to figure out some way of passing the size information along with the array when you call the function. Normally this is accomplished two ways:

- Pass the size as an explicit parameter to the function call.
- Make sure that the array is always terminated by a unique marker value, so that the function can tell when the end of the data has been reached.

How Do Native Arrays Work?

A native array in C++ isn't an object, but is simply a collection of values strung together in memory. So a 10-element array of integers consists of 10 integers one after the other in memory. The name of the array is a pointer to the first element, so when you declare an array like this:

```
int foo[10];
```

you are telling the compiler to reserve memory large enough to hold 10 integers and return you the address as *foo*. When you access an array element, you're actually specifying the offset from this address, so that *foo[1]* means "offset one *int* from the address foo and use what is stored there." This explains why array indexing starts from zero: an index of zero denotes an offset of zero from the start address, and thus means the first element.

Once it has allocated the space, pretty much all the compiler knows about an array is its starting address. When you provide an offset in terms of an array index, the compiler generates code to access that piece of memory. And if you've got it wrong and stepped outside the bounds of the array, you can end up reading or writing somewhere inappropriate. In fact, deliberately accessing outside the bounds of arrays has been the basis for many security attacks on programs and systems over the years.

To finish this brief explanation, note that there's a close link between arrays and pointers. So close, in fact, that any array access can be written using pointer notation instead of array notation, as shown here:

```
// These two are equivalent
n = arr[3];
n = *(arr + 3);
```

In the second example, the compiler is being told to de-reference a point three *ints* away from address *arr*.

Let's investigate passing an array over to a function.

1. Continue with the project from the previous exercise, reopening it if necessary.
2. Add the following function definition immediately after the *using namespace System;* line:

```
void func(int arr[], size_t size)
{
  for(size_t i=0; i<size; i++)
    Console::WriteLine(arr[i]);
}
```

The first argument to the function tells the compiler that the address of an array is going to be passed. This is equivalent to passing a pointer, and it is very common to see *int** used instead. The second argument passes the size of the array—in effect, the amount of memory pointed to by the first argument. The *size_t* type is a *typedef* for *unsigned int*, and it is good practice to use this type for integer arguments that denote sizes, lengths, or dimensions. The function prints out the array by using the size, just as before.

3 Call the function from the *_tmain* routine like this:

```
func(arr, 10);
```

What if the array size was changed at some point? You can make your code more robust by calculating the number of elements in the array automatically using the *sizeof* operator, like this:

```
func(arr, sizeof(arr)/sizeof(arr[0]));
```

Sizeof returns the size of its argument in bytes, where the argument can be a variable name or a type name. Using *sizeof* on an array returns the total size of the array in bytes, in this case, 40 bytes. When divided by the size of one element—four bytes—you're left with the number of elements in the array.

Initialization of Arrays

It's possible to initialize arrays at the point of declaration, as shown in the following syntax fragment:

```
int arr[4] = { 1, 2, 3, 4 };
```

The values to be used for initialization are provided as a comma-separated list in braces ({}) on the right-hand side of an assignment; these values are known as an *aggregate initializer*. The compiler is clever enough to figure out how many values are in the list, and it will dimension the array to fit if you don't provide a value:

```
// Dimension the array automatically
int arr[] = { 1, 2, 3, 4 };
```

If you give a dimension and then provide too many values, you'll get a compiler error. If you provide too few values, the initial values you give will be used to initialize the array starting from element zero, and the remaining elements will be set to zero.

Multidimensional Arrays

Multidimensional arrays in C++ are an extension of the single-dimension variety, in that a two-dimensional array is actually an array of single-dimension arrays. So in C++, arrays of higher dimensions are all built out of single dimension arrays. The following short exercise shows how to create and use a two-dimensional array:

1 Open Visual Studio and create a new Managed C++ Application project called MultiD.

2 Open the source file MultiD.cpp and add the following code to the *_tmain* function:

```
int _tmain(void)
{
  Console::WriteLine(S"Multidimensional Arrays");

  // Create a 2D array
  int arr[2][3];

  // Fill the array
  for(int i=0; i<2; i++)
    for(int j=0; j<3; j++)
      arr[i][j] = (i+1)*(j+1);

  return 0;
}
```

Note that a two-dimensional array is declared by using two sets of square brackets. You don't put the two values inside one set of brackets, as you do in many other languages, and for higher order arrays, you simply add more sets of square brackets. As with single-dimension arrays, you have to give the size at compile time, and the indices of each dimension vary from zero to one less than the declared size. Array elements are also accessed using two sets of square brackets.

3 Print out the array using an extension of the method for printing out the elements of the single-dimension array as follows:

```
// Print the array content
for(int i=0; i<2; i++)
{
  for(int j=0; j<3; j++)
    Console::Write("{0} ", __box(arr[i][j]));

  Console::WriteLine();
}
```

Notice that one row of the array gets printed on one line. The inner loop prints a single row using repeated calls to *Console::Write*. To format the output, the array element has to be boxed using a call to the *__box* keyword. After each row has been output, a call to *Console::WriteLine* outputs a new line.

To pass a multidimensional array to a function, use two empty sets of square brackets (for example, *int arr[][]*) and specify the dimension information as before.

Dynamic Allocation and Arrays

So far, all arrays in this chapter have had a fixed size allocated at compile time. It is possible—and very common—to create arrays dynamically at run time using the *new* operator. The array you create still has a fixed size, but this size can be specified at run time when you know how many elements you need. The following exercise shows how to create an array dynamically, and then use it:

1 Open Visual Studio and create a new Managed C++ Application project called Dynamic.

2 Open the source file Dynamic.cpp and add the following code to the *_tmain* function:

```
int _tmain(void)
{
    Console::WriteLine(S"Dynamic Arrays");

    // Create an array dynamically
    int* pa = new int[10];

    // Fill the array
    for(int i=0; i<10; i++)
        pa[i] = i*2;

    // Print the array content
    for(int j=0; j<10; j++)
        Console::WriteLine(pa[j]);

    // Get rid of the array once we're finished with it
    delete pa;

    return 0;
}
```

> You've previously used the *new* operator to create .NET reference types, but the operator is also used in traditional C++ code to allocate memory dynamically at run time. The syntax is *new*, followed by the type of the array and the dimension in square brackets. Once the array has been created, you're returned a pointer to the start of the array.

You can see that dynamic arrays are accessed in exactly the same way as statically allocated arrays, using the square brackets notation. This use of a pointer with array notation underlines the relationship between pointers and arrays, as explained in the sidebar "How Do Native Arrays Work?"

Note the call to *delete* just before the program exits. Allocating an array dynamically in traditional C++ doesn't create a managed object, so there is no garbage collection associated with this array. This means that to use memory efficiently, you have to remember to deallocate memory once you've finished with the array. Strictly speaking the call is unnecessary here, because all allocated memory is freed up when the program exits. However, in any real-world program, you need to manage your memory carefully to make sure all memory is freed up at an appropriate point.

note

Once you've called *delete* on a pointer, you must not use the pointer again because the memory it points to is no longer allocated to you. If you try to use a pointer after freeing up the memory it points to, you can expect to get a run-time error.

Problems with Manual Memory Management

Manual memory management is widely considered to be the single biggest cause of bugs in C and C++ programs, and it is the driving force behind the development of the garbage collection mechanisms in languages such as C#. If it is up to the programmers to call *delete* on every piece of memory they allocate, mistakes are going to be made.

Two main problems are associated with manual memory management:

- **Not freeing up memory.** This is normally the less serious of the two, and results in a program taking up more memory than it needs, a process known as memory leakage. In extreme cases, the amount of extra memory consumed by an application can reach the point where memory leakage starts to interfere with other applications or even the operating system.
- **Freeing up memory inappropriately.** In a complex program, it might not be obvious where a particular piece of memory should be freed up or whose responsibility it is to free it. If *delete* gets called too soon and another piece of code tries to use the dynamically allocated array, you can expect a run-time error. The same is true if anyone attempts to call *delete* on the same pointer more than once.

Although manual memory allocation using *new* and *delete* lets you do some very clever things, these two problems were the impetus behind the development of garbage collectors, which make the system track the use of dynamically allocated memory and free it up when no one else is using it.

__gc Arrays

The .NET Framework has extended the C++ array model by adding *__gc* arrays. As you might expect from the use of the *__gc* keyword, a *__gc* array is a dynamic array that is allocated on the .NET heap, and is subject to the usual garbage collection rules.

> **note**
>
> Unlike standard C++ arrays, subscripting in *__gc* arrays is not a synonym for pointer arithmetic.

You can create a *__gc* array in a very similar way to a traditional dynamic array:

```
Int32 gcArray[] = new Int32[10];
```

Note that the array type is the .NET *Int32* rather than the built-in *int* type. Note also the way that *gcArray* has been declared: it is no longer a pointer, as with traditional arrays, but is a managed object. All *__gc* arrays inherit from *System::Array*, so any method or property of *System::Array* can be directly applied to the *__gc* array. See the next section for details about *System::Array* and how to use it.

Using *__gc* and *__nogc* keywords

You can use the *__gc* and *__nogc* keywords to determine whether a managed or unmanaged array is going to be created. Normally, creating an array of primitive types will result in an unmanaged array. You can, however, use the *__gc* keyword to create a managed array of a primitive type, as shown in the following code:

```
// Create an unmanaged array of ints
int* arr = new int[10];

// Create a managed array of int
int arr1 __gc[] = new int __gc[10];
```

The *__gc[]* syntax will create an array of primitive types that is subject to the usual garbage collection mechanism.

In a similar way, you can use *__nogc* to create "traditional" unmanaged arrays of .NET types, provided that the type corresponds to one of the C++ primitive types.

```
// Create an unmanaged array of Int32
Int32 arr1 __nogc[10];
```

This array is not a managed array object, and it won't be garbage collected. In addition, because it isn't an array object, it does not support any of the functionality of the *System::Array* class.

Arrays and Reference Types

Because reference types are always accessed using references, creating and initializing arrays of reference types is slightly different than creating arrays of value types. The following exercise shows how to create and use an array of reference types. In this example, you'll use *System::String* as the reference type, but you can easily substitute a reference type of your own.

1. Open Visual Studio and create a new Managed C++ Application project called RefArray.
2. Open the RefArray.cpp source file and add the following code to the *_tmain* function:

```
int _tmain(void)
{
  Console::WriteLine(S"Arrays of Reference Types");

  // Create an array of String references
  String* pa[] = new String*[5];

  // Explicitly assign a new String to element zero
  pa[0] = new String("abc");
  // Implicitly assign a new String to element one
  pa[1] = "def";

  // Print the array content
  for(int i=0; i<5; i++)
  {
    if (pa[i] == 0)
      Console::WriteLine("null");
    else
      Console::WriteLine(pa[i]);
  }

  return 0;
}
```

3. Compile and run the code.

   You should see the two strings "abc" and "def": printed, followed by three "null" entries.

The declaration of *pa* creates a new array of string references, and not of the strings themselves. The references in the array are initialized with nulls, and you need to create objects and assign them to the references in the array. In the example, you've assigned values to the first two out of five values, so when you print the array out you see the two strings printed, followed by three nulls.

Multidimensional *__gc* Arrays

The Managed Extensions provide a new model for creating multidimensional *__gc* arrays, as shown in the following code fragment:

```
// Create a multidimensional array of String references
Int32 pn[,] = new Int32[3,2];

// Initialize two members
pn[0,0] = 3;
pn[1,1] = 4;
```

The declaration of the array reference—in this case *pn*—uses square brackets containing zero or more commas to denote the number of dimensions in the array. There's always one fewer comma than the number of dimensions, so if you wanted to create a three-dimensional array, you'd declare it as *Int32 p3d[,,]*. The *new* operator also uses square brackets, but with the list of dimensions inside one set of brackets. This makes it easy to tell when you're dealing with a multidimensional managed array as opposed to a traditional multidimensional array.

You'll meet multidimensional *__gc* arrays later in the chapter, when we talk about the *System::Array* class in more detail.

The .NET Array Class

Managed arrays in the .NET Framework all inherit from *System::Array*, and this means that every managed array has a number of useful properties and methods. These properties and methods are summarized in the following two tables.

Property	Description
IsFixedSize	Returns *true* if the array has a fixed size. Always returns *true*, unless overridden by a derived class
IsReadOnly	Returns *true* if the array is read-only. Always returns *false*, unless overridden by a derived class.
IsSynchronized	Returns *true* if the array is thread-safe (synchronized). Always returns *false*, unless overridden by a derived class.
Length	Returns the total number of elements in all dimensions of the array.
Rank	Returns the number of dimensions in the array.
SyncRoot	Returns a pointer to an object that can be used to synchronize access to the array.

Method	Description
BinarySearch	Searches a single-dimension array for a value, using a binary search algorithm.
Clear	Sets all or part of an array to zero or a null reference.
Clone	Creates a shallow copy of the array.
Copy	Static method that copies all or part of one array to another array, performing type downcasting as required.
CopyTo	Method that copies all or part of one array to another.
GetEnumerator	Returns an enumerator for the array. See later in the section for details on enumerators.
GetLength	Returns the number of elements in a specified dimension as an integer.
GetLowerBound	Returns the lower bound of a specified dimension as an integer.
GetUpperBound	Returns the upper bound of a specified dimension as an integer.
GetValue	Returns the value at a specified position in a single- or multidimensional array.
IndexOf	Returns the index of the first occurrence of an element in an array or part of an array.
Initialize	Initializes an array of value types by calling the default constructor of the value type. This method must not be used on arrays of reference types.
LastIndexOf	Returns the index of the last occurrence of an element in an array or part of an array.
Reverse	Reverses the order of the elements in all or part of a single-dimension array.
SetValue	Sets an array element to a specified value.
Sort	Sorts the elements in a single-dimension array.

Basic Operations on Arrays

Unlike traditional C++ arrays, managed arrays are objects, and they "know" how many dimensions they have and how many elements they contain. The following exercise introduces you to some of the basic functionality in the *System::Array* class:

1. Open Visual Studio if it isn't already open, and create a new C++ Managed Application project called SysArray.
2. At the top of the *_tmain* function, add declarations for some loop counters and a two-dimensional array of 32-bit integers, like this:

```
// Declare loop counters
```

```
int i,j,k;
// Create a multidimensional array of Int32
Int32 pn[,] = new Int32[3,2];
```

This is the array that you'll use for exploring the features of the *System::Array* class in the rest of this section.

3 Because this is a managed array, it inherits directly from *System::Array*, so you can use the Rank and Length properties of the *Array* class to find out the rank (number of dimensions) and total length of the array:

```
Console::WriteLine("Rank is {0}", __box(pn->Rank));
Console::WriteLine("Length is {0}",
                    __box(pn->get_Length()));
```

When you run this code, you should find that the rank is two and the total length is six, which matches the declaration.

note

The *get_Length* method is used here rather than just the Length property. This appears to be a bug in the pre-release version used when writing this book.

4 The *GetLength* method—not to be confused with the Length property—returns the size of any one dimension of the array, so you can print out the sizes of each dimension like this:

```
// Print out the array dimension information
for (i=0; i<pn->Rank; i++)
    Console::WriteLine("Dimension {0} is of size {1}",
__box(i),
                 __box(pn->GetLength(i)));
```

Now that you've got an array and can find out how large each dimension is, you need to know how to get and set elements in the array.

5 Carrying on with the previous example, add the following nested loops to the end of your code:

```
// Fill the array with values
for (j=0; j<pn->GetLength(0); j++)
    for (k=0; k<pn->GetLength(1), k++)
      pn[j,k] = (j+1)*(k+1);
```

The outer loop iterates over the rows, while the inner loop iterates over the columns, and the [x,y] notation is used to reference the array elements. The

Array class also has the *SetValue* method, which provides an alternative way of setting values for those languages that don't support C++-style array notation:

```
// Put '10' in array element [1,1]
pn->SetValue(__box(10), 1, 1);
```

Note that when using *SetValue,* you have to box the value to be inserted into the array because *SetValue* expects a pointer to a reference type.

6 Print out the values in the array by using a similar pair of nested loops:

```
// Print out the array data
for (j=pn->GetLowerBound(0); j<=pn->GetUpperBound(0); j++)
  for (k=pn->GetLowerBound(1); k<=pn->GetUpperBound(1); k++)
      Console::WriteLine("pn[{0},{1}] = {2}", __box(j),
                     __box(k), __box(pn[j,k]));
```

Once again, the outer loop iterates over the rows while the inner loop iterates over the columns. In this case, the *GetLowerBound* and *GetUpperBound* methods return the indices of the lower and upper bounds. The argument to *GetUpperBound* and *GetLowerBound* is the dimension of the array whose bound you want to find. In C++ the lower bound is invariably zero, and the upper bound can be obtained using the *GetLength* method, so these are mainly useful in other languages where it might be common to have arrays with arbitrary lower and upper bounds.

All the integer values have to be boxed before they can be printed out. As an alternative to boxing the array value, you can use the *GetValue* method to access an array element, which returns an object reference:

```
Console::WriteLine("pn[{0},{1}] = {2}", __box(i),
                           __box(k), pn->GetValue(i,j));
```

More Advanced Array Operations

You can now create arrays, find out how many dimensions they have and how large they are, and set and retrieve values. This section introduces some of the more advanced operations supported by the *Array* class, such as copying, searching, and sorting.

Copying Array Elements

The following exercise shows you how to use the *Copy* method to copy part of one array to another:

1 Open the project you were using in the previous exercise if you've closed it.

2 At the end of the *_tmain* function, create a second two-dimensional array the same size and type as the original:

```
// Create another multidimensional array of Int32
Int32 pn2[,] = new Int32[3,2];
```

3 Add some code to fill the new array with a constant value:

```
// Fill the array with a constant value
for (j=0; j<pn2->GetLength(0); j++)
    for (k=0; k<pn2->GetLength(1); k++)
      pn2[j,k] = 47;
```

4 To copy some values over from the first array to the second, use the static *Copy* method.

```
// Copy two values from pn to pn2
System::Array::Copy(pn,0, pn2,2, 2);
```

This method lets you copy all or part of one array into another. The first two arguments are the source array and the index at which to start copying; the second two are the destination array and the starting index from which elements are to be replaced; and the final argument is the number of elements to be copied. In this case, you've copied two elements from *pn* into the middle of *pn2,* which you'll be able to see if you add code to print out the contents of *pn2*.

Searching

It is common to want to search an array to see whether it contains a specific entry, and you can do this using the *IndexOf* and *LastIndexOf* methods.

1 Create a new Managed C++ Application project called Strings.

2 Open the Strings.cpp source file, and add code to the top of the *_tmain* function to create an array of strings:

```
// Create an array of strings
String* sa[] = { S"Dog", S"Cat", S"Elephant", S"Gerbil",
S"Dog",
    S"Horse", S"Pig", S"Cat" };

// Check the length
Console::WriteLine("sa has length {0}",
                    __box(sa->get_Length()));
```

3 The *IndexOf* and *LastIndexOf* functions both let you search to see whether a particular object occurs in the array. Add the following code the *_tmain* function:

```
// Search for a value
String* s = S"Dog";

int pos = Array::IndexOf(sa, s);
Console::WriteLine("Index of s in sa is {0}", __box(pos));

// Search for the next occurrence
pos = Array::IndexOf(sa, s, pos+1);
Console::WriteLine("Next index of s in sa is {0}",
__box(pos));
```

The call to *IndexOf* finds the first occurrence of string "Dog" in the array, and returns its index, which in this case is zero. The second call, to an overload of *IndexOf*, searches for an occurrence beginning at a given offset. Since the search is starting just past the first occurrence, the index returned is that of the second occurrence, which is 4. A third overload lets you search within a portion of the array.

note

If the value isn't found, the index returned will be one less than the lower bound of the array, which in C++ will tend to mean a value of -1.

LastIndexOf works in the same way, but starts searching from the other end of the array.

Sorting

The static *Array::Sort* method and its overloads give you a way to sort an array or part of an array, while *Array::Reverse* lets you reverse the order of elements. Try adding the following code to the *_tmain* routine:

```
Array::Sort(sa);
Array::Reverse(sa);
for (int i=0; i<sa->get_Length(); i++)
    Console::WriteLine(sa[i]);
```

When you run the program, you should get the elements of the array printed in reverse order, from "Pig" back to "Cat."

One valuable overload to *Sort* lets you provide two arrays, one of which contains keys used to define the sort order. Here's an example to show you how this works.

1 Continue with the same Strings project. The *sa* array currently contains the following entries:

```
Pig
Horse
Gerbil
Elephant
Dog
Dog
Cat
Cat
```

2 After the calls to *Sort* and *Reverse*, add a new array:

```
Int32 keys[] = { 6, 4, 3, 5, 2, 2, 1, 1 };
```

This array contains the keys that you're going to use to sort the array of animal names. They reflect my preferences—cats are number one, while pigs come in at number six—so feel free to change them if you like.

3 Add another call to *Sort*, specifying both arrays:

```
Array::Sort(keys, sa);
```

The *keys* array is sorted, and the elements in *sa* are sorted into exactly the same order. When you run the code and print out the array, you'll find that the elements have been sorted from "Cat" to "Pig."

The *IComparable* Interface

Any type that wants to be used in the *Sort* method has to implement the *IComparable* interface, which has one member, *CompareTo*. When *CompareTo* is invoked on an object, it gets passed a reference to another object. The function returns zero if the two instances are equal, a negative value if the object passed in is greater, and a positive value if the object passed in is less.

Enumerators

The *GetEnumerator* method returns an enumerator that allows you to iterate over the elements of the collection, in rather the same way that *For Each* iterates over collections in Microsoft Visual Basic or *foreach* in C#.

An enumerator provides programmers with a high-level way to iterate over the items in a collection without having to know about how the collection is actually implemented. This means that you can use an enumerator to iterate over the contents of an array or a linked list in exactly the same way, without knowing exactly how you get from one element to another in the underlying data structures. Many of the collections in the .NET Framework support the enumerator model.

A call to *GetEnumerator* returns you a pointer to an *IEnumerator*, which has two methods and one property that you can use:

- *MoveNext* advances the enumerator to the next element in the collection.
- *Reset* moves the enumerator back to just before the first element in the collection.
- Current returns a reference to the current element.

In this next exercise, you'll use an enumerator to list the elements in the *String* array.

1 Continue with the Strings project, and add the following *using* declaration to the start of the program:

```
using namespace System::Collections;
```

The *IEnumerator* interface is defined in the *System::Collections* namespace, so it makes it easier to use enumerators if you add a *using* declaration for the namespace.

2 Add the following code to the end of the *_tmain* function:

```
IEnumerator* ie = sa->GetEnumerator();
while (ie->MoveNext())
    Console::WriteLine(ie->Current);
```

You'll notice several things about this code. To begin with, the enumerator starts off positioned before the first element, so you need to call *MoveNext* once to get to the first element. When there are no more elements to retrieve, calls to *MoveNext* return *false*. The property Current retrieves the current object, but doesn't move the pointer, so you'll get the same value back until you call *MoveNext* again. The Current property also returns a general *Object** pointer, so you will often need to cast this to the actual type of the object, using the C++ *dynamic_cast* or the .NET equivalent keyword, *__try_cast*. (See Chapter 11 for details on how to use *__try_cast*.)

What isn't obvious from the preceding code is that the enumerator gets a snapshot of the underlying collection. This means that enumerators are designed for read-only access to collections, and that you can have several independent enumerators active on the same collection at one time. If any changes are made to the underlying collection, the snapshot will get out of sync, and if this happens the *IEnumerator* will throw an *InvalidOperationException* to tell you that it no longer reflects the underlying data.

The *IEnumerable* and *IEnumerator* Interfaces

Any type that wants to provide enumerator access to its members must implement the *IEnumerable* interface. This has the one method, *GetEnumerator*, which returns a pointer to some object that implements the *IEnumerator* interface.

Other .NET Collection Classes

The *System::Collections* and *System::Collections::Specialized* namespaces contain a number of very useful collection classes that can be used in C++ programs. Some of the most commonly used ones are listed in the following table. A couple of them will be examined later in more detail to give you an idea of how they work.

Class	Description
ArrayList	A dynamically growable array
Stack	Accesses a list of elements from the top only
Queue	Stores a list of elements, and accesses them in the same order they were stored
StringCollection	Stores a list of strings and retrieves them by index (in *System::Collections::Specialized*)
HashTable	A collection that stores elements by key
StringDictionary	A *HashTable* with the key strongly typed to be a string (in *System::Collections::Specialized*)
SortedList	A collection that extends *HashTable*, allowing you to retrieve elements by index as well

The ArrayList Class

The *ArrayList* class, defined in the *System::Collections* namespace, is a dynamically growable (and shrinkable) array. By default, instances of this class are resizable and writable, but the class provides two shared methods that let you create read-only and fixed-size *ArrayLists*.

The following exercise shows you how to create an *ArrayList* and manipulate it:

1 Open Visual Studio and create a new Managed C++ Application project called ArrayList.

2 Open the ArrayList.cpp source file and add the following line immediately after the *using namespace System;* line:

```
using namespace System::Collections;
```

The *ArrayList* class is defined in the *System::Collections* namespace, and by inserting a *using* directive, you can use the name without having to fully qualify it every time.

3 Add some code to the *_tmain* function:

```
int _tmain(void)
{
  Console::WriteLine(S"ArrayList Demo");

  // Create a default ArrayList
  ArrayList* pal = new ArrayList();

  // Look at the count and capacity
  Console::WriteLine("Capacity={0}", __box(pal-> Capacity));
  Console::WriteLine("Count={0}", __box(pal-> Count));

  // Adjust the capacity
  pal->set_Capacity(10);
  Console::WriteLine("Capacity={0}", __box(pal-> Capacity));

  // Add some elements
  pal->Add(__box(0));
  pal->Add(__box(2));
  pal->Add(__box(3));
  pal->Insert(1, __box(1));
  Console::WriteLine("Count is now {0}",
                     __box(pal-> Count));

  return 0;
}
```

The default *ArrayList* constructor creates an empty *ArrayList*. The next two lines use the Capacity and Count properties to print out the current capacity of the *ArrayList* and a count of how many objects it currently contains. You'll find if you run this code that the count is zero—not surprising because we haven't added anything yet—and that the capacity is 16. The default capacity of an *ArrayList* is 16, which means that you can add up to 16 items before the object has to go back to the operating system for more memory. An alternative constructor lets you specify a different initial capacity, as shown here:

```
// Create an ArrayList with a capacity of ten elements
ArrayList* pal = new ArrayList(10);
```

If you exceed the capacity when adding elements, it will automatically be doubled. If your array is too large, you can reduce its capacity to match the actual number of elements stored by calling *TrimToSize*. You can also reset the capacity of the *ArrayList* at any time by using its Capacity property.

The *ArrayList* doesn't contain any elements until you add some using the *Add* or *Insert* functions. *Add* adds a new item to the end of the list, while *Insert* takes a zero-based index and inserts a new item at that position. Note once again that, to add an *int* to the *ArrayList*, I have to box it to obtain an *Object** pointer.

> **note**
>
> Because *ArrayLists* store any object that inherits from *Object*—and that means all .NET types—you can store mixed types in a single *ArrayList*.

4 You can print out the contents of the *ArrayList* in two ways: explicitly, using the *get_Item* function, or by using an enumerator. Add this code to print the contents using the Item property:

```
for (int i=0; i<pal->Count; i++)
    Console::WriteLine("Item({0}) = {1}", __box(i),
                       pal->get_Item(i));
```

The *get_Item* method returns a reference to the item at a given index in the collection, and it will throw an *ArgumentOutOfRangeException* if the argument is less than zero or greater than the current count. You can obtain and use an enumerator in exactly the same way as you did in the "Enumerators" section earlier in the chapter.

5 The syntax for removing items from the *ArrayList* is similar to that used for retrieving them:

```
// Remove item at index 2
pal->RemoveAt(2);
```

If you want to remove more than one element, the *RemoveRange* function takes a starting index and a number of elements to remove. In addition, if you have stored a pointer to an object in the collection, you can use the *Remove* function, which will search the *ArrayList* and remove the first occurrence.

Other *ArrayList* Operations

The *ArrayList* class implements the same interfaces as the *System::Array* class discussed earlier in the chapter, and this means that it provides much of the same functionality:

- The *IList* interface provides the *Add, Clear, Contains, IndexOf, Insert, Remove,* and *RemoveAt* methods, plus the Item, IsFixedSize, and IsReadOnly properties.
- The *ICollection* interface provides the *CopyTo* method, plus the Count, IsSynchronized, and SyncRoot properties.
- The *IEnumerable* interface provides the *GetEnumerator* method.
- The *ICloneable* interface provides the *Clone* method.

These interfaces are used to specify common functionality for the collection classes, and once you know how the interface methods work, it becomes easier to use other collection classes.

The *SortedList* Class

The *SortedList* class, also defined in the *System::Collections* namespace, represents a collection of keys and values. A *SortedList* is very similar to a *HashTable*, which also maintains key/value pairs, but the *SortedList* maintains its data in sorted key order, and allows you to access items by index as well as by key. In this section, you'll see how the *SortedList* class works, and you'll be able to apply what you learn to *HashTables* as well.

> **note**
>
> Because of the need to maintain a sort order, operations on a *SortedList* are usually slower than on an equivalent *HashTable*, so only use a *SortedList* if you also need access to elements by key.

SortedList sorts its entries two ways:

- The objects stored in the *SortedList* can implement the *IComparable* interface with its one *CompareTo* method. All the value types, such as number and string classes, implement this interface, and you should implement it on any other user-defined types whose values can be ordered.
- An external "comparer" object can be provided, which implements the *IComparer* interface with its one *Compare* method.

The following exercise shows you how to create a *SortedList* and manipulate it. As an example, suppose you wanted to maintain a list of employees' names together with their phone extensions. A *SortedList* would work well in this case, using the name as the key and the extension as the value.

1. Open Visual Studio and create a new Managed C++ Application project called SortedList.
2. Open the SortedList.cpp source file and add the following line immediately after the *using namespace System;* line:

   ```
   using namespace System::Collections;
   ```

   The *SortedList* class is defined in the *System::Collections* namespace, and by inserting a *using* directive, you can use the name without having to fully qualify it every time.
3. Add the following code to the *_tmain* function, to create a *SortedList* and add some data to it:

   ```
   SortedList* psl = new SortedList();

   psl->Add(new String("Dilbert"), __box(1044));
   psl->Add(new String("Wally"), __box(2213));
   psl->Add(new String("Ted"), __box(1110));
   psl->Add(new String("Alice"), __box(3375));
   ```

   As with the *ArrayList* discussed in the previous section, a *SortedList* has a default capacity, and will automatically increase its capacity as necessary. Alternative constructors let you create *SortedLists* with particular initial capacities, and you can trim excess using the *TrimToSize* function.

   You can also use the *set_Item* method to add a key/value pair. This has the same syntax as *Add,* and in C++ there is no difference between using *set_Item* and *Add*.

> **note**
>
> Keys can't be null pointers, but you can use null pointers as values.

4 Add some code to print out the contents of the *SortedList*.

```
for (int i=0; i<psl->get_Count(); i++)
    Console::WriteLine(psl->GetByIndex(i));
```

The loop uses the *GetByIndex* function to retrieve each value in turn, and you'll find when you run the code, that the values are printed in the order 3375-1044-1110-2213, which reflects the alphabetical ordering of the keys.

5 In addition to retrieving values by index, you can retrieve them by key, like this:

```
Console::WriteLine("Value for key 'Alice' is {0}",
    psl->get_Item(new String("Alice")));
```

The *get_Item* method checks its argument, and returns the associated value if a match is found. If no match is found, a *null* pointer is returned.

6 Modify entries in the list by key or by value.

```
// Change the value associated with key 'Alice'
psl->set_Item(new String("Alice"), __box(5555));

// Change the value at index 3
psl->SetByIndex(3, __box(1010));
```

The *set_Item* method stores a value against a key. If the key already exists, its associated value is overwritten; if it doesn't exist, a new key/value pair is created. *SetByIndex* will work only on existing keys, and replaces the value at a given index.

Other Operations on SortedLists

You can use the *IndexOfKey* and *IndexOfValue* methods to return the index of a given key or value, and both of them will return -1 if the key or value you specify doesn't exist in the collection. Likewise, the *ContainsKey* and *ContainsValue* functions will return *true* if the collection contains a given value or key.

If you want to delete items from the collection, *Remove* can be used to remove an item by key, while *RemoveByIndex* does the same thing by index, and *Clear* can be used to remove all entries.

The *StringCollection* Class

The *StringCollection* class, defined in the *System::Collections::Specialized* namespace, represents a collection of strings. *StringCollections* lets you access elements by index, and add, remove, and insert items.

Because the *StringCollection* class implements the *ICollection, IEnumerable,* and *IList* interfaces, the class implements the methods associated with those interfaces, and so it provides a lot of functionality that you've already met, such as *Clear, Count, Contains,* and *CopyTo.*

In the following brief exercise, you'll create a *StringCollection* and see how to use it.

1. Open Visual Studio and create a new Managed C++ Application project called StringCollection.
2. Open the StringCollection.cpp source file and edit the first few lines of the file so that they look like this:

   ```
   #using <mscorlib.dll>
   #using <system.dll>
   #include <tchar.h>

   using namespace System;
   using namespace System::Collections::Specialized;
   ```

   The *StringCollection* class is defined in the *System::Collections::Specialized* namespace. To use it, you have to add a *#using* directive for the system.dll file, which is where the classes physically live.
3. Add the following code to the *_tmain* function to create a *StringCollection* and add some data to it:

   ```
   StringCollection* psc = new StringCollection();

   psc->Add(new String("Rhyl"));
   psc->Add(new String("Prestatyn"));
   psc->Add(new String("Abersoch"));
   psc->Add(new String("Nefyn"));
   ```

   Unlike *ArrayList* and *SortedList, StringCollection* objects are created with no initial capacity, and simply grow as more items are added.

4 Since *StringCollection* implements the *ICollection, Ilist,* and *IEnumerable* interfaces, it supports much of the same functionality as the other classes we've discussed, including the ability to use enumerators. Add some code to the end of *_tmain* to print out the contents of the collection:

```
StringEnumerator* ie = psc->GetEnumerator();
while (ie->MoveNext())
    Console::WriteLine("string is {0}", ie->Current);
```

Chapter 12 Quick Reference

To	Do This
Create a fixed-size array of C++ built-in types	Use a native C++ array.
Create a managed array of C++ built-in types	Use the *__gc* keyword when creating the array, for example: `int arr1 __gc[] = new int __gc[10];`
Create an unmanaged array of .NET types	Use the *__nogc* keyword when creating the array, for example: `Int32 arr2 __nogc[22];`

Iterate over the members of a managed array	Either use the Count property with a loop, for example:
	`int arr1 __gc[] = new int __gc[10];`
	`for (int i=0; i<arr1->Count; i++)`
	`    // do something`
	Or get an enumerator, and use the *MoveNext* method and Current property, for example:
	`IEnumerator* ie = sa->GetEnumerator();`
	`while (ie->MoveNext())`
	`    Console::WriteLine(ie->Current);`

Create a dynamic array	Use the *ArrayList* class.
Maintain a list of key/value pairs	Use the *SortedList* or *Hashtable* classes.
Maintain a list of strings	Use the *StringCollection* class.

CHAPTER 13

Properties

In this chapter, you'll learn

- ✔ *What properties are*
- ✔ *The properties supported by the Managed Extensions for C++*
- ✔ *How properties are implemented*

Properties have been available in some programming languages—such as Microsoft Visual Basic—for some time, but the .NET Framework has added support for them into Intermediate Language (IL), so that they can easily be implemented in any .NET programming language. You'll see in this chapter that properties can often lead to a more natural style of programming without sacrificing robustness or violating principles of object-oriented programming.

What Are Properties?

A long-accepted tenet of object-oriented programming is that it's a bad idea to give users direct access to the data members that make up your classes. There are two main reasons for this:

- If users directly access data members, they're required to know about the implementation of the class, and that might limit your ability to modify the implementation later.
- Users of your classes might—deliberately or accidentally—corrupt the data in objects by using inappropriate values, possibly leading to program failures or other undesirable results.

So it is recommended that you hide data members, making them private and giving indirect access to them by using member functions. In traditional C++ this has often been done using *get* and *set* members, so that a data member called *date* might be accessed using a pair of member functions called *set_date* and *get_date*. This works fine, but client code always has to call the *get* and *set* functions directly.

Properties in the .NET Framework give you a way to implement a virtual data member for a class. You implement the *get* and *set* properties, and the compiler converts them into calls to the *get* or *set* method as appropriate:

```
MyClass* pmc = new MyClass;
pmc->Name = "fred";          // calls pmc->set_Name("fred")
s = pmc->Name;               // calls pmc->get_Name()
```

It appears to the user that MyClass has a real data member called *Name*, and the property can be used in exactly the same way as a real data member.

If you've programmed in Visual Basic, the idea of implementing properties using the *get*, *set*, and *let* methods should be familiar to you. In the .NET Framework, properties can be created and used in any .NET language, so that you can create a class in Visual Basic and still use its properties in a C++ program, and vice versa.

The Two Kinds of Properties

Two kinds of properties are supported by the Managed Extensions: scalar properties and indexed properties.

A scalar property gives access to a single value by using *get* and *set* methods. For example, a *name* property would implement *get_Name* and *set_Name* functions to give access to the underlying name data. It is important to note that a property doesn't have to represent a simple data member of the managed class. A property can represent derived values, so that if a class has a *date of birth* member, it would be possible to implement an *age* property that calculates the age. Properties can also represent far more complex values, which might involve using data from other sources, such as searching databases or accessing URLs.

An indexed property allows a property to be accessed as if it is an array, using the traditional C++ square bracket ([]) notation.

> **note**
>
> If you've ever come across the overloaded [ ]operator in traditional C++, you'll find that indexed properties provide similar functionality, but you don't have to code the operator overload yourself.

Indexed properties still use *get* and *set* methods for implementation, and the compiler automatically generates the required code so that clients can use the square bracket notation. This means that if the compiler sees a property that can be implemented as an indexed property, it will automatically generate the code so that this happens.

The next two sections in this chapter demonstrate how to implement both scalar and indexed properties.

Implementing Scalar Properties

As mentioned in the previous section, a scalar property is one that gives you access to a single data member using *get* and *set* methods. The following exercise shows you how to implement scalar properties on a managed class, using a simple *Person* class containing *name* and *age* members.

1. Start Microsoft Visual Studio .NET and open a new Managed C++ Application project called Person.
2. Add the following class definition after *using namespace System;* and before the *_tmain* function:

```
__gc class Person
{
    String* name;
    int age;
public:
    // Person class constructors
    Person() { name = 0; age = 0; }

    // The Name property
    __property String* get_Name() { return name; }
    __property void set_Name(String* s) { name = s; }

    // The Age property
    __property int get_Age() { return age; }
    __property void set_Age(int n) { age = n; }
};
```

   The class has two private data members that hold the name and age of the person. Properties are implemented using *get_* and *set_* methods, and you tell the compiler that these are property methods (as opposed to some other methods that just happen to start with *get_* and *set_*) using the *__property* keyword.

The compiler uses the part of the name after *get_* or *set_* to generate the virtual data member that clients will use. In the preceding code, *get_Name* and *set_Name* will result in the class getting a virtual data member called *Name*.

note

You can't use *get_name* and *set_name* as the names of your property methods because this would result in a virtual member called *name*, which would clash with the existing real data member called *name*. However, it is common to use the name of an existing data member with different case as the name of a property.

3 You can use the property from C++ code as if it were a real data member of the class. Add the following code to *_tmain* to test the property:

```
int _tmain(void)
{
    // Create a Person object
    Person* pp = new Person();

    // Set the name and age using properties
    pp->Name = "fred";
    pp->Age = 77;

    // Access the properties
    Console::WriteLine("Age of {0} is {1}", pp->Name, __box(pp->Age));
    return 0;
}
```

Once a *Person* object has been created and initialized, the *name* and *age* members can be accessed through the *Name* and *Age* virtual data members that have been generated by the compiler.

Errors in Properties

What happens if a property *get* or *set* method encounters an error? Consider the following code:

```
// Set the name and age using properties
pp->Name = "spiro";
pp->Age = -31;
```

This is a good situation in which to use exceptions, which were discussed in Chapter 11. The property *set* method needs to communicate that the value passed in isn't acceptable, and exceptions provide the best way to do this. You could therefore modify the *set_Age* function to check its argument like this:

```
__property void set_Age(int n)
{
    if (n < 0)
        throw new ArgumentException("Negative ages aren't allowed");
    age = n;
}
```

If anyone tries to set the age to a negative value, an *ArgumentException* that has to be caught in the calling code will be thrown.

Rules for Constructing Scalar Properties

A number of rules govern how scalar properties are created in Managed C++. First, all properties must be declared using the *__property* keyword. Properties are implemented using *get* and *set* methods, and any method whose name starts with *get_* or *set_* must define a property *get* or *set* method.

The names of the *get* and *set* methods must be the same except for the prefix, and as you've already seen, you can't use a name that resolves to the same name as another member of the class. The access level to *get* and *set* methods can be different, so that a class can have a public *get* method and a protected *set* method, for example.

Properties can be virtual and even pure virtual, and it isn't necessary for both the *get* and *set* methods to have the same virtual specifier.

Read-Only and Write-Only Properties

You don't always have to provide *get* and *set* methods for a property. If you don't provide a *set* method, you end up with a read-only property. If you omit the *get* method, you'll have a write-only property (which is possible, but a lot less common than the read-only variety).

This exercise shows how to implement a read-only property, and also illustrates how to create a derived property. You'll change the *Person* class from the previous exercise so that it includes a date of birth rather than an age. The derived

Age property will then calculate the person's age from the date of birth; it is obviously a derived property because you can't change someone's age without changing their date of birth as well.

1 Either start a new Managed C++ Application project, or modify the one from the previous exercise.

2 Enter or edit the definition of the *Person* class so it looks like the following code. Place it after *using namespace System;* and before the *_tmain* method:

```
__gc class Person
{
    String* name;
    int dd, mm, yyyy;

public:
    // Person class constructors
    Person() { name = 0; dd = 0; mm = 0; yyyy = 0; }
    Person(String* n, int d, int m, int y)
    {
        name = n;
        dd = d; mm = m; yyyy = y;
    }

    // The Name property
    __property String* get_Name() { return name; }
    __property void set_Name(String* s) { name = s; }

    // The read-only Age property
    __property int get_Age()
    {
        DateTime now = DateTime::get_Now();

        return now.get_Year() - yyyy;
    }
};
```

The class now has four data members: a *String* for the name and three integers to hold the date of birth. A second constructor for the class is used to create an object with the date of birth set from the arguments.

note

It would be neater to use a *System::DateTime* object to represent the date of birth, but you can't have pointers to managed types as members of a *__gc* class.

The *Age* property now has only a *get* method, which retrieves a *DateTime* object representing the current date and time and calculates the age from the difference between the current year and the stored year.

3 Use the *Name* and *Age* properties as you did in the previous example:

```
int _tmain(void)
{
    // Create a Person object
    Person* pp = new Person("fred", 4,9,1955);

    // Access the Name and Age properties
    Console::WriteLine("Age of {0} is {1}", pp->Name, __box(pp->Age));
    return 0;
}
```

You can't set the *Age* property because you haven't provided a *set_Age* function.

Implementing Indexed Properties

Now that you know how to implement a scalar property, let's move on to consider indexed properties, also known as *indexers*. These are useful for classes that have data members that are collections of items, and where you might want to access one of the items in the collection.

The Bank Example

An example might be a *Bank* class that maintains a collection of *Accounts*. If you're not using properties, you'd tend to see code like this being used to access members of the *Bank* class:

```
// Get a pointer to one of the Accounts held by the Bank
Account* pacc = theBank->getAccount(1234567);
```

An indexed property will let you access the *Account* members using array notation, like this:

```
// Get a pointer to one of the accounts held by the Bank
Account* pacc = theBank->Account[1234567];
```

You can implement *get* and *set* methods for indexed properties, so that you can use them on both sides of the equal sign (=). The following code fragment uses two properties, with the first indexed property giving access to an account, and the second giving access to an overdraft limit:

```
// Set the overdraft limit for one of the accounts
theBank->Account[1234567]->OverDraft = 250.0;
```

The following longer exercise walks you through implementing the *Bank* and *Account* classes, and shows you how to create and use the scalar and indexed properties.

Implementing the *Bank* Class

1. Start Visual Studio .NET and open a new Managed C++ Application project called Banker.
2. Add the definition for a new class called *Bank* by right-clicking on the project name in the Solution Explorer, choosing Add from the pop-up menu, and then choosing Add Class from the hierarchical menu that appears.
3. This brings up the Add Class dialog box, where you choose the type of class you're going to add. Make sure the Generic C++ Class icon is selected before you click Open:

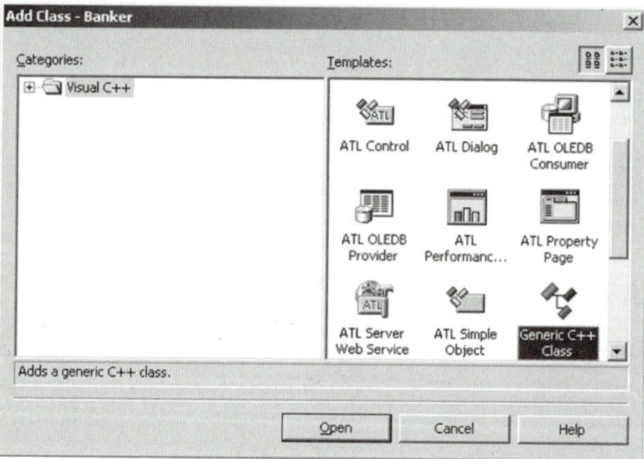

4. The Generic C++ Class Wizard constructs the skeleton of a new class for you. Fill in the fields as shown in the following graphic, and then click Finish:

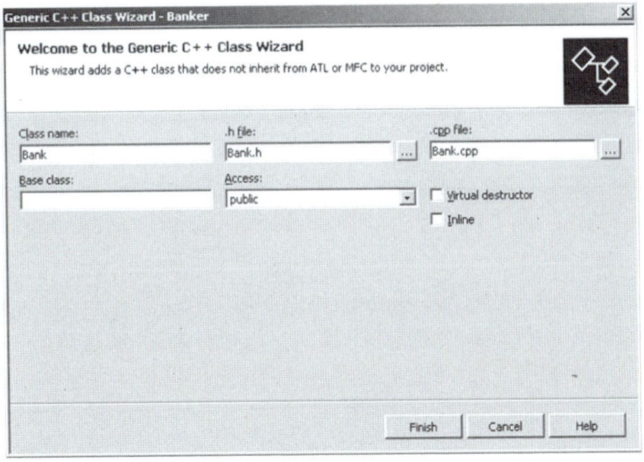

The wizard creates a generic class that simply consists of a constructor and a destructor. The class definition will be in file Bank.h and the class implementation in file Bank.cpp.

5 You need to edit the class code to fit this application. First, open the header file Bank.h and perform the following three edits:

- Delete the destructor definition from the class.
- Add the *__gc* keyword to the class definition, because you need a managed class.
- Type a line **#using <mscorlib.dll>** immediately after the *#pragma once* declaration. This is needed when defining managed types.

You should end up with a header file that looks like this:

```
#pragma once
#using <mscorlib.dll>

__gc class Bank
{
public:
    Bank();
};
```

6 Open the implementation file Bank.cpp, and make the corresponding changes:

- Remove the destructor implementation.
- Add a call to *Console::WriteLine* in the constructor, so you can verify that it has been called.
- Add **using namespace System;** after the *#using* line, so that *Console* and other classes in the *System* namespace can be used without further qualification.

The file should look like this when you've finished editing:

```
#include "StdAfx.h"
#include "bank.h"
#using <mscorlib.dll>
using namespace System;

Bank::Bank()
{
    Console::WriteLine("Bank: constructor");
}
```

7 To ensure that everything is correct, open the Banker.cpp file, and add code to the *_tmain* function to create a *Bank* object:

```
int _tmain(void)
{
    Console::WriteLine("Bank Example");

    // Create a Bank object
    Bank* theBank = new Bank();

    return 0;
}
```

8 You must also *#include* Bank.h from the Banker.cpp file so the compiler will know where to locate the declaration of the *Bank* class. Add the following code to Banker.cpp after the *#include "stdafx.h"* line:

```
#include "Bank.h"
```

Compile and run this code, and you should see the constructor message being printed on the console.

Adding the *Account* Class

The next stage involves creating the *Account* class, using the Generic C++ Class Wizard in very much the same way.

1 Add a class called *Account* to the project, in exactly the same way as you added the *Bank* class.

2 Make the same edits to the *Account* class as you did to the *Bank* class. You should end up with a header file Account.h that looks like this:

```
#pragma once
#using <mscorlib.dll>
```

```
__gc class Account
{
public:
    Account();
};
```

and an implementation file Account.cpp that looks like this:

```
#include "StdAfx.h"
#include "account.h"
#using <mscorlib.dll>
using namespace System;

Account::Account()
{
    Console::WriteLine("Account: constructor");
}
```

3 Add some structure to the *Account* class. Accounts will have a name, a balance, and an overdraft limit, so add three private members to the *Account* class definition in Account.h, like this:

```
long accNumber;    // the account number
double balance;    // the current balance
double limit;      // the overdraft limit
```

4 Edit the constructor definition and implementation as follows so that three values are passed in and used to initialize these three variables:

```
Account::Account(long num, double bal, double lim)
{
    Console::WriteLine("Account: constructor");
    // Basic sanity checks
    if (num < 0 || lim < 0)
       throw new ArgumentException("Bad arguments to constructor");

    // Initialize values
    accNumber = num;
    balance = bal;
    limit = lim;
}
```

The basic sanity check simply checks that the account number and overdraft limit aren't negative, and throws an *ArgumentException* if they are.

Creating *Account* Class Properties

Once the *Account* class has been constructed, you can add properties to allow access to the three data members. All these use scalar properties and are easy to implement.

1. Add a public *get* method to Account.cpp to allow read-only access to the account number, as shown here:

```
__property long get_AccountNumber()
{
    return accNumber;
}
```

   You can add the function definition inline in the class definition. Remember to put it in the public section!

2. You also need to add a read-only property for the balance member, as in real life you don't want people simply modifying the balances in their accounts from code.

```
__property double get_Balance()
{
    return balance;
}
```

3. Add a read-write property for the overdraft limit, because it is quite possible that the limit might get changed from time to time.

```
__property double get_Limit()
{
    return limit;
}

__property void set_Limit(double lim)
{
    if (lim < 0)
        throw new ArgumentException("Limit can't be negative");

    limit = lim;
}
```

   If you choose to make these inline in the class definition, you'll need to add a *using namespace System;* line or fully qualify the name of *ArgumentException* before the code will compile.

4. Test out your implementation by adding some code to the *_tmain* function in Banker.cpp to create a new *Account* object and access its properties. Include the Account.h file, and then add code to create an *Account* object, like this:

```
// Create an Account object
Account* theAccount = new Account(123456, 0.0, 0.0);
```

Adding Accounts to the *Bank* Class

The purpose of the *Bank* class is to hold *Accounts*, so the next step is to modify the *Bank* class to hold a collection of *Account* objects. Rather than design something from scratch, you'll use the *System::Collections::ArrayList* class (which you met in Chapter 12) to hold the *Accounts*.

Implementing *Add* and *Remove* Methods

The *Add* and *Remove* methods provide a way to manipulate the collection of *Accounts* held by the *Bank* class.

1 Open the Bank.h header file. Add the following two lines of code immediately after the *#using <mscorlib.dll>* line at the top of the file:

```
using namespace System::Collections;
#include "Account.h"
```

The *using* declaration will make it easier to use *ArrayList* in the *Bank* class, and you'll need to reference the *Account* class later on.

2 Add an *ArrayList* variable to the *Bank* class, making sure that it is private.

```
ArrayList* accts;
```

3 Add the following line of code to the *Bank* constructor to create the *ArrayList* member:

```
accts = new ArrayList();
```

4 Add the code for the *Add* method inline in the header file, as follows:

```
bool Add(Account* pAcc)
{
    // check if account is in list
    if (accts->Contains(pAcc))
        return false;
    else
        accts->Add(pAcc);
    return true;
}
```

Add takes a pointer to an *Account* object and then uses the *ArrayList* *Contains* method to check whether the account already exists in the collection. If it doesn't, *Add* adds the *Account* to the collection.

Remove is very similar:

```
bool Remove(Account* pAcc)
{
    // check if account is in list
    if (accts->Contains(pAcc))
    {
        accts->Remove(pAcc);
        return true;
    }
    else
        return false;
}
```

Remove checks whether an *Account* is in the *ArrayList* and removes it if the account is there. It isn't necessary to call *Contains*, because *Remove* will silently do nothing if you try to remove an item that isn't in the list. Users, though, might be interested in knowing that the account they're trying to remove isn't in the collection already.

Implementing an Indexed Property to Retrieve Accounts

You can now manipulate the collection of *Accounts*, adding and removing items. If you want to look up a particular account, you'll probably want to do it by the account number, and an indexed property provides a good way to do this. You'll only need to retrieve *Account* references using the property, so you'll implement a read-only indexed property.

1 Open the Bank.h header file, if it isn't already open.
2 Add the following code to implement the property:

```
__property Account* get_Acct(long number)
{
    IEnumerator* ie = accts->GetEnumerator();
    while (ie->MoveNext())
    {
        Account* pa = dynamic_cast<Account*>(ie->get_Current());
        if (pa->AccountNumber == number)
            return pa;
    }
    throw new ArgumentOutOfRangeException("Bad account number");
}
```

You might wonder why the property isn't called *get_Account*. The problem is that this would result in a virtual data member called *Account* being added to the *Bank* class, and this would clash with the name of the *Account* class.

The function uses an enumerator—discussed in Chapter 12—to iterate over the *Accounts* in the *ArrayList*. As long as there are more elements in the collection, *MoveNext* moves to the next element, which can then be accessed using the *Current* method. The pointer returned by *Current* is a generic *Object**, so it needs to be cast into an *Account** before you can get at the account number. The cast is done using a dynamic cast, but you don't need to check the return from the cast in this case, because you can be certain that there is nothing except *Account** pointers in the collection.

When you find an account whose number matches the one passed in, the pointer is returned. If no such account is found, an exception is thrown because trying to access a non-existent account is equivalent to reading off the end of an array: it's a serious error that should be signaled to the caller.

3 Test out the *Bank* class by adding some code to the *_tmain* function in Banker.cpp. You'll need to start by making sure that the Bank.h and Account.h header files are included. Next, add some code so that your *_tmain* function is similar to the following:

```
int _tmain(void)
{
    Console::WriteLine(S"Bank example");

    // Create a bank
    Bank* theBank = new Bank();

    // Create some accounts
    Account* accountOne = new Account(123456, 100.0, 0.0);
    Account* accountTwo = new Account(234567, 1000.0, 100.0);
    Account* accountThree = new Account(345678, 10000.0, 1000.0);

    // Add them to the Bank
    theBank->Add(accountOne);
    theBank->Add(accountTwo);
    theBank->Add(accountThree);

    // Use the indexed property to access an account
    Account* pa = theBank->Acct[234567];
    Console::WriteLine("Balance is {0}", __box(pa->get_Balance()));

    return 0;
}
```

After creating a *Bank* and a number of *Accounts*, you add the *Accounts* to the *Bank*'s collection by calling *Add*. You can then use the indexed property to access an account by number and use that pointer to display the balance. Test the property by passing in an account number that doesn't exist, and check that an exception is thrown.

Chapter 13 Quick Reference

To	Do This

Create a property for a C++ class	Use the *__property* keyword with *get* and *set* methods. For example:
	`__property void set_Weight(int n) { ...}`
	`__property int get_Weight() { ... }`

Implement a read-only property	Implement only the *get* method.
Implement a write-only property	Implement only the *set* method.

Implement an indexed property	Implement a property whose *get* and *set* methods take parameters that are used to determine which value to get or set.
	For example:
	`__property void set_Pay(Person*, Amount*);`
	`__property Amount* get_Pay(Person*);`

Delegates and Events

In this chapter, you'll learn

- ✔ *What delegates are*
- ✔ *How to create and use delegates*
- ✔ *What events are*
- ✔ *How to create and use events*

Delegates and events are extremely powerful and important constructs in the Microsoft .NET Framework. Events in particular are used widely in GUI programs as a means of communicating between components, but both delegates and events can be used to good effect in non-GUI code.

What Are Delegates?

The function pointer mechanism in C and C++ has been used by programmers for many years, and it is a very useful way of implementing mechanisms such as event handlers. Unfortunately, function pointers are a C++ language feature, so they're of no use in the .NET environment, where features need to be accessible from many languages. If you're interested in knowing more about function pointers and how they work, see the following sidebar, "What Are Function Pointers?"

Delegates are the .NET equivalent of function pointers, and they can be created and used from any .NET language. They can be used by themselves, and they also form the basis for the .NET event mechanism discussed in the second part of this chapter.

What Are Function Pointers?

A normal pointer lets you access a variable through a pointer containing its address. A function pointer lets you execute a function using the address of the routine. In exactly the same way that you can use a pointer to hold the addresses of different variables, you can use the same function pointer to invoke different functions. And in the same way that normal pointers must have a type associated with them (so that you can only point at doubles with a *double** pointer, for instance), function pointers must have a function signature associated with them.

The following line of code shows how you declare a function pointer in C++:

```
long (*pf)(int, int);
```

The code declares a function pointer called *pf*, which can be used to invoke any function that takes two *int* parameters and returns a *long*. The following function prototype has the right signature:

```
long func1(int, int);
```

This means that you can invoke the function indirectly like this:

```
pf = func1;          // assign address of func1 to pf
long l = pf(3,4);    // invoke func1() through pf
```

Remember that in C++ the name of a function without any parentheses evaluates to its address, so the first line takes the address of the function and stores it in *pf*. The second line uses *pf* to invoke the function.

You can use a function pointer to invoke any function that matches its signature, and that's what makes function pointers useful for event handling. You can define a function pointer to represent the event handler and then hook up the actual function to the pointer later.

What Do Delegates Do?

A delegate is a class that lets you invoke one or more methods that have a particular signature. Here's a simple example to show when you might want to use a delegate.

Imagine that I want to be able to perform operations on numbers by passing a number into a function and getting a transformed value back, like this:

```
double d = 3.0;
double result = square(d);
result = cube(d);
```

```
result = squareRoot(d);
result  = tenToThePowerOf(d);
```

In each case, I'm calling a function that has the same signature: one that takes a *double* and returns a *double* as its result.

With delegates, I can define a mechanism that will let me call any of those methods, because they all have the same signature. Not only can I call any of the four methods above, I can also define other methods and can call them through the delegate—provided that the signature matches. This makes it possible for one class or component to define a delegate, and for other classes to attach functions to the delegate and use it. You'll see examples of this use of delegates later in the chapter when we cover events.

In this case, I want to use the delegate to call one method at a time, but it is possible to attach more than one function to a delegate, and all of the functions would get called in order when the delegate was invoked. The .NET Framework defines the *System::Delegate* as the base for delegates that call a single method, and *System::MulticastDelegate* as the base for delegates that can call more than one method. All delegates in Managed C++ are multicast delegates.

Defining Delegates

This exercise uses the numerical operations example from the previous section to show you how to create and use a simple delegate in Managed C++ code.

1. Open Microsoft Visual Studio .NET if it isn't already open, and create a new Managed C++ Application project called Delegate1.
2. Open the Delegate1.cpp source file and add the definition of a delegate to the top of the file, immediately after the *using namespace System;* line:

   ```
   __delegate double NumericOp(double);
   ```

   The *__delegate* keyword is used to define a delegate. It might look as though this is a function prototype for a function called *NumericOp*, but it is actually defining a delegate type that inherits from *System::MulticastDelegate*. This delegate, called *NumericOp*, can be bound to any function that takes one *double* as an argument and returns a *double*.

Implementing Delegates

Now that you have defined a delegate, you can write code to use it to call functions. One of the rules for using delegates is that you can only use a delegate to call functions that are members of managed C++ classes; you can't use a delegate to call a global function or a function that's a member of an unmanaged C++ class.

14

Delegates and Events

Calling Static Member Functions Using Delegates

Let's start by looking at the simplest case: calling static member functions using a delegate.

1 All the functions we want to call need to be static members of a class, so add a class to your source code file, above the *_tmain* function, which looks like this:

```
__gc class Ops
{
public:
    static double square(double d)
    {
        return d*d;
    }
};
```

The class definition has to use *__gc* to make it a managed class, and it contains one public static method, which simply takes a number and returns its square.

2 Create a delegate in the *_tmain* function of the program, as shown here:

```
// Declare a delegate
NumericOp* pOp = new NumericOp(0, &Ops::square);
```

When you declared the delegate, you created a new reference type called *NumericOp*, so you can now create a *NumericOp* object. The constructor takes two arguments. The first one is a pointer to an object, used when calling non-static members, so in this example it is a *null* pointer. The second argument is the address of the function that is to be associated with the delegate, so you use the & operator to specify the address of *Ops::square*.

The object pointed to by *pOp* is now set up so that it will call the *square* function when it is invoked, and it will take exactly the same arguments (and return the same type) as *Ops::square*.

note

You can't change the function that a delegate invokes once it's been created. In this respect, delegates differ from C++ function pointers.

3 Every delegate has an *Invoke* method that you use to call the function that has been bound to the delegate. *Invoke* will take the same arguments and

return the same type as the function being called. Add the following lines to use *pOp* to call the *square* function:

```
// Call the function through the delegate
double result = pOp->Invoke(3.0);

Console::WriteLine("Result is {0}", __box(result));
```

4 You can now easily create another static member, create a delegate, and call the function. Test this out by adding a second static member to the *Ops* class, called *cube*:

```
static double cube(double d)
{
    return d*d*d;
}
```

5 Create another delegate in the same way as the first, but this time pass it the address of the *cube* function in the constructor:

```
// Declare a second delegate
NumericOp* pOp2 = new NumericOp(0, &Ops::cube);
```

When you call *Invoke* on this delegate, it will call the *cube* function for you, as seen here:

```
// Call the function through the delegate
double result2 = pOp2->Invoke(3.0);

Console::WriteLine("Result of cube() is {0}",
__box(result2));
```

Calling Non-Static Member Functions Using Delegates

You can also call non-static member functions of classes by using delegates. By definition, a non-static member function has to be called on an object, so you need to tell the delegate the function it is going to call, and the object it is going to use. This is done in the delegate's constructor, like this:

```
// Declare a delegate bound to a non-static member
MyDelegate* pDel = new MyDelegate(pMyObject, &MyClass::myFunction);
```

The constructor specifies the address of an object, *pMyObject*, and a member function belonging to the class to which *pMyObject* belongs. When *Invoke* is called on this delegate, it is equivalent to a direct call to *pMyObject->myFunction*.

Using Multicast Delegates

We've seen how it is possible to use a delegate to call a single function, but it is also possible for a delegate to call more than one function with a single call to *Invoke*. A delegate that does this is called a multicast delegate and is derived from the *System::MulticastDelegate* class.

> **note**
>
> All the delegates that you create in C++ using the *__delegate* keyword are multicast delegates.

All delegate objects have an invocation list that holds the functions to be called. The invocation list for a normal delegate has one member, and you manipulate the invocation lists for multicast delegates using the *Combine* and *Remove* methods.

If you look at the documentation for the *Combine* method, you'll see that it takes two or more *Delegate* objects as its arguments. You don't build up a multicast delegate by specifying more functions to add to its invocation list. Instead, a multicast delegate is built up by combining other delegates, which can in turn be single or multicast delegates themselves.

The following exercise shows you how to create and use a multicast delegate.

1. Open Visual Studio .NET if it isn't already open, and create a new Managed C++ Application project called Multicast.
2. Open the Multicast.cpp source file and add the definition of a delegate to the top of the file, immediately after the *using namespace System;* line:

   ```
   __delegate void NotifyDelegate(int);
   ```

   This delegate, called *NotifyDelegate*, can be bound to any function that takes one *int* as an argument and returns *void*.
3. You're going to call two functions through the multicast delegate. Since all functions called by delegates have to be members of a managed class, define two classes at the start of your project, each of which contains a static member function:

   ```
   __gc class Client1
   {
   public:
       static void NotifyFunction1(int n)
       {
   ```

```
        Console::WriteLine("Client1: got value {0}", __box(n));
    }
};

__gc class Client2
{
public:
    static void NotifyFunction2(int n)
    {
        Console::WriteLine("Client2: got value {0}", __box(n));
    }
};
```

These two classes are almost identical, both defining a single static member function that has the signature required by the delegate.

4 You want to call the two static member functions through one delegate, but you can't create a delegate to bind to two functions directly. Instead, you need to create two normal delegates (as you did in the previous exercise) and combine them into a multicast delegate. So define two delegates in the *_tmain* function, each of which binds to one of the static methods.

```
Console::WriteLine("Multicast Delegates");

// Declare two delegates
NotifyDelegate *pDel1, *pDel2;

// Bind them to the functions
pDel1 = new NotifyDelegate(0, &Client1::NotifyFunction1);
pDel2 = new NotifyDelegate(0, &Client2::NotifyFunction2);
```

At this stage you could use *Invoke* to use both of the delegates, just as you did in the previous exercise.

5 Build a multicast delegate from *pDel1* and *pDel2* by using the *Delegate* class's static *Combine* method, like this:

```
// Combine the invocation lists of the two delegates
NotifyDelegate *pDel3 =
    dynamic_cast<NotifyDelegate*>(Delegate::Combine(pDel1, pDel2));
```

Combine is a static member of the *Delegate* class that takes pointers to two delegates, and returns you a new delegate whose invocation list combines the entries from both delegates.

You need to use a cast because the pointer returned from *Combine* is simply a *Delegate**, and it needs to be cast into a *NotifyDelegate** before it can be used.

note

In other .NET languages, such as Microsoft Visual Basic and C#, the syntax is simpler but multicast delegates are still being created using the same mechanism.

6 The multicast delegate is now used in exactly the same way as the normal delegates, using the *Invoke* method:

```
// Invoke the multicast delegate
pDel3->Invoke(3);
```

When you build and run the program, you should see two lines of output, as shown in the following screenshot:

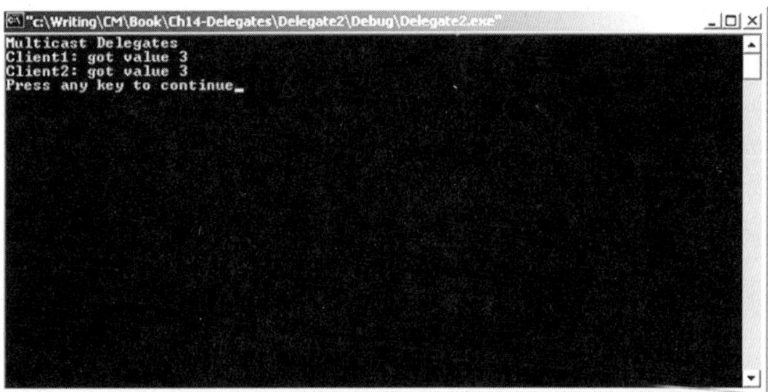

Note that the functions are called in the order in which the delegates are combined, so if you want to change the ordering, you'll need to change the way you create the multicast.

7 You can use this multicast delegate as the basis for making up another one.

```
// Create a second multicast delegate
NotifyDelegate *pDel4 =
    dynamic_cast<NotifyDelegate*>(Delegate::Combine(pDel3,
pDel3));
```

In this case, you're combining the invocation list of *pDel3* twice, which means that you'll get the following output when you invoke it:

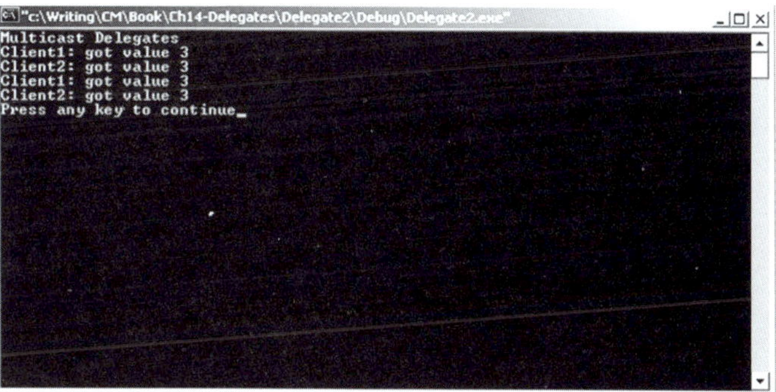

8 As the final part of this exercise, you can use the *Remove* method to remove an item from a multicast delegate's invocation list. Here's how:

```
// Remove an item
NotifyDelegate *pDel5 =
    dynamic_cast<NotifyDelegate*>(Delegate::Remove(pDel3, pDel1));
```

The *Remove* function takes two arguments: the delegate to be operated on, and the item to remove. If the item to be removed exists in the invocation list of the first delegate, it is removed. In this example, *pDel1* is being removed from the invocation list of *pDel3*, leaving only *pDel2*. If you invoke this delegate, you'll see that you get only the output from *pDel2*.

What Are Events?

Most, if not all, GUI platforms support the idea of events, and they are very heavily used in GUI programming. As an example, consider a button. Buttons don't exist on their own, but are used as part of a user interface and are contained by some other item. This is usually a form, but it could also be some other control such as a toolbar.

The whole point of having a button on a form is so the user can click it in order to tell the program something. For example, the user clicked the OK button, so dismiss the dialog box; or the user clicked the Print button on the toolbar, so print the document.

Events provide a formalized, standard mechanism that lets event sources (such as a button) hook up with event receivers (such as a form). Events in the .NET Framework implement a publish-and-subscribe mechanism, where event sources make public the events that they will raise—they publish them—and event receivers tell the source which events they're interested in—they subscribe to events. Event receivers can also unsubscribe when they no longer want to receive a particular event.

Events in the .NET Framework are based on multicast delegates, and it isn't too hard to see how this will work. An event source could declare a delegate for each event it wanted to generate, such as *Click*, *DoubleClick*, and so on. An event receiver could then define suitable methods and pass them over to the event source, which would use *Combine* to add them to its multicast delegates. When the time comes to fire the event, the event source could call *Invoke* on the delegate, thus calling the requisite functions in the receivers.

The actual event mechanism simplifies the syntax so that you don't have to deal with delegates directly, and is designed to fit in with the event mechanism that already exists in Visual Basic. The following exercise takes you through creating an event source class and event receiver classes that register themselves with the source and use the events when they're fired.

Implementing an Event Source Class

1 Open Visual Studio. NET if is isn't already open, and create a new Managed C++ Application project called Event1.

   Event sources and receivers use delegates, so the first step is to define a delegate for each of the events raised by the source.

2 In this example, two events will be used, so open the Event1.cpp source file, and define the following two delegates immediately after the *using namespace System;* line:

```
// Delegates
__delegate void FirstEventHandler(String*);
__delegate void SecondEventHandler(String*);
```

   The delegates define the signatures of the methods that event receivers have to implement to handle the events, so they're often given names that end with Handler. Each of these events will simply pass a string as the event data, but you can make the data passed over as complex as you want.

3 Add the implementation of the event source class to the source file like this:

```
// Event source class
__gc class EvtSrc
{
public:
    // Declare the events
    __event FirstEventHandler* OnFirstEvent;
    __event SecondEventHandler* OnSecondEvent;

    // Event raising functions
    void RaiseOne(String* pMsg)
```

```
    {
        OnFirstEvent(pMsg);
    }

    void RaiseTwo(String* pMsg)
    {
        OnSecondEvent(pMsg);
    }
};
```

The first thing to note is the use of the *__event* keyword to declare two events. You need one *__event* declaration for each event that you want to raise, and its type is that of the delegate associated with the event. So in the case of the first event object, the type is *FirstEventHandler** to match the *FirstEventHandler* delegate. Using the *__event* keyword causes the compiler to generate a lot of delegate handling code for you; if you're interested in exactly what's going on, see the following sidebar, "How Does the *__event* Keyword Work?"

You can then use the event objects in the *EvtSrc* class to raise the events, simply by using them as if they were function calls and passing the appropriate argument.

How Does the *__event* Keyword Work?

The *__event* keyword isn't only used in managed code, but can also be used to describe events in native C++ classes and COM events.

When you declare an *__event* member for a class in managed code, the compiler generates code to implement the underlying delegate mechanism. For the *OnFirstEvent* event object in the exercise, you'd get the following methods generated:

- *add_OnFirstEvent*, a public method that calls *Delegate::Combine* to add a receiver to this event's invocation list. Rather than calling *add_OnFirstEvent* directly, you use '+=' operator on the event object, which calls the function for you.
- *remove_OnFirstEvent*, a public method that calls *Delegate::Remove* to remove a receiver from this event's invocation list. As with the *add_* function, you don't call this directly but use the '-=' operator on the event object.
- *raise_OnFirstEvent*, a protected method that calls *Delegate::Invoke* to call all the methods on this event's invocation list.

The raise method is protected so that it can be called only through the proper channels and not directly by client code.

Implementing an Event Receiver

You now have a class that can be used to fire events, so the next thing you need is a class that will listen for events and act on them when they've been generated.

1 Add a new class to the project called EvtRcv1:

```
// Event receiver class
__gc class EvtRcv1
{
    EvtSrc* theSource;
public:
};
```

The receiver has to know the event sources it is working with to be able to subscribe and unsubscribe, so add an *EvtSrc** member to the class to represent the one source you'll be working with.

2 Add a constructor to the class that takes a pointer to an *EvtSrc* object, and check that it isn't null. If it is OK, save it away in the *EvtSrc** member.

```
EvtRcv1(EvtSrc* pSrc)
{
    if (pSrc == 0)
       throw new ArgumentNullException("Must have event source");
    // Save the source
    theSource = pSrc;
}
```

3 Define the handler functions that *EvtSrc* is going to call. As you know from our discussion of delegates, the signatures of these methods will have to match the signatures of the delegates used to define the events, as shown here:

```
// Handler functions
void FirstEvent(String* pMsg)
{
    Console::WriteLine("EvtRcv1: event one, message was {0}",
                       pMsg);
}

void SecondEvent(String* pMsg)
{
    Console::WriteLine("EvtRcv1: event two, message was {0}",
                       pMsg);
}
```

FirstEvent is the handler for the *FirstEventHandler* delegate, and *SecondEvent* is the handler for the *SecondEventHandler* delegate. Each of them simply prints out the string that they've been passed.

4 Once you have the handlers defined, you can subscribe to the event source. Edit the constructor for the *EvtRcv1* class so it looks like the following code:

```
EvtRcv1(EvtSrc* pSrc)
{
   if (pSrc == 0)
       throw new ArgumentNullException("Must have event source");
   // Save the source
   theSource = pSrc;

   // Add our handlers
   theSource->OnFirstEvent +=
        new FirstEventHandler(this, &EvtRcv1::FirstEvent);
   theSource->OnSecondEvent +=
        new SecondEventHandler(this, &EvtRcv1::SecondEvent);
}
```

You subscribe to an event using the += operator. In the code, you're creating two new delegate objects, which will call back to the *FirstEvent* and *SecondEvent* handlers on the current object. This is exactly the same syntax you'd use if you were manually creating a delegate. The difference is in the += operator, which combines the newly created delegate with the event source's multicast delegate.

As you read in the preceding sidebar , += calls the compiler-generated *add_OnFirstEvent* method, which in turn calls *Delegate::Combine*.

Although you've subscribed to all the events automatically in the constructor, you could also use member functions to subscribe to individual events as required.

5 A matching -= operator lets you unsubscribe from events. Add the following member function, which will unsubscribe from the first event:

```
// Remove a handler
void RemoveHandler()
{
    // Remove the handler for the first event
    theSource->OnFirstEvent -= new FirstEventHandler(this,
      &EvtRcv1::FirstEvent);
}
```

The syntax for using the -= operator to unsubscribe is exactly the same as that for the += operator to subscribe.

Hooking It All Together

Now that you've written the event source and event receiver classes, you can write some code to test them out.

1 Edit the *_tmain* function to create event source and receiver objects:

```
int _tmain(void)
{
    Console::WriteLine(S"Event Example");

    // Create a source
    EvtSrc* pSrc = new EvtSrc();

    // Create a receiver, and bind it to the source
    EvtRcv1* pRcv = new EvtRcv1(pSrc);

    return 0;
}
```

The *EvtSrc* constructor takes no arguments, while the *EvtRcv1* constructor has to be passed a valid *EvtSrc* pointer. At this point, the receiver is set up, listening for events to be fired from the source.

```
int _tmain(void)
{
    Console::WriteLine(S"Event Example");

    // Create a source
    EvtSrc* pSrc = new EvtSrc();

    // Create a receiver, and bind it to the source
    EvtRcv1* pRcv = new EvtRcv1(pSrc);

    // Fire events
    Console::WriteLine("Fire both events:");
    pSrc->RaiseOne(S"Hello, mum!");
    pSrc->RaiseTwo(S"One big step");

    return 0;
}
```

Calls to the source's *RaiseOne* and *RaiseTwo* functions tell it to fire both events. When you run this code, you should see output like this:

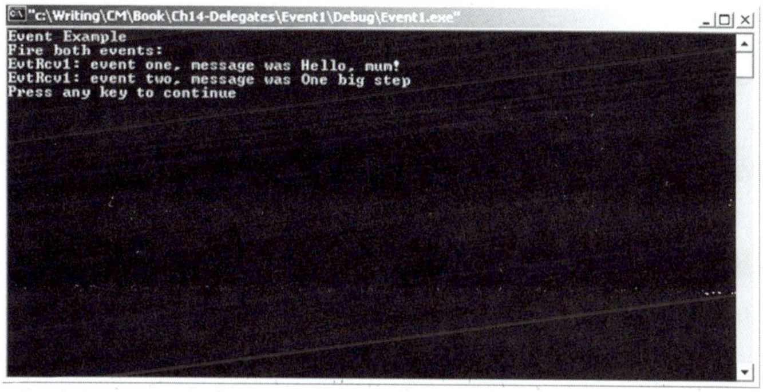

```
"c:\Writing\CM\Book\Ch14-Delegates\Event1\Debug\Event1.exe"
Event Example
Fire both events:
EvtRcv1: event one, message was Hello, mum!
EvtRcv1: event two, message was One big step
Press any key to continue
```

The receiver has had both handlers called and so has printed both the messages associated with the events.

2 Insert some code to call the *RemoveHandler* function of the receiver, and try firing both events again:

```
// Remove the handler for event one
pRcv->RemoveHandler();

// Fire events again
Console::WriteLine("Fire both events:");
pSrc->RaiseOne(S"Hello, mum!");
pSrc->RaiseTwo(S"One big step");
```

This time you should only see the second message printed, because the receiver is no longer handling the first event.

Chapter 14 Quick Reference

To	Do This
Define a delegate	Use the *__delegate* keyword with a function prototype. For example: `__delegate void DelegateOne(double d);`
Create a delegate bound to a static class member	Use *new* to create a *Delegate* object, passing 0 for the first parameter and the address of the static function as the second parameter. For example: `DelegateOne* pDel = new DelegateOne(0, &MyClass::MyFunc);`
Create a delegate bound to a non-static class member	Use *new* to create a *Delegate* object, passing a pointer to the instance for the first parameter and the address of the member function as the second parameter. For example: `DelegateOne* pDel = new DelegateOne( pMyObject, &MyClass::MyOtherFunc);`
Execute the function bound to a delegate	Use the delegate's *Invoke* function, passing any parameters required. For example: `pDel->Invoke(22.7);`
Create an event	First, define a delegate to define the handler routine for this event, as follows: `__delegate void ClickHandler(int, int);` Then in the event source class, use the *__event* keyword to define an event object: `__event ClickHandler* OnClick;`
Raise an event	Use the event object as if it were a function, passing any parameters. For example: `OnClick(xVal, yVal);`
Subscribe to an event	Use the += operator. For example: `mySrc->OnClick += new ClickHandler(this, &myHandler);`
Unsubscribe from an event	Use the -= operator. For example: `mySrc->OnClick -= new ClickHandler(this, &myHandler);`

PART 4

Using The .NET Framework

15

The .NET Framework Class Library

In this chapter, you'll learn

- ✔ *What the Microsoft .NET Framework consists of*
- ✔ *The major components of the .NET Framework*
- ✔ *The main namespaces that make up the .NET Framework Class Library*

In previous chapters, you learned how to use Managed C++ to build simple applications. Now it's time to move on to learn how to build real Microsoft .NET applications that involve GUIs, databases, Web servers, and all the other mechanisms needed by the modern Microsoft Windows application. And that's where the .NET Framework comes in.

The .NET Framework is the new library of classes that you use to build Windows applications. It is large, quite complex, and far-reaching in its scope. This chapter will give you an overview of what the .NET Framework is and what it can do, before we cover some of its features in more detail in later chapters.

What Is the .NET Framework?

The .NET Framework is a computing platform that has been designed by Microsoft to simplify the development of modern applications, such as:

- Applications that use sophisticated GUI front ends
- Applications that use the Internet
- Applications that are distributed over more than one computer
- Applications that make sophisticated use of databases

There are two main components to the .NET Framework: the Common Language Runtime (known as the CLR) and the .NET Framework Class Library. We'll examine both of these in this chapter.

The Common Language Runtime

You've already met the Common Language Runtime, because this is the part of .NET that provides the "management" in the Managed Extensions for C++. The CLR is a run-time execution engine that is responsible for executing code within the .NET environment, providing services such as security, memory management, and remoting (communication between objects in different domains, processes, or computers). Code that is run by the CLR is known as managed code; code that executes outside the control of the CLR is unmanaged code. All Microsoft Visual Basic and C# code is managed, but it is possible to write both managed and unmanaged code in Microsoft Visual C++, and to have both types of code working together in the same program.

Intermediate Language

All .NET languages compile down into an intermediate form called Intermediate Language, or IL. It is sometimes also known as MSIL, for Microsoft Intermediate Language.

IL is similar to Java bytecode, in that it is an intermediate form of code produced by the compiler that can't be directly executed on a target system. IL code is also portable. In contrast to Java, however, IL code is always converted into native code before it is executed, and this is done by a Just-In-Time (or JIT) compiler. This conversion might happen on demand, function-by-function as a program executes, or all at once when a program is installed.

One of the great innovations of IL is that it isn't simply a low-level, machine-independent object code. In fact, support for object-oriented functionality—such as the ideas of classes, encapsulation and data hiding, polymorphism, and inheritance—is built into IL, so that you can view it as a type of object-oriented assembler language. This makes it far more powerful than Java bytecode, and it allows you to do cross-language object-oriented programming, easily calling members in Managed C++ classes from Visual Basic and vice-versa, and even inheriting from a Managed C++ class in Visual Basic.

> **note**
>
> If you're interested in seeing what IL looks like, you can use the IL Disassembler tool, ILDASM, to open a .NET executable and show you the code in IL. There's an example of how to do this later in the chapter.

The Common Type System

The Common Type System (or CTS) provides a specification for how types are defined, managed, and used, and this is an important part of the .NET cross-language integration. The CTS provides a set of rules that languages must obey, which helps to ensure that types created in different languages can interoperate with one another.

The Common Language Specification

The Common Language Specification (or CLS) is a set of rules and constraints that compiler and library writers need to follow to be sure that the languages and code they produce will interoperate with other .NET languages. The CLS forms a subset of the CTS, and if a language or library is CLS-compliant, it will completely interoperate with other CLS-compliant languages.

You'll see in the online documentation that some .NET member functions are marked as not CLS-compliant, which means that they might not be accessible from some .NET languages. For example, functions that use unsigned integers are not CLS-compliant because unsigned integers are not included in the types specified by the CLS, and they can't be called from Visual Basic.

The .NET Framework Class Library

The .NET Framework Class Library is an object-oriented library of classes that provides all the tools you need to write a wide variety of programs.

Over the years since Windows was first released, programmers have written Windows applications using the Windows API (Application Programming Interface). This gives you a large number—several thousand—of C functions that you can call from your programs in order to interact with Windows. However, there are two main problems with the Windows API: first, it isn't object-oriented, and second, it's a C library, so it can't easily be used from every language.

One of the benefits of object-oriented programming is the help that it gives in structuring and managing large-scale projects. The Windows API has grown to several thousand functions, and it gets harder and harder to manage such a large collection of unstructured routines. In addition to its other benefits, such as encapsulation and polymorphism, object-oriented programming lets you impose a structure onto code, so that a *Dialog* class can contain all the functions relating to dialogs. This makes it much easier to use a library the size of the Windows API.

The second problem with the Windows API is that it is basically written for C programmers, so it uses many features that are unique to C, such as pointers and null-terminated strings. This makes it hard—and sometimes impossible—to use some functionality from languages other than C or C++. It also means that you tend to need a lot of ugly "plumbing" to interface between languages such as Visual Basic and the API.

The .NET Framework Class Library provides a set of classes that can be used from any .NET language, because it works at the IL level. All .NET languages compile down to the same intermediate code, and because they all use references and agree on the basic set of value types, they can all use the classes defined in the Class Library. This is a huge step forward and provides language interoperability on a scale never seen before. In the past, compiler vendors who supported more than one language—such as TopSpeed or Salford—have added features to their compilers to make it simple to mix their languages in multi-language applications, but no one has produced a language-independent programming framework on the scale of the .NET Framework before.

> **note**
>
> The first release of the .NET Framework is on the Windows platform, but it has been designed so that it can be ported to other platforms in the future.

Metadata

.NET classes are self-describing, in that they carry descriptive information with them in the EXE or DLL. This information, called metadata, includes the following information:

- The name, version, and culture-specific information (such as the language and calendar used) for the assembly
- The types that are exported by the assembly
- Other assemblies that this one depends on
- Security permissions needed to run
- Information for each type in the assembly: name, visibility, base class, interfaces implemented, and details of members
- Additional attribute information

Most of the metadata is standard and is created by the compiler when it produces the IL code, but you can use attributes to add extra metadata information.

The following exercise shows you how to modify the standard metadata produced by the compiler.

1. Create a Managed C++ Application project called Meta1. Open the Solution Explorer and look at the Source Files folder, and you'll see that the project contains three C++ source files. Meta1.cpp is the code for the application, while AssemblyInfo.cpp contains definitions of the standard metadata items that you can modify, and StdAfx.cpp is there to include the StdAfx.h header file.

2. Open AssemblyInfo.cpp. You'll see that the file contains a number of lines that look like the following:

```
[assembly:AssemblyTitleAttribute("")];
[assembly:AssemblyDescriptionAttribute("")];
[assembly:AssemblyConfigurationAttribute("")];
[assembly:AssemblyCompanyAttribute("")];
[assembly:AssemblyProductAttribute("")];
[assembly:AssemblyCopyrightAttribute("")];
[assembly:AssemblyTrademarkAttribute("")];
[assembly:AssemblyCultureAttribute("")];
```

   Metadata is added to C++ code by enclosing declarations in square brackets ([]). The *assembly:* part at the start means that this is an attribute that applies to an assembly, as opposed to a type within an assembly. There is a set of standard attributes that you can use to change the metadata compiled into an assembly, and most of them are listed in AssemblyInfo.cpp.

3. Edit the *AssemblyCompanyAttribute* line to contain some suitable name, like this:

```
[assembly:AssemblyCompanyAttribute("Acme Rocket Sled,
Inc.")];
```

4. Now build the project, which automatically creates the assembly for you. How can you be sure that the metadata in the assembly reflects your change? One way to find out is to use ILDASM, the IL disassembler. ILDASM is part of the .NET SDK, and as of beta 2, it is located in the \Program Files\Microsoft.NET\FrameworkSDK\Bin directory. You can either start it from there or open a Microsoft Visual Studio .NET command prompt using the Programs, Microsoft Visual Studio .NET 7.0, Visual Studio .NET Tools, Visual Studio .NET command prompt entry on the Start menu. This will open a console window that has the path set to include all the Visual Studio .NET and .NET SDK directories, so you can simply type **ildasm** to start the program.

5. When the ILDASM window opens, use the File menu to browse for the Meta1.exe executable, and open it. You should see something like this:

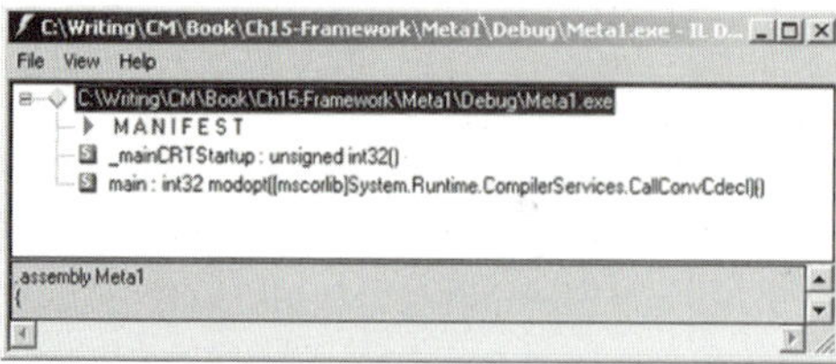

6 Double-click on MANIFEST, which will open a separate window displaying the assembly metadata. Scroll down until you find the *AssemblyCompanyAttribute* line, which should read something like this:

```
.custom instance void
[mscorlib]System.Reflection.AssemblyCompanyAttribute::.ctor(string)
 = ( 01 00 16 41 63 6D 65 20 52 6F 63 6B 65 74 20 53   //
...Acme Rocket S
        6C 65 64 2C 20 49 6E 63 2E 00 00 )                //
led, Inc...
```

Although the contents are given in hex, you can see that the metadata does reflect the change you made to the project.

Assemblies

Assemblies are the basic building blocks from which .NET applications are constructed, and they are the fundamental unit of deployment and versioning. Assemblies contain IL code, metadata that describes the assembly and its contents, and any other files needed for run-time operation. An assembly is therefore much more self-contained than a standard Windows executable or COM object because there is no reliance on external sources of information such as the Windows Registry. Every .NET type is part of an assembly, and no .NET type can exist outside an assembly.

I just mentioned that assemblies are fundamental units within the .NET world. There are several ways in which this applies:

- **Versioning.** The assembly is the smallest unit to which versioning is applied, and the assembly manifest describes the assembly's version together with the versions of any assemblies on which it depends. This information means that it is possible to check that components with the wrong version information aren't being used at run time.
- **Deployment.** Assemblies are loaded only as needed, which makes them highly suitable for distributed applications.
- **Type.** A type's identity includes the assembly in which it lives. Two types with the same name living in two different assemblies are considered to be two completely different types.

- **Security**. The assembly boundary is where security permissions are checked.

The .NET Framework Namespaces

The .NET Framework Class Library is made up of a set of classes, interfaces, structures, and enumerations that are contained in almost 100 namespaces. This section begins by explaining how to use namespaces in Managed C++ code and then goes on to list the major .NET namespaces, together with brief details of their function and content.

You've already encountered .NET namespaces in use in Managed C++ code when you've used the C++ *using* keyword, as in the following example:

```
using namespace System::Collections;
```

As with traditional C++ namespaces, .NET namespaces provide an additional level of scoping that helps you organize code and guard against name clashes. Two classes with the same name can be used in a program, provided that they belong to different namespaces. A type name that includes the namespace information is called the fully qualified name, as in the examples shown here:

```
System::Collections::ArrayList  // the ArrayList class from
System::Collections
System::Threading::Thread        // the Thread class from
System::Threading
```

Namespace names in .NET typically consist of more than one word. In Managed C++, the components of the name are separated by the scope resolution operator ::. In other .NET languages such as C# and Visual Basic, the components are separated using a period (.), so that in Visual Basic, the preceding examples would be:

```
System.Collections.ArrayList
System.Threading.Thread
```

All classes, interfaces, structures, and enumerations that are part of the .NET Framework Class Library belong to a namespace. All the namespaces provided by Microsoft begin with one of two prefixes. Those that start with System have been developed as part of the .NET Framework Class Library, while those beginning with Microsoft have been developed by other product groups within Microsoft.

Namespace names can have any number of components, but there's no hierarchical relationship implied in names that contain the same root components.

The hierarchical nature of namespace names simply gives you a way to organize your classes, so that *System::Collections::Specialized* and *System::Collections* both contain collections, yet they aren't necessarily related in any other way.

> **note**
>
> Note to Java programmers: although .NET namespaces look very much like Java package names, there's no relationship between namespace names and directory paths as there is in Java.

There's no requirement that all the classes belonging to one namespace are defined in the same DLL, or that a single DLL contains classes from only one namespace.

Using Namespaces in C++ Programs

Managed C++ programs use the *#using* preprocessor directive to import metadata into a program using the Managed Extensions for C++. Remember that metadata is information that describes the types in an assembly, and it includes the fully qualified names of all the types. For example, suppose the compiler sees a line such as:

```
#using <mscorlib.dll>
```

It loads the DLL and reads the metadata for all the types that are defined there. Because mscorlib.dll contains most of the core .NET Framework classes, this imports the metadata for a very large number of types.

> **note**
>
> You can currently use only *#using* to reference assemblies defined in DLLs. This restriction might be lifted at a later date, but for now you can reference only in-process components.

The *#using* keyword means that you have to know which DLL holds the class or classes you want to use. Your normal source for this information will be the online help, and whenever I mention a namespace in the rest of this chapter, I'll also say which DLL it belongs to.

Some of the fully-qualified names can get rather long. Thus, it is common to use a traditional *using* directive to specify namespace names, so that you can use unqualified names, as shown here:

```
// Read the metadata for MSCORLIB
#using <mscorlib.dll>

// Import all the names
using namespace System::Collections;

// Now you can use ArrayList without having to qualify it
ArrayList* pal = new ArrayList();
```


The *System* Namespace

The *System* namespace, defined in mscorlib.dll, contains a lot of fundamental classes, including:

- Base classes for commonly used value and reference types, plus the base class for arrays
- Events and event handlers
- Delegates and interfaces
- Attributes
- Exceptions
- Math
- Application environment management
- Garbage collection
- Local and remote program invocation
- Data type conversion

You've already met a lot of types from *System* in earlier chapters, and some of the other classes are rather obscure, so I won't go through them in detail. There are a few points that are worth mentioning about some of the classes in *System*, and they are covered in the following sections.

Basic Types

System implements all the basic types defined by the Common Type System, and you can find these listed in the following table, which you first saw in Chapter 9.

Value Type	Description	Managed C++ Equivalent Type
Byte	A 8-bit unsigned integer	*char*
SByte	An 8-bit signed integer	*signed char*
Int16	A 16-bit signed integer	*short*
Int32	A 32-bit signed integer	*int* or *long*
Int64	A 64-bit signed integer	*__int64*
UInt16	A 16-bit unsigned integer	*unsigned short*
UInt32	A 32-bit unsigned integer	*unsigned int* or *unsigned long*
UInt64	A 64-bit unsigned integer	*unsigned __int64*
Single	A single-precision 32-bit floating point number	*float*
Double	A double-precision 64-bit floating point number	*double*
Boolean	A Boolean value	*bool*
Char	A 16-bit Unicode character	*wchar_t*
Decimal	A 96-bit decimal value	*Decimal*
IntPtr	A signed integer whose size depends on the platform	No built-in type
UIntPtr	An unsigned integer whose size depends on the platform	No built-in type

Note that several of the types—namely the unsigned integer types and *SByte* aren't CLS-compliant, so be wary of using them when you're writing code that is going to be used from other .NET languages.

All .NET languages map these types onto native types, so that Managed C++ maps *int* onto *System::Int32*, but you can also use the types directly if you want.

Floating Point Types

The *Single* and *Double* types implement IEEE-754 floating-point arithmetic. For the uninitiated, this means that every operation has a defined result, so you never get a divide-by-zero error when doing floating-point math; instead, you get an answer of infinity. The floating-point classes have values to represent positive and negative infinity and "not a number" as well as methods to test for them, as shown in the following example:

```
double top = 1.0;
double bottom = 0.0;

double result = top/bottom;

if (result == Double::PositiveInfinity)
  Console::WriteLine("+infinity");
else if (result == Double::NegativeInfinity)
  Console::WriteLine("-infinity");
else if (result == Double::Nan)
  Console::WriteLine("NaN");
```


The Collections Namespaces

You've already met the collections namespaces, *System::Collections* and *System::Collections::Specialized*, in Chapter 12. *System::Collections* is implemented in mscorlib.dll, while *System::Collections::Specialized* is implemented in system.dll, so if you want to use both, you'll have to use two *#using* statements like the following:

```
#using <mscorlib.dll>
#using <system.dll>
```

The following table lists the main classes that you'll find in the *System::Collections* namespace.

Class	Description
ArrayList	A dynamically growable array
BitArray	A class that stores a number of Boolean values as the individual bits of an integer
Hashtable	A hash table that stores objects by hash key
Queue	A list where objects are added at one end and retrieved from the other end
SortedList	A linked list whose members are maintained in sorted order
Stack	A first-in last-out stack

The following table shows the main classes that you'll find in the *System::Collections::Specialized* namespace.

Class	Description
BitVector32	A class that stores a number of Boolean values as the individual bits of a 32-bit integer
ListDictionary	A dictionary implemented using a singly-linked list
NameValueCollection	A sorted collection of string keys and values
StringCollection	An unsorted collection of strings
StringDictionary	A hash table with the key strongly typed to be a string rather than an object
StringEnumerator	An enumerator to work with *StringCollection*

The Collections Interfaces

The *System::Collections* namespace also defines a series of interfaces that are used to define the behavior of the collection classes. The collection classes themselves implement one or more of these interfaces, and you can use them as the basis for writing your own collection classes. The main interfaces are listed in the following table.

Interface	Description
ICollection	Defines the size, enumerator, and synchronization methods for all collections.
IComparer	Defines a method for comparing two objects.
IDictionary	Implemented by collections that manage key/value pairs, such as *HashTable* and *ListDictionary*.
IDictionaryEnumerator	Defines methods for enumerating over the items in a dictionary.
IEnumerable	Defines the *GetEnumerator* method, which returns an *IEnumerator*. Implemented by almost all collections.
IEnumerator	Defines the properties and methods of enumerators
IHashCodeProvider	Implemented by classes that provide hash code values.
IList	Implemented by classes that define indexed collections of objects.

The Diagnostics Namespace

System::Diagnostics provides a number of classes to:

- Trace program execution
- Interact with the debugger

- Use the system event log
- Start system processes
- Monitor system performance

All the classes in *System::Diagnostics* are implemented in system.dll.

The IO Namespace

The *System::IO* namespace, defined in mscorlib.dll, provides the classes that implement the .NET I/O functionality. The main classes in this namespace are described in the following table.

Class	Description
BinaryReader	Reads .NET primitive types from a byte stream
BinaryWriter	Writes .NET primitive types to a byte stream
Directory	Contains static methods for operating on directories
DirectoryInfo	Represents a path to a directory, and contains methods for operating on the directory path
File	Contains static methods for operating on files
FileInfo	Represents a path to a file, and contains methods for operating on the file path
FileStream	Reads and writes to files using streams
FileSystemInfo	The base class for *FileInfo* and *DirectoryInfo*
FileSystemWatcher	Watches for changes in the file system and fires events when changes occur
IOException	The exception thrown when I/O errors occur
MemoryStream	Reads and writes streams of bytes to and from memory
Path	Represents directory strings in a platform-independent way
Stream	The abstract base for the stream classes
StreamReader	Reads Unicode characters from a byte stream
StreamWriter	Writes Unicode characters to a byte stream
StringReader	Reads Unicode characters from a string
StringWriter	Writes Unicode characters to a string
TextReader	The base class for *StreamReader* and *StringReader*
TextWriter	The base class for *StreamWriter* and *StringWriter*

As with all the .NET Framework Class Library classes, these classes are language-independent. They can be used alongside or in place of the C++ stream classes. You'll find out more about some of the *System::IO* classes in Chapter 18.

15 Class Library

The Drawing Namespaces

A number of namespaces provide all the graphics functionality for the .NET Framework:

- *System::Drawing*, which encapsulates the basic GDI+ drawing functionality. The namespace provides simple two-dimensional pixel-oriented graphics.
- *System::Drawing::Design*, which extends *System::Drawing* to add design-time functionality so that you can extend the Visual Studio .NET interface with custom items.
- *System::Drawing:Drawing2D*, which provides more advanced two-dimensional and vector graphics.
- *System::Drawing::Imaging*, which adds image processing functionality to GDI+.
- *System::Drawing::Printing*, which allows you to customize and control the printing process.
- *System::Drawing::Text*, which adds advanced typography support to GDI+, including the ability to create and use collections of fonts.

The original set of Windows graphics routines was called GDI, for Graphical Device Interface. It provided a very simple set of two-dimensional graphics primitives, so that you could draw lines, circles, rectangles, and other simple shapes, as well as strings of text. The .NET Framework has built on this functionality, and its graphics library is called GDI+.

You'll learn more about GDI+ in Chapter 18.

The Forms Namespace

Visual Basic programmers have been used to programming with forms for some time. GUI applications in Visual Basic consist of a number of forms, each of which is a separate top-level window. Developers select controls—such as buttons and list boxes—from the toolbox and drop them onto the form. Every control has properties and methods associated with it; the Visual Basic property editor allows interactive modification of properties at design time, and both methods and properties can be accessed from code at run time.

The *System::Windows::Forms* namespace, which you'll learn more about in Chapters 16 and 17, provides Visual Basic-style form-based development to all .NET languages, including C++. This namespace is huge, containing over 300 classes, structures, and enumerations. The following table lists some of the most important classes to give you a feel for what is available.

Class	Description
Application	Provides methods and properties for managing applications
AxHost	Wraps ActiveX controls so that they can be used as Windows Forms controls
Button	Represents a Windows *Button* control
CheckBox	Represents a Windows *CheckBox* control
CheckedListBox	Represents a *ListBox* control that has a check box to the left of each item
Clipboard	Gives access to the system clipboard
ColorDialog	Displays a standard color picker dialog box
ComboBox	Represents a Windows *ComboBox* control
Control	The base class for all controls
Cursor	Represents a cursor
DataGrid	Displays Microsoft ADO.NET data in a scrollable grid
DateTimePicker	Represents a Windows date-time picker control
DomainUpDown	Represents a Windows up-down control that displays string values
FileDialog	Displays a standard file open or save dialog box
Form	Represents a window or dialog box that makes up part of an application's user interface
Label	Represents a Windows *Label* control
ListBox	Represents a Windows *ListBox* control
ListView	Displays a list of items in one of four views
Panel	Represents a Windows *Panel* control
RichTextBox	Represents a Windows *RichTextBox* control
StatusBar	Represents a Windows *StatusBar* control
TextBox	Represents a Windows *Textbox* control
ToolBar	Represents a Windows *ToolBar* control

The Net Namespaces

Networking support is provided by the *System::Net* and *System::Net:Sockets* classes. *System::Net* provides an interface to many of the protocols commonly used today, such as manipulating IP addresses, making DNS lookups, talking to HTTP and FTP servers, managing cookies, and authentication.

System::Net::Sockets provides an implementation of the Berkeley Sockets protocol and provides a .NET wrapper around the Windows WinSock API.

The XML Namespaces

XML is heavily used throughout the .NET Framework, and several namespaces provide support for creating and manipulating XML:

- *System::Xml*, which provides the basic classes needed for processing XML
- *System::Xml::Schema*, which provides support for XML Schemas
- *System::Xml::Serialization*, which lets you serialize .NET objects to and from XML
- *System::Xml::XPath*, which contains the XPath parser and evaluation engine
- *System::Xml::Xsl*, which contains the XSL processor

Using these classes, it is possible to perform all the manipulation of XML that you'll ever need to do. These classes make the .NET Framework one of the most productive environments for XML programming.

The Data Namespaces

The *System::Data* namespaces hold the classes that implement ADO.NET, a new version of Microsoft Active Data Object technology optimized to work with the .NET Framework, which enables you to build components that manage data from a number of data sources. Data from different data sources is provided by data providers, of which there are two shipped with the .NET Framework. The OLEDB data provider uses Microsoft COM-based technology that makes it possible to use many different kinds of data sources—such as relational database tables, Excel spreadsheets, and even text files—as if they were databases. The SQLClient data provider works with data from Microsoft SQL Server.

The most important class in the *System::Data* namespaces is *DataSet*, which represents an in-memory cache of data retrieved from a data source. A *DataSet* consists of one or more *DataTable* objects, and these in turn consist of a collection of *DataColumn* objects.

The Web Namespaces

Because one of the main reasons for introducing the .NET Framework was to make it easier to build Web applications, it is perhaps no surprise that the .NET Framework contains a number of namespaces related to Web programming. These are all related to Microsoft ASP.NET, the latest version of Microsoft Active Server Pages technology that is optimized to work in the .NET environment.

The most significant of the Web namespaces are listed here:

- *System::Web*, which provides the basic functionality for browser-to-server communication over HTTP, including the *HttpRequest* and *HttpResponse* classes that enable an ASP.NET page to exchange data with the client using HTTP
- *System::Web::Mail*, which lets you prepare and send e-mail attachments using the SMTP service built into Windows 2000
- *System::Web::Security*, which provides classes that implement security in ASP.NET
- *System::Web::Services*, which provides the classes that let you build Web Services
- *System::Web::UI*, which contains all the classes that let you build server-side controls

The features provided by two of these namespaces merit particular mention. Web Services, in particular, are a great new feature introduced by the .NET Framework. A Web Service is a programmable entity living on a Web server that can be accessed using standard Internet protocols. What this means in practice is that you can expose a function on a Web server that others can call. Communication between client and server uses standard protocols, such as HTTP, and data is usually passed to and from the Web Service in XML format using SOAP (the Simple Object Access Protocol). The use of XML over HTTP makes it possible to access Web Services easily from clients written in just about any programming language on any platform. It is also possible to find out what services a Web server supports, and it is very easy in Visual Studio .NET to write clients that make use of Web Services.

The *System::Web::UI* namespaces let you build server-side controls. You program these as if they were normal controls, but their code executes on the server. The *System::Web::UI::HtmlControls* namespace contains classes that represent HTML server controls that map directly onto standard HTML elements, such as buttons and forms. *System::Web::UI::WebControls* is more abstract and lets you program server-side controls that may not map directly onto HTML.

Chapter 15 Quick Reference

To	Do This
Use data structures such as dynamic arrays, lists, and hash tables	Use the classes in the *System::Windows::Collections* and *System::Windows::Collections::Specialized* namespaces.
Create a form-based application	Use the classes in *System::Windows::Forms*, and derive a class from *System::Windows::Forms::Form*.
Work with XML	Look at the classes in the *System::XML* namespace.
Trace program execution, interact with the event log, or monitor system performance	Use the classes in the *System::Diagnostics* namespace.
Work with databases using ADO.NET	Look at the *System::Data* namespaces.

16

Introducing Windows Forms

In this chapter, you'll learn

- ✔ *What Windows Forms is*
- ✔ *What the* System.Windows.Forms *namespace contains*
- ✔ *How to create and use forms in applications*
- ✔ *How to handle events*
- ✔ *How to use the basic controls*
- ✔ *How to use menus*
- ✔ *How to execute and debug Windows Forms applications*

Windows Forms is a powerful feature of the Microsoft .NET Framework that provides a set of classes for building GUI applications. In contrast to most other GUI libraries, Windows Forms can be used from any .NET language, and you can now easily build mixed language graphical applications.

Windows Forms is a large and complex subject, encapsulating the whole of writing GUI applications. The subject is worth a book in its own right, so the following two chapters can only scratch the surface to give you a flavor of how Windows Forms operates and how you can use it to write GUI applications.

What Is Windows Forms?

If you've ever programmed in Microsoft Visual Basic, the idea behind Windows Forms will be familiar to you. In fact, for the .NET Framework, Microsoft has taken the Visual Basic GUI programming model, complete with forms, controls and properties, and generalized it so that it can be used from any .NET language.

A Windows Forms application consists of one or more windows, called forms. These may be top-level windows, child windows, or dialog boxes, and an application may support many different forms. You place controls—such as buttons and list boxes—onto a form in order to build the GUI for your program. A simple form is shown in the following figure:

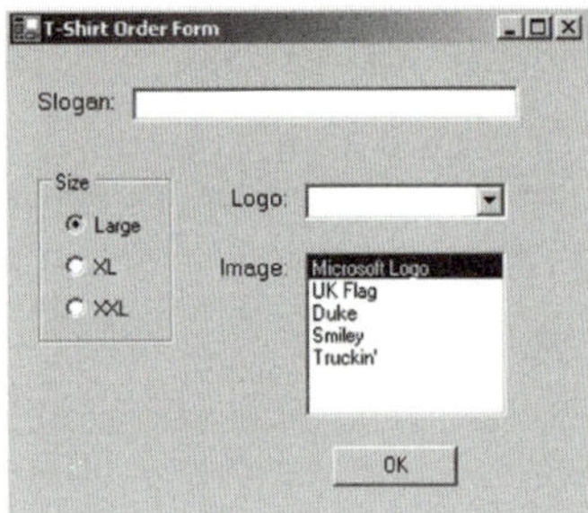

This form is a top-level window that is resizable and has a title bar; it also has Minimize, Maximize, and Close buttons on the right, and a system menu button on the left. It contains a selection of common controls, including a button, radio buttons, a group box, and a combo box.

note

You can also draw on forms using the classes in the *System.Drawing* namespace; we'll cover this in Chapter 18.

Windows Forms and Designers

If you're a Visual Basic or C# programmer, you can use designers to create the user interface. Microsoft Visual Studio .NET supports graphical GUI construction using designers, which put a form on the screen and let you drag components from a toolbox and drop them onto the form. A property editor lets you set the properties of forms and controls—such as color and text—and makes it easy to add event handlers.

Forms are always constructed at run time by executing code, and designers simply take what you do on the screen and generate code underneath, which will create the user interface for you at run time. If you open a Visual Basic or C# project and look at the source code, you'll see a section labeled "Windows Form Designer generated code," which contains that code.

Unfortunately, there is no designer for Microsoft Visual C++ included in the first release of Visual Studio .NET, so you have to create and populate forms yourself by writing code. Don't worry, though, because it is perfectly possible to create sophisticated GUI applications without designers.

Windows Forms vs. MFC

Since its earliest days, Visual C++ has shipped with a library called MFC (Microsoft Foundation Classes). This library is used for writing C++ applications for Microsoft Windows, and it encapsulates mostly that part of the Windows API that deals with GUI programming, along with some other areas such as databases and networking.

MFC has become a standard for writing Windows applications in Visual C++, the latest version ships with Visual Studio .NET, and there is a lot of MFC code still around. It has nothing to do with .NET, however, and you probably won't want to use it for new Windows development in C++.

However, you still might need to use MFC when:

- You have an MFC application, and you aren't updating it (or can't update it) to use Windows Forms.
- You've got to use some existing MFC components.
- You really like the MFC Document-View architecture, which isn't supported in the .NET Framework.

In the vast majority of cases, though, you'll want to use the .NET Framework. The object-oriented coverage of the Windows API is more complete, and it is better object-oriented code. Plus, you can do mixed-language programming easily using .NET.

A Word About ATL

While on the subject of C++ libraries for Windows programming, I'll also mention the other major Microsoft offering, ATL. The Active Template Library is a C++ library for writing the smallest, fastest COM objects possible. As such, it is a very specialized library, and few people will need to use it now that the .NET Framework has made COM less of a mainstream technology.

note

The .NET Framework makes it less necessary for developers to know about and use COM, because it provides technologies that make some of the traditional uses of COM (for example, general components and ActiveX controls) less necessary. This means that COM has been pushed more into the background as a specialized, mainly server-side technology.

The *System.Windows.Forms* Namespace

The Windows Forms classes are provided in two namespaces: *System.Windows.Forms* and *System.Windows.Forms.Design*. The second of these contains classes for design-time use, which typically means customizing and extending the designers used in Visual Studio .NET. Because Visual C++ doesn't use any of these designers, I won't mention this namespace again.

System.Windows.Forms is a very large namespace, containing over 300 classes and enumerations. The following table shows some of the major members of this namespace, and you'll meet lots more during the rest of this chapter.

Name	Description
Application	Provides static methods to manage applications, including starting and stopping them, and getting information about them.
AxHost	Provides a way to host ActiveX controls in Windows Forms applications.
BorderStyle	An enumeration that specifies the border style for controls. BorderStyle has three members: *Fixed3D* for three-dimensional borders, *FixedSingle* for simple line borders, and *None* for no border.
Button	Represents a Windows button control.
ButtonState	An enumeration that specifies the appearance of a button. Members include *Inactive*, *Pressed*, and *Normal*.
CheckBox	Represents a Windows check box control.
Clipboard	Lets you place data onto and retrieve it from the system clipboard.
ColorDialog	Displays a standard dialog box to let the user pick a color.
ComboBox	Represents a Windows combo box control.
Cursor	Represents a cursor.
DataGrid	Displays ADO.NET data in a scrollable grid.
DateTimePicker	Represents a Windows date-time picker control.

Form	Represents a window or dialog box.
HscrollBar	Represents a Windows horizontal scroll bar control.
ImageList	Represents a collection of images typically used by toolbars.
Label	Represents a Windows label control.
ListBox	Represents a Windows list box control.
ListView	Displays a list of items in one of four views.
Menu	Represents a menu.
MessageBox	Displays a message box.
Panel	A control that can contain other controls.
ProgressBar	Represents a Windows progress bar control.
RadioButton	Represents a Windows radio button control.
Splitter	Provides splitter functionality to a window.
StatusBar	Represents a Windows status bar control.
TextBox	Represents a Windows edit control.
ToolBar	Represents a Windows toolbar control.

Creating and Using Forms

If this were a book about C# or Visual Basic programming using Visual Studio .NET, I'd switch at this point to lots of screen shots of the development environment, showing you how to use the designers to build GUIs by dragging components from the toolbox and dropping them onto forms. Unfortunately, as I remarked above, Visual C++ .NET doesn't yet support designers, so you're going to have to construct GUI code by hand.

> **note**
>
> Writing code by hand has the advantage—not always apparent when using visual tools—that you'll understand what all the code is actually doing.

Creating a Simple Form

The following exercise shows you how to create and display a simple form.

1. Start Visual Studio .NET, and open a new Managed C++ Application project called CppForm.
2. Open the CppForm.cpp file, and add the following two lines immediately after the line *#using <mscorlib.dll>*:

```
#using <System.dll>
#using <System.Windows.Forms.dll>
```

These two DLLs hold assemblies needed by Windows Forms applications.

3 Add the following two lines after the line *using namespace System*:

```
using namespace System::ComponentModel;
using namespace System::Windows::Forms;
```

The *System::Windows::Forms* namespace holds the classes used in building forms. *System::ComponentModel* provides classes that manage the design-time and run-time behavior of components and controls, and it is usually needed when working with forms.

4 The next step is to define a form class, so add the following simple class definition to the code immediately after the *using* lines:

```
__gc public class CppForm : public Form {
public:
   CppForm() {}
};
```

The class is a managed class, as shown by the *__gc* keyword, and it inherits from the *System::Windows::Forms::Form* class. You're not adding any functionality yet, so just provide a do-nothing constructor, which will get filled in with more functionality later.

5 Now you need to show the form, so add code to the project's *main* function so that it looks like this:

```
int main(void)
{
    Console::WriteLine(S"Forms Example");

   // Create a form
    Application::Run(new CppForm());
    return 0;
}
```

The *Application* class is part of the *System::Windows::Forms* namespace, and contains static methods that you can use to manage Windows applications, including the *Run* method, which is used to display a form and start running a message loop on the current thread. See the following sidebar "What's a Message Loop?" for more details.

6 Compile and run the code. You should see the usual Console window displaying the text "Forms Example," and then a window should be displayed, as shown in the following figure.

You can see how the form has all the attributes of a window: it has a title bar and a system menu button on the left, it has Minimize, Maximize and Close buttons, and you can resize it. It doesn't have a caption because you haven't yet given it one, and because you haven't specified a particular size, it is created with the default size of 300 by 300 pixels.

7 Click the Close button—the one marked with an "x" on the far right of the title bar—to close the window. This terminates message processing, and closes the window. Within a second or so, you should see the message "Press Any Key To Continue" displayed on the Console window, showing you that the application has exited.

What's a Message Loop?

If you don't know how a Windows application works, here is a quick introduction.

A message loop is at the heart of every Windows application, providing the "pump" that drives the execution of the program. The parts of a Windows application, such as the forms, buttons, and scrollbars, communicate with each other, with other applications, and with the system by passing messages. In the world of Windows programming, a message is a small packet of data that is sent to a component to tell it something has happened. These somethings, called events, could include a timer going off, a key being pressed on the keyboard, or the user clicking on a button. A message is a structure that describes an event, and Windows delivers the message to the appropriate application, placing it in the application's message queue.

There are a tremendous number of events being delivered to a Windows application all the time, even when nothing much appears to be happening. At the heart of the application sits the message loop, a tight loop of code that removes one message at a time from the message queue and sends each off to the right part of the application for processing.

In prehistoric times, when the only tools programmers had for writing Windows programs were a C compiler and a copy of the Windows SDK (Software Development Kit), you had to code up the message loop manually and understand the architecture behind message processing. Nowadays, we have development frameworks—such as MFC and the .NET Framework—which do all the housekeeping for you, so you don't need to get into the details of how message processing happens. You can if you want to do advanced and clever things, but you don't have to for the vast majority of applications.

So when you want to run a form as the GUI for your application, you need to start up a message loop so that the form can process messages. You do this using the *Application::Run* function, which has the effect of both starting a message loop and displaying the form.

The message loop keeps running until it receives a quit message. This can be sent from application code, or it can be sent by the operating system as a result of the user physically closing the window. In either case, the message loop terminates, the window closes, and the application exits.

Using Form Properties

Now that you've mastered the basics of displaying a form, let's move on to see how you can affect the way the form looks and behaves.

The *Form* class has 39 properties and 20 methods, the most important of which are summarized in the following table.

Name	Method or Property?	Description
AcceptButton	P	Gets or sets a reference to the button control that corresponds to the user pressing Enter.
Activate	M	Activates the window, bringing it to the front of the application's collection of windows.
ActiveForm	P	Gets the currently active form for this application, meaning the one at the front of the application's collection of windows.
AutoScale	P	Gets or sets a Boolean value indicating whether the form adjusts its size to fit the height of the font used on the form and scales its controls accordingly. The default is *true*.
AutoScroll	P	Gets or sets a value indicating whether the form displays scroll bars when controls fall outside the displayable area. The default is *true*.
CancelButton	P	Gets or sets a reference to the button control that corresponds to the user pressing Esc.
ClientSize	P	Gets or sets the size of the client area of the form. (The client area is the portion of the form that excludes the title bar and borders.)
Close	M	Closes the form and frees any resources the form has used.
DesktopLocation	P	Gets or sets the location of the form on the Windows desktop.
FormBorder	P	Gets or sets the border style of the form. The default is *FormBorderStyle.Sizeable*.
HelpButton	P	Gets or sets a Boolean value indicating if the form is to display a Help button on the title bar. The default is *false*.
Icon	P	Gets or sets the icon associated with the form.

(continued)

(continue)

Name	Method or Property?	Description
MaximizeBox	P	Gets or sets a Boolean value that indicates if the form is displaying a Maximize box on the title bar. The default is *true*.
Menu	P	Gets or sets a reference to the menu that is displayed on this form.
MinimizeBox	P	Gets or sets a Boolean value that indicates if the form is displaying a Minimize box on the title bar. The default is *true*.
OwnedForms	P	Holds the collection of child forms owned by this form, if any.
SetDesktopLocation	M	Sets the location of the form on the desktop.
ShowDialog	M	Shows the form as a modal dialog box
ShowInTaskBar	P	Gets or sets a Boolean value, which is *true* if the form is to be shown in the Windows taskbar. The default is *true*.
Size	P	Gets or sets the form's size.
SizeGripStyle	P	Determines how (or even whether) the sizing grip is shown at the bottom right of the form. The default is
SizeGripStyle.Hide.		
TopLevel	P	Gets or sets a Boolean value, which is true if the form is a top-level window, meaning it has no parent other than the Windows desktop. The default is *true*.
TopMost	P	Gets or sets a Boolean value, which is true if the form is a topmost window, meaning it is always displayed on top of other windows, even when it doesn't have the focus. The default is *false*.
WindowState	P	Gets or sets the form's window state, which determines how the form is displayed: minimized, maximized, or normal. The default is *FormWindowState.Normal*.

The *Form* class also has a very large number of methods and properties that it inherits from its base classes, which are shown here:

```
Object
  MarshalByRefObject
    Component
      Control
        ScrollableControl
          ContainerControl
            Form
```

Notice especially the *Component* class, which forms the basis for all components that can be used with forms, and *Control*, which provides the base class for all visual components. All the base classes between them provide *Form* with approximately 110 properties, 180 methods, and 70 events! There are far too many to list here, so I suggest that you consult the .NET Framework documentation for more details. When I use inherited properties in the exercises or examples in this chapter, I'll tell you which base class they come from.

The following exercise will show you how to set the properties of a form so that you can make it appear where and how you want.

1 Continue with the previous application. First, let's provide a caption to go on the title bar, so add code to the CppForm constructor so that it looks like this:

```
CppForm()
{
  // Set the form caption
  Text = S"Test Form";
}
```

The *Text* property is inherited from *Control*, and it is being used here to set the text associated with the control. Many controls have some notion of an associated piece of text. In the case of an edit control, it's the text in the control; in the case of a button, it is the legend on the button. In the case of a form, it is the title displayed on the title bar of the form.

If you rebuild and run the code, you'll see that the form now displays a caption.

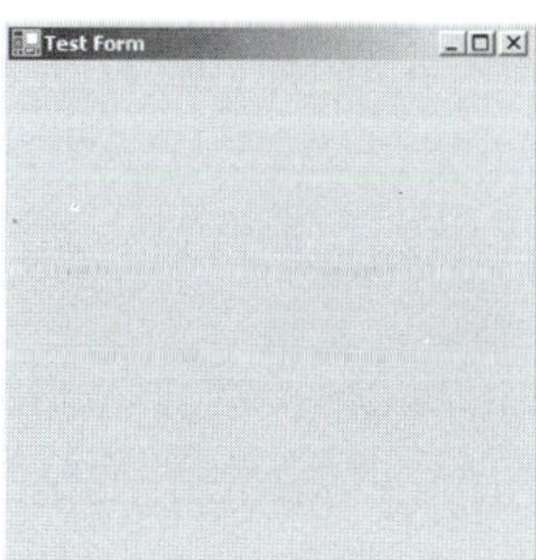

2 The form border is represented by the *FormBorder* property, which takes its value from the *FormBorderStyle* enumeration. The default border style is *FormBorderStyle::Sizeable*, which provides a simple border whose outline you can drag to change the size of the form.

```
CppForm()
{
  // Set the form caption
  Text = S"Test Form";
  // Set the border style to 3D fixed
  FormBorderStyle = FormBorderStyle::Fixed3D;
}
```

3 Compile and run the code, and you'll see that the border style has changed and you can no longer resize the window, as shown in the following illustration:

Experiment with other Form properties to change the look and feel of the form.

Form Relationships

Any form can create other forms—think of displaying a dialog box—and by default these will be independent of one another, so that you can minimize them and close them separately. There will be a parent/child relationship between them, but apart from that relationship, they are independent. Top-level forms, which are usually used for an application's main window, either do not have a parent form or have the desktop as a parent.

It is also possible for one top-level form to be the owner of another top-level form, in which case there is a relationship between the two forms such that:

- The owned form is minimized, maximized, and hidden along with its owner.
- The owned form is closed when the owner form is closed.
- The owned form never displays behind the owner form.

Think of the Find and Replace dialog box in Microsoft Word. This window appears when you want to find something in the document and hovers over the Word window until you close it. If you minimize Word, the dialog box is minimized, and it disappears when you close Word.

Placing Controls on the Form

Now that you know how to create forms and set their properties, let's examine how to add controls to a form. The following exercise will walk you through adding two buttons to the form, and the same procedure can be applied to many other controls.

1 Continue with the same Windows Forms project that was used in the previous two exercises.

2 Add a private *Button** member to the *CppForm* class, like this:

```
private:
  Button* btn1;
```

Button is a member of the *System::Windows::Forms* namespace and represents a Windows button control.

3 Before doing any more with the button, you're going to need to access the *System::Drawing* namespace, so add the following *#using* and *using* lines to the appropriate places at the start of the code:

```
#using <System.Drawing.dll>
using System::Drawing;
```

You need *System::Drawing* because it contains the *Point* and *Size* classes that you're going to use to define the location and size of the button.

4 Now you need to create and set the properties of the button. So that the constructor doesn't get too large and crowded with code, create another private member function of the class called *Setup_Buttons* as follows:

```
private:
    void Setup_Buttons()
    {
    }
```

5 Add a call to this function in the *CppForm* constructor, right after you've set the *Text* and FormBorderStyle properties, as shown here:

```
// Set up the buttons on the form
Setup_Buttons();
```

6 Now fill in the *Setup_Buttons* function like so:

```
void Setup_Buttons()
{
    // Add a button
    btn1 = new Button();
    btn1->Text = S"OK";

    btn1->Size = System::Drawing::Size(70,25);
    btn1->Location = Point(130,225);
}
```

This code creates a button object and then uses its Text property to set the caption on the button to "OK". The *Size* and *Location* properties are then used to specify the size of the button in pixels and where it is going to be placed on the screen. The coordinates for *Location* are in pixels, relative to the top-left corner of the form containing the button.

Note that you have to fully qualify the *Size* type, because the *Form* class also has a *Size* member, and if you just say Size(120,40), the compiler thinks you mean *Form::Size,* and you'll get a compiler error.

7 The last task is to make the form aware of the button. You do this by adding the button to the form's collection of controls. Add this line to *Setup_Buttons* after you've set the button's location:

```
Controls->Add(btn1);
```

Every container (such as a form) has a *Controls* property that contains references to all the controls currently hosted by the form. By adding a control to the collection, you make sure that the form will display it and will treat is as an owned window.

8 Add a second button, btn2, duplicating the code in *Setup_Buttons* that you added for btn1. Make it display "Cancel" for the text, and make the size the same, but change the *Location* so that this one displays at (210,225). Make sure you add this second button to the *Controls* collection!

Compile and run the code, and you should see two buttons displayed on the form, as shown in the following graphic:

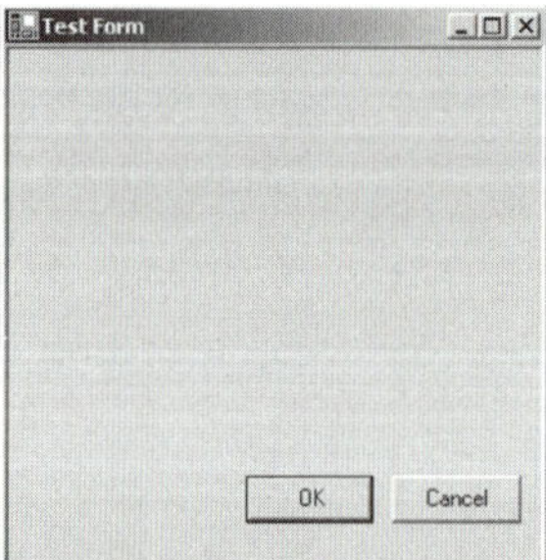

A Word About Layout

It may seem rather unsatisfactory to have to enter the coordinates and size of every control you want to place on a form. Surely this is going to make constructing sophisticated user interfaces a chore? Well, if you're using Visual Basic or C#, you have designers in Visual Studio .NET that calculate the coordinates for you from the controls that you drop onto a form. And forms in the Java language have an associated layout manager, an object that takes care of laying out the controls in a container for you.

However, we don't have either of those sophistications in Visual C++ yet, so I'm afraid that you'll have to carefully calculate the coordinates of the controls and write the code to place them on the form.

Handling Events

It isn't much use placing buttons on a form unless you can make them do something, so let's take a look at how to handle the events that are fired by controls. The .NET event mechanism was covered in Chapter 14, so you might review that material now if you want to refresh your memory.

To handle an event, you need to create an event handler function and attach it to the event source. In Chapter 14, you saw how to do this with custom event source and receiver classes, and I'll now show you how to do it with standard event sources in the form of controls.

note

Once again, users of Visual Basic and C# get help from Visual Studio .NET when implementing event handlers, but C++ programmers have to do the job by hand.

The following exercise, which follows on from the last one, shows you how to add event handlers for the buttons on the form.

1 Continue with the project from the previous exercise. The form currently contains two buttons, and the most common occurrence is when a user clicks on the button and a *Click* event is raised. You're going to add handlers for the *Click* events associated with the two buttons.

2 Add the following skeleton for an event handler function to the *CppForm* class immediately after the constructor:

```
private:
    void Btn1_Clicked(Object* pSender, EventArgs* pArgs)
    {
    }
```

The event handler function is private; it isn't intended that it will be called from anywhere outside the class. The function is called *Btn1_Clicked*; there's nothing special about the name, but it is a popular convention when naming event handlers that you include the names of the event source object and the event being handled.

The first argument to the handler function is a pointer to the object that originated the event. You can use one event handler to handle events from a number of sources, so you could use this parameter to tell which source the event came from. You can also use it to access the methods and properties of the sender, if you need to.

The second argument is a pointer to an *EventArgs* object that contains information about the event. In the case of a button click, there isn't any data, and *EventArgs* is the base class for all events and as such doesn't contain any information. Other event types used by other controls might want to pass you extra information, and you'll meet some of these event types later in the chapter.

3 This function is called when the button is clicked, and just to prove that the handler is called, add a line to display a message box, as shown here:

```
    void Btn1_Clicked(Object* pSender, EventArgs* pArgs)
    {
        MessageBox::Show(S"It worked!", S"Message...");
    }
```

The *MessageBox* class is part of the *Forms* namespace, and its one *Show* method is used to display a standard Windows message box. *Show* has a dozen overloads that take different combinations of arguments, and the one I'm using only specifies the message and title. This message box will display without an icon and with a single OK button.

4 The final task is to make the button aware of the handler. Add the following line of code to the *Setup_Buttons* function just after you've set the button's location and size:

```
btn1->Click += new EventHandler(this,
&CppForm::Btn1_Clicked);
```

From the discussion of events in Chapter 14, you'll recall that event handlers are connected with event sources by delegates. There are several different event handlers associated with controls (we'll meet some of them later in the chapter), but the delegate used for controls that don't pass back any data is called *EventHandler*, and this event delegate passes back a plain *EventArgs* object.

So to connect an event handler to the button object, you create a new *EventHandler* and pass it a pointer to the object and the address of the function within the object that is going to handle the event. In this case, you're handling the event within the *CppForm* object, so pass the *this* pointer for the first argument and the address of the *Btn1_Clicked* function as the second.

The event handler is registered with the source by using the += operator to link the handler to the button's *Click* event.

note

Remember that if you wanted to cancel the event handling later, you could use the -= operator to unlink the handler.

5 Try building and testing the application. You should see a message box like the one below when you click OK:

Note that the message box is modal: you can't return to the application until you've sent the message box away by clicking OK.

6 Try adding a similar handler for the Cancel button.

Using Controls

Now that you've seen the basics of adding controls to forms and handling events, let's look at some of the controls that are available for you to use in Windows Forms applications. This section will look at the most fundamental controls, and the following chapter will deal with other controls in more detail. All these controls inherit from the *Component* and *Control* classes, which gives them a very large number of methods and properties in common.

Controls and Events

Although some controls—such as icons and labels—can be used in a purely decorative way or to present information to the user, many controls are used to enable the user to interact with the application. They do this by firing events when the user interacts with them in some way, such as clicking a button, moving a scrollbar, or choosing a date from a calendar control.

Exactly what and how many events can be fired varies from control to control. Buttons, for example, only tend to fire *Click* events when the user clicks on them. A complex control such as a tree control, for example, can fire many different events, because there are many ways in which a user can interact with the tree. When using a control, you need to consult the .NET Framework documentation to find out what events can be fired, and what handler functions you need to provide.

note

You can also create your own controls to use on forms, but that is outside the scope of this book.

Label

A *Label* is a control that is used to provide descriptive text on a form. Users don't normally interact with *Label* controls, and these controls don't usually receive the input focus, so it is unusual for programs to handle events originating from *Labels*.

Using *Labels* mainly consists of creating them, and then setting the Label properties. The following table shows the most commonly used properties of the *Label* class:

Label Property	Description
AutoSize	Determines whether the label automatically resizes itself to fit the text.
BackColor (inherited from *Control*)	Represents the background color of the label.
BorderStyle	Gets or sets the style of the label border: three-dimensional, single, or none.
FlatStyle	Determines whether the label is has a flat appearance.
Font (inherited from *Control*)	Represents the font for the control.

Label Property	Description
ForeColor (inherited from *Control*)	Represents the foreground color of the label.
Image	Gets or sets the image associated with the label.
ImageAlign	Represents the alignment of the image on the label. The default is centered.
ImageIndex	The index of the image to be used from the associated *ImageList*.
ImageList	The *ImageList* to be used as a source of images for this label.
PreferredHeight	Gets the height necessary to display one line of text.
PreferredWidth	Gets the width necessary to display the current text.
RenderTransparent	Determines whether the container's background will be displayed as the background to the label.
TabStop	Determines whether the user can tab to this control.
Text	Represents the text of the label.
TextAlign	Gets or sets the text alignment. The default is left aligned.
UseMnemonic	Determines whether ampersand (&) characters in the text should be interpreted as access keys.

There are a couple of items in the table worth explaining in more detail.

Labels do participate in the tab order on forms but don't usually receive the focus. If you want to give the focus to a label for some reason, set the *TabStop* property to *true*. In addition, ampersand (&) characters normally aren't interpreted as access keys as they are in menus, where the presence of an ampersand underlines the following character rather than displaying the ampersand. If you want ampersands to be interpreted as access keys, set the UseMnemonic property to *true*.

Labels can display an image as well as (or instead of) text, and the *Image* property represents the image currently associated with the label. You can also use images stored in *ImageList* controls, via the *ImageList* and *ImageIndex* properties.

The following exercise shows you how to add a label to a form and how to manipulate the label's properties.

1 Continue using the *CppForm* project. Add a private *Label* member to the class, as shown here:

```
Label* theLabel;
```

2 Add a function called *Setup_Label* to the class, and call it from the constructor after the calls to *Setup_Buttons*, like this:

```
private:
    void Setup_Label()
    {
    }
```

3 Add code to *Setup_Label* to create the *Label* and set the text as shown here:

```
void Setup_Label()
{
    theLabel = new Label();
    theLabel->AutoSize = true;

    theLabel->Text = S"    Acme Consulting, Inc.";
}
```

Note the spaces before the word Acme. You're going to display an image at the left of the label, and you need to leave space so that it doesn't overlap with the start of the text. Setting the *AutoSize* property to *true* means that the label will resize itself to contain whatever text is assigned to it.

4 Now set up the font details for the label by adding this code at the end of *Setup_Label*:

```
// Set the font
theLabel->Font = new System::Drawing::Font(S"Verdana",
                                   16, FontStyle::Italic);
theLabel->ForeColor = Color::Black;
```

Fonts are represented by *System::Drawing::Font* objects. There are several ways of constructing *Font* objects, and here I'm using the font family (Verdana), the point size (25 points), and the style (Italic). Again, you have to fully qualify the name of the *Font* class so that it doesn't get confused with the *Font* property of *Form*.

Colors are represented by members of the *System::Drawing::Color* class, and there are a large number of predefined colors that are defined as static members of *Color*.

5 Set the size and the location of the label on the form, as shown here:

```
// Set location and size
theLabel->Location = Point(20,20);
theLabel->Size = System::Drawing::Size(theLabel-
>PreferredWidth,
                                        theLabel-
>PreferredHeight);
```

The label is going to be displayed at (20,20) on the form. The size is calculated from the *PreferredWidth* and *PreferredHeight* properties, which are calculated from the *Text* and *Font* settings.

> **note**
> If you're simply going to use *PreferredWidth* and *PreferredHeight* for the size of the label, you don't need to set the *Size* property, because these are taken as the defaults. I've used them here to show how the size is calculated.

6 Now add an image to the label, as follows:

```
// Add an image
Bitmap* theImage = new Bitmap("floppy.bmp");
theLabel->Image = theImage;
theLabel->ImageAlign = ContentAlignment::MiddleLeft;
```

Bitmap images are represented by the *Bitmap* class. The constructor simply takes a reference to a suitable image (which can be a BMP, GIF, or JPG file). The *Bitmap* object is assigned to the *Image* property of the label and its alignment set to *MiddleLeft*. Alignments are members of the *ContentAlignment* enumeration, and *MiddleLeft* specifies middle alignment vertically and left alignment horizontally.

7 Finally, don't forget to add the label to the collection of controls on the form, like this:

```
Controls->Add(theLabel);
```

8 Build and run the program, and you'll see a label containing text and an image being displayed at the top of the form, as shown here:

Button

You've already met the *Button* class earlier in the chapter and you've seen how to add buttons to forms. A *Button* represents a Windows button on a form and, next to *Label*, it is probably the simplest of the commonly used Windows controls.

The most frequently used properties of the *Button* class are listed in the following table.

Button Property	Description
DialogResult	Represents the value that is returned to the parent form when the button is clicked.
FlatStyle (inherited from *ButtonBase*)	Determines whether the button is drawn with a flat style.
Image (inherited from *ButtonBase*)	Gets or sets the image displayed on the button.
ImageAlign (inherited from *ButtonBase*)	Gets or sets the image alignment. The default value is *MiddleCenter*.
IsDefault (inherited from *ButtonBase*)	Determines whether the button is the form's default button.
TextAlign (inherited from *ButtonBase*)	Gets or sets the alignment of the text on the button.

A button on a form can be designated the default button, in which case it is displayed with a darker border than other buttons on the form. If the user presses Enter, it is taken to be equivalent to clicking on the default button.

Forms that are used as dialog boxes use buttons to close the dialog box and return a value to the caller. The *DialogResult* property can be used to assign a result code (such as OK or Cancel) to the form, and clicking on a button that has a *DialogResult* set will close the parent form without your having to hook up any event handlers.

CheckBox and *RadioButton*

If you look at the .NET Framework documentation, you'll find that *Button*, *CheckBox*, and *RadioButton* all have the same base class, *ButtonBase*. This is because all three classes are different types of button, each sharing the same on/off functionality, but contributing their own special characteristics.

Property	Description
AutoCheck	Determines whether the appearance of the control automatically changes when the user clicks it (as opposed to being set from code).
CheckAlign	Represents the alignment of the check box. The default is *MiddleLeft*.
Checked	Represents the check state of the control, with *true* representing checked.
CheckState (*CheckBox* only)	Represents the state of the checkbox: checked, unchecked, or indeterminate (appears dimmed).
Image (inherited from *ButtonBase*)	Gets or sets the image displayed on the button.

Property	Description
ImageAlign (inherited from *ButtonBase*)	Gets or sets the image alignment. The default value is *MiddleCenter*.
ThreeState (*CheckBox* only)	If true, the checkbox can display three states: checked, unchecked, or indeterminate.

CheckBox and *RadioButton* can both fire events when the *Appearance* and *Checked* properties change, and *CheckBox* also fires an event if the *CheckState* changes.

Using Radio Buttons as a Group

It is common to use radio buttons to let users select one of a set of options. To do this, you provide a set of radio buttons inside a *GroupBox* control; the *GroupBox* not only encloses the buttons visually but also makes them act as a group, ensuring that when any one is selected, the others are deselected.

The following exercise shows you how to set up a group box containing radio buttons on a form.

1. Continue with the *CppForm* project. Add some new members to the *CppForm* class to represent the group box and the three radio buttons it contains, as shown here:

```
GroupBox* gbox;
RadioButton* rb1;
RadioButton* rb2;
RadioButton* rb3;
```

2. Add a function called *Setup_Group* to create and set up the group box.

```
private:
    void Setup_Group()
    {
    }
```

   Add a call to this function from the *CppForm* constructor.

3. Add the following code to create the group box and set its title and location:

```
void Setup_Group()
{
    gbox = new GroupBox();
    gbox->Text = S"Language";
    gbox->Location = Point(20,60);
}
```

You can also set the size of the group box, but the default size of 200 pixels wide by 100 pixels high will be sufficient for this exercise.

4 Now create the three radio buttons and set their properties with the following code:

```
rb1 = new RadioButton();
rb1->Text = S"Visual Basic";
rb1->Location = Point(10,15);

rb2 = new RadioButton();
rb2->Text = S"C#";
rb2->Location = Point(10,40);

rb3 = new RadioButton();
rb3->Text = S"C++";
rb3->Location = Point(10,65);
rb3->Checked = true;
```

Each of the three radio buttons has its *Text* and *Location* properties set. Note that the location is in pixels relative to the top left of the group box, not the form itself. The third button has its *Checked* property set to *true*, so this radio button will be checked when the application starts.

5 Connect all the controls by adding the radio buttons to the group box, and the group box to the form, like this:

```
gbox->Controls->Add(rb1);
gbox->Controls->Add(rb2);
gbox->Controls->Add(rb3);

Controls->Add(gbox);
```

6 Build and test the application. You should see the radio buttons displaying inside the group box, and find that when you select one button, all the others are unchecked.

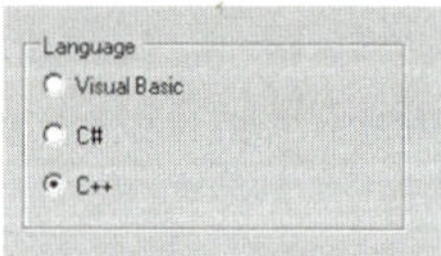

ListBox and *ComboBox*

List boxes and combo boxes are common features of Windows applications, each representing a scrollable list of items. The *ComboBox* class differs from the *ListBox* class in being able to display an item in a *TextControl* above the list.

These two classes have many features in common, because they both derive from the *ListControl* class, which provides some common functionality.

The table below shows commonly used properties of the *ListBox* class.

Property	Description
ColumnWidth	Determines whether the appearance of the control automatically changes when the user clicks it (as opposed to being set from code).
HorizontalScrollbar	Represents the alignment of the check box. The default is *MiddleLeft*.
IntegralHeight	Set to *true* if the *ListBox* should resize itself so it doesn't show partial items.
Items	Represents the collection of items held in the list box.
MultiColumn	Set to *true* if the list box supports multiple columns. The default is *false*.
PreferredHeight	Gets the combined height of all items in the list box. You can use this to resize the list box so all items display without vertical scroll bars.
ScrollAlwaysVisible	If set to *true*, the vertical scroll bar will always be visible.
SelectedIndex	Represents the 0-based index of the currently selected item, or -1 if there is no selection.
SelectedIndices	For multi-selection list boxes, represents a collection of the indexes of all the items currently selected in the list box.
SelectedItem	Gets or sets the currently selected object in the list box.
SelectedItems	For multi-selection list boxes, represents a collection of all the items currently selected in the list box.
SelectionMode	Represents the selection mode of the list.
Sorted	Set to *true* if the items in the list box are to be sorted. The default is *false*.
Text	Represents the text of the currently selected item in the list box. If you set this property to a *String*, the control searches for the first item that matches the string and selects it.
TopIndex	The index of the top item visible in the control.

The *SelectionMode* property represents the way users can select items from the list and can take one of the following values from the *SelectionMode* enumeration:

- *SelectionMode::None*, meaning the user cannot select any items
- *SelectionMode::One*, meaning the user can select one item at a time
- *SelectionMode::MultiSimple*, meaning the user can select more than one item at a time

- *SelectionMode::MultiExtended*, meaning that the user can use the Shift, Ctrl, and arrow keys to make selections

ListBox also supports a number of methods, the most commonly used of which are summarized in the table below.

Method	Description
BeginUpdate, *EndUpdate*	*BeginUpdate* prevents the list box redrawing until *EndUpdate* is called. This improves the performance when adding several items.
ClearSelected	Deselects all the items in a list box.
FindString, *FindStringExact*	Finds the first item in the list box that starts with a given string or which exactly matches a given string.
GetSelected	Returns *true* if the item with the specified index is selected.
SetSelected	Sets or clears the selection for an item in the list box.
Sort	Sorts the items in the list box alphabetically.

The main event fired by the *ListBox* class is the *SelectedIndexChanged* event, fired when a user selects a new item in the list.

The *ComboBox* class has a similar set of methods and properties, as outlined in the two tables below.

Property	Description
DropDownStyle	Represents the style of the combo box.
DropDownWidth	Represents the width in pixels of the drop-down box.
DroppedDown	Set to *true* if the list portion is currently displayed.
IntegralHeight	Set to *true* if the combo box should resize itself so it doesn't show partial items.
Items	Represents the collection of items held in the combo box.
MaxDropDownItems	Represents the maximum number of items in the drop-down list. The value must be between 1 and 100.
MaxLength	Represents the maximum length of the text in the text box.
SelectedIndex	Gets or sets the 0-based index of the currently selected item. The value is -1 if there is no selection.
SelectedItem	Gets or sets the currently selected item.
SelectedText	Represents the currently selected text in the *TextBox* portion of the *ComboBox* control.
SelectionStart, *SelectionLength*	Gets or sets the start position and length of the selected text in the *TextBox* portion of the *ComboBox* control.
Sorted	Determines whether the list in the combo box is sorted.
Text	Gets or sets the text in the *TextBox* portion of the *ComboBox* control.

A combo box can have one of three styles:

- *ComboBoxStyle::DropDown*, where the text box can be edited and the user must click the arrow to display the list
- *ComboBoxStyle::DropDownList*, which is the same as *DropDown*, with the exception that the text box can't be edited
- *ComboBoxStyle::Simple*, where the text box can be edited and the list is always visible

Method	Description
BeginUpdate, *EndUpdate*	*BeginUpdate* prevents the combo box redrawing until *EndUpdate* is called. This improves the performance when adding several items.
FindString, *FindStringExact*	Finds the first item in the combo box that starts with a given string or which exactly matches a given string.
Select	Selects a range of text in the *TextBox* portion of the combo box.
SelectAll	Selects all the text in the *TextBox* portion of the combo box.

As with *ListBox*, the main event fired by the *ComboBox* class is the *SelectedIndexChanged* event, fired when a user selects a new item in the list.

The exercise that follows will show you how to set up a combo box and respond to the events it fires, and you'll find that list boxes work in very much the same way.

1 Open the *CppForm* project if it isn't already open.

2 Add a *ComboBox* member to the class, making sure that it is private, like this:

```
private:
    ComboBox* combo1;
```

3 Add a function called Setup_Combo to set up the combo box.

```
private:
    void Setup_Combo()
    {
    }
```

Call it from the constructor along with all the other set-up functions.

4 Add the following code to *Setup_Combo* to create a new combo box and set its style and location:

```
combo1 = new ComboBox();
combo1->DropDownStyle = ComboBoxStyle::DropDownList;
combo1->Location = Point(20,180);
```

The style is set to *DropDownList*, which means that the user has to click the button to the right of the text box in order to display the list, and that the text in the text box can't be edited.

5 The combo box will display with a default width, but it would be tidy if the control were sized to fit the longest string that's going to be displayed. You can do this as shown here:

```
Label* l1 = new Label();
l1->Text = S"Intermediate";
combo1->Width = l1->PreferredWidth + 20;
```

The *PreferredWidth* property of the *Label* class tells you the width in pixels of the label's text, so it can be used to size the combo box. The extra 20 is an allowance for the drop-down button to the right of the edit control.

6 Finish this function by adding some strings to the combo box, and adding the combo box to the form's collection of controls, like this:

```
combo1->Items->Add(S"Beginner");
combo1->Items->Add(S"Intermediate");
combo1->Items->Add(S"Advanced");
combo1->SelectedIndex = 0;

Controls->Add(combo1);
```

After adding the strings, the *SelectedIndex* is set to 0 so that the first one is displayed when the application starts.

7 The *SelectedIndexChanged* event will be fired whenever the user selects a new item in the drop-down list. Add a handler function to *CppForm* as shown here:

```
void Combo_SelChanged(Object* pSender, EventArgs* pArgs)
{
    if (pSender == combo1)
    {
        String* ps = String::Concat(S"New index is ",
                           __box(combo1->SelectedIndex)-
>ToString());
        MessageBox::Show(ps, S"Index Change");
    }
}
```

The function checks that the sender was *combo1*, and if that was so, it builds a *String* containing the index of the new selection. The *String* is built using the static *Concat* function from the *String* class, and in order to convert the *SelectedIndex* value from an integer to a *String*, it is first boxed so that *ToString* can be called on the resulting object. The final string is displayed in a message box, so that you can be sure the selection has happened.

8 The final task is to link the handler up to the combo box in the normal way, using the following code:

```
combo1->SelectedIndexChanged +=
        new EventHandler(this, &CppForm::Combo_SelChanged);
```

9 Build and run the project, and you'll see a combo box on the form that displays three items. You should also get a message box displayed whenever you select a new item.

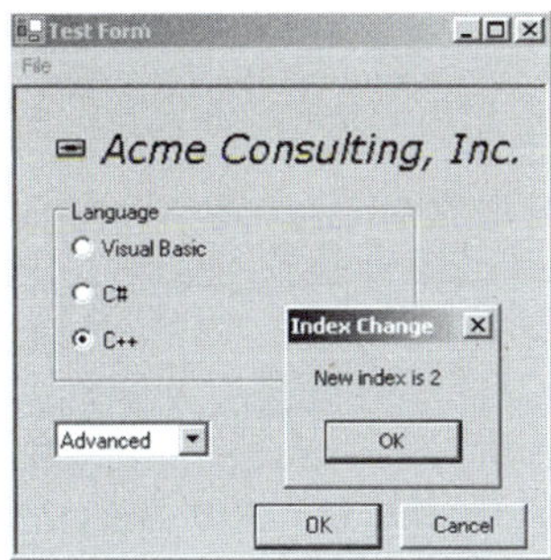

TextBox

The *System::Windows::Forms* namespace has two edit control classes, both of which are derived from *TextBoxBase*. I'll look at *TextBox* in this section, and you'll find the more advanced *RichTextBox* class covered in the next chapter.

A *TextBox* is a Windows edit control, that provides a number of methods and properties to manipulate the text inside the control. *TextBox* actually inherits most of its methods and properties from *TextBoxBase*, and the following two tables list some of the most commonly used inherited members.

Property	Description
AcceptsTab	If *true*, the Tab key will enter a tab character into the control instead of moving to the next control in the tab order. The default is *false*.
AutoSize	If *true*, the control automatically resizes itself to fit its text. The default is *true*.
BackColor, *ForeColor*	Represents the background and foreground colors.

(continued)

(continued)

Property	Description
BorderStyle	Represents the border style. The default is *Fixed3D*.
CanUndo	Set to *true* if the last operation can be undone.
HideSelection	If *true*, selected text in the control is dimmed when the focus passes to another control.
Lines	Gets or sets the collection of lines in a text box as an array of *Strings*.
MaxLength	Represents the maximum number of characters that can be typed into a control. The default value is 0, which means that the length is limited only by the available memory.
Modified	Gets or sets a Boolean value representing whether the control's content has been modified.
Multiline	If *true*, the control is a multi-line *TextBox*.
PreferredHeight	Gets the preferred height in pixels for the current font. This enables you to size the text box so it displays text correctly.
ReadOnly	Gets or sets the read-only status of the control.
SelectedText	Represents the currently selected text.
SelectionLength	Gets or sets the length of the selection.
SelectionStart	Gets or sets the start of the selection.
Text	Gets or sets the text displayed in the control.
TextLength	Gets the length of the text in the control.
WordWrap	If *true*, multi-line text boxes will word-wrap as necessary. If *false*, they will scroll horizontally until a newline character is reached.

Method	Description
AppendText	Appends text to the control
Clear	Clears the text in the control
ClearUndo	Clears the most recent operation from the control's undo buffer
Copy	Copies the selected text to the clipboard
Cut	Cuts the selected text to the clipboard
Paste	Replaces the current selection with the contents of the clipboard
ScrollToCaret	Scrolls the control so that the caret is visible
Select	Selects text in the control
SelectAll	Selects all the text in the control
Undo	Undoes the last clipboard or text change operation

Text boxes can be single-line or multi-line, controlled by the *Multiline* property. Multi-line text controls will use newline characters to break lines, whereas single-line controls will display them as control characters (which usually display as a short vertical bar). The *Lines* property holds an array of *Strings* that can be used to represent the lines in a multi-line edit control.

Text controls maintain an undo buffer, so it is possible to undo changes. Because it is possible to clear the undo buffer, you should check the *CanUndo* property before trying to undo operations.

The *TextBox* class adds several properties to the ones it inherits from *TextBoxBase*, as shown in the following table:

Property	Description
AcceptsReturn	If *true*, the Enter key will create a new line in a multi-line text box instead of activating the default button for the form. The default is *true*.
CharacterCasing	Determines whether the control modifies the case of characters as they are entered. The values may be *CharacterCasing::Normal* (the default), *CharacterCasing::Upper*, or *CharacterCasing::Lower*.
PasswordChar	If set to a value other than 0, masks the characters with the specified value as they are typed. The default is 0.
ScrollBars	Determines whether a multi-line text box displays with scrollbars. The default is no scrollbars.
TextAlign	Represents the text alignment. The default is *HorizontalAlignment.Left*.

This exercise shows you how to add an edit control to the form and manipulate the text it contains.

1 Open the *CppForm* project, if it isn't already open. The form was created with the default size of 300 by 300 pixels. In order to create more space to display a text box, set the size of the form in the *CppForm* constructor, with the following code:

```
Size = System::Drawing::Size(450,300);
```

An extra 150 pixels horizontally will give enough space to display the text box next to the group box.

2 Add a *TextBox* member to the class, making sure that it is private.

```
private:
    TextBox* text1;
```

3 Add a private function called *Setup_Text*, as shown here:

```
private:
  void Setup_Text()
  {
  }
```

Add a call to this function from the *CppForm* constructor.

4 Fill in the *Setup_Text* function to create a text box and set its properties:

```
void Setup_TextBox()
{
    text1 = new TextBox();
    text1->Location = Point(250,60);
    text1->Size = System::Drawing::Size(100,150);
    text1->Multiline = true;

    Controls->Add(text1);
}
```

The text box is positioned just to the right of the group box and is 100 by 150 pixels in size. It is a multi-line text box, so it can display more than one line of text.

5 Let's arrange for the text in the text box to be filled in automatically when the user clicks on the radio buttons. To do this, you need to add a handler for the radio buttons, like this:

```
void Radio_Clicked(Object* pSender, EventArgs* pArgs)
{
    if (pSender == rb1)
        text1->Text = "You have selected the Visual Basic
option.";
    else if (pSender == rb2)
        text1->Text = "You have selected the C# option.";
    else if (pSender == rb3)
        text1->Text = "You have selected the C++
option.\r\n\r\n"
                         "Here is another line";
}
```

The handler checks which of the radio buttons has originated the event and puts some appropriate text into the text box. The third radio button puts two lines of text into the text box, separated by a blank line; the \r\n sequence acts as a line break.

note

If you haven't seen it before, putting two string literals next to one another on adjacent lines isn't an error. If the C++ preprocessor sees two literals next to one another, it automatically concatenates them into one before sending the string to the compiler. This makes a neat way to split long string literals across lines.

6 Connect the handler routine to the radio buttons in the *Setup_Group* function like this:

```
rb1->Click += new EventHandler(this,
&CppForm::Radio_Clicked);
rb2->Click += new EventHandler(this,
&CppForm::Radio_Clicked);
rb3->Click += new EventHandler(this,
&CppForm::Radio_Clicked);
```

Despite the fact that all the radio buttons are going to have the same handler, you have to connect the controls to the handler one by one.

7 Build and run the program. You should now be able to click the radio buttons on the form and see text displayed in the text box.

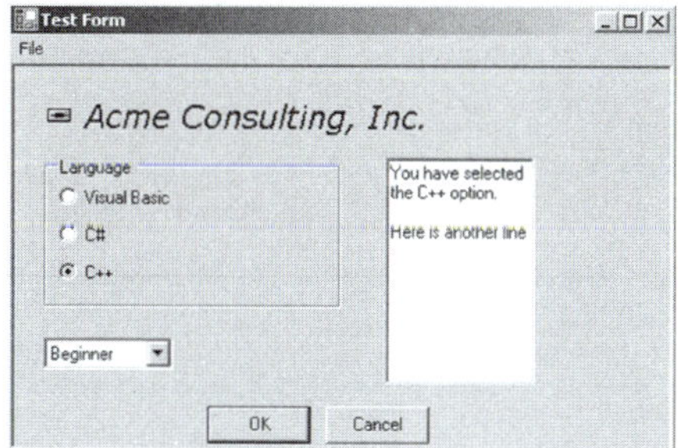

Using Menus

Menus are a well-known feature of most GUI programs, and the *Forms* namespace contains a complete set of classes for building and working with menus.

Menus in Windows Forms applications are represented by two main classes: *MainMenu* represents the menu bar that sits at the top of a form, while *MenuItem* represents all the items that make up the menus attached to a *MainMenu*. A *MainMenu* has a collection of *MenuItems*, and in order to model the hierarchical nature of menus, *MenuItems* themselves can have collections of other *MenuItems*.

In use, menu items bear some similarity to buttons; they are both distinguished by their text, and both fire a *Click* event when they are selected. It probably won't surprise you to learn that you set up handlers for menu items in exactly the same way as you do for buttons.

Menu Design

There are a number of well-established guidelines relating to how menus ought to be constructed and presented to the user, and I'll give a brief outline of some of the more important ones here.

First, it is convention that the leftmost menu on the menu bar is called File, and the last item on the File menu is the one that exits from the program. It is usually called Exit. Likewise, the rightmost item on the menu bar should be the Help menu, which will contain entries to help the user access the Help system, and probably an entry to show the program's About box. Menu items that are going to display a dialog box should end with an ellipsis (...); for example, About.... Menu items that are going to have an immediate action, such as exiting the application, shouldn't use an ellipsis.

To help users navigate around menus, assign access keys to menus by putting an ampersand before one of the letters in the menu caption; for example, &File associates the access key F with this menu item. Users can navigate through menus by holding down Alt and typing the access keys. You can also assign shortcuts to individual menu items, such as Ctrl+P for print, and these should be added to the most frequently used menu items.

Drop-down menus shouldn't be too long; any more than 10 entries is probably excessive. Consider using hierarchical menus.

Menus shouldn't let the user do anything that isn't sensible. For example, if there are no files open, an application shouldn't let the user select the Print option. There's nothing to print, so it is just confusing to be able to select the item. It is good practice to dim (disable) menu items that don't apply in the current context. Some applications dynamically add and remove menu items, but this tends to lead to confusion as users can't remember how to make a particular menu item reappear!

The following exercise will show you how to add a simple menu to the application's main form.

1 Continue working with the same project you've been using throughout this chapter.

2 Add a function called *Setup_Menu* in the same way that you did for *Setup_Buttons*:

```
private:
    void Setup_Menu ()
    {
    }
```

3 Add a call to this function in the *CppForm* constructor, just before the call to *Setup_Buttons*.

4 Now you need to assemble the menu from *MainMenu* and *MenuItem* objects. You're going to add a menu bar containing one drop-down menu, which in turn contains two menu items. This means that you'll need one *MainMenu* and three *MenuItem* objects, so add them as members of the *CppForm* class, remembering to make them private, as shown here:

```
MainMenu* menuBar;
MenuItem* fileMenu;
MenuItem* item1;
MenuItem* item2;
```

The menu bar object is *menuBar*, *fileMenu* will represent the drop-down, and *item1* and *item2* will be the two menu items.

5 You can now fill in the *Setup_Menu* function to create the objects and link them together with the following code:

```
void Setup_Menu()
{
    // Create the main menu bar
    menuBar = new MainMenu();

    // Create the File menu
    fileMenu = new MenuItem("&File");
    menuBar->MenuItems->Add(fileMenu);

    // Create menu items and add them
    item1 = new MenuItem("&About...");
    item2 = new MenuItem("E&xit");

    fileMenu->MenuItems->Add(item1);
    fileMenu->MenuItems->Add(item2);

    // Add the main menu to the form
    Menu = menuBar;
}
```

The *MainMenu* object is created by a call to its default constructor, while the constructors for the *MenuItem* objects take a string which is the text that will appear on the menu at run time. You're eventually going to use the About menu item to display an About dialog box, so make sure that the menu item text finishes with three periods (...), because it is conventional to add an ellipsis to menu items that are going to display dialog boxes.

MainMenu and *MenuItem* objects both have a *MenuItems* collection, which represents the collection of *MenuItems* belonging to the object. You add a new object to the collection using the *Add* function, and you can see in the code how the *fileMenu* object is added to *menuBar*, and *item1* and *item2* are added to the *fileMenu* object. The final task is to assign the *menuBar* to the form's Menu property. If you forget to do this, you won't see a form displayed on the screen!

note

It doesn't matter whether you create all the menu items first and then use *Add* to link them together at the end, or create and link them as you go. Do whichever you find easiest to code.

6 You provide menu items so that the user can select them and execute code. To make this work, you add handler functions for menu items in exactly the same way that you do for buttons. Earlier, you added a separate handler function for each of the two buttons. In this exercise, you'll add a single handler that will be called for both menu items, and you'll use the parameters passed into the handler to determine which menu item was called.

Add the following handler code to the *CppForm* class:

```
void MenuItem_Clicked(Object* pSender, EventArgs* pArgs)
{
    if (pSender == item1)
        MessageBox::Show(S"The About menu item", S"Menu");
    else if (pSender == item2) {
        // Exit from the application
        Application::Exit();
    }
    else
        MessageBox::Show(S"Some other menu item", S"Menu");
}
```

Once again, the name of the handler function, *MenuItem_Clicked*, reflects the source of the events and the event type. Note how the *pSender* argument is checked to see which of the menu items was chosen. If it was *item1*, the program currently displays a message box, and we'll use this to display a dialog box later in the chapter. If the selected item was *item2*, the call to *Application::Exit* is used to close the form and exit from the program.

7 The final task is to connect the handler to the menu items, and this is done in exactly the same way as it is for buttons. Add the following two lines to the *Setup_Menu* function immediately before you set the *Menu* property of the form:

```
item1->Click += new EventHandler(this,
&CppForm::MenuItem_Clicked);
item2->Click += new EventHandler(this,
&CppForm::MenuItem_Clicked);
```

Note how both *MenuItem* objects use the same handler function. Unfortunately, there's no way that you can associate the same handler with a number of objects without setting up each one individually.

8 Build and run the program. You should see that the form now has a menu bar at the top, and you should be able to select the menu items.

More About Menus

Now that you've mastered the basics of adding menu support to programs, I'll briefly mention some of the other features of the menu classes.

First, you can create hierarchical menus by adding *MenuItem* objects to the *MenuItems* collection of any existing item. The following code fragment shows how you do this:

```
actionMenu = new MenuItem("Action");
menuBar->MenuItems->Add(actionMenu);

submenu1 = new MenuItem("Do");
actionMenu->MenuItems->Add(submenu1);
anotherItem = new MenuItem("Whatever...");
actionMenu->MenuItems->Add(anotherItem);

// Create menu items and add them
item1_1 = new MenuItem("This...");
item1_2 = new MenuItem("That...");

submenu1->MenuItems->Add(item1_1);
submenu1->MenuItems->Add(item1_2);
```

A drop-down menu called actionMenu gets added to the menu bar, and then two items—submenu1 and anotherItem—are added to the drop-down menu. Two other items are then added to the *MenuItems* collection for the submenu1 item, to build the structure shown in the following screen shot:

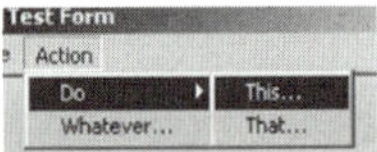

To add a separator bar to a menu, add a *MenuItem* whose text consists of a single hyphen (-), like this:

```
actionMenu->MenuItems->Add(new MenuItem("-"));
```

Note that I don't save the pointer to the separator item. Menu separators can't be selected, so I'm not going to need to refer to it again in the program. The effect of adding a separator to the Action menu is shown in the following screen shot:

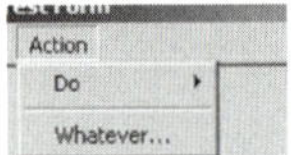

The *Checked* and *Enabled* properties can be used to display a checkmark next to a menu item, and to dim menu items that aren't currently active. Simply set the requisite property to *true* or *false*, as required.

Displaying a Context Menu

Most GUI applications nowadays use context menus—small menus that pop up when you right-click over a window and are used to provide menu items specific to that part of the GUI. You can easily add a context menu to a form by creating a *ContextMenu* object, adding menu items to it, and then assigning it to the form's ContextMenu property.

The following exercise shows you how to add a context menu to a form.

1. Continue working with the same project you've been using throughout this chapter.
2. Add a function called *Setup_Context_Menu* in the same way that you did for *Setup_Menu*:

   ```
   private:
       void Setup_Context_Menu ()
       {
       }
   ```

3. Add a call to this function in the *CppForm* constructor, just before the call to *Setup_Buttons*.

4 Assemble the menu from *ContextMenu* and *MenuItem* objects. The context menu is going to contain three menu items, which means that you'll need one *ContextMenu* and three *MenuItem* objects. Add them as members of the *CppForm* class, remembering to make them private, as shown here:

```
System::Windows::Forms::ContextMenu* popupMenu;
MenuItem* item_p1;
MenuItem* item_p2;
MenuItem* item_p3;
```

You need to give the fully qualified name for the *ContextMenu* class, because the *Form* class also has a ContextMenu property.

5 Add the following code to the *Setup_Context_Menu* function to create the context menu:

```
// Create the context menu
popupMenu = new System::Windows::Forms::ContextMenu();

// Create the items in the context menu
item_p1 = new MenuItem("One");
popupMenu->MenuItems->Add(item_p1);
item_p2 = new MenuItem("Two");
popupMenu->MenuItems->Add(item_p2);
item_p3 = new MenuItem("Three");
popupMenu->MenuItems->Add(item_p3);

ContextMenu = popupMenu;
```

You can see how creating a context menu is exactly the same as creating a main menu, and you have all the same methods and properties to work with. Once again, you need to use the fully qualified name for *ContextMenu* in order to avoid a name clash with the *Form::ContextMenu* property. To associate the pop-up menu with the form, assign the *ContextMenu* to the form's *ContextMenu* property.

6 Build and run the code. You'll find that you can display the context menu by right-clicking on the form.

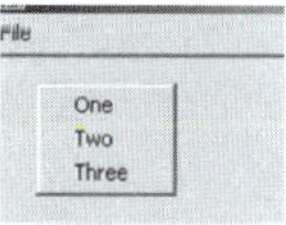

You use handlers with items on context menus in exactly the same way as with main menus.

Chapter 16 Quick Reference

To	Do This
Create a form	Derive a class from *System::Windows::Forms::Form*.

Add controls to a form	Create a control object and add it to the form's *Controls* collection. For example:
	`Button* btn1 = new Button();`
	`btn1->Text = S"OK";`
	`Controls->Add(btn1);`

Handle events	Create an *EventHandler* object and use += to attach it to an event on the required object. For example:
	`btn1->Click +=     new EventHandler`
	`(this, &handlerFunction);`

Add a menu to a form	Create a *MainMenu* item and add *MenuItems* to it, and then assign the *MainMenu* to the Menu property of the form. For example:
	`MainMenu* mm = new MainMenu();`
	`MenuItem* item1 = new MenuItem("File");`
	`mm->MenuItems->Add(item1);`
	`myForm->Menu = mm;`

Add a context menu	Create a *ContextMenu* and add it to a form, in exactly the same way that you'd add a *MainMenu*.

Dialog Boxes and Controls

In this chapter, you'll learn how to

- ✔ *Create and use dialog boxes*
- ✔ *Use the Windows common dialog boxes*
- ✔ *Use more of the controls provided by the Microsoft .NET Framework*

Chapter 16 introduced you to the world of Windows Forms and showed you how you can use the classes in the *System.Windows.Forms* namespace to build GUI applications.

This chapter looks at more features of Windows Forms. It starts by showing you how to create and use dialog boxes in GUI applications and then goes on to look at more of the controls provided by the *System.Windows.Forms* namespace.

Using Dialog Boxes

You've met dialog boxes before—the About dialog box possessed by just about every application, for example, or the Insert Table dialog box in Microsoft Word.

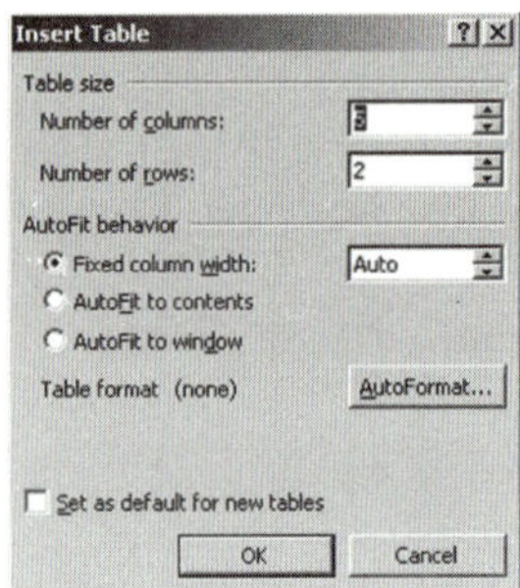

In the .NET Framework, the difference between dialog boxes and other kinds of windows is rather blurred and a dialog box is just another form, but that hasn't always been the case in Microsoft Windows programming. Before .NET, dialog boxes had several special properties:

- They were windows that were optimized to work with controls.
- They usually had a fixed border so that you couldn't resize them.
- They could be described in data using a dialog box template, and be automatically created and populated with controls at run time. This data was attached to the executable as a binary Windows resource.
- They could be created as modal dialog boxes, in which case the application was blocked until the dialog box was sent away, or as modeless dialog boxes, in which case the dialog box window floated on top of its parent window and you could use both.

Windows Forms has some of these properties already; you can easily use controls on forms, and you can set the border so the form can't be resized. However, you can't use dialog box templates, because .NET doesn't work that way and doesn't use resources. You have to build dialog boxes in code, just like any other form. To help you design forms that work like modal dialog boxes, the *Form* class has a *ShowModal* function that displays a form modally, so you have to close the form before you can use the rest of the application.

The following exercise continues the *CppForm* project that you began in the previous chapter and shows you how to create an About dialog box for your application.

> **note**
>
> If you haven't worked through the examples in Chapter 16, you'll find the code for the CppForm project on the CD-ROM. You can use this as the basis for the exercises in this chapter.

Dialog Box Design

As with menus, you should be aware of a couple of design guidelines when designing dialog boxes. If the dialog box simply exists to display some data—such as a reminder—to the user, it should include a button that the user can use to dismiss the dialog box. This button should be labeled with OK, Done, or another word indicating that the user is finished with the dialog box.

If the user enters data into the dialog box, it should include two buttons. One button will accept the changes and dismiss the dialog box, and is conventionally labeled OK, while the other button will discard the changes before dismissing the dialog box, and is normally labeled Cancel. These buttons are usually placed in a horizontal row at the bottom of the dialog box.

On a more general note, don't make dialog boxes too cluttered. It is better to have several dialog boxes that do one thing well than one giant dialog box that is a mess of controls. You might also want to consider investigating tabbed dialog boxes, which can help to reduce clutter. To see some examples of good and bad dialog box design, take a look at *http://www.iarchitect.com/*.

1 Open the *CppForm* project if it isn't already open.

2 Add a new class called *AboutBox* to the start of the source code, before the definition of *CppForm*:

```
__gc public class AboutBox : public Form {
public:
    AboutBox()
    {
    }
};
```

A dialog box is simply another form, and the main difference from the application's main form lies in how you display it, as you'll see shortly.

3 Set the properties for the dialog box form in the constructor, like this:

```
AboutBox()
{
    // Set some form parameters
    Text = S"About CppForm";
    FormBorderStyle = FormBorderStyle::Fixed3D;
    Size = System::Drawing::Size(300,150);
}
```

Dialog boxes usually aren't resizable, so the constructor sets the border style to *Fixed3D* to make a non-resizable border.

4 The dialog box is going to show two labels and an OK button, so add a private *Button* member to the class, as shown here:

```
Button* OKButton;
```

Once the labels have been created, you won't refer to them again, so there's no need to have them as members of the class.

5 Add the following code to the constructor to create two labels and add them to the form:

```
// Add the labels
Label* label1 = new Label();
label1->Text = "The CppForm Application";
label1->Size = System::Drawing::Size(label1->PreferredWidth,
                                     label1->PreferredHeight);
label1->Location = Point(20, 30);

Label* label2 = new Label();
label2->Text = "Julian Templeman, 2001";
label2->Size = System::Drawing::Size(label1->PreferredWidth,
                                     label1->PreferredHeight);
label2->Location = Point(20, 30+label1->PreferredHeight+10);

// Add the controls to the form
Controls->Add(label1);
Controls->Add(label2);
```

Note the use of the *PreferredWidth* and *PreferredHeight* properties to automatically size the labels to the text they contain, and the use of *PreferredHeight* to calculate the position of the second label.

6 Construct and add the button with the following code:

```
// Add the OK button
OKButton = new Button();
OKButton->Text = S"OK";
OKButton->Size = System::Drawing::Size(40,25);
OKButton->Location = Point(240,85);

// Set up a handler
OKButton->Click += new EventHandler(this,
&AboutBox::OKButton_Clicked);
```

```
// Add the button to the form
Controls->Add(OKButton);
```

There's nothing new here: create a button, set its properties, and then link in an event handler.

Here's the code for the event handler function:

```
void OKButton_Clicked(Object* pSender, EventArgs* pArgs)
{
    // Close the form
    Close();
}
```

The handler function simply closes the form when the button is clicked.

7 The last step is to arrange for the dialog box to be displayed when the About menu item is selected. Locate the *CppForm::MenuItem_Clicked* function, and edit the code as follows, adding the lines shown in **bold** in the following listing:

```
void MenuItem_Clicked(Object* pSender, EventArgs* pArgs)
{
    if (pSender == item1) {
        AboutBox* box = new AboutBox();
        box->ShowDialog();
    }
    else if (pSender == item2) {
        Application::Exit();
    }
    else
        MessageBox::Show(S"Some other menu item", S"Menu");
}
```

When the About menu item is chosen, create an *AboutBox* object, and then call its *ShowDialog* function. This has the effect of displaying the form as a modal dialog box, so that it has to be closed before you can continue working with the application.

8 Build and run the application. When you select the About item on the File menu, you should see the About dialog box displayed.

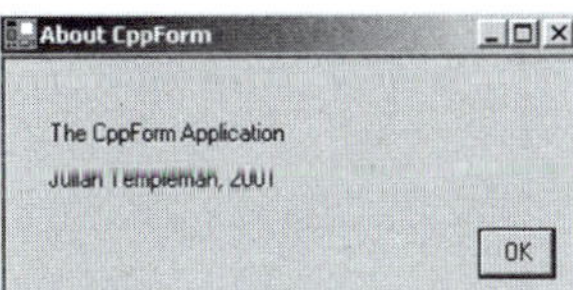

The *DialogResult* Property

It is common for dialog boxes to contain a set of buttons—such as Yes, No, and Cancel, or Abort, Retry, and Ignore—which the user can use to pass information back to the application. The *DialogResult* property is used to pass a value back to the calling code that shows which button was clicked to dismiss the dialog box. The property will take one of the values from the *DialogResult* enumeration, whose values are shown in the following table.

Member	Description
Abort	Represents the return value *Abort*, and is usually set by a button labeled Abort
Cancel	Represents the return value *Cancel*, and is usually set by a button labeled Cancel
Ignore	Represents the return value *Ignore*, and is usually set by a button labeled Ignore
No	Represents the return value *No*, and is usually set by a button labeled No
None	Nothing is returned from the dialog box, and the modal dialog box continues running
OK	Represents the return value *OK*, and is usually set by a button labeled OK
Retry	Represents the return value *Retry*, and is usually set by a button labeled Retry
Yes	Represents the return value *Yes*, and is usually set by a button labeled Yes

You might be slightly puzzled by the description of the None entry, and I need to explain how *DialogResult* works.

A user will typically dismiss a dialog box by clicking a button, and you've already seen how the handler for the OK button was used to close the About box in the previous exercise. If you want to pass back a return value from a modal dialog box, assign one of the values from the table to the form's *DialogResult* property. This, however, has the effect of assigning the value *and* immediately closing the form. So you could replace the OK button handler in the previous exercise with the following code:

```
void OKButton_Clicked(Object* pSender, EventArgs* pArgs)
{
    // Send back 'OK' and close the form
    DialogResult = System::Windows::Forms::DialogResult::OK;
}
```

The caller can check the value returned from *ShowDialog* to find out what the dialog box returned.

In fact, it can be even easier to close the form and send a value back to the caller. You can set the *DialogResult* property on the button itself, and when the button is clicked, it closes the parent form and sends the appropriate result back. To do this in the example code, modify the code where you set up the button, as shown here:

```
// Add the OK button
OKButton = new Button();
OKButton->Text = S"OK";
OKButton->DialogResult =
System::Windows::Forms::DialogResult::OK;
OKButton->Size = System::Drawing::Size(40,25);
OKButton->Location = Point(240,85);
```

You can now delete the line that hooks up the handler and the handler function itself, and the program will work the same as before.

Using Data with Dialog Boxes

It's common to use dialog boxes to obtain information from the user. This often means that you have to load data into the dialog box before displaying it and then extract the data that the user entered, usually when the user clicks OK. Here's an example of a dialog box that displays information, lets the user change it, and then reads the changes when it is dismissed.

1 Open the *CppForm* project if it isn't already open. Add a new class called *MyDialog* to the top of the project, before the definition of *CppForm* itself.

```
__gc public class MyDialog : public Form {
public:
  MyDialog()
  {
  }
};
```

2 The dialog box is going to contain controls to gather a user's personal details, which in this case will be name, phone number, and department. Each of these will need a control and a label, and you'll also need OK and Cancel buttons to dismiss the dialog box. Add the following eight private data members to the *MyDialog* class:

```
Label* nameLabel;
TextBox* nameBox;
Label* phoneLabel;
```

```
TextBox* phoneBox;
Label* deptLabel;
ComboBox* deptCombo;

Button* OKBtn;
Button* CancelBtn;
```

The name and phone fields are represented by *TextBox* controls, and the department is represented by a *ComboBox* control.

3 Setting up the form and the controls takes quite a few lines of code. Start with the *Form* parameters, adding the following code to the *MyDialog* constructor:

```
// Set the form parameters
Text = S"Personal Details";
FormBorderStyle = FormBorderStyle::Fixed3D;
Size = System::Drawing::Size(280,200);
```

The border style is set to *Fixed3D* so that the dialog box can't be resized.

4 Add the following code to create all the controls:

```
// Create the controls
nameLabel = new Label();
nameBox = new TextBox();
phoneLabel = new Label();
phoneBox = new TextBox();
deptLabel = new Label();
deptCombo = new ComboBox();
OKBtn = new Button();
CancelBtn = new Button();
```

5 Create and set up the name field and its label, as shown here:

```
// nameLabel
nameLabel->Location = Point(16, 24);
nameLabel->Size = System::Drawing::Size(48, 16);
nameLabel->Text = "Name:";
nameLabel->TextAlign = ContentAlignment::MiddleRight;

// nameBox
nameBox->Location = Point(72, 24);
nameBox->Size = System::Drawing::Size(152, 20);
nameBox->Text = "";
```

There's nothing new here: the label and text box are placed next to one another, and the text box contains no initial text.

The code to set up the phone field and its label looks very similar:

```
// phoneLabel
phoneLabel->Location = Point(16, 56);
phoneLabel->Size = System::Drawing::Size(48, 16);
phoneLabel->Text = "Phone:";
phoneLabel->TextAlign = ContentAlignment::MiddleRight;

// phoneBox
phoneBox->Location = Point(72, 56);
phoneBox->Size = System::Drawing::Size(152, 20);
phoneBox->Text = "";
```

6 Add the following code for the combo box holding department information, and its label:

```
// deptLabel
deptLabel->Location = Point(16, 88);
deptLabel->Size = System::Drawing::Size(48, 16);
deptLabel->Text = "Dept:";
deptLabel->TextAlign = ContentAlignment::MiddleRight;

// deptCombo
deptCombo->DropDownWidth = 121;
deptCombo->Location = Point(72, 88);
deptCombo->Size = System::Drawing::Size(121, 21);
deptCombo->Items->Add(S"IT");
deptCombo->Items->Add(S"Admin");
deptCombo->Items->Add(S"R&D");
deptCombo->Items->Add(S"Catering");
deptCombo->Items->Add(S"Manufacturing");
```

The combo box holds five items, none of which is selected by default.

7 Add the following code for the OK and Cancel buttons:

```
// OKButton
OKBtn->Location = Point(104, 136);
OKBtn->Name = "OKButton";
OKBtn->Text = "OK";
OKBtn->DialogResult = DialogResult::OK;

// CancelButton
CancelBtn->Location = Point(192, 136);
CancelBtn->Name = "CancelButton";
```

```
CancelBtn->Text = "Cancel";
CancelBtn->DialogResult = DialogResult::Cancel;
```

The two buttons have default sizes, and each has its *DialogResult* member set. This means that when they're clicked, they'll both dismiss the dialog box and return a *DialogResult* to the calling code.

8 Add all the controls to the form, with the following code:

```
// Add the controls
Controls->Add(nameBox);
Controls->Add(phoneBox);
Controls->Add(nameLabel);
Controls->Add(phoneLabel);
Controls->Add(deptLabel);
Controls->Add(deptCombo);
Controls->Add(OKBtn);
Controls->Add(CancelBtn);

AcceptButton = OKBtn;
CancelButton = CancelBtn;
```

The final two lines set up the *AcceptButton* and *CancelButton* properties of the form. If set, the *AcceptButton* holds a reference to the button that is the default button on the form. Pressing the Enter key has the same effect as clicking the default button, and since we've got the *DialogResult* set to OK on *OKBtn*, pressing Enter will dismiss the dialog box and send *DialogResult::OK* back to the caller. The *CancelButton* property holds a reference to the button that maps onto the Esc key.

9 To let the calling code get and set the values in the controls, add some public *get* and *set* functions to the class, like this:

```
public:
    void setName(String* theName) { nameBox->Text = theName; }
    String* getName() { return nameBox->Text; }
    void setPhone(String* thePhone) { phoneBox->Text = thePhone; }
    String* getPhone() { return phoneBox->Text; }
    void setDept(int theDept) { deptCombo->SelectedIndex = theDept; }
    int getDept() { return deptCombo->SelectedIndex; }
```

There is a pair of *get* and *set* methods for each field in the dialog box, and these will let the user of the *MyDialog* class manipulate the data without giving them complete access to the *TextBox* and *ComboBox* objects.

10 Add the code to display the dialog box. First, declare a new private *MenuItem* member for the *CppForm* class called *item11* with the following code:

```
private:
    MenuItem* item11;
```

11 In the *Setup_Menu* function, add another item to the File menu, and link it in to the same handler as the other menu items:

```
item1 = new MenuItem("&About...");
item11 = new MenuItem("&MyDialog...");
item2 = new MenuItem("E&xit");

fileMenu->MenuItems->Add(item1);
fileMenu->MenuItems->Add(item11);
fileMenu->MenuItems->Add(item2);

item1->Click += new EventHandler(this,
&CppForm::MenuItem_Clicked);
item11->Click += new EventHandler(this,
&CppForm::MenuItem_Clicked);
item2->Click += new EventHandler(this,
&CppForm::MenuItem_Clicked);
```

12 Edit the *MenuItem_Clicked* function to respond to the new menu item. The code already checks for two menu items, so add another *else if* clause to check for the new one:

```
else if (pSender == item11) {
    // Create the dialog
    MyDialog* box = new MyDialog();

    // Fill in the initial data
    box->setName(S"Joe Bloggs");
    box->setPhone(S"555-0155");
    box->setDept(1);

    // Show the dialog
    if (box->ShowDialog() == DialogResult::OK)
    {
        // If it came back with OK, display the name
        MessageBox::Show(box->getName(), S"Name was...");
    }
}
```

After the dialog box object has been created, you use the *set* methods to put the initial data into the controls. The dialog box is then shown to the user using *ShowDialog*, and when it returns, you can check the return value and see whether it was *DialogResult::OK* or *DialogResult::Cancel*. If it was OK, you can then use the *get* methods to extract the final data from the dialog box object.

13 Build and run the code, and when you select the MyDialog menu item, you should see the dialog box display with its initial data.

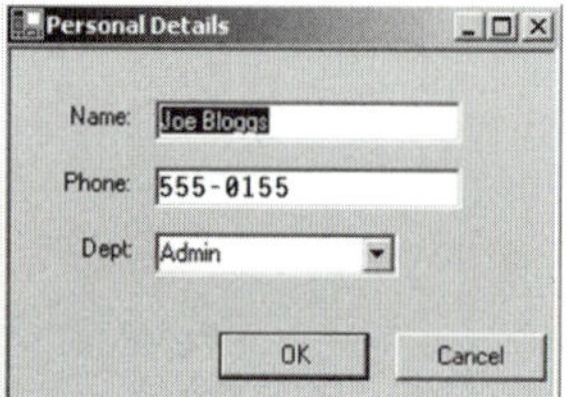

Tab Ordering

You can use the Tab key to move from control to control on a form. By default, the order in which you move between controls follows the order in which they're created, but you can impose your own order by assigning a 0-based value to the *TabIndex* property of any control.

It isn't an error for two controls to have the same *TabIndex* value, but the order in which they are selected will then depend on the order in which they are displayed on the screen.

Using Common Dialogs

There are a number of dialog boxes that many programs need to use. Examples include File Open and File Save dialog boxes, font pickers, and color choosers. Windows has always provided a set of these Common Dialogs, and they are available for you to use with Windows Forms.

Using the Common Dialogs has several advantages:

- Programmers don't have to keep reinventing the same dialog boxes.
- You get fully functional dialog boxes for free, and some of these are difficult to write.
- Users see a familiar set of dialog boxes, so they don't have to figure out just how the File Open dialog box works in your program, for example.
- Dialog boxes are displayed to suit the operating system. Display a File Open dialog box on a Windows 2000 computer, and you'll see the Windows 2000 version. Do the same on a Windows XP system, and the XP version will be displayed.

Windows Forms provides you with the common dialog boxes listed in the following table:

Class	Purpose
ColorDialog	Displays a dialog box to let the user pick a color
FileDialog	The base class for the *OpenFileDialog* and *SaveFileDialog* classes
FontDialog	Displays a dialog box to let the user pick a font
OpenFileDialog	Displays a standard File Open dialog box
PageSetupDialog	Displays a dialog box to let the user manipulate page settings, such as margins and page orientation
PrintDialog	Displays a dialog box to let the user select a printer and the portion of the document to print
SaveFileDialog	Displays a standard File Save dialog box

All these dialog boxes inherit from *CommonDialog*, which provides members that are used only by inherited classes, not by you.

These classes are used just like any other dialog box: You create a dialog box object, set its properties, and then display it by calling *ShowDialog*. The following exercise shows you how to use a Font dialog box to choose a font, and then use it to set the font of the *Label* control on the form.

1. Open the *CppForm* project if it isn't already open.
2. Add a *Font* member to the *CppForm* class:

   ```
   System::Drawing::Font* labelFont;
   ```

   You have to give the fully qualified name of the *Font* class, or else it will conflict with the form's *Font* property.
3. Add a new item to the File menu with the text "Choose Font...." As you've done with other menu items, this requires you to add a *MenuItem* member to the class, create the item, add it to the File menu, and hook it into the handler for all the menu items:

   ```
   MenuItem* fontDlgItem;
   ...
   fontDlgItem = new MenuItem("&Choose Font...");
   ...
   fileMenu->MenuItems->Add(fontDlgItem);
   ...
   fontDlgItem->Click += new EventHandler(this,
   &CppForm::MenuItem_Clicked);
   ```

   I haven't gone through each of the steps in detail because you should be used to adding new menu items by this stage.

4 Edit the code in the *Setup_Label* function so that the *Font* is saved in the *labelFont* object, as shown here:

```
// Set the font
labelFont = new System::Drawing::Font(S"Verdana", 16,
FontStyle::Italic);
theLabel->Font = labelFont;
theLabel->ForeColor = Color::Black;
```

This code is very similar to what you already have, except that the pointer to the *Font* is now stored away in the *labelFont* member.

5 Edit the *MenuItem_Clicked* handler function, adding an *else if* clause to handle the new menu item, like this:

```
else if (pSender == fontDlgItem)
{
    FontDialog* fd = new FontDialog();
    fd->Font = labelFont;

    if (fd->ShowDialog() == DialogResult::OK)
    {
        MessageBox::Show(fd->Font->Name, S"Name was...");
        labelFont = fd->Font;
        theLabel >Font = labelFont;
    }
}
```

The code creates a *FontDialog* object and then initializes it with the current font represented by *labelFont*. *ShowDialog* displays the dialog box, and if it returns a *DialogResult::OK* status, it sets the font of the label to reflect the user's choice. The *Label* control will immediately update itself to use the new font.

6 Build and run the code, and you should be able to display a Font selection common dialog box, as shown here.

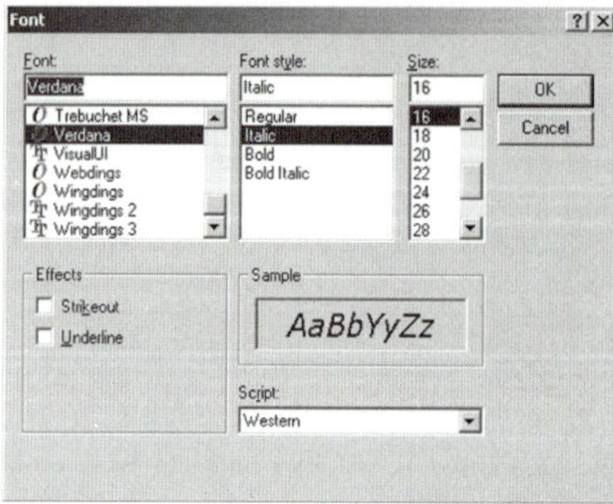

More About Controls

The *System::Windows::Forms* namespace provides you with a large number of controls that you can use to build program GUIs. The following table lists the major controls in the namespace.

Control	Description
CheckedListBox	A *ListBox* control with a *CheckBox* on each item.
Clipboard	Not strictly a control, but a class that lets you interact with the Windows clipboard.
DataGrid	A grid control that works with ADO.NET datasets.
DateTimePicker	A control that lets the user select a date and time.
DomainUpDown	An up-down control that displays strings.
ErrorProvider	Works with other controls to show that a control has errors associated with it.
Help	Encapsulates the HTML Help engine.
ImageList	A control that manages a list of images. Frequently used with toolbars and other controls that need multiple images.
LinkLabel	A label that can display hyperlinks.
ListView	Displays a list of items in one of four views: small icon, large icon, list, and details. Think of the right panel of Windows Explorer.
MonthCalendar	Lets the user select a date using a visual display.
NumericUpDown	An up-down control that displays numbers.
Panel	A control that can contain other controls.
PictureBox	A control that can display images from image files.
ProgressBar	A control that displays the progress of an operation.
PropertyGrid	A control that lets you browse the properties of an object.
RichTextBox	A *TextBox* control that supports formatting and other word processing features.
ScrollBar	A control that encapsulates a standard Windows scrollbar. If you want a control to act as a slider, use a *TrackBar* instead of a *ScrollBar*.
Splitter	A control for resizing docked controls at run time.
StatusBar	A control that represents the status bar at the bottom of a window.
TabControl and *TabPage*	Controls that let you create and manage tabbed dialog boxes.
Timer	A control that implements a timer.
ToolBar	A control that implements a standard toolbar.
TrackBar	A control that implements a slider.
TreeView	A control for displaying a hierarchical collection of items as a tree. Think of the left panel of Windows Explorer.

There are far too many to cover here in detail, so I'll show you how to use some of the major ones.

Using the *TreeView* Control

TreeView controls, which display a hierarchy of items as a tree, will be familiar to anyone who has used Windows Explorer. The *System.Windows.Forms.TreeView* control wraps the Windows *TreeView* control and makes it simple to create and manipulate trees of items. Let's look at the methods and properties provided by the class, and then the exercise will show you how to create and use a *TreeView*.

A *TreeView* is formed of nodes, represented by *TreeNode* objects, which exist in a parent/child relationship. Root nodes have no parent, and it is possible for a *TreeView* to contain more than one root node. The following graphic shows a typical *TreeView*.

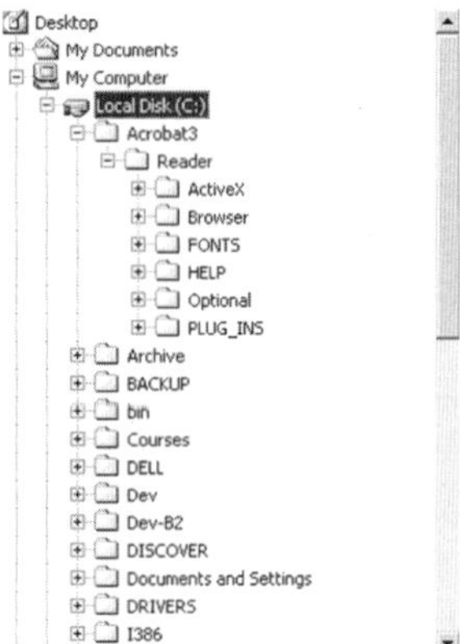

In this example, Desktop is the root node. Each node can have a label and an icon associated with it, and might have lines joining it to sibling and parent nodes. If a node has child nodes, it might display a button next to it that shows a plus sign (+). Clicking on the plus sign—or double-clicking on the node label or icon—will expand the tree to show the child nodes, in which case the plus sign changes to a minus sign (-). Nodes can have a pair of images associated with them, which are used to show expanded and collapsed nodes.

Creating a *TreeView* is a matter of setting the control's properties and then creating the *TreeNode* objects and linking them to form the tree. Both the *TreeView* and *TreeNode* classes have a Nodes property that holds a collection of child nodes.

TreeViews are complex controls, so the class has a lot of properties, methods, and events, the most commonly used of which are summarized in the following tables.

Property	Description
BorderStyle	Represents the border style of the control. The default is *Fixed3D*.
CheckBoxes	Determines whether check boxes are displayed next to nodes. The default is *false*.
FullRowSelect	Determines whether selecting a node highlights the entire width of the control or only the label. The default is *false*.
HideSelection	Determines whether the selected node will remain highlighted when the control loses the focus. The default is *true*.
HotTracking	Determines whether labels take on the appearance of a hyperlink when the mouse pointer is over them. The default is *false*.
ImageIndex	Represents the 0-based index of the image in the associated *ImageList* that is used as the default image for nodes.
ImageList	Represents the *ImageList* control that holds the list of images used by the *TreeView*.
Indent	Represents the distance each level of child nodes is indented, in pixels.
LabelEdit	Determines whether the user can edit the labels on nodes. The default is *false*.
Nodes	Represents the collection of nodes in the control.
Scrollable	Determines whether the control displays scroll bars when they are needed. The default is *true*.
SelectedImageIndex	Represents the 0-based index of the image in the associated *ImageList* that is used as the image for selected nodes.
SelectedNode	Gets or sets the currently selected node.
ShowLines	Determines whether lines are drawn between nodes in the tree.
ShowPlusMinus	Determines whether plus and minus signs are displayed next to nodes that have child nodes.
ShowRootLines	Determines whether lines are drawn between nodes at the root of the tree.
Sorted	Determines whether the nodes in the tree are sorted alphabetically.
TopNode	Returns a reference to the first fully visible node.
VisibleCount	Gets the number of nodes that are fully visible in the tree.

Method	Description
BeginUpdate	Disables redrawing of the *TreeView*. Use this if you're going to add several items, because it prevents the control redrawing itself after each item is added.
CollapseAll	Collapses all nodes in the tree.
EndUpdate	Enables redrawing of the *TreeView*.
ExpandAll	Expands all nodes in the tree.
GetNodeAt	Gets the node at a particular set of coordinates.
GetNodeCount	Gets the number of nodes attached to the control.

Event	Description
AfterCheck	Occurs after a *TreeNode* check box is checked
AfterCollapse	Occurs after a *TreeNode* is collapsed
AfterExpand	Occurs after a *TreeNode* is expanded
AfterLabelEdit	Occurs after a *TreeNode* label is edited
AfterSelect	Occurs after a *TreeNode* has been selected
BeforeCheck	Occurs before a *TreeNode* check box is checked
BeforeCollapse	Occurs before a *TreeNode* is collapsed
BeforeExpand	Occurs before a *TreeNode* is expanded
BeforeLabelEdit	Occurs before a *TreeNode* label is edited
BeforeSelect	Occurs before a *TreeNode* has been selected
ItemDrag	Occurs when an item is dragged onto the *TreeView* control

The following exercise will show you how to create and populate a *TreeView* control. We have several controls to discuss in the rest of this chapter, so you'll use the controls to put together a Windows Explorer-like file browser. It's not a very sophisticated one, to be sure, but it will serve to show you the basics of working with these controls in a real application.

1 Start a new Managed C++ Application project, and call it CppControls.

2 Add the *#using* and *using* statements for the namespaces that you'll need for a Windows Forms application, as shown here:

```
#using <System.dll>
#using <System.Drawing.dll>
#using <System.Windows.Forms.dll>

using namespace System::Drawing;
using namespace System::ComponentModel;
using namespace System::Windows::Forms;
```

3 Add a new managed class to represent the main form for the application, and call it *CppWindow*.

```
__gc class CppWindow : public Form
{
public:
  CppWindow()
  {
  }
};
```

4 You need to show the form, so add code to the project's *_tmain* function so that it looks like this:

```
int _tmain(void)
{
    Console::WriteLine(S"Controls Example");

    // Create a form
    Application::Run(new CppWindow());
    return 0;
}
```

5 Add a *TreeView* as a member of the *CppWindow* class, like this:

```
private:
  TreeView* treeView1;
```

6 Create a private function called *Setup_TreeView*, which will be used to create and set up the *TreeView* control.

```
void Setup_TreeView()
{
}
```

Add a call to this function from the *CppWindow* constructor.

7 Add the following code to *Setup_TreeView* to create the control:

```
void Setup TreeView()
{
    // Create the control
    treeView1 = new TreeView();
    treeView1->Dock = DockStyle::Left;
    treeView1->Size = System::Drawing::Size(121, 273);

    // Add a sample node
    treeView1->Nodes->Add(new TreeNode("Root"));
}
```

The *Dock* property determines whether the *TreeView* is going to dock itself against any of the sides of the container. The default value of this is *DockStyle::None*, so controls don't dock by default. By setting the value to *DockStyle::Left*, the control will dock against the left side of the container, and the docked edge will also be resized to match that of the form. This means that, although you need to set the size of the control, the height you give is ignored.

The final line adds one node to the tree, just so that you can see at this early stage that it is working correctly. The Nodes property represents a collection of *TreeNode* objects; *TreeNode* has several constructors, but the simplest just takes a string to represent the label on the node.

8 Now add the *TreeView* control to the form's list of controls, by placing this line at the end of the constructor:

```
Controls->Add(treeView1);
```

Don't put this line in the *Setup_TreeView* function. There's a good reason for this, which I'll explain when you add a splitter bar to the application.

9 Build and run the program. You should see something like the following graphic.

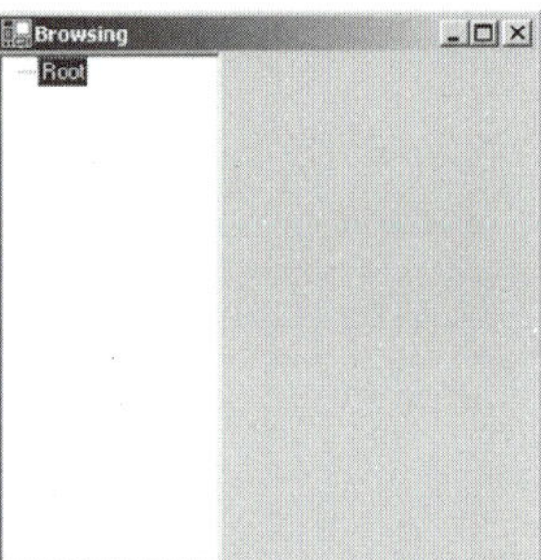

The *TreeView* is docked to the left side and has one member, which is highlighted.

Adding Directory Browsing

Now that the *TreeView* has been set up, let's make it display some useful information. Adding directory browsing capabilities will show you how to add nodes to the control and how to respond to *TreeView* events.

1 Now that you know the *TreeView* displays correctly, remove the line from *Setup_TreeView* that added the sample Root node.

2 The first step in displaying directory information is to add a list of drive letters to the control. You'll be using classes from the *System::IO* namespace, so add a *using* directive to the list at the top of the code, as shown here:

```
using namespace System::IO;
```

3 Add the following code to the end of *Setup_TreeView*:

```
// get the logical drives
String* drives[] = Directory::GetLogicalDrives();
for(int i=0; i<drives->Count; i++)
{
    String* name = dynamic_cast<String*>(drives->get_Item(i));
    TreeNode* tn = new TreeNode(name);
    treeView1->Nodes->Add(tn);
    tn->Nodes->Add(new TreeNode("<dummy>"));
}
```

The *Directory* class is one of the file system access classes provided in *System::IO*, and it has a number of static methods that help you to work with directories. The first member of *Directory* that you'll use is *GetLogicalDrives*, which returns an array of strings containing the names of all the logical drives. Note that the function returns a .NET managed array rather than a C++ native array, so you use the *Count* property to see how many elements the array contains, and the *get_Item* method to access an element. Since *get_Item* returns a plain *Object**, *dynamic_cast* is used to cast the pointer to a *String**.

note

In most cases, you ought to check the pointer returned by *dynamic_cast* at run time in case the cast has failed. Here, I know that *GetLogicalDrives* always returns an array of *Strings*, so I'm not expecting the cast ever to fail.

I construct a new *TreeNode* for every item in the array, initialized with the drive name and added to the *TreeView*. By adding them all directly to the *TreeView*, I'm creating multiple root nodes, which is quite reasonable in this application.

The final line of code adds one child element labeled <dummy> to each of the new nodes. You have seen tree controls showing the plus and minus signs, which you use to expand and collapse the tree. These signs aren't displayed unless the *TreeNode* has child nodes. The problem is that I don't want to create the child entries until the user clicks on a plus sign, but the parent node doesn't get a plus sign unless the children are already in place. One quick and simple solution is to add a dummy child node: If coded correctly, the user will never see this, but the parent node will have a plus sign. When the user expands the node, the dummy node is deleted and replaced by the real child nodes.

4 If you build and run the code at this point, you should see the *TreeView* containing a list of the logical drives, each of which has a plus sign next to it.

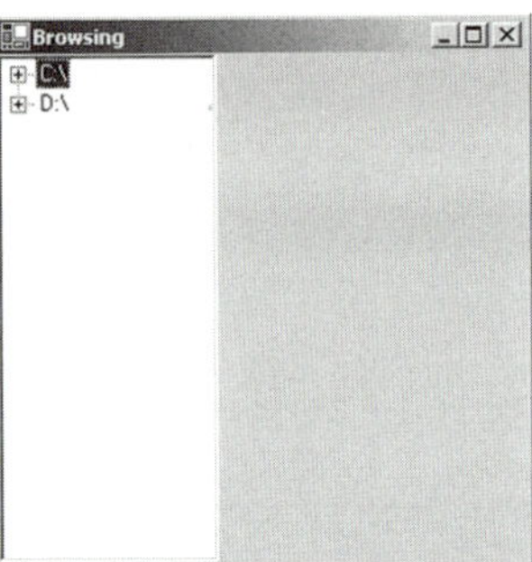

5 The obvious next step is to add another level of detail when the user clicks on one of the plus signs. Looking at the table of events above, you'll probably agree that the best event to handle is the *BeforeExpand* event, which is fired before a *TreeNode* is expanded. Add an event handler declaration to *Setup_TreeView*, just before the code to get the logical drives:

```
treeView1->BeforeExpand += new TreeViewCancelEventHandler(
                        this,
&CppWindow::TreeView_BeforeExpand);
```

The *BeforeExpand* event needs a *TreeViewCancelEventHandler*. The Cancel part of the name reflects the fact that this event is fired *before* the expansion is done, and it would be possible for the code to decide to cancel the expansion.

6 Add the handler function itself to the *CppWindow* class, like this:

```
void TreeView_BeforeExpand(Object* pSender,
                           TreeViewCancelEventArgs* pe)
{
    // First zap the dummy node, assuming there is one
    if (pe->Node->Nodes->Count != 0)
        pe->Node->Nodes->RemoveAt(0);
}
```

As usual, the function name reflects the control and the event, and the handler gets passed two arguments. Unlike the previous event handlers for buttons and menus that you've seen, this one gets passed a *TreeViewCancelEventArgs* object, which contains extra information about the event (specifically, the *TreeNode* that is about to be expanded).

Before adding any child nodes to the tree, you need to remove the dummy node that was added so that the plus sign would display. The *Node* property of the *TreeViewCancelEventArgs* object holds a pointer to the node that the event refers to. This node's collection of children is accessed via the *Nodes* property, and an element can be removed by passing a 0-based index to the *RemoveAt* method. Before doing so, however, you need to check that there is a node to be removed, by checking the number of child nodes.

7 Add the following code to display the contents of a directory:

```
void TreeView_BeforeExpand(Object* pSender,
                           TreeViewCancelEventArgs* pe)
{
    // First zap the dummy node, assuming there is one
    if (pe->Node->Nodes->Count != 0)
        pe->Node->Nodes->RemoveAt(0);

    // Get a list of subdirectories
    String* dirs[];
    try
    {
        dirs = Directory::GetDirectories(pe->Node->FullPath);
    }
    catch(System::Exception* pe)
    {
        MessageBox::Show(pe->Message, "Error");
        Return;
    }

    // Add a child node for each one
    for(int i=0; i<dirs->Count; i++)
    {
        String* dirName = dynamic_cast<String*>(dirs-
>get_Item(i));
        TreeNode* tn = new
TreeNode(Path::GetFileName(dirName));
        pe->Node->Nodes->Add(tn);
        // Add a dummy child node
        tn->Nodes->Add(new TreeNode("<dummy>"));
    }
}
```

Given a path that points to a directory, the *Directory::GetDirectories* function returns an array of strings containing the names of all subdirectories. As before, this is a managed array and not a native C++ array. The *FullPath* property of *TreeNode* returns a string that represents the path from the root to the node, and it does this by concatenating all the labels of the node's parents, separated by a separator character. This is very useful when dealing with directory trees, because if every label is a directory name and the separator character is a backslash (\), the full path to the directory can be built with very little trouble when the user expands a node.

Note the *try* and *catch* blocks around the call to *GetDirectories*. What if you click on the drive letter for a CD or floppy drive that doesn't contain a disk? *GetDirectories* will throw a "device not ready" exception, so you need to be prepared to catch it if you don't want the program to fail.

The *for* loop creates a *TreeNode* for every directory name and adds it as a child of the current node. The names returned by *Directory::GetDirectories* are full path names, but you don't want to use the full path as a name. The *Path::GetFileName* will strip off everything up to (and including) the final backslash in a path, leaving just the directory name.

And finally, a dummy node is added to each child so that the plus sign will display properly.

> **note**
>
> You can, of course, remove *TreeNodes* from the *Nodes* collection using *Remove*. And if you're going to add or remove a lot of nodes at one time, consider using the *BeginUpdate* and *EndUpdate* functions to stop the control redrawing itself every time the *Nodes* collection changes.

8 The application works as it is, but let's add images to the items in the tree to make it look more professional. To do this, you need to use an *ImageList* control. As its name implies, an *ImageList* is simply a control that manages a series of images, and they're used by controls that might end up using a lot of images, such as *TreeViews*, *ListViews*, and *ToolBars*. Add the following code to *Setup_TreeView* before the line that sets up the *BeforeExpand* event handler:

```
// Set up the ImageList
ImageList* il = new ImageList();
il->Images->Add(new Bitmap("Folder.bmp"));
il->Images->Add(new Bitmap("Folder_Open.bmp"));

treeView1->ImageList = il;
treeView1->ImageIndex = 0;
treeView1->SelectedImageIndex = 1;
```

ImageLists hold *Images*, and because *Bitmap* is a subclass of *Image*, you can use *Bitmaps* here. I created the two small icons at left to represent open and closed folders by copying the icons from Windows Explorer.

The *Images* property of the *ImageList* is a standard collection that holds pointers to the *Image* objects, and as usual, *Add* is used to add the *Images* to the collection. The next three lines set this *ImageList* as the one the *TreeView* will use, and define the images that are used by default for unselected and expanded nodes. In this case, image zero is being used for unselected nodes, and image one for selected nodes.

9 Build and run the application. You should see the tree being displayed with images.

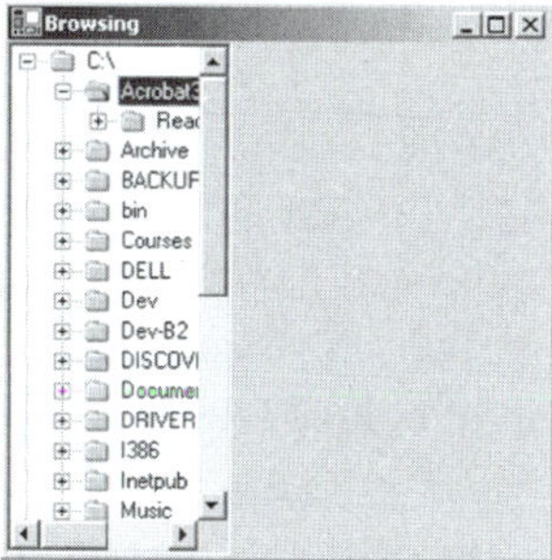

Using the *ListView* Control

A *ListView* is a control that is used to display a list of items; unlike the *TreeView*, there's no hierarchical structure in the data being displayed. An item in a *ListView* can have several items of text and icons associated with it, and can be displayed in one of four views:

- Large Icon view, which displays a large icon with text underneath. Items are arranged in a grid in Large Icon view.
- Small Icon view, which displays a small icon with text alongside. Items are arranged in columns in Small Icon view.
- List view, which displays the text associated with the item, one item per line.
- Details view, which displays columns, each of which contains a text item.

You can see what these views look like by opening Windows Explorer and using the View menu to change the appearance of the *ListView*.

Like *TreeView*, *ListView* is a complex class with many properties, methods, and events. The following tables summarize the most important ones.

Property	Description
Alignment	Represents how items align in the *ListView*. The default is to align to the top of the control.
AllowColumnReorder	Determines whether the user can drag column headers to reorder the columns. This property is meaningful only in Details view. The default is *false*.
AutoArrange	Determines whether items are automatically arranged according to the alignment. The default is *true*.
BackColor	Represents the background color of the control.
BorderStyle	Represents the border style of the control. The default is *Fixed3D*.
CheckBoxes	Determines whether each item will have a check box next to it. The default is *false*.
CheckedIndices	Gets the indexes of the currently checked list items.
CheckedItems	Gets the currently checked list items.
Columns	The collection of columns used in Details view.
FocusedItem	Gets the item that currently has the focus.
ForeColor	Represents the foreground color of the control.
FullRowSelect	Determines whether clicking an item will select just the item or the entire row it is in. Used only in Details view. The default is *false*.
GridLines	Determines whether gridlines are drawn between items. The default is *false*.
HeaderStyle	Gets or sets the column header style: clickable, non-clickable, or no header.
HideSelection	Determines whether the highlighting of selected items is hidden when the control loses the focus. The default is *true*.
HoverSelection	Determines whether items can be selected by hovering over them with the mouse. The default is *false*.
Items	The *ListView*'s collection of items.
LabelEdit	Determines whether the user can edit item labels. The default is *false*.
LabelWrap	Determines whether item labels wrap in icon view. The default is *true*.
LargeImageList	The *ImageList* used in Large Icon view.
MultiSelect	Determines whether the *ListView* allows selection of more than one item at a time. The default is *true*.
Scrollable	Determines whether scrollbars are visible. The default is *true*.
SelectedIndices	A collection holding the indexes of currently selected items.
SelectedItems	A collection holding pointers to the currently selected items.
SmallImageList	The *ImageList* used in Small Icon view.

Sorting	Represents the sort order of the items: ascending, descending, or none.
TopItem	Returns the item at the top of the list.
View	Represents the view that the *ListView* is currently displaying: Large Icon, Small Icon, List, or Details.

Method	Description
ArrangeIcons	Arranges icons in Small Icon or Large Icon view.
BeginUpdate	Disables redrawing of the *ListView*. Use this if you're going to add several items, because it prevents the control redrawing itself after each item is added.
Clear	Removes all items and columns from the *ListView*.
EndUpdate	Re-enables redrawing of the *ListView*.
EnsureVisible	Ensures that a particular item is visible, scrolling the list if necessary.
GetItemAt	Gets the item at specific X-Y coordinates.
GetItemRect	Gets the bounding rectangle for an item.
IsInputKey	Handles special input keys, such as Page Down and the arrow keys.

Event	Description
AfterLabelEdit	Occurs after a label is edited.
BeforeLabelEdit	Occurs before a label is edited.
ColumnClick	Occurs when the user clicks on a column.
ItemActivate	Occurs when an item is activated.
ItemCheck	Occurs when the user checks an item. Applies only if the CheckBoxes property is set to true.
ItemDrag	Occurs when an item is dragged and dropped.
SelectedIndexChanged	Occurs when the user clicks on an item.

The items displayed in a *ListView* are represented by the *ListViewItem* class. A *ListViewObject* can contain a number of data items:

- A label
- An image index, which determines which image from the Large and Small *ImageLists* will be used for this item
- Foreground and background colors
- A tag, which can be any .NET object that you want to attach to the item
- A collection of subitems, which are used to provide the data for the columns when the control is in Details view

To show you how to use a *ListView*, the following exercise continues working with the CppControls project and adds a *ListView* control to the right-hand side of the main form. This will display the details of any directory you select in the *TreeView* control.

1. Add a private *ListView* member to the *CppWindow* class, as shown here:

```
private:
ListView* listView1;
```

2. Add a *Setup_ListView* member function to the class, which will be used to create and set up the *ListView* control.

```
void Setup_ListView()
{
    // Create the ListView and set its properties
    listView1 = new ListView();
    listView1->Dock = DockStyle::Fill;
    listView1->Location = Point(124, 0);
    listView1->Size = System::Drawing::Size(168, 273);
}
```

3. Add a call to this function from the CppWindow constructor. The ListView is created so it is positioned just to the right of the TreeView. Its *Dock* property is set to *Fill*, which means it will fill up all the remaining space on the form.

4. As a test, create a couple of *ListViewItem* objects and add them to the *ListView*, like this:

```
// Create a couple of test items to go in the ListView
ListViewItem* listViewItem1 = new ListViewItem("Foo");
ListViewItem* listViewItem2 = new ListViewItem("Bar");

// Add them to the ListView
listView1->Items->Add(listViewItem1);
listView1->Items->Add(listViewItem2);
```

ListViewItems can be created in a number of ways, but the simplest is to use the constructor that requires only a label.

5. In the *CppWindow* constructor, add the *ListView* to the form's collection of controls. Make sure that you add the *ListView* before you add the *TreeView*.

```
Controls->Add(listView1);
Controls->Add(treeView1);
```

I'll explain why this is necessary when we discuss splitter bars later in the chapter.

6. Build and run the application. You should see the *ListView* and items displayed as shown in the following graphic.

The items are being displayed in the default Large Icon view, but because there are no icons, you see only the labels.

Displaying Directory Details

Now that you've seen how to create a *ListView*, let's use it in practice to display the details of a directory that's been selected in the *TreeView*. For simplicity, this example will support only the Details view, but you could add code to support the other three views.

1. Delete the code at the end of *Setup_ListView* that creates the two sample items. Now that you know the application works, you no longer need the samples.
2. Add the following line of code to the *Setup_ListView* function to switch to Details view:

```
// Set to use Details view
listView1->View = View::Details;
```

3. To use Details view, you need to set up columns to display the data. This information is held in the *Columns* collection of the *ListView*, which holds *ColumnHeader* objects. Add the following code to *Setup_ListView*, following from the previous addition:

```
// Set up the columns for use with Details view
ColumnHeader* col1 = new ColumnHeader();
col1->Text = S"Type";
col1->Width = 40;

ColumnHeader* col2 = new ColumnHeader();
col2->Text = S"Name";
col2->Width = 85;

ColumnHeader* col3 = new ColumnHeader();
col3->Text = S"Size";
col3->Width = 65;
```

```
listView1->Columns->Add(col1);
listView1->Columns->Add(col2);
listView1->Columns->Add(col3);
```

Each *ColumnHeader* has a label, set through the Text property, and a width in pixels. In this example, we display only the type of the item (file or directory), its name, and its size. You can add more columns if you want to display more information.

4 That's all the setting up. You can run the program now, and you'll see an empty *ListView* on the form. The next step is to add the code to fill the *ListView* with file and directory information. As you'll see, this process is very similar to creating the *TreeView* nodes. Add a private member function called *Fill_ListView* to the *CppWindow* class, like this:

```
void Fill_ListView(String* path)
{
}
```

The argument is the directory path whose contents we want to display.

5 Add a call to *Fill_ListView* to the end of the *TreeView_BeforeExpand* handler function, as shown here:

```
// Fill the ListView with details of the current node
Fill_ListView(pe->Node->FullPath);
```

When the child nodes have been constructed and added to the *TreeView*, the full directory path is passed to *Fill_ListView* so that it can fill in the *ListView*.

6 Now let's start coding *Fill_ListView*. The first task is to clear out the existing items to make way for the new directory listing.

```
// Clear everything from the ListView
listView1->Items->Clear();
```

Make sure that you call *Clear* on the Items property, and don't call *listView1->Clear* instead, because that will clear everything from the *ListView*, including the column headers you just added!

7 In true Windows Explorer style, the *ListView* will list the directories first, followed by the files. Add this code to get the subdirectories of the current path:

```
// Start with the directories
String* dirs[];
try
{
    dirs = Directory::GetDirectories(path);
}
catch(System::Exception* pe)
{
```

```
        MessageBox::Show(pe->Message, "Error");
        return;
    }
```

This code uses the same *Directory::GetDirectories* function that you used when creating *TreeView* entries. Once again the call is enclosed in a *try* and *catch* block, although in this case there's much less chance that an exception will be thrown.

8 Once you've got the list of directory names, create *ListViewItems* to represent them, and add them to the *ListView*, as follows:

```
// Create new ListViewItem objects to represent the directories
for(int i=0; i<dirs->Count; i++)
{
    String* pathName = dynamic_cast<String*>(dirs-
>get_Item(i));
    String* dirName = Path::GetFileName(pathName);

    // Create an array of String* to hold the subitems
    String* subItems[] = new String*[3];
    subItems[0]= S"Dir";
    subItems[1] = dirName;
    subItems[2] = S" ";

    // Create the ListViewItems from the subitems
    ListViewItem* itm = new ListViewItem(subItems);
    // Add the ListViewItem to the ListView
    listView1->Items->Add(itm);
}
```

The *get_Item* function retrieves an item from the array, and *GetFileName* splits off the final component from the path. We need a *ListViewItem* that has three text fields, one for each of the three columns in the *ListView*. There is a constructor for *ListView* that takes an array of *Strings*, so it is a simple matter to create an array of three *Strings*, initializing them to the type of item (*Dir* for directory), the name of the directory, and a blank string for the size, because we don't report sizes for directories.

note

If you want to get more sophisticated, investigate creating *ListViewSubItems* and using them to build a *ListViewItem*. *ListViewSubItem* lets you assign icons, fonts, and colors to each individual item.

The last few lines create a *ListViewItem* from the *String* array and then add the *ListViewItem* to the *ListView*.

9 Follow the same process to add details of the files. Here's the code. It is long, but there's little here you haven't seen before.

```
// Now follow with the files
String* files[];
try
{
    files = Directory::GetFiles(path);
}
catch(System::Exception* pe)
{
    MessageBox::Show(pe->Message, "Error");
    return;
}

// Create new ListViewItem objects to represent the files
for(int i=0; i<files->Count; i++)
{
    String* pathName = dynamic_cast<String*>(files->get_Item(i));
    String* dirName = Path::GetFileName(pathName);

    // Create an array of String* to hold the subitems
    String* subItems[] = new String*[3];
    subItems[0]= S"File";
    subItems[1] = dirName;

    // Find the file size
    FileInfo* f = new FileInfo(pathName);
    subItems[2] = __box(f->Length)->ToString();

    // Create the ListViewItems from the subitems
    ListViewItem* itm = new ListViewItem(subItems);
    // Add the ListViewItem to the ListView
    listView1->Items->Add(itm);
}
```

The code is almost exactly the same as the code for adding directory details, except for the lines that find the file size. The *System::IO::FileInfo* class represents a file path, and it is used here to get the length of the file in bytes. The long value returned by the property is boxed so that you can call *ToString* on it, and the resulting string is added to the list of subitems.

10 If you build and run the application, you should be able to list directory contents.

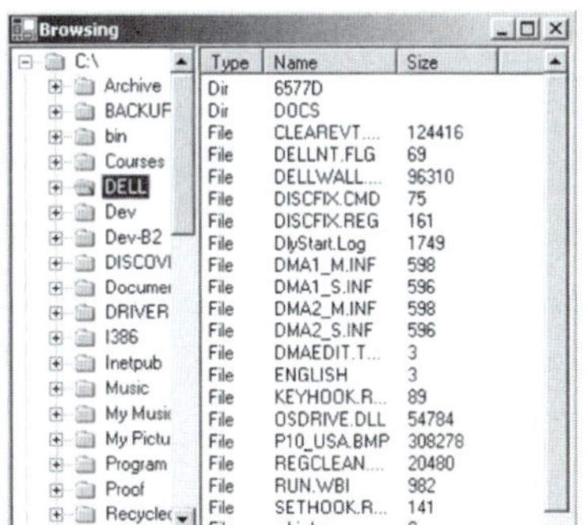

11 The *ListView* gets updated only when you expand a tree node, but it would be good if it was updated whenever you select a node. Do this by adding a handler for the *BeforeSelect* event and linking it to the *TreeView_BeforeExpand* function. Linking both events to the same handler is what we want here, because we want both events to take the same action. Add this line of code to *Setup_TreeView*, after the existing event handler:

```
treeView1->BeforeSelect += new
TreeViewCancelEventHandler(this,
                              &CppWindow::TreeView_BeforeExpand);
```

You'll now find that the *ListView* gets updated whenever you select or expand a node.

Using Splitters

The application now works adequately, but it would be good if you could resize the *TreeView* and *ListView* controls rather than having to use the scrollbars. The *Splitter* control gives users the ability to resize docked controls at run time, and you'll shortly see how to add one to the *CppWindow* form so that users can resize the two view controls.

Splitter doesn't have many properties or methods that you use in code. Once you've added a *Splitter* to a form, the user interacts with it by dragging it from side to side; when the mouse moves over the splitter, the cursor changes to a double-headed arrow to show that the splitter can be dragged. It is possible to handle the events that are fired when the splitter is moved, but this isn't often needed.

Many people find it difficult to make splitters work on forms, because the way you set them up isn't particularly intuitive. The secret lies in the order in which you add the controls to the form, because this order depends on the Z-order of the form's control. In computer graphics terminology, Z-order refers to the front-to-back ordering of graphical objects that might overlap one another. The buttons, list boxes, and other objects that you use to make up user interfaces don't normally overlap, but they still have a Z-order based on the order in which you add them to the form. When using graphical GUI designers, you can change the Z-order using bring-to-front and send-to-back commands.

A splitter works with the object immediately before it in the Z-order, so to associate it with a *TreeView*, you have to add the controls to the form in the following order:

```
Controls->Add(listView1);
Controls->Add(splitter1);
Controls->Add(treeView1);
```

The *ListView* will be at the bottom (or back) of the Z-order, with the splitter in the middle and the *TreeView* at the top (or front). If you add them in any other order, the application won't work as you expect.

The following exercise shows how to add a splitter to the main form. The splitter will be attached to the *TreeView*, and because the *ListView*'s Dock property is set to *Fill*, it will automatically resize to fill the remainder of the form whenever you resize the *TreeView*.

1. Add a *Splitter* as a private member of the *CppWindow* class, like this:

   ```
   private:
     Splitter* splitter1;
   ```

2. Add a private member function to the class called *Setup_Splitter*, which will be used to create and set up the splitter.

   ```
   void Setup_Splitter()
   {
       splitter1 = new Splitter();
       splitter1->Location = Point(121, 0);
       splitter1->Size = System::Drawing::Size(3, 273);
       // Don't include this control in the tab order
       splitter1->TabStop = false;
   }
   ```

   The splitter is positioned just to the right of the *TreeView* and sized to extend the full height of the form. Add a call to this function from the *CppWindow* constructor.

3. Move to the *CppWindow* constructor, and add the *Splitter* control to the form's collection of controls. Make sure to add the controls in the correct order:

```
Controls->Add(listView1);
Controls->Add(splitter1);
Controls->Add(treeView1);
```

4 Build and run the application. You'll find that you can now move the splitter bar to resize the *TreeView* control.

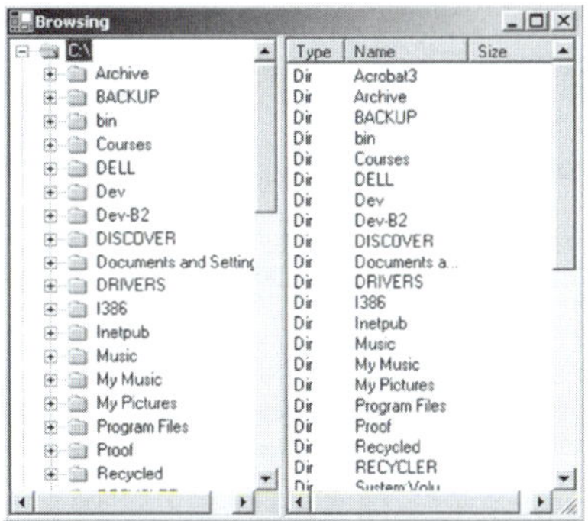

Using Toolbars

Toolbars are a standard feature of just about every GUI application, and the *ToolBar* class provides everything you need to add toolbar functionality to an application.

The *ToolBar* class has a number of properties, as summarized in the following table:

Property	Description
Appearance	Represents the appearance of the *ToolBar*, which can be *Normal* or *Flat*. The default is *Normal*.
AutoSize	Determines whether the *ToolBar* automatically resizes itself to fit the buttons. The default is *true*.
BorderStyle	Represents the border style of the *ToolBar*. The default is *None*.
Buttons	Gets the collection of *ToolBarButton* objects hosted by this *ToolBar*.
ButtonSize	A *Size* value that represents the size of the buttons on the *ToolBar*. The default is 24 pixels wide by 22 pixels high.
Divider	Determines whether this *ToolBar* displays a divider. The default is *true*.
DropDownArrows	Determines whether arrows are displayed next to drop-down buttons. The default is *true*.
ImageList	The list of images used on this *ToolBar*.

(continued)

(continued)

Property	Description
ImageSize	Gets a *Size* object representing the size of the images in the *ImageList*.
ShowToolTips	Determines whether ToolTips are shown for buttons.
TextAlign	Represents how the text aligns with respect to the images on buttons. The default is *ToolBarTextAlign::Underneath*.
Wrappable	Determines whether buttons will wrap to the next line if the *ToolBar* becomes too narrow. The default is *true*.

Buttons on a toolbar are represented by *ToolBarButton* objects, and this class also has several useful properties, which are summarized in the following table.

Property	Description
DropDownMenu	Represents the menu associated with a drop-down button.
Enabled	Determines whether this button is enabled. The default is *true*.
ImageIndex	Represents the index of the image in the *ToolBar*'s *ImageList* that will be used for this button. The default is -1 (no image).
Parent	Gets a pointer to the *ToolBar* that is hosting a button
PartialPush	Determines whether a toggle-style button is partially pushed. The default is *false*.
Pushed	Determines whether a button is currently pushed. The default is *false*.
Rectangle	Gets the bounding rectangle for a button.
Style	Represents the button's style. The default is *PushButton*.
Tag	Represents any object that you want to be associated with the button.
Text	Represents the text on the button, if any.
ToolTipText	Represents the text to be displayed for this button's ToolTip. The parent *ToolBar*'s ShowToolTips property must be true for ToolTips to be displayed.
Visible	Determines whether the button is visible. The default is *true*.

ToolBarButtons can be displayed with one of four styles:

- *PushButton* (the default), where the button simply acts as a pushbutton
- *DropDownButton*, where clicking on the button drops down a menu
- *ToggleButton*, where the button toggles between its up and down states

- *Separator*, where the button acts as a separator between two other buttons. Like the separator on a menu, this style of button can't be selected.

The *ToolBar* class has two events: *ButtonClick*, which is fired when a button is clicked, and *ButtonDropDown*, which is fired when the menu of a drop-down button is about to be displayed.

This exercise will add a *ToolBar* to the form. The bar will host two buttons: the first is a drop-down button with a menu, while the second is a standard pushbutton. You'll also add a handler for the second button, to learn how handlers are used with *ToolBars*.

1 Add a private *ToolBar* member to the *CppWindow* class from the previous exercise, along with three *ToolBarButton* members, as shown here:

```
private:
    ToolBar* toolBar1;
    ToolBarButton* button1;
    ToolBarButton* button2;
    ToolBarButton* button3;
```

2 Add a private function to the class called *Setup_ToolBar*, which will be used to create and set up the *ToolBar* control.

```
void Setup_ToolBar()
{
    toolBar1 = new ToolBar();
    toolBar1->ShowToolTips = true;
}
```

The *ShowToolTips* property determines whether a ToolTip will be displayed when the mouse pointer hovers over a button. Add a call to this function from the *CppWindow* constructor.

3 Add the *ToolBar* to the form's collection of controls in the *CppWindow* constructor. It doesn't matter where you put this one in the list, so you might as well add it to the end.

```
Controls->Add(toolBar1);
```

4 Edit *Setup_ToolBar* to create the *ImageList* object that will hold the bitmaps displayed on the buttons, using the following code:

```
void Setup_ToolBar()
{
    toolBar1 = new ToolBar();
    toolBar1->ShowToolTips = true;
```

```
    // Set up the imagelist
    ImageList* il = new ImageList();
    il->Images->Add(new Bitmap("view.bmp"));
    il->Images->Add(new Bitmap("exit.bmp"));

    // Set the toolbar to use the imagelist
    toolBar1->ImageList = il;
}
```

You've seen an *ImageList* used like this before. The *Add* function is used to add a bitmap object to the *ImageList*'s *Images* collection, and the *ToolBar*'s *ImageList* property is used to let the *ToolBar* know which *ImageList* object it is using.

5 Create the buttons, set their properties, and add them to the *ToolBar*. Here's the code for the first button:

```
// Create the first button
button1 = new ToolBarButton();
button1->Style = ToolBarButtonStyle::DropDownButton;
button1->ImageIndex = 0;
button1->ToolTipText = "View";

System::Windows::Forms::ContextMenu* cm = new
System::Windows::Forms::ContextMenu();
MenuItem* item1 = new MenuItem("Details");
cm->MenuItems->Add(item1);
button1->DropDownMenu = cm;
```

The button is going to have *DropDownButton* style, so that a menu will be displayed when the button is clicked. It is going to use image zero from the *ToolBar*'s *ImageList*, and "View" is going to be displayed in the ToolTip. The *ContextMenu* holds the menu for the *DropDownButton*, and it is assigned to the *DropDownMenu* property of the button. I've only added one item to the menu, but you can easily add others.

Note that you need to used the fully qualified name for *ContextMenu*, or it will conflict with the form's *ContextMenu* property.

6 Add the following code to make the middle button a separator:

```
button2 = new ToolBarButton();
button2->Style = ToolBarButtonStyle::Separator;
```

Setting the style to *Separator* makes this display as a gap in the button set, and this object doesn't then play any more part in the program's user interface. It can't fire events, and the user can't interact with it.

7 Add the following code to make the third button display as a normal pushbutton:

```
button3 = new ToolBarButton();
// PushButton is the default style, so you don't need to set
it
button3->Style = ToolBarButtonStyle::PushButton;
button3->ImageIndex = 1;
button3->ToolTipText = "Exit";
```

As the comment says, the default style is *PushButton*, so there's no need to include it specifically. I've done so here so that you can see the style of each button. The button will use image one from the *ImageList*, and its ToolTip will display "Exit." You'll soon add a handler for this button, which will cause the application to exit.

8 Add all the buttons to the *ToolBar*.

```
toolBar1->Buttons->Add(button1);
toolBar1->Buttons->Add(button2);
toolBar1->Buttons->Add(button3);
```

9 Add a handler for the third button. Add the following line of code to the end of *Setup_ToolBar*:

```
// Set up the handler
toolBar1->ButtonClick += new
ToolBarButtonClickEventHandler(this,
                              &CppWindow::ToolBar_Click);
```

The *ToolBarButtonClick* event has its own handler class, so you need to be careful to create the right type of handler object.

10 The *ToolBar_Click* function handles events coming from *ToolBar* buttons.

```
void ToolBar_Click(Object* pSender,
ToolBarButtonClickEventArgs* pe)
{
    if (pe->Button == button3)
    {
        Application::Exit();
    }
}
```

The handler function gets passed a *ToolBarButtonClickEventArgs* object that contains details of which button was clicked. The function checks the *Button* member of this object, which holds a pointer to the button that originated the event. If it was *button3*, the application exits.

Note that you don't check the *pSender* argument: this holds a pointer to the *ToolBar* itself, not to the button. It would be useful if the application contained more than one *ToolBar*.

note

To handle the user selecting an item from the menu associated with a drop-down button, simply attach an event handler to the menu item, just as you would for any menu item. We covered how to do this in the previous chapter.

11 Build and run the application. You should see a *ToolBar*, which should contain two buttons with a gap between them. Clicking the right-hand button should cause the application to exit.

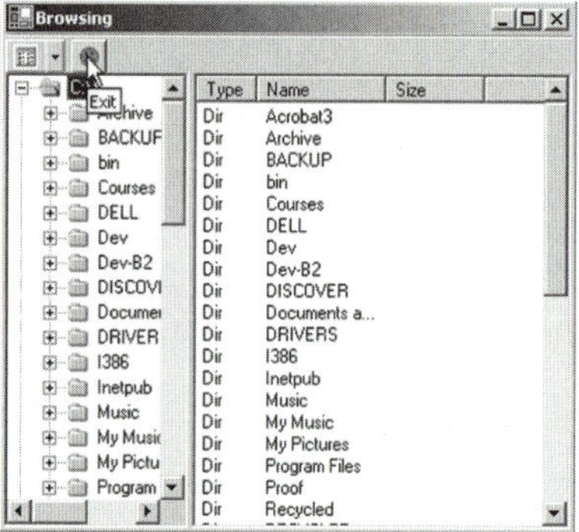

Using Status Bars

The *StatusBar* class represents the standard status bar that you see at the bottom of many application windows. As its name implies, the purpose of a status bar is to present status information to the user. Simple status bars display one or more text items, and if you want a more advanced display, you can take over part or all of the drawing of the status bar in order to display bitmaps, progress controls, or other UI elements. Because this chapter is presenting an introduction to controls, I'll concentrate on showing you how to display text on a status bar.

note

Although you can add a status bar to any form, they are not usually added to dialog boxes.

The following exercise shows how to add a status bar to a form and how to use the status bar to display information.

1 Add a private *StatusBar* member to the *CppWindow* class from the previous exercise:

```
private:
  StatusBar* statusBar1;
```

2 Add a private function to the class called *Setup_StatusBar*, which will be used to create and set up the status bar control.

```
void Setup_StatusBar()
{
    statusBar1 = new StatusBar();
}
```

For the time being, use all the default properties for the *StatusBar*. Add a call to this function from the *CppWindow* constructor.

3 Add the *StatusBar* to the form's collection of controls in the *CppWindow* constructor. It doesn't matter where you put this one in the list.

```
Controls->Add(statusBar1);
```

4 You can easily use the *StatusBar* to display the path whose contents are currently being listed in the *ListView*. To do this, add a line to the start of the *Fill_ListView* function, like this:

```
void Fill_ListView(String* path)
{
    // Put the path in the status bar
    statusBar1->Text = path;
...
```

Whatever is assigned to the *Text* property of the *StatusBar* will be displayed, left-justified, on the control.

5 Build and run the application, and select a directory. You should see the path displayed on the status bar.

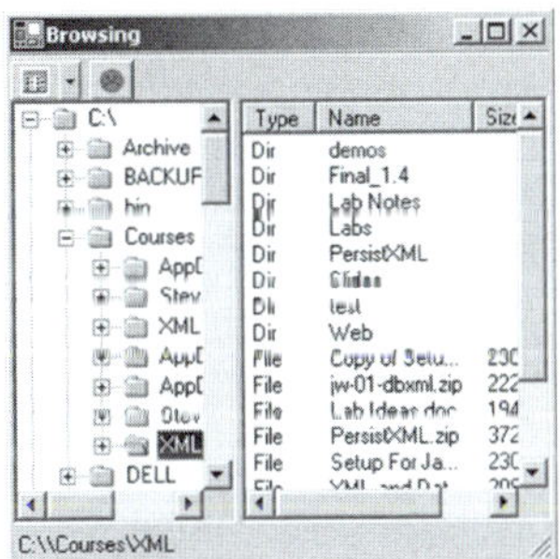

A *StatusBar* can display a *sizing grip* to the bottom right, which users can use to resize the window. This is displayed by default, but you can turn it off by setting the *SizingGrip* property to *false*.

note

You might notice that the path displayed has two backslashes as the first separator. This is because the root directory name is returned as C:\, and when the *TreeView* builds the full path for you, it uses a backslash as the path separator. Having two backslashes instead of one makes no difference to using the path, but if you want to tidy up the path, you can easily remove one from the root name.

You can display more than one piece of information on a status bar, as shown here:

Each of the sunken areas on the status bar is called a panel, and you can add as many panels as you want to the bar. A *StatusBar* object will display either text or panels, and you use the ShowPanels property to determine which is to be displayed at any given time. By default, ShowPanels is *false*, so that text is displayed.

Here's how to modify the *StatusBar* to support two panels, and display the current path in one of them.

1 Add two private *StatusBarPanel* members to the *CppWindow* class, as follows:

```
private:
    StatusBarPanel* statusBarPanel1;
    StatusBarPanel* statusBarPanel2;
```

Each panel on a *StatusBar* is represented by a *StatusBarPanel* object.

2 Edit the *Setup_StatusBar* function to create and add the two panels.

```
void Setup_StatusBar()
{
    statusBar1 = new StatusBar();

    // Set the bar to use panels...
    statusBar1->ShowPanels = true;

    statusBarPanel1 = new StatusBarPanel();
    statusBarPanel1->Width = 200;

    statusBarPanel2 = new StatusBarPanel();
    statusBarPanel2->Width = 100;
```

```
    statusBar1->Panels->Add(statusBarPanel1);
    statusBar1->Panels->Add(statusBarPanel2);
}
```

Setting *ShowPanels* to *true* means that the *StatusBar* will display panels instead of text. The next step is to create two *StatusBarPanel* objects, set their widths to 200 and 100 pixels respectively, and add them to the *StatusBar*'s *Panels* collection in the usual way.

3. Display the path in the first panel by changing the code in *Fill_ListView* to set the *Text* property of the *StatusBarPanel* rather than the *StatusBar*:

```
// Put the path in the first panel on the statusbar
statusBarPanel1->Text = path;
```

4. If you build and run the application now, you'll see the *StatusBar* displaying two panels.

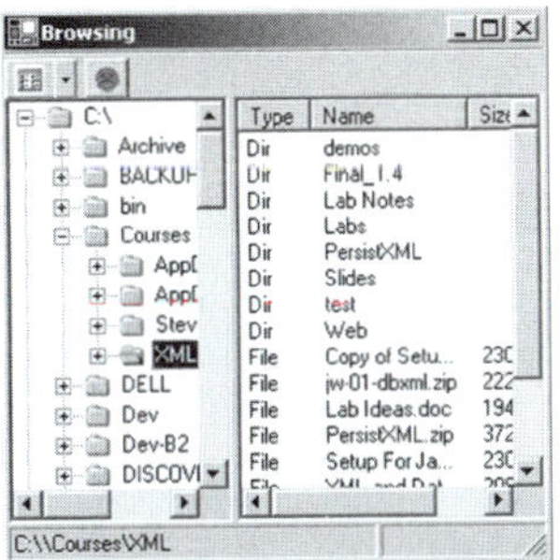

Chapter 17 Quick Reference

To	Do This
Create and display a modal dialog box	Create a class that derives from *Windows::Forms*, and display it using the *ShowDialog* function.
Return a status code from a dialog box	Set the *DialogResult* property for the form. For example: `DialogResult = DialogResult::OK` Alternatively, set the *DialogResult* property of the buttons you want to use to close the form.
Create a Common Dialog	Create a dialog box object of the appropriate type, set its properties, and then display it using *ShowModal*.
Create and use a *TreeView*	Create an object of the *TreeView* class and add it to the form's *Controls* collection.

(continued)

(continued)

To	Do This
	For example: `TreeView* tv = new TreeView();` Controls->Add(tv); Then create *TreeNode* objects and add them to the *TreeView*'s *Nodes* collection. `TreeNode* tn = new TreeNode("A Node"); Tv->Nodes->Add(tn);`
Create and use a *ListView*	Create an object of the *ListView* class and add it to the form's *Controls* collection. For example: `ListView* lv = new ListView(); Controls->Add(lv);` Then create *ListViewItem* objects and add them to the *ListView*'s *Items* collection: `ListViewItem* lvi = new ListViewItem("A Node"); lv->Items->Add(lvi);`
Add a splitter to a form	Create an object of the *Splitter* class, and add it to the form's collection of controls. Make sure that the splitter is added immediately before the control you want it to resize.
Add a toolbar to a form	Create an object of the *ListView* class, and add it to the form's *Controls* collection. For example: `ToolBar* tb = new ToolBar(); Controls->Add(tb);`
Add buttons to a toolbar	Create *ToolBarButton* objects, set their properties, and add them to the *ToolBar*'s *Buttons* collection. For example: `ToolBarButton tbb = new ToolBarButton(); tb->Buttons->Add(tbb);`
Add a status bar to a form	Create an object of the *StatusBar* class and add it to the form's *Controls* collection. For example: `StatusBar* stb = new StatusBar();` You can then assign strings to the *Text* property in order to have them display on the *StatusBar*.
Add panels to a status bar	Set the *ShowPanels* property of the *StatusBar* to *true*. Now create *StatusBarPanel* objects and add them to the *StatusBar*'s *Panels* collection: `StatusBarPanel p1 = new StatusBarPanel(); p1->Width = 200; // pixels stb->Panels->Add(p1);` You can now assign strings to the *Text* property in order to have them display in the panel.

18 Graphical Output

In this chapter, you'll learn how to

- ✔ *Use GDI+ to draw on forms*
- ✔ *Use color*
- ✔ *Use fonts*
- ✔ *Display images on forms*
- ✔ *Print from applications*

Chapters 16 and 17 introduced you to the world of Windows Forms, and showed you how to use the classes in the *System::Windows::Forms* namespace to build GUI applications. This chapter introduces the drawing mechanisms that underlie all the Windows Forms functionality. You're going to learn how to draw on forms, how to display images, and how to print.

Graphics with GDI+

The Microsoft .NET subsystem that handles graphical output is called GDI+. GDI (or Graphical Device Interface) was the original Windows graphics model introduced with Microsoft Windows 3.0. It remained much the same through the versions of Windows that followed, but it has been greatly improved for the .NET Framework, hence the addition of the plus sign (+) to the name.

GDI+ provides a library of classes for performing simple two-dimensional graphics, such as drawing lines and simple shapes, displaying text and bitmaps, and printing. Although GDI+ is much improved compared to the original GDI, it is still essentially a very simple two-dimensional graphics library, with no advanced features like animation or three-dimensional effects.

The *System::Drawing* Namespaces

The GDI+ functionality is spread across several namespaces:

- *System::Drawing* provides the basic functionality.
- *System::Drawing::Drawing2D* provides more advanced two-dimensional and vector graphics.
- *System::Drawing::Imaging* provides functionality for image processing.
- *System::Drawing::Text* provides more typographic functionality than in *System::Drawing*.
- *System::Drawing::Printing* handles printing.

In this chapter, we'll mainly be looking at the features offered by the basic *System::Drawing* namespace, as well as the printing functionality provided by *System::Drawing::Printing*.

The main classes in *System::Drawing* are listed in the following table:

Class	Description
Bitmap	Represents a bitmap. This class can work with several common formats, including BMP, GIF, and JPG.
Brush	Brushes are used to fill the interiors of shapes.
Brushes	A collection of predefined brushes.
Color	Represents a color.
Font	Represents a font.
FontFamily	Represents a family of fonts.
Graphics	Represents a drawing surface.
Icon	Represents an icon.
Image	The base for the other image classes, such as *Bitmap* and *Metafile*.
Pen	Used for drawing the outlines of shapes.
Pens	A collection of predefined pens.
Point, *PointF*	Integer and floating-point structures that represent an X-Y point.
Rectangle, *RectangleF*	Integer and floating-point structures that represent a rectangle.
Region	Represents a region. Regions don't have to be rectangular.
Size, *SizeF*	Integer and floating-point structures that represent a size.
SolidBrush	A brush that fills a shape with a solid color.
StringFormat	Encapsulates a set of text layout information, such as alignment and line spacing.

SystemBrushes	A collection of *Brushes* representing the system colors.
SystemColors	A collection of *Color* objects representing the system colors.
SystemIcons	A collection of icons, mainly representing those used in *MessageBoxes*.
SystemPens	A collection of *Pens* representing the system colors.
TextureBrush	A brush that uses an image to fill shapes.

The *Graphics* Class

If you want to draw on a form, there are a lot of things you need to consider first. For instance, your program might run on a PDA or WAP phone, so is the display monochrome or color? How many colors can the display support? What's the display resolution? And what about output to printers—can they be color or black and white, support different paper sizes and orientations, and have a range of resolutions?

However, GDI+ isolates you from these worrying about these factors through the *Graphics* class, which represents an idealized drawing surface. As you'll see shortly, the *Graphics* class supports a lot of drawing operations: you use these to draw, and the *Graphics* object renders them on the actual output device, effectively isolating you from the characteristics of the output device.

note

If you have come across the idea of a Windows device context, then you know what a *Graphics* object is, because the *Graphics* class is the .NET way of encapsulating a device context.

In addition to being the place where you send graphical output, a *Graphics* object can also tell you about the device it is using. In this way, a *Graphics* object is an intermediary between you and the output device. The rest of this chapter will show you how to make use of the *Graphics* class to produce graphical output.

Creating *Graphics* Objects

If you look at the documentation for the *Graphics* class, you'll see that it doesn't have any constructors. You don't create a *Graphics* object directly, but instead use the form's *CreateGraphics* function to obtain one:

```
// Create a Graphics object
Graphics* pg = myForm->CreateGraphics();
```

The reason for this is that a *Graphics* object represents an underlying Windows data structure called a device context. Whether you get a new or a cached object is not your problem, because using a factory method like *CreateGraphics* hides the details of how the *Graphics* object is actually obtained.

A *Graphics* object uses system resources, and these will be released when the object is garbage collected. Since you don't know when this will be, it is a good idea to free up resources when you've finished by calling the object's *Dispose* method:

```
// Release the resources held by the Graphics object
pg->Dispose();
```

It is good programming practice to hold on to *Graphics* objects for as short a time as possible, because the supply of graphics resources on some systems might be limited. You should, therefore, call *Dispose* as soon as you've finished with the object.

Drawing Objects

Basic drawing operations are performed using *Pen* and *Brush* objects. *Pens* are used to draw lines and the outlines of shapes, while *Brushes* are used to fill the interior of shapes.

Pens

Simple *Pens* are created by specifying a line width in pixels and a color:

```
// Create a black pen with default width of one pixel
Pen* pen1 = new Pen(Color::Black);

// Create a red pen two pixels wide
Pen* pen2 = new Pen(Color::Red, 2.0);
```

The *Color* arguments are specified using static members of the *Color* class. We'll discuss *Color* in more detail later in the chapter.

If you want to create more advanced *Pens*, you can specify a *Brush* instead of a *Color*. This gives you the option of filling the lines with images or patterns.

Brushes

Brushes come in several varieties, all of which inherit from the *Brush* base class. The simplest is the *SolidBrush*, which fills an area with a solid color:

```
// Create a blue brush
SolidBrush* br1 = new SolidBrush(Color::Blue);
```

The *TextureBrush* class uses an image to fill shapes. If the image is smaller than the shape, it can be tiled:

```
// Create a TextureBrush which will tile
TextureBrush* br2 = new TextureBrush(new Bitmap("brush.bmp"),
                                 WrapMode::Tiled);
```

Standard Pens and Brushes

The *Pens* class has properties that define over 140 pens representing the full range of system-defined colors. Each of these has a width of one pixel. The *Brushes* class does exactly the same for brushes:

```
// Create a one-pixel wide red pen
Pen* redPen = Pens::Red;

// Create a standard blue brush
Brush* blueBrush = Brushes::Blue;
```

The *SystemPens* and *SystemBrushes* classes are very similar, but their properties reflect the standard system colors that are used to draw UI components:

```
// Create a pen the color of window frames
Pen* redPen = SystemPens::WindowFrame;

// Create a brush which has the standard color of 3D controls
Brush* blueBrush = SystemBrushes::Control;
```

The values associated with these pens and brushes might change if the user uses the Control Panel to change the desktop color scheme.

Drawing Operations

Now let's put together what you've learned so far, and do some drawing on a form. The *Graphics* class has a lot of drawing methods, the most common of which are summarized in the table below:

Method	Description
Clear	Fills the entire drawing area with a color
DrawArc	Draws an arc representing a portion of an ellipse
DrawBezier	Draws a Bezier curve
DrawClosedCurve, *FillClosedCurve*	Draws or fills a closed curve defined by an array of points
DrawCurve	Draws a curve

(continued)

(continued)

Method	Description
DrawEllipse, *FillEllipse*	Draws or fills an ellipse defined by a bounding rectangle
DrawIcon	Draws an icon
DrawImage	Draws an image
DrawLine	Draws a line
DrawLines	Draws a set of lines connecting an array of points
DrawPie, *FillPie*	Draws or fills a pie segment defined by an ellipse and two radial lines
DrawPolygon, *FillPolygon*	Draws or fills a polygon defined by an array of points
DrawRectangle, *FillRectangle*	Draws or fills a rectangle
DrawString	Draws a string
FillRegion	Fills a region defined by a *Region* object

Note how there are separate *draw* and *fill* calls. If you want to draw a rectangle outlined in black and filled with red, you'll have to call both *DrawRectangle* and *FillRectangle*.

The following exercise will show you how to draw some simple shapes on a form:

1 Start a new Managed C++ Application project called CppDraw.

2 Change the declaration of the main function to look like this:

```
void __stdcall WinMain(void)
```

If you use *WinMain* instead of *main*, you won't get a Console window displayed. This is better for Windows applications that don't need to use a Console, but when developing it can be useful to have a Console available because you can use *Console::WriteLine* to display log information.

3 Add all the *#using* and *using* statements to the top of the code, so that it looks like this:

```
#include "stdafx.h"

#using <mscorlib.dll>
#using <System.dll>
#using <System.Drawing.dll>
#using <System.Windows.Forms.dll>

using namespace System;
```

```
// Needed for drawing classes
using namespace System::Drawing;
using namespace System::Drawing::Drawing2D;
// These two are needed for Windows Forms
using namespace System::ComponentModel;
using namespace System::Windows::Forms;
```

You'll find that you end up with the same set of namespaces imported in just about every Windows Forms application.

4 Before the *WinMain* function, add a managed class called *CppWindow* to represent the main form of the application:

```
__gc class CppWindow : public Form
{
public:
    CppWindow()
    {
        Text = S"Drawing";
        ClientSize = System::Drawing::Size(300, 300);
    }
};
```

The class inherits from *Form*, as you'd expect, and the size of the client area is set to 300 by 300 pixels.

note

The client area is that part of the form that you are responsible for maintaining, and represents the area of the form inside the scrollbars and frame.

5 Add a button to the form, along with a handler:

```
CppWindow()
{
    Text = S"Drawing";
    ClientSize = System::Drawing::Size(300, 300);

    // Add a button
    Button * drawBtn = new Button();
    drawBtn->Text = S"Draw";
    drawBtn->Location = Point(200,220);
    Controls->Add(drawBtn);
    // Add an event handler
    drawBtn->Click += new EventHandler(this, &CppWindow::Btn_Click);
}
```

You've seen how to add buttons and set up handlers before, but refer back to Chapter 16 if you need to refresh your memory. The button is positioned toward the bottom right of the window, and when it is clicked, graphics code will execute.

6 Here's the code for the handler:

```
void Btn_Click(Object* pSender, EventArgs* pe)
{
    // Get a Graphics object
    Graphics* pg = CreateGraphics();

    // Get a Pen
    Pen* pen1 = new Pen(Color::Black);

    // Draw a line
    pg->DrawLine(pen1, 20,20, 100,100);

    // Dispose of the Graphics object
    pg->Dispose();
}
```

When the button is clicked, a *Graphics* object is created, along with a one-pixel-wide black pen. The *DrawLine* method takes a pointer to a *Pen*, plus the beginning and end coordinates of the line in pixels. Once the line has been drawn, you no longer need the *Graphics* object, so you can call its *Dispose* method.

Coordinates are in pixels, with (0,0) at the top left of the form. So X coordinates increase to the right, while Y coordinates increase downward.

7 Add the following line to the WinMain function:

```
Application::Run(new CppWindow());
```

8 Build and run the program. You should see a line drawn on the screen when you click the button.

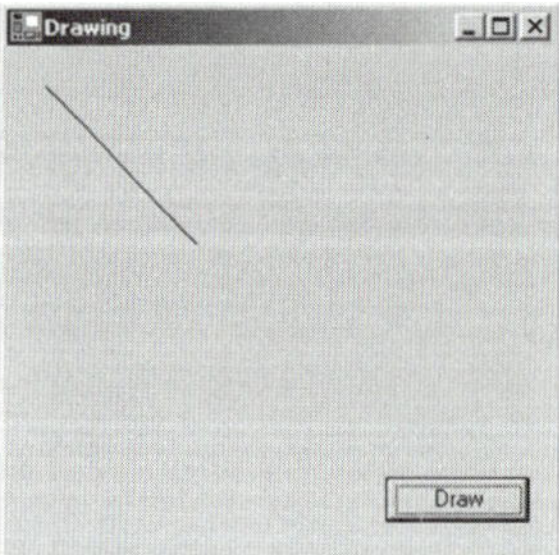

9 You can now add a few more calls to *Graphics* drawing methods. Make sure you put these after the first call to *DrawLine* in the *Btn_Click* method and before the call to *Dispose*:

```
// Draw a styled line
Pen* pen2 = new Pen(Color::Blue, 3.0);
pen2->DashStyle = DashStyle::Dash;
pg->DrawLine(pen2, 20,120, 100,60);

// Draw a filled rectangle
SolidBrush* sb1 = new SolidBrush(Color::Red);
pg->FillRectangle(sb1, 60,30, 40,40);

// Draw a filled and outlined rectangle
SolidBrush* sb2 = new SolidBrush(Color::Yellow);
pg->FillRectangle(sb2, 90,40, 45,45);
pg->DrawRectangle(pen1, 90,40, 45,45);

// Draw a filled ellipse
SolidBrush* sb3 = new SolidBrush(Color::Green);
pg->FillEllipse(sb3, 30,100, 65,50);
```

The line uses a new *Pen* that draws dashed lines. There are several members of the *DashStyle* enumeration, and you can also produce your own custom dashed lines by defining the dash pattern. Two rectangles are drawn, one red and one yellow, and the second one is outlined in black.

10 Build and run the application. You should get output like this when you click the Draw button.

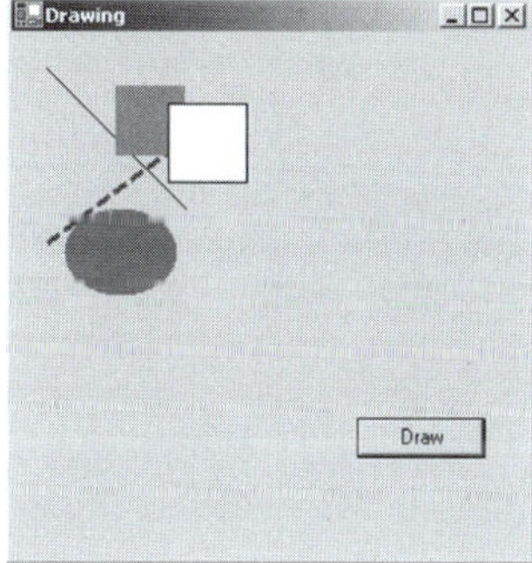

Paint Events

Try running the program, then minimize the window to the taskbar and bring it back by clicking on the taskbar button. You'll find that all the graphics have disappeared, and you'll also find that the same thing happens if you let another window display on top of the Drawing application window. You can regenerate the graphics by clicking the Draw button again, but why does the drawing disappear?

What's happening here is quite normal. Windows takes care of refreshing the components on the form—the form itself, the title bar, and the button—but it is your responsibility to refresh anything you have drawn on the client area of the form.

Whenever a window needs refreshing, the operating system will send it a *paint* event. If you handle these *paint* events, you can ensure that the form will always display its data.

The following exercise shows you how to handle *paint* events, and also how to interact with the mouse. The program will capture *MouseDown* and *MouseUp* events when you click and release the mouse button, and will draw a line between the point where you clicked the button and the point where you release it.

1. Continue with the CppDraw application from the previous exercise. You can remove the *Button* and handler code as you won't be requiring it in this exercise, but it will do no harm to leave it in.
2. Add two *Point* members to the *CppWindow* class:

   ```
   Point p1, p2;
   ```

   Since *Point* is a value type, these are declared as variables and not as pointers.
3. The *MouseDown* event is fired when any mouse button is clicked down while the mouse is over a control; the *MouseUp* event is fired when the mouse button is released. Arrange for handler functions to be called for the *MouseDown* and *MouseUp* events on the form, by adding the following lines to the *CppWindow* constructor:

   ```
   // Add mouse event handlers
   MouseDown += new MouseEventHandler(this, &CppWindow::Form_MouseDown);
   MouseUp += new MouseEventHandler(this, &CppWindow::Form_MouseUp);
   ```

   The *MouseDown* event handler will save away the position of the mouse pointer at the time the button was clicked:

```
void Form_MouseDown(Object* pSender, MouseEventArgs* pe)
{
    p1.X = pe->X;
    p1.Y = pe->Y;
}
```

The handler functions for *mouse* events get sent *MouseEventArgs* objects, which contain information about the event. *MouseEventArgs* has several useful properties:

- *Button* tells you which mouse button was clicked.
- *Clicks* tells you the number of mouse clicks that triggered the event.
- *Delta* tells you the number of notches the wheel on a wheel-equipped mouse was rotated.
- *X* and *Y* tell you the X and Y coordinates of the mouse when the event was fired.

In this example, you're saving away the X and Y values in the variable *p1*.

note

Because *p1* is a value type, you have to use dot notation to access its members.

The *MouseUp* handler is similar, in that it also stores away the coordinates:

```
void Form_MouseUp(Object* pSender, MouseEventArgs* pe)
{
    p2.X = pe->X;
    p2.Y = pe->Y;

    Graphics* gr = CreateGraphics();
    Pen* pen1 = new Pen(Color::Black);

    gr->DrawLine(pen1, p1.X,p1.Y, p2.X,p2.Y);

    gr->Dispose();
}
```

Once the coordinates have been stored away, the function draws a line between the two points.

If you build and run the application at this point, you should be able to draw lines on the form using the mouse. You'll find, however, that they disappear whenever the form needs repainting, just like in the previous exercise. In the rest of this exercise, you'll save coordinates of the lines as you draw them, and then redraw the collection of lines whenever the form needs repainting.

4 Add a *using* declaration for *System::Collections* to the top of the program:

```
using namespace System::Collections;
```

You're going to store the line information in an *ArrayList*, which is part of the *System::Collections namespace*.

5 Add a private *ArrayList* member to the *CppWindow* class:

```
ArrayList* list;
```

6 Create the *ArrayList* object in the *CppWindow* constructor:

```
list = new ArrayList();
```

7 Add a new managed struct called *Line* to the top of the program, before *CppWindow*:

```
__gc struct Line
{
   Point p1;
   Point p2;
};
```

This struct simply holds two *Points* that represent the endpoints of the line. You could easily extend this type to hold other information, such as color and line style.

8 Every time you draw a line, create a new *Line* object and add it to the *ArrayList*. Add the following code to the end of the *Form_MouseUp* function, after the call to *DrawLine* and before the call to *Dispose*:

```
// Add a new line to the list
Line* pline = new Line();
pline->p1 = p1;
pline->p2 = p2;

list->Add(pline);
```

The *Line* object simply holds the *Points* that represent the endpoints of the line.

9 To handle *paint* events, you need to add a handler, so add the following code to the *CppWindow* constructor, after the *mouse* event handlers:

```
// Add paint event handler
Paint += new PaintEventHandler(this, &CppWindow::Form_Paint);
```

Paint events need a *PaintEventHandler*, which sends a *PaintEventArgs* object to describe the event.

10 Add the code for the *paint* event handler:

```
void Form_Paint(Object* pSender, PaintEventArgs* pe)
{
    Graphics* gr = pe->Graphics;
    Pen* pen1 = new Pen(Color::Black);

    for(int i=0; i<list->Count; i++)
    {
        Line* pline = dynamic_cast<Line*>(list->get_Item(i));
        gr->DrawLine(pen1, pline->p1.X,pline->p1.Y,
                                        pline->p2.X,pline->p2.Y);
    }
}
```

The function first gets a *Graphics* object and creates a *Pen*. When you're handling a *repaint* event, you get a *Graphics* object as part of the *PaintEventArgs* argument; use this one, and don't create your own. Likewise, don't call *Dispose* on this object when you finish with it; you didn't create it, so it isn't your responsibility to dispose of it.

The code then loops over all the items in the *ArrayList*, retrieving each one and casting it from an *Object** back to *a Line**. Once this is done, you can use the coordinates in the *Line* object to draw the lines.

11 Build and run the program now. You'll find that the lines you draw persist through minimizing, maximizing, and other window events that cause a repaint.

Using Color

Colors are represented by the *System::Drawing::Color* structure, and are formed from four components: Red, Green, Blue, and Alpha. The first three represent the proportions of red, green, and blue in the color, and are specified as an integer with a value from 0 (none) to 255 (maximum). Pure red would therefore have a value of (255,0,0). The *Alpha* value represents the transparency of the color, and can vary from 0 (fully transparent) to 255 (fully opaque).

Like *Graphics*, the *Color* structure doesn't have a constructor. You create *Colors* by using one of the three static factory methods:

18 Graphical Output

- *FromARGB*, which creates a *Color* from a set of Alpha, Red, Green, and Blue values.
- *FromKnownColor*, which creates a *Color* from a member of the *KnownColor* enumeration (see below).
- *FromName*, which creates a color given a name.

The *Color* class defines a large number of properties that represent system-defined colors, ranging from AliceBlue to YellowGreen.

The *KnownColor* enumeration defines a list of system-defined colors. These include the standard colors defined in *Color* (such as AliceBlue) as well as values representing colors used in the Windows GUI, such as *ActiveCaption* (the color of the title bar on an active window) and *WindowText* (the color of the text in a window). The values of these colors might change if the user alters the desktop color scheme using the Control Panel.

Here are some examples showing how to create colors:

```
// Pure red, fully opaque
Color c = Color::FromARGB(255, 255, 0, 0);

// The 'CornSilk' standard color
Color c1 = Color::FromKnownColor(KnownColor::CornSilk);

// Another way to get CornSilk
Color c3 = Color::CornSilk;
```

Note that once a *Color* has been constructed, you can't change its values. If you need to change a *Color*, you'll have to create a new *Color* based on the existing one:

```
// Pure red, fully opaque
Color c = Color::FromARGB(255, 255, 0, 0);

// Pure red, semi-transparent
Color c4 = Color::FromARGB(127, c.R, c.G, c.B);
```

The A, R, G, and B properties can be used to access the components of the *Color*.

Using Fonts

Two classes in *System::Drawing* are used to represent fonts: *Font* and *FontFamily*. A *Font* object represents a single font and specifies the font name, the size, and the style attributes. A *FontFamily* defines a set of fonts that share many characteristics, but which might differ in font style.

The following table lists the major properties of the *Font* class. Note that they are all read-only: Once created, a *Font* cannot have its properties changed.

Property	Description
Bold	True if the font has bold style.
FontFamily	Gets the font family that this font belongs to.
Height	Gets the height of the font in the current units.
Italic	True if the font has italic style.
Name	Gets the name of the font.
Size	Gets the size of the font in the current units.
SizeInPoints	Gets the size of the font in points (1/72").
Strikeout	True if the font has strikeout style.
Style	Gets the style information for the font.
Underline	True if the font has underline style.
Unit	Gets the unit of measure for this font. By default, this will be pixels.

The Style is composed of one or more values from the *FontStyle* enumeration, which has the members *Bold*, *Italic*, *Regular*, *Strikeout*, and *Underline*.

The following short exercise will demonstrate how to create and use a *Font* to draw text on a form. You'll enhance the existing application so that using the left button will draw lines, while the right button will draw a text string.

1. Add a *Font* member to the *CppWindow* class:

```
private:
    System::Drawing::Font* font1;
```

   You'll need to use the fully qualified name, or else the declaration will conflict with the form's Font property.

2. Create a *Font* object in the *CppWindow* constructor:

```
// Create the Font
font1 = new System::Drawing::Font("Verdana", 8,
                   FontStyle::Regular, GraphicsUnit::Millimeter);
```

Once again, you need to use the fully qualified name to avoid name clashes. The first argument is the name of the font, followed by the size. What the size represents depends on the last argument, which represents the units to be used. The *GraphicsUnit* enumeration contains all the valid units, which can be any of the following:

- *Display*, which uses 1/75" as the unit of measure
- *Document*, which uses document units (1/300")
- *Inch*
- *Millimeter*
- *Pixel*
- *Point*, which uses printer's points (1/72")
- *World*, which uses world coordinates

In this case, I'm specifying 16 millimeters, which will be easily visible on the form. The font style can be any of the values from the *FontStyle* enumeration, combined with the OR operator (|) if you want to use more than one of them.

3 Edit the *Form_MouseUp* function so that it differentiates between the left and right mouse buttons:

```
void Form_MouseUp(Object* pSender, MouseEventArgs* pe)
{
    Graphics* gr = CreateGraphics();
    Pen* pen1 = new Pen(Color::Black);

    if (pe->Button == MouseButtons::Left)
    {
        // Draw lines
        p2.X = pe->X;
        p2.Y = pe->Y;

       gr->DrawLine(pen1, p1.X,p1.Y, p2.X,p2.Y);

        // Add a new line to the list
        Line* pl = new Line();
        pl->p1 = p1;
        pl->p2 = p2;

        list->Add(pl);
    }
    else if (pe->Button == MouseButtons::Right)
```

```
        {
            // Draw text
            gr->DrawString(S"text", font1, Brushes::Black, pe->X, pe->Y);
        }

        gr->Dispose();
    }
```

The function now checks which mouse button gave rise to the event. If it is the left button, a line gets drawn. If it is the right button, a string is drawn at the mouse position using the font you just created. The third argument to *DrawString* is a *Brush*, which defines the fill color or pattern for the text.

4 Build and run the application. You should be able to draw lines and text using the left and right mouse buttons.

Note that the text isn't persistent: unlike the lines, it will disappear when the window gets repainted.

Handling Images

The *Image* class provides the base class for all the image classes in *System::Drawing*, especially the *Bitmap* class, which is used to represent and manipulate images in a number of formats.

Bitmap has a number of useful properties and methods, which are summarized in the following two tables:

Property	Description
Height	Gets the height of the bitmap in pixels
HorizontalResolution	Gets the horizontal resolution, in pixels per inch
Palette	Gets or sets the color palette used by this image
PixelFormat	Gets or sets the *PixelFormat* value that describes the color format of the pixels

(continued)

(continued)

Property	Description
Size	Gets the width and height of this bitmap as a *Size* object
VerticalResolution	Gets the vertical resolution, in pixels per inch
Width	Gets the width of the bitmap in pixels

Method	Description
FromFile	Creates a bitmap from data in a file
FromHbitmap	Creates a bitmap from a Windows HBITMAP
FromStream	Creates a bitmap from data from a stream
RotateFlip	Rotates and/or flips the image
Save	Saves the image in a given format

You can see the formats that are supported by looking at the *ImageFormat* enumeration.

The following exercise illustrates how to display a bitmap on a form:

1. Find the *Form_Paint* function that handles *paint* events. You need to display the bitmap in the *paint* event handler so that it gets redisplayed when the form needs to refresh itself. Add the following code to *Form_Paint*:

```
// Draw the image
Bitmap* bmp = new Bitmap(S" ramp1.gif");
gr->DrawImage(bmp, 10,10);
```

   The code simply creates a *Bitmap* object that reads data from a GIF file. The call to *DrawImage* then draws the image at position (10,10) on the form. The image I've used forms a vertical stripe down the left side of the form.

note

You'll find the ramp1.gif file on the CD that accompanies this book. Copy it from the CD into the project directory to use it in this code.

2 Build and run the application. You'll now see a bitmap displayed on the form.

Printing

The *System::Drawing::Printing* namespace contains the classes that implement the printing functionality within GDI+. Printing isn't particularly hard, but it can be a rather involved process because of the number of classes involved.

The first class you'll meet when printing is *PrintDocument*. A *PrintDocument* object represents your link with a printer, and can be used for more than one print job. *PrintDocument* has four properties:

- *DefaultPageSettings*, which gets or sets a *PageSettings* object that represents the default page settings.
- *DocumentName*, which represents the document name.
- *PrintController*, which gets or sets a *PrintController* object that controls the printing process.
- *PrinterSettings*, which gets or sets a *PrinterSettings* object that controls where and how the document is printed.

The *PrinterSettings* and *PageSettings* classes hold data about the printer to be used—such as paper trays—and the *PageSettings* holds data about the setup of the document, such as orientation and number of copies.

The exercise that follows shows you how to use the printing functionality within GDI+. You'll use the existing application you've been developing during this chapter, and add a menu item that will let you print the contents of the form.

1 You need to add a menu to the form, so start by adding some menu members to the *CppWindow* class:

```
MainMenu* mnu;          // the main menu for the form
MenuItem* fileMenu;     // the File dropdown menu
MenuItem* printItem;    // the Print item on the File menu
MenuItem* exitItem;     // the Exit item on the File menu
```

2 Create a function called *Setup_Menu*, and add a call to it in the *CppWindow* constructor:

```
void Setup_Menu()
{
}
```

3 Add the code to *Setup_Menu* to create the menu items and link them together:

```
void Setup_Menu()
{
    // Create the MainMenu
    mnu = new MainMenu();
    // Create the File menu and add it to the MainMenu
    fileMenu = new MenuItem("&File");
    mnu->MenuItems->Add(fileMenu);

    // Create the menu items and add them to the File menu
    printItem = new MenuItem("&Print...");
    exitItem = new MenuItem("E&xit");
    fileMenu->MenuItems->Add(printItem);
    fileMenu->MenuItems->Add(new MenuItem("-"));
    fileMenu->MenuItems->Add(exitItem);

    // Set the MainMenu to be the Form's menu
       Menu = mnu;
}
```

note

Setting up menus like this should be familiar to you by now. If you need to refresh your knowledge of how menus work, see Chapter 16.

4 Set up the event handlers for the Print and Exit menu items:

```
printItem->Click += new EventHandler(this, &CppWindow::MenuItem_Click);
exitItem->Click += new EventHandler(this, &CppWindow::MenuItem_Click);
```

5 Add the code for the *MenuItem_Click* handler function:

```
void MenuItem_Click(Object* pSender, EventArgs* pe)
{
    if (pSender == printItem)
    {
        // The PrintDocument holds the settings
        PrintDocument* pdoc = new PrintDocument();
        // Create a dialog and attach it to the document
        PrintDialog* pd = new PrintDialog();
        pd->Document = pdoc;

        // Show the dialog
        if (pd->ShowDialog() == DialogResult::OK)
        {
            // Add the page handler
            pdoc->PrintPage += new PrintPageEventHandler(this,
                                         &CppWindow::PrintAPage);
            // Print the page
            pdoc->Print();
        }
        else
            MessageBox::Show("Print cancelled", "Information");
    }
    else if (pSender == exitItem)
        Application::Exit();
}
```

The handler code determines which menu item raised the event. If it was the Exit item, the application exits. If it was the Print item, a *PrintDialog* gets displayed; *PrintDialog* is one of the Common Dialogs, and will display the familiar printer selection dialog shown here.

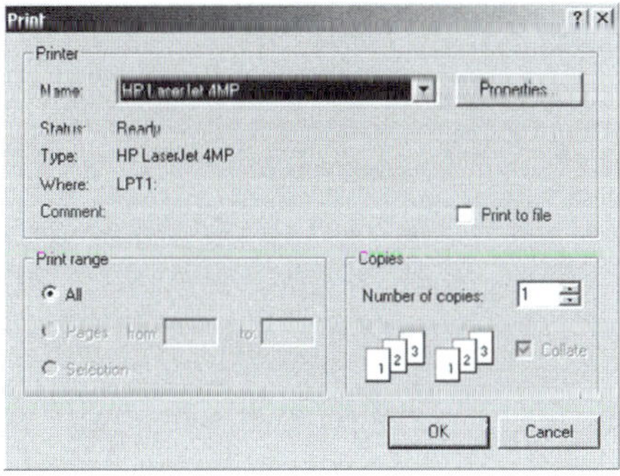

The purpose of this dialog is to gather the information needed for the printing process; this information is stored in a *PrintDocument* object for later use. So before you display the *PrintDialog*, you need to create a *PrintDocument* object and assign it to the dialog's Document property. You can then show the *PrintDialog*, and when the user dismisses the dialog box, check the return value to see whether you should continue printing.

The *PrintDocument* controls the printing process, so you call its *Print* function to start printing. You also need to provide a *callback* function that *PrintDocument* will call once for each page that needs to be printed. You add the *callback* in the normal way, by adding an event handler to the *PrintDocument*.

Here's the code for the *callback* function:

```
void PrintAPage(Object* pSender, PrintPageEventArgs* pe)
{
    Graphics* gr = pe->Graphics;
    Pen* pen1 = new Pen(Color::Black);

    // Draw the image
    Bitmap* bmp = new Bitmap(S"c:\\temp\\ramp1.gif");
    gr->DrawImage(bmp, 10,10);

    for(int i=0; i<list->Count; i++)
    {
        Line* pl = dynamic_cast<Line*>(list->get_Item(i));
        gr->DrawLine(pen1, pl->p1.X,pl->p1.Y, pl->p2.X,pl->p2.Y);
    }
}
```

Notice that the code is exactly the same as that in the *paint* event handler. In this case, I'm taking a very simple-minded approach to printing and simply dumping the content of the form straight to the printer. In real life, you'd probably want to add headers and footers and perhaps format the output differently.

note

What if your output fits on more than one page? The page handler function is going to be called once for each page, and it is up to you to keep track of where you are, and what needs to be printed. As long as there are more pages to print, set the HasMorePages property of the *PrintPageEventArgs* object to *true* before returning from the handler function, and it will get called again.

6 Add a *using* declaration for *System::Drawing::Printing* to the top of the program: using System::Drawing::Printing;

7 Build and run the application. Draw some lines and text on the screen, and verify that you can send the output to your printer.

note

You'll find that the lines appear on the printed output, but the text doesn't. This is because the data for the lines was saved so that it could be redrawn in PrintAPage; the text data wasn't saved, so it won't be redrawn.

Chapter 18 Quick Reference

To	Do This
Draw on a form	Create a *Graphics* object using the form's *CreateGraphics* function: `Graphics* gr = myForm->CreateGraphics();` Remember to call *Dispose* on the *Graphics* object when you've finished with it: `gr->Dispose();`
Draw lines and the outlines of shapes	Create *Pen* objects and use them in calls to *Graphics* class drawing functions. Use the *Pens* and *SystemPens* classes to obtain *Pens* with standard colors.
Fill shapes	Create *Brush* objects and use them in calls to *Graphics* class drawing functions. Use the *Brushes* and *SystemBrushes* classes to obtain *Brushes* with standard colors.
Use colors	Create *Color* objects and use them when constructing *Pens* and *Brushes*.
Display images	Create a *Bitmap* object, passing it the name of an image file. Then use the *Graphics* class *DrawImage* function to render it.
Print from an application	Create a *PrintDialog*. Create a *PrintDocument* and assign it to the *PrintDialog*'s *Document* property. Show the dialog box, and check whether it returns *DialogResult::OK*. Create a *callback* function and attach it to the *PrintDocument*'s *PrintPage* event, and then call the *PrintDocument*'s *Print* function to print the page.

19

Working with Files

In this chapter, you'll learn

- ✔ *How the Microsoft .NET Framework does input/output*
- ✔ *The classes that make up the* System::IO *namespace*
- ✔ *How to perform text input/output*
- ✔ *How to read and write files*
- ✔ *How to work with files and directories*
- ✔ *How to perform binary input/output*

You've already used the *Console* class to perform input/output (I/O) to and from the Console. This chapter will introduce you to the *System::IO* namespace, which contains the classes, structures, and enumerations that implement the Microsoft .NET I/O model.

note

If you know anything about the Java I/O mechanism as implemented in the java.io package, you'll find it easy to start working with .NET I/O, because the two have many similarities.

The *System::IO* Namespace

The *System::IO* namespace contains all the classes that are used for binary and text I/O, as well as classes that help you to work with files and directories. The following table lists the main classes in the namespace.

Class	Description
BinaryReader	Reads primitive data types as binary values
BinaryWriter	Writes primitive data types as binary values
BufferedStream	A stream class that buffers reads and writes to another stream
Directory	Has static methods for working with directories
DirectoryInfo	Has non-static methods for working with directories
File	Has static methods for working with files
FileInfo	Has non-static methods for working with files
FileStream	A class for reading and writing files using a stream
FileSystemInfo	The abstract base class for *DirectoryInfo* and *FileInfo*
FileSystemWatcher	Watches for changes to the file system
IOException	The exception thrown by classes in the *System::IO* namespace
MemoryStream	A stream class that reads and writes memory
Path	Helps you work with directory strings in a platform independent manner
Stream	The abstract base class for all the stream classes
StreamReader	A *TextReader* that reads characters from a byte stream
StreamWriter	A *TextWriter* that writes characters to a byte stream
StringReader	A *TextReader* that reads from a string
StringWriter	A *TextWriter* that writes to a string
TextReader	The abstract base class for *StreamReader* and *StringReader*
TextWriter	The abstract base class for *StreamWriter* and *StringWriter*

The I/O-oriented classes in *System::IO* can be divided into three groups:

- The *Stream* classes, which are designed for input and output of streams of bytes
- The *BinaryReader* and *BinaryWriter* classes, which are used to input and output .NET primitive types, such as *Int32* and *Double*, in binary form
- The *TextReader* and *TextWriter* classes, which are used for character-mode I/O

This chapter focuses on the latter two groups.

Text Input/Output Using Readers and Writers

TextReader and *TextWriter* are the abstract base classes for a group of classes that are used to read and write characters. There are four classes in *System::IO* that derive from these two bases—*StreamReader*, *StreamWriter*, *StringReader*, and *StringWriter*—along with several other much more specialized writer classes in other namespaces.

Using *TextWriters*

The *TextWriter* class has a number of useful methods, as summarized in the following table.

Method	Description
Close	Closes the writer and releases any resources it's using
Dispose	Releases the resources used by the writer
Flush	Causes all buffered data to be written to the underlying device
Synchronized	Creates a thread-safe wrapper for the writer
Write	Writes text without a newline
WriteLine	Writes text with a newline

As you might guess from the inclusion of the *Write* and *WriteLine* functions in the table, the *Console* class uses a *TextWriter* object to perform output.

Let's look at how you use the *StreamWriter* class, to show you how the I/O classes work together. Before we start, though, it is important that you understand how the .NET Framework implements I/O. Rather than create a number of classes that each do an end-to-end I/O task, .NET implements a number of smaller general-purpose classes that you can plug together to get the effect you want. So .NET doesn't have a "write characters to a file" class and a "write characters to the screen" class. Instead, it has a "write characters to a byte stream" class and a "read bytes and write them to a file" class; if you plug the output from the first into the input of the second, you end up writing characters to a file.

This model is flexible, because you can take binary or character data and convert it into bytes and then pass the bytes to any of several classes to output them to files, memory, or a string. Data is transferred between the classes as streams of bytes, a method that provides a flexible base on which to build. The basic functionality for handling byte streams is provided by the *Stream* class, and you can build your own specialized I/O classes on top of *Stream* if you need to.

With that information in mind, the following exercise will show you how to write character data to a text file using a *TextWriter*. Using the Plug and Play model for I/O that the .NET Framework uses, you need to create two objects:

- A *FileStream* object that takes bytes as input and writes them to a file
- A *StreamWriter* object that takes text and converts it to a byte stream

Here's the exercise.

1. Start a new Managed C++ Application project called CppWriter.
2. The *TextWriter* and file I/O classes are part of *System::IO*, so include a *using* declaration at the start of the program, like this:

```
using namespace System::IO;
```

3. In the *_tmain* function, create a *FileStream* object to write to a file.

```
// Create a FileStream
try
{
    FileStream* fs = new FileStream("c:\\temp\\output.txt",
FileMode::Create);
}
catch(System::Exception* pe)
{
    Console::WriteLine(pe->ToString());
}
```

The *FileStream* constructor takes a file name and a mode; in this case, the file is going to be created if it doesn't exist, and overwritten if it does.

> **note**
>
> See the section "The *FileStream* Class" for more details on how to construct *FileStreams*.

The code is enclosed in a *try* block, because there are a lot of things that could go wrong when trying to open this file.

4. Create a *StreamWriter* that uses the *FileStream*, as shown here:

```
try
{
    // Create a FileStream
```

```
    FileStream* fs = new FileStream("output.txt",
FileMode::Create);

    // Create a StreamWriter
    StreamWriter* sw = new StreamWriter(fs);
}
catch(System::Exception* pe)
{
    Console::WriteLine(pe->ToString());
}
```

The *StreamWriter* constructor takes a pointer to a *Stream* object as its one argument.

5 You can now use the *Write* and *WriteLine* functions to output text to the file. Put the following lines inside the *try* block:

```
sw->WriteLine(S"First line");
sw->WriteLine(S"Second line");
sw->WriteLine(S"Third line");
```

6 Make sure that all output is flushed to the file, and close the stream.

```
sw->Flush();
sw->Close();
```

note

WriteLine performs buffered output, which means that it doesn't necessarily write lines to the file every time you call the function. Instead, it maintains an internal buffer and writes the buffer to disk as necessary. One disk access per buffer is more efficient than writing individual lines, but you need to call *Flush* at the end of the code in order to make sure that output currently in the buffer is transferred to the file.

7 Build and run the application.

A text file called output.txt should appear in the CppWriter project directory. The file contains the three lines of text written by the CppWriter application.

The *FileStream* Class

FileStream is used to pass bytes from some other class—such as *StreamWriter*—to a file. There are several overloaded constructors to this class, which let you specify combinations of the following:

- The filename
- The file mode, which determines how the file is going to be opened
- The type of access required
- The sharing options

The file mode is represented by members of the *FileMode* enumeration, which are listed in the following table:

Member	Description
Append	Opens an existing file or creates a new file and appends text to the end
Create	Creates a new file or opens an existing one and overwrites it
CreateNew	Creates a new file, throwing an exception if the file already exists
Open	Opens an existing file
OpenOrCreate	Opens an existing file or creates a new one
Truncate	Opens an existing file and truncates its size to 0 bytes. An exception will be thrown if the file doesn't exist.

The access is represented by members of the *FileAccess* enumeration, as listed in the following table:

Member	Description
Read	Represents read access
ReadWrite	Represents read/write access
Write	Represents write access

Similarly, the sharing access is specified by the *FileShare* enumeration:

Member	Description
None	No sharing
Read	Represents shared read access
ReadWrite	Represents shared read/write access
Write	Represents shared write access

The following example shows how to construct a *FileStream* using these permissions:

```
FileStream* fs2 = new FileStream(
    "foo.txt",                  // the filename
    FileMode::Create,           // create or overwrite
```

```
FileAccess::ReadWrite,  // request read/write access
FileShare::Read);       // allow shared reading
```

note

Although you'll usually use the *FileStream* class with other writer classes, you can use its *Read* and *Write* methods to input and output bytes directly.

Using *TextReader*

The structure and operation of the *TextReader* class parallels that of *TextWriter*. The following table lists the methods provided for you by *TextReader*:

Method	Description
Close	Closes the reader and releases any resources it's using
Dispose	Releases the resources used by the reader
Peek	Returns the next character from the input stream without removing it
Read	Reads one or more characters from the input stream
ReadBlock	Reads a block of characters
ReadLine	Reads a line
ReadToEnd	Reads to the end of the input stream
Synchronized	Provides a thread-safe wrapper for *TextReader* objects

As with *TextWriter*, you use *TextReader* by plugging a reader into an object that is going to act as a source of bytes. There are several of these, including the one you've already met, *FileStream*.

The exercise that follows show you how to write a program similar in functionality to the UNIX "more" command, which will read a file and echo its contents to the screen a few lines at a time. After it has displayed some lines, the user has the choice of pressing the Enter key to continue or pressing Q to quit.

1. Start a new Managed C++ Application project called CppReader.
2. Include a *using* declaration for *System::IO* at the top of the project.

   ```
   using namespace System::IO;
   ```

3. Because the user is going to enter the name of the file to be listed on the command line, change the declaration of the *_tmain* function to include the command line parameter arguments, as shown here:

```
int _tmain(int argc, char* argv[])
```

note

If you haven't met command-line arguments in a C or C++ program before, the *_tmain* function can optionally take two arguments. The first—traditionally named *argc*—is the number of command line arguments, while the second—traditionally named *argv*—is an array of strings.

4 Add code to *_tmain* to ensure that the user has entered a filename.

```
// Check for required arguments
if (argc < 2)
{
    Console::WriteLine(S"Usage: CppReader path");
    return 0;
}

String* path = new String(argv[1]);
```

If the user hasn't given two arguments, an error message is printed and the program exits. If the user has, the second argument is saved for later use.

5 It's wise to check that the path represents an existing file before continuing, so add this code:

```
if (!File::Exists(path))
{
    Console::WriteLine("Invalid filename!");
    return -1;
}
```

The *File::Exists* method checks whether a file with the specified name exists, returning *false* if it doesn't. It will also return *false* if you give the name of a directory rather than a file.

6 Start to list the file. The first step is to create a *FileStream*, and then connect it to a *StreamReader*:

```
try
{
    FileStream* fs = new FileStream(path, FileMode::Open);

    StreamReader* sr = new StreamReader(fs);
}
```

```
catch(System::Exception* pe)
{
    Console::WriteLine(pe->ToString());
}
```

In this case, you're opening the file using *FileMode::Open*, which will throw an exception if the file doesn't already exist.

7 Listing the file is done in this loop, which you should place after creating the *StreamReader* object, like this:

```
int count = 0;
for(;;)
{
    String* line  = sr->ReadLine();
    count++;
    // If there are no more lines, break out of the loop
    if (line == 0) break;

    Console::WriteLine(line);

    if (count % 20 == 0)
    {
        Console::Write("--more--");
        String* response = Console::ReadLine();
        if (response->Equals(S"q")) break;
        count = 0;
    }
}

Console::WriteLine("-- end --");
```

The *count* variable is going to be used to count the lines as they're read, so that the program knows where to break. The loop reads a line into a *String* using the *StreamReader's ReadLine* function; if there are no more lines to read, a *null* pointer will be returned. The line is then echoed to the Console and the count checked. I've set the number of lines displayed at one time to an arbitrary value of 20; when the count is exactly divisible by 20, the program writes "--more—" to the Console and waits for the user to input something. If the user presses Q, the program stops; otherwise, it outputs the next set of lines.

8 Build and run the program, giving the name of a suitable text file as the argument.

Working with Files and Directories

The *System::IO* namespace contains several classes to help you work with files and directories.

Getting Information About Files and Directories

The *Directory* and *DirectoryInfo* classes provide you with functions to help you work with directories. The difference between them is that *Directory* only contains only static methods, while *DirectoryInfo* contains non-static instance methods. Why the need for two different classes? It is necessary for .NET to perform a security check before allowing you access to a directory or file: the *Directory* class performs this check every time you use one of its static methods, which can be time-consuming. Objects of the *DirectoryInfo* class, on the other hand, work with one directory, and the security check is done once when the object is constructed. It can therefore be a lot more efficient to use *DirectoryInfo* if you're going to perform multiple operations on one directory.

The following table lists the main methods of the *Directory* class.

Method	Description
CreateDirectory	Creates a directory
Delete	Deletes a directory, and optionally its subdirectories
Exists	Checks whether a directory exists
GetCreationTime	Gets the creation time of a directory
GetCurrentDirectory	Returns a string representing the path to the current directory
GetDirectories	Gets an array of strings representing the names of subdirectories in a given directory
GetDirectoryRoot	Returns the root portion of a path
GetFiles	Gets an array of strings representing the names of the files in a given directory
GetFileSystemEntries	Gets an array of strings representing the names of the files and directories in a given directory
GetLastAccessTime	Gets the last access time for the directory
GetLastWriteTime	Gets the last write time for the directory
GetLogicalDrives	Gets a list of the logical drives on the computer
GetParent	Gets the parent directory of a specified directory
Move	Moves a directory and its contents
SetCreationTime	Sets the creation time for a directory
SetCurrentDirectory	Sets the current directory
GetLastAccessTime	Sets the last access time for the directory
GetLastWriteTime	Sets the last write time for the directory

The following two tables list the methods and properties of the *DirectoryInfo* class.

Property	Description
Exists	Value is *true* if the directory path exists
Name	Represents the name of the directory
Parent	Gets a *DirectoryInfo* object representing the parent of this directory
Root	Gets a *DirectoryInfo* object representing the root portion of a directory path

Method	Description
Create	Creates a directory
CreateSubdirectory	Creates one or more subdirectories
Delete	Deletes a directory and its contents
GetDirectories	Gets an array of *DirectoryInfo* objects representing the subdirectories of this directory
GetFiles	Gets an array of *FileInfo* objects representing the files in this directory
GetFileSystemInfos	Gets an array of *FileSystemInfo* objects representing the directories and files in this directory
MoveTo	Moves the directory and its contents
ToString	Returns the fully-qualified path as a string

Two classes, *File* and *FileInfo*, are used to work with files. Like the classes discussed earlier, *File* contains static methods, while *FileInfo* contains non-static instance methods. The following tables list the methods and properties exposed by these classes.

Method	Description
AppendText	Appends text to a file, creating the file if it doesn't already exist
Copy	Copies a file
Create	Creates a new file
CreateText	Creates a new text file
Delete	Deletes a file
Exists	Returns true if a file exists
GetAttributes	Returns the file attributes
GetCreationTime	Returns the file's creation time

(continued)

(continued)

GetLastAccessTime	Returns the file's last access time
GetLastWriteTime	Returns the file's last write time
Move	Moves a file to a new location
Open	Opens a *FileStream* for read/write access to a file
OpenRead	Opens a *FileStream* for read-only access to a file
OpenText	Opens a *FileStream* to read from a text file
OpenWrite	Opens a *FileStream* for read/write access to a file
SetAttributes	Sets the file attributes
SetCreationTime	Sets the file's creation time
SetLastAccessTime	Sets the file's last access time
SetLastWriteTime	Sets the file's last write time

Property	Description
Directory	Returns a *DirectoryInfo* object representing the file's parent directory
DirectoryName	Returns a string representing the file's full path
Exists	Returns true if the file exists
Length	Returns the length of the file in bytes
Name	Returns the name of the file

Method	Description
AppendText	Creates a *StreamWriter* to append text to a file
CopyTo	Copies a file to another location
Create	Creates a new file and a *FileStream* to write to it
CreateText	Creates a *StreamWriter* to write to a new text file
Delete	Deletes a file
MoveTo	Moves a file to a new location
Open	Returns a *FileStream* with a specified level of access to a file
OpenRead	Returns a *FileStream* with read access to a file
OpenText	Creates a *StreamReader* to read from an existing file
OpenWrite	Returns a *FileStream* with read/write access to a file
ToString	Returns the file path as a string

The following example illustrates the use of the directory and file manipulation classes. You'll construct a simple directory-listing program similar in functionality to the MS-DOS "dir" command.

Here's how it will work:

- If the path represents a file, the details of the file will be printed.
- If the path represents a directory, the contents of the directory will be listed.
- In addition to the name, the user can choose to display size, last modification date, and/or attributes. For directories, only the last modification date applies.

1 Start a new Managed C++ Application project called CppFiles.

2 Because all the file and directory classes are part of *System::IO*, include a *using* declaration at the start of the program, as follows:

```
using namespace System::IO;
```

3 The user will use the command-line to give options and a path to list, so edit the definition of the *_tmain* function to include the command line argument parameters, just as you did in the CppReader exercise.

```
int _tmain(int argc, char* argv[])
```

4 The user can call the program with a path, or with options plus a path. Add this, and all the code that follows, to the *_tmain* function:

```
// Check for required arguments
if (argc < 2)
{
    Console::WriteLine(S"Usage: CppFiles [options] [path]");
    return 0;
}
```

The array of command line arguments includes everything on the command line, so the first item will always be the program name. This means that we always want at least two arguments if we want the user to include a path.

5 If the user has specified options, we need to find out what they are. Each option is specified by a single letter, and the set of options chosen is represented by a string of option letters. The options supported in this simple program are *s* for the size, *d* for the last modification date, and *a* for attributes. It doesn't matter what order options are given in, so *sa* and *as* would both print the size and attributes.

Here's the code to check the arguments and save the path and the options that the user has specified:

```
String* options = 0;
String* path = 0;
bool bGotOptions = false;
```

```
// Split out the arguments
if (argc == 3)
{
    bGotOptions = true;
    options = new String(argv[1]);
    path = new String(argv[2]);
}
else if (argc == 2)
    path = new String(argv[1]);
```

If there are three command-line arguments, interpret the first one as an option string.

6 See which options the user has selected, using the following code:

```
bool bSize = false;
bool bDate = false;
bool bAtts = false;

// If we have options, check them. The default is to list
// the name only
// Possible options are:
//   v      verbose listing, gives name, size & access time
//   s      list size
//   d      list last access date
//   a      list attributes
if (bGotOptions)
{
    options = options->ToLower();

    if (options->IndexOf('v') != -1)
    {
        bSize = true;
        bDate = true;
        bAtts = true;
    }
    else
    {
        if (options->IndexOf('s') != -1) bSize = true;
        if (options->IndexOf('d') != -1) bDate = true;
        if (options->IndexOf('a') != -1) bAtts = true;
    }
}
```

Three Boolean variables represent the option choices. If *v* for *verbose* has been entered, all options are set. Otherwise the individual option letters are checked, and the corresponding *bool* variables set accordingly.

7 Determine whether the path that has been entered is a file or a directory. Here's the code to do it:

```
bool bItsAFile = false;
bool bItsADirectory = false;

FileInfo* fi = new FileInfo(path);
DirectoryInfo* di = new DirectoryInfo(path);

if (fi->Exists)
    bItsAFile = true;
else if (di->Exists)
    bItsADirectory = true;

if (!bItsAFile && !bItsADirectory)
{
    Console::WriteLine(S"No such file or directory");
    return(-1);
}
```

It isn't as straightforward to check this as you might expect. You have to use the *Exists* property of the *FileInfo* and *DirectoryInfo* classes to check whether the path you have is a file or a directory. If it is a file, *Exists* will return *true* for *FileInfo* and *false* for *DirectoryInfo*, and vice versa if it is a directory. Either *bItsAFile* or *bItsADirectory* might be set. If you end up with neither set, the path specified on the command line cannot be found; the application displays a message and exits, returning *-1* as an error code.

8 Now that you know what sort of object you have and what options the user wants, you can print out the details. The first case will be the details for a single file.

```
if (bItsAFile)
{
  Console::Write(fi->Name);
  if (bSize)
    Console::Write(" {0}", __box(fi->Length));
  if (bDate)
    Console::Write(" {0}",
      File::GetLastAccessTime(fi->ToString()).ToString());
  if (bAtts)
  {
```

```
        FileAttributes fa =
          File::GetAttributes(fi->ToString());
        Console::Write(" ");
        if (fa & FileAttributes::Normal)
          Console::Write("<normal>");
        else
        {
          if (fa & FileAttributes::Archive)
            Console::Write("a");
          if (fa & FileAttributes::Hidden)
            Console::Write("h");
          if (fa & FileAttributes::System)
            Console::Write("s");
          if (fa & FileAttributes::ReadOnly)
            Console::Write("r");
        }
      }
    Console::WriteLine();
    }
```

The program always echoes the file name and then displays other information based on the options required by the user. The *Length* property needs to be boxed before it can be printed using *Write*. You have to get the last access time using one of the static methods of the *File* class, which takes the file path as an argument; the easiest way to get the path is to use *FileInfo*'s *ToString* method.

If the user has requested attributes, use the *GetAttributes* static member of *File* to get a *FileAttributes* object, and then use the bitwise AND operator & (an ampersand) to match it against the various permissions defined in *FileAttributes*. This code is checking only four attributes; it would be easy to extend it to check more.

9 If the user has entered a directory path, list the contents of the directory. The following code lists subdirectories first and files second, and it lists directory names in uppercase and files in lowercase; you can obviously change this to display things however you prefer. Let's start with the code for listing the subdirectories:

```
else if (bItsADirectory)
{
  // List the directory contents - subdirs first, then
  // files
  String* dirs[] =
    Directory::GetDirectories(di->ToString());
```

```
for(int i=0; i<dirs->Count; i++)
{
  DirectoryInfo* sdi =
    new DirectoryInfo(
      dirs->get_Item(i)->ToString());
  // Directories list in upper case
  String* dirName = sdi->Name->ToUpper();
  Console::Write("{0,30}",dirName);
  // no size, so put a few blanks
  String* ss = S"--";
  Console::Write("{0,12}",ss);

  // last mod date is OK
  if (bDate)
    Console::Write(" {0}",
      Directory::GetLastAccessTime(
        sdi->ToString()).ToString());
  // no attributes, either
  // finish the line
  Console::WriteLine();
}
```

The *Directory::GetDirectories* function returns an array of strings representing the names of the subdirectories in the current directory. Because this is a .NET array, you can use the *Count* property to determine how many elements it has. For each element, you create a *DirectoryInfo* object; this is easy, because the *ToString* method will return the path name when called for an array element.

The name is converted to uppercase and then printed out. Note the use of a field width in the *Write* statement: format specifiers can take an optional field width after the field number. If this value is positive, the item is right-justified in the field; if it is negative, the item is left-justified. A field width of 30 characters should be wide enough for most directory names. Directories don't have a size, so output two hyphens as the size field. They do have a last access time, which can be obtained from the *Directory* class.

10 Process the file entries. This code follows the same pattern as that for the subdirectories but also includes some of the code from the single-file case:

```
// Now do the files
String* files[] = Directory::GetFiles(di->ToString());
for(i=0; i<files->Count; i++)
{
    FileInfo* fci =
```

```
                new FileInfo(files->get_Item(i)->ToString());
            // Files list in lower case
            String* fileName = fci->Name->ToLower();
            Console::Write("{0,30}",fileName);
            if (bSize) Console::Write("{0,12}",
                    __box(fci->Length));
            if (bDate) Console::Write("  {0}",
                File::GetLastAccessTime(
                    fci->ToString()).ToString());

            // Attributes
            if (bAtts)
            {
                FileAttributes fa =
                    File::GetAttributes(fci->ToString());
                Console::Write("  ");
                if (fa & FileAttributes::Normal)
                    Console::Write("<normal>");
                else
                {
                    if (fa & FileAttributes::Archive)
                        Console::Write("a");
                    if (fa & FileAttributes::Hidden)
                        Console::Write("h");
                    if (fa & FileAttributes::System)
                        Console::Write("s");
                    if (fa & FileAttributes::ReadOnly)
                        Console::Write("r");
                }
            }
            // finish the line
            Console::WriteLine();
        }
    }
```

The *Directory::GetFiles* static method returns an array of strings representing the files in the current directory. As before, you construct an object to represent each file and then query it. You do this exactly the same way as for the single-file case earlier in the exercise.

11 Build the application, then open a Console window, change to the project's *Debug* directory, and run the program with a suitable command line, such as:

```
CppFiles sa C:\
```

You should see output similar to the following screenshot:

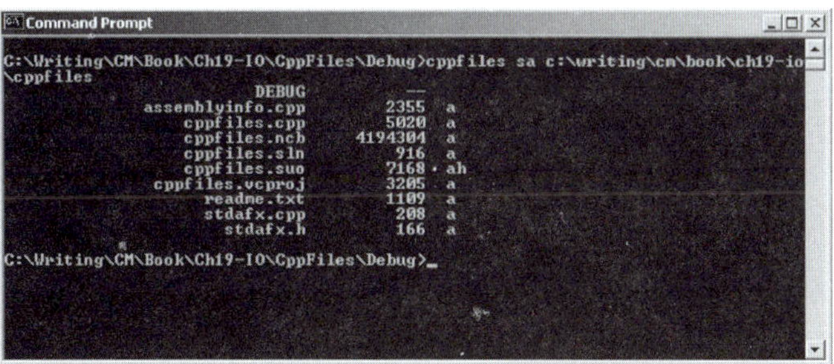

Binary I/O

Binary I/O in the .NET Framework uses the *BinaryReader* and *BinaryWriter* classes, which read and write .NET primitive types in binary format. As with the *TextReader* and *TextWriter* classes, the binary I/O classes use an underlying *Stream* object to provide a byte stream. Both *BinaryReader* and *BinaryWriter* have a *BaseStream* property that gives access to the underlying *Stream*.

The *BinaryWriter* Class

The following table lists the methods provided by *BinaryWriter*.

Method	Description
Close	Closes the writer and the underlying *Stream*
Dispose	Releases the resources used by the writer
Flush	Causes all buffered data to be written to the underlying device
Seek	Sets the seek position within the underlying *Stream*
Write	Writes a value to the *Stream*
Write7BitEncoded	Writes a 32-bit integer in a compressed format

If you look at the documentation, you'll see that the *Write* function has no fewer than 18 overloads for you to cope with when writing the various basic types provided by the .NET Framework. Because not all of the types provided by .NET are CLS-compliant, you need to be careful when using some of the *Write* methods if you intend the data to be read from code written in other .NET languages.

> **note**
>
> The Common Language Subset (CLS) defines types that all .NET languages must support. The signed byte and unsigned integer types are not included in the CLS, and so might not be usable from some .NET languages. The most important of these is Microsoft Visual Basic .NET, which doesn't support any of the non-CLS-compliant types.

The *BinaryReader* Class

The following functions are provided by *BinaryReader*:

Method	Description
Close	Closes the writer and the underlying *Stream*.
Dispose	Releases the resources used by the writer.
FillBuffer	Fills the internal buffer with a number of bytes read from the underlying stream.
PeekChar	Reads the next character but doesn't advance the seek pointer.
Read	Reads one or more bytes or characters from the *Stream*.
Read7BitEncoded	Reads a 32-bit integer that was written in a compressed format.
ReadBoolean	Reads a Boolean from the *Stream*.
ReadByte, *ReadBytes*	Reads one or more *Bytes* from the *Stream*.
ReadChar, *ReadChars*	Reads one or more *Chars* from the *Stream*.
ReadDecimal	Reads a *Decimal* from the *Stream*.
ReadDouble, *ReadSingle*	Reads a double or single precision floating point value from the *Stream*.
ReadInt16, *ReadInt32*, *ReadInt64*	Reads an integer type from the *Stream*.
ReadSByte	Reads a signed byte from the *Stream*. This method is not CLS-compliant.
ReadString	Reads a *String* from the *Stream*.
ReadUInt16, *ReadUInt32*, *ReadUInt64*	Reads an unsigned integer type from the *Stream*. These methods are not CLS-compliant.

Unlike *BinaryWriter*, *BinaryReader* provides separate functions to read each of the basic types.

The exercise that follows shows you how to use the *BinaryReader* and *BinaryWriter* classes to write binary data to a file and read it back. It uses a class, *Customer*, which represents a bank customer who has a name, an account number, and a current balance. The program writes customer details to a file in binary, and reads them back.

1 Create a new Managed C++ Application project called CppBinRead.

2 Add the *using* declaration for *System::IO* to the start of the code, like this:

```
using namespace System::IO;
```

3 Add a new class definition before the *_tmain* function:

```
__gc class Customer
{
    String* name;
    long accNo;
    double balance;
public:
    // Constructors
    Customer() : name(0), accNo(0), balance(0.0) {}
    Customer(String* s, long l, double b) :
        name(s), accNo(l), balance(b) {}

    // Write object data to a BinaryWriter
    void Write(BinaryWriter* bw)
    {
        bw->Write(name);
        bw->Write(accNo);
        bw->Write(balance);
    }

    // Read object data from a BinaryReader
    void Read(BinaryReader* br)
    {
        name = br->ReadString();
        accNo = br->ReadInt32();
        balance = br->ReadDouble();
    }

    // Properties to retrieve the instance variables
    __property String* get_Name() { return name; }
    __property long get_Account() { return accNo; }
    __property double get_Balance() { return balance; }
};
```

The class has three data members: a *String* for the name, a *long* for the account number, and a *double* for the balance. There are constructors to create default and fully populated objects, and a set of read-only properties to allow access to the data members.

The *Read* and *Write* functions use *BinaryReader* and *BinaryWriter* objects to read and write the state of the object in binary format.

4 Edit the *_tmain* function so that it uses the command line argument parameters, as follows:

```
int _tmain(int argc, char* argv[])
```

5 Add the following code to *_tmain* to check that the user passes in a filename, and save the path away as a *String*:

```
// Check for required arguments
if (argc < 2)
{
    Console::WriteLine(S"Usage: CppBinRead path");
    return -1;
}

String* path = new String(argv[1]);
```

This code is very similar to the argument-handling code that has been used in other exercises in this chapter. Note that for simplicity I'm not checking the path for validity, but it is easy—and advisable—to add such a check in a real application.

6 Create some *Customer* objects.

```
Customer* c1 = new Customer(S"Fred Smith", 1234567, 100.0);
Customer* c2 = new Customer(S"Bill Jones", 2345678, 1000.0);
Customer* c3 = new Customer(S"Dave Davies", 3456789,
5000.0);
```

7 To write the objects out, you need a *BinaryWriter* and a *FileStream* to do the output to the file.

```
try
{
    // Create a FileStream
    FileStream* fstrm = new FileStream(path,
FileMode::Create,
                                        FileAccess::ReadWrite);

    // Create a BinaryWriter to use the FileStream
```

```
    BinaryWriter* binw = new BinaryWriter(fstrm);
}
catch(System::Exception* pe)
{
    Console::WriteLine(pe->ToString());
}
```

The *FileStream* will write to a file, creating it if necessary, and the file will be opened with read/write access, because you'll be reading from it later in the program. Once again, it is good practice to put the I/O class creation code in a *try* block to catch any problems that may occur.

8 Writing the object data to the file is simply a case of calling the *Write* function, passing in a pointer to the *BinaryWriter*. Add the following code at the end of the *try* block:

```
c1->Write(binw);
c2->Write(binw);
c3->Write(binw);
```

9 Because the file was opened with read/write access, you can now read from the file. To do this, create a *BinaryReader* object and attach it to the same *FileStream*, as shown here:

```
// Create a BinaryReader that reads from the same FileStream
BinaryReader* binr = new BinaryReader(fstrm);
```

10 Before you can read from a file that you've written to, you have to move the position of the *seek* pointer.

```
// Move back to the beginning
binr->BaseStream->Seek(0, SeekOrigin::Begin);
```

Note that this uses the BaseStream property to get at the underlying *Stream* object. If you haven't met *seek* pointers before, see the explanation in the following sidebar .

Streams and *seek* Pointers

Every stream in .NET has a *seek* pointer associated with it, which represents the position in the *Stream* at which the next read or write operation will take place. This pointer is automatically repositioned when you use *Stream* class methods to read or write the *Stream*, but it is also possible to move it yourself if you need to (and if you know what you're doing).

The most likely time you'll need to do this is when you open a *Stream* for read/write access. Once you've written to the *Stream*, the *seek* pointer will be positioned at the end, ready for the next write. If you want to read from the *Stream*, you'll have to reposition the pointer.

You do this by using the *Seek* method of the *Stream* object, giving it an offset in bytes and a position where the offset should be applied. Offsets can be positive or negative, the sign reflecting whether the offset should move towards the start (negative) or end (positive) of the stream. The possible positions are members of the *SeekOrigin* enumeration, and they can be *SeekOrigin::Current* (the current position), *SeekOrigin::Begin* (the start of the *Stream*), or *SeekOrigin::End* (the end of the *Stream*).

11 Create a new *Customer*, and read its details from the file, as follows:

```
Customer* c4 = new Customer();
c4->Read(binr);
Console::WriteLine("Balance for {0} (a/c {1}) is {2}",
        c4->Name, __box(c4->Account), __box(c4->Balance));
```

The new *Customer* object has all its fields set to default values. The call to *Read* tells it to read its data from the current position in the file.

The obvious potential problem is that the *Read* function will read from wherever the *BinaryReader* is currently positioned. If it isn't at the beginning of a *Customer*'s data, you can expect to get an exception thrown.

tip

If you want to save the state of objects in a real-world program, you wouldn't do it manually like this. The *System::Runtime::Serialization* namespace contains classes that help you save and restore the state of objects in an efficient way.

12 Build and run the application, providing a suitable file name.

Chapter 19 Quick Reference

To	Do This

Write text to a file	Create a *StreamWriter* that outputs to a *FileStream*, and then use the *Write* and *WriteLine* members of *StreamWriter*. For example:
	`FileStream* fs =`
	`    new FileStream("foo.txt");`
	`StreamWriter* sw =`
	`    new StreamWriter(fs);`
	`sw->WriteLine(S"Some text");`
	Flush and close the *StreamWriter* when you're finished with it. For example:
	`sw->Flush(); sw->Close();`

Read text from a file	Create a *StreamReader* that reads from a *FileStream*, and then use the *ReadLine* member of *StreamReader*. For example:
	`FileStream* fs =`
	`    new FileStream("foo.txt");`
	`StreamReader* sr =`
	`    new StreamReader(fs);`
	`String* line = sr->ReadLine();`

Write binary values to a file	Create a *BinaryWriter* that outputs to a *FileStream*, and then use the overloaded *Write* members of *BinaryWriter*. For example:
	`FileStream* fs =`
	`    new FileStream("bar.dat");`
	`BinaryWriter* bw =`
	`    new BinaryWriter(fs);`
	`bw->Write(S"Some text");`
	`bw->Write(100.00);`

Read binary values from a file	Create a *BinaryReader* that reads from a *FileStream*, and then use the ReadXxx members of *BinaryReader*. For example:
	`FileStream* fs =`
	`    new FileStream("foo.txt");`
	`BinaryReader* br =`
	`    new BinaryReader(fs);`
	`String* line = br->ReadString();`
	`Double d = br->ReadDouble();`

Find out about a file	Use the static functions provided by the *File* class. If you're going to do several operations on the same file, consider creating a *FileInfo* object and using that instead.
Find out about a directory	Use the static functions provided by the *Directory* class. If you're going to do several operations on the same file, consider creating a *DirectoryInfo* object and using that instead.

PART 5

Data Access

20

Reading and Writing XML

In this chapter, you'll learn

- ✔ *Why XML is so important to Microsoft .NET*
- ✔ *The classes that make up the .NET XML namespaces*
- ✔ *How to parse XML files using* XmlTextReader
- ✔ *How to validate XML using* XmlValidatingReader
- ✔ *How to write XML using* XmlTextWriter
- ✔ *How to use the* XmlDocument *to manipulate XML in memory*

This is the first of two chapters that introduce you to the XML capabilities of the Microsoft .NET Framework. XML plays a major role in .NET as an enabling technology, and the .NET Framework provides full support for just about everything you'll need to do with XML.

note

This chapter assumes that you already know something about XML. You should be comfortable with elements, attributes, validation, namespaces, and all the other paraphernalia that surrounds XML.

There isn't space to give you a grounding in XML and the XML technologies, so if you haven't met XML before, you might want to consult a book such as *XML Step by Step Second Edition* by Michael Young (Microsoft Press, 2002) before reading further.

XML and .NET

One of the major features of the .NET Framework is that it enables you to easily produce distributed applications that are language-independent, and that will be platform-independent when .NET is ported to other platforms. XML plays a major part in this plan by acting as a simple, portable glue layer that is used to pass data around in distributed applications.

Microsoft has XML-enabled many parts of the .NET Framework, and I'll list a few of the main ones to give you a flavor of where and how they are used:

- It is possible for the results of database queries to be returned as XML, so that they are far more portable than ADO recordset objects. It is also possible to interact with databases more fully using XML.
- Calls can be made to Web Services using SOAP (Simple Object Access Protocol), an XML–based protocol for making remote procedure calls.
- Finding out what a Web Service provider can do for you involves using UDDI, the Universal Description, Discovery, and Integration service. When you query a UDDI service, you post a query in XML, and a description of what is available comes back as more XML.

The .NET XML Namespaces

The .NET Framework contains a number of namespaces supporting XML functionality, as summarized in the following table:

Namespace	Description
System::Xml	The overall namespace for XML support
System::Xml::Schema	Supports for W3C and the Microsoft XDR schemas
System::Xml::Serialization	Supports serializing objects to and from XML
System::Xml::XPath	Supports XPath parsing and evaluation
System::Xml::Xsl	Supports XSLT transformation

This chapter will be mainly concerned with the *System::Xml* namespace and will touch on some of the capabilities of *System::Xml::Schema*. Chapter 21 will cover using the XPath and XSL namespaces.

The XML Processing Classes

There are four main classes in the *System::Xml* namespace for processing XML. I'll briefly list their capabilities and functionality here, before getting into more detailed examination in the rest of the chapter.

- The *XmlTextReader* class is used for fast, forward-only parsing without validation. It will check documents for well-formedness using a DTD (Document Type Definition), but doesn't use it for validating. "Forward only" means that you parse the document from start to finish, and you can't back up in order to reparse an earlier part of the document.
- *XmlValidatingReader* implements a forward-only parser that provides more functionality than *XmlTextReader*, in particular the ability to validate input using DTDs, W3C XSD schemas, or Microsoft XDR schemas. Both *XmlTextReader* and *XmlValidatingReader* are derived from the abstract class *XmlReader*, which provides much of the basic functionality.
- *XmlTextWriter* provides a fast, forward-only way to write XML to streams or files. The XML produced conforms to the W3C XML 1.0 specification, complete with namespace support.
- *XmlDocument* implements the W3C Document Object Model, providing an in-memory representation of an XML document.

Parsing XML with *XmlTextReader*

Let's start by looking at how you can parse XML with the *XmlTextReader* class. *XmlTextReader* provides you with a way to parse XML data that minimizes resource usage. It does this by reading forwards through the document, recognizing elements as it reads. Very little data is cached in memory, but the forward-only style has two main consequences. The first is that it isn't possible to go back to an earlier point in the file without starting to read again from the top. The second consequence is slightly more subtle: elements are read and presented to you one by one, with no context. So if you need to keep track of where an element occurs within the document structure, you'll need to do it yourself. If either of these sound like limitations to you, you might need to use the *XmlDocument* class, which is discussed later in the chapter.

XmlTextReader uses a "pull" model, which means that you call a function to get the next node when you're ready. This is in contrast to the widely used SAX (Simple API for XML Parsing) API, which uses a "push" model, firing events at callback functions that you provide.

The following tables list the main properties and methods of the *XmlTextReader* class.

Property	Description
AttributeCount	Returns the number of attributes on the current node
Depth	Returns the depth of the current node in the tree
Encoding	Returns the character encoding of the document
EOF	Returns *true* if the reader is at the end of the stream
HasValue	Returns *true* if the current node can have a value
IsEmptyElement	Returns *true* if the current element has no value
Item	Gets the value of an attribute
LineNumber	Returns the current line number
LinePosition	Returns the character position within the current line
LocalName	Returns the name of the current element without a namespace prefix
Name	Returns the full name of the current element
Namespaces	Determines whether the parser should use namespaces
NamespaceURI	Gets the namespace URI for the current node
NodeType	Gets the type of the current node
Prefix	Returns the current namespace prefix
ReadState	Returns the state of the reader (for example, closed, at the end of the file, or still reading)
Value	Gets the value for the current node
XmlLang	Gets the current *xml:lang* scope

Method	Description
Close	Changes the state of the reader to *Closed*, and closes the underlying stream
GetAttribute	Gets the value of an attribute
MoveToAttribute	Moves to the attribute with a specified index or name
MoveToElement	Moves to the element that contains the current attribute
MoveToFirstAttribute, *MoveToNextAttribute*	Iterates over the attributes for an element
Read	Reads the next node from the stream
ReadAttributeValue	Processes attribute values that contain entities
ReadBase64, *ReadBinHex*	Reads content encoded as Base64 or BinHex
ReadChars	Reads character content
ReadString	Reads the content of an element or text node as a string

The most important function in the second of these tables is *Read*, which tells the *XmlTextReader* to fetch the next node from the document. Once you've got the node, you can use the NodeType property to find out what you have. You'll get one of the members of the *NodeType* enumeration, whose members are listed in the following table.

Node Type	Description
Attribute	An attribute, for example, *type=hardback*
CDATA	A CDATA section
Comment	An XML comment
Document	The document object, representing the root of the XML tree
DocumentFragment	A fragment of XML that isn't a document in itself
DocumentType	A document type declaration
Element	An XML element
EndElement	The end of an XML element
Entity	An entity declaration
EndEntity	The end of an entity declaration
EntityReference	An entity reference (for example, <)
None	Used if the node type is queried when no node has been read
Notation	A notation entry in a DTD
ProcessingInstruction	An XML processing instruction
SignificantWhitespace	White space in a mixed content model document, or when *xml:space=preserve* has been set
Text	The text content of an element
Whitespace	White space between markup
XmlDeclaration	The XML declaration at the top of a document

The following exercise will show you how to read an XML document using the *XmlTextReader* class. Here's the sample XML document used by this and the other exercises in this chapter, which lists details of three volcanoes, and which contains many common XML constructs:

```
<?xml version="1.0" ?>
<!-- Volcano data -->
<geology>
  <volcano name="Erebus">
    <location>Ross Island, Antarctica</location>
    <height value="3794" unit="m"/>
    <type>stratovolcano</type>
```

```
    <eruption>constant activity</eruption>
    <magma>basanite to trachyte</magma>
  </volcano>
  <volcano name="Hekla">
    <location>Iceland</location>
    <type>stratovolcano</type>
    <height value="1491" unit="m"/>
    <eruption>1970</eruption>
    <eruption>1980</eruption>
    <eruption>1991</eruption>
    <magma>calcalkaline</magma>
    <comment>The type is actually intermediate between crater row
    and stratovolcano types</comment>
  </volcano>
  <volcano name="Mauna Loa">
    <location>Hawaii</location>
    <type>shield</type>
    <height value="13677" unit="ft"/>
    <eruption>1984</eruption>
    <magma>basaltic</magma>
  </volcano>
</geology>
```

1. Create a new Managed C++ Application project, and call it CppTextReader.
2. Add the following two lines to the top of CppTextReader.cpp:

   ```
   #using <System.xml.dll>
   using namespace System::Xml;
   ```

   The code for the XML classes lives in System.xml.dll, so this needs to be included via a *#using* directive. It is also going to be easier to use the classes if you include a *using* directive for the *System::Xml* namespace, as shown here.
3. Because you're going to supply the name of the XML document when you run the program from the command line, change the declaration of the *_tmain* function to include the command line argument parameters, as follows:

   ```
   int _tmain(int argc, char* argv[])
   ```

4. Add this code to the start of the *_tmain* function to check the number of arguments and save the path away:

   ```
   // Check for required arguments
   ```

```
if (argc < 2)
{
    Console::WriteLine(S"Usage: CppTextReader path");
    return -1;
}

String* path = new String(argv[1]);
```

5 Now that you've got the path, create an *XmlTextReader* to parse the file.

```
try
{
    // Create the reader...
    XmlTextReader* rdr = new XmlTextReader(path);
}
catch (Exception* pe)
{
    Console::WriteLine(pe->ToString());
}
```

The *XmlTextReader* constructor takes the name of the document you want to parse. It's a good idea to catch exceptions here, as several things can go wrong at this stage, including passing the constructor a bad path name. You can build and run the application from the command line at this stage if you want to check that the file opens correctly.

Note that *XmlTextReader* isn't limited to reading from files. Alternative constructors let you take XML input from URLs, streams, strings, and other *TextReader* objects.

Parsing the file simply means making repeated calls to the *Read* function until the parser runs out of XML to read. The simplest way to do this is to put a call to *Read* inside a *while* loop.

6 Add this code to the end of the *try* block:

```
// Read nodes
while (rdr->Read())
{
    // do something with the data
}
```

The *Read* function returns *true* or *false* depending on whether there are any more nodes to read.

7 Each call to *Read* positions the *XmlTextReader* on a new node, and you query the NodeType property in order to find out which of the node types listed in the preceding table you are dealing with. Add the following code,

which checks the node type against several of the most common types:

```
// Read nodes
while (rdr->Read())
{
    switch (rdr->NodeType)
    {
    case XmlNodeType::XmlDeclaration:
        Console::WriteLine("-> XML declaration");
        break;
    case XmlNodeType::Document:
        Console::WriteLine("-> Document node");
        break;
    case XmlNodeType::Element:
       Console::WriteLine("-> Element node, name={0}", rdr->Name);
       break;
    case XmlNodeType::EndElement:
        Console::WriteLine("-> End element node, name={0}",
                             rdr->Name);
        break;
    case XmlNodeType::Text:
       Console::WriteLine("-> Text node, value={0}", rdr->Value);
       break;
    case XmlNodeType::Comment:
       Console::WriteLine("-> Comment node, name={0}, value={1}",
                            rdr->Name, rdr->Value);
        break;
    case XmlNodeType::Whitespace:
        break;
    default:
        Console::WriteLine("** Unknown node type");
        break;
    }
}
```

Every time a new node is read, the *switch* statement checks its type against members of the *XmlNodeType* enumeration. I haven't included the cases for every possible node type, but only those that occur in the sample document.

You'll notice that the Name and Value properties are used for some node types. Whether a node has a Name and a Value depends on the node type. For example, elements have names and can have values, while comments have a value (the comment text) but don't have names. Processing instructions normally have both names and values.

Also notice that nodes of type *XmlNodeType::Whitespace* are simply discarded. The volcanoes.xml file contains plenty of white space to make it readable to humans, but the CppTextReader program isn't really interested in white space, so the program prints nothing when it encounters a white space node.

8 Build the application and run it from the command line, giving the name of an XML file:

```
CppTextReader volcanoes.xml
```

The first few lines of the output should look like this:

```
-> XML declaration
-> Comment node, name=, value= Volcano data
-> Element node, name=geology
-> Element node, name=volcano
-> Element node, name=location
-> Text node, value=Ross Island, Antarctica
-> End element node, name=location
-> Element node, name=height
-> Element node, name=type
-> Text node, value=stratovolcano
-> End element node, name=type
-> Element node, name=eruption
-> Text node, value=constant activity
```

The first node is the XML declaration at the top of the document, and that is followed by a comment, whose value is the comment text. Each XML element in the document will produce a matching pair of Element and EndElement nodes, with the content of a node represented by a nested Text node.

You can see that the nodes are presented to you in linear sequence, so if you want to keep track of the hierarchical structure of the document, you're going to have to put code in place to do it yourself.

Verifying Well-Formed XML

XML that is correctly constructed is called well-formed XML. This means that elements will be correctly nested and that every element tag will have a matching end element tag.

If the *XmlTextReader* encounters badly formed XML, it will throw an *XmlException* to tell you what it thinks is wrong. As with all parsing errors, the place where it is reported might be some distance from the real site of the error!

Handling Attributes

XML elements can include attributes, which consist of name/value pairs, and which are always string data. In the sample XML file, the *volcano* element has a *name* attribute, while the *height* element has *value* and *unit* attributes. Here's how to process the attributes on an element:

- Add code to the Element case in the *switch* statement so that it looks like this:

```
case XmlNodeType::Element:
    Console::WriteLine("-> Element node, name={0}", rdr->Name);
    if (rdr->AttributeCount > 0)
    {
        Console::Write("  ");
        while (rdr->MoveToNextAttribute())
           Console::Write(" {0}={1}", rdr->Name, rdr->Value);
       Console::WriteLine();
    }
    break;
```

  The *AttributeCount* property will tell you how many attributes an element has, and the *MoveToNextAttribute* method will let you iterate over the collection of elements, each of which has a name and a value. Alternatively, you could use the *MoveToAttribute* function to position the reader on a particular attribute by specifying either a name or a 0-based index.

Attributes are read along with the element node that they're part of. When reading attributes, you can use the *MoveToElement* method to position the reader back to the parent element. When you run the code, you should see output similar to this for nodes that have attributes:

```
-> Element node, name=height
   value=13677 unit=ft
```

Parsing XML with Validation

XML documents can be checked for validity in a number of ways, and the *XmlValidatingReader* lets you validate XML using the three most common standards:

- Document Type Definitions (DTDs)
- W3C schemas
- Microsoft XDR schemas

XmlValidatingReader has the same set of methods and properties as *XmlTextReader*, with a few additional properties to support validation. These are listed in the following table:

Property	Description
CanResolveEntities	Returns a value indicating whether this reader can resolve entities. *XmlValidatingReader* always returns *true*.
EntityHandling	Specifies the type of entity handling: whether to expand all entities (the default) or to expand character entities and return general entities as nodes.
Reader	A pointer to the underlying *XmlReader*.
Schemas	Returns the collection of schemas used for validation.
SchemaType	Gets a schema type object for the element currently being read. Returns a null reference if called when vali dation is using a DTD.
ValidationType	Specifies the type of validation to perform: none, DTD, Schema, XDR, or Auto. The default is Auto, which will determine the type of validation required from data in the file.

There is one extra method over and above those supported by *XmlTextReader*, and that is *ReadTypedValue*, which gets a .NET CLR type corresponding to a type in validated XML.

You can create an *XmlValidatingReader* to parse XML document fragments from a string or stream, but it is most common to base the validating reader on an underlying *XmlTextReader* object.

The following exercise modifies the *XmlTextReader* program to validate the XML as it is parsed. In order to do validation, you need to have a DTD or schema to validate against. Here's a DTD for the volcano XML data, which I've stored in a file called geology.dtd:

```
<!ELEMENT geology (volcano)+>
<!ELEMENT volcano (location,height,type,eruption+,magma,comment?)>
<!ATTLIST volcano name CDATA #IMPLIED>
<!ELEMENT location (#PCDATA)>
<!ELEMENT height EMPTY>
<!ATTLIST height value CDATA #IMPLIED
                 unit CDATA #IMPLIED>
<!ELEMENT type (#PCDATA)>
<!ELEMENT eruption (#PCDATA)>
<!ELEMENT magma (#PCDATA)>
<!ELEMENT comment (#PCDATA)>
```

note

I've used a DTD for simplicity, but a schema can be used in exactly the same way.

Edit the volcanoes.xml file to add a DOCTYPE reference at the top of the file.

```
<?xml version="1.0" ?>
<!DOCTYPE geology SYSTEM "geology.dtd">
<!-- Volcano data -->
```

If you check the sample XML document against the DTD, you'll notice that there is a problem. The element ordering for the second volcano, Hekla, is location-type-height rather than the location-height-type order demanded by the DTD. So when you parse this XML with validation, you'd expect a validation error from the parser.

1. Add a *using* declaration to the top of the code, as shown here:

   ```
   using namespace System::Xml::Schema;
   ```

   Some of the classes and enumerations are part of the *System::Xml::Schema* namespace, and the inclusion of this *using* declaration will make it easier to refer to them in code.

2. Create an *XmlValidatingReader* based on the existing *XmlTextReader*, like this:

   ```
   // Create the reader...
   XmlTextReader* rdr = new XmlTextReader(path);

   // Create the validating reader and set the validation type
   XmlValidatingReader* xvr = new XmlValidatingReader(rdr);
   xvr->ValidationType = ValidationType::Auto;
   ```

   The constructor for the *XmlValidatingReader* takes a reference to the *XmlTextReader*, which it uses to perform the basic parsing tasks. The last line sets the validation type to Auto, which means that the *XmlValidatingReader* will decide for itself what type of validation to use, based on the references to DTDs or schemas it finds in the XML document.

note

It's not really necessary to set the *ValidationType* in this case because *Auto* is the default, but I included it to show you how to control the validation.

3 Edit all the code that parses the XML to use the *XmlValidatingReader xvr* rather than the *XmlTextReader rdr*, as follows:

```
// Read nodes from the XmlValidatingReader
while (xvr->Read())
{
    switch (xvr->NodeType)
    {
    case XmlNodeType::XmlDeclaration:
        Console::WriteLine("-> XML declaration");
        break;
    case XmlNodeType::Document:
        Console::WriteLine("-> Document node");
        break;
    case XmlNodeType::Element:
        Console::WriteLine("-> Element node, name={0}", xvr->Name);
        break;
    case XmlNodeType::EndElement:
        Console::WriteLine("-> End element node, name={0}",
                            xvr->Name);
        break;
    case XmlNodeType::Text:
        Console::WriteLine("-> Text node, value={0}", xvr->Value);
        break;
    case XmlNodeType::Comment:
        Console::WriteLine("-> Comment node, name={0}, value={1}",
                            xvr->Name, xvr->Value);
        break;
    case XmlNodeType::Whitespace:
        break;
    default:
        Console::WriteLine("** Unknown node type");
        break;
    }
}
```

Because *XmlValidatingReader* provides a superset of *XmlTextReader's* functionality, it is a simple matter to swap between the two.

4 If you now build and run the program, it should throw an exception when it finds the invalid element ordering in the document, plus several more lines of stack trace information.

```
System.Xml.Schema.XmlSchemaException: Element 'volcano' has
invalid
  content. Expected 'height'. An error occurred at
  file:///C:/XMLFiles/volcanoes.xml(14, 2).
   at
System.Xml.XmlValidatingReader.InternalValidationCallback(
                   Object sender, ValidationEventArgs e)
```

Note that the error message gives the line and character position where the parser found the problem, which in this case is line 14, character 2. By default, the parser will throw an exception if it finds a validation error, and if you don't handle it, the program will terminate.

You can improve on this by installing an event handler. The parser fires a *ValidationEvent* whenever it finds something to report to you, and if you install a handler for this event, you'll be able to handle the validation errors yourself and take appropriate action.

5 Event handler functions must be members of a managed class, so create a new class specially to host a static handler function. Add this code before the *_tmain* function:

```
__gc class ValHandler
{
public:
static void ValidationHandler(Object* pSender,
                              ValidationEventArgs* pe)
    {
       Console::WriteLine("Validation Event: {0}", pe->Message);
    }
};
```

The *ValHandler* class contains one static member, which is the handler for a *ValidationEvent*. As usual, the handler has two arguments: a pointer to the object that fired the event, and an argument object. In this case, the handler is passed a *ValidationEventArgs* object that contains details about the parser validation error. This sample code isn't doing anything except printing the error message, but in practice you'd decide what action to take, based on the *Severity* property of the *ValidationEventArgs* object.

6 Link up the handler to the *XmlValidatingReader* in the usual way:

```
XmlValidatingReader* xvr = new XmlValidatingReader(rdr);
xvr->ValidationType = ValidationType::Auto;
```

```
// Set the handler
xvr->ValidationEventHandler +=
    new ValidationEventHandler(0,
&ValHandler::ValidationHandler);
```

Make sure that you set up the handler before you call *Read* to start parsing the XML!

7 Build and run the program once again. This time you won't get the exception message and stack trace, but you will see the messages printed out from the event handler as it finds validation problems.

8 Correct the ordering of the elements in the XML file and run the program again. You shouldn't see any validation messages this time through.

Writing XML Using *XmlTextWriter*

If you've read about XML, you're probably aware that the XML 1.0 specification from W3C describes the serialized form of XML—the way that XML appears when rendered as text—complete with angle brackets, start tags and end tags, and namespace and XML declarations. If you've got some data that you want to write out as XML, it isn't hard to do it manually, but the .NET Framework provides you with the *XmlTextWriter* class to help with a lot of the formatting chores, such as keeping track of indentation and inserting namespace information everywhere it is needed.

The following tables list the properties and methods of the *XmlTextWriter* class.

Property	Description
Formatting	Determines whether the XML is output with indentation. The default is *Formatting::None*.
Indentation	Determines the indentation level. The default is 2.
IndentChar	Represents the indentation character. The default is a space.
Namespaces	Determines whether to support namespaces. The default is *true*.
QuoteChar	Represents the character used to quote attribute values. The value must be a single or double quotation mark, and the default is double.
WriteState	Gets the state of the writer.
XmlLang	Gets a string that represents the value of the *xml:lang* attribute. The value will be null if there is no *xml:lang* attribute in the current scope.
XmlSpace	Represents the value of the *xml:space* attribute.

The state of the writer tells you what the writer is doing at the point you query the property. It will report one of the values from the *WriteState* enumeration, such as *Start* (no write methods have been called yet), *Closed*, *Attribute* (it is writing an attribute), or *Content* (it is writing element content).

Method	Description
Close	Closes the writer and the underlying stream
Flush	Flushes whatever is in the buffer
LookupPrefix	Returns the current namespace prefix, if any
WriteBase64, *WriteBinHex*	Encodes binary bytes as Base64 or BinHex and writes the text
WriteCData	Writes text out as a CDATA section
WriteCharEntity	Writes a Unicode character as a hexadecimal character entity
WriteChars	Writes text
WriteComment	Writes text as an XML comment
WriteDocType	Writes a DOCTYPE declaration
WriteEntityRef	Writes an entity reference
WriteFullEndElement	Writes a full end element tag
WriteName	Writes a name, making sure it is a valid XML name
WriteProcessingInstruction	Writes an XML processing instruction
WriteQualifiedName	Writes an XML qualified name
WriteRaw	Writes raw markup manually
WriteStartAttribute, *WriteEndAttribute*	Writes the start and end of an attribute
WriteStartDocument, *WriteEndDocument*	Writes the start and end of a document
WriteStartElement, *WriteEndElement*	Writes the start and end of an element
WriteString	Writes text
WriteWhitespace	Writes white space

As you can see from the preceding table, writing elements, attributes, and documents needs you to call a *start* and an *end* function. When using *XmlTextWriter*, you don't simply write an element; you write the start tag, then write its content, and then write the end tag. This means that you have to keep track of where you are in the document to ensure that you call the correct *end* functions at the correct time.

This exercise shows you how to write a simple XML document using *XmlTextWriter* and uses most of the major member functions of the class.

1 Start a new Managed C++ Application project, and call it CppXmlWriter.

2 Add to the top of CppXmlWriter.cpp the following two lines that reference the XML DLL and help you access the namespace members:

```
#using <System.xml.dll>
using namespace System::Xml;
```

3 You're going to supply the name of the XML document to write when you run the program from the command line, so change the declaration of the *_tmain* function to include the command line argument parameters, as follows:

```
int _tmain(int argc, char* argv[])
```

4 Add this code to the start of the *_tmain* function to check the number of arguments and save the path away:

```
// Check for required arguments
if (argc < 2)
{
    Console::WriteLine(S"Usage: CppXmlWriter path");
    return -1;
}

String* path = new String(argv[1]);
```

5 Creating an *XmlTextWriter* is very similar to creating an *XmlTextReader*, as follows:

```
try
{
    // Create the writer...
    // Use the default encoding
    XmlTextWriter* writer = new XmlTextWriter(path, 0);
}
catch (Exception* pe)
{
    Console::WriteLine(pe->ToString());
}
```

The writer is created by specifying the path for the new file and the character encoding that should be used. Passing a *null* pointer means that the writer will use the default UTF-8 encoding, which is a good default choice.

note

If you want to use another encoding, such as UTF-7 or ASCII, you can specify a *System::Text::Encoding* object of the appropriate type.

6 Let's write the XML declaration to the file. Add the following code to the end of the *try* block:

```
// Set the formatting
writer->Formatting = Formatting::Indented;

// Write the standard document start
writer->WriteStartDocument();

// Flush and close
writer->Flush();
writer->Close();
```

XmlTextWriter can produce output indented or without formatting. The default is no formatting, so you need to set the *Formatting* property if you want indentation. The defaults for the indentation character (a space) and the indentation level (two characters) are usually quite acceptable.

WriteStartDocument produces a standard XML declaration, and in order to make sure that all the text is output to the file, you should call *Flush* and *Close* before exiting.

7 Write the root element to the document, as shown here:

```
// Write the standard document start
writer->WriteStartDocument();

// Write the start and end of the root element
writer->WriteStartElement("geology");
writer->WriteEndElement();
```

The content of the root element will go between the calls to *WriteStartElement* and *WriteEndElement*. There isn't any content in this case, but you still need both calls. Build and run the application at this stage, giving the name of the XML file.

```
CppXmlWriter foo.xml
```

You'll see that the program writes an empty root element.

```
<?xml version="1.0"?>
<geology />
```

8 Add one of the volcano entries to the root element, to see how some of the other methods of *XmlTextWriter* are used, as shown here:

```
// Start the root element
writer->WriteStartElement("geology");

// Start the volcano element
writer->WriteStartElement("volcano");

// Do the name attribute
writer->WriteAttributeString("name", "Mount St.Helens");

// Write the location element
writer->WriteStartElement("location");
writer->WriteString(S"Washington State, USA");
writer->WriteEndElement();

// Write the height element
writer->WriteStartElement("height");
writer->WriteAttributeString("value", "9677");
writer->WriteAttributeString("unit", "ft");
writer->WriteEndElement();

// Write the type element
writer->WriteStartElement("type");
writer->WriteString(S"stratovolcano");
writer->WriteEndElement();

// Write the eruption elements
writer->WriteStartElement("eruption");
writer->WriteString(S"1857");
writer->WriteEndElement();

writer->WriteStartElement("eruption");
writer->WriteString(S"1980");
writer->WriteEndElement();

// Write the magma element
writer->WriteStartElement("magma");
writer->WriteString(S"basalt, andesite and dacite");
writer->WriteEndElement();
```

```
// Close the volcano element
writer->WriteEndElement();

// Close the root element
writer->WriteEndElement();
```

I've left in the root element code so that you can see how everything nests. Adding extra elements isn't hard, but it is rather long-winded, and you have to be careful to nest all the calls correctly.

9 Build and run the program, providing it with a suitable filename. The file should contain XML that looks very much like this:

```
<?xml version="1.0"?>
<geology>
  <volcano name="Mount St.Helens">
    <location>Washington State, USA</location>
    <height value="9677" unit="ft" />
    <type>stratovolcano</type>
    <eruption>1857</eruption>
    <eruption>1980</eruption>
    <magma>basalt, andesite and dacite</magma>
  </volcano>
</geology>
```

You can see how all the elements contain their attributes, how they are nested correctly, and how everything is properly indented.

Using *XmlDocument*

Our handling of XML so far has been forward-only, which is very light on resource usage but isn't so useful if you need to be able to move around within the XML document. The *XmlDocument* class is based on the W3C Document Object Model, and it is the class that you want to use if you need to browse, modify, or create an XML document.

What Is the W3C Document Object Model?

The Document Object Model (DOM) is a specification for an API that lets programmers manipulate XML held in memory. The DOM specification is language-independent, and bindings are available for many programming languages, including C++. *XmlDocument* is based upon the DOM, with Microsoft extensions.

Because it works with XML in memory, it has several advantages and disadvantages over the *XmlTextReader* forward-only approach.

One advantage is that, in reading the entire document and building a tree in memory, you have access to all the elements and can wander through the document at will. You can also edit the document, changing, adding, or deleting nodes, and write the changed document back to disk again. It is even possible to create an entire XML document from scratch in memory and write it out—serialize it—and this is a useful alternative to using *XmlTextWriter*.

The main disadvantage is that the whole of an XML document is held in memory at once, so the amount of memory needed by your program is going to be proportional to the size of the XML document you're working with. This means that if you're working with a very large XML document—or have limited memory—you might not be able to use *XmlDocument*.

The *XmlDocument* class has a number of properties, methods, and events, the most important of which are summarized in the following three tables.

Property	Description
DocumentElement	Returns the root element for the document.
DocumentType	Returns the DOCTYPE node, if one is present.
InnerXml	Gets or sets the markup representing the children of the current node.
IsReadOnly	Gets a value indicating whether the current node is read-only.
LocalName	Gets the name of the current node without a namespace prefix.
Name	Gets the fully-qualified name of the current node.
NodeType	Gets the type of the current node. The node type will be one of the *XmlNodeType* values listed in the table on page 447.
OwnerDocument	Gets the *XmlDocument* to which the current node belongs.
PreserveWhitespace	Determines whether white space should be regarded as significant. The default is false.

Method	Description
CloneNode	Creates a duplicate of the current node
CreateAttribute	Creates an *XmlAttribute* object
CreateCDataSection	Creates an *XmlCDataSection* object
CreateComment	Creates an *XmlComment* object
CreateDefaultAttribute	Creates a default *XmlAttribute* object
CreateDocumentType	Creates an *XmlDocumentType* object
CreateElement	Creates an *XmlElement* object
CreateEntityReference	Creates an *XmlEntityReference* object
CreateNavigator	Creates an *XPathNavigator* for navigating the object and its contents
CreateNode	Creates a plain *XmlNode*
CreateProcessingInstruction	Creates an *XmlProcessingInstruction* object
CreateTextNode	Creates an *XmlText* object
CreateXmlDeclaration	Creates an *XmlDeclaration* object
GetElementsById	Returns an XML element with the specified ID attribute
GetElementsByTagName	Gets a list of descendent nodes matching a name
ImportNode	Imports a node from another document
Load	Loads XML from a file, URL, *Stream*, or *Reader* object
LoadXml	Loads XML from a *String*

ReadNode	Creates an *XmlNode* based on the current position of an *XmlReader*
Save	Saves the XML document to a file, *Stream*, or *Writer*
WriteContentTo	Saves all the children of the *XmlDocument* node to a *Writer*
WriteTo	Saves the *XmlDocument* to a *Writer*

Event	Description
NodeChanged	Fired when the value of a node has been changed
NodeChanging	Fired when the value of a node is about to be changed
NodeInserted	Fired when a node has been inserted
NodeInserting	Fired when a node is about to be inserted
NodeRemoved	Fired when a node has been removed
NodeRemoving	Fired when a node is about to be removed

The *XmlNode* Class

You'll notice a lot of references to nodes in the preceding tables. The DOM tree that an *XmlDocument* object builds in memory is composed of nodes, each of which is an object of a class that inherits from the abstract *XmlNode* base class. Just about everything in an XML document is represented by a node. For example:

- Elements are represented by the *XmlElement* class.
- Attributes are represented by the *XmlAttribute* class.
- The text content of elements is represented by the *XmlText* class.
- Comments are represented by the *XmlComment* class.

The *XmlNode* class provides common functionality for all these node types, and because this functionality is so important when working with *XmlDocument*, I've listed the properties and methods of *XmlNode* in the following two tables.

Property	Description
Attributes	Gets the collection of attributes for the node.
ChildNodes	Gets all the children of the node as an *XmlNodeList*.
FirstChild, *LastChild*	Gets a pointer to the first and last children of the node.
HasChildNodes	Value is *true* if a node has child nodes.
InnerText	Represents the concatenated values of the node and all its children.
InnerXml, *OuterXml*	InnerXml gets or sets the markup representing the children of the node. OuterXml includes the node and its children.
IsReadOnly	Returns the read-only status of the node.
Item	Gets a child element by name.
Name, *LocalName*, *Prefix*	The name of the node, with or without namespace information.
NextSibling, *PreviousSibling*	Gets a pointer to the node immediately following or preceding a node.
NodeType	Returns an *XmlNodeType* value representing the type of the node.
OwnerDocument	Gets a pointer to the *XmlDocument* that owns this node.
ParentNode	Gets the node's parent node.
Value	Gets or sets the value of the node. What the value represents will depend on the node type.

Method	Description
AppendChild, *PrependChild*	Adds a child to the end or beginning of a node's list of child nodes
Clone, *CloneNode*	Clones a node
CreateNavigator	Creates an *XPathNavigator* for navigating the object and its contents
GetEnumerator	Returns an enumerator for the collection of child nodes
InsertAfter, *InsertBefore*	Inserts a node after or before a specified node
Normalize	Normalizes the tree so that there are no adjacent *XmlText* nodes
RemoveAll	Removes all children and/or attributes of a node
RemoveChild	Removes a specified child node
ReplaceChild	Replaces a specified child node

SelectNodes	Selects a list of nodes matching an XPath expression
SelectSingleNode	Selects the first node that matches an XPath expression
Supports	Tests whether the underlying DOM implementation supports a particular feature
WriteContentTo	Saves all children of the current node
WriteTo	Saves the current node

Perhaps the most important descendent of *XmlNode* is *XmlElement*, which represents an element within a document. This class adds a number of methods to *XmlNode*, most of which are concerned with getting, setting, and removing attributes.

The final exercise in this chapter shows you how to use *XmlDocument*. You'll write a program that reads the volcano XML file into memory and then inserts a new element into the structure.

1 Start a new Managed C++ Application project, and call it CppDom.

2 Add to the top of CppDom.cpp the two following lines that reference the XML DLL and help you access the namespace members:

```
#using <System.xml.dll>
using namespace System::Xml;
```

3 You're going to supply the name of the XML document to read when you run the program from the command line, so change the declaration of the *_tmain* function to include the command line argument parameters, as shown here:

```
int _tmain(int argc, char* argv[])
```

4 Add this code to the start of the *_tmain* function to check the number of arguments and save the path away:

```
// Check for required arguments
if (argc < 2)
{
    Console::WriteLine(S"Usage: CppXmlWriter path");
    return -1;
}

String* path = new String(argv[1]);
```

5 Create a new managed class called *XmlBuilder*, and give it an *XmlDocument** as a data member:

```
__gc class XmlBuilder
{
    XmlDocument* doc;
};
```

You need a managed class because it will be necessary to pass the *XmlDocument* pointer around between functions. You could do this explicitly in the argument list of each function, but it is better to make it a member of a class, so that it can be accessed by all the member functions.

6 Add a constructor that creates an *XmlDocument* object and tell it to load the file that was specified on the command line:

```
public:
XmlBuilder(String* path)
{
    // Create the XmlDocument
    doc = new XmlDocument();

    // Load the data
    doc->Load(path);
    Console::WriteLine("Document loaded");
}
```

Unlike *XmlTextReader*, the *XmlDocument* class reads and parses the file when it is constructed. Note that you're not catching exceptions here: Something might go wrong when opening or parsing the file, but exceptions are left for the caller to handle.

7 Add some code to the *_tmain* function to create an *XmlBuilder* object. Make sure you are prepared to handle any exceptions that occur.

```
try
{
    XmlBuilder* pf = new XmlBuilder(path);
}
catch(Exception* pe)
{
    Console::WriteLine(pe->Message);
}
```

You can try building and running the code at this point; if you see the "Document loaded" message displayed, you know that the document has been loaded and parsed.

The next step is to access the nodes in the tree. The current XML document contains three *volcano* elements; what you'll do is find the second element and insert a new element after it. There are a number of ways in which you could do this, and I'll just illustrate one method. It isn't the most efficient way to do the job, but it does show how to use several *XmlDocument* and *XmlNode* methods and properties.

1 Start working with the tree by getting a pointer to its root. As you'll use this several times, add an *XmlNode** member to the *XmlBuilder* class to hold the root, like this:

```
private:
    XmlNode* root;
```

2 Add the following code to the constructor to get the root node:

```
// Get the root of the tree
root = doc->DocumentElement;
```

DocumentElement returns you the top of the DOM tree. Note that this is not the root element of the XML document, which is one level down.

3 You also need to get the list of child nodes for the root. As you'll be using this again, add an *XmlNodeList** member to the class to hold the list.

```
private:
    XmlNodeList* xnl;
```

4 The following code shows how you can get a list of child nodes and iterate over it. Add this code to the constructor:

```
// get the child node list
xnl = doc->ChildNodes;
IEnumerator* ie = xnl->GetEnumerator();

while (ie->MoveNext() == true)
    Console::WriteLine("Child: {0}",
        (dynamic_cast<XmlNode*>(ie->Current))->Name);
```

The ChildNodes property returns a list of child nodes as an *XmlNodeList*. This is a typical .NET collection class, which means that you can get an enumerator to iterate over the nodes. The code iterates over the child nodes, printing the name of each. Note that, because *Current* returns an *Object** pointer, it has to be cast to an *XmlNode** before you can use the Name property.

5 The *IEnumerator* interface is part of the *System::Collections* namespace, so you need to add the following near the top of the CppDom.cpp file, after the other *using* directives:

```
using namespace System::Collections;
```

If you run this code on the volcanoes.xml file, you should see output similar to the following:

```
Document loaded
Child: xml
Child: geology
Child: #comment
Child: geology
```

The root of the tree has four child nodes: the XML declaration, the DOCTYPE declaration, a comment, and the root node.

note

Once you've verified the existence of the child nodes, you can remove the lines that declare and use the enumerator, as you won't need them again. Make sure you don't remove the line that assigns the value to *xnl*!

6 Now that you've got the root of the tree, you need to find the root element of the XML. That's done by a function called *processChildNodes*, as shown here:

```
void processChildNodes()
{
    // Declare an enumerator
    IEnumerator* ie = xnl->GetEnumerator();

    while (ie->MoveNext() == true)
    {
        // Get a pointer to the node
       XmlNode* pNode = dynamic_cast<XmlNode*>(ie->Current);

        // See if it is the root
        if (pNode->NodeType == XmlNodeType::Element &&
            pNode->Name->Equals(S"geology"))
        {
            Console::WriteLine("  Found the root");
            processRoot(pNode);
        }
    }
}
```

The function creates an enumerator and iterates over the children of the root node. The root XML element will be identified by the fact that it will be of type *XmlNodeType::Element*, and will have the name "geology." Once we've identified that element, the function *processRoot* is then used to process the children of the root XML element.

Here's the *processRoot* function:

```
void processRoot(XmlNode* rootNode)
{
    XmlNode* pVolc =
       dynamic_cast<XmlNode*>(rootNode->ChildNodes->Item(1));

    // Create a new volcano element
    XmlElement* newVolcano = createNewVolcano();

    // Link it in
    root->InsertBefore(newVolcano, pVolc);
}
```

The function is passed in the root node. I know that the file I'm working with has more than two *volcano* elements, and I know that I want to insert a new one before the second element. So I can get a direct reference to the second element by using the Items property on *ChildNodes* to access a child node by index. In real code, you'd obviously need to put in a lot more checking to make sure you were retrieving the desired node.

Once the node has been retrieved, you call *createNewVolcano* to create a new *volcano* element, and then use *InsertBefore* to insert the new one immediately before the node you just retrieved by index.

7 Now add the *createNewVolcano* function, which creates a new *volcano* element. To save space, I haven't given the code for creating the whole element, but just enough that you can see it working.

```
XmlElement* createNewVolcano()
{
    // Create a new element
    XmlElement* newElement = doc->CreateElement("volcano");

    // Set the name attribute
    XmlAttribute* pAtt = doc->CreateAttribute("name");
    pAtt->Value = S"Mount St.Helens";
    newElement->Attributes->Append(pAtt);
```

```
    // Create the location element
    XmlElement* locElement = doc->CreateElement("location");
    XmlText* xt = doc->CreateTextNode(S"Washington State, USA");
    locElement->AppendChild(xt);

    newElement->AppendChild(locElement);

    return newElement;
}
```

The function creates a new *XmlElement* for the volcano. Note that the node classes—*XmlElement*, *XmlComment*, and so on—don't have public constructors, so you need to create them by calling the appropriate factory method. The *name* attribute gets appended to the element's collection of attributes, and then the *location* element is created with its content. Building DOM trees like this is simply a process of creating new nodes and appending them to one another.

8 It would be useful to be able to print out the modified tree, so add a function called *printTree* to the class, as shown here:

```
void printTree()
{
    XmlTextWriter* xtw = new XmlTextWriter(Console::Out);
    xtw->Formatting = Formatting::Indented;

    doc->WriteTo(xtw);
    xtw->Flush();
    Console::WriteLine();
}
```

You've already seen the use of *XmlTextWriter* to create XML manually. You can also use it to output XML from a DOM tree, by linking it up to an *XmlDocument* as shown here.

9 Add calls to *processChildNodes* and *printTree* to the *_tmain* function, and you can build and test the program.

```
try
{
    XmlBuilder* pf = new XmlBuilder(path);
    pf->processChildNodes();

    pf->printTree();
}
```

```
catch(Exception* pe)
{
    Console::WriteLine(pe->Message);
}
```

When you run the program, you'll be able to see that the new node has been added to the tree.

Chapter 20 Quick Reference

To	Do This
Parse XML without validation	Create an *XmlTextReader* and pass it the name of a file. Then use the *Read* method to read nodes from the file.
Parse XML with validation	Create an *XmlTextReader*, and then use it to initialize an *XmlValidatingReader*. Create a handler function for validation events, and attach it to the *ValidationEventHandler* event of the *XmlValidatingReader*.
To work with XML in memory	Create an *XmlDocument*, and use its *Load* or *LoadXml* functions to parse XML into a DOM tree in memory.

21

Transforming XML

In this chapter, you'll learn how to

- ✔ *Use* XPathNavigator *to traverse DOM trees*
- ✔ *Use XPath to select nodes from a document*
- ✔ *Use XSL to transform XML*

The XPath and XSL technologies give you a powerful way to transform XML into other forms. This chapter gives you an introduction to how these technologies are implemented in the Microsoft .NET Framework.

Transforming XML

XML is proving to be a useful way of storing and exchanging data, but it isn't very often that you want to use the data in XML format. You usually need to transform the data into some other form to present it to the end user or use it in programs.

By using the classes in the XML namespaces, such as *XmlTextReader* and *XmlDocument*, you can obviously write programs that parse XML and turn it into other forms. The problem is that this requires programming skills, and in the Web world a lot of people want to manipulate XML but don't have such skills.

XSL (the Extensible Stylesheet Language) was developed to provide a way of transforming XML that doesn't rely on programming skills. Anyone who understands XML syntax can write a style sheet, which is then applied to an XML document to transform it into some other form.

note

If you've encountered cascading style sheets (CSS) when putting a Web site together, you already know how style sheets can be used to manipulate data. XSL is far more fully featured than CSS and permits a much greater range of transformations.

XSLT (XSL Transformations) adds extra constructs to XSL to make it into a simple (and cumbersome!) programming language, and this greatly increases the scope and complexity of the transformations that you can perform. XSL and XSLT are not normally thought of as separate entities, so when I talk about XSL in the rest of this chapter, you can assume that I'm including XSLT as well.

XSL is used for several different types of text-based transformations:

- **Transforming XML into HTML for display.** This is perhaps the most common use for XSL, where data stored in XML is transformed into HTML to be displayed on a browser. One advantage of this approach is that different style sheets can be developed to suit different clients: one for a Pocket PC, one for a desktop browser, one for a WAP phone, and so on. Generating the data is simply a matter of applying the correct style sheet to the data.
- **Transforming XML to XML.** You might need to extract some data from a document, reorder or reformat, or convert between different schemas. For example, two companies might want to exchange customer details in XML, but it is likely that the formats they use will be different. A style sheet could be used to convert XML documents from one format to the other.
- **Transforming XML to other text-based formats, such as PDF or RTF.** This area is still under development, and few tools are available at present.

To use XSL, you create a style sheet and then pass the XML document and the style sheet through an XSL engine, which performs the transformation. An XSL engine is included with the Microsoft MSXML parser, and because this parser is installed with Microsoft Internet Explorer, you don't need to install anything extra to start using XSL.

Before getting into specifics, I'll mention XPath. It is very common in XSL to want to pick out particular elements or groups of elements. For instance, I might want to display all the *title* elements as <h1> HTML headings, or all *author* elements in bold. XPath (the XML Path Language) provides a syntax for selecting elements based on their names, relationships within the document, and other criteria.

> **note**
>
> If you've met regular expressions in text editors or programming languages, you have an idea of how XPath works: XPath is used to select elements, rather than text, from a document.

Using XPath

XPath provides a way to specify selection criteria for elements, such as "all the items that cost more than $30" or "the invoices that are more than 30 days old." XPath expressions are normally used in XSL style sheets but can also be used from code to select elements from a Document Object Model (DOM) tree.

The *XPathNavigator* Class

Before you can try using XPath, let me introduce the *XPathNavigator* class, which is part of the *System::Xml::XPath* namespace. In the previous chapter, you encountered two ways of parsing XML. *XmlTextReader* provided a simple, forward-only mechanism, where you used the *Read* method to read the elements in sequence. *XmlDocument* read the entire document into memory, but you had to walk through the tree manually. One of the main differences between these two classes is that *XmlTextReader* always has the idea of a current node, but *XmlDocument* does not. *XPathNavigator* is a class that sits on top of an *XmlDocument* and navigates through the document for you. Like *XmlTextReader*, it has the notion of a current position, but unlike *XmlTextReader*, you aren't restricted to moving forward through the document.

The following tables list the most commonly used properties and methods of the *XPathNavigator* class. You'll notice that there is a certain amount of overlap with the *XmlDocument* class.

Property	Description
HasAttributes	Set to *true* if the current element has attributes.
HasChildren	Set to *true* if the current node has children.
IsEmptyElement	Set to *true* if the current element has no content.
Name, *LocalName*	The name of the current node, with or without a namespace prefix.
NodeType	The node type. This will be one of the *XmlNodeType* values listed on page 447.
Prefix	The current namespace prefix, if any.
Value	The value of the current node.
XmlLang	The value of the *xml:lang* attribute.

Method	Description
Clone	Creates a new *XPathNavigator* positioned to the same point.
ComparePosition	Compares the position of two navigators.
Compile	Compiles an XPath expression into an *XpathExpression* object.
Evaluate	Evaluates an XPath expression.
GetAttribute	Gets the value of a named attribute.
GetNamespace	Gets the value of a namespace node corresponding to a local name.
IsDescendant	Returns *true* if an XPathNavigator is a descendant of the current navigator. One navigator is a descendant of another if it is positioned on a descendant node.
IsSamePosition	Returns *true* if two navigators are positioned on the same node.
Matches	Returns *true* if the current node matches an XPath expression.
MoveTo	Moves a navigator to the same position as another navigator.
MoveToAttribute	Positions the navigator on a given attribute.
MoveToFirst, *MoveToNext*, *MoveToPrevious*	Moves between nodes at the same level in the tree (sibling nodes).
MoveToFirstAttribute, *MoveToNextAttribute*	Moves to the first and subsequent attributes of an element.
MoveToFirstChild	Moves to the first child element. Returns *false* if there are no children.
MoveToId	Moves to a node with the specified ID attribute.

MoveToNamespace, *MoveToNextNamespace*	Moves to namespace nodes.
MoveToParent	Moves up one level in the tree.
MoveToRoot	Moves to the root of the tree.
Select	Selects zero or more nodes based on an XPath expression.
SelectAncestors	Selects ancestors of the current node.
SelectChildren	Selects children of the current node.
SelectDescendants	Selects descendants of the current node.

Using *XPathNavigator*

This exercise will show you how to create an *XPathNavigator* and use it to move around a document. It uses the same volcanoes.xml file used in the exercises in Chapter 20.

1 Create a new Managed C++ Application project. Call it CppNavigator.

2 Add the following three lines to the top of CppNavigator.cpp:

```
#using <System.xml.dll>
using namespace System::Xml;
using namespace System::Xml::XPath;
```

The code for the XML classes lives in System.xml.dll, so this needs to be included by means of a *#using* directive. It is also going to be easier to use the classes if you include *using* directives for the *System::Xml* and *System::Xml::XPath* namespaces, as shown here.

3 You're going to supply the name of the XML document when you run the program from the command line, so change the declaration of the *_tmain* function to include the command line argument parameters, like this:

```
int _tmain(int argc, char* argv[])
```

4 Add this code to the start of the *_tmain* function to check the number of arguments and save the path away:

```
// Check for required arguments
if (argc < 2)
{
    Console::WriteLine(S"Usage: CppNavigator path");
    return -1;
}

String* path = new String(argv[1]);
```

21 Transforming XML

5 Now that you've got the path, create an *XmlDocument* to parse the file and load it into a DOM tree.

```
try
{
    // Create the XmlDocument to parse the file
    XmlDocument* doc = new XmlDocument();

    // Load the file
    doc->Load(path);
    Console::WriteLine("Document loaded");
}
catch(Exception* pe)
{
    Console::WriteLine(pe->Message);
}
```

As I explained in the *XmlDocument* example in the previous chapter, it is a good idea to be prepared to catch exceptions when using *XmlDocument*, because it will throw exceptions if it has problems opening the file and if it finds any parsing errors.

6 Create an *XPathNavigator* that uses the *XmlDocument*. Add this, and following code in this exercise, to the end of the *try* block:

```
// Create the navigator
XPathNavigator* nav = doc->CreateNavigator();
```

The navigator will let you navigate over the tree created by the *XmlDocument*.

> **note**
>
> It is also possible to create *XPathNavigators* to work with fragments of XML documents, by using an alternative constructor that takes a pointer to a node somewhere in the document.

7 The following lines of code show how you use the navigator to walk through the document:

```
// Move to the top of the tree and print details
nav->MoveToRoot();
Console::WriteLine("top: name={0}, type={1}, value={2}",
                   nav->Name,
```

```
                    __box(nav->NodeType)->ToString(),
                    nav->Value);
// Move to the first child, which is a comment
nav->MoveToFirstChild();
Console::WriteLine("first child: name={0}, type={1}",
                    nav->Name,
                    __box(nav->NodeType)->ToString());
// Move to the next element, which is the root element
nav->MoveToNext();
Console::WriteLine("next child: name={0}, type={1}",
                    nav->Name,
                    __box(nav->NodeType)->ToString());
// Move to the next element, which will be the first
// volcano
nav->MoveToFirstChild();
Console::WriteLine("next child: name={0}, type={1}",
                    nav->Name,
                    __box(nav->NodeType)->ToString());
if (nav->HasAttributes)
{
    nav->MoveToFirstAttribute();
    Console::WriteLine(" attribute: name={0}, type={1}",
                        nav->Name, nav->Value);
    nav->MoveToParent();
}
```

The navigator isn't positioned on any node initially, so you need to call *MoveToRoot* to move it to the top of the tree. As with *XmlDocument*, this isn't the root element of the XML, but the top of the DOM tree.

Move around the tree by calling the various *Move* methods. You need to be careful to distinguish between sibling and child nodes: *MoveToNext* and *MoveToPrevious* will move between sibling nodes at the same level in the tree, whereas *MoveToFirstChild*, *MoveToNextChild*, and the other *Child* functions move down a level to work with child nodes. You can use *MoveToParent* to move back up a level when you've finished processing child nodes.

In this example, *MoveToRoot* positions the *XPathNavigator* object at the root of the DOM tree. If you look at the output from this code, you'll see that the root doesn't have a name. Its type is *Root*, and its value is a long string of text, which represents the concatenated values of all its child nodes. This is not very useful, but it *is* logical, because the value of an element consists of its value plus the value of all its children.

This code uses the *Name*, *NodeType*, and *Value* properties; Whether the node has a *Name* and a *Value* will depend on the NodeType.

You're navigating down to the first *volcano* element, and because it has a *name* attribute, the code prints out the details of the first attribute. Note the call to *MoveToParent* after the attribute details have been printed: Attributes are children of their parent node, so when you've finished processing the attributes, you have to move one level up in order to point the navigator back at the parent element.

8 Experiment with adding more code to the program to print out selected elements and attributes, and make sure that you're getting the results you expect!

Using XPath with *XPathNavigator*

Now that you know how to create and use an *XPathNavigator*, let's move on to XPath itself. The XPath expression language is very complex and capable of defining extremely precise matches. This chapter isn't the place for anything like a full explanation of XPath expressions, but you'll find an introduction to the topic in the following sidebar, "Basic XPath Syntax." For more details about XPath, consult the XML SDK documentation provided by the Microsoft Developer Network (MSDN) at *http://msdn.microsoft.com/library*.

Basic XPath Syntax

In case you haven't encountered XPath before, here is an introduction to the very simplest XPath syntax.

XPath uses pattern matching to create expressions that match one or more elements within a document. You create basic expressions using element names, with child relationships denoted by forward slash marks (/). The syntax is very similar to specifying file and directory paths. For example,

```
foo/bar
```

specifies *bar* as a child of *foo*. When passed to an XPath processor and evaluated, it will match all *bar* elements that are children of *foo* elements. A leading slash mark means that the search should begin at the root, an asterisk matches any element, and two slash marks (//) will match any number of levels in the tree. Here are a few more examples:

```
books//price      -- match price elements any number of levels below
       books
books/*/author   -- match author elements that are grandchildren of books
/company          -- match company elements that occur at the root
```

Simple conditionals can be represented with square brackets ([]), so that

```
order[subtotal]
```

will match *order* elements that have a child *subtotal* element. To match attributes, use an at sign (@) sign, short for attribute. The following line

```
volcano[@name]
```

will match all *volcano* elements that have a *name* attribute.

When an XPath engine evaluates an expression, it returns a list of the nodes that match, and this list might contain zero, one, or more nodes. It's important to note that these nodes are now completely out of context, and you can't tell where in the document they occur, or what relationship they have to one another.

You can use XPath to select a set of nodes using *XPathNavigator*'s *Select* function, as demonstrated in the following brief exercise.

1. Continue with the same project. Add the following code, which will set the *XPathNavigator* back to the top of the document tree:

```
// Move back to the root
Console::WriteLine(S"XPath test...");
nav->MoveToRoot();
```

2 The following code will select all the *volcano* elements that are children of *geology*:

```
XPathNodeIterator* xpi = nav->Select("/geology/volcano");
Console::WriteLine(S"Select returned {0} nodes",
                   __box(xpi->Count));
```

The *Select* function takes a string representing an XPath expression and passes it to the XPath engine. The function returns an *XPathNodeIterator** that you can use to iterate over the set of nodes retrieved by the XPath engine. You can find out how many nodes were retrieved by using the Count property on the *XPathNodeIterator*.

XPathNodeIterator is basically an enumerator, so it supports the *MoveNext* method and the Current property. The following code will print out details of all the elements in the node list:

```
while (xpi->MoveNext())
{
    XPathNavigator* xpn = xpi->Current;
    Console::Write("node: name={0}, type={1}", xpn->Name,
                   __box(xpn->NodeType)->ToString());
    xpn->MoveToFirstAttribute();
    Console::WriteLine(", name={0}", xpn->Value);
}
```

As usual, *MoveNext* moves from item to item in the collection. You might expect Current to return you a pointer to a node, but it actually returns a pointer to another *XPathNavigator*, which you use to investigate the tree of elements under the current item. The *Write* statement writes out the node name and type, and then you retrieve the first attribute, which holds the name of the volcano.

3 Build and run the program. This part should give you the following output:

```
XPath test...
Select returned 3 nodes
node: name=volcano, type=Element, name=Erebus
node: name=volcano, type=Element, name=Hekla
node: name=volcano, type=Element, name=Mauna Loa
```

4 Modify the expression to return only those *volcano* elements that have a *comment* child element, as shown here:

```
XPathNodeIterator* xpi = nav->Select("/geology/
volcano[comment]");
```

You should now get only one child node returned.

note

If you're going to use the same XPath expression several times, you can compile it to produce an *XPathExpression*. This object can be used in *Select* statements instead of a string, and it cuts out the text parsing step.

Using XSL

To transform a document using XSL, you need to create a style sheet that defines the transformation and then pass the style sheet to the XSL processor. The first important thing to note is that XSL style sheets are simply XML documents: They have all the familiar syntax and are written, structured, and processed in just the same way as any other XML document.

XSL transformations are handled using the *XslTransform* class from the *System::Xml::Xsl* namespace. The class has only three members and is very simple to use. Here's the typical sequence you follow to apply a transformation:

1. Create an *XslTransform* object.
2. Use its *Load* method to load the style sheet from a file, a URL, an *XmlReader*, or an *XPathNavigator*.
3. Call the *Transform* method to perform the transformation. You can input and output data in a number of ways, as you'll see in the example.

The following short exercise will show you how to process XML using an XSL style sheet. Like XPath, XSL is too complex to introduce in any detail here, but if you haven't met XSL before, you'll find basic details in the following sidebar, "The Basics of XSL Style Sheets."

The Basics of XSL Style Sheets

This brief explanation of how XSL style sheets work should help you understand the one used in the exercise. First, XSL style sheets are simply another type of XML document, so they have to obey all the usual rules: They start with an XML declaration, they contain a single root element, and all elements must nest and be closed correctly.

An XSL style sheet is defined by a *stylesheet* element, which has to define the XSL namespace and the version attribute. This namespace has to use the correct URL; otherwise, the element won't be recognized as an XSL style sheet. It is normal for the namespace prefix to be "xsl," but this isn't essential.

XSL works by specifying templates that use XPath expressions to match sets of nodes in the document. The following example sheet defines one template that matches the root element. When the style sheet is processed, the XSL engine looks at the body of the template and applies it to the node list. Any other XSL commands are processed, and anything it doesn't recognize as an XSL command gets echoed to the output. In this example, the HTML isn't recognized as XSL commands, so it is echoed to the output.

Note that content—such as the HTML—is still processed by the XSL processor, so it has to be valid XML. All elements must be correctly nested and must have closing tags.

There are a number of XSL commands, two of which are used in the example. The *xsl:for-each* command provides a looping construct which loops over all the nodes that match the current template. The *xsl:value-of* command typically retrieves the value of an element or attribute. You can see in the example how the two attributes of the *height* element are used to build the contents of the table cell.

Here's the style sheet that I'll use to transform the XML. It contains one template that matches the root element and then prints out some of the fields for each *volcano* element in a table.

```
<?xml version="1.0" ?>
<xsl:stylesheet xmlns:xsl="http://www.w3.org/1999/XSL/Transform"
version="1.0">

<xsl:template match="/geology">
<html>
```

```
<head><title>Volcanoes</title></head>
<body>
<h1>Volcanoes</h1>
<table width="75%" border="1">
<tr>
  <th>Name</th>
  <th>Location</th>
  <th>Height</th>
  <th>Type</th>
</tr>
<xsl:for-each select="volcano">
  <tr>
  <td><xsl:value-of select="@name"/></td>
  <td><xsl:value-of select="location"/></td>
  <td><xsl:value-of select="height/@value"/>
              <xsl:value-of select="height/@unit"/></td>
  <td><xsl:value-of select="type"/></td>
  </tr>
</xsl:for each>
</table>
</body>
</html>
</xsl:template>
</xsl:stylesheet>
```

Here's how to use this style sheet to transform the XML.

1 Create a new Managed C++ Application project, and call it CppXsl.

2 Add the following four lines to the top of CppXsl.cpp:

```
#using <System.xml.dll>
using namespace System::Xml;
using namespace System::Xml::XPath;
using namespace System::Xml::Xsl;
```

The code for the XML classes lives in System.xml.dll, so this needs to be included via a *#using* directive. It's easier to use the classes if you include *using* directives for the three XML namespaces, as shown here.

3 You're going to supply the names of the XML document to transform and the style sheet to use when you run the program from the command line, so change the declaration of the *_tmain* function to include the command line argument parameters, like this:

```
int _tmain(int argc, char* argv[])
```

4 Add the following code to the start of the *_tmain* function to check the number of arguments and save the path away:

```
// Check for required arguments
if (argc < 3)
{
    Console::WriteLine(
          S"Usage: CppXsl xml-file stylesheet");
    return -1;
}

String* path = new String(argv[1]);
String* xslpath = new String(argv[2]);
```

5 Now that you've got the path, create an *XmlDocument* to parse the file and load it into a DOM tree.

```
try
{
    // Create the XmlDocument to parse the file
    XmlDocument* doc = new XmlDocument();

    // Load the file
    doc->Load(path);
    Console::WriteLine("Document loaded");
}
catch(Exception* pe)
{
    Console::WriteLine(pe->Message);
}
```

As before, it is a good idea to be prepared to catch exceptions when using *XmlDocument*, because it will throw exceptions if it encounters any problems with opening or parsing the file.

6 Now create an *XPathNavigator* that uses the *XmlDocument*, and position it at the root. Add this, and following code in this exercise, to the end of the *try* block:

```
// Create the navigator and position it
XPathNavigator* nav = doc->CreateNavigator();
nav->MoveToRoot();
```

7 Create an *XslTransform* object and load the style sheet, as shown here:

```
// Create the XslTransform and load it
XslTransform* xslt = new XslTransform();
xslt->Load(xslpath);
```

The *Load* function loads the style sheet, parsing it just like any other XML document. Always put calls to *Load* inside a *try* block to catch file loading and parsing errors.

> **note**
>
> *Load* can also take its input from an *XmlReader* or an *XPathNavigator*.

8 The output from this transformation is going to be HTML, so it would be useful to output it properly formatted. As you saw in the previous chapter, *XmlTextWriter* is used to output formatted XML, so you can create an *XmlTextWriter* to write its output to the Console, using the following code:

```
// Create a writer for output
XmlTextWriter* xtw = new XmlTextWriter(Console::Out);
xtw->Formatting = Formatting::Indented;
```

9 Now you can do the transformation, like this:

```
// Do the transformation
xslt->Transform(nav, 0, xtw);
```

The first argument to *Transform* is the source of the XML, which in this case is an *XPathNavigator*. The second argument, which we're not using, lets you pass data into the transform using an *XslArgumentList* object. The third argument specifies the destination for the output, which is the Console via the *XmlTextWriter*.

10 Build and run the program from the command line, specifying the names of the XML and XSL files. You should see HTML output like this:

```
<html>
  <head>
    <title>Volcanoes</title>
  </head>
  <body>
    <h1>Volcanoes</h1>
    <table width="75%" border="1">
      <tr>
        <th>Name</th>
        <th>Location</th>
```

```
        <th>Height</th>
        <th>Type</th>
      </tr>
      <tr>
        <td>Erebus</td>
        <td>Ross Island, Antarctica</td>
        <td>3794m</td>
        <td>stratovolcano</td>
      </tr>
      <tr>
        <td>Hekla</td>
        <td>Iceland</td>
        <td>1491m</td>
        <td>stratovolcano</td>
      </tr>
      <tr>
        <td>Mauna Loa</td>
        <td>Hawaii</td>
        <td>13677ft</td>
        <td>shield</td>
      </tr>
    </table>
  </body>
</html>
```

The data has been extracted from the XML file and merged with HTML to create the output. Here's how the output looks in a browser:

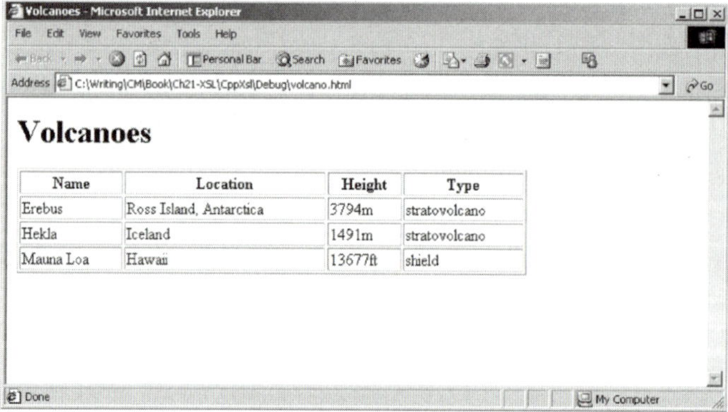

Chapter 21 Quick Reference

To	Do This
Navigate forward and back over an *XmlDocument*	Create an *XPathNavigator*.
Select nodes based on XPath expressions	Use the *XPathNavigator Select* function.
Transform XML using an XSL style sheet	Create an *XslTransform* object, load the style sheet using the *Load* method, and then call the *Transform* method to perform the transformation.

CHAPTER

22

Using ADO.NET

In this chapter, you'll learn how to

- ✔ *Connect to a Microsoft SQL Server database*
- ✔ *Execute SQL statements to query the database*
- ✔ *Execute SQL statements to update the database*
- ✔ *Create disconnected applications, which use a* DataSet *to cache tables in memory*
- ✔ *Create a report displaying data from the database*

ADO.NET is the data access API from Microsoft for the Microsoft .NET Framework. ADO.NET has been optimized to work with .NET to enable distributed applications and services to exchange data easily and reliably.

ADO.NET offers two distinct programming models, depending on the type of application you need to build:

- If your application can obtain and maintain a direct connection to a data source, you can use classes such as *SqlConnection*, *SqlCommand*, and *SqlDataReader* to exchange data with the data source. These classes are superficially similar to previous versions of ADO, but you'll find many differences when you look into the details.
- If your application is disconnected from a data source, you can use a *DataSet* to represent an in-memory cache of data from the data source. *DataSet* is the most important new class in ADO.NET, because it enables you to freely pass data between applications and services residing on different tiers in your architecture.

In this chapter, you will learn how to use ADO.NET to connect to a data source, execute queries, and perform database update operations.

You will also learn how to use *DataSets* in a disconnected application. You will see how to fill a *DataSet* with data from a database and display the data in a *DataGrid*.

> **note**
> ADO.NET provides access to any kind of database. The examples in this chapter describe how to use Microsoft SQL Server 2000.

What Is ADO.NET?

ADO.NET is a strategic API from Microsoft for data access in the modern era of distributed, Internet-based applications. ADO.NET contains a set of interfaces and classes that enable you to work with data from a wide range of databases, including SQL Server, Oracle, Sybase, Microsoft Access, and so on.

ADO.NET Data Providers

ADO.NET uses the concept of a data provider to provide efficient access to different types of databases. Each data provider includes classes to connect to a particular type of database. The .NET Framework includes two data providers, as shown in the following table.

Data provider	Description
SQL Server .NET data provider	Contains classes that give optimized access to Microsoft SQL Server 7.0 and later
OLE DB .NET data provider	Contains classes that give access to Microsoft SQL Server 6.5 and earlier. Also provides access to databases such as Oracle, Sybase, Access, and so on.

ADO.NET Namespaces

The classes in ADO.NET are divided into the six namespaces shown in the following table.

Namespace	Description
System::Data	This is the core namespace in ADO.NET, and contains generic classes that are used for any type of data source. For example, the *DataSet* class is defined in this namespace.
System::Data::Common	Defines common interfaces that are implemented appropriately by each data provider.
System::Data::SqlClient	Defines classes for the SQL Server data provider. These classes include *SqlConnection*, *SqlCommand*, *SqlParameter*, *SqlDataReader*, *SqlTransaction*, and *SqlDataAdapter*. (A data adapter is a special object that enables you to load and save data in a *DataSet*; you will learn more about data adapters later in this chapter.)
System::Data::OleDb	Defines classes for the OLE DB data provider. These classes include *OleDbConnection*, *OleDbCommand*, *OleDbParameter*, *OleDbDataReader*, *OleDbTransaction*, and *OleDbDataAdapter*.
System::Data::SqlTypes	Defines classes that represent native SQL Server data types.
System::Xml	Defines XML–related classes. ADO.NET is tightly integrated with XML. For example, there is a class named *XmlDataDocument* in the *System::Xml* namespace that enables you to treat relational data as if it were an XML document. See *XmlDataDocument* in Microsoft Visual Studio .NET Help for details.

ADO.NET Assemblies

The majority of ADO.NET classes are in the *System::Data* assembly (one notable exception is the *XmlDataDocument* class, which is in the *System::Xml* assembly). To use these assemblies, include the following statements in your application:

```
#using <System.Data.dll>  // This assembly contains ADO.NET classes
#using <System.Xml.dll>   // This assembly contains XML classes,
                          //   such as XmlDataDocument
```

Once you have imported these assemblies, you can import the required namespaces for your application. For example, if you need to access a SQL Server 2000 database, you need the following *using* statement:

```
using System::Data::SqlClient;
```

Creating a Connected Application

In the next few pages, you will create a Managed C++ application that connects to a SQL Server 2000 database. You will use a *SqlConnection* object to establish this connection.

Once you are connected, you will create a *SqlCommand* object to represent a SQL statement. You will then perform the following tasks:

- Execute a statement that returns a single value. *SqlCommand* has an *ExecuteScalar* method for this purpose.
- Execute a statement that updates the database. *SqlCommand* has an *ExecuteNonQuery* method to do this.
- Execute a statement that queries the database. *SqlCommand* has an *ExecuteReader* method to do this. *ExecuteReader* returns a *SqlDataReader* object, which provides fast forward-only access to the rows in the result set. You will use this *SqlDataReader* object to process the result set.

Connecting to a Database

In this exercise, you will create a new application to perform all the operations described above. The first step is to connect to the database.

1. Create a Managed C++ Application project called ConnectedApplication.
2. Open the Solution Explorer, and look at the Source Files folder. Double-click ConnectedApplication.cpp to view it in the code editor.
3. After the statement *#using <mscorlib.dll>*, add the following statement:

```
#using <System.dll>         // For Console I/O
#using <System.Data.dll>    // For ADO.NET
```

   This enables you to use classes that reside in the *System.Data.dll* assembly.

4. After the statement *using namespace System*, add the following statements:

```
using namespace System::Data;              // Generic ADO.NET
                                           // definitions
using namespace System::Data::SqlClient;   // Specific
                                           // definitions
                                           // for SQL
                                           // Server data
                                           // provider
```

note

The SQL Server data provider supports SQL Server 7.0 and later. If you want to access a different type of database, you must use the OLE DB data provider instead. To do so, use the following statement:

```
using namespace System::Data::OleDb;
```

5 In the *_tmain* function, create a *SqlConnection* object as follows:

```
SqlConnection * cnPubs = new SqlConnection();
```

note

If you are using the OLE DB data provider, create an *OleDbConnection* object instead of a *SqlConnection* object.

This is a general issue that applies throughout this example. If you are using the SQL Server .NET data provider, use classes prefixed as *Sql** (for example, *SqlException*). If you are using the OLE DB data provider, use classes prefixed as *OleDb** (for example, *OleDbException*).

6 The *SqlConnection* object has a ConnectionString property, which enables you to specify the server, database, and security credentials (and many other connection properties, too). Set the ConnectionString property as follows:

```
cnPubs->ConnectionString =
    S"data source=(local);integrated security=true;"
    S"initial catalog=Pubs";
```

This connection string defines a connection to the local SQL Server instance. The *integrated security=true* parameter instructs SQL Server to use integrated Microsoft Windows authentication to authenticate the user, rather than SQL Server authentication. The *initial catalog=Pubs* parameter indicates that we want to access data in the *Pubs* database.

note

If you want to use SQL Server authentication rather than integrated Windows authentication, specify the following information in the connection string:

```
"integrated
security=false;userid=theUser;password=thePassword"
```

7 Open the database connection as follows:

```
try
{
     cnPubs->Open();
    Console::WriteLine(
       S"Connected to database successfully!");
}
catch (SqlException * Xcp)
{
     Console::Write(S"Error occurred: ");
     Console::WriteLine(Xcp->Message);
}
```

Just about everything you do with databases can generate an exception. Therefore, you should always enclose your database code in a *try* and *catch* block, as shown in the code above.

8 At the end of the *_tmain* function, close the database connection as follows:

```
if (cnPubs->State != ConnectionState::Closed)
{
     cnPubs->Close();
}
Console::WriteLine(
   S"The database connection is now closed");
```

The State property indicates the current state of the connection. The allowable values for this property are defined in the *ConnectionState* enumerated type, which is located in the *System::Data* namespace.

9 Build your program, and fix any compiler errors.

10 Run the program. If all is well, you'll see the following message displayed on the Console:

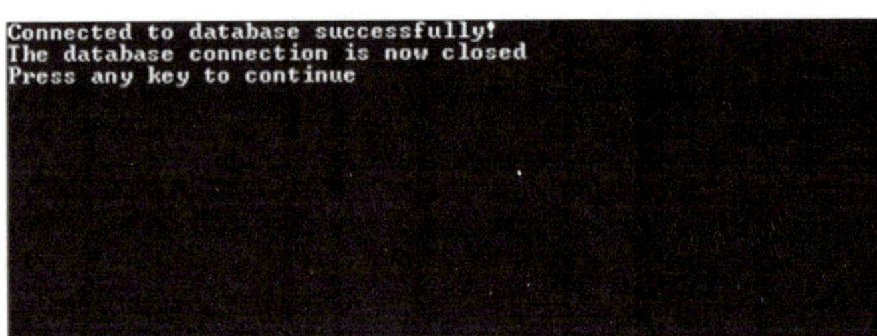

Creating and Executing a Command

In this exercise, you will create a *SqlCommand* object that represents the following SQL statement:

```
SELECT COUNT(*) FROM titles
```

This statement returns an integer indicating how many rows are in the *titles* table. You will execute this statement by using the *ExecuteScalar* method on the *SqlCommand* object.

1 Continue using your Managed C++ Application project from the previous exercise.

2 In the *_tmain* function, add the following code to the *try* block (after the statement that opens the database connection):

```
SqlCommand * cmTitles = new SqlCommand();
cmTitles->CommandText = S"SELECT COUNT(*) FROM Titles";
cmTitles->CommandType = CommandType::Text;
cmTitles->Connection = cnPubs;
```

This code creates and configures a *SqlCommand* object to encapsulate a SQL statement. The *CommandText* property defines the SQL to be executed or the name of a stored procedure. The *CommandType* property indicates whether *CommandText* is a SQL statement (*CommandType::Text*) or a stored procedure name (*CommandType::StoredProcedure*). The *Connection* property specifies which database connection to use when executing the command.

note

You could write the previous code sample more concisely, as follows:

```
SqlCommand * cmTitles = new SqlCommand(S"COUNT(*) FROM
Titles", cnPubs);
```

3 Add the following code to execute the SQL statement and display the results on the Console:

```
Object * numberOfTitles = cmTitles->ExecuteScalar();
Console::Write(S"Number of titles: ");
Console::WriteLine(numberOfTitles);
```

4 Build your program, and fix any compiler errors.

5 Run the program. The following message should be displayed on the Console:

```
Connected to database successfully!
Number of titles: 18
The database connection is now closed
Press any key to continue
```

Executing a Command that Modifies Data

In this exercise, you will execute a command that increases the price of all books by 5 percent. You will use the following SQL statement:

```
UPDATE titles SET price = price * 1.05 WHERE price IS NOT NULL
```

You will use the *ExecuteNonQuery* method to execute this statement. *ExecuteNonQuery* returns an integer to indicate how many rows were affected by the statement.

> **note**
>
> The *WHERE* clause in the SQL statement is required in this example, because some titles have a *NULL* price. The publisher hasn't decided the price of these books yet, so we must not try to increase these prices.

1. Continue using your Managed C++ Application project from the previous exercise.
2. Find the code you wrote in the previous exercise, and add the following line of code:

   ```
   cmTitles->CommandText = S"UPDATE titles SET price = "
      S"price * 1.05 WHERE price IS NOT NULL";
   ```

   This reuses the *SqlCommand* object from the previous exercise but specifies a different SQL statement.
3. Add the following code to execute the SQL statement and display the results on the Console:

   ```
   int rowsAffected = cmTitles->ExecuteNonQuery();
   Console::Write(S"Number of titles increased in price: ");
   Console::WriteLine(rowsAffected);
   ```

4. Build your program, and fix any compiler errors.

5 Run the program. The following message should be displayed on the Console:

```
Connected to database successfully!
Number of titles: 18
Number of titles increased in price: 16
The database connection is now closed
Press any key to continue
```

Notice that there are 18 titles, but only 16 have increased in price. This is because two books do not yet have an assigned price.

Executing Queries and Processing the Results

In this exercise, you will execute a command that queries information from the database. You will use the following SQL statement:

```
SELECT title, price FROM titles
```

You will use the *ExecuteReader* method to execute this statement. *ExecuteReader* returns a *SqlDataReader* object, which is a fast forward-only reader through the rows in the result set.

1 Continue using your Managed C++ Application project from the previous exercise.

2 Find the code you wrote in the previous exercise, and add the following line of code:

```
cmTitles->CommandText = S"SELECT title, price FROM titles";
```

This reuses the *SqlCommand* object from the previous exercise but specifies a different SQL statement.

3 Add the following code to execute the SQL statement and retrieve the results into a *SqlDataReader* object:

```
SqlDataReader * reader = cmTitles->ExecuteReader();
```

4 Add the following code to loop through the results one row at a time. For each row, output column 0 (the *title*) as a *string* value, and output column 1 (the *price*) as a *decimal* value.

```
Console::WriteLine(S"\n----------------------------------");
while (reader->Read())
{
    Console::Write(reader->GetString(0));
    Console::Write(S", ");
```

```
        if (reader->IsDBNull(1))
        {
            Console::WriteLine(S"No price yet");
        }
        else
        {
            Console::WriteLine(reader->GetDecimal(1));
        }
    }
    Console::WriteLine(S"-------------------------------------");
```

The *Read* method steps through the record set a row at a time. For each row, we use the strongly typed methods *GetString* and *GetDecimal* to get the values of columns 0 and 1, respectively.

Notice the *IsDBNull* test on column 1. This tests whether the *price* column is *NULL* or contains a real value.

5 After the loop, close the *SqlDataReader* as follows:

```
reader->Close();
```

6 Run the program. The following message should be displayed on the Console (you might get different values that we've shown here):

```
Connected to database successfully!
Number of titles: 18
Number of titles increased in price: 16

-------------------------------------
The Busy Executive's Database Guide, 34.1899
Cooking with Computers: Surreptitious Balance Sheets, 20.4386
You Can Combat Computer Stress!, 5.1139
Straight Talk About Computers, 34.1899
Silicon Valley Gastronomic Treats, 34.1899
The Gourmet Microwave, 5.1139
The Psychology of Computer Cooking, No price yet
But Is It User Friendly?, 39.2525
Secrets of Silicon Valley, 34.2068
Net Etiquette, No price yet
Computer Phobic AND Non-Phobic Individuals: Behavior Variations, 36.9264
Is Anger the Enemy?, 18.7283
Life Without Fear, 11.9724
Prolonged Data Deprivation: Four Case Studies, 34.1899
Emotional Security: A New Algorithm, 13.6659
Onions, Leeks, and Garlic: Cooking Secrets of the Mediterranean, 35.8316
Fifty Years in Buckingham Palace Kitchens, 20.4386
Sushi, Anyone?, 25.638
-------------------------------------
The database connection is now closed
Press any key to continue
```

Creating a Disconnected Application

For the rest of the chapter, we'll turn our attention to disconnected applications. A disconnected application is one that does not have a permanently available connection to the data source. For example, a salesperson might require an application that can access data in the central database, even when they are out of the office.

ADO.NET provides the *DataSet* class to enable you to achieve data access in disconnected applications. The following illustration shows the *DataSet* object model:

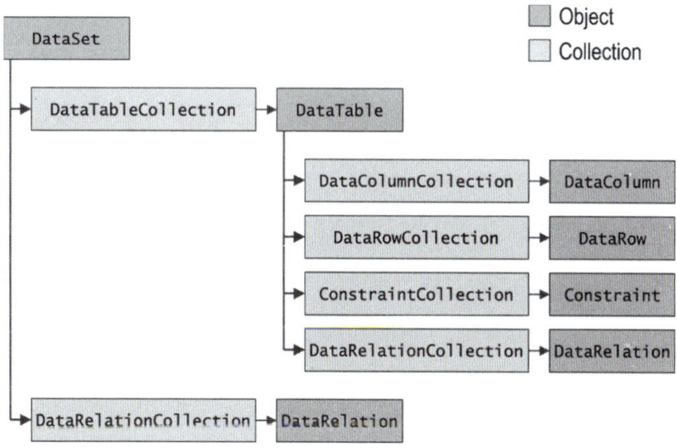

A *DataSet* is an in-memory collection of *DataTable* objects and relationships between these *DataTable*s. You can create many *DataTable*s in a *DataSet* to hold the results of numerous SQL queries.

Each *DataTable* has a collection of *DataColumn* objects. These *DataColumn*s contain metadata about the columns, such as the column name, data type, default value, and so on.

Each *DataTable* also has a collection of *DataRow* objects. These *DataRow*s contain the data for the *DataSet*.

To fill a *DataSet* with data, you must use a data adapter object. If you are using the SQL Server .NET data provider, you will use *SqlDataAdapter*. If you are using the OLE DB .NET data provider, you will use *OleDbDataAdapter*.

The following illustration shows how data adapters work with *DataSets*:

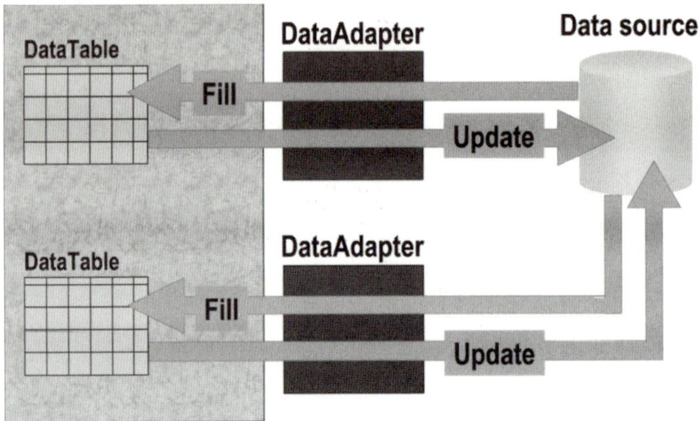

Each data adapter works with a single *DataTable* in a *DataSet*. You call the *Fill* method on a data adapter to fill the *DataSet* with data from the database. You call the *Update* method on a data adapter to save any changes in the *DataSet* back to the database.

Internally, the data adapter has four command objects to achieve data access on behalf of the *DataSet*. The data adapter uses these command objects to retrieve data from the database and to update the database with any modifications. If the data adapter is using the SQL Server data provider, these commands will be *SqlCommand* objects. If the data adapter is using the OLE DB data provider, these commands will be *OleDbCommand* objects.

The following table describes these command objects.

Command object in a data adapter	Description
SelectCommand	Contains a SQL *SELECT* statement to retrieve data from the database into the *DataSet* table
InsertCommand	Contains a SQL *INSERT* statement to insert new rows from the *DataSet* table into the database
UpdateCommand	Contains a SQL *UPDATE* statement to modify existing rows in the database
DeleteCommand	Contains a SQL *DELETE* statement to delete rows from the database

To illustrate these capabilities, you will create a new application that performs the following tasks:

- Create a *SqlDataAdapter* to access the *titles* table in the *Pubs* SQL Server database
- Use the *SqlDataAdapter* to fill a *DataSet*

- Bind the *DataSet* to a *DataGrid* on a form to display the information retrieved from the database

Creating the Form

In this exercise, you will create a new application to perform all the operations described above. The first step is to create the form.

1. Create a Managed C++ Application project called DisconnectedApplication.
2. Open the Solution Explorer, and look at the Source Files folder. Double-click DisconnectedApplication.cpp to view it in the code editor.
3. After the statement *#using <mscorlib.dll>*, add the following statements:

```
#using <System.dll>                  // For Console I/O
#using <System.Data.dll>             // For ADO.NET
#using <System.Xml.dll>              // For serialization support
                                        //   in DataSet
#using <System.Windows.Forms.dll>      // For the form
#using <System.Drawing.dll>             // Also for the form
```

4. After the statement *using namespace System*, add the following statements:

```
using namespace System::Data;           // Generic ADO.NET
                                       // definitions, such as
                                       // DataSet
using namespace System::Data::SqlClient;  // SQL Server data
                                           // provider
                                           // definitions
using namespace System::ComponentModel;   // .NET GUI classes
using namespace System::Windows::Forms;   // .NET forms
```

5. The next step is to define a form class, so add the following class definition to the code immediately after the *using* lines:

```
// Form to display titles from the Pubs database
__gc public class TitlesForm : public Form
{
public:
    TitlesForm()
    {
        // Set form properties
        this->Text = "Book titles from Pubs database";
        this->Size = System::Drawing::Size(310, 300);

        // Set Button properties
```

```
            btnFill = new Button();
            btnFill->Text = S"Fill";
            btnFill->Size = System::Drawing::Size(80, 25);
            btnFill->Location = System::Drawing::Point(210,
                                                    230);

            // Set DataGrid properties
            dgTitles = new DataGrid();
            dgTitles->Size = System::Drawing::Size(280, 200);
            dgTitles->Location = System::Drawing::Point(10, 10);

            // Add controls to form
            this->Controls->Add(btnFill);
            this->Controls->Add(dgTitles);
        }
    private:
        Button * btnFill;
        DataGrid * dgTitles;
    };
```

6 In the *_tmain* function, create a form for the disconnected application, like this:

```
Application::Run(new TitlesForm());
```

7 Build your program, and fix any compiler errors.

8 Run the program. If all is well, a form should appear as follows:

Creating and Configuring the Data Adapter

In this exercise, you will add a *SqlDataAdapter* and a *SqlConnection* to your form class. You will configure these objects so that the *SqlDataAdapter* queries all the data in the *titles* table in the *Pubs* database.

1. Continue using your Managed C++ Application project from the previous exercise.
2. Add two data members to the *TitlesForm* class, as follows:

```
SqlConnection * cnPubs;      // Connection to Pubs database
SqlDataAdapter * daTitles;  // Data adapter for the
                            // "titles" table
```

3. Add the following code to the form constructor to create and configure these objects:

```
this->cnPubs = new SqlConnection(S"data source=(local);"
    S"integrated security=true;initial catalog=Pubs");
this->daTitles = new SqlDataAdapter(S"SELECT * FROM Titles",
                                    cnPubs);
```

The *SqlDataAdapter* constructor takes two parameters. The first parameter specifies the *SELECT* statement for the *SqlDataAdapter*, which implicitly creates a *SqlCommand* object for the data adapter's *SelectCommand* property. The second parameter specifies which database connection to use to perform queries and updates.

4 Build your program, and fix any compiler errors.

Creating and Filling the DataSet

In this exercise, you will add a *DataSet* to your form class. You will create this object in the form constructor and fill the *DataSet* with data when the user clicks the *Fill* button on the form.

1 Continue using your Managed C++ Application project from the previous exercise.

2 Add the following data member to the *TitlesForm* class:

```
DataSet * dsTitles;         // DataSet, containing in-memory
                            // cache of data
```

3 Add the following code to the form constructor to create the *DataSet* object:

```
this->dsTitles = new DataSet("Titles");
```

4 Register an event handler method for the button-click event on the *Fill* button, as follows:

```
this->btnFill->Click += new EventHandler(this,
    &TitlesForm::BtnFill_Clicked);
```

5 Implement the button-click event handler method as follows:

```
void BtnFill_Clicked(Object* pSender, EventArgs* pArgs)
{
    this->daTitles->Fill(this->dsTitles);
    this->dgTitles->DataSource =
        this->dsTitles->Tables->Item[0]->DefaultView;
}
```

The first statement tells the data adapter to fill the *DataSet*. The data adapter will implicitly invoke the SQL statement in its SelectCommand property and load the data into the *DataSet*.

The second statement binds the *DataSet* to the *DataGrid*. This will cause the *DataSet* data to be displayed in the *DataGrid*.

6 Build your program, and fix any compiler errors.

7 Run the program and click *Fill*. The *DataGrid* should display all the data from the *titles* table in the *Pubs* database.

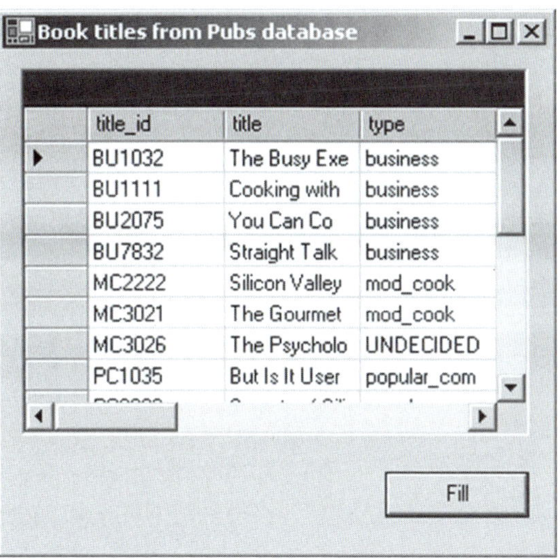

Chapter 22 Quick Reference

To	Do This

Use ADO.NET classes	Import the ADO.NET assemblies, and use the required ADO.NET namespaces. For example:
	`#using <System.Data.dll>`
	`using System::Data;`
	`using System::Data::SqlClient;`

Connect to a database	Create a *SqlConnection* or *OleDbConnection* object, and configure its ConnectionString property. For example:
	`SqlConnection * cnPubs =`
	`    new SqlConnection();`
	`cnPubs->ConnectionString =`
	`    S"data source=(local);integrated "`
	`    S"security=true;initial catalog=Pubs";`

Create a command object	Create a *SqlCommand* or *OleDbCommand* object, and configure its CommandText, CommandType, and Connection properties. For example:
	`SqlCommand * cmTitles =`
	`    new SqlCommand();`
	`cmTitles->CommandText =`
	`    S"SELECT title FROM Titles";`
	`cmTitles->CommandType =`
	`    CommandType::Text;`
	`cmTitles->Connection = cnPubs;`

(continued)

(continued)

<table>
<tr><td>Execute a command</td><td>If the command returns a scalar value, call ExecuteScalar. If the command modifies the database, call ExecuteNonQuery. If the command performs a query, call ExecuteReader. Assign the result to a SqlDataReader or OleDbReader object, and use this reader to loop through the result set. For example:<pre>
SqlDataReader * reader =
    cmTitles->ExecuteReader();
while (reader->Read())
{
    Console::Write(reader->GetString(0));
}
</pre></td></tr>
<tr><td>Use data in a disconnected application</td><td>Create a SqlDataAdapter (or OleDbAdapter), and specify commands to access the database. Create a DataSet, and fill the DataSet by using the data adapter. For example:<pre>
daTitles = new SqlDataAdapter(
    S"SELECT * FROM Titles", cnPubs);
dsTitles = new DataSet("Titles");
daTitles->Fill(dsTitles);
</pre></td></tr>
<tr><td>Display a DataSet in a DataGrid</td><td>Use the DataSource property. For example:<pre>
dgTitles->DataSource =
    dsTitles->Tables->Item[0]->DefaultView;
</pre></td></tr>
</table>

PART 6

Creating Distributed Applications

23

Building a Web Service

In this chapter, you'll learn

- ✔ *What Web Services are*
- ✔ *How Web Services work*
- ✔ *How to create a simple Web Service*
- ✔ *How to use a Web Service from a browser*

Web Services are an exciting feature of Microsoft .NET that make writing distributed applications much easier than before. They will change the way in which Web-based applications are written, and this chapter will show you how to get started.

What Are Web Services?

Web Services are a new feature of the .NET Framework that let client code access software components across networks using standard protocols such as SMTP and HTTP.

Over the past few years, Microsoft Windows programmers have become used to COM (the Component Object Model) and its role in producing software components. COM allows programmers to produce self-contained, language-independent components which can be built together into systems, and which can be used to form the basis of flexible distributed applications. Other component systems are also in widespread use, such as CORBA and Java's RMI.

Although COM is very useful, it has some shortcomings. First, writing COM components can be difficult, requiring a wealth of arcane knowledge on the part of the programmer. Second, COM uses a proprietary binary protocol to communicate between components running remotely, and this makes it hard to use

COM components anywhere outside of a pure Microsoft environment. Integrating a COM system with components that use CORBA or RMI is not at all simple.

Web Services help in two ways. First, you don't need much specialized knowledge to write Web Services, and it is often very easy to provide a Web Service interface to existing code. The second advantage is that Web Services use standard Internet data formats and protocols for communication, so it is a lot easier to build heterogeneous distributed systems. If you want to talk to some Windows-based components written in C++ from a remote client written in Java, you're going to have a *much* easier time if you do it using Web Services.

A Web Service Scenario

Here's a simple scenario to show you how Web Services can make the development of distributed services much easier.

Imagine that on one page of your Web site, you need to present some data on currency exchange rates. How do you get up-to-date exchange rate data? In the past, you might have had to use a proprietary online service to access the data, or even extract the data from HTML scraped off the appropriate Web page. If the bank provides the appropriate Web Service, you can simply make a call to the remote method, passing in the currency details and getting back the exchange rate. The Web Service acts as a remote procedure call, allowing you to call a function exposed by a remote Web server, and the use of standard Web protocols irons out any computer or language dependencies. So you could access the Service from client code written in anything from Microsoft VBScript to C++.

Web Services and The Future

Web Services provide a way to move towards a service-based computing model. As the world becomes more and more interconnected, it will become increasingly common to make use of Web Services to build distributed applications. This might happen on many scales, from the micro to the macro. At the micro level, a programmer could use a Web Service to provide a small parcel of functionality to his or her application. Someone writing a word–processing program might use Web Services to provide access to specialized spell checkers, or the writer of a spreadsheet might use them to give access to financial information.

On the macro scale, entire applications could be exposed as Web Services, so that users would subscribe to software rather than buying it. In the future, it might be possible to pay Microsoft to subscribe to Microsoft Office rather than buy it. Nothing would be installed on your computer, and every time you wanted to write a document, you would connect to the remote Office service.

Web Service Architecture

Several pieces of infrastructure are needed in order to make Web Services work:

- Data formats and protocols to enable Web Services to communicate in a language- and platform-independent manner.
- A standard way for Web Services to describe themselves.
- A way for clients to discover Web Services.

Let's look at this infrastructure in more detail.

Data Formats and Protocols

One of the major advantages of the Web Service model over COM and CORBA is the use of standard data formats and protocols over proprietary offerings.

Clients can communicate with Web Services in three ways:

- Using HTTP GET commands.
- Using HTTP POST commands.
- Using SOAP.

The first two methods use HTTP in a way that will be familiar to anyone who has written code to talk to a Web server. The use of the HTTP GET command (which adds request data to the end of the URL sent to the server) and the POST command (which passes data in the body of the HTTP message) means that you can talk to Web Services from almost any language. The third method uses the SOAP protocol that is being developed by Microsoft, IBM, and several other authorities. The advantage of SOAP over HTTP is that it enables clients and servers to exchange more highly structured information than is possible with the HTTP commands.

What Is SOAP?

The Simple Object Access Protocol (SOAP) provides a way to call methods using XML and HTTP. The details of the method you want to call and any arguments you need to supply are formatted as an XML SOAP packet. The server parses the contents of the packet, makes the call, and sends back a reply packet, which is also in XML. This means that SOAP gives you, in effect, an XML- and HTTP-based RPC (remote procedure call) mechanism. SOAP relies on W3C schemas to define the content of SOAP packets, and the use of schemas makes it possible to define and pass over structured data.

SOAP isn't a Microsoft invention, although Microsoft gives a lot of input to the committee that is defining the SOAP standard. There are SOAP bindings to many languages, and a growing number of applications are using SOAP to provide language- and platform-independent access to services.

Binary protocols such as DCOM and CORBA often find it hard to work through firewalls, but SOAP is much easier to work with in normal commercial distributed environments because it uses HTTP to send and receive data.

All three communication methods use HTTP as the transport mechanism, which means that Web Services integrate very well with existing Web-based solutions.

Web Service Description

Clients need to be able to obtain a description of how to interact with a Web Service, such as the name of the service and what arguments it requires. Anyone who has worked with COM will be familiar with the idea of the COM type library, which contains a description of a COM object, its interfaces, and the methods they support.

The equivalent of the type library in the .NET Framework is provided by the Web Service Description Language (WSDL). It describes the methods exposed by a Web Service and the in and out parameters they require, and as you might expect by now, it provides the information using XML. The format of WSDL files is quite complex, and because of the tools provided for you in Microsoft Visual Studio .NET, you won't need to work with it directly, so I won't mention it further.

Web Service Discovery

You might want to advertise the Web Services that your server supports so that clients can find your service from elsewhere on the Web. DISCO (Discovery of Web Services) is a SOAP-based protocol that defines a format for description data, together with a protocol for retrieving it. If you want to advertise your Web Services, you post DISCO files on your server. Clients can use these files to navigate to the appropriate WSDL files that describe the Web Services in detail.

You can choose to advertise your services by static or dynamic advertising. Static advertising makes use of DISCO files that point to WSDL documents:

```
<?xml version="1.0"?>
<disco:discovery
    xmlns:disco="http://schemas.xmlsoap.org/disco"
    xmlns:scl="http://schemas.xmlsoap.org/disco/scl">
<scl:contractRef ref="http://myServer/myService.asmx?WSDL"/>
<scl:discoveryRef ref="http://someotherServer/serviceDir.disco"/>
</disco:discovery>
```

DISCO documents always contain a *discovery* element as the root and define the *disco* namespace (which is used to tag the *discovery* element) and the *scl* namespace, which is used to tag the *contractRef* elements that point to WSDL files, as well as *discoveryRef* elements that point to DISCO files on linked sites.

Dynamic advertising means that all Web Services under a URL will be advertised automatically if you include a dynamic discovery file in the directory. Dynamic discovery files look like this:

```
<?xml version="1.0"?>
<dynamicDiscovery
    xmlns:disco="urn://schemas-dynamic:disco.2000-03-17"/>
```

If you place this file in the root directory of a Web server, all Web Services under the root will be automatically advertised. However, you can use *exclude* elements to omit some directories from the search path, like this:

```
<?xml version="1.0"?>
<dynamicDiscovery
  xmlns:disco="urn://schemas-dynamic:disco.2000-03-17">
    <exclude path="_vti_cnf" />
</dynamicDiscovery>
```

The *exclude* element can be used to speed up the search by omitting directories that don't need to be searched, as well as to hide Web Services that aren't publicly available.

note

If you create Web Services using Visual Studio .NET, you'll get a dynamic discovery file created for you.

The Web Services Namespaces

Web Services are supported by several namespaces in the .NET Framework.

Namespace	Description
System::Web::Services	Contains the classes used to build and use Web Services
System::Web::Services::Description	Contains the classes that let you describe Web Services using WSDL
System::Web::Services::Discovery	Contains classes that let client code locate Web Services elsewhere on the Web
System::Web::Services::Protocols	Contains classes that define the protocols used in Web Services

The *System::Web::Services* namespace contains the classes that you use to create and use Web Services. It isn't a large namespace, and the three main classes are listed in the following table.

Class	Description
WebMethodAttribute	An attribute that marks a method as callable from remote Web clients
WebService	An optional base class used to build Web Services
WebServiceAttribute	An attribute that is used to add additional information to a class that implements a Web Service

Web Services will often derive from *WebService*, but this is necessary only if you want access to the common Microsoft ASP.NET objects, as listed in the following table.

Property	Description
Application	Gets the application state object, which is common to all sessions.
Context	Gets the ASP.NET *HttpContext* object for the current HTTP request.

Server	Returns an *HttpServerUtility* object that provides utility methods for working with the Web server.
Session	Gets the *HttpSessionState* object for the current request.
User	Returns an ASP.NET *User* object representing the current user. This object can be used for authentication purposes.

If you don't need access to these properties, you don't need to derive a class from *WebService*.

Creating a Simple Web Service

Because you might often want to expose C++ code as Web Services, Visual Studio .NET contains tools to help you build and deploy Web Services. This exercise will show you how to create and deploy a simple service that implements methods to convert temperatures between Fahrenheit and Celsius:

1 Create a new project, and make sure that it is a Managed C++ Web Service project. Call it Converter.

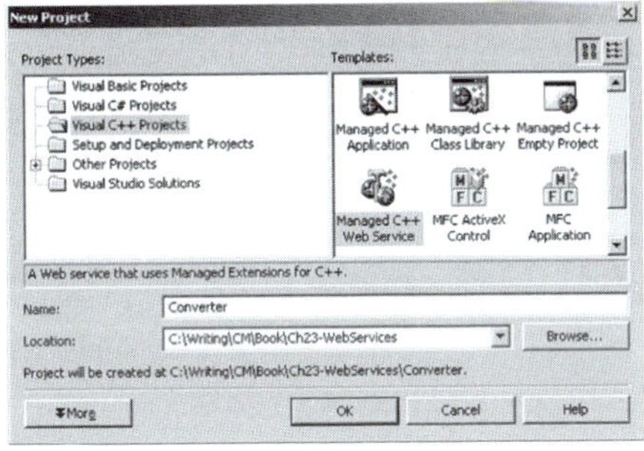

2 When you look at the project details, you'll find an .asmx file as well as the more familiar C++ source files. This file contains details that tell the Web server which class contains the implementation of the Web Service. Open the file and take a look at the content:

```
<%@ WebService Class=Converter.Class1 %>
```

The single line tells the Web server that the *Converter* Web Service is implemented by *Converter.Class1*, the class called *Class1* in namespace *Converter*. If you now open the Converter.h file, you'll see the class and namespace defined there. *Class1* isn't a very descriptive name, so change it to *TemperatureConverter* in Converter.h, and also edit the .asmx file so it now reads:

```
<%@ WebService Class=Converter.TemperatureConverter %>
```

Building a Web Service 23

The project also contains a .vsdisco file, which is the dynamic discovery file used to advertise the Web Service to remote clients.

The sample class in the *Converter* namespace currently has one method called *HelloWorld*, which shows you how to add methods to a *WebService* class.

3 You can use *HelloWorld* to test out a Web Service, but let's replace the function with a real one. Change the name of the sample class to *TemperatureConverter*, and edit the class definition in Converter.h to add the two conversion functions, making sure that you remove the dummy *HelloWorld* function:

```
namespace Converter
{
    [WebServiceAttribute(
      Namespace="http://VCSBS/WebServices/",
      Description="A Web Service for converting"
      "temperatures between Fahrenheit and Celsius")]
  public __gc class TemperatureConverter : public
    WebService
  {
  public:
      [WebMethod(Description=
      "Converts temperatures from Fahrenheit to Celsius")]
      double ConvertF2C(double dFahrenheit);
      [WebMethod(Description=
      "Converts temperatures from Celsius to Fahrenheit")]
      double ConvertC2F(double dCelsius);
  };
}
```

note

The *Description* of the *WebServiceAttribute* has been declared, with string literals on two separate lines. If the C++ preprocessor sees two adjacent string literals, it will concatenate them. This provides an easy way to split long strings over more than one line.

Web Services are a very good advertisement for the use of attributes, and you can see here how attributes are used to add the necessary metadata to ordinary C++ classes and members. The *WebServiceAttribute* attribute provides a description and an XML namespace for the service that is used to distinguish it from other services on the Web. You can also use this attribute to supply a name, if you want the service name to be different from that of the namespace and class.

note

The default namespace is *http://tempuri.org* (for "temporary URI"), and while this can be used for development, it should be changed when services are going to go live.

The *WebMethod* attribute shows that these two methods are exposed by the Web Service.

4 Implement the *ConvertC2F* and *ConvertF2C* functions by editing the Converter.cpp file so it looks like this:

```
namespace Converter
{
    double TemperatureConverter::ConvertF2C(double dFahrenheit) {
        return ((dFahrenheit - 32) * 5) / 9;
    }

    double TemperatureConverter::ConvertC2F(double dCelsius) {
        return (9/5 * dCelsius) + 32;
    }
}
```

5 Build the project.

This will compile the code, and will automatically deploy the Web Service onto your Web server. You can verify that the service has been installed by looking at the Web server's Inetpub\wwwroot directory, where you should see a virtual directory with the same name as the project.

And that's all there is to it. Some Web Services will obviously be more complicated, but creating a Web Service can be as simple as adding some attributes to a class!

Using the Web Service from a Browser

You can use a Web browser to invoke the Web Service methods, and the following short exercise will show you how to do it:

1 Start Microsoft Internet Explorer.

2 Type the URL for the Web Service's .asmx file into the Address bar. If you've called the Web Service "Converter" and installed it on IIS on your local computer in the default virtual directory, the address will be:

```
http://localhost/Converter/Converter.asmx
```

note

If you've installed the service on a remote computer or used another virtual directory, you'll have to amend the address accordingly.

When you press Enter, the Web server will return you details of the *Converter* service and the methods it supports:

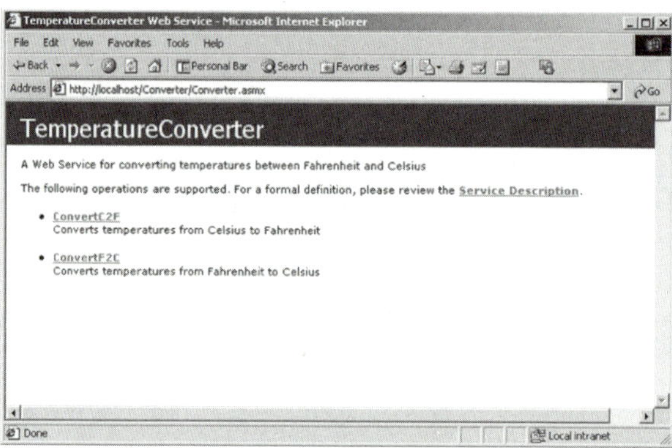

You can see how metadata has been extracted from the class and used to provide a description of the service.

3 Click one of the two methods.

This sends an HTTP GET command to the server, which results in the server auto-generating a Web Service consumer and sending it back to the browser:

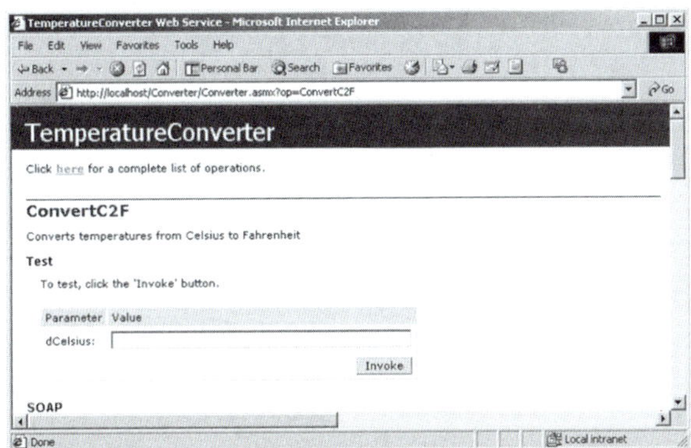

The consumer takes the form of an HTML page that contains a description of the service, a way of testing the method, and descriptions of how to use the service using HTTP GET, HTTP POST, and SOAP.

4 Test the method by entering a suitable value into the text box and clicking Invoke.

The Web Service will invoke the method and return the answer as XML:

```
<?xml version="1.0" encoding="utf-8" ?>
<double xmlns="http://VCSBS/WebServices/">42</double>
```

The *double* element identifies the value as a double, and the namespace is used to identify the Web Service that is returning the result.

Using the Web Service from Code

Before you can use a Web Service, you obviously need to locate it and find out how you need to use it. Visual Studio .NET uses Web References to represent Web Services, wherever they are located. It also has tools to locate services, and you can browse your local computer, a UDDI server, or the Internet in general.

note

UDDI (Universal Description, Discovery, and Integration) is a mechanism for Web Service providers to advertise the existence of their services, and for clients to locate Web Services of interest.

When you find a service that you want to use, Visual Studio .NET will use the DISCO discovery service to retrieve the WSDL file that describes the service. Client code needs to be able to find the Web Service at run time and to communicate with it. Adding a Web Reference to your project uses the

WSDL information to create a proxy class that takes care of finding and communicating with the service, so all you have to do is work with a local object that exposes the same methods as the remote service.

> **note**
>
> If you've ever used remote COM objects from C++ code in Visual C++, you'll see similarities in the way you use Web Services.

The following exercise shows you how to use the Web Service that you created earlier in the chapter. This exercise assumes that you have built and installed the service and that it is running on a local Web server.

1. Create a new Managed C++ Application project called TempClient. Leave the definition of the *main* function as it is because you won't require any command line arguments, and this is going to be a Console application.
2. Add a Web Reference to the project, either by choosing Add Web Reference on the Project menu, or by right-clicking on the project in the Solution Explorer and selecting Add Web Reference from the shortcut menu.

   This will bring up the Add Web Reference dialog box:

   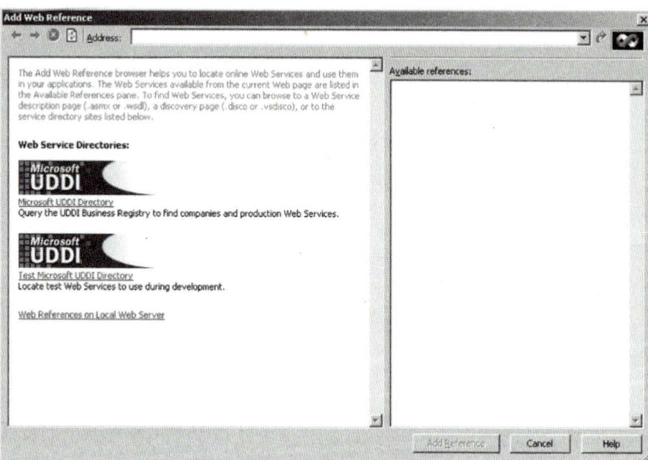

   You have three ways to locate the Web Service. First, if it is registered with the Microsoft UDDI service, you can click on the UDDI link. If you know the location of the service, you can enter a URL in the Address bar. In this case, the service lives on the local server, so you can use the third option and click Web References On Local Web Server to display locally registered services.

> **note**
>
> It might take several seconds to activate this link while the server uses dynamic discovery to build its list of services.

This will display details of the dynamic DISCO file for the local server, which links through to the local Web Services. As you'll see from the following figure, I have a number of experimental Web Services installed on my computer:

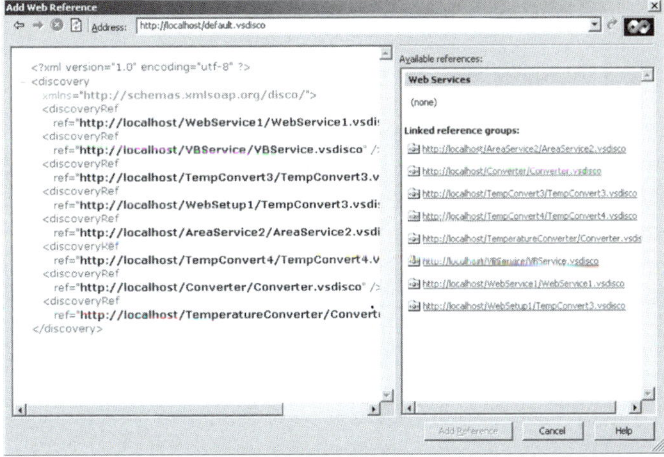

If you look at the XML in the left pane, you'll see that all the entries in the DISCO file refer to the local DISCO files for the Web Services, so you need to navigate further to get details of a particular service.

3 In the right pane, click on the link to the Converter.vsdisco file, which will display the contents in the usual two-pane, XML-on-the-left layout:

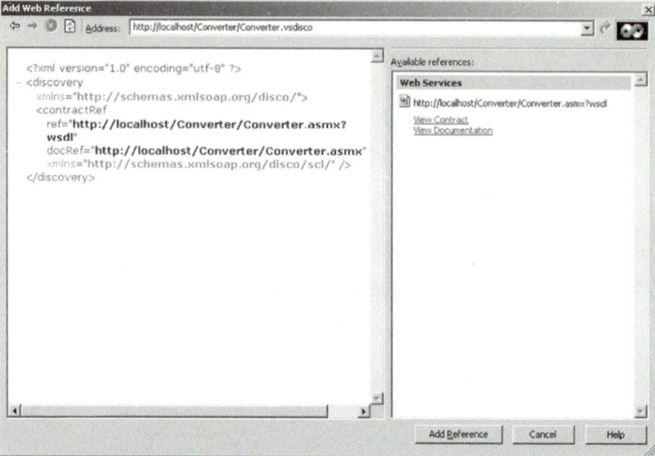

You can click View Contract and View Documentation to retrieve more information about the service. View Contract displays the contents of the WSDL file that describes the Web Service, while View Documentation shows you the same information window that you displayed in the browser in the previous exercise.

4 Click Add Reference to create the reference proxy.

When the process has finished, you'll find that a new file called WebService.h has been added to the project. This defines *#using* directives for the proxy class (which has been built into a DLL called Converter.dll) and any .NET Framework DLLs that are needed. In TempClient.cpp, add a *#include* for WebService.h in the *main* function just after the *#include* for stdafx.h:

```
#include "stdafx.h"
#include "WebService.h"
```

The proxy code has been generated in C#, and if you want, you can look at the file Converter.cs that has been added to your project directory. This is built into Converter.dll as part of the project build process.

5 Add code to the *main* function to create and access the Web Service:

```
int main(void)
{
    Console::WriteLine(S"Web Service Test");
    try
    {
        // Create a proxy object
        TemperatureConverter* conv = new TemperatureConverter();
        // Call a conversion method...
```

```
        double fahrVal = conv->ConvertC2F(10.0);
        Console::WriteLine("10C is {0}F", __box(fahrVal));
    }
    catch(Exception* pe)
    {
        Console::WriteLine(pe->Message);
    }

    return 0;
}
```

The proxy class that has been provided by you has the same name as the deployment project, so the class name here is *TemperatureConverter* and not *Converter*.

You can create a new *TemperatureConverter* object just like any other .NET object, and call its *ConvertC2F* method to convert a value. This might not seem like a particularly impressive demonstration, but remember that the Web Service could be installed anywhere else on the Internet and could be written in any language. In fact, it's not even necessary for the service to be written using the .NET Framework at all.

Debugging Web Services

Debugging a Web Service is quite simple. First, make sure that you've built a debug version of the Web Service code. This is the default build, so if you haven't changed anything, you'll have a debug version. To debug a Web Service, place a breakpoint in the C++ code at the place you want to start debugging by clicking in the gray margin to the left of the code window. A red dot will show you where the breakpoint is located. Now press F5 to run the service under the debugger. After a few seconds, Internet Explorer starts, displaying the documentation of the Web Service. You can now interact with the Internet Explorer window just as you did in the "Using the Web Service from a Browser" section above.

Select the method that you want to debug, and bring up the test page, as shown in the graphic on page 522. When you click Invoke, you'll find yourself back in the Visual Studio .NET environment, where you can debug the C++ code in the normal way.

If You're Not Using Visual Studio .NET

You can still use Web Services even if you're not using Visual Studio .NET. The wsdl.exe command line tool supplied as part of the .NET Framework

SDK will generate a proxy for you in exactly the same way as the wizard does in Visual Studio .NET.

The following command line shows how you could create a proxy for talking to the Converter service by hand:

```
wsdl /l:cs /protocol:SOAP http://localhost/Converter/Converter.asmx?WSDL
```

The */l* (or */language*) argument determines the language the proxy will be written in. You've got a choice of Microsoft Visual Basic (VB), Microsoft JScript (JS), or C# (CS). The default is CS if you don't specify a language. The */protocol* argument defines the protocol that is going to be used to talk to the service; I've chosen SOAP, but you can also specify *httpPost* or *httpGet*. The final argument is the URL of the Web Service, and you can also specify a WSDL file if you have one available.

You can then build the proxy code into a DLL using the following command line:

```
csc /t:library /r:system.web.services.dll /r:system.xml.dll
   /r:system.data.dll  Converter.cs
```

The command line tells the C# compiler to compile Converter.cs into a DLL, and gives the references to the DLLs containing the .NET classes that will be used. Once you've build this DLL, you can add *#using* to any project in order to use the Web Service.

Chapter 23 Quick Reference

To	Do This

Create a class that acts as a Web Service	Create a Managed C++ class, and add the *WebServiceAttribute* to the class definition. For example:
	`[WebServiceAttribute]`
	`class MyClass {...};`
	Add the *WebMethod* attribute to the member functions that you want your Web Service to expose. For example:
	`[WebMethod]`
	`String* GetMyName() {...}`

Create a class that acts as a Web Service and gives access to the standard ASP.NET objects	Create a Managed C++ class that inherits from *System::Web::Services::WebService*.

Add a description to a Web Service class or Web method	Add a *Description* attribute to the *WebServiceAttribute* or *WebMethod* attribute. For example:
	`[WebServiceAttribute (Description=`
	`"My Service")]`
	`class MyClass {...};`

Provide a unique identifier for your Web Service	Use the *Namespace* attribute on the *WebServiceAttribute* for the Web Service class to define a unique namespace URL. For example:
	`[WebServiceAttribute (Namespace=`
	`"http://myServiceUrl")]`
	`class MyClass {...};`

Use a Web Service from Managed C++ code	Add a Web Reference to the project by choosing Add Web Reference on the Project menu, or by right-clicking on the project name in Solution Explorer and selecting Add Web Reference.
Debug a Web Service	Build and install a debug version of the project. Place a breakpoint in the code, and then press F5 to execute the code under the debugger. An Internet Explorer window will be displayed for you to interact with the service, and you will be returned to the Visual Studio .NET environment when the breakpoint in the code is hit.
Create a proxy to a Web Service when you're not using Visual Studio .NET	Use the wsdl.exe tool from the .NET Framework SDK to create a proxy from the WSDL description of the service, and then compile the code into a proxy DLL.

Introduction to ATL Server

In this chapter, you'll learn

- ✔ *What ATL Server is*
- ✔ *How to create Web-based applications with ATL Server*
- ✔ *How to create Web Services with ATL Server*

In the previous chapter, you learned how to create Web Services using Managed C++. In this chapter, you're going to learn how to the ATL Server library to create Web Services and Web-based applications.

What Is ATL Server?

ATL Server is a set of extensions to the Active Template Library (ATL) included with Microsoft Visual Studio .NET. It's provided to let you develop Web-based code using unmanaged C++. The ATL Server library is different from the original ATL, because the new code in ATL Server has little to do with COM but concentrates on Web development instead.

The ATL Server library provides a lot of functionality and contains classes for:

- Writing ISAPI extensions
- Writing Web Services
- Writing filters and CGI servers
- Handling cookie-based sessions
- Caching session state in memory or to database tables

- Working with sockets and HTTP
- Working with SMTP
- Writing SOAP clients and servers
- Handling MIME types and encoding/decoding using various schemes, such as Base64
- Formatting HTML
- Monitoring performance
- Working with files, memory-mapped files, and IStream-like access to files
- Manipulating paths
- Using crypto and security API wrappers

In addition, ATL Server offers many utility classes, including classes for image and date manipulation, and a number of new container classes, including red/black trees, hashes, lists, and maps.

ATL Server is designed to be used with ASP.NET to provide parts of a Web Application when performance is critical and when you need fine-grained control over areas such as threading and caching. However, ATL Server might not be needed in the majority of cases, where normal .NET Web-based applications and Web Services offer enough performance.

There's far too much in ATL Server to cover in this chapter, so I'm going to concentrate on how you can use ATL Server to build two types of projects:

- ISAPI Web applications, where fixed HTML content is modified by active content supplied by an ATL Server DLL. These Web applications are ATL-based alternatives to ASP.NET Web-based applications.
- XML–based Web Services in Microsoft Visual C++, where clients can talk to ATL Services using HTTP.

In the past, ISAPI programming has often been difficult and tedious. ATL Server has been developed to make the task simpler and more intuitive, using minimalist classes built in the ATL style and wizards in the development environment. There is also support for ATL Server in Visual C++, including deployment functionality and debugging support.

What Is ISAPI?

The Internet Server API (ISAPI) lets Microsoft Windows programmers write extensions to Microsoft Internet Information Server (IIS) to generate HTML pages dynamically. ISAPI extensions are implemented as DLLs that implement a set of entry points. When you request the DLL as part of a URL, IIS chooses a pooled thread, loads the DLL, and passes the extension information about the page request by calling these entry points. The extension code can then get access to data passed through POST, GET, or HTTP headers. IIS also passes the extension a function pointer that the extension can use to "write" the output page.

ISAPI is flexible, produces fast code, and is relatively easy to use. If your application is simple, ISAPI works well, because all you need to do is read the data that is passed to the ISAPI extension, process it, and write a response back to the client. When applications get more complicated, ISAPI doesn't offer much more functionality; for example, it has no database access, nor can it handle session information or cookies, or help with encryption or the generation of e-mail messages.

Coding with ATL Server

If you've coded with ATL before, you'll be familiar with fact that ATL is not for the faint-hearted. It demands a good level of familiarity with fairly advanced C++ template techniques as well as an in-depth knowledge of COM. Many C++ developers have put off using ATL for these reasons.

ATL Server takes a different approach and uses some of the new features introduced in Visual C++ .NET to make coding ATL simpler. Instead of presenting you with complex implementation details, most of the work in an ATL Server project is done using attributes. You add attributes to classes to mark them as ATL Server classes and to set properties for the classes, and the compiler processes the attributes at compile time and generates the required implementation code. This means that if you're using Visual Studio .NET to write ATL Server applications, you'll seldom see the sort of template code you're used to in ATL.

Creating Web-Based Applications Using ATL Server

In this section, we'll look at the first type of project you can build with ATL Server: Web-based applications. First I'll give you an overview of the server architecture, and then you'll see how to build a sample application.

ATL Server Architecture

The architecture of ATL Server applications is shown in the following illustration:

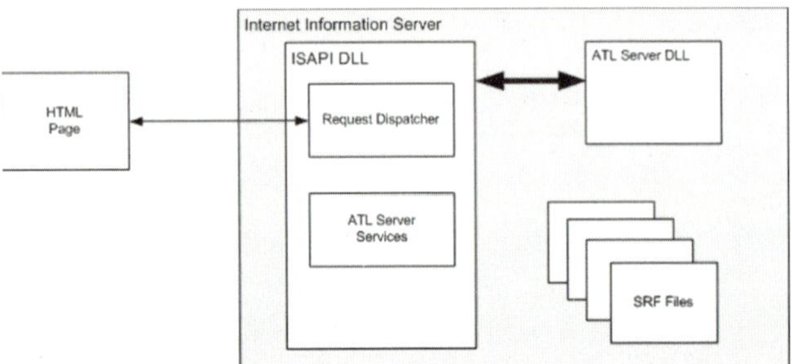

There is one ATL Server ISAPI DLL per Web server, acting as an extension to IIS, forwarding requests to the Web-based applications.

Browser clients use the URL of a Server Response File (SRF) to connect to the server. SRFs define the layout of the page and how the methods exposed by ATL Server are going to be used. The ISAPI DLL is registered as the default handler for SRFs, so it processes the file, making use of ATL Server to provide dynamic content. See the exercise below for details about what an SRF looks like.

SRFs are similar to ASP pages, containing a mixture of HTML and references to functionality within the ATL server. The tags—within double braces ({{}})—are called replacement tags. As with ASP pages, the dynamic content is separated from the static layout.

SRFs are either passed in as part of the requested URL or held as resources. They contain three pieces of information:

- The name of the handler class and the DLL it lives in
- Static HTML for the returned page
- Placeholder tags in the HTML which are replaced with dynamic content at run time

Here's a very simple Server Response File:

```
{{handler mydll.dll/Default}}
<html><body>
{{aCommand}}
</body></html>
```

The placeholders are enclosed in double braces, because as far as HTML is concerned, they are plain text, so they won't be processed by intelligent tools such as Microsoft FrontPage.

SRFs are processed by the stencil processor code that is part of ATL Server. Once SRFs have been parsed by the processor, they are cached so that they can be used again without the need for additional parsing.

The stencil processor loads the handler DLL specified in the {{handler}} placeholder and looks for the handler class whose name is specified after the slash. A single ATL Server DLL can contain many handler classes, one of which can be identified as the Default handler. The ATL Server DLL also contains a handler map that links handler names to ATL classes within the DLL. Here's a typical handler map:

```
BEGIN_HANDLER_MAP()
   HANDLER_ENTRY("Default:", CMyHandler)
   HANDLER_ENTRY("Handler2", CMyHandler2)
END_HANDLER_MAP()
```

The map associates class names with the handler names that are used in the SRFs.

Here's a simple definition of a handler class:

```
[request_handler="Default"]
class CMyHandler
{ public:
    DWORD ValidateAndExchange();
    [tag_name="aCommand"]
    DWORD OnCommand();
};
```

This is the simplest way to set up a handler class. If you want more of a challenge, you can do it the traditional ATL way by manually deriving a handler class from the requisite ATL base classes (in this case, *CRequestHandlerT<>*), but attributes make life a lot easier in Visual C++ .NET.

The *request_handler* attribute marks this class as a handler and establishes its name. Methods within the class can be tagged with a *tag_name* attribute that matches a method with a name used in a placeholder tag in an SRF.

The *ValidateAndExchange* method is used to validate any parameters passed in through HTTP and to perform any initialization needed by the handler.

More About Server Response Files

Putting a tag name in an SRF file will result in the corresponding method being called. There are also some other commands that let you do more complex processing.

The {{include}} command lets you refer to another SRF, which the processor will load and parse. The {{if}}, {{else}}, and {{endif}} tags let you perform conditional processing, calling a command that returns HTTP_SUCCESS or TTP_S_FALSE to denote logical *true* or *false* values. This means that you can put text like this within an SRF:

```
{{if CardNumberIsValid}}
<p>Card validated.
{{else}}
<p>Card number invalid.
{{endif}}
```

Here's the code for the method:

```
DWORD CardNumberIsValid()
{
  DWORD retval = HTTP_S_FALSE;

  LPCSTR pszNumberToCheck =
    m_HttpRequest.m_pFormVars->Lookup("CardNumber");

  if (pszNumberToCheck && pszNumberToCheck[0])
  {
    // check the number
    if (ok)
      retval = HTTP_SUCCESS;
  }

  return retval;
}
```

The code assumes that the calling form contains an input field called CardNumber. It then retrieves the content of the field from the HTTP header using the *m_HttpRequest* object that represents the HTTP request stream. If you need to write HTML output back to the client, you can use the *Write* method of the *m_HttpResponse* object.

The value returned by the function will determine what HTML is included in the response.

Writing a Web Application Using ATL Server

The following exercise shows you how to create a Web Application using ATL Server.

1. On the File menu, select New and then Project to open the New Project dialog box.
2. Select Visual C++ Projects in the leftpane, and click ATL Server Project in the right pane. Call the project MyAtlServer.

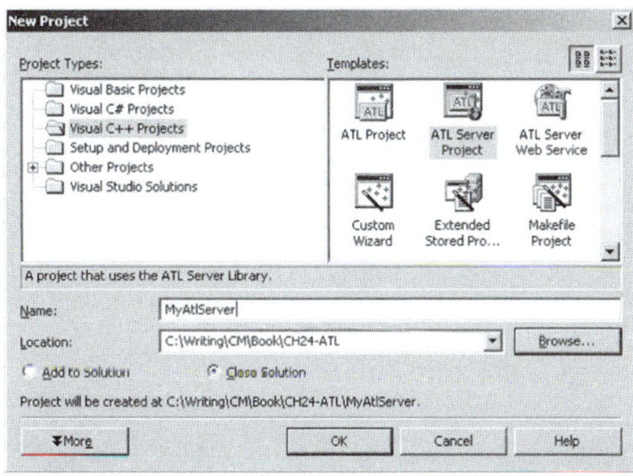

3. Click OK to bring up the ATL Server Project Wizard.

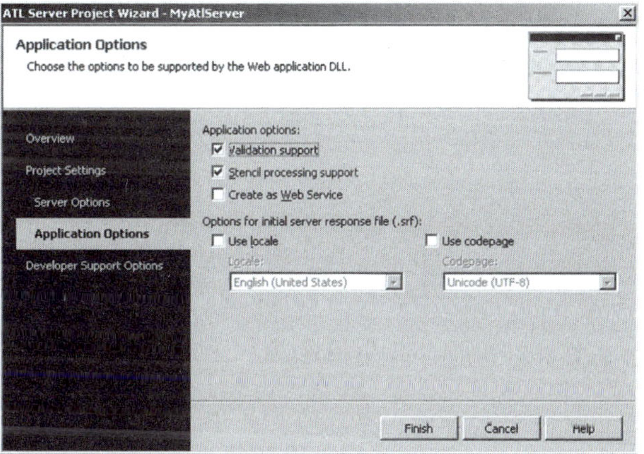

This wizard has several pages; the illustration shows the Application Options page. Although there are a number of options that you can customize, for this simple example you can accept all the default settings. For details about some of the other options available through the wizard, see the following sidebar, "ATL Server Project Options."

ATL Server Project Options

The ATL Server Project Wizard has four pages of options: Project Settings, Server Options, Application Options, and Developer Support Options.

The Project Settings page lets you choose whether to create separate or combined DLLs. ATL Server is an ISAPI extension for a Web server, so it has both an ISAPI part and an ATL part: these can either be created as two separate DLLs or be combined into one. The other major option on this page allows you to select deployment support, which means your project will be automatically deployed to the server.

The Server Options page lets you set various support options, such as adding performance counters and data caching support, and also lets you set up session state services so you can persist data across requests to the service.

Nothing on the Application Options page applies to Web Service projects, but the Developer Support Options page lets you set three options to help you work with the project: adding TODO comments, adding debug support so that the service can be debugged using the WebDbg utility, and whether specifying attributes are used in the generated Visual C++ code.

4. Click Finish to create the project files.

   You'll find that two projects have been created for you in two separate directories: one for the ATL Server files and one for the ISAPI extension files.

5. The ATL Server project already contains a sample function that returns a "Hello World" string. Add another method that will return the current date and time as a string. Start by adding the *include* file for the C++ date and time functionality to the top of the MyAtlServer.h file, as seen here:

   ```
   #include <ctime>
   ```

   This includes the standard ctime header file, which in standard C++ simply includes the old C time.h header.

6. Add the new method to the *CMyAtlServerHandler* class with the following code:

   ```
   [ tag_name(name="GetDate") ]
   HTTP_CODE OnGetDate(void)
   {
       time_t theTime;
       time(&theTime);
       tm* loctm = localtime(&theTime);
   ```

```
    m_HttpResponse << asctime(loctm);
    return HTTP_SUCCESS;
}
```

The function gets the current time and stores it into a *time_t* variable, then uses the *localtime* function to convert to the local time zone. The *asctime* function is used to render the local time as a string, which is passed back to the *m_HttpResponse* object.

Note that *tag_name* is set to GetDate, which is how you'll refer to this command in the SRF file.

7 Edit the SRF file to use the new command. Open the SRF file in Visual Studio .NET, and make sure that you use the tabs at the bottom of the code window to change to HTML view. Edit the SRF code so that it looks like this:

```
<html><HEAD></HEAD>
<BODY>
{{// A simple SRF file}}
{{handler MyAtlServer.dll/Default}}
<h2>Time Server</h2>
The current date and time is: {{GetDate}}
</BODY>
</html>
```

The {{// ...}} line is an SRF comment, and you can use as many as you like to document your SRF files. The {{handler}} command establishes the DLL and handler to be used for this SRF file, and the {{GetDate}} command will call the function in the DLL whose output will be merged with the fixed content.

8 Build the project. This will result in both ATL and ISAPI DLLs being built and deployed to the Web server. If you look in the output window, you should see something like this:

```
------ Build started: Project: MyAtlServer,
                                     Configuration: Debug Win32
----

Compiling...
StdAfx.cpp
Compiling...
MyAtlServer.cpp
Linking...
Creating library Debug/MyAtlServer.lib and object
```

```
                    Debug/MyAtlServer.exp
Deploying the web files...
Copied file from c:\MyAtlServer\MyAtlServer.srf
                    to
c:\inetpub\wwwroot\MyAtlServer\MyAtlServer.srf
Copied file from c:\MyAtlServer\Debug\MyAtlServer.dll
                    to
c:\inetpub\wwwroot\MyAtlServer\MyAtlServer.dll

Build log was saved at "file://
c:\MyAtlServer\Debug\BuildLog.htm"
MyAtlServer - 0 error(s), 0 warning(s)


------ Build started: Project: MyAtlServerIsapi,
                              Configuration: Debug Win32 ------

Compiling...
StdAfx.cpp
Compiling...
MyAtlServerIsapi.cpp
Compiling resources...
Linking...
Creating library Debug/MyAtlServerIsapi.lib and
                          object Debug/MyAtlServerIsapi.exp
Deploying the web files...
stopping W3SVC......
starting
W3SVC...............................................
Copied file from
c:\MyAtlServerIsapi\Debug\MyAtlServerIsapi.dll
        to
c:\inetpub\wwwroot\MyAtlServer\MyAtlServerIsapi.dll

Build log was saved at "file://
c:\MyAtlServerIsapi\Debug\BuildLog.htm"
MyAtlServerIsapi - 0 error(s), 0 warning(s)
```

Both projects are built, and the requisite files are copied to the correct virtual directory on the server. Note how the Web server is stopped and restarted when the ISAPI DLL is installed, just in case the DLL is already in use.

Using the Web Application from a Browser

The application can be used very easily from a browser: simply enter the URL of the SRF file into the browser's Address field. In this case, the URL is *http://localhost/MyAtlServer/MyAtlServer.srf*. When the SRF file has been processed, you'll see the output in the browser window.

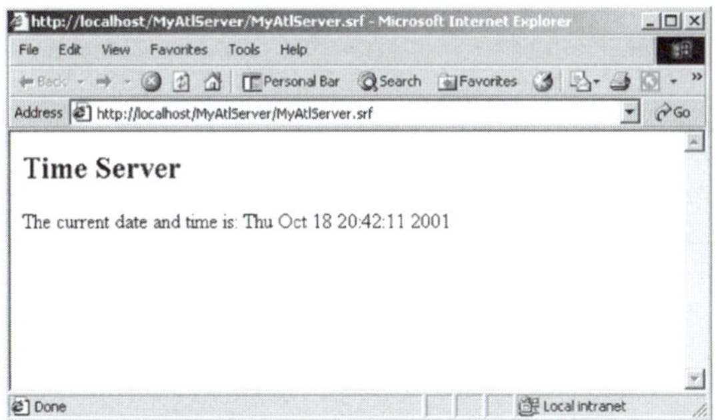

Creating Web Services Using ATL

ATL Server is a set of native—not Managed—C++ classes that developers can use to create Web-based applications, Web Services, and other server applications.

Writing a Web Service in ATL

Now that I've introduced ATL and its role in writing Web server components, let's move on to see how to write a Web Service in ATL. So that you can compare and contrast Managed C++ Web Services and those written in ATL, the following exercise will create another version of the TemperatureConverter Web Service from Chapter 23 written in ATL.

Creating the Code Skeleton

1. On the File menu, select New and then Project to open the New Project dialog box.
2. Select Visual C++ Projects in the left pane, and click ATL Server Web Service in the right pane. Call the project AtlConverter.

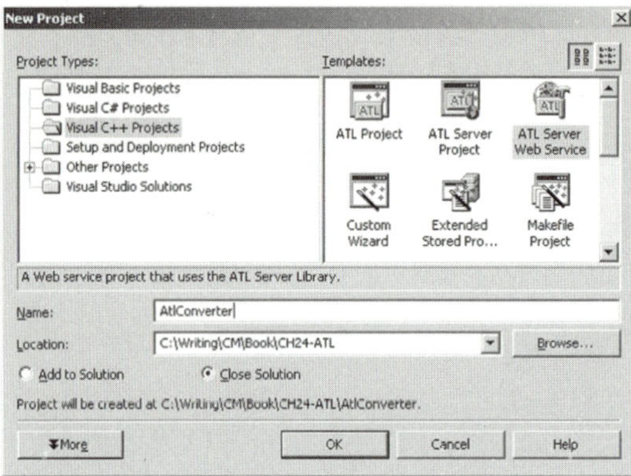

3 Click OK to bring up the ATL Server Project Wizard.

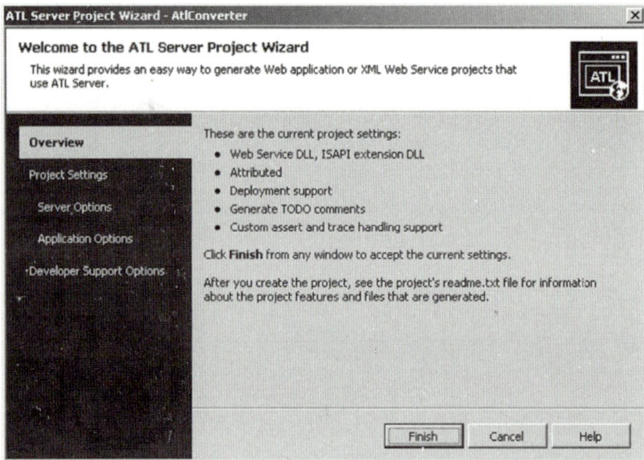

This wizard has several pages that let you configure the ATL Server code and build options, and some of the most important are described in the sidebar "ATL Server Project Options" earilier in this chapter. In this case, you'll use the default options, so simply click Finish to tell the wizard to generate the files.

Modifying the Interface

If you open the Solution Explorer, you'll see that the solution contains two projects, one for the ISAPI part and the other the COM ATL part. We're going to concentrate on the ATL part of the project, because there are no changes that need to be made to the ISAPI project.

As I've already explained, the behavior of COM objects is defined by the interfaces they expose. When you create a COM object in an ATL project, the wizard creates a single custom interface for you that will define the methods your

COM object is going to expose. Here's the listing from AtlConverter.h for the skeleton interface created by the wizard:

```
[
    uuid("2863F2DA-E84A-4B14-8FDF-3C1669558950"),
    object
]
__interface IAtlConverterService
{
    // HelloWorld is a sample ATL Server web service method.
    // It shows how to declare a web service method and its
    // in-parameters and out-parameters
    [id(1)] HRESULT HelloWorld([in] BSTR bstrInput,
        [out, retval] BSTR *bstrOutput);
    // TODO: Add additional web service methods here
};
```

The *__interface* keyword introduces an interface definition, and the interface is called *IAtlConverterService*.

> **note**
>
> By convention, COM interface names begin with the letter I.

The interface has two attributes; in this case, they are part of the metadata needed by the COM object rather than by the .NET Framework. The UUID is the unique identifier that COM uses to identify this interface; it is automatically generated by the wizard. The *object* attribute is used to identify this interface as a COM interface.

Interfaces provide the definition of functionality without providing any implementation, so all the interface contains is a function prototype. Notice how this function uses COM types rather than .NET Framework types; this is because ATL produces COM objects and not .NET objects.

The *id(1)* attribute before HRESULT assigns a dispatch ID, so this method can be used as an *Automation* object, and the *in*, *out*, and *retval* attributes control the marshalling of data into and out of the method.

The following example shows you how to add the temperature conversion methods to the interface.

1. Open the AtlConverter.h header file and locate the *IAtlConverterService* interface definition. Comment out the existing definition of the *HelloWorld* method.
2. Add two method definitions to the *IAtlConverterService* definition so that it looks like this:

```
__interface IAtlConverterService
{
    [id(1)] HRESULT ConvertF2C([in] double dFahr,
                               [out, retval] double*
dCelsius);
    [id(2)] HRESULT ConvertC2F([in] double dCelsius,
                               [out, retval] double* dFahr);
};
```

These are typical COM method definitions: both return HRESULTs, the only type that COM methods are allowed to return. Input parameters are marked with *in* attributes, and anything that is returned must be declared as a pointer and have the *out* attribute. You can't use the return value from a COM method to return anything other than a COM status return, so if you want a method that will act like a function in languages like Microsoft Visual Basic, you have to mark an *out* parameter with the *retval* attribute to show that it can be used as a function return value.

The two *id* attributes are used to allow these methods to be called via automation from languages that need automation support.

Providing the Implementation

Now you need to add the implementation of the methods. All the implementation is in the *CAtlConverterService* class, which is derived from *IAtlConverterService*. This means that it has to implement all the methods defined in the interface.

> **note**
>
> A C++ class can inherit from an interface, which means that it inherits the function definitions defined by the interface. Because the interface doesn't provide any implementation itself, it is up to the derived class to implement all the necessary methods.

Note the attributes at the top of the *CAtlConverterService* class implementation:

```
[
   request_handler(name="Default", sdl="GenAtlConverterWSDL"),
    soap_handler(
         name="AtlConverterService",
         namespace="urn:AtlConverterService",
         protocol="soap"
    )
]
```

The *request_handler* attribute is added to a class to make it an ATL Server class that can handle HTTP requests, and it causes the compiler to add the correct base classes to the code. The *name* parameter specifies the name of the handler, and the *sdl* parameter gives the name of the compiler-generated handler that will return the WSDL for this request handler.

The *soap_handler* attribute is applied to a class to provide the methods for handling SOAP method calls and for exposing information about the class by means of WSDL. The *name* parameter specifies the name of the Web Service, and the default is to use the project name with "Service" appended. The *namespace* parameter provides a unique namespace for the service, and if none is provided, the name of the class is used instead. The *protocol* parameter defines the protocol that is going to be used to access this service; the only one supported at present is SOAP, and it is taken as the default.

1. Open the AtlConverter.h header file if it isn't already open, and locate the *CAtlConverterService* class definition. Comment out or remove the existing implementation of the *HelloWorld* method.
2. Add the implementation for the *ConvertF2C* and *ConvertC2F* methods to the class, as shown here:

```
[soap_method]
HRESULT ConvertF2C(/*[in]*/ double dFahr,
                   /*[out, retval]*/ double* dCelsius)
{
    // Check the return value
    if (dCelsius == 0) return E_POINTER;

    *dCelsius = ((dFahr - 32) * 5) / 9;
    return S_OK;
}
```

```
[soap_method]
HRESULT ConvertC2F(/*[in]*/ double dCelsius,
                   /*[out, retval]*/ double* dFahr)
{
    // Check the return value
    if (dFahr == 0) return E_POINTER;

    *dFahr = (9/5 * dCelsius) + 32;
    return S_OK;
}
```

Both methods are prefixed with the *soap_method* attribute, which is attached to methods in a Web Service. Adding this attribute exposes the method as a Web method with a corresponding WSDL description. The calculations are the same for the .NET Web Service, but the results are returned through the *out* parameters. Because these are pointers, both output parameters are checked before assignment, and a COM E_POINTER error code is returned if either pointer has a null value.

Both methods also return the S_OK COM return code, indicating that the function completed successfully.

3 Build the project. Provided you haven't made any coding errors, you'll find that the project is compiled, linked, and automatically deployed to the virtual directory of the Web server. Here are the appropriate entries from the build log for my service:

```
Compiling...
AtlConverter.cpp
Linking...
Creating library Debug/AtlConverter.lib and object
                Debug/AtlConverter.exp
Deploying the web files...
Copied file from c:\AtlConverter\AtlConverter.disco to
            c:\inetpub\wwwroot\AtlConverter\AtlConverter.disco
Copied file from c:\AtlConverter\AtlConverter.htm to
              c:\inetpub\wwwroot\AtlConverter\AtlConverter.htm
Copied file from c:\AtlConverter\Debug\AtlConverter.dll to
              c:\inetpub\wwwroot\AtlConverter\AtlConverter.dll
```

The files that are copied over are slightly different from those that are copied for a .NET Web Service. There are two DLLs, for the ATL Server and ISAPI parts of the project, a DISCO file that contains details of how to get the WSDL for the service, and an HTML page that provides basic information about the service.

If you open the DISCO file, you'll see that it looks like this:

```
<?xml version="1.0" ?>
<discovery xmlns="http://schemas.xmlsoap.org/disco/">
<contractRef xmlns="http://schemas.xmlsoap.org/disco/scl/"
   ref="http://localhost/AtlConverter/AtlConverter.dll?
        Handler=GenAtlConverterWSDL"
    docRef="http://localhost/AtlConverter/AtlConverter.htm"/>
</discovery>
```

When a client wants the WSDL, the ATL Server DLL will be asked to provide it by passing it the name of the compiler-generated WSDL handler, and the name given is the same as in the *request_handler* attribute for the *CAtlConverterService* class.

Using ATL Server

You can now use the Web Service in the same way that you'd use a .NET Web Service. The following steps show you how to access an ATL Server Web Service from code.

1. Create a new Managed C++ Application project, and call it UseAtlServer.
2. Add a Web Reference to the project by right-clicking on the project name in the Solution Explorer, and selecting Add Web Reference from the context menu. This will display the Add Web Reference dialog, which is illustrated in Chapter 23.
3. Type the address of the DISCO file of your service into the Address field. If you've called the project AtlConverter and installed it on the local computer, the URL will be:

   http://localhost/AtlConverter/AtlConverter.disco

> **note**
>
> You can't just click on the Web References On The Local Server link and expect to see ATL Service, because it isn't installed with quite the same mechanism as .NET Web Services.

4. This will display the DISCO information for the service.

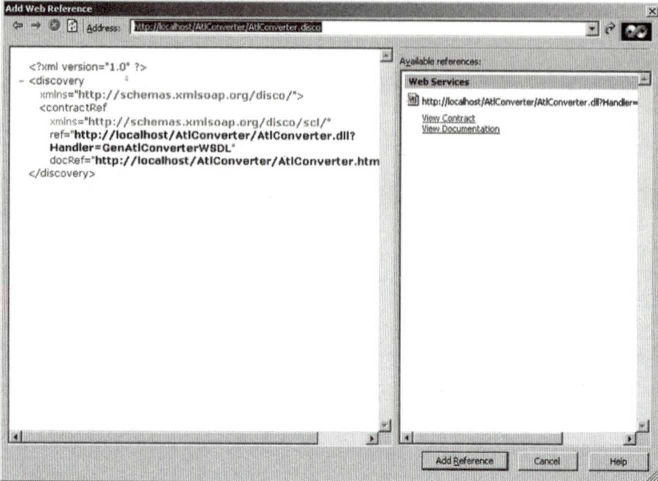

I explained the content of the DISCO file in the previous section, so now you can simply click Add Reference to add a reference to the project.

When the code generation has finished, you'll find that your project has a new header file, WebService.h, which contains the *#using* statements for all the DLLs that are needed to use the service. If you haven't already read it, refer to Chapter 23 for details about how the proxy class is generated in C# and built into a proxy DLL. This Web Service DLL is very similar in function to traditional COM proxy DLLs. You need to add the following *#include* directive to the top of UseAtlServer.cpp so code in that module will be able to use the proxy DLL:

```
#include "WebService.h"
```

5 To use the Web Service, modify the *_tmain* function in UseAtlServer.cpp as follows:

```
try
{
    AtlConverterService* ps = new AtlConverterService();
    double d = ps->ConvertF2C(47.5);
    Console::WriteLine("47.5F is {0}C", __box(d));
}
catch(Exception* pc)
{
    Console::WriteLine(pc->Message);
}
```

The proxy class is called *AtlConverterService*, which was the name given for the service in the *soap_handler* attribute of the ATL Server class. You can call the methods exposed by the service in the same way you would any COM object.

6 Build the project and run it from the command line. If all is working correctly, you should see the converted temperature displayed as the program's output.

Chapter 24 Quick Reference

To	Do This
Create an ATL Server Web Application	Create an ATL Server Project in Visual Studio .NET. Add methods to the implementation class, giving them suitable *tag_name* attributes. Edit the SRF file to reference the methods you've defined in the implementation class.
Access an ATL Server Web Application	Use the URL of the application's SRF file.
Create an ATL Server Web Service	Create an ATL Server Web Service project in Visual Studio .NET. Add method definitions to the interface, and then add method implementations to the ATL implementation class.
Access an ATL Server Web Service from code	Use the Add Web Reference menu item to add a Web Reference to your service

PART 7
Advanced Topics

CHAPTER

25

Working with Unmanaged Code

In this chapter, you'll learn

- ✔ *The issues that affect managed and unmanaged code*
- ✔ *How to use managed objects in unmanaged code*
- ✔ *How to use the Platform Invoke mechanism to call unmanaged functions in DLLs*

Although this book is concerned with using Managed C++ with the Microsoft .NET Framework, at times you'll have to call functions outside the .NET environment.

The *System::Runtime::InteropServices* namespace contains classes and structures to help with interoperation between .NET and the outside world. In this chapter, I'll introduce one feature of the namespace: the Platform Invoke mechanism for calling unmanaged functions within DLLs, and will investigate some of the other issues that surround interacting with unmanaged code. The final chapter will consider interoperating between COM and .NET.

Managed vs. Unmanaged Code

Code and data that live in the .NET world are called *managed*, because locations and lifetimes are managed by the Common Language Runtime (CLR). Code and data that exist outside of .NET are called *unmanaged*, because there is no central mechanism for managing their lifetimes. Sometimes you have to mix the two, calling existing unmanaged code from within .NET. This section introduces some of the issues and techniques that you'll need to consider in this situation.

Mixed Classes

Although managed classes are normally composed of other managed types, it is possible to mix managed and unmanaged types as members of classes under some circumstances. It is also possible to have a pointer to an unmanaged object as a member of a managed class, as in this example:

```
__gc class ManagedClass
{
  UnmanagedClass* puc;
  ...
};
```

Because the member is unmanaged, it's up to you to manage the lifetime of the object at the other end of the pointer. You should handle this carefully: unmanaged objects sometimes need explicit deletion at a particular point in the code, and this might not fit well with the .NET garbage collection model. However, you can declare destructors for managed classes and use *delete* on objects of managed types, so it's possible to arrange for correct object deallocation in most circumstances.

You can't have an unmanaged object as a member of a managed class:

```
__gc class ManagedClass
{
  UnmanagedClass obj;    // compiler error
  ...
};
```

An unmanaged object will work as a member class only if the host object is explicitly deleted at some point: at the end of the enclosing block for an automatic variable, at the end of the process for a global variable, or when *delete* is called on a pointer. Managed objects don't work in this way, and the garbage collector can't collect an unmanaged object.

It's impossible to have a pointer to a managed type as part of an unmanaged class:

```
class UnmanagedClass
{
  ManagedClass* pObj;    // compiler error
  ...
};
```

Because the unmanaged object doesn't exist in the .NET world, the pointer to the object is invisible to the garbage collector, so it doesn't know who has a reference to the object or when it can be garbage collected.

GCHandle

There is a way to use a managed type as part of an unmanaged class, and that is to use the *GCHandle* type provided in the *System::Runtime::InteropServices* namespace. *GCHandle* asks the run time to give you a "handle" to refer to a managed object from unmanaged code. You use the *GCHandle::Alloc* static method to create the handle, and the handle's *Free* method to release it again. Here's how you'd use *GCHandle* if you wanted to pass a pointer to a managed object to unmanaged code:

- Create a *GCHandle* to refer to your object. *GCHandles* can be converted to and from integers for ease of passing them between functions.
- Pass the *GCHandle* to the unmanaged code. As long as the handle hasn't been freed, the run time won't collect the object.
- Call *Free* on the handle when the unmanaged code no longer needs it. At this point, the run time is free to collect the object if no one else is using it.

To help you use *GCHandles* within unmanaged code without having to get into the details of using *Alloc* and *Free*, Microsoft provides a helper template class called *gcroot*. The following short exercise shows you how to include a pointer to a managed type as part of an unmanaged class using *gcroot*.

1. Create a new Managed C++ Application project called Manage.
2. Add an *include* directive for the gcroot.h system include file just below the stdafx.h *include* directive:

   ```
   #include <gcroot.h>
   ```

   This system header file defines the *gcroot* helper class.
3. Add a *#using* statement to the top of the code to make it easier to use the *System::Runtime::InteropServices* namespace:

   ```
   using namespace System::Runtime::InteropServices;
   ```

4. Add the definition of a simple managed class to the code:

```
__gc class MClass
{
public:
    int val;
    MClass(int n) { val=n; }
};
```

This class simply wraps an integer, whose value is set in the constructor.

5. Add the definition of an unmanaged class called *UClass*:

```
class UClass
{
public:
    gcroot<MClass*> mc;

    UClass(MClass* pmc)
    {
        mc = pmc;
    }

    int getValue()
    {
        return mc->val;
    }
};
```

The definition of the *mc* variable is an example of using a template class. Templates aren't as widely used in Managed C++ as they are in traditional C++. If you want to know more about them, consult the following sidebar "Templates in C++." The definition effectively creates a *gcroot* variable that wraps a *GCHandle* to an *MClass** pointer. The *GCHandle* is created when the *gcroot* object is created, and freed when the *gcroot* object is destroyed.

Templates in C++

Templates are an advanced feature of standard C++ that can be used in managed code, but which aren't needed much in code written for .NET. This sidebar only provides a brief introduction to their use in the *GCHandle* exercise. It doesn't cover constructing template classes; if you're interested in that, you should consult an intermediate-to-advanced text on traditional C++.

Templates provide a way to write generic classes. What does this mean? Imagine you have a class that holds a pointer to some type. At times you might want to use an *int**, at other times a *double** or a *char**. A pointer is simply a variable that holds an address, and all pointers are the same size, so how can you arrange for your class to hold a pointer to anything? Templates give you a way to write classes that contain one or more "wildcard" types so that the actual type will be provided at run time.

The *gcroot* class has been written to accept a pointer to any type of object, and when you create a *gcroot* object, you must specify the type that this instance will contain. You do this by specifying the type in angle brackets after the type name:

```
// Create a gcroot to hold an MClass*
gcroot<MClass*> mc;

// Create a gcroot to hold a Foo*
gcroot<Foo*> ff;
```

You can't specify the *gcroot* type without something in the angle brackets, as the declaration isn't complete unless you've specified the type that's going to take the place of the wildcard.

A *UClass* object is passed a pointer to a managed *MClass* object when it is created, and this pointer is stored away in the *gcroot* object. The *getValue* function simply returns the public *val* member from the *MClass* object, so you can verify that the code really lets you access a managed object from an unmanaged context.

6 Modify the *_tmain* function to use the classes:

```
int _tmain(void)
{
    Console::WriteLine(S"Testing...");

    // Create a managed object
    MClass* pm = new MClass(3);

    // Create an unmanaged object
    UClass uc(pm);

    int v = uc.getValue();
    Console::WriteLine("Value is {0}", __box(v));

    return 0;
}
```

The code first creates a managed object and initializes it with an integer. The pointer to this object is then used to initialize an unmanaged object, and the *getValue* function is used to extract the value from the managed object before printing it out. When the *UClass* object goes out of scope, the *gcroot* is destroyed and this frees the *GCHandle*, which in turn frees up the managed object.

Pinning and Boxing

This section discusses two Managed C++ keywords, *__pin* and *__box*, and shows you how they're used in code.

Pinning Pointers

In .NET, you normally leave the CLR to manage all the details of memory allocation and management, and it assumes that it can move managed objects around in the managed heap as and when it wants. At times, however, you might have to tell it to leave objects where they are. For example, if you want to pass a pointer to a managed object to an unmanaged function, you don't want the CLR to move the object around in memory while it's being used by the unmanaged code.

Pinning gives you a way to tell the CLR to leave an object where it is in memory: the object is pinned in place until the pin is removed. The *__pin* keyword lets you create a *pinning pointer*, which can be used to pin an object in memory; any object referred to through a pinning pointer won't be moved until it is no longer pointed to by the pinning pointer. This will occur when the pinning pointer goes out of scope, or if 0 is explicitly assigned to the pointer.

You can use pinning on all or part of a managed object. If you pin a member of a managed object, it results in the whole object being pinned. The following code fragment shows the creation and use of a pinning pointer:

```
// A class that contains an integer
__gc class MyClass
{
public:
    int val;
};

// Create a managed object
MyClass* pObject = new MyClass();

// Create a pinning pointer
MyClass __pin *pPinned = pObject;

// Pass the integer member to an unmanaged function
someFunc(&pPinned->val);

// Zero out the pinning pointer
pPinned = 0;
```

Once the object has been pinned, you can pass the address of the *int* member to an unmanaged function, confident that the *int* won't be moved around in memory. Assigning 0 to the pinning pointer frees up the *MyClass* object so that it can be moved.

Boxing and Unboxing

Boxing and unboxing allow value types to be treated as objects. We talked about value types way back in Chapter 9, where you learned that they are fundamentally different from reference types. To reiterate, value types have three particular properties:

- Value types are stored on the stack, unlike references, which are stored on the run-time heap.
- Instances of value types are always accessed directly, unlike reference types, which are accessed through references. This means that you don't use the *new* operator when creating instances.
- Copying value types copies the value, rather than the reference.

Anything that wraps around a simple value, such as a Boolean or an integer, and that is less than about 16 bytes in size is a good candidate for making a value type, and value types can be far more efficient than the equivalent reference types.

The efficiency stems from the fact that value types aren't accessed via references, so they can't be regarded as objects in the same way that reference types can. This becomes a problem when you want to use a value type in a context where an object reference is needed. For example, consider the overload of the *Console::WriteLine* function that performs formatted output, whose prototype is shown here:

```
static void WriteLine(String*, Object*);
```

The *String** parameter is the format string, and the second is a pointer to any .NET reference type. Since value types aren't accessed by references, you can't directly specify a value type. If you try this:

```
int foo = 12;
Console::WriteLine("foo is {0}", foo);
```

you'll get the following compiler error:

```
error C2665: 'System::Console::WriteLine' :
        none of the 19 overloads can convert parameter 2 from type 'int'
```

Boxing

Boxing wraps a value type in an object box, so that it can be used where an object reference is needed. In Managed C++, it is done using the *__box* keyword.

> **note**
>
> You've already seen this keyword used many times in the book, so I won't present an exercise here.

You can fix the *WriteLine* code like this:

```
int foo = 12;
// Box the value so it can be printed
Console::WriteLine("foo is {0}", __box(foo));
```

When you use the *__box* keyword, three things happen:

- A managed object is created on the CLR heap.
- The value of the value type is copied bit by bit into the managed object.
- The address of the managed object is returned.

Note that the managed object contains a copy of the value type; this means that any modifications you might make to the managed wrapper don't propagate back to the original value.

note

C# supports implicit boxing, in which the compiler boxes values when it determines that boxing is necessary. This isn't supported in Managed C++ for performance reasons, so you have to use the *__box* keyword explicitly in order to box values.

Unboxing

What if you want to copy the value back out of a boxed object? In C# this is done automatically for you by the compiler, but in Managed C++ you have to do it yourself. There is no *__unbox* keyword to correspond to *__box*, so you must unbox manually.

The following exercise shows you how to get the value back out of a boxed object using a dynamic cast.

1. Create a new Managed C++ Application project called Boxing.
2. Edit the *_tmain* function to create an integer and box it:

```
int _tmain(void)
{
    Console::WriteLine(S"Boxing Example");

    // Create an int
    int foo = 12;

    // Box it
    Object* pFoo = __box(foo);
```

```
    // Use the boxed object
    Console::WriteLine("Value of foo is {0}", pFoo);

    return 0;
}
```

3 Add the following code to get the value back out of the box:

```
// Unbox the value
int fooTwo = *dynamic_cast<__box int*>(pFoo);

Console::WriteLine("fooTwo is {0}", __box(fooTwo));
```

The *dynamic_cast* checks to see if a boxed *int* is on the other end of the *pFoo* pointer, and if it is, it returns an *int* pointer which is dereferenced by the first asterisk. See the following sidebar "Casting in C++" for more details on the *dynamic_cast* operator.

Casting in C++

The *dynamic_cast* operator is a mechanism for casting variables in C++. Casting has been around in C for many years as a means for the programmer to explicitly convert between types, and it is usually used to perform conversions that the compiler otherwise wouldn't do. Here's an example:

```
int width = 640;
int height = 480;
double ratio = width / height;
```

Dividing two integers gives an integer result, so the answer is 0, which wasn't intended. This code will give the correct result:

```
double ratio = double(width) / height;
```

The cast tells the compiler to treat width as a *double*, which results in a floating-point division operation. There are two equivalent syntaxes for casting, both of which have exactly the same effect:

```
double ratio = (double)width / height;  // older style C cast
double ratio = double(width) / height;  // C++ function-style
cast
```

Explicit C-style casting like this is dangerous, because it enables the programmer to perform risky and inappropriate conversions like this:

```
char* pc = ...;
int* pi = (int*)pc;
```

Here, a character pointer is being cast to an integer pointer. Since they're both pointers and simply contain addresses, this will work, but is it likely that the address of a character or string can also be used as the address of an integer? This is probably an error on the programmer's part.

Casting is often used with object pointers, especially when inheritance is involved. Consider the following code:

```
Car* pc = new Car();
Vehicle* pv = pc;
```

If *Car* derives from *Vehicle*, then it is quite safe to assign *pc* to *pv*. *Car* inherits all the members of *Vehicle*, so you can use a *Car* through a *Vehicle* pointer. However, what if later in the program you want to go back the other way?

```
Car* pMyCar = pv;
```

The compiler will complain if you try this, typically giving you error C2440: "Cannot convert from Vehicle* to Car*." It's fine to go from *Car* to *Vehicle*, because a car is a vehicle, but if you try to assign from a *Vehicle* to a *Car*, how does the compiler know that the object on the other end of the *Vehicle* pointer is a *Car*? It could be any kind of *Vehicle*, such as a *Bus*, *Truck*, or *Motorcycle*. Casting up the hierarchy—upcasting from *Car* to *Vehicle*—is inherently safe, while downcasting from *Vehicle* to *Car* is inherently unsafe.

You can use an explicit cast to tell the compiler what to do, like this:

```
Car* pMyCar = (Car*)pv;
```

This gets rid of the error message, but it is error prone: What if the object on the other end of *pv* isn't a *Car*? There's no way the compiler can warn you, and your program can get into serious trouble later on. C++ provides four casting operators for these situations: *const_cast*, *static_cast*, *dynamic_cast*, and *reinterpret_cast*. These are designed to make casting more explicit and safer.

(continued)

(continued)

The *const_cast* operator is used to remove *const* from pointers; if *pcc* is a *const char** pointer, then the following two lines of code are equivalent:

```
char* pc = (char*)pcc;
char* pc = const_cast<char*>(pcc);
```

Const_cast checks that the type of the pointer and the type given in the angle brackets differ only by *const*. If they're any more different than that—say *int** and *const char**—you'll get a run-time error.

The *static_cast* operator converts between types in an expression, using only the type information available in the expression. This is often used for converting between built-in types (such as *int* to *double*), and might not be safe. Here's an example of a static cast:

```
double d = static_cast<double>(anInt);
```

You can use *static_cast* to cast between derived and base types (for example, from *Car** to *Vehicle**), but it isn't usually necessary as the compiler will do this automatically as required.

The *dynamic_cast* operator converts between objects in a hierarchy when the check needs to be done at run time.

```
Car* pc = dynamic_cast<Car*>(pVehicle);
```

A check is done at run time to see whether the object on the other end of the *pVehicle* pointer is indeed a *Car*. If it is, a *Car** pointer is returned, but if it isn't, the result is a *null* pointer. This gives you a simple way to check whether the wrong pointer has been used:

```
Car* pc = dynamic_cast<Car*>(pVehicle);
if (pc == 0)
    // pVehicle wasn't pointing to a Car
```

The final operator, *reinterpret_cast*, allows any pointer type to be converted to any other pointer type, and allows integer types to be converted to and from pointers. Here's an example:

```
unsigned int ui = reinterpret_cast<unsigned int>(pVehicle);
```

The address in the *Vehicle* pointer will be used to initialize an unsigned integer. Although there are legitimate reasons for needing to do this, it isn't something you'll want to do very often, if at all!

If you need to use casting in C++ code, make sure you use the C++ casting operators rather than the traditional C-style casts. Using C-style casts leaves you open to all sorts of errors, many of which can be caught by the more modern operators available.

Using P/Invoke to Call Functions in the Win32 API

Although it's possible to do a great deal using the functionality provided in the .NET Framework, at times you'll need to make use of code that wasn't written for .NET. For example:

- You need to call a Microsoft Windows API function that doesn't have a .NET equivalent.
- You have some code in a DLL that originated outside .NET and can't be rewritten.
- You have code that needs to be written in a language that's not yet supported by the .NET Framework.

Whatever the reason, the code you're calling exists outside the .NET managed environment, so you need a way to pass function calls into and out of .NET. The mechanism is called P/Invoke (for Platform Invoke), and is provided to let you call functions in DLLs.

Using P/Invoke involves adding a prototype to your code that uses attributes to tell .NET about the function you're proposing to call. In particular, you need to tell it the name of the DLL containing the function, the name of the function, what arguments the function takes, and what it returns.

A mechanism such as P/Invoke is necessary because work needs to be done to communicate between managed and unmanaged code. Take strings as an example: A string in Managed C++ is a pointer to a *String* object, but in unmanaged C++, a string isn't represented by an object. Instead, it is a pointer to a series of memory locations that contain characters and is terminated by a null. If you're going to pass string data between managed and unmanaged code, something has to convert between the corresponding managed and unmanaged data types. This conversion process is called *marshaling*, and it is one of the tasks that P/Invoke performs for you.

Identifying Functions

There are two points that you need to be aware of when identifying functions to call using P/Invoke. Although you usually identify functions in DLLs by name, you can also assign functions in a DLL a number that can be used to execute the function at run time. If you need to, you can identify DLL functions to P/Invoke using these ordinal numbers.

When you call Windows API functions, you can also have two or more versions of functions that take characters or strings as arguments. This happens because Windows can support more than one character encoding; for example, standard Windows 2000 supports both the ASCII (one byte per character) and Unicode (two bytes per character) character encodings. This means that there need to be ASCII and Unicode versions of each function, identified by an "A" or a "W" added to the end of the function name (for example, *MessageBoxW*). Although you can call the different versions directly, the C++ compiler will map a call to *MessageBox* onto the correct function depending on whether you're using ASCII or Unicode in your program.

As you'll discover in the exercise later in this section, you can specify which version of a function you want to use with P/Invoke. If you don't explicitly pick one, the ASCII version will be chosen.

The following exercise shows you how to call an unmanaged function in one of the Windows system DLLs. The obvious candidate for this exercise is *MessageBox* for two reasons: first, it's a stand-alone function and doesn't require any setting up, and second, it's obvious whether the call has worked or not!

The *MessageBox* function—or rather, the *MessageBoxA* and *MessageBoxW* functions—live in the User32.dll system DLL. Three system DLLs contain the unmanaged Windows API code:

- User32.dll, which contains functions for message handling, timers, menus, and communications.
- Kernel32.dll, which contains low-level operating system functionality for memory management and resource handling.
- GDI32.dll, which contains the GDI graphics subsystem code.

How do you know which DLL holds a particular system function? If you look the function up in the Platform SDK, you'll usually find a clue in the "Requirements" section at the end of the topic. For example, the Help topic for *MessageBox* has the following line:

```
Library: Use User32.lib
```

This line tells you that if you want to use *MessageBox* in traditional C++ code, you'll have to link with a library called User32.lib, and the name User32 tells you that the code actually lives in User32.dll.

Now that we know where the *MessageBox* function can be found, here's the exercise:

1. Start a new Managed C++ Application project called Message.
2. Add a *using namespace* statement to the top of the project:

   ```
   using namespace System::Runtime::InteropServices;
   ```

   The attribute class that you'll be using is part of the *System::Runtime::InteropServices* namespace, and it's much easier to use if you declare the namespace.
3. Add the prototype for the *MessageBox* function before the *_tmain* routine:

   ```
   // Declare the HWND typedef
   typedef void* HWND;

   // Set up the import
   [DllImportAttribute("User32.dll", CharSet=CharSet::Auto)]
   extern "C" int MessageBox(HWND hw, String* text,
                             String* caption, unsigned int type);
   ```

   HWND is one of the traditional Windows data types and is simply a *typedef* for a *void** pointer. The prototype for the *MessageBox* function is declared using the *DllImportAttribute* attribute class. The two parameters passed to the attribute are the name of the DLL housing the function, and (because this is a function that uses characters or strings) an indication of which version to use. *CharSet::Auto* leaves it up to the target platform to decide which version to call and how to convert the string arguments.

   The actual Windows API function is a C function rather than a C++ function, so *extern "C"* is used to ensure that the compiler generates the correct calling sequence. Note how *String** pointers are used to pass string information, where the original function would require a Windows LPTSTR type. The P/Invoke marshaling will automatically convert the data when making the call.
4. Add code to the *_tmain* function to call *MessageBox*:

```
int _tmain(void)
{
   Console::WriteLine(S"P/Invoke Example");

   String* theText = S"Hello World!";
   String* theCaption = S"A Message Box...";
   MessageBox(0, theText, theCaption, 0);

   return 0;
}
```

When you build and run the code, you'll see a *MessageBox* displayed on the screen:

The *DllImportAttribute* Class

You used the *DllImportAttribute* class in the previous exercise to provide a prototype for an unmanaged function. This class has a number of fields that can be used when constructing the prototype, and they're listed in the following table:

Field	Description
CallingConvention	Defines the calling convention used when passing arguments to the unmanaged function
CharSet	Defines how characters and strings are to be handled
EntryPoint	Indicates the name or ordinal number of the DLL function to be called
ExactSpelling	Indicates whether the name of the entry point should be modified to correspond to the character set in use
PreserveSig	Used for COM methods, this field should be set to *true* if that the return values from methods shouldn't be altered in any way
SetLastError	If *true*, the caller can use the Win32 *GetLastError* function to determine whether an error occurred

Let's look at the more common fields in detail. The *CallingConvention* defines how arguments are passed between the managed and unmanaged code, and will take one of the values in the *CallingConvention* enumeration. Different languages use different ways of passing arguments, so Windows supports a number of different calling conventions. C and C++ normally use the C calling convention, often known as *cdecl*, while many other Windows languages use the standard calling convention, often abbreviated to *stdcall*. You call Windows API functions using *stdcall*, and it's the default unless you use the *CallingConvention* field to choose another.

CharSet lets you specify how characters and strings are to be marshaled, and takes one of the values from the *CharSet* enumeration. You can specify *CharSet::Ansi*, in which case all characters and strings are converted to one-byte ANSI characters and an "A" is appended to the name of the DLL entry point. Choosing *CharSet::Unicode* converts characters and strings to use two-byte Unicode characters and appends a "W" to the entry point name. However, it's usually sufficient to specify *CharSet::Auto*, which chooses the best option for the host system.

The *EntryPoint* field lets you specify the name or ordinal number of the entry point in the DLL. If you don't specify this field, as in the exercise above, the entry point name is taken to be the function name given in the prototype. A name given using the *EntryPoint* field takes precedence over the prototype name, so this gives you the ability to provide synonyms for unmanaged functions if you want to refer to them by another name when calling them in your code. The following code fragment shows how you could define a synonym for the *MessageBox* function:

```
[DllImportAttribute("User32.dll", EntryPoint="MessageBox",
                   CharSet=CharSet::Auto)]
extern "C" int WindowsMessageBox(HWND hw, String* text,
                        String* caption, unsigned int type);
```

You call the function as *WindowsMessageBox*, and the call is mapped onto the *MessageBox* entry point in User32.dll.

Passing Structures

You'll often need to pass structured data to arguments to unmanaged functions, and you must do this carefully. In particular, you need to specify the way structures are laid out in memory to be sure that they are passed around correctly. You specify the layout of structures and classes using the *StructLayoutAttribute* and *FieldOffsetAttribute* classes.

You add *StructLayoutAttribute* to managed types to define a formatted type with a particular layout. There are three possible layout types that you can specify for a formatted type:

- Automatic layout, where the run time might reorder the members if it is more efficient. You *never* use automatic layout for types that are going to be used with P/Invoke, because you need to be sure that everything stays in the same order.
- Explicit layout, where members are ordered according to byte offsets specified by *FieldOffset* attributes on each field.
- Sequential layout, where members appear in unmanaged memory in the same order that they do in the managed definition.

The following exercise shows how to call an unmanaged Windows API function that needs to be passed a structure. The function is *GetSystemPowerStatus*, which reports on the AC and battery status of the system. The Windows API defines a structure SYSTEM_POWER_STATUS, which contains the status information. The definition of this unmanaged structure is shown here:

```
typedef struct _SYSTEM_POWER_STATUS {
    BYTE ACLineStatus;
    BYTE  BatteryFlag;
    BYTE  BatteryLifePercent;
    BYTE  Reserved1;
    DWORD  BatteryLifeTime;
    DWORD  BatteryFullLifeTime;
} SYSTEM_POWER STATUS, *LPSYSTEM_POWER_STATUS;
```

The prototype for the *GetSystemPowerStatus* function in the API documentation is:

```
BOOL GetSystemPowerStatus(
  LPSYSTEM_POWER_STATUS lpSystemPowerStatus  // status
);
```

The function takes a pointer to a SYSTEM_POWER_STATUS structure, fills it in, and hands back the filled structure, returning a Boolean value to let you know whether it worked or not. Your task is to call this function, passing over a structure, and display the results.

1. Create a new Managed C++ Application project called PowerMonitor.
2. Add the following line after *using namespace System*:

   ```
   using namespace System::Runtime::InteropServices;
   ```

   This will make it easier to refer to the attributes we'll be using later.
3. Define a managed equivalent for the structure:

```
[StructLayoutAttribute(LayoutKind::Sequential)]
__gc class PStat {
public:
    System::Byte ACLineStatus;
    System::Byte BatteryFlag;
    System::Byte BatteryLifePercent;
    System::Byte Reserved1;
    System::UInt32 BatteryLifeTime;
    System::UInt32 BatteryFullLifeTime;
};
```

Our equivalent of SYSTEM_POWER_STATUS is a managed class called *PStat*. The original definition contains two Windows data types: BYTE represents a one-byte integer, and so can be represented by the *System::Byte* type, while DWORD is a 32-bit unsigned integer, and so is represented by *System::UInt32*. The *StructLayoutAttribute* is attached to the class, and *LayoutKind::Sequential* is specified so that the layout of the members will remain the same as the data is passed through P/Invoke.

4 Define the prototype for the *GetSystemPowerStatus* function:

```
// Define the BOOL type
typedef int BOOL;

// Prototype for the function
[DllImportAttribute("Kernel32.dll", CharSet=CharSet::Auto)]
BOOL GetSystemPowerStatus(PStat* ps);
```

BOOL is a Windows type representing a Boolean value, and is actually a *typedef* for an integer. It has been widely used in the Windows API because C lacks a true Boolean type. The prototype uses the real name of the function as it occurs in Kernel32.dll, and the single argument is given as a pointer to our managed type.

5 Write the code to call the function. Edit the *_tmain* function to create a *PStat* object and use it to call the function:

```
int _tmain(void)
{
    Console::WriteLine(S"Power Status Test...");
    PStat* ps = new PStat();

    BOOL b = GetSystemPowerStatus(ps);
    Console::WriteLine(S"Got status, return was {0}", __box(b));

    return 0;
}
```

If the call worked, the return value should be non-zero, which represents a Boolean *true* value.

6 Add code to report on the members of the class:

```
// Report on the AC line status
Console::Write(S"AC line power status is ");
switch(ps->ACLineStatus) {
case 0:
    Console::WriteLine("'off'");
    break;
case 1:
    Console::WriteLine("'on'");
    break;
case 255:
    Console::WriteLine("'unknown'");
    break;
}

// Report on the battery status
Console::Write(S"Battery charge status is ({0})",
               __box(ps->BatteryFlag));
if (ps->BatteryFlag & 1)
    Console::Write(" 'high'");
if (ps->BatteryFlag & 2)
    Console::Write(" 'low'");
if (ps->BatteryFlag & 4)
    Console::Write(" 'critical'");
if (ps->BatteryFlag & 8)
    Console::Write(" 'charging'");
if (ps->BatteryFlag & 128)
    Console::Write(" 'no system battery'");
Console::WriteLine();

// What's the percentage charge left in the battery?
Console::WriteLine(S"Battery life is {0}%",
   __box(ps->BatteryLifePercent));

// How many seconds battery life is left?
if (ps->BatteryLifeTime == -1)
    Console::WriteLine("Battery life in seconds: Unknown");
else
```

```
Console::WriteLine(S"Battery seconds remaining: {0} secs",
                   __box(ps->BatteryLifeTime));
```

The first check is on the *ACLineStatus* field, which will have the value 0 (on), 1 (off), or 255 (unknown). The second check is on the status of the battery, and this value can be made up of one or more of the values 1 (high charge), 2 (low charge), 4 (critically low charge), 8 (charging), and 128 (no battery present). Each of these represents a particular bit position within the result, and the *bitwise OR* operator is used to check which bits are set.

The final two checks print out the percentage lifetime left in the battery and the number of seconds. If the function can't determine the number of seconds, it will return -1 in this field.

7 Build and run the program. This illustration shows the output that I got when I ran the program on my laptop:

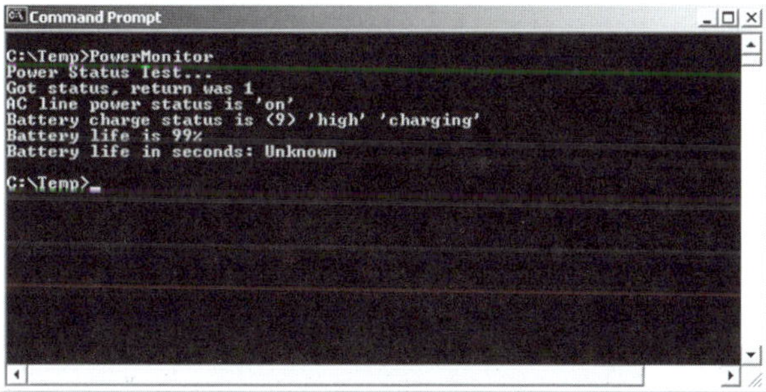

```
Command Prompt
C:\Temp>PowerMonitor
Power Status Test...
Got status, return was 1
AC line power status is 'on'
Battery charge status is (9) 'high' 'charging'
Battery life is 99%
Battery life in seconds: Unknown

C:\Temp>_
```

Chapter 25 Quick Reference

To	Do This

Obtain a safe handle to a managed object so that it won't be garbage collected while being used by	Use the *System::Runtime::InteropServices::GCHandle::Alloc* function to wrap a pointer to a managed object in a *GCHandle*. The easiest way to do this is to use the *gcroot* helper class. For example:
	`Foo* ff = new unmanaged code Foo();`
	`gcroot<Foo*> pf = ff;`
	This code wraps the pointer to the *Foo* object with a *GCHandle*, and handles cleanup when the *gcroot* is destroyed.

Fix all or part of a managed object in memory so it can safely be used by unmanaged code	Use the *__pin* keyword to create a pinning pointer. For example: `Foo __pin * ptr = new Foo();` The managed *Foo* object won't be moved in memory or garbage collected until the pinning pointer goes out of context or has 0 assigned to it.
Convert a value type to an object so that it can be used where an object is required	Use the *__box* keyword to create an object wrapper. For example: `int n = 3; Object* po = __box(n);` Note that the value in the box is a copy of the original.
Retrieve the value from a boxed object	Use *dynamic_cast* to cast the boxing object to the correct type, and then dereference the pointer. For example: `int myVal = *dynamic_cast<__box int*>(po);`
Call an unmanaged function in a DLL	Use the Platform Invoke mechanism by declaring a prototype for the unmanaged function that uses the *DllImportAttribute* class to specify the DLL in which the function lives and other optional parameters

26

Attributes and Reflection

In this chapter, you'll learn

- ✔ *What attributes are*
- ✔ *How to use attributes to add metadata to managed types*
- ✔ *How to create your own attribute types*
- ✔ *How to access attribute metadata from code*

This chapter introduces metadata and attributes, and shows you how to start defining and manipulating metadata for your own .NET types.

Metadata and Attributes

The concept of metadata is central to the way the .NET Framework works, so to be an effective .NET programmer, you need to know what it is and how to work with it.

Metadata is data attached to .NET data types that carries information about those types. A lot of metadata contains information that can't be specified in the programming language itself, and it offers a useful—many people would say essential—way to provide all the extra information needed by the .NET run time.

One of the major advantages of metadata is that it is stored along with the code, so that extra data doesn't need to be stored separately. For example, with COM objects, all manner of extra data has to be stored in the Microsoft Windows registry. One of the main problems with configuring and using COM objects is ensuring that the data in the registry doesn't get corrupted or otherwise out of step with the COM code.

Another major advantage of metadata is that it provides a way to add version information to the code, so that you know the version of a component you're using. This solves a whole lot of problems that have plagued programmers since the early days of Windows, and is a huge step forward.

The compiler always attaches metadata to the output code to describe it, and the Common Language Runtime (CLR) uses the metadata to control the loading and execution of the code. You can also attach metadata to code using attributes, special syntax elements that can be attached to classes and class members. You'll see how to use attributes later in this chapter.

You can see some of the metadata that the compiler attaches to your code if you use the Intermediate Language (IL) disassembler tool, ildasm.exe, included with the .NET Framework SDK (which you'll find in Program Files, Microsoft Visual Studio .NET, FrameworkSDK, bin, if you've installed to the default location). The following example shows you how to use ildasm.exe to examine a simple program:

1. Create a new Managed C++ Application project called Hello.
2. Add a new managed class to the program:

   ```
   __gc class Hello
   {
   public:
       static void SayHello()
       {
           Console::WriteLine("Hello, world");
       }
   };
   ```

   The class doesn't really have to do anything particular, as it is simply here so that you can disassemble it to look at the metadata.
3. Build the program to generate the executable.
4. Run the ildasm.exe program. This program doesn't appear on the Start menu, so you need to run it from the command line. To do this, start a Visual Studio .NET command prompt, which has the path set up to let you run all the tools from the Visual Studio and .NET Framework directories. You'll find Visual Studio .NET Command Prompt under Visual Studio .NET Tools on the Microsoft Visual Studio .NET menu. Start a command prompt and type **ildasm** to run the tool. You should see a window like this:

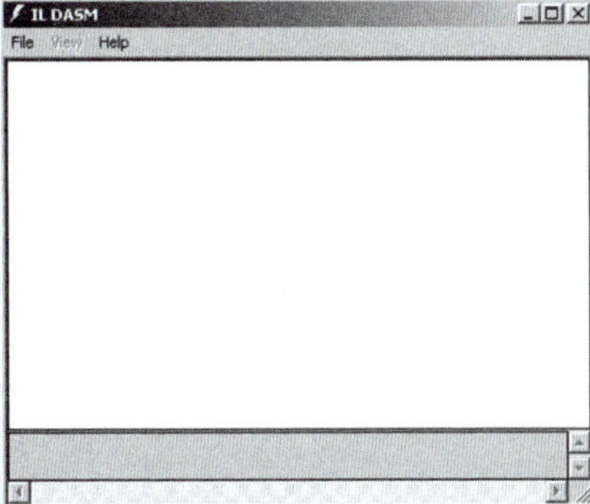

5 Select Open from ildasm's File menu, navigate to the Hello.exe executable, and open it. The display should now look like this:

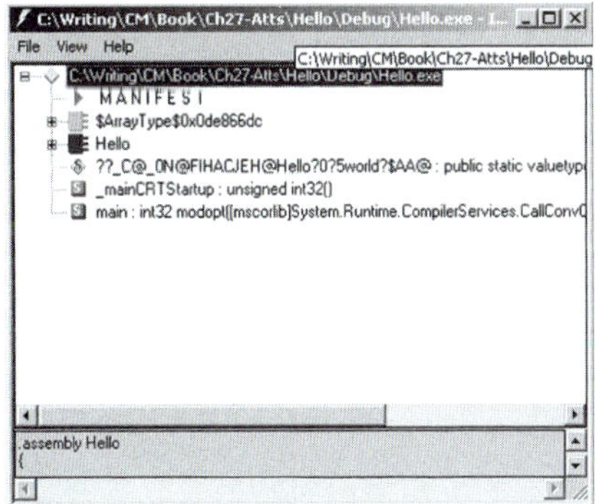

6 We're interested in the managed type *Hello*, which is indicated by the blue component symbol. Click on the plus sign (+) to expand the tree for Hello, and the details of the class will be displayed:

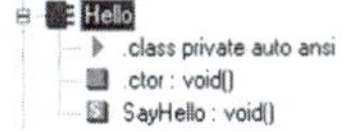

The type has three entries: the details of the class itself, and the entries for two methods, which are the *SayHello* method you added, and the default constructor provided by the compiler.

7 Double-click on the red triangle to bring up the class information, and you'll see a window like this:

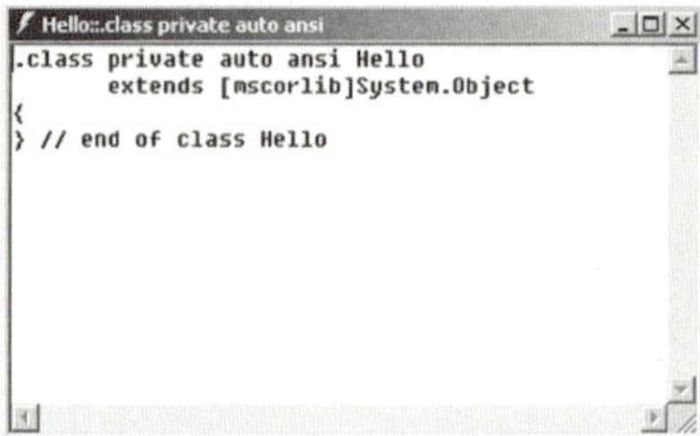

The definition of the managed class—which extends *System::Object*—is marked as *private auto ansi*. These keywords represent items of metadata that have been added by the compiler to describe the class. You can open the other methods in this class to see what metadata is attached to them.

You can enquire about attributes at run time using reflection, a feature of the .NET Framework that allows programmers to find out information about the objects they are using, such as what class they belong to, what methods they support, and what metadata is attached to them. Using attributes in code is very powerful, because it effectively gives you a way to extend the programming language, introducing new properties for your classes that don't exist in the base language.

Later in the chapter, you'll see how to create custom attributes, and how to use code to look at the attributes attached to classes.

Using Predefined Attributes

In this section, we'll discuss how to use the attributes that are predefined by the .NET Framework. You can use these attributes in two ways: by editing the AssemblyInfo.cpp file that comes as part of a Managed C++ project, and by attaching attributes to managed elements in your code.

The AssemblyInfo.cpp File

Every Managed C++ project includes an AssemblyInfo.cpp file that contains code affecting the attributes applied to the assembly. You can edit this file in order to customize the assembly attributes, and these will be used to set the metadata in the assembly at build time. The following exercise shows you how to modify assembly attributes:

1 Create a new Managed C++ Application project called AssemblyAttributes.

2 Open the AssemblyInfo.cpp file and examine its contents. You'll see that the file contains a number of entries of the form:

```
[assembly:AssemblyTitleAttribute("")];
```

Most of these have empty strings as arguments.

3 Find the version number attribute, and edit it to produce a new version:

```
[assembly:AssemblyVersionAttribute("1.1.105.3")];
```

This number would correspond to version 1.1, build 105, revision 3.

4 Compile and build the program. If you now look at the assembly using the ILDASM tool, you can see the version in two places. First, it will show in the pane at the bottom of the ILDASM main window:

You can also see it if you double-click on the MANIFEST entry in the main window, and scroll down to the bottom of the data window which is opened as a result. The line starting with ".ver" lists the version metadata:

```
.ver 1:1:105:3
```


It is possible to check this version number in applications that use this assembly, although how to do so is beyond the scope of this book.

Using the Predefined Attribute Classes

Although much of the metadata produced by the compiler is predefined and you can't alter it, there are a number of optional standard attributes provided by various .NET Framework namespaces. The following table lists some of the standard attributes you might want to use in your own projects:

Class	Description
System::AttributeUsageAttribute	Specifies the usage of another attribute class
System::CLSCompliantAttribute	Indicates whether a program element is CLS-compliant
System::Diagnostics::ConditionalAttribute	Indicates that a method can be called if a preprocessor symbol is defined
System::Diagnostics::DebuggableAttribute	Modifies code generation for run-time JIT (Just In Time) debugging
System::Diagnostics::Debugger HiddenAttribute	Indicates for a method that breakpoints can't be set in the code, and that debuggers will not stop in the method

(continued)

(continued)

System::Diagnostics::DebuggerStepThroughAttribute	Indicates for a method that the debugger will not stop in this method, although breakpoints can be set
System::FlagsAttribute	Indicates that an enumeration is to be used as a set of flags, and can be represented by a bit field
System::MTAThreadAttribute	Indicates that the default threading model for an application is MTA (multi-threaded apartment)
System::NonSerializedAttribute	Indicates that a field of a serializable class should not be serialized
System::ObsoleteAttribute	Indicates program elements that are no longer in use
System::ParamArrayAttribute	Indicates that a method accepts a variable number of arguments
System::SerializableAttribute	Indicates that a class can be serialized
System::STAThreadAttribute	Indicates that the default threading model for an application is STA (single-threaded apartment)

You'll meet a lot of attributes when working with COM in Managed C++, because they are used to define all the metadata needed by COM objects that is specified in IDL for unmanaged COM C++ code.

The following exercise will show you how to use one of the standard attributes in code. You'll use the *ObsoleteAttribute* class to mark a class method as obsolete, and see how the compiler gives a warning when you use the obsolete method. This exercise will also show you how to build a Managed C++ DLL and use it in code. If you want to know more about DLLs, see the following sidebar, "DLLs in Windows."

DLLs in Windows

Windows executable code can be parceled up in two forms: as an executable, or as a DLL. Dynamic Link Libraries, or DLLs, contain executable code, but can't run on their own. A DLL contains functions or classes used by other code in a process, and a DLL is loaded at run time so that the function or class code is accessible.

There are both advantages and disadvantages to using DLLs. Here are some advantages:

- DLLs can be loaded and unloaded on demand, so applications can control their memory use.
- They can be shared by more than one process, so they are a good way to provide shared functionality such as printer drivers.
- Using DLLs means that it is possible to upgrade or fix part of an application without having to redistribute or reinstall everything.

There is also one major drawback to DLLs in the traditional Windows world: an application might use the wrong version of a DLL. This is especially true of Windows system DLLs, because you can easily end up with multiple versions of the same DLL on one computer. This can lead to problems that are hard to debug, and users with applications that don't work because somewhere a DLL is out of date.

However, this isn't so much of a problem for .NET programmers, because assemblies—the fundamental building blocks of .NET applications—have version information built in, and it is possible to specify in code exactly what versions of an assembly are acceptable. If code does end up running on a computer with the wrong version of an assembly, the result will be a precise error message rather than odd behavior.

In the .NET world, DLLs provide one way to package up assemblies. If an assembly contains a standard entry point—such as *main* or *WinMain*—it can be built into an assembly with an .exe extension that can be executed from the command line. If the assembly doesn't contain an entry point, it can be built into a library assembly containing types that can be referenced from other assemblies, but that has no entry point to begin execution.

note

There is a bug in the beta and Release Candidate versions which means that the compiler only recognizes the *Obsolete* attribute in managed types that have been loaded from a separate assembly. If you put all the code from the exercise into one file and build a single executable, you'll find that the compiler doesn't act on the *ObsoleteAttribute* settings.

The Solution consists of two projects: a Managed C++ Application that holds the *_tmain* function, and a Managed C++ Library project that holds a managed class called *Hello*. The *_tmain* function will create a *Hello* object and call methods on it, which will need the DLL assembly to be loaded at run time.

1 Create a new Managed C++ Application project, and call it UseAttributes. You'll add code to this project later.

2 Right-click on the Solution name in the Solution Explorer window, choose Add from the shortcut menu, and then New Project.

 This will bring up the familiar New Project dialog box.

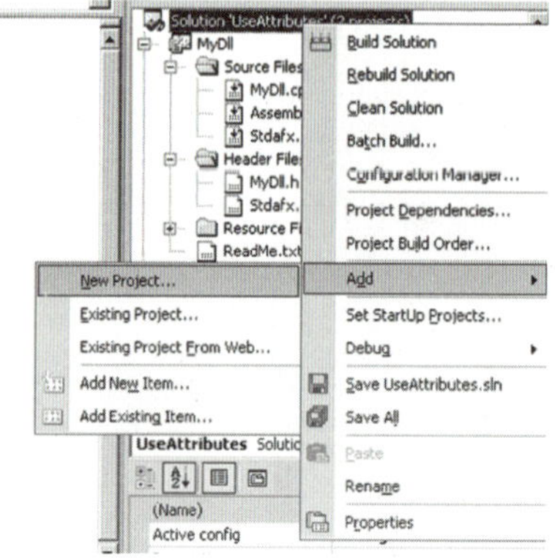

3 Make sure the project type is set to Managed C++ Class Library, and call the project MyDll. Click OK.

4 Open the MyDll.h file from Solution Explorer, and you'll see the skeleton of a namespace containing a single class. Edit the class definition so that it contains two methods, as shown here:

```
// MyDll.h

#pragma once
```

```
using namespace System;

namespace MyDll
{
    public __gc class Hello
    {
    public:
        [ObsoleteAttribute("Don't use this", true)]
        void SayHello()
        {
            Console::WriteLine("Hello");
        }

        void SayHello2()
        {
            Console::WriteLine("Hello again");
        }
    };
}
```

The two methods simply write a line of text to the Console. The difference between them is that the first has an *ObsoleteAttribute* attached to it, indicating that this method is out of date and shouldn't be used. The first argument to *ObsoleteAttribute* is a string giving the reason the method is obsolete and telling the user what alternative action to take. Many compilers (although unfortunately not Microsoft Visual C++) will display this string as part of a compiler warning or error message. The second argument is a Boolean value that determines whether use of this function is to be regarded as an error (*true*) or a warning (*false*) by the compiler.

5 Build the DLL project by right-clicking on the project name in the Solution Explorer and choosing Build from the shortcut menu.

6 Open the UseAttributes.cpp source file. Because the *Hello* class is located in another assembly, you need to add a *#using* statement so that the compiler can locate the assembly at compile time. Add the following line immediately after the existing *#using* statement:

```
#using <MyDll.dll>
```

It will also be easier to use the *Hello* class if you don't have to use fully qualified names, so add a *using* declaration for the namespace:

```
using namespace MyDll;
```

7 Edit the *_tmain* function to create an object and call the obsolete method:

```
int _tmain(void)
{
    Console::WriteLine(S"Attribute test");

    Hello* ph = new Hello();
    ph->SayHello();

    return 0;
}
```

8 Before compiling the project, you need to let the compiler know where it can find the DLL. Right-click UseAttributes in the Solution Explorer, then select Properties from the shortcut menu. This will display the project's Property Pages dialog box:

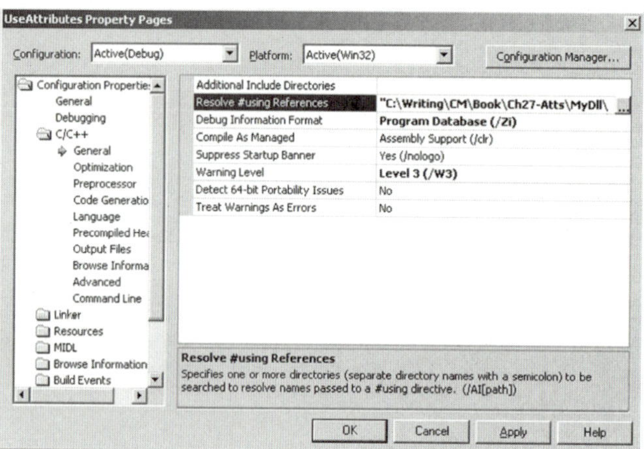

Add the path to the directory where the DLL lives by clicking the Ellipsis (...) button to bring up the Resolve #using References dialog box:

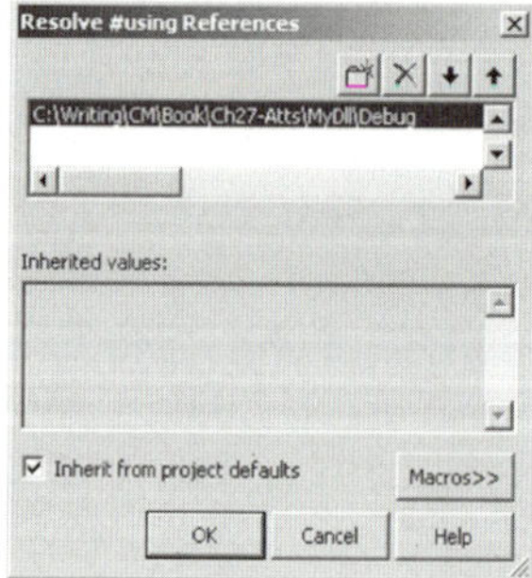

Click the New Line button (it has a picture of a folder on it), then click the Ellipsis button that appears to browse to the MyDll debug directory and add it to the list. Click OK, then click OK again to exit the UseAttributes Property Pages dialog box.

9 Build the project. The compiler will see the *ObsoleteAttribute* attached to the *SayHello* method, and will issue a compiler warning:

```
UseAttributes.cpp(19) : warning C4996:
'MyDll::Hello::SayHello' was
  declared deprecated
```

Managed C++ doesn't treat *ObsoleteAttribute* quite the same way as the C# and Visual Basic .NET compilers do: it doesn't print the message associated with the attribute and it takes no notice of the second parameter, flagging all obsolete methods as warnings only.

Defining Your Own Attributes

As you'll see in this section, you can easily define custom attributes and use them in your projects. Custom attributes are quite simple to write, because an attribute is simply represented by a class that has properties and methods that represent the attribute parameters. For example, suppose you had the following attribute attached to a class designed to control the generation of logging information at run time:

```
[LogAttribute("myfile.log", type=LogAttribute::AllMethods)]
__gc class MyClass...
```

The attribute has two parameters, one for the log filename and a second that determines the level of logging. It's represented by a class called *LogAttribute* whose members contain the filename and type information. Information about the attribute class is included with the metadata for *MyClass*, and a *LogAttribute* object can be queried at run time to retrieve its parameters. You'll see how to query attributes in code in the final section of this chapter.

You can use any .NET class to represent an attribute, but you'll tend to use a class that derives from the *System::Attribute* base class because that will give you a number of convenient methods.

Attribute Targets

Attributes can be used at all levels in .NET, so you can apply them to whole assemblies, to .NET types, or to individual methods and properties within types. An attribute usually isn't applicable at all levels, so there needs to be some way to restrict the items to which an attribute can be attached.

The *AttributeUsage* attribute, represented by the *System::AttributeUsageAttribute* class, is a meta-attribute: an attribute that is applied to attributes. You attach an *AttributeUsageAttribute* to the class that implements an attribute to say where it can be used. Here's an example:

```
[AttributeUsageAttribute(AttributeTargets::Method)]
```

This attribute would be attached to an attribute class to show that it can only be used on methods. The table below lists the members of the *AttributeTargets* enumeration that control where attributes are valid.

Member	Description
All	The attribute can be applied to any element
Assembly	The attribute can be applied to an assembly
Class	The attribute can be applied to a class
Constructor	The attribute can be applied to a type constructor
Delegate	The attribute can be applied to a delegate
Enum	The attribute can be applied to an enumeration
Event	The attribute can be applied to an event
Field	The attribute can be applied to a field
Interface	The attribute can be applied to an interface
Method	The attribute can be applied to a method
Module	The attribute can be applied to a PE (Portable Executable) module
Parameter	The attribute can be applied to a parameter
Property	The attribute can be applied to a property
ReturnValue	The attribute can be applied to a return value
Struct	The attribute can be applied to a struct, for example, a value type

If you want to specify more than one target, you can combine two or more members together with the bitwise OR operator (|), as you'll see in the exercise.

Attribute Class Properties

Although some attributes can be used without parameters, most will specify at least one. Attribute parameters fall into two groups:

- Positional parameters, which are identified simply by their position in the parameter list.
- Named parameters, which are specified as a name/value pair.

Consider the example of a custom attribute I gave earlier at the start of the "Defining Your Own Attributes" section:

```
[LogAttribute("myfile.log", type=LogAttribute::AllMethods)]
```

This attribute has one positional parameter and one named parameter called *type*. Positional parameters always appear before named parameters, and are passed to the class constructor. Named parameters are implemented as properties in the attribute class.

Design Criteria for Attribute Classes

Before moving on to the exercise, here are a few design criteria you should bear in mind when you write a custom attribute class:

- Always add "Attribute" to the class name for an attribute (for example, call a class *DocumentationAttribute* rather than *Documentation*).
- Use positional arguments for required parameters.
- Use named arguments for optional parameters.
- Provide a read-only property for each positional argument.
- Provide a read/write property for each named argument. Be sure the name of the property differs in case from that of the argument (for example, for an argument called *type*, provide a property called *Type*).

Writing a Custom Attribute

This exercise will show you how to create a custom attribute that can be used to document methods and properties. In the next section, you'll see how to write code that makes use of this attribute.

1. Create a new Managed C++ Class Library project, and call it CustomAtt. The custom attribute needs to be created as a DLL so that it can be used in other projects.

2 Open the CustomAtt.h header file, and edit the skeleton class as follows:

```
namespace CustomAtt
{
   [AttributeUsageAttribute(AttributeTargets::Method |
                    AttributeTargets::Property)]
   public __gc class DocumentationAttribute
   {
   };
}
```

Our class is called *DocumentationAttribute*; the name follows the convention of having the class name for an attribute end with "Attribute." The class is tagged with an *AttributeUsageAttribute* that limits its use to class methods and properties. Note how you can use more than one member of the *AttributeTargets* enumeration by combining them with the bitwise OR operator (|). This class doesn't inherit from *System::Attribute* because we don't need any of the features it provides.

3 The attribute will include three pieces of data: the documentation text, which will be a positional parameter, and author and date strings, which will be optional (and thus implemented as named parameters). Add the declarations for the three members to the class:

```
namespace CustomAtt
{
   [AttributeUsageAttribute(AttributeTargets::Method |
                    AttributeTargets::Property)]
   public __gc class DocumentationAttribute
   {
       String* text;     // documentation text
       String* author;   // optional author field
       String* date;     // optional date field
   };
}
```

4 Add the constructor:

```
public:
   DocumentationAttribute(String* txt)
   {
       // Save the text away
       text = txt;
   }
```

The constructor takes a string as its only argument, which is saved away as the documentation text.

5 Add a read-only property so that users can retrieve the text at run time:

```
// Read-only property to return the text
__property String* get_Text() { return text; }
```


note

A read-only property is one that implements a *get* method without also implementing a matching *set* method.

6 Add read/write properties to allow access to the two named parameters:

```
// Properties for the positional parameters
__property String* get_Author() { return author; }
__property void set_Author(String* au) { author = au; }

__property String* get_Date() { return date; }
__property void set_Date(String* dt) { date = dt; }
```

Remember that in Managed C++ the name of the property function needs to match the name you want to give to the parameter, so a parameter called *Date* will be implemented by property methods called *get_Date* and *set_Date*. The two *set* functions simply save away the strings they are passed; in real code, you'd probably want to perform some validation.

7 Build the project to check that you haven't made any errors.

8 Add some code that will use the new attribute. Right-click on the Solution name in the Solution Explorer window, choose Add from the shortcut menu, and then New Project. Make sure the project type is set to Managed C++ Application, and call the project TestAtts. Click OK.

9 To give easy access to the DLL containing the attribute code, copy the CustomAtt.dll file from the CustomAtt project debug directory into the TestAtts project directory.

10 Open the TestAtts.cpp file and add *#using* and *using namespace* lines to the top of the file:

```
#using <mscorlib.dll>
#include <tchar.h>
#using <CustomAtt.dll>

using namespace System;
using namespace CustomAtt;
```

The *#using* directive causes the compiler to load and access the CustomAtt DLL, and the *using* declaration makes it possible to use the attribute class without having to fully qualify the class name.

11 Define a managed class that uses the new custom attribute:

```
// A class to test the attribute
__gc class TestAtts
{
    int val;
public:
    [DocumentationAttribute(
      "The TestAtts class constructor takes an integer",
      Author="julian", Date="10/10/01")]
    TestAtts(int v)
    {
        val = v;
    }
    [DocumentationAttribute(
      "The read-only Value property returns the value of"
      " the int class member", Author="julian")]
    __property int get_Value() { return val; }
};
```

The *DocumentationAttribute* has been attached to the two members of this class. The constructor uses all three possible parameters, while the property only uses the text and the *Author* named parameter.

> **note**
>
> Remember that you can split a string literal over two lines, and as long as there is nothing between the closing and opening double quotation marks except white space characters, the preprocessor will concatenate them for you.

12 Build the project to make sure it compiles cleanly. You can now use ILDASM to see how the attribute data is held in the class.

13 Run ILDASM as before, and open the TestAtts.exe file. Click the plus sign (+) next to the blue component symbol labeled *TestAtts*, and double-click on the .ctor entry. This will bring up the disassembly for the constructor, as shown here:

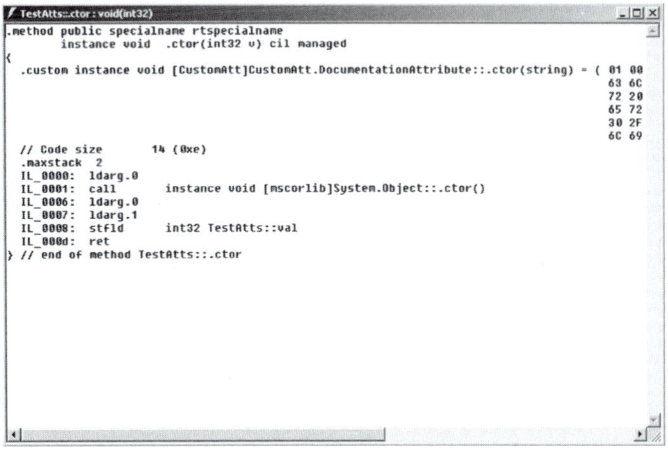

TestAtts::.ctor : void(int32)

```
.method public specialname rtspecialname
        instance void  .ctor(int32 v) cil managed
{
  .custom instance void [CustomAtt]CustomAtt.DocumentationAttribute::.ctor(string) = ( 01 00
                                                                                         63 6C
                                                                                         72 20
                                                                                         65 72
                                                                                         30 2F
                                                                                         6C 69
  // Code size       14 (0xe)
  .maxstack  2
  IL_0000:  ldarg.0
  IL_0001:  call       instance void [mscorlib]System.Object::.ctor()
  IL_0006:  ldarg.0
  IL_0007:  ldarg.1
  IL_0008:  stfld      int32 TestAtts::val
  IL_000d:  ret
} // end of method TestAtts::.ctor
```

You can see how the code creates a *DocumentationAttribute* object that then forms part of the *TestAtts* object. You can access this attribute object from code, and you'll see how to do this in the next section.

14 Before leaving this exercise, try adding the *DocumentationAttribute* to the class, like this:

```
[DocumentationAttribute("The TestAtts class",
Author="julian")]
__gc class TestAtts
{
    ...
}
```

When you compile this code, the compiler will give you an error message because the attribute cannot be applied to classes:

```
c:\Code\TestAtts\TestAtts.cpp(14): error C3303:
    'CustomAtt::DocumentationAttribute': attribute can only be
       used on 'methods, properties'
```

Using Reflection to Get Attribute Data

The final section of this chapter shows you how to use attributes at run time by enquiring about what attribute data an object contains. Querying attribute data is only one aspect of reflection, a feature of the .NET Framework that lets you find out a lot of detail about objects and the classes they belong to at run time. I can't cover every aspect of reflection in this chapter, but we'll cover enough to let you query attribute data.

The *Type* Class

Before I talk about reflection and how it relates to attributes, you need to know something about the *Type* class. *System::Type* is a class that represents type declarations. This means you can get a *Type* object to represent any object to which you have a reference, and you can then use that object to find out many details about the type. You can obtain *Type* objects to represent value types, arrays, classes, interfaces, and enumerations. It is the primary way to access metadata, and the way in which you use reflection. Although the *Type* class is used mainly by language tool writers, you might find it useful at times, such as when you want to access class attributes.

System::Type has a lot of members (over 40 properties and almost 50 methods). The two tables below list a selection of properties and methods from this class to show you the sort of information you can access through a *Type* object.

Property	Description
Assembly	Gets a reference to the assembly where the type is defined
AssemblyQualifiedName	Gets the fully qualified name of the type, including the name of the assembly it was loaded from
Attributes	Returns a *TypeAttributes* object representing the collection of attributes for this type
BaseType	Returns a *Type* for the type from which this object directly inherits
FullName	Returns the fully qualified name of the type, including namespace
GUID	Returns the GUID associated with the type, if any
IsAbstract	Returns *true* if the type is abstract
IsArray	Returns *true* if the type is an array
IsByRef	Returns *true* if the type is passed by reference
IsClass	Returns *true* if the type is a reference type (and not an interface or value type)
IsComObject	Returns *true* if the type is a COM object
IsInterface	Returns *true* if the type is an interface
IsValueType	Returns *true* if the type is a value type
Module	Gets a reference to the module (the DLL) in which the type is defined
Namespace	Gets the namespace of the type as a string
UnderlyingSystemType	Gets a reference to the *Type* representing the CLR type underlying this language-specific type

Member	Description
GetConstructor, *GetConstructors*	Gets information about one or all of the constructors for the type
GetEvent, *GetEvents*	Gets information about one or all of the events defined for the type
GetField, *GetFields*	Gets information about one or all of the fields defined for the type
GetInterface, *GetInterfaces*	Gets information about one or all of the interfaces implemented by the type
GetInterfaceMap	Returns an *InterfaceMap* showing how interface methods are mapped onto actual class methods
GetMember, *GetMembers*	Gets information about one or all of the members of the type
GetMethod, *GetMethods*	Gets information about one or all of the methods of the type
GetProperty, *GetProperties*	Gets information about one or all of the properties defined by the type
GetType	A static function that returns a *Type* object
GetTypeFromCLSID, *GetTypeFromProgId*	Gets a *Type* object representing a COM object
InvokeMember	Invokes a member of the current type
ToString	Returns the *Type*'s name as a string

You might think you need to use the Attributes property to find out about custom attribute properties, but this only allows access to standard system attribute data.

Accessing Standard Attributes

You can use the *Type* class's Attributes property to find out about the standard attribute settings for classes. This property returns you a *TypeAttributes*, which is a value type; it's a set of flags describing which standard attributes are set for the type. This enumeration has nearly 30 members, and the following table shows you some of the common attributes that form part of *TypeAttributes*:

Member	Description
Abstract	Specifies that the class is abstract
AnsiClass	Specifies that strings are using ANSI character encoding
AutoClass	Specifies that the string encoding is automatically decided
Class	Specifies that the type is a class
HasSecurity	Specifies that the type has security information associated with it
Import	Specifies that the type has been imported from another assembly
Interface	Specifies that the type is an interface
NotPublic	Specifies that the type is not public
Public	Specifies that the type is public
Sealed	Specifies that the type cannot be extended by inheritance
Serializable	Specifies that the type can be serialized
UnicodeClass	Specifies that strings are using Unicode character encoding

You can find out whether a type has an attribute set by using the bitwise AND operator (&), as shown in the following code fragment:

```
if (tt->Attributes & TypeAttributes::Public)
    Console::WriteLine("Type is public");
```

If you want to check the whether the type is a class, a value type, or an interface, you need to use the *ClassSemanticsMask* member:

```
if ((tt->Attributes & TypeAttributes::ClassSemanticsMask) ==
    TypeAttributes::Class)
    ole::WriteLine("Type is a class");
```

Accessing Custom Attribute Data

Custom attribute data is accessed using the static *GetCustomAttribute* and *GetCustomAttributes* members of the *Attribute* class. As you'd expect, the first retrieves information about one attribute, while the second returns you an array containing details of all the custom attributes for a type. This exercise will show you how to use the *Type* class and the *GetCustomAttributes* method to retrieve the attribute settings from the class you created in the previous exercise.

1 Continue using the TestAtts project that you started in the previous exercise. You need to create a *Type* object to use reflection to find out about custom attributes, so add this code to the start of the *_tmain* function:

```
int _tmain(void)
{
    Console::WriteLine(S"Testing Attributes");
```

```
    // Create an object and get its type
    TestAtts* ta = new TestAtts(3);
    Type* tt = ta->GetType();

    return 0;
}
```

You obtain a *Type* object using the *GetType* method that every .NET type inherits from *System::Object*.

2 You can see whether there are any custom attributes on a class by using the *GetCustomAttributes* method on the *Type* object, like this:

```
// See if there are any custom attributes on the class
Object* patts[] = tt->GetCustomAttributes(true);
int n = patts->Length;
Console::WriteLine(
    "Number of custom attributes on the class is {0}",
__box(n));
```

We know that the class doesn't have any custom attributes, so you'd expect a count of 0.

3 The attributes are actually on the class members, not on the class itself, so get a list of the class members and query them:

```
// Get info on the class members
MemberInfo* pmi[] = tt->GetMembers();
int nMembers = pmi->Count;
Console::WriteLine("Number of class members is {0}",
    __box(nMembers));
```

Calling *GetMembers* on the *Type* object returns an array of *MemberInfo* objects that describe the members. Running this code on the *TestAtts* class tells you that there are seven members.

note

The seven members are: the constructor, the private data value, the property *get* method, and four methods inherited from the *Object* base class (*Equals*, *GetHashCode*, *GetType*, and *ToString*).

4 Loop over the list of class members, and get the custom attributes for each one:

```
for (int i=0; i<pmi->Count; i++)
{
    Object* pMemberAtts[] = pmi[i]->GetCustomAttributes(true);

    if (pMemberAtts->Count > 0)
    {
        Console::WriteLine("Attributes for member {0}:", pmi[i]);
        for(int j=0; j<pMemberAtts->Count; j++)
        {
            Console::WriteLine(" attribute is {0}", pMemberAtts[j]);
        }
    }
}
```

The outer loop considers each member in turn, and calls *GetCustomAttributes* on the *MemberInfo* object to get a list of attribute objects. If there are any for this member, we print them out. As you'd expect, just passing an array element to *WriteLine* results in calling the appropriate *ToString* method, which normally prints out the name of the class.

5 There are several ways to figure out whether a member has the *Documentation* custom attribute, and the code below shows one of them. Modify the code for the inner loop in step 4 so that it looks like this:

```
for (int j = 0; j < pMemberAtts->Count; j++)
{
    Console::WriteLine("  att is {0}", pMemberAtts[j]);
    DocumentationAttribute* pda =
        dynamic_cast<DocumentationAttribute*>(pMemberAtts[j]);
    if (pMemberAtts[j]->GetType()->Equals(pda->GetType()))
    {
        Console::WriteLine(
            "The member has the Documentation attribute");
        Console::WriteLine("Text is '{0}'", pda->Text);
    }
}
```

The loop first uses *dynamic_cast* to cast the current attribute as a *DocumentationAttribute* pointer. Then the *Equals* method compares the *Type* object of the current attribute against that of the *DocumentationAttribute* class to see if they are the same. If they are, the loop retrieves the *Text* member of the current attribute and prints it.

6 Build and run the program. You should see Console output similar to that shown here, listing the attributes present on class members, and showing the values of the documentation text:

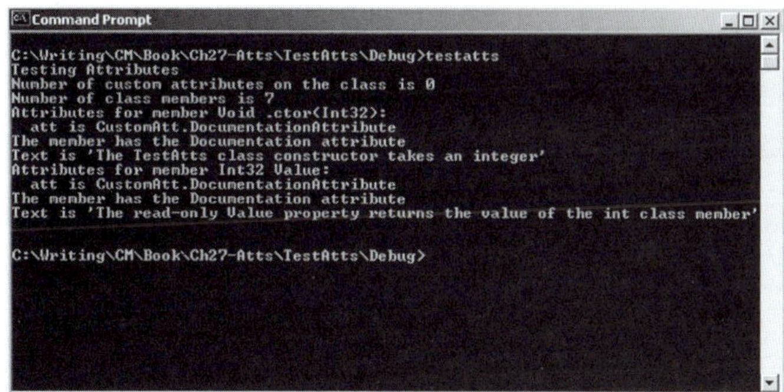

Chapter 26 Quick Reference

To	Do This
Modify the assembly-level attributes in a class	Edit the entries in the AssemblyInfo.cpp file that is generated for all Managed C++ projects in Visual Studio .NET

Find out about the standard attributes of a type	Use the Attributes property on a *Type* object that represents the type, and use the bitwise AND operator (&) to compare the value with members of the *TypeAttributes* enumeration. For example:
	`if (t->Attributes &`
	`    TypeAttributes::Public)`

Create a custom attribute	Create a class to represent an attribute, and use the *AttributeUsage* attribute to control where your attribute can be applied. For example:
	`[AttributeUsageAttribute(`
	`    AttributeTargets::Method)]`
	`public __gc class MyAttribute`
	`{ ... };`

Represent mandatory parameters for a custom attribute	Add arguments to the class constructor or constructors, plus read only properties to give access to the values
Represent optional parameters for a custom attribute	Add a property to represent each optional parameter

(continued)

(continued)

Find out which custom attributes are attached to a class	Create a *Type* object and use its *GetCustomAttributes* method to retrieve an array of objects representing the attributes attached to the class.
	For example:
	`Type* tt = myObject->GetType();`
	`Object* patts[] =`
	`  tt->GetCustomAttributes(true);`

Find out which custom attributes are attached to a class member	Create a *Type* object and use its *GetMembers* method to retrieve an array of *MemberInfo* objects representing the class members. Then call *GetCustomAttributes* on each *MemberInfo* object. For example:
	`Type* tt = myObject->GetType();`
	`MemberInfo* pmi[] = tt->GetMembers();`
	
	`for (int i=0; i<pmi->Count; i++)`
	`{`
	` Object* pMemberAtts[] =`
	`    pmi[i]->GetCustomAttributes(true);`
	
	` if (pMemberAtts->Count > 0)`
	`{`
	` // Do something`
	`}`

CHAPTER

27

Living with COM

In this chapter, you'll learn

- ✔ *How .NET lets you use COM objects from .NET projects*
- ✔ *How to use COM objects through early and late binding*
- ✔ *How to use ActiveX controls in Windows Forms projects*
- ✔ *How to expose .NET objects as COM objects*

Although the types provided within the Microsoft .NET Framework are sufficient for the vast majority of programs, there are times when you'll need to interact with existing components, in particular COM components and ActiveX controls. This chapter shows you how the worlds of .NET and COM can interoperate so you can make best use of new and existing technologies.

note

This chapter assumes that you know what COM objects are, and something about how to use them outside the .NET world. If words like GUID, HRESULT, *IUnknown*, *IDispatch*, and type library don't mean anything to you, then you should learn more about COM before proceeding with this chapter.

COM Components and COM Interop

The designers of the .NET Framework recognized that, although it is easier to use and more flexible than COM for many applications, the .NET Framework won't replace COM any time soon. For this reason, they provided the COM Interop facility to let .NET and COM objects interact. Why does the .NET Framework need to worry about COM? There are several reasons:

- Developers are already using COM components, and a .NET equivalent might not be available.
- Even where COM components have been developed in-house, for economic or technical reasons, it might not be feasible to rewrite them as .NET objects.
- Some operating system services, such as the enterprise services offered by COM+, are firmly COM-based.

As you'll see shortly, it is very easy to use a COM object or an ActiveX control from .NET code, and this gives .NET developers access to hundreds of existing .NET objects. It is also possible to use a .NET object from COM code, although I'd expect this to be a less common occurrence.

Using COM Components from .NET Code

To use a COM object from .NET code, you first create a Runtime-Callable Wrapper, or RCW. You need the RCW because there are several major differences between COM and .NET, which are summarized in the following table:

COM	.NET
Clients must manage the lifetimes of COM objects they create.	The Common Language Runtime (CLR) manages the lifetime of .NET objects.
Clients use *QueryInterface* or browse the object's type information to find out whether a particular interface is supported.	Clients can use reflection to query an object.
COM objects are accessed through raw pointers and are therefore fixed in memory.	.NET objects are accessed through references and can be moved around by the CLR for performance reasons.

Wrapper classes are necessary to bridge these differences so that a COM object can appear as a .NET object and vice versa.

How Do RCWs Work?

The wrapper takes the form of a proxy class that does all the work of creating and talking to the COM object for you so that you can use COM objects just as if they were .NET objects. You can see how this works in the following diagram. The RCW does all the housekeeping by interacting with the Microsoft Windows Registry, creating the object, forwarding calls to the object, and managing its lifetime. The primary goal of the RCW is to hide the complexity of

COM objects from .NET programmers so that in some cases, .NET programmers might not even know they are using a COM object.

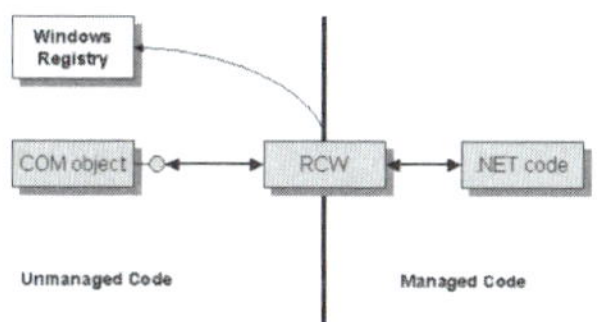

The wrapper class maintains a cache of interface pointers on the object it is using and releases these pointers when the object is no longer needed. The RCW itself is governed by the usual .NET garbage collection rules, because it is a managed object.

Because data types often differ in the .NET and COM worlds, the RCW performs standard marshaling so that both sides can use data types that are familiar to them. For example, when passing string data through an RCW, the .NET side works with *String* objects, but the COM side will probably use COM's BSTR type; the RCW automatically converts between the two as necessary.

If you've used COM objects from C++, you're aware that COM objects implement several standard interfaces—such as *IUnknown* and *IDispatch*—that COM client programmers have to know about. The RCW simplifies the process of using COM objects by automatically handling many of the standard interfaces, as listed in the following table.

Interface	Description
IUnknown	The RCW uses *IUnknown* for object identity checking, type coercion via *QueryInterface*, and lifetime management.
IDispatch	Used for late binding to COM objects using reflection (see below).
IErrorInfo	Used for providing error information.
IProvideClassInfo	If the COM object being wrapped implements this interface, the RCW uses it to provide better type identity.
IConnectionPoint and *IConnectionPointContainer*	If the COM object uses connection points, the RCW implements delegate-style events.
IDispatchEx	If the COM object implements *IDispatchEx*, the RCW exposes and implements the .NET *IExpando* interface.
IEnumVARIANT	The RCW enables COM types that expose this interface to be treated as .NET collections.

Creating and Using RCWs

You can create RCW classes in two ways:

- If you're using Microsoft Visual Studio .NET with either Microsoft Visual Basic or C#, you can use a wizard to create the RCW for you.
- If you're using Managed C++ or compiling code from the command line, the .NET Framework contains a tool called tlbimp.exe (for Type Library Importer) that reads a COM type library, and creates a wrapper class based on the information it finds.

The following exercise shows you how to use tlbimp.exe to create a wrapper for a COM object and then use the object.

> **note**
>
> I've created a simple COM object for use in this exercise. It is called *TConverter* and implements the same simple temperature conversion functionality that I demonstrated in the Web Service chapter. You'll find the source and executable for the Converter project, plus directions for installing it, on the CD that accompanies this book. Make sure *TConverter* has been installed before starting this exercise.

1. Create a new Managed C++ Application project, and call it ComWrapper.
2. Open a Console window to run the tlbimp.exe tool. If you use a Visual Studio Command Prompt window, you'll have the path set up automatically to let you run tlbimp from any directory.

> **tip**
>
> You can open a Visual Studio Command Prompt window from the Visual Studio .NET Tools menu.

3. Change to the directory containing the type library for the Converter project, where you'll find the file _Converter.tlb. All the files in this directory whose names start with an underscore have been produced automatically during the build process, and you shouldn't edit them yourself. You can, however, read the type library to generate a wrapper.

4 Run the tlbimp.exe tool on the type library to generate the wrapper code:

```
tlbimp _Converter.tlb
```

Running the tool with no arguments except the type library name will produce a wrapper using all the defaults. In this case, it produces an assembly called Converter.dll that contains the wrapper class. The following table summarizes the options that can be used with the tlbimp tool:

Options	Description
/asmversion:*number*	Specifies the version number to be given to the assembly.
/delaysign	Signs the resulting assembly using delayed signing, where the assembly isn't properly signed until late in the development process.
/help	Displays Help for the command.
/keycontainer: *containername*	Signs the assembly with the key pair found in the specified key container.
/keyfile:*filename*	Signs the assembly with the key pair found in the specified key file.
/namespace:*name*	Specifies the namespace for the assembly.
/nologo	Runs the command without any startup banner.
/out:*file*	Specifies the name for the output file. By default, the name is the type library name given in the IDL.
/primary	Produces a primary interop assembly, indicating that this assembly was produced by the publisher of the COM component. Primary interop assemblies must by signed with a strong name.
/publickey:*file*	Signs the assembly with the specified public key. This option is used for testing and delayed signing.
/reference:*file*	Gives the name of a file to be used to resolve references to types defined outside the current type library.
/silent	Suppresses the display of success messages.
/strictref	Does not import a type library if the tool cannot resolve all the references within it.
/sysarray	Imports COM style *SafeArrays* as .NET *System::Array* types.
/unsafe	Produces interfaces without .NET security checks. It introduces security risks, so it should only be used when known to be necessary.
/verbose	Displays additional information about the conversion process.

Names and Signing

Assemblies are normally identified by their name, version number, and possibly locale information. This is adequate for private assemblies that are going to be used only within a single application. However, it isn't good enough for those that will be used more widely, because two people could use the same name for their assemblies with lots of potential for confusion.

To make assemblies unique, they should be given a strong name, which consists of the text name, version, and locale information, plus a public key and a digital signature. Every key generated using Public Key Encryption is unique, so using keys and digital signatures serves both to provide a unique identifier for an assembly and as a way to verify the assembly owner or creator.

COM requires that components can be uniquely identified, and it uses GUIDs to accomplish this. .NET strong names fulfill the requirement for unique component identification, and they also provide information about the component's originator, which GUIDs do not.

Because the wrapper assembly is going to be used only in one project, the signing options aren't needed. Remember that shared assemblies that are going to live in the Global Assembly Cache have to be signed with a strong name. Delayed signing can be useful in large organizations with strictly controlled access to private encryption keys. Using this option, the assembly is only signed with the public key, and the full signing with the private key is delayed until late in the development process (typically just before shipping).

5 Open ILDASM from the Visual Studio .NET Console window, and use it to examine Converter.dll.

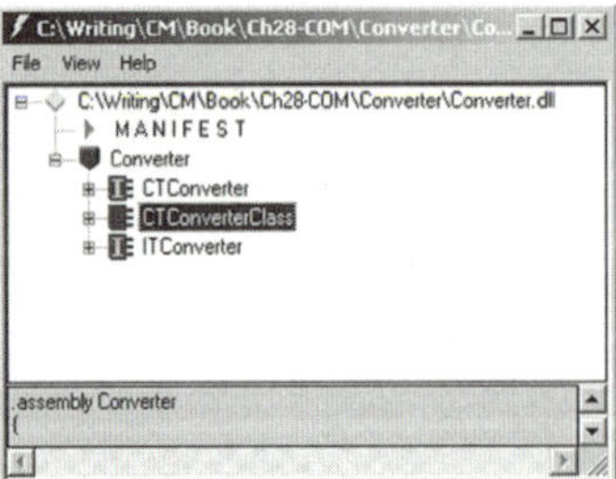

The shield-like symbol with the red top represents a namespace, so the namespace you need to import is *Converter*. You can see that the assembly contains three types. *CTConverter* and *ITConverter* represent the original

COM coclass and interface definitions respectively, and they're marked with an "I" to show that they are interfaces. *CTConverterClass* is a real type, and the Runtime-Callable Wrapper is produced by tlbimp.

So to deduce the name of the wrapper class without using ILDASM, take the name of the COM coclass, put a "C" on the front and "Class" on the end.

6 Add code to the ComWrapper project to use the COM object. First, you need to set the project properties so that the compiler can find the wrapper assembly file. Right-click on the project name in Solution Explorer, and choose Properties from the shortcut menu to bring up the Property Pages for the project.

7 Select the C/C++ General tab in the tree in the left-hand pane, and then highlight the Resolve #using References entry in the table in the right-hand pane. Use the ellipsis button on the right to bring up the Resolve #using References dialog box. Then use the Create New Folder button to display a File Open dialog box; use it to navigate to the folder containing the wrapper DLL.

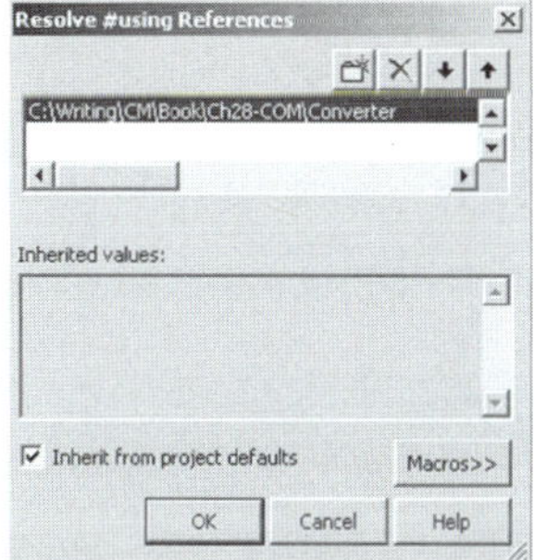

Click OK to dismiss the dialog box, and click OK again to dismiss the project Property Pages.

8 Add *#using* and *using* directives to your code:

```
#using <Converter.dll>
using namespace Converter;
```

Because the compiler knows where to look for the assembly, you don't need to use a full path.

9 Add code to create a wrapper object, and use it to call methods on the COM object:

```
int _tmain(void)
{
    Console::WriteLine(S"COM Interop Sample");
```

```
    // Create a COM object
    CTConverterClass* pt = new CTConverterClass();

    // Call a conversion method and print the result
    double d = pt->ConvertC2F(27.0);
    Console::WriteLine("27C is {0}F", __box(d));

    return 0;
}
```

Note how the wrapper is created just like any other managed object, and methods are called on it in exactly the same way as normal. There's no way to tell from this code that you're using a COM object, and the wrapper performs all the lifetime management for you.

Handling COM Errors

You know COM methods return status and error information using 32-bit HRESULTs. The RCW converts all error HRESULTs into exceptions that you can catch in your code. The test Converter project returns an error if the conversion methods are passed any values less than –273°C or –241°F, because temperatures less than absolute zero have no meaning. Here's the COM code:

```
STDMETHODIMP CTConverter::ConvertC2F(double dCelsius, double* dFahr)
{
    if (dFahr == 0) return E_POINTER;

    // Temperatures below -273C are meaningless...
    if (dCelsius < -273.0) return E_INVALIDARG;

    *dFahr = (9/5 * dCelsius) + 32;
    return S_OK;
}
```

This code might return two error HRESULTs: the first, E_POINTER, will occur if the pointer to the result variable is 0, which won't happen when called by the RCW. The second, E_INVALIDARG, will occur if an invalid temperature is passed.

These will be converted to exceptions by the RCW, and as usual, you need to catch them to prevent your program from terminating. Here's what you'll see on the Console if you pass an invalid temperature:

```
Unhandled Exception:
   System.ArgumentException: The parameter is incorrect.
```

```
  at Converter.CTConverterClass.ConvertC2F(Double dCelsius)
  at main() in c:\code\comwrapper\comwrapper.cpp:line 20
```

You can handle this by adding a *try* and *catch* block to the code in the *_tmain* function:

```
try
{
    double d = pt->ConvertC2F(-280.0);
    Console::WriteLine("-280C is {0}F", __box(d));
}
catch(Exception* pe)
{
    Console::WriteLine("Exception from COM object: {0}", pe->Message);
}
```


Late Binding to COM Objects

Runtime-Callable Wrappers implement early binding connections to COM objects, because you have all the details of what the COM object can do available to you at compile time. If you want to use a COM object that implements *IDispatch*, you can also call it at run time, but it is a little more complex.

This exercise will show you how to use the *Converter* object with late binding. This COM object was created with a dual interface, so it can be accessed via both early binding and late binding.

1. Create a new Managed C++ Application project called LateBind.
2. Get a *Type* object that represents the COM component. (Consult the previous chapter, "Attributes and Reflection," for more details of the *Type* class and its uses.)

```
// Get a type representing the COM object
Type* t = Type::GetTypeFromProgID(S"Converter.TConverter");
if (t == 0)
{
    Console::WriteLine("Error getting type for TConverter");
    return -1;
}
Console::WriteLine("Got type for TConverter");
```

The *GetTypeFromProgID* static method takes a COM *progID* as a string and creates a *Type* object to represent the coclass. If there is a problem creating the *Type* object, because the *progID* can't be found or there's some other registry-related problem, a *null* pointer will be returned. Overloads of this function let you specify that an exception will be thrown instead of getting a *null* pointer, if that suits your code better.

3 Use the *System::Activator* class to create the COM object for you:

```
// Use System::Activator to create an instance
Object* pObj = Activator::CreateInstance(t);
```

The *Activator* class creates instances of local or remote objects for you. The reference returned is a general object reference; you don't need to cast it to any specific type, as this will be taken care of for us later.

4 Build the parameter list before you call a conversion method on the object. This takes the form of an array of *Objects*:

```
// Make up the argument list
Object* pArgs[] = { __box(27.0) };
```

Here, the array contains only one value, the temperature to be converted. As you know by now, built-in types have to be converted before they can be used as objects, so you need to box the value.

5 Call the conversion method dynamically, using the *InvokeMember* method of the *Type* class:

```
// Invoke the method
try
{
    Object* pa = t->InvokeMember(S"ConvertC2F",
           Reflection::BindingFlags::InvokeMethod, 0, pObj, pArgs);

    double d = Convert::ToDouble(pa);
    Console::WriteLine(S"27C is {0}F", __box(d));
}
catch(Exception* pe)
{
    Console::WriteLine("Exception from Invoke: ", pe->Message);
}
```

InvokeMember, as its name implies, dynamically invokes a member of an object. The arguments supplied to the function are the name of the member to be invoked, the type of operation (in this case, you're invoking a method rather than accessing a property or field), a pointer to a *Binder* object (which you're not using), a pointer to the object on which the operation is to be invoked, and a pointer to the argument array.

If the call works, you'll be passed back an *Object* reference representing the result, which is then converted to the appropriate type using one of the static methods of the *Convert* class.

Using ActiveX Controls in Windows Forms Projects

Any serious COM application makes use of one or more ActiveX controls, and GUI applications commonly use many third-party components that have been implemented as ActiveX controls.

note

The current definition of an ActiveX control is any COM object that implements at least *IUnknown* and that handles its own registry entries on installation and removal. This includes just about any modern COM object, so it isn't a very useful definition. In this section, I'm talking about ActiveX controls in the original sense, meaning components (often graphical) that can be used in a form-based programming environment.

Traditional ActiveX controls are among the most complex COM objects in common use, and only expert COM programmers should deal with raw ActiveX controls. Fortunately, GUI programming environments such as Visual Studio usually hide the complexity of ActiveX controls so that you can easily use them in your projects.

ActiveX controls are accessed via a Runtime-Callable Wrapper just like any COM object, but because they are usually used in Windows Forms projects, the *System::Windows::Forms* namespace contains a special class, *AxHost*, that forms the basis of RCWs used to talk to ActiveX controls. *AxHost* also takes care of interacting with the development environment so that the control wrapper can appear in the toolbox, be dragged onto forms, and have its properties edited in the normal way.

As with plain RCWs, there are two ways to create an RCW for an ActiveX control.

- If you're using Visual Studio .NET and coding in Visual Basic or C#, you can simply add a reference to a COM object as if it were a .NET object. Visual Studio automatically generates an appropriate wrapper class derived from *AxHost* for you.
- If you're building from the command line or using Managed C++, the .NET Framework provides you with a tool called AxImp.exe that generates the RCW for you.

The exercise that follows shows you how to generate an RCW for an ActiveX control and use it in a Windows Forms project. The usual control I use for this exercise is the Microsoft Calendar control that is installed with Microsoft Office; it is widely available and easy to program, and it is easy to see whether or not it appears correctly on the form.

1 Create a new Managed C++ Application project, and call it AxImport.

2 Open a Console window to run the aximp.exe tool. If you use a Visual Studio Command Prompt window, you'll have the path set up automatically so that you can run aximp from any directory.

> **tip**
>
> You can open a Visual Studio Command Prompt window from the Visual Studio .NET Tools menu.

3 Change to the directory containing the Calendar ActiveX control. The file you want is called MSCAL.OCX, and it usually lives in the Office subdirectory of the Microsoft Office directory tree.

4 Run the aximp.exe tool, giving the name of the OCX as the only argument:

```
aximp mscal.ocx
```

As with the tlbimp.exe tool, there are numerous options that can be specified when running aximp.exe, but you don't require any of them for this exercise. You'll find that the tool generates two DLLs: MSACAL.dll and AxMSACAL.dll. The first is the plain RCW that lets you interface to the COM types defined in the OCX, while the second holds the wrapper class derived from *AxHost* that lets you use the control on a form.

5 Open the AxMSACAL.dll file with ILDASM. You'll see that the namespace is called *AxMSACAL* and that the main *Calendar* control class is called *AxCalendar*.

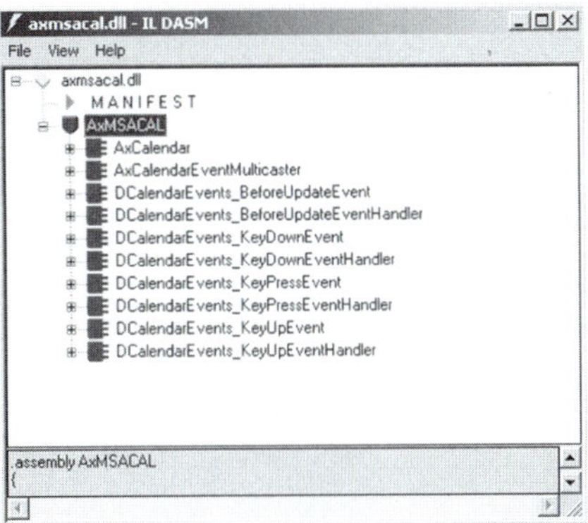

6 Add code to the AxImport project to use the *Calendar* control. First, you need to set the project properties so that the compiler can find the wrapper assembly file. Right-click on the project name in Solution Explorer, and choose Properties from the shortcut menu to bring up the Property Pages for the project.

7 Select the C/C++ General tab in the tree in the left-hand pane, and then highlight the Resolve #using References entry in the table in the right-hand pane. Use the ellipsis button on the right to bring up the Resolve #using References dialog box. Then use the Create New Folder button to display a File Open dialog box; use it to navigate to the folder containing the wrapper DLL.

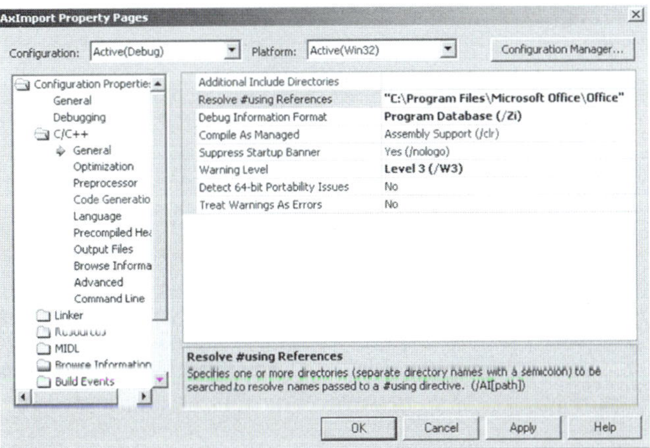

8 Because this is a Windows Forms example program, you'll need to set up the project to use Windows Forms. You will also need to reference the AxMSACAL.dll that you created in Step 4. Add four *#using* lines to reference the two DLLs that hold the Windows Forms code:

```
#using <System.dll>
#using <System.Drawing.dll>
#using <System.Windows.Forms.dll>
#using <AxMSACAL.dll>
```

It will also make life easier if you add four *using* directives:

```
using namespace System::ComponentModel;
using namespace System::Windows::Forms;
using namespace System::Drawing;
using namespace AxMSACAL;
```

The *System::Windows::Forms* namespace holds the classes used in building forms. *System::ComponentModel* provides classes that manage the design-time and run-time behavior of components and controls, and it tends always to be needed when working with forms. *System::Drawing* holds various types used in GUI construction, in particular the *Size* and *Point* types used to specify the size and location of components.

9 Create a class that inherits from *System::Windows::Forms::Form* to represent the form on the screen.

Add the following code to the AxImport.cpp source file to create a simple Form class:

```
// A simple form class
__gc class SimpleForm : public Form
{
public:
    SimpleForm()
    {
    }
};
```

tip

If you need to know more about Windows Forms and how to use them in Managed C++, consult Chapter 16.

10 Set a few properties in the *Form* constructor so that the form displays correctly on the screen:

```
SimpleForm()
{
```

```
    // Set the form caption
    Text = S"ActiveX Test";

    // Set the border style to 3D fixed
    FormBorderStyle = FormBorderStyle::Fixed3D;

    // Set the size
    Size = System::Drawing::Size(400,350);
}
```

11 Add a reference to a *Calendar* control as a member of the class so that you can refer to it later:

```
private:
    AxCalendar* pac;
```

12 Create a *Calendar* control and add it to the form by adding this code to the constructor after you've set the form size:

```
// Create a Calendar Control
pac = new AxCalendar();

// Set size and position
pac->Size = System::Drawing::Size(350,300);
pac->Location = Point(10,10);

// Add the control to the form
Controls->Add(pac);
```

The code creates a new wrapper, which in turn creates the *Calendar* control. The size and location are set as for any other .NET control, and the control is added to the form in the usual way, by a call to *Add*.

13 Add the following code to *_tmain* to invoke the *SimpleForm* class:

```
Application::Run(new SimpleForm());
```

14 Build and run the project, and you'll see a form that displays a *Calendar* control, like this:

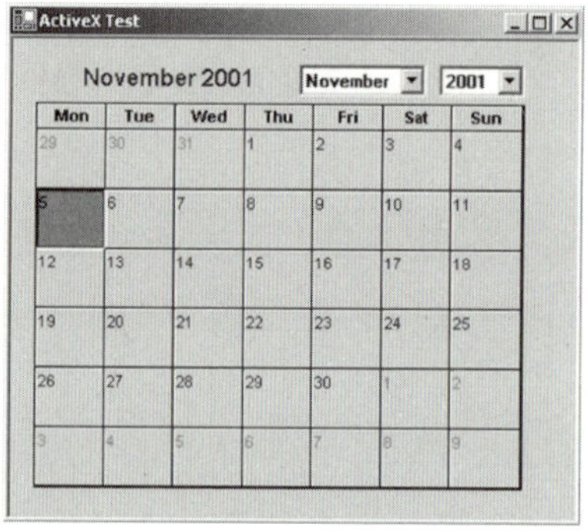

Calling Control Methods

You can call methods on the control just as you would on any other .NET control. C# and Visual Basic programmers can see what methods and properties the wrapper exposes in Visual Studio, but C++ users don't have the same level of interaction with the wrapper. The easiest way to see what you can call is to use ILDASM to list the methods exposed by the wrapper. The following short exercise shows you how to interact with the *Calendar* component:

1 Continue with the same project, but increase the size of the form to (400,400).

2 Add two buttons to the form, for stepping the calendar to the next or previous month:

```
// Add the 'next month' button
Button* bNext = new Button();
bNext->Text = S"Next";
bNext->Size = System::Drawing::Size(40,20);
bNext->Location = Point(40,340);

Controls->Add(bNext);

// Add the 'Previous month' button
Button* bPrev = new Button();
bPrev->Text = S"Previous";
bPrev->Size = System::Drawing::Size(60,20);
bPrev->Location = Point(100,340);

Controls->Add(bPrev);
```

The two buttons are added to the bottom of the form.

3 Now add handler functions for the two buttons:

```
private:
    void NextButton_Clicked(Object* pSender, EventArgs* pArgs)
    {
        pac->NextMonth();
    }

    void PrevButton_Clicked(Object* pSender, EventArgs* pArgs)
    {
        pac->PreviousMonth();
    }
```

These buttons call the *NextMonth* and *PreviousMonth* methods on the *Calendar* control, neither of which takes any arguments.

4 Link the handlers to the controls at the end of the *SimpleForm* constructor:

```
// Add Handlers
bNext->Click +=
        new EventHandler(this, &SimpleForm::NextButton_Clicked);
bPrev->Click +=
        new EventHandler(this, &SimpleForm::PrevButton_Clicked);
```

tip

If you need more information about attaching handler functions to controls, consult Chapter 16.

5 Build and run the project, and you'll be able to step the Calendar through the months.

Using .NET Components as COM Components

In addition to using COM objects from .NET clients, you can use .NET objects in the COM world. The process for exposing .NET classes as COM objects is complex, because interacting with COM at the C++ level is difficult. For this reason, this section introduces the topic, but leaves practical implementation of .NET to COM code for more advanced texts.

Once again, wrapper classes are used, only this time they are called COM-Callable Wrappers (CCWs). In effect, a CCW puts a COM layer onto a .NET object so that the .NET object behaves in exactly the way a COM object is expected to behave. The process is shown below:

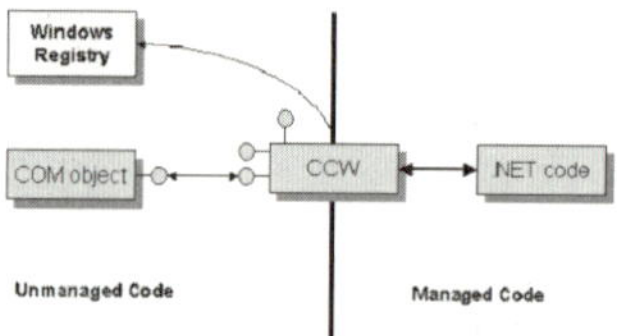

The CCW exposes all the interfaces expected by clients using COM, such as *IUnknown* and *IDispatch*, and lets the client code manage its lifetime in the normal COM manner.

What Must .NET Types Implement to Be Used as COM Objects?

COM objects have a particular set of characteristics, and .NET types need to follow some rules if they're to be exposed as COM objects using COM Interop. Here's a summary of what the .NET type has to do:

- It has to supply a default constructor, meaning one that doesn't take arguments, because COM objects are always created uninitialized and there's no standard way to pass over initialization data. For this reason, it must be possible to create .NET objects uninitialized if they're going to be used as COM objects.
- The type's assembly must be signed with a strong name. See the sidebar "Names and Signing" for details on strong names and how to use them.
- The type's assembly must be placed where the CLR can find it. See the sidebar "Installing Assemblies" for more details.
- The correct COM-related registry entries must be made for the .NET object. This is done for you if you're using Visual Studio.

Installing Assemblies

Assemblies are typically installed in one of two places. Private assemblies, intended for use by a single application, can be placed in the directory where the executable lives or any directory directly underneath. Shared assemblies are installed into the Global Assembly Cache (also known as the GAC), which is a per-computer repository for assemblies that need to be shared. You don't manually copy assembly files into the GAC, but instead use the tools provided by the .NET Framework for managing the cache (such as gacutil.exe).

Assemblies must live in one of these two locations, because these are where the CLR looks for assemblies when it needs to load them at run time.

Chapter 27 Quick Reference

To	Do This
Use a COM object from .NET code	Use the tlbimp.exe tool to generate a Runtime-Callable Wrapper for the COM object, and then reference the wrapper in your code as you would any other .NET class.
Use a COM object via late binding	Use the static *GetTypeFromProgID* or *GetTypeFromCLSID* methods of the *Type* class to generate a *Type* object representing the COM object. Then use the *CreateInstance* static method on the *System::Activator* class to create an instance of the object. Finally, use *InvokeMethod* on the *Type* object to invoke your chosen method.
Use an ActiveX control from a Windows Forms project	Use the aximp.exe tool to generate a Runtime-Callable Wrapper for the ActiveX control, and then reference the wrapper assembly in your Windows Forms project. Use the wrapper object as you would any other control.

About the Authors

Julian Templeman

Julian Templeman first touched fingers to keypunch in 1972, punching Fortran code onto cards at college in London. Soon after, he moved on to Macro-11 programming on PDP-11s. This qualifies him as a Real Programmer, and until recently, he had a PDP-11 in his garage to remind him of better times. Since then, he's programmed systems of all types and sizes, from single-chip computers for instrumentation to Cray and CDC supercomputers. In the course of these endeavors, he has (he is confident to assert) forgotten more programming languages than most of the readers of this book will ever learn: SNOBOL, SPITBOL, Babbage, Forth, TRAC, flavors of LISP, flavors of Basic (the A$ sort), several dialects of JCL (//DD SYSIN * and all that jazz), TECO, Macro11, Z80 assembler, various other assemblers, WATFOR, WATFIV, Icon—the list is, if not endless, then at least reasonably long. Of course, being a Real Programmer, he has never programmed in COBOL, RPG, or any other of those languages beloved by suits and bean-counters, or done anything serious involving SQL.

Julian now runs a consultancy and training company in London, specializing in COM, Java, and now Microsoft .NET. He also writes computer books. You can reach him at *julian@groucho.demon.co.uk*.

Andy Olsen

Andy Olsen is a freelance consultant engaged in training, consultancy, and development services in C++, C#, and related .NET Framework technologies. Andy has been developing Microsoft applications for more than 15 years and has been using C++ since the late 1980s. He is a keen football and rugby supporter and also enjoys running and skiing, but not all at the same time. Andy now lives by the sea in Swansea, South Wales.

Tyrone Howe (Chapter 1)

Tyrone Howe received a degree in computational science from the University of Hull. He has worked as a software engineer for GEC Avionics and as a project manager for Dover Harbour Board. In 1994, he started his own company, Computerco, which specializes in software development, training, and consulting. In his spare time, Tyrone writes music and flies microlight aircraft.

Mike Hudson (Chapters 2 and 3)

Mike Hudson has been programming computers professionally for over 15 years. Having made the transition from Z80 assembler and the AI languages—from LISP and Prolog to C++ via C—he has spent the last 10 years developing systems in C++. Mike lives in a small village in Cornwall, England.

Index

D

V

W

X

Y

Z

Stepladder

A ladder is a portable piece of equipment with rungs attached to sides made of metal, wood, or rope, used for climbing up or down. A **stepladder** is a folding ladder that has flat broad steps and a hinged supporting frame. Remember: Do not stand on the top two rungs of any ladder, and do not try to "walk" a ladder by rocking it. Climb down the ladder, and then move it.

At Microsoft Press, we use tools to illustrate our books for software developers and IT professionals. Tools are an elegant symbol of human inventiveness, and a powerful metaphor for how people can extend their capabilities, precision, and reach. From basic calipers and pliers to digital micrometers and lasers, our stylized illustrations of tools give each book a visual identity and each book series a personality. With tools and knowledge, there are no limits to creativity and innovation. Our tag line says it all: *The tools you need to put technology to work.*

Get a ***Free***
e-mail newsletter, updates, special offers, links to related books, and more when you
register on line!

Register your Microsoft Press® title on our Web site and you'll get a FREE subscription to our e-mail newsletter, *Microsoft Press Book Connections.* You'll find out about newly released and upcoming books and learning tools, online events, software downloads, special offers and coupons for Microsoft Press customers, and information about major Microsoft® product releases. You can also read useful additional information about all the titles we publish, such as detailed book descriptions, tables of contents and indexes, sample chapters, links to related books and book series, author biographies, and reviews by other customers.

Registration is easy. Just visit this Web page and fill in your information:

http://www.microsoft.com/mspress/register

Microsoft®

Proof of Purchase

Use this page as proof of purchase if participating in a promotion or rebate offer on this title. Proof of purchase must be used in conjunction with other proof(s) of payment such as your dated sales receipt—see offer details.

Microsoft® Visual C++® .NET Step by Step

0-7356-1567-5

____

CUSTOMER NAME

Microsoft Press, PO Box 97017, Redmond, WA 98073-9830

MICROSOFT LICENSE AGREEMENT

Book Companion CD

IMPORTANT—READ CAREFULLY: This Microsoft End-User License Agreement ("EULA") is a legal agreement between you (either an individual or an entity) and Microsoft Corporation for the Microsoft product identified above, which includes computer software and may include associated media, printed materials, and "online" or electronic documentation ("SOFTWARE PRODUCT"). Any component included within the SOFTWARE PRODUCT that is accompanied by a separate End-User License Agreement shall be governed by such agreement and not the terms set forth below. By installing, copying, or otherwise using the SOFTWARE PRODUCT, you agree to be bound by the terms of this EULA. If you do not agree to the terms of this EULA, you are not authorized to install, copy, or otherwise use the SOFTWARE PRODUCT; you may, however, return the SOFTWARE PRODUCT, along with all printed materials and other items that form a part of the Microsoft product that includes the SOFTWARE PRODUCT, to the place you obtained them for a full refund.

SOFTWARE PRODUCT LICENSE

The SOFTWARE PRODUCT is protected by United States copyright laws and international copyright treaties, as well as other intellectual property laws and treaties. The SOFTWARE PRODUCT is licensed, not sold.

1. **GRANT OF LICENSE.** This EULA grants you the following rights:

   a. **Software Product.** You may install and use one copy of the SOFTWARE PRODUCT on a single computer. The primary user of the computer on which the SOFTWARE PRODUCT is installed may make a second copy for his or her exclusive use on a portable computer.

   b. **Storage/Network Use.** You may also store or install a copy of the SOFTWARE PRODUCT on a storage device, such as a network server, used only to install or run the SOFTWARE PRODUCT on your other computers over an internal network; however, you must acquire and dedicate a license for each separate computer on which the SOFTWARE PRODUCT is installed or run from the storage device. A license for the SOFTWARE PRODUCT may not be shared or used concurrently on different computers.

   c. **License Pak.** If you have acquired this EULA in a Microsoft License Pak, you may make the number of additional copies of the computer software portion of the SOFTWARE PRODUCT authorized on the printed copy of this EULA, and you may use each copy in the manner specified above. You are also entitled to make a corresponding number of secondary copies for portable computer use as specified above.

   d. **Sample Code.** Solely with respect to portions, if any, of the SOFTWARE PRODUCT that are identified within the SOFTWARE PRODUCT as sample code (the "SAMPLE CODE"):

      i. **Use and Modification.** Microsoft grants you the right to use and modify the source code version of the SAMPLE CODE, *provided* you comply with subsection (d)(iii) below. You may not distribute the SAMPLE CODE, or any modified version of the SAMPLE CODE, in source code form.

      ii. **Redistributable Files.** Provided you comply with subsection (d)(iii) below, Microsoft grants you a nonexclusive, royalty-free right to reproduce and distribute the object code version of the SAMPLE CODE and of any modified SAMPLE CODE, other than SAMPLE CODE, or any modified version thereof, designated as not redistributable in the Readme file that forms a part of the SOFTWARE PRODUCT (the "Non-Redistributable Sample Code"). All SAMPLE CODE other than the Non-Redistributable Sample Code is collectively referred to as the "REDISTRIBUTABLES."

      iii. **Redistribution Requirements.** If you redistribute the REDISTRIBUTABLES, you agree to: (i) distribute the REDISTRIBUTABLES in object code form only in conjunction with and as a part of your software application product; (ii) not use Microsoft's name, logo, or trademarks to market your software application product; (iii) include a valid copyright notice on your software application product; (iv) indemnify, hold harmless, and defend Microsoft from and against any claims or lawsuits, including attorney's fees, that arise or result from the use or distribution of your software application product; and (v) not permit further distribution of the REDISTRIBUTABLES by your end user. Contact Microsoft for the applicable royalties due and other licensing terms for all other uses and/or distribution of the REDISTRIBUTABLES.

2. **DESCRIPTION OF OTHER RIGHTS AND LIMITATIONS.**

   - **Limitations on Reverse Engineering, Decompilation, and Disassembly.** You may not reverse engineer, decompile, or disassemble the SOFTWARE PRODUCT, except and only to the extent that such activity is expressly permitted by applicable law notwithstanding this limitation.
   - **Separation of Components.** The SOFTWARE PRODUCT is licensed as a single product. Its component parts may not be separated for use on more than one computer.
   - **Rental.** You may not rent, lease, or lend the SOFTWARE PRODUCT.
   - **Support Services.** Microsoft may, but is not obligated to, provide you with support services related to the SOFTWARE PRODUCT ("Support Services"). Use of Support Services is governed by the Microsoft policies and programs described in the

user manual, in "online" documentation, and/or in other Microsoft-provided materials. Any supplemental software code provided to you as part of the Support Services shall be considered part of the SOFTWARE PRODUCT and subject to the terms and conditions of this EULA. With respect to technical information you provide to Microsoft as part of the Support Services, Microsoft may use such information for its business purposes, including for product support and development. Microsoft will not utilize such technical information in a form that personally identifies you.

- **Software Transfer.** You may permanently transfer all of your rights under this EULA, provided you retain no copies, you transfer all of the SOFTWARE PRODUCT (including all component parts, the media and printed materials, any upgrades, this EULA, and, if applicable, the Certificate of Authenticity), **and** the recipient agrees to the terms of this EULA.
- **Termination.** Without prejudice to any other rights, Microsoft may terminate this EULA if you fail to comply with the terms and conditions of this EULA. In such event, you must destroy all copies of the SOFTWARE PRODUCT and all of its component parts.

3. **COPYRIGHT.** All title and copyrights in and to the SOFTWARE PRODUCT (including but not limited to any images, photographs, animations, video, audio, music, text, SAMPLE CODE, REDISTRIBUTABLES, and "applets" incorporated into the SOFTWARE PRODUCT) and any copies of the SOFTWARE PRODUCT are owned by Microsoft or its suppliers. The SOFTWARE PRODUCT is protected by copyright laws and international treaty provisions. Therefore, you must treat the SOFTWARE PRODUCT like any other copyrighted material **except** that you may install the SOFTWARE PRODUCT on a single computer provided you keep the original solely for backup or archival purposes. You may not copy the printed materials accompanying the SOFTWARE PRODUCT.

4. **U.S. GOVERNMENT RESTRICTED RIGHTS.** The SOFTWARE PRODUCT and documentation are provided with RESTRICTED RIGHTS. Use, duplication, or disclosure by the Government is subject to restrictions as set forth in subparagraph (c)(1)(ii) of the Rights in Technical Data and Computer Software clause at DFARS 252.227-7013 or subparagraphs (c)(1) and (2) of the Commercial Computer Software—Restricted Rights at 48 CFR 52.227-19, as applicable. Manufacturer is Microsoft Corporation/One Microsoft Way/Redmond, WA 98052-6399.

5. **EXPORT RESTRICTIONS.** You agree that you will not export or re-export the SOFTWARE PRODUCT, any part thereof, or any process or service that is the direct product of the SOFTWARE PRODUCT (the foregoing collectively referred to as the "Restricted Components"), to any country, person, entity, or end user subject to U.S. export restrictions. You specifically agree not to export or re-export any of the Restricted Components (i) to any country to which the U.S. has embargoed or restricted the export of goods or services, which currently include, but are not necessarily limited to, Cuba, Iran, Iraq, Libya, North Korea, Sudan, and Syria, or to any national of any such country, wherever located, who intends to transmit or transport the Restricted Components back to such country; (ii) to any end user who you know or have reason to know will utilize the Restricted Components in the design, development, or production of nuclear, chemical, or biological weapons; or (iii) to any end user who has been prohibited from participating in U.S. export transactions by any federal agency of the U.S. government. You warrant and represent that neither the BXA nor any other U.S. federal agency has suspended, revoked, or denied your export privileges.

DISCLAIMER OF WARRANTY

NO WARRANTIES OR CONDITIONS. MICROSOFT EXPRESSLY DISCLAIMS ANY WARRANTY OR CONDITION FOR THE SOFTWARE PRODUCT. THE SOFTWARE PRODUCT AND ANY RELATED DOCUMENTATION ARE PROVIDED "AS IS" WITHOUT WARRANTY OR CONDITION OF ANY KIND, EITHER EXPRESS OR IMPLIED, INCLUDING, WITHOUT LIMITATION, THE IMPLIED WARRANTIES OF MERCHANTABILITY, FITNESS FOR A PARTICULAR PURPOSE, OR NONINFRINGEMENT. THE ENTIRE RISK ARISING OUT OF USE OR PERFORMANCE OF THE SOFTWARE PRODUCT REMAINS WITH YOU.

LIMITATION OF LIABILITY. TO THE MAXIMUM EXTENT PERMITTED BY APPLICABLE LAW, IN NO EVENT SHALL MICROSOFT OR ITS SUPPLIERS BE LIABLE FOR ANY SPECIAL, INCIDENTAL, INDIRECT, OR CONSEQUENTIAL DAMAGES WHATSOEVER (INCLUDING, WITHOUT LIMITATION, DAMAGES FOR LOSS OF BUSINESS PROFITS, BUSINESS INTERRUPTION, LOSS OF BUSINESS INFORMATION, OR ANY OTHER PECUNIARY LOSS) ARISING OUT OF THE USE OF OR INABILITY TO USE THE SOFTWARE PRODUCT OR THE PROVISION OF OR FAILURE TO PROVIDE SUPPORT SERVICES, EVEN IF MICROSOFT HAS BEEN ADVISED OF THE POSSIBILITY OF SUCH DAMAGES. IN ANY CASE, MICROSOFT'S ENTIRE LIABILITY UNDER ANY PROVISION OF THIS EULA SHALL BE LIMITED TO THE GREATER OF THE AMOUNT ACTUALLY PAID BY YOU FOR THE SOFTWARE PRODUCT OR US$5.00; PROVIDED, HOWEVER, IF YOU HAVE ENTERED INTO A MICROSOFT SUPPORT SERVICES AGREEMENT, MICROSOFT'S ENTIRE LIABILITY REGARDING SUPPORT SERVICES SHALL BE GOVERNED BY THE TERMS OF THAT AGREEMENT. BECAUSE SOME STATES AND JURISDICTIONS DO NOT ALLOW THE EXCLUSION OR LIMITATION OF LIABILITY, THE ABOVE LIMITATION MAY NOT APPLY TO YOU.

MISCELLANEOUS

This EULA is governed by the laws of the State of Washington USA, except and only to the extent that applicable law mandates governing law of a different jurisdiction.

Should you have any questions concerning this EULA, or if you desire to contact Microsoft for any reason, please contact the Microsoft subsidiary serving your country, or write: Microsoft Sales Information Center/One Microsoft Way/Redmond, WA 98052-6399.

PN 097-0002296